U.S. Laws, Acts, and Treaties

MAGILL'S CHOICE

U.S. LAWS, ACTS, AND TREATIES

Volume 2

1929-1970

edited by

Timothy L. Hall

University of Mississippi School of Law

co-editor

Christina J. Moose

SALEM PRESS, INC.

Pasadena, California   Hackensack, New Jersey

∞ The paper used in these volumes conforms to the American National Standard for Permanence of Paper for Printed Library Materials, Z39.48-1992 (R1997).

Parts of this publication previously appeared in the following publications, copyrighted by Salem Press, Inc.: *Great Events from History: Human Rights* (© 1992), *Great Events from History: Business and Commerce*
(© 1994), *Great Events from History: Ecology and the Environment* (© 1995),
Ready Reference: American Justice (c 1996), *Great Events from History: Revised North American Series* (c 1997), *Ready Reference: Censorship* (© 1997),
Ready Reference: Women's Issues (© 1997), *Natural Resources* (© 1998),
Encyclopedia of Family Life (© 1999), *Racial and Ethnic Relations in America*
(© 1999), *The Sixties in America* (© 1999), *Aging* (© 2000), *Encyclopedia
of Environmental Issues* (© 2000), *Encyclopedia of the U.S. Supreme Court*
(© 2001), *Magill's Choice: American Indian History* (© 2002), and *Magill's
Choice: The Bill of Rights* (© 2002). New material has been added.

Library of Congress Cataloging-in-Publication Data
U.S. laws, acts, and treaties / edited by Timothy L. Hall.
    p. cm. — (Magill's choice)
Includes bibliographical references and index.
    ISBN 1-58765-098-3 (set : alk. paper) — ISBN 1-58765-099-1 (vol. 1 :
alk. paper) — ISBN 1-58765-100-9 (vol. 2 : alk. paper)— ISBN
1-58765-101-7 (vol. 3 : alk. paper)
    1. United States. Laws, etc. 2. Law—United States. 3. United
States—Foreign relations—Treaties. I. Title: US laws, acts, and
treaties. II. Hall, Timothy L. III. Series.
    KF385.A4U152 2003
    348.73′2—dc21

                                                      2002156063

Third Printing

PRINTED IN THE UNITED STATES OF AMERICA

CONTENTS

Contents

Contents by Popular Name

U.S. Laws, Acts, and Treaties

AGRICULTURAL MARKETING ACT

DATE: June 15, 1929

U.S. STATUTES AT LARGE: 46 Stat. 11

U.S. CODE: 12 § 1141

CATEGORIES: Agriculture; Banking, Money, and Finance; Business, Commerce, and Trade

This act established the Federal Farm Board to make loans to farm co-operatives and to control surpluses of farm commodities.

In order to understand the impact of the Agricultural Marketing Act of 1929, it is necessary to understand what happened to the American farm sector early in the twentieth century. The second decade of the twentieth century was a good one for farmers. The world had experienced rapid industrial expansion, causing incomes and spending to rise. Demand for agricultural commodities had expanded, giving farmers high prices for their crops. Farmers in the United States were producing large crops and exporting large parts of them to foreign markets. A fixed quantity of good agricultural land caused land prices to go up, making farmers feel wealthier. There was no end in sight to the prosperity.

Things began to change in 1919. European farmers were producing more as they recovered from World War I, and prices started to fall. In 1921, wheat and cotton were selling for half their prices of 1920, and farmers realized that hard times had returned. By 1923, agricultural commodity prices had started to rise slowly, and farm conditions began to improve. Things were getting better, but conditions for farmers still were unfavorable. Mechanization of farm work promised to help farmers by cutting production costs but was soon to contribute to problems of overproduction.

EARLY ATTEMPTS TO HELP FARMERS

Agriculture was an important sector in the United States economy in the early 1920's, and Congress believed that help was needed for farmers, even though farm prices were edging up after the drastic drop in the early 1920's. A major attempt to help was embodied in the five McNary-Haugen bills introduced in Congress from 1924 to 1928. These bills called for an export corporation, which would purchase agricultural crops in large enough amounts to keep their prices at acceptably high levels. These purchases were not to be sold domestically but were to be sold in foreign markets. The bills also called for an import tariff to discourage foreign farmers from sending agricultural goods to the United States to compete with domestic products. The first three McNary-Haugen bills did not pass Congress. The last two bills passed Congress but were vetoed by President Calvin Coolidge. Herbert Hoover, Coolidge's secretary of commerce, was influential in advising Coolidge to veto the bills.

The Agricultural Marketing Act of 1929 differed from these bills in that it focused on improved marketing as a means of aiding farmers. The government, under this act, would encourage formation of national cooperative marketing organizations but would not run them.

As director of the Food Administration and as secretary of commerce, Hoover had participated in the many agricultural policy debates of the late 1910's and the 1920's. In 1928, he campaigned for president, promising to call a special session of Congress to deal with farm problems. Hoover had grown up on an Iowa farm and believed that an improved marketing process was the solution to the farm problem. Despite his strong feelings about the issue, once in the office of president he sent no specific legislation of his own to Congress, not wanting to interfere with Congress's legislative prerogative. Even so, Congress knew what Hoover wanted. It passed the Agricultural Marketing Act, which became law on June 15, 1929.

PROVISIONS OF THE ACT

The overall goal of the act was to put agriculture on an equal footing with other business sectors in the country. The objectives specified to carry this out were to decrease agricultural surpluses, stabilize prices for agricultural commodities and thereby cut down on speculation, and provide help in marketing agricultural commodities. The act called for the establishment of the Federal Farm Board, which was to have a budget of $500 million.

THE FEDERAL FARM BOARD

The Federal Farm Board was directed to set up national farmer cooperatives as a means of achieving its goals. These cooperatives were to be controlled by farmers and were to be used primarily to improve the marketing of crops. It was believed that the coming together of farmers into a comprehensive organization that could bargain on behalf of farmers would give farmers the power to prevent drastic price declines. The Federal Farm Board was authorized to make loans to the cooperatives to increase their size and efficiency. These loans could be used to build new facilities or for expenses of marketing agricultural crops. Farmers could obtain loans at low rates of interest.

President Hoover persuaded Alexander Legge to leave his $100,000-per-year job as chairman of International Harvester to become the first chairman of the Federal Farm Board. Seven other board members were appointed, representing the major farm commodities. Arthur M. Hyde, as Hoover's secretary of agriculture, was an ex officio member.

By October of 1929, the Federal Farm Board had succeeded in setting up the Farmers National Grain Associations, which were stock companies in each of the major commodities. Stock in the associations was owned by the larger local grain cooperatives. The goal of each of these corporations was to become a large, centralized organization to facilitate marketing for the particular commodity it represented. It was hoped that their sheer size and the coordination of the marketing process they offered would increase the efficiency of marketing agricultural crops, thus stabilizing prices at the desired high levels. The National Grain Associations were also supposed to control agricultural surpluses. Unfortunately, the government also had in place county extension agents, whose job was to help increase production. Getting farmers to control production was difficult, and the Federal Farm Board never succeeded in this task. The government thus, to some extent, operated at cross purposes, trying to keep prices high while also encouraging production.

THE GREAT DEPRESSION

In 1930, the Federal Farm Board decided that its efforts were not succeeding. A surplus of major commodities kept agricultural prices low. Several factors contributed to the surpluses. The United States and Europe had had a few years of abundant harvests, and other countries were restricting imports from the United States and imposing tariffs in retaliation for the Smoot-Hawley Tariff of 1930. Farmers were particularly hurt by these retaliatory tariffs because they had long used exports as a means for eliminating agricultural surpluses. Finally, the Great Depression caused everyone to suffer. Low incomes meant that people were buying less of everything, including farm products.

The surplus in wheat was particularly troubling. Wheat prices fell dramatically, and in response the Federal Farm Board set up Grain Stabilization Boards in February of 1930. The Grain Stabilization Boards hoped to control grain prices by encouraging farmers to reduce their output. Chairperson Legge of the Federal Farm Board and Secretary of Agriculture Hyde toured the country trying to get farmers to participate in the production control process. They were unsuccessful in getting farmers to cooperate with these programs, so the Grain Stabilization Boards, started buying surplus wheat. The purchase program was intended to be temporary, as no one recognized that the Great Depression was going to last for many years. Grain prices continued to fall, and by 1931 farm incomes were at the lowest levels of the century. The Federal Farm Board decided that it could no longer afford to buy grain or to store the grain it had already purchased. Fearing that the grain already purchased would rot in storage, the Federal Farm Board began to sell the grain it owned. This had a further dampening effect on prices and enraged farmers. The public outcry against the sale was so large that Legge eventually resigned as chair of the Federal Farm Board.

INEVITABLE FAILURES

The national cooperatives never emerged as the force that Hoover had hoped they would be. They were poorly managed and suffered from the same inefficiencies as the rest of the agricultural sector. They had little lasting effect on American agriculture, and most of them did not survive to the end of the 1930's.

The price stabilization portion of the Federal Farm Board's efforts fared no better than did the national cooperatives. The Federal Farm Board found that it could not stop the slide in agricultural prices by buying surplus grains, as illustrated by the case of wheat. Not only did it fail to keep prices from going down, it spent $400 million in taxpayers' money and disrupted commodity markets. Stabilization was a relatively new idea that was to be used in later legislation; some credit needs to be given to the Federal Farm Board for innovative thinking.

Hoover did not recognize immediately that his farm plans were not working, so no adjustments to the plans were made during his presidential administration. His top farm advisers shared Hoover's vision of how to help the farmers and so did not offer alternative plans. In Hoover's defense, it is likely that the McNary-Haugen plans introduced in the 1920's would not have fared much better. The onset of the Great Depression, coinciding with increased production made possible by the mechanization of farm production, made the Federal Farm Board's goals nearly impossible to achieve.

Hoover had high hopes for solving farm problems with voluntary participation by farmers. He had seen what had happened to farmers in the Soviet Union and did not want the government to intervene on such a large scale. Farmers did not choose to participate in Hoover's plans, however, and even if they had, the low budgets available to the Federal Farm Board doomed the stabilization plans to failure.

NEW LEGISLATION

Congress became disenchanted with the Federal Farm Board and cut its 1932-1933 budget by 60 percent. Hoover lost the 1932 election, in which Franklin D. Roosevelt was elected president. Roosevelt had his own ideas about what should happen in the farm sector. He abolished the Federal Farm Board in 1933, effectively ending the influence of the Agricultural Marketing Act of 1929. In 1933, Congress passed the Agricultural Adjustment Act, which was the New Deal's attempt to help farmers.

By 1935, farm income was 50 percent higher than it had been in 1932. Key elements of the 1933 act were declared unconstitutional in January of 1936. Later that year, new farm legislation was passed. As was suggested by the Federal Farm Board, production controls were a key element in the new plans.

Eric Elder

SOURCES FOR FURTHER STUDY

Benedict, Murray. *Farm Policies of the United States, 1790-1950*. New York: Twentieth Century Fund, 1953.
Davis, Joseph S. *On Agricultural Policy, 1926-1938*. Stanford, Calif.: Food Research Institute, 1939.

Hamilton, David. *From New Day to New Deal.* Chapel Hill: University of North Carolina Press, 1991.

Kirkendall, Richard. *Social Scientists and Farm Politics in the Age of Roosevelt.* Ames: Iowa State University Press, 1982.

Nourse, Edwin G. *Marketing Agreements Under the AAA.* Washington, D.C.: Brookings Institution, 1935.

Rasmussen, Wayne, and Gladys Baker. "A Short History of Price Support and Adjustment Legislation and Programs for Agriculture, 1933-65." *Agriculture Economics Research* 18 (1966): 68-79.

Tweeten, Luther. *Foundations of Farm Policy.* 2d rev. ed. Lincoln: University of Nebraska Press, 1979.

SEE ALSO: Hundred Days legislation (1933); Tennessee Valley Authority Act (1933); Taylor Grazing Act (1934).

SMOOT-HAWLEY TARIFF ACT

ALSO KNOWN AS: Hawley-Smoot Tariff Act; Tariff Act of 1930
DATE: June 17, 1930
U.S. STATUTES AT LARGE: 46 Stat. 741
U.S. CODE: 19 § 1202-1527
CATEGORIES: Business, Commerce, and Trade; Tariffs and Taxation

By signing the Smoot-Hawley Tariff Act, Herbert Hoover sparked foreign retaliation against American products, which precipitated a temporary collapse of the international trading system.

The Smoot-Hawley Tariff raised average U.S. tariff rates by approximately 18 percent. The largest increases were on agricultural products, on which average tariff rates increased by about 57 percent. President Herbert Hoover's signing of the tariff bill on June 17, 1930, climaxed a political struggle that had lasted more than a year. Proponents of higher tariff rates had hoped in particular to give relief to farmers, whose incomes generally had lagged during the prosperity of the 1920's. More generally, they hoped that protection from foreign competition would allow U.S. producers to avoid production cutbacks and layoffs as the Great Depression began to unfold.

TARIFFS: PROS AND CONS

Opponents of higher tariffs had three main concerns. First, they feared that higher tariffs would end up protecting inefficient domestic producers and thereby result in higher prices for consumers. Second, they were afraid that an increase in U.S. tariffs would spark foreign retaliation, hurting the U.S. export sector. Finally, opponents were afraid that if the United States reduced its purchases of goods from other countries (particularly in Europe) that were heavily indebted to the United States, then it would become difficult for those countries to continue to make payments on their debt. The result might be the undermining of the international financial system.

While serving as secretary of commerce during the Warren G. Harding and Calvin Coolidge administrations, Hoover had become known as a strong proponent of protective tariffs. The 1928 Republican Party platform called for increased duties on agricultural products, and Hoover made this promise a central part of his presidential campaign. Although Hoover did not come out in favor of a general increase in tariff rates, he did state during the campaign that the United States should largely confine its imports to those products that could not be produced domestically. This position makes more understandable Hoover's eventual willingness to accept a general increase in tariff rates.

PASSAGE AND PROVISIONS

Shortly after assuming office, Hoover called a special session of Congress to convene on April 15, 1929, for the express purpose of raising tariff duties on agricultural products. The House of Representatives quickly passed a new tariff bill. As a result of political trading during the legislative process, it contained substantial increases in duties on nonagricultural products as well. Because it was a revenue measure, the bill originated in the House and was known formally as the Hawley-Smoot bill. Willis Hawley of Oregon was the chairman of the House Ways and Means Committee. The legislation is more popularly known as the Smoot-Hawley bill because of the greater political prominence of Reed Smoot of Utah, the chairman of the Senate Finance Committee. The Senate was much slower to act, and the special session of Congress concluded in November without passage of a new tariff bill. When Congress reconvened in April, 1930, a compromise was worked out. The final version of the bill was passed on June 14.

The bill achieved final passage in the House fairly easily, by a vote of 222 to 153. It was largely a party line vote, with 208 Republicans voting for the bill and only 20 against it; 133 Democrats voted against the bill and only 14 for it. The vote in the Senate was much closer, 44-42 for passage, as a group of eleven so-called "insurgent" Republicans led by senators William Borah, George W. Norris, and Robert La Follette voted against passage.

Because the increase in tariff rates embodied in the bill went well beyond Hoover's initial call for an increase in agricultural duties, there was some hope among the bill's opponents that the president might veto it. Among those arguing in favor of a veto were prominent members of the banking and financial community, some leading industrialists including Henry Ford, the editors of many prominent newspapers including *The New York Times*, and perhaps most famously, a group of more than a thousand economists who signed a petition urging a veto. Prominent among those arguing in favor of signing the bill were most farm organizations and the American Federation of Labor.

Hoover's decision to sign the bill was probably most dependent on three considerations. First, as his statements during the 1928 presidential campaign had made clear, he had a strongly protectionist philosophy. Second, he doubted that a better bill could be procured from Congress, and he believed that the failure to pass any tariff bill would be seen, particularly by farmers, as his having failed to carry through on an important campaign promise. Finally, he managed to get included in the bill a provision allowing the United States Tariff Commission to modify tariff duties in the future. Hoover expected that this provision would put an effective end to congressional tariff making. With Hoover's signature on June 17, the bill went into effect with the new fiscal year that began on July 1, 1930.

CANADIAN RETALIATION

The hope of proponents of Smoot-Hawley that the act would lead to increased income and employment in the United States was dependent upon its not leading to excessive foreign retaliation against American products. Most of the United States' major trading partners did increase tariffs following the passage of Smoot-Hawley; but whether these increases were mainly in response to the U.S. action is difficult to know with certainty. In some cases, including that of Canada, at that time the largest trading partner of the United States, it seems reasonably clear that tariff increases were enacted in large part as retaliation for Smoot-Hawley. In other cases, the role of retaliation is less clear. This is true of Great Britain, at that time the second largest trading partner of the United States.

At the time Hoover took office, the Canadian government, under Liberal Prime Minister William Lyon Mackenzie King, was committed to lower tariffs. There is some reason to believe that King might have planned to include tariff reductions in his budget announcement of March, 1929, but this possibility was foreclosed by anticipation of Hoover's announcement of the special session of Congress to consider tariff increases.

As time passed and the likelihood of general tariff increases in the United States grew, King came under pressure from Conservative Party leader Richard Bedford Bennett. Bennett argued in favor of using tariffs to shift Canada's economic relations away from the United States and toward the British Empire. In a widely publicized speech in November, 1929, King warned that if tariff increases adversely affecting Canada were passed by the U.S. Congress, some reaction would surely follow. King still had hopes that either no new tariff bill would make it through Congress or that if one did pass, Hoover would somehow manage to shield Canada from its worst effects.

By the spring of 1930, King felt obliged to include in his budget tariff adjustments that reflected the changing political realities. The duties on 270 goods imported from within the British Empire were reduced, and there were small increases in duties on certain imports from the United States. The budget included countervailing duties on sixteen products, under which the Canadian duty would be raised to match any increase in duties on those products levied by other countries.

Perhaps buoyed by the initially favorable domestic response to the new budget, King announced that a general election would be held in July. Most observers believed the key issue in the campaign to be the proper Canadian response to the Smoot-Hawley Tariff

Act. Bennett accused the United States of attempting to steal the jobs of Canadian workers through tariff increases and reiterated his view that Canada should adjust its tariff structure so as to encourage trade with other countries in the British Empire at the expense of the United States. On the defensive, King attempted to play up what he claimed was the alarm in the United States over the mild tariff increases enacted by Canada in May.

Although many expected the election to be close, the Conservatives won a large victory, securing their only majority in the Canadian parliament in any election between 1911 and 1958. The key to the size of the Conservative victory was their unexpectedly strong showing in Quebec, where resentment against increased U.S. duties on dairy products was very strong, and the provinces of Alberta, Manitoba, and Saskatchewan, where increased U.S. duties on wheat led to a strong political reaction. Once in power, Bennett fulfilled his promise to increase duties on U.S. products and reorient Canadian trade toward the British Empire.

The tariff war with Canada cost U.S. exporters dearly. In 1929, 18 percent of U.S. merchandise exports had gone to Canada, and the United States had enjoyed a $445 million merchandise trade surplus with Canada. By 1933, only 13 percent of U.S. merchandise exports were going to Canada, and the United States ran a surplus of only $26 million with Canada.

BRITISH RESPONSE

The reaction of the British government and public to the Smoot-Hawley bill is somewhat difficult to disentangle from general developments in British politics at the time. From the middle of the nineteenth century, Britain had been strongly committed to free trade. As the Great Depression began, Prime Minister Ramsay MacDonald's Labor government attempted to maintain this commitment to free trade. Rising unemployment, however, helped to reinforce those calling for a turn toward protectionism. The passage of Smoot-Hawley further undermined support for free trade, particularly within the Conservative Party.

The Conservative Party had been home to a substantial protectionist wing dating back at least to Joseph Chamberlain's campaign in 1903 to raise British tariffs and to negotiate reciprocal tariff preferences with members of the British Empire. The majority view within the party, probably reflecting the majority view of the British public, remained in favor of free trade. The Conservative defeat in the 1929 general election was attributed by some to the party's failure to adopt an aggressive protectionist policy as an offset to the Labor Party's natural appeal during a time of rising unemployment. It was only following the passage of Smoot-Hawley and increases in tariffs in several British dominions, notably Canada, that Stanley Baldwin, the leader of the Conservative Party, came out in favor of increased British tariffs. Baldwin argued that although he remained opposed to protectionism, he had become convinced that only by raising its own tariffs would Britain obtain the bargaining power necessary to successfully negotiate a multilateral reduction in tariff rates.

In September, 1931, Ramsay MacDonald, having lost much of the support of his own party, formed a coalition government, relying heavily on Conservative support. Running on a platform that included pledges of higher tariffs, the government won a large victory in October, 1931. A general increase in tariffs was then passed by the House of Commons in February, 1932. This was followed by further tariff increases following the Ottawa conference of July, 1932, at which Britain and its dominions and colonies agreed to further tariff increases on non-Empire imports and reductions in tariffs on imports from within the British Empire.

The net negative impact on the U.S. economy from the unraveling of the world trade system in the face of retaliatory tariff increases was considerable. Measured in today's dollars, the United States had a surplus of exports of goods and services over imports of goods and services of approximately 5 billion. By 1933, this had become a deficit of nearly 2 billion. The League of Nations estimated that the volume of world trade declined in real terms by more than 65 percent between 1929 and 1933. Not until the General Agreement on Tariffs and Trade was successfully negotiated in 1947 was the world trading system restored to a sound footing. Willis Hawley and Reed Smoot were both defeated in the 1932 elections.

Anthony Patrick O'Brien

SOURCES FOR FURTHER STUDY
Ball, Stuart. *Baldwin and the Conservative Party: The Crisis of 1929-1931.* New Haven Connecticut: Yale University Press, 1988.

Eichengreen, Barry, and Roger Ransom, eds. "The Political Economy of the Smoot-Hawley Tariff." In *Research in Economic History.* Vol. 12. Westport, Conn.: JAI Press, 1989.

Hoover, Herbert. *The Memoirs of Herbert Hoover: The Cabinet and the Presidency, 1920-1933.* New York: Macmillan, 1952.

Jones, Joseph M., Jr. *Tariff Retaliation Repercussions of the Hawley-Smoot Bill.* Philadelphia: University of Pennsylvania Press, 1934.

Kindleberger, Charles P. *The World in Depression, 1929-1939.* Berkeley: University of California Press, 1975.

Pastor, Robert A. *Congress and the Politics of U.S. Foreign Policy, 1929-1976.* Berkeley: University of California Press, 1980.

Schattschneider, E. E. *Politics, Pressures, and the Tariff.* New York: Prentice Hall, 1935.

SEE ALSO: Dingley Tariff (1897); Payne-Aldrich Tariff Act (1909); General Agreement on Tariffs and Trade of 1947 (1947).

HOOVER-STIMSON DOCTRINE

ALSO KNOWN AS: Stimson Doctrine
DATE: Issued January 7, 1932
CATEGORIES: Asia or Asian Americans; Foreign Relations

The United States expressed its moral disapproval of the Japanese aggression against China but failed to deter that aggression.

In the late 1920's, some Japanese leaders, especially junior officers of the Kwantung Army stationed in Manchuria, favored expansion. They viewed China's growing nationalism and its progress toward unification under the Nationalist (Kuomintang) government with fear. Their solution was to seize Chinese territory before China became sufficiently strong to defend itself. This policy was especially favored by officers of the Kwantung Army, a unit of the Japanese army created in 1905 to safeguard Japanese imperialist interests in its leased territories and railroads in China's northeastern provinces, known in the West as Manchuria. Officers of the Kwantung

Army were prominent in the Black Dragon Society, an ultranationalist officers' organization dedicated to expansion on the Asian mainland. Capitalizing on the devastating floods along the Yangtze River Valley, the communist revolt, and other domestic problems in 1931, Kwantung Army officers, defying an order from the Japanese cabinet to desist, attacked a dozen cities in Manchuria simultaneously on the night of September 18, 1931. Called the September 18, or Manchurian, incident, this was the first shot that culminated in World War II in Asia.

CALLS FOR ENDING JAPANESE AGGRESSION

Militarily unready, the Chinese government felt that resistance would have given Japan an excuse to widen its aggression and therefore would have been suicidal. Instead, it appealed to the League of Nations, and to the United States under the 1928 Kellogg-Briand Pact. This pact, cosponsored by then-U.S. secretary of state Frank Kellogg and signed by the United States, China, Japan, and sixty-one other nations, renounced aggressive war as an instrument of national policy. Repeated League of Nations resolutions ordering Japan to halt its advances, agreed to by the Japanese cabinet, were ignored by the Kwantung Army, which completed conquering Manchuria early in 1932.

U.S. RESPONSE

In response, the United States secretary of state Henry Stimson announced on January 7, 1932, a nonrecognition doctrine, which stated that the United States would not recognize territorial changes created by means contrary to the Kellogg-Briand Pact:

> [T]he American Government . . . cannot admit the legality of any situation de facto nor does it intend to recognize any treaty or agreement entered into between [the Japanese and the Chinese governments] . . . which may impair the treaty rights of the United States [or] which may be brought about by means contrary to the covenants and obligations of the Pact of Paris of August 27, 1928 [the Kellogg-Briand Pact].

This Hoover-Stimson Doctrine, also known simply as the Stimson Doctrine, became the cornerstone of U.S. policy in Asia in response to Japanese aggression. In 1932 the League of Nations created a special commission headed by British diplomat Lord Lytton to study the Manchurian incident. The ensuing Lytton Report (1933) charged Japan with aggression, declared the Japanese puppet state of Manchukuo a sham, and demanded that Japan restore Manchuria to China. The report was unanimously endorsed by the League Assembly, and Japan immediately resigned from the league.

Beset by the effects of the Great Depression and by isolationism, the United States did not attempt to force Japan to give up its conquests and lent no more than moral support to China. Burdened by neither military threat nor economic sanctions, Japan ignored international condemnation and continued its aggressions against China and other nations. No nation, except Japan's later Axis allies Germany and Italy, recognized Japan's conquests, and the situation eventually resulted in World War II.

Jiu-Hwa Lo Upshur

Sources for Further Study

Christopher, James W. *Conflict in the Far East: American Diplomacy in China from 1928-33.* Leiden, The Netherlands: E. J. Brill, 1950.

Morison, Elting E. *Turmoil and Tradition: A Study of the Life and Times of Henry L. Stimson.* Boston: Houghton Mifflin, 1960.

Rappaport, Armin. *Henry L. Stimson and Japan, 1931-1933.* Chicago: University of Chicago Press, 1963.

Smith, Sara R. *The Manchurian Crisis, 1931-1932: A Tragedy in International Relations.* New York: Columbia University Press, 1948.

Stimson, Henry L. *The Far Eastern Crisis: Recollections and Observations.* New York: Council on Foreign Relations, 1936.

Yoshihashi, Takehiko. *Conspiracy at Mukden: The Rise of the Japanese Military.* New Haven, Conn.: Yale University Press, 1963.

SEE ALSO: Kellogg-Briand Pact (1928).

NORRIS-LA GUARDIA ACT

DATE: March 23, 1932
U.S. STATUTES AT LARGE: 47 Stat. 70
U.S. CODE: 29 § 101
CATEGORIES: Labor and Employment

> *By curbing the use of injunctions in labor disputes, extending unions'*
> *exemption from antitrust laws, and prohibiting "yellow dog" con-*
> *tracts, the Norris-La Guardia Act made it easier to organize and*
> *operate labor unions.*

As industry developed rapidly in the United States in the late nineteenth century, widespread efforts were undertaken to organize labor unions and to engage employers in collective bargaining.
Many employers resisted these efforts. The Norris-La Guardia Act
of March 23, 1932, was passed in order to free labor unions from
antiunion actions involving three related elements: the Sherman
Antitrust Act, the injunction, and the "yellow dog" contract.

ANTIUNION STRATEGIES

One instrument for such resistance was the Sherman Antitrust Act
of 1890, which outlawed "every contract . . . or conspiracy, in re-
straint of trade or commerce. . . ." Union actions such as strikes and
boycotts could be penalized through employer lawsuits for triple
damages, as in the Danbury Hatters' (*Loewe v. Lawlor*) case of 1908.
Antiunion employers often were able to obtain court injunctions
against union actions. An injunction is a court order primarily intended to forbid someone from taking actions that could cause severe injury to another. Courts had wide latitude in issuing injunctions. Violating an injunction could bring the offender under
severe penalties for contempt of court, again with wide discretion
for the court.

   Another antiunion instrument was the so-called "yellow dog"
contract, whereby a worker was required, as a condition of employment, to explicitly agree not to join a union and to renounce any
current union membership. Efforts by legislatures to outlaw such
contracts had been overruled by the United States Supreme Court.
A company whose workers had signed such contracts could seek an

injunction against any union organizer who might try to persuade workers to breach their contracts.

THE CLAYTON ACT

The Clayton Act of 1914 ostensibly established the principle that the existence and operation of labor unions were not illegal under the Sherman Act. Further, the law forbade the federal courts to issue injunctions against a long list of union activities, vaguely worded but clearly referring to strikes and boycotts.

Union jubilation that the Clayton Act would expand labor's scope of organized activity was short-lived, however. In 1917, the Supreme Court held in the *Hitchman Coal Company v. Mitchell* case that issuing an injunction was an appropriate remedy against a union organizer trying to persuade workers to breach their "yellow dog" contracts. Even more striking was the *Duplex Printing Company v. Deering* case of 1921. The Duplex company had attempted to obtain court action against a system of union boycotts intended to force it to become unionized. Federal district and appeals courts refused to uphold the Duplex claim, but the Supreme Court overruled them in 1921. The decision held that the union's actions could be in violation of the Sherman Act and did not constitute a "labor dispute" protected by the specific terms of the Clayton Act. Furthermore, issuing an injunction was appropriate to prevent harm to the employer. In a dissenting opinion, Justice Louis D. Brandeis pointed out that the majority opinion appeared to deny the intent of the Clayton Act.

A strong antiunion trend persisted in Supreme Court decisions during the 1920's. In 1921, the Court upheld use of an injunction against picketing when there were elements of intimidation and when "outsiders" to the direct dispute were involved, in *American Steel Foundries v. Tri-City Central Trades Council*. Also in 1921, the Court held unconstitutional an Arizona statute establishing the right to peaceful picketing in *Truax v. Corrigan*. The case of *Bedford Cut Stone Company v. Journeymen Stone Cutters' Association* (1927) involved concerted refusal by union stonecutters to work on the products of a nonunion firm. The Court held that this action could be considered a violation of the Sherman Antitrust Act and that an injunction was an appropriate form of relief. In a vigorous dissent, Justice Brandeis pointed out the lack of parallel between the union activities and the business monopoly actions against which the antitrust laws were directed.

DEPRESSION YEARS

The prosperous conditions of the 1920's did not produce much union militancy; in fact, union membership showed a declining trend. After 1929, the economy headed into severe depression. As workers faced wage reductions, layoffs, or reduced hours, many perceived an increased need for the protection of union members and collective bargaining. Workers brought increasing political pressure to overrule the antiunion legal doctrines. In Congress, their cause was taken up by Senator George W. Norris, a Republican progressive from Nebraska. With the aid of a panel of distinguished labor law experts, including Felix Frankfurter of Harvard Law School, Norris drafted a bill to achieve the intent of the Clayton Act. Fiorello Henry La Guardia of New York, also a progressive, introduced the bill into the House of Representatives. As the worsening depression created a sense of panic among many legislators who became eager to show concern for workers, the Norris-La Guardia Act passed both houses of Congress by overwhelming margins and became law on March 23, 1932.

PROVISIONS OF LA GUARDIA

Sections 3 and 4 of the law stated that contracts whereby workers agreed not to join a union were not to be enforced and could not be the basis for injunctions. Section 4 directed federal courts not to issue injunctions against concerted refusals to work (that is, strikes), joining or remaining in a union, giving financial or other aid to a union or strike, publicizing a labor dispute by picketing or other methods, or assembling peaceably to organize or promote a labor dispute. Further, such actions were not to be held to constitute violations of the antitrust laws. Section 13 gave a broad definition of a labor dispute, allowing disputes to involve persons other than an employer and his or her workers, thus broadening the range of union activities protected by the law. Section 6 provided that no union officer or member could be held liable for financial damages for the separate and independent actions of other union members or officers.

The Norris-La Guardia Act removed obstacles to the formation of unions and to their activities, particularly organizing, striking, and boycotting. The law did not commit the government directly to the promotion of unions. Such promotion, however, was soon forthcoming. After the election of 1932, Franklin D. Roosevelt's New Deal swept aside the Republican administration and many Republican members of Congress, including La Guardia. One of the first acts of the New Deal was passage of the National Industrial Recovery Act (NIRA) of 1933.

Its section 7a guaranteed workers the right to form and join unions of their own choosing and obliged employers to bargain with those unions. Similar provisions were contained in the Railway Labor Act of 1934. When the NIRA was held unconstitutional in 1935, Congress enacted the National Labor Relations Act (Wagner Act) of 1935. This affirmed a "right" to unionize and created the National Labor Relations Board (NLRB) to make this right effective. Whereas the Norris-La Guardia Act merely protected union activities from damage suits and injunctions, the Wagner Act protected unions from a long list of "unfair" labor practices. These included employer interference with union organizing activities or union operations, discrimination against union members, and refusal to bargain collectively "in good faith" with certified unions. The NLRB was authorized to conduct elections to determine if a group of workers should be represented by a union.

EFFECT ON LABOR RELATIONS
As a consequence of this legislation, much of the focus in labor relations shifted away from the private lawsuits with which the Norris-La Guardia Act was concerned. Union organizers undertook vigorous campaigns for new members, sparked by the Congress of Industrial Organizations (CIO) under the leadership of John L. Lewis. Union membership, which had fallen below three million in 1933, passed ten million in 1941.

Organizing efforts continued to meet with strong opposition, and employers still tried to enlist the courts to assist them, without much success. In 1938, the Supreme Court upheld the constitutionality of the Norris-La Guardia Act in the case of *Lauf v. E. G. Shinner and Company.* The Court affirmed the legality of union picketing activities directed against a nonunion employer. In the case of *Apex Hosiery Company v. Leader,* the Supreme Court in 1940 refused to consider a union sitdown strike to be a violation of the antitrust laws. The case arose from a violent incident in 1937 when union members broke into the company's plant and physically took possession of it. The Court noted that the union's actions were clearly unlawful but argued that the appropriate remedies lay in channels other than the antitrust laws. In the case of *United States v. Hutcheson* (1941), the Supreme Court again refused to permit antitrust prosecution to be brought against union officials. The carpenters' union that was the target of the lawsuit was trying to use a boycott to induce Anheuser-Busch Brewing Company to reverse a decision that certain work should be performed by machinists. It was a no-win situation for the company, since it could be similarly attacked by the machinists if it reversed its decision. The Supreme Court simply affirmed that the union actions should not be viewed as a violation of the Sherman Antitrust Act.

The great spread of unionization in the late 1930's helps explain why hourly wage rates in manufacturing increased about 30 percent between 1935 and 1941 at a time when more than 10 percent of workers remained unemployed. Some economists noted that while union workers were benefiting, their gains were raising business costs and thus slowing the rise of job openings for the unemployed. Union membership continued to increase during World War II, but developments led many observers to believe that unions held too much power. Strikes by coal miners led by John L. Lewis during the war were particularly damaging to the image of unions. In November, 1946, Lewis provoked a confrontation with the government, which was then nominally operating the mines under wartime legislation. A federal court issued an injunction against a work stoppage by the union and then imposed heavy fines on Lewis and the union when they did not comply. In March, 1947, the Supreme Court upheld the injunction, ruling that the Norris-La Guardia Act did not apply when the government was in the role of employer. In 1945, the Supreme Court established that some labor union actions could be considered to violate the Sherman Antitrust Act, if the union acted in collusion with employers in a manner that promoted monopoly conditions in markets for business products.

The belief that unions had gained too much power ultimately led to adoption of the Taft-Hartley Act in 1947. That act prohibited a long list of "unfair" practices by unions. By that time, many of the issues confronted by the Norris-La Guardia Act had faded from significance. Under the protection of the Wagner Act, unions had been organized and certified in most of the areas in which workers wanted them. "Yellow dog" contracts had disappeared, and harassment of union organizers had diminished. A major consequence of the Norris-La Guardia Act was to shift the bulk of litigation involving labor union activities to state courts. Picketing and related activities associated with strikes and other labor disputes often primarily involved state laws, local ordinances, and local police. Private business firms largely lost the opportunity to bring civil lawsuits to halt or penalize nonviolent strikes and other labor union activities.

Paul B. Trescott

SOURCES FOR FURTHER STUDY

Bernstein, Irving. *The Lean Years: A History of the American Worker, 1920-1933*. Boston: Houghton Mifflin, 1960

_____. *Turbulent Years: A History of the American Worker, 1933-1941*. Boston: Houghton Mifflin, 1970.

Dougherty, Carroll R. *Labor Problems in American Industry*. Boston: Houghton Mifflin, 1941.

Gregory, Charles O., and Harold A. Katz. *Labor and the Law*. 3d ed. New York: W. W. Norton, 1979.

Kintner, Earl W., ed. *Federal Antitrust Laws and Related Statutes: A Legislative History*. 11 vols. Buffalo, N.Y.: William S. Hein, 1978, 1982-1985.

Lieberman, Elias. *Unions Before the Bar*. New York: Harper and Brothers, 1950.

Limpus, Lowell M., and Burr Leyson. *This Man La Guardia*. New York: E. P. Dutton, 1938.

Mason, Alpheus T. *Brandeis: A Free Man's Life*. New York: Viking Press, 1946.

Norris, George W. *Fighting Liberal*. New York: Macmillan, 1945.

SEE ALSO: Sherman Antitrust Act (1890); Clayton Antitrust Act (1914); Railway Labor Act (1926); National Labor Relations Act (1935); Fair Labor Standards Act (1938); Labor-Management Relations Act (1947).

TWENTIETH AMENDMENT

ALSO KNOWN AS: Lame-Duck Amendment
DATE: Ratified January 23, 1933; certified February 6, 1933
U.S. STATUTES AT LARGE: 47 Stat. 745
CATEGORIES: Constitutional Law; Government Procedure and Organization

The Twentieth Amendment addressed an outdated provision of the Constitution that had led, in modern times, to "lame-duck" congressional sessions.

Under the original Constitution, Congress was to meet on the first Monday in December; newly elected members did not take office until the following March. Consequently, unless a special session were called, new members of Congress did not normally begin their service until the next December session—thirteen months after their election. These dates were undoubtedly originally established to meet transportation and communication problems of the late eighteenth century. The result was that every two years there was a "lame-duck" session of Congress in which members who had been defeated for reelection in November continued their service until March. Outrageous pork-barrel legislation was commonly passed during these lame-duck sessions: Having nothing to lose, defeated representatives would exercise their power during the year following an election to ensure appropriations for their favorite projects. Congress's work during the session was frequently characterized by "logrolling" (vote trading) and, in the Senate, prolonged filibusters.

The amendment was the last of the great constitutional reforms promoted by the Progressive movement, the Sixteenth through Twentieth Amendments. It was introduced by Senator George W. Norris of Nebraska. Congress proposed it to the state legislatures in March, 1932; eventually it was ratified by all the states, but it achieved the constitutionally required three-fourths early in 1933 and was proclaimed as the Twentieth Amendment by the secretary of state on February 6, 1933.

PROVISIONS

The main thrust of the Amendment is found in its first two sections, which adjust the dates of the terms of the president, senators, and representatives. The first section changes the dates of the terms. Inauguration of a new president and vice president was moved from March to January 20, thus limiting the amount of time to be served by an outgoing administration. The terms of senators and representatives were set to begin or end at noon on January 3. The second section of the amendment does away with the December session of Congress altogether. Under its terms Congress is required to meet at least once a year beginning on January 3.

Sections 3 and 4 of the amendment provide for the case of the death of a president-elect and give Congress the power to decide what will happen should neither the president-elect nor the vice-president-elect have qualified by the beginning of the next presidential term. These sections also authorize Congress to establish by law the presidential succession in the event of the deaths of both the president and vice president. Except under the most extraordinary, and perhaps dangerous, conditions, the later provisions of the Twenty-fifth Amendment, which allow the president to nominate a new vice president should the latter office become vacant, diminish the importance of this part of the Twentieth Amendment.

The Twentieth Amendment successfully did away with the evils of the prolonged lame-duck session of Congress. The service of defeated members of Congress lasts from election day until adjournment at the end of the session in December. It is further shortened by the Thanksgiving and Christmas recesses. As a practical matter, more than 90 percent of congressional incumbents are returned every election day anyway, so the lame-duck session has now become largely a phenomenon of the past.

Robert Jacobs

SOURCES FOR FURTHER STUDY

Corwin, Edward S., ed. *Constitution of the United States of America.* Washington, D.C.: Government Printing Office, 1953.

Farber, Daniel A., and Suzanna Sherry. *History of the American Constitution.* Belmont, Calif.: Wadsworth, 1999.

Peltason, J. W. *Corwin and Peltason's Understanding the Constitution.* 14th ed. New York: Harcourt Brace, 1997.

Vile, John R. *Encyclopedia of Constitutional Amendments, Proposed Amendments, and Amending Issues, 1789-1995.* Santa Barbara, Calif: ABC-CLIO, 1996.

SEE ALSO: Twelfth Amendment (1804); Presidential Succession Act (1947); Twenty-fifth Amendment (1967).

HUNDRED DAYS LEGISLATION

DATE: March-June, 1933

CATEGORIES: Agriculture; Banking, Money, and Finance; Business, Commerce, and Trade; Energy; Health and Welfare; Housing; Labor and Employment

Fifteen major laws were passed during the hundred days following Franklin Roosevelt's rise to the presidency as legislators negotiated compromises to address the economic and social emergency created by the Great Depression.

On November 8, 1932, Franklin D. Roosevelt was elected president of the United States. Few people knew what to expect from Roosevelt, a consummate politician who once described himself as "a Christian and a Democrat." One thing, however, was clear: Immediate action of some kind was imperative to stop the nation from slipping further into economic chaos. Perhaps out of desperation, the people were impressed with the expressions of confidence embodied in Roosevelt's inaugural address and his promise of action. The problem facing the new administration was how to sustain this sense of movement and confidence in a new order.

EMERGENCY COMPROMISE

On March 9, 1933, a special session of Congress met and sat until June 16. During that period, later to be known as the Hundred

Days, fifteen major resolutions became law and the United States underwent a revolutionary change. The legislation was the product of no single person or particular group. The essence of the program was emergency compromise, with Roosevelt standing above the various interests and masterminding them.

BANKING LEGISLATION

The immediate problem was to do something about the paralyzed banking system and to restore business confidence. As a preliminary measure, Roosevelt issued an executive order on March 5, proclaiming a national bank holiday. During the holiday, cash from the Federal Reserve replenished bank vaults. The closing of the banks had the therapeutic effect of convincing many people that, having reached rock-bottom, the situation had to improve. Roosevelt submitted to Congress on March 9, 1933, an Emergency Banking Relief Act, which was passed immediately. The act gave the president power over gold transactions, outlawed hoarding, and provided for the gradual reopening of the banks under the supervision of the secretary of the Treasury. This was followed the next day by the Economy Act, which, despite threatened congressional revolt, reduced federal expenditures drastically by cutting government salaries and veterans' payments. On March 12, Roosevelt gave his first radio address in a series that came to be known as "fireside chats." He emphasized that most of the banks were sound and would reopen in a few days. When the banks did reopen, people rushed to deposit money rather than to make withdrawals. The banking crisis subsided.

Roosevelt next attempted to eradicate some abuses in the nation's banking and financial practices. The Securities Act of May 27, 1933, called for close supervision by the Federal Trade Commission of the issue of new stock, and held stock sellers liable if they provided false information. A complementary measure was the Glass-Steagall Banking Act of June 16, 1933, which differentiated between commercial banking and investment banking. An important corollary of this act was the creation of the Federal Deposit Insurance Corporation (FDIC) to insure individual bank deposits up to five thousand dollars. The insurance on deposits was a significant step in restoring public confidence and bringing currency back into the banks.

AGRICULTURAL LEGISLATION

Another pressing problem was agriculture. In preparing his legislation, Roosevelt relied heavily upon the advice of his secretary of agriculture, Henry A. Wallace. A former farm editor and horticulturist, Wallace advocated a domestic allotment plan designed to combat overproduction and declining prices by restricting acreage and leasing to the government land left idle. The scale of payments was aimed at establishing parity between farm prices and the cost of manufactured goods, based on figures for the years 1909 to 1914. Not all farming interests accepted this idea of production control; many demanded cheap money as a remedy. When the Agricultural Adjustment Act (AAA) was finally signed into law on May 12, 1933, it provided for various other options to control production besides government leasing of idle land. Additional New Deal legislation provided for loans through the Farm Credit Administration, aid to very poor farmers with the Resettlement Administration, and a means for all rural areas to receive power through the Rural Electrification Administration.

THE NEW DEAL

The unemployed and the middle class also received benefits under the new legislation, which later became known collectively as the New Deal. The unemployed were helped through the Civilian Conservation Corps (CCC), one of Roosevelt's most popular measures. The act, passed on March 29, 1933, provided for a civilian army of young men to work in reforestation and conservation projects. In the nine-year life span of the CCC, a total of 250,000 jobless men between the ages of eighteen and twenty-five were given an opportunity to move forward in life. Enactment of the Federal Emergency Relief Act on May 12, 1933, and the subsequent creation of the Federal Emergency Relief Administration (FERA) provided for direct federal grants to states for purposes of relief and brought about a cooperative effort between federal and state agencies. FERA, headed by Harry Hopkins, promoted the idea of work relief instead of the "dole" (as welfare was often called at the time) and stipulated that there would be no discrimination of any kind concerning recipients.

To meet the problems of the middle-class homeowners facing mortgage foreclosures, the Home Owners Refinancing Act, passed in June, 1933, provided for the exchange of defaulted mortgages for guaranteed government bonds, but it appeared to give more assistance to mortgage companies than to hard-pressed homeowners. Homeowners benefited later, when it became government policy to refinance loans where possible instead of taking possession of homes.

One of the most successful programs of the Roosevelt administration was the enactment of the Tennessee Valley Authority Act (TVA) on May 18, 1933. The act provided for a regional authority that would build dams designed to control disastrous flooding in the states of the Tennessee River basin, bring electricity to rural areas, and replant forests. Eventually, the TVA became the largest utility company in the United States.

LABOR LEGISLATION
When organized labor demanded action to relieve unemployment, Senator Hugo L. Black of Alabama proposed a thirty-hour work week, and his proposal received considerable support from labor interests. Roosevelt regarded the bill proposed by Black to be both unconstitutional and unworkable, but he had to meet the growing demand for relief by industry and industrial workers. He therefore ordered his advisers to prepare an omnibus labor and industry measure to attack the root causes of depression in those fields. A draft was prepared under the direction of Raymond Moley, economist and assistant secretary of state. The passage of the National Industrial Recovery Act (NIRA) on June 16, 1933, provided for industrial self-government through the use of universal codes regulating production, wages, and hours, but negated enforcement of the antitrust laws. Although the program was short-lived, these codes benefited nearly four million women workers through wage and hour provisions. The program did not, however, set up codes for agricultural or domestic laborers, three-fourths of whom were African American.

The Roosevelt administration hoped that the act would eliminate inefficiency and raise prices. The provision that all codes must be submitted for government approval pleased advocates of government control, such as Rexford Guy Tugwell, a member of Roosevelt's Brain Trust—a group of distinguished individuals serving as advisers to the president. Organized labor received legal guarantees that all codes would have to provide for collective bargaining before they could be recognized. Finally, the unemployed were assured of aid from a vast program of public works connected with the NIRA and financed from additional money through increased federal spending.

UNPRECEDENTED ACHIEVEMENT

On June 16, 1933, Congress adjourned after its historic session. Never in the nation's history had so much new legislation been enacted in so short a time. With Roosevelt's support from both houses, bills originating from the president's White House office were passed nearly every day in order to give the country help during the emergency of the Depression. The hasty legislation that was adopted during the Hundred Days helps to explain why so many measures subsequently had to be drastically amended or abandoned altogether.

George Q. Flynn, updated by
Marilyn Elizabeth Perry

SOURCES FOR FURTHER STUDY

Davis, Kenneth S. *FDR: The New Deal Years, 1933-1937.* New York: Random House, 1986.

Freidel, Frank. *Franklin D. Roosevelt: A Rendezvous with Destiny.* Boston: Little, Brown, 1990.

Leuchtenburg, William E. *Franklin D. Roosevelt and the New Deal, 1932-1940.* New York: Harper & Row, 1963.

Morgan, Ted. *FDR: A Biography.* New York: Simon & Schuster, 1985.

Schlesinger, Arthur Meier. *The Coming of the New Deal.* Vol. 2 in *The Age of Roosevelt.* Boston: Houghton Mifflin, 1959.

Sitkoff, Harvard, ed. *Fifty Years Later: The New Deal Evaluated.* Philadelphia: Temple University Press, 1985.

SEE ALSO: Tennessee Valley Authority Act (1933); Banking Act of 1933 (1933); National Industrial Recovery Act (1933).

GOOD NEIGHBOR POLICY

DATE: Issued March 4, 1933
CATEGORIES: Foreign Relations

> *A new articulation of U.S. relations with Latin American nations replaced military interventionism with mutual respect and cooperation.*

In his first inaugural address, President Franklin D. Roosevelt promised that the United States would conduct itself in international relations as a good neighbor. After he applied the term specifically to relations with Latin America and pledged his opposition to armed intervention, the phrase "good neighbor" came to be identified with his Latin American foreign policy.

Following the Spanish-American War (1898), the United States intervened militarily in Central America and the Caribbean. Asserting its right to exercise a police power in the Americas under the 1904 Roosevelt Corollary to the Monroe Doctrine, U.S. presidents sent troops into Cuba, Haiti, the Dominican Republic, Nicaragua, Mexico, and Panama to stabilize conditions, prevent European intervention, and protect U.S. lives and property. After a brief incursion in 1909, a contingent of U.S. Marines was stationed in Nicaragua almost continuously from 1912 to 1933.

LATIN AMERICANS SEEK A NONINTERVENTION RESOLUTION

Seeking to prevent future interventions, several Latin American jurists proposed the adoption of doctrines against intervention or the use of force or diplomatic recognition to protect the interests of foreign nations in Latin America or to change Latin American governments. At the Sixth Inter-American Conference, held in Havana, Cuba, in 1928, the Latin American representatives tried, but failed, to obtain U.S. support for a nonintervention resolution. There was also increasing opposition in the United States to the policy of sending troops to protect U.S. interests in Central America and the Caribbean.

In 1928, president-elect Herbert Hoover made a series of goodwill trips to Latin America, and in 1930 he repudiated the Roosevelt Corollary to the Monroe Doctrine. Resisting pressure to intervene to protect U.S. investors, Hoover prepared to withdraw troops from Haiti and removed the marines from Nicaragua. His goodwill gestures were undermined, however, by the Great Depression and the high duties imposed by the Smoot-Hawley Tariff Act of 1930.

ROOSEVELT ISSUES THE POLICY

On March 4, 1933, Franklin D. Roosevelt, in his inaugural address, declared that in foreign policy he wished to "dedicate this nation to the policy of the good neighbor . . . who respects himself and . . . the rights of others." After his inauguration, Roosevelt undertook specific measures to improve relations with Latin America and stimulate economic recovery. In 1933, at the Seventh International Conference of American States, in Montevideo, Uruguay, Secretary of State Cordell Hull accepted the principle of nonintervention and signed a convention declaring that no state had the right to intervene in the internal and external affairs of other countries, with a vague reservation. Hull also proposed the reduction of tariffs and trade agreements to stimulate trade. In 1936, at an inter-American conference in Buenos Aires, the United States signed an expanded resolution renouncing intervention and agreed to the principle of consultation in the event of a war between American nations or an external threat to the peace of the Americas.

CUBA

In 1933, Roosevelt had also dispatched Assistant Secretary of State Sumner Welles to a revolutionary Cuba, where Welles orchestrated the resignation of dictator Gerardo Machado. When Welles's personally designated successor was overthrown by a sergeant's revolt, however, Welles persuaded Roosevelt to withhold recognition from the nationalistic government of Ramón Grau San Martín. With U.S. naval vessels offshore, this policy of nonrecognition encouraged a second revolt, bringing to office a series of presidents controlled by Colonel Fulgencio Batista y Zaldívar.

Despite clear interference in Cuban politics, President Roosevelt had refrained from using armed force in Cuba, and in 1934 the United States and Cuba agreed to the removal of the Platt Amendment (1903), which, following the Spanish-American War, asserted the U.S. right both to intervene in Cuba to protect Cuban independence and to maintain a military base on the island. Similar agreements were concluded with Panama and the Dominican Republic.

The United States and Cuba also signed reciprocal trade agreements that lowered duties on Cuban sugar, guaranteed access to the U.S. market for Cuban agricultural exports, and reduced duties on hundreds of U.S.-manufactured goods exported to Cuba.

OIL INTERESTS

When Bolivia, Mexico, and Venezuela threatened to nationalize U.S. oil companies in 1937 and 1938, the Good Neighbor Policy faced a direct challenge. President Roosevelt not only resisted the pressure to intervene but also accepted the right of these countries to seize the assets of the companies or increase government revenues from their operations, as long as they made immediate and just compensation. Concerned about the war in Europe, Roosevelt also continued economic assistance and signed new trade agreements with Bolivia and Mexico after a brief suspension. By refusing to intervene to protect the oil companies, Roosevelt demonstrated his adherence to the principle of nonintervention and the concept of the Good Neighbor. In addition to renouncing the use of military force in the Caribbean and Central America, the United States provided credits to struggling countries through the newly created Export-Import Bank and negotiated a series of reciprocal trade agreements to lower barriers to trade between the United States and Latin America.

LONG-RANGE IMPACT

Because of its renunciation of intervention and the withdrawal of troops, the Good Neighbor Policy fostered an era of good relations and cooperation between Latin America and the United States on the eve of World War II. In a series of agreements drawn up at prewar conferences, nations of Latin America and the United States agreed to cooperate and form an alliance of mutual protection. Following the attack on Pearl Harbor, all Latin American countries but Argentina joined the Allied war effort, cracking down on Axis sympathizers and supplying strategic materials, airbases, and troops for the Allies. Although Argentina was eventually pressured to declare war on the Axis, the public efforts by the U.S. ambassador to influence or change the government in Buenos Aires not only backfired but also raised the specter of past interventions.

While the unity and cooperation between the United States and Latin America survived the war, the death of Roosevelt on April 12,

1945, and the departure of the architects of the Good Neighbor Policy from the State Department contributed to its demise. Differences between Latin America and the United States had already surfaced at wartime and postwar conferences, and with the advent of the Cold War the United States turned its attention to the economic recovery of Europe and the defense of the West.

After 1945, therefore, Latin American requests for economic cooperation and assistance were ignored until the triumph of Fidel Castro's revolution in Cuba in 1959. When the Central Intelligence Agency conducted a covert action to overthrow the democratically elected government of Guatemala in 1954, it appeared that the United States had abandoned nonintervention in favor of military intervention to protect the interests of a U.S. company, thereby ending the era of the good neighbor. Subsequent attempts to overthrow Castro, U.S. invasions of the Dominican Republic, Grenada, and Panama, the overthrow of Salvador Allende in Chile, and the support of military forces in Central America also violated the principle of nonintervention and the Good Neighbor Policy.

The Good Neighbor Policy did not promote freedom and democracy. After the removal of U.S. troops, the commanders of the national guards trained by the United States seized power and established long-term dictatorships. Since these regimes guaranteed stability, protected foreign investments, and were anticommunist, they received U.S. economic and military aid. Although the reciprocal trade agreements stimulated trade, they also reinforced a dependency on the U.S. market and prevented economic development through diversification. Nevertheless, the Good Neighbor Policy fostered a period of goodwill among the nations of the Western Hemisphere, as well as a sense of political hegemony against potential aggressors. The United States demonstrated its growing role in world affairs and safeguarded its long-range interests in both the economic well-being and political autonomy of its Latin American neighbors.

D. Anthony White

SOURCES FOR FURTHER STUDY

Aguilar Monteverde, Alonso. *Pan-Americanism from Monroe to the Present: A View from the Other Side.* Translated by Asa Zatz. New York: Monthly Review Press, 1968.

Blasier, Cole. *The Hovering Giant: U.S. Responses to Revolutionary Change in Latin America, 1910-1985.* Rev. ed. Pittsburgh: University of Pittsburgh Press, 1985.

Gellman, Irwin F. *Good Neighbor Diplomacy: United States Policies in Latin America, 1933-1945.* Baltimore: The Johns Hopkins University Press, 1979.

LaFeber, Walter. *Inevitable Revolutions: The United States in Central America.* New York: W. W. Norton, 1984.

Wood, Bryce. *The Dismantling of the Good Neighbor Policy.* Austin: University of Texas Press, 1985.

_____. *The Making of the Good Neighbor Policy.* New York: Columbia University Press, 1961.

SEE ALSO: Treaty of Paris (1898); Platt Amendment (1903); Panama Canal Act (1912); Smoot-Hawley Tariff Act (1930); Bretton Woods Agreement (1944); General Agreement on Tariffs and Trade of 1947 (1947); Inter-American Treaty of Reciprocal Assistance (1948); Panama Canal Treaties (1978); North American Free Trade Agreement (1993); General Agreement on Tariffs and Trade of 1994 (1994).

TENNESSEE VALLEY AUTHORITY ACT

DATE: May 18, 1933
U.S. STATUTES AT LARGE: 48 Stat. 58
U.S. CODE: 16 § 831
CATEGORIES: Agriculture; Energy; Environment and Conservation

After decades of debate over government versus private ownership of electric power, Congress created the Tennessee Valley Authority, demonstrating the critical relationship between economic and environmental decisions.

On May 18, 1933, President Franklin D. Roosevelt signed the bill creating the Tennessee Valley Authority (TVA) as the first public regional development agency in the nation. The history of the founding of the TVA is also the history of an enduring national debate over the appropriateness of publicly versus privately owned electric power generation. This controversy illustrates the critical links among economic development, environmental use, and the role of the federal government in economic and environmental decisions.

HYDROELECTRIC POWER, PROGRESSIVISM, AND PINCHOT

The debate originated in the nineteenth century and pitted conservationists and Progressive politicians against the electric power industry. Unregulated capitalist ventures in the 1880's and 1890's had caused widespread environmental destruction for economic gain. The conservation movement emerged, urging that natural resources be regulated by the federal government, that is, that resources be protected and carefully used. Conservation meant controlled economic development in the first half of the twentieth century. Pioneering conservationist Gifford Pinchot developed the concept of multiple-use management first for the conservation of forest resources, then extended the idea to water resources. He argued that private power companies' exploitation of only the hydroelectric power of rivers would waste the rivers' potential for flood control and increased navigation. Conservationists were also motivated by changes in technology. Steam-electric power generated by burning coal or oil had been the main source of power since the 1880's. For the first time, power transmission technology made possible the transport of electric power from remote rivers to cities. Ownership and control of electric power generation was a critical issue because of the enormous amounts of power needed to run the production processes on which the economy depended.

Progressive politicians supported the regulation of industry for environmental and social purposes. Progressives such as Republican senator George W. Norris of Nebraska accepted the utility of the multipurpose use of natural resources. More important, the Progressive politicians feared that if private utilities monopolized hydroelectric resources, they would soon control all industry and, ultimately, the country. Believing that regulatory policy would not be enough, Progressives emphasized the need for competition from public power.

MUSCLE SHOALS

An important focal point for the controversy over public versus private power was the development of the federally owned Muscle Shoals site on the Tennessee River. Near Florence, Alabama, the Tennessee River falls 137 feet in thirty-seven miles. Known as Muscle Shoals, this series of rapids, pools, and rocks constituted an obstruction to navigation. Near the end of the century, the water power potential of the shoals was recognized. In 1906, the Muscle Shoals Hydroelectric Power Company began a ten-year attempt to secure congressional approval for a joint navigation and power project at Muscle Shoals in which the government was to bear a substantial portion of the cost. The company failed. Other private developers also tried and failed to purchase the site from the government.

In 1916, the passage of the National Defense Act mandated that Muscle Shoals was to be used by the government to produce the nitrates needed for explosives in the anticipated war effort. Muscle Shoals was chosen primarily because it was both technically plausible and politically desirable. Additionally, the nitrate plants could be used in peacetime to produce the nitrates required for cheap fertilizer needed by southern farmers.

The Army Corps of Engineers constructed a steam-electric plant to provide power for the nitrate facilities because it was important to begin nitrate production sooner than the time needed to construct a hydroelectric dam would allow. President Woodrow Wilson ordered the dam—eventually named Wilson Dam—built in addition to the steam plants. The nitrate plants never worked, however, and the dam was not completed until 1925. For ten years, little use was made of Wilson Dam's power-producing capacity.

After the war, President Wilson attempted to carry out the mandate of the National Defense Act of 1916 to produce peacetime nitrates for fertilizer, but his plan became enmeshed in the dispute over public versus private operation of hydroelectric plants. The electric power industry expanded rapidly in the decade after the war, and companies were eager to buy Muscle Shoals. In 1921, Henry Ford offered to purchase the site. Several other companies made bids to buy it, but their efforts were consistently foiled by Senator Norris.

POWER GOES PUBLIC

In 1926, Norris proposed his first bill for the multipurpose development of the Tennessee River watershed. Congress passed the bill in 1928, but President Calvin Coolidge pocket-vetoed it. Congress passed Norris's second bill in 1930, but President Herbert Hoover vetoed it amid charges that it was socialist.

The Democratic Party's 1932 platform reflected the public-versus-private-power debate by advocating the conservation, development, and use of the nation's water power in the public interest. Franklin D. Roosevelt took office in March, 1933, with 15 million people unemployed and the banks closed by executive order to prevent collapse. As governor of New York, Roosevelt had taken a strong position on the power question, attempting to increase the effectiveness of state regulation. Soon after taking office, he called Congress into special session and asked for legislation similar to Norris's to create the TVA. He signed the bill as part of his New Deal legislation to bolster economic development and appointed Arthur E. Morgan, a renowned engineer, as the first chairman of the TVA Board of Directors. The TVA was administered by the chairman and two directors who answered to Congress.

The TVA was created as the first public regional development agency charged with planning regional economic development while protecting natural resources in order to create wealth for the people from the resources of the valley. The act defines the TVA region as the area drained by the Tennessee River, which includes parts of Alabama, Georgia, Kentucky, Mississippi, North Carolina, Tennessee, and Virginia. The agency was granted three major powers: to construct dams for flood control and hydroelectric power, to deepen the river channel to aid navigation, and to produce and distribute electricity and fertilizer.

LONG-TERM TRENDS

It has been said that the seeds for the TVA were planted in World War I and fertilized by World War II, but that the agency mushroomed in the Cold War. In the late 1980's, however, many of the TVA's nuclear power plants were idled by technical problems or by protest. The agency's impact has nevertheless been significant in the history of environmental policy in both immediate effects and long-term trends.

The most important immediate effect of the creation of the TVA was the agency's control over the 650-mile-long Tennessee River. Dams constructed for flood control and for hydroelectric power to electrify the rural hinterlands also created large lakes for recreation that brought land developers and tourist dollars to the region.

At least three important long-term trends emanated from the creation of the TVA. The first is that, although the TVA's establishment did not stop the public-versus-private-power debate, it gave it form and served as a concrete symbol of the continuing debate. Private-power advocates lost the battle for the Tennessee Valley but won a qualified victory in the war against public power. The continuing debate is apparent in court cases in which private utility companies challenge the constitutionality of the TVA's selling power. It is also apparent in various presidential actions. President Dwight Eisenhower wanted to sell the TVA but believed it politically unfeasible. He tried to limit the agency's freedom of operation but failed. In Barry Goldwater's 1964 presidential campaign, he vowed to sell the TVA. Ronald Reagan's administration also wanted to sell the TVA but settled for the appointment of noted businessman Marvin Runyon as TVA chairman.

A second important long-term trend concerns the exposure of the fundamental relationship between economic growth and environmental use. The TVA represents an organizational effort to promote economic growth and conserve resources. Conflicts have been generated by the TVA's attempts to carry out these seemingly contradictory tasks. The most notable clash concerned the building of Tellico Dam and the protection of the snail darter from extinction.

In 1963, the TVA announced plans to build the Tellico Dam to create a 16,500-acre reservoir for recreation and industrial development and to deliver forty thousand jobs. The TVA bought or had condemned thirty-eight thousand acres of land, more than twice that needed for the reservoir itself, much of it fertile farm land taken from families under threat of eminent domain. Construction was halted when an endangered species of fish, the snail darter, was discovered in the Tennessee River. The TVA's fight to build Tellico Dam became a *cause célèbre*. In 1980, President Jimmy Carter signed a congressional bill exempting the Tellico Dam project from all federal laws and mandating its completion. It was a hollow victory for the TVA: Conceding that industrial development was unlikely, the agency sold the land to a county agency that sold it at auction to prospective homeowners. The TVA's experiences have been paralleled in conflicts between lumber mills and protectors of the spotted owl in the northwest United States and also in Brazil, where thousands of acres of rain forest are destroyed each day, along with unknown species of plants and animals, in the service of economic growth and development.

A third important long-term impact of the TVA is the precedent the agency set for government intervention in power technology. With the government's participation in the development of hydroelectric power and its emphasis on electric power as important to national defense, the way was paved for federal direction of nuclear technology. The government's Manhattan Project was designed to research and develop the atomic bomb for use in World War II. Oak Ridge, Tennessee, was chosen as one of three secret sites constructed for working on the bomb, in part because of its proximity to an enormous source of electric power: the TVA. In its postwar bid to control the development of nuclear technology, the federal government again turned to the TVA. In 1946, Director David Lilienthal left the TVA to become the first chairman of the Atomic Energy Commission (AEC), the federal regulatory agency for nuclear technology. TVA was complicit in creating the Cold War nuclear arms race, buying coalfields, increasing their stripmining operations, and building a vast coal-fired power system to power the federal nuclear operations.

Building on the TVA as its instrument in promoting nuclear technology in the name of national defense, the government in the 1960's proceeded to build nuclear-fueled electric power plants. Instead of fighting private enterprise, the government this time subsidized the construction and operation of nuclear power plants for private industry and legislatively limited industry's liabilities in the event of a nuclear accident. This close alliance between government and private forces in the development of commercial nuclear power became a contentious issue in the aftermath of the Three Mile Island accident, and in the 1980's (as a result of the energy crises of the late 1970's as well as environmental concerns), nuclear development was curtailed in favor of efficiency measures.

CURRENT STATUS

TVA's effects have been varied, both in their consequences and in their capacity for social progress. The agency set an important precedent, however, in becoming the first organization to seek the protection of public resources as defined by regional, rather than legal, boundaries, resulting in planned efforts toward coastal management, wetlands management, and the protection of the Everglades. After managing to survive the deregulation of the electric utilities industry during the 1990's, the TVA imposed efficiency measures, ending its nuclear plant building program and responding to environmental concerns in 1998 with a new clean-air strategy to reduce the pollutants that cause ozone and smog.

Sherry Cable and
Thomas E. Shriver

SOURCES FOR FURTHER STUDY

Chandler, William U. *The Myth of TVA: Conservation and Development in the Tennessee Valley, 1933-1983.* Cambridge, Mass.: Ballinger, 1984.

Creese, Walter L. *TVA's Public Planning: The Vision, the Reality.* Knoxville: University of Tennessee Press, 1990.

Grant, Nancy L. *TVA and Black Americans: Planning for the Status Quo.* Philadelphia: Temple University Press, 1990. A scholarly examination of TVA's policies toward black people as employees and residents of the Tennessee Valley. Concludes that TVA's reform impulse effectively was stifled by the need to work within the political establishment.

Hargrove, Erwin C. *Prisoners of Myth: The Leadership of the Tennessee Valley Authority, 1933-1990.* Princeton, N.J.: Princeton University Press, 1994. Examines the mentality of TVA's upper management, their concept of the role TVA should play in the development of the region, and the limitations of that role.

Hubbard, Preston J. *Origins of the TVA: The Muscle Shoals Controversy, 1920-1932.* Nashville, Tenn.: Vanderbilt University Press, 1961. Documents the various attempts to deal with the Army Corps of Engineers project at Muscle Shoals. Useful for understanding the roots of TVA in the Progressive ideology of the early twentieth century.

Lilienthal, David E. *Democracy on the March.* New York: Harper & Brothers, 1944. A charter member of the TVA's Board of Directors and first chairman of the Atomic Energy Commission, the author presents his own vision of what the TVA should be. Important historical document that illuminates the author's feud with TVA Chairman Arthur E. Morgan.

McCraw, Thomas K. *Morgan vs. Lilienthal: The Feud Within the TVA.* Chicago: Loyola University Press, 1970. Detailed analysis of the feud between TVA Chairman Arthur E. Morgan and TVA Director David E. Lilienthal. The feud and its outcome determined the shape that the agency would take.

_____. *TVA and the Power Fight, 1933-1939.* New York: J. B. Lippincott, 1971. Good, nuanced study of the continuation of the debate over publicly versus privately owned electric power after the TVA was founded, and the role of the TVA in that debate. Particular emphasis on the lawsuits brought against the TVA.

McDonald, Michael J., and John Muldowny. *TVA and the Dispossessed.* Knoxville: University of Tennessee Press, 1982. Examines resettlement of the population in Norris after construction of Norris Dam. Good analysis of how the TVA used the power of eminent domain as a threat to force residents to sell their land.

Selznick, Philip. *TVA and the Grass Roots: A Study in the Sociology of Formal Organization.* New York: Harper Torchbooks, 1966. Classic sociological work that analyzes the TVA's operations as a formal organization, particularly its failure to use democratic decision making in questions of economic development in the valley.

Wheeler, William Bruce. *TVA and the Tellico Dam, 1936-1979: A Bureaucratic Crisis in Post-Industrial America.* Knoxville: University of Tennessee Press, 1986. The story of the big dam and the little fish: Tellico Dam and the snail darter. Good historical analysis of the conflict.

SEE ALSO: National Defense Act (1916); Federal Power Act (1920); Natural Gas Act (1938); Atomic Energy Act of 1954 (1954); Niagara Power Act (1957); Price-Anderson Act (1957); Energy Policy and Conservation Act (1975); Public Utility Regulatory Policies Act (1978).

BANKING ACT OF 1933

DATE: June 16, 1933
U.S. STATUTES AT LARGE: 48 Stat. 162
PUBLIC LAW: 73-66
CATEGORIES: Banking, Money, and Finance

The Banking Act established deposit insurance, regulated interest paid on deposits, prohibited underwriting of corporate securities by commercial banks, and restricted loans to buy securities.

Failure of hundreds of American banks each year in the 1920's, and then thousands of them at the beginning of the Great Depression in the period 1930-1933, dramatized the inadequacies of the existing banking and financial oversight system. Senator Carter Glass began pushing for reform of the system in 1931. The Senate Banking Committee, when it reported out the bill that became the Banking Act of 1933, explained that "a completely comprehensive measure for the reconstruction of our banking system" had been deferred. The purposes of the committee's emergency bill were more modest: "to correct manifest immediate abuses, and to bring our banking system into a stronger condition." The new law significantly amended the Federal Reserve Act (1913) and the National Bank Act of 1864 and added the Federal Deposit Insurance Corporation (FDIC) to those agencies already regulating and monitoring the banking system.

COUNTERING SPECULATION

The collapse of the stock market, with share prices on average falling to one-sixth of their 1929 value by 1932, was blamed in large part on excessive loans to stockbrokers and, through them, to stock speculators. Generous credit to stock speculators had fueled the Wall Street boom in the late 1920's. A major purpose of the Banking Act of 1933, signed into law on June 16 of that year, was to prevent the "undue diversion of funds into speculative operations."

Banks belonging to the Federal Reserve System (member banks) were forbidden to act as agents to brokers and dealers on behalf of nonbank lenders. The Federal Reserve Board, a presidentially appointed group that governed the Federal Reserve System, was to ascertain whether bank credit was being used unduly for speculative purposes. It could limit the amount of member banks' loans that could be secured by stock and bond collateral. Member banks fostering speculation through their lending policies would be denied the privilege of borrowing from the Federal Reserve Bank of their district. Congress was concerned that businesses engaged in agriculture, industry, and commerce would be deprived of adequate credit. Most of the loans financing speculation in stocks and bonds had been made by banks in financial centers; there is no evidence that these banks turned down requests by business firms for short-term loans. Moreover, corporations could finance expansion through the sale of new securities.

Commercial banks in the 1920's began large-scale development of affiliates that dealt in securities. By 1930, these affiliates brought more than half of all new securities issues to market, in successful competition with established investment banks. Extensive hearings on affiliates' practices conducted by Ferdinand Pecora, counsel to the Senate Banking Committee, generated negative publicity regarding abuses. One section of the Banking Act of 1933, often referred to as the Glass-Steagall Act (although this name was originally attached to the entire Banking Act of 1933), ordered the separation of deposit taking from investment banking activities within a year. Financial institutions had to choose to be either commercial banks or investment houses; investment banks could no longer accept deposit accounts and member banks could no longer underwrite securities issues of business corporations. Banks with national charters were, however, permitted to underwrite and deal in securities issued by all levels of government in the United States for resale to the investing public. Separation of commercial banking and investment banking was expected to contribute to the soundness of commercial banks and to increase the overall stability of the economy.

There is little evidence to support the idea, which prevailed in 1933, that many bank failures were the result of the securities activities of affiliates. Many failures of small banks were blamed on the poor results of their securities portfolios, purchased on the advice of larger "correspondent" banks eager to promote issues held by their affiliates. As a result of this perception of blame, member banks were forbidden to invest in corporate stock. They could continue to buy corporate bonds for their investment portfolios, provided that those bonds were of investment, rather than speculative, quality.

PROVISIONS OF GLASS-STEAGALL
Senator Glass was convinced that banks should confine their activities to short-term lending to businesses. His belief in short-term lending stemmed from the fact that the deposits of banks were largely payable on demand. He believed that banks should not lock themselves into long-term loans when their deposits, the source of funding for loans, could be withdrawn quickly.

Banks were believed to have taken on riskier loans and investments than in the past so that they could offer higher interest rates to their depositors (a situation believed to have recurred in the 1970's and 1980's). To encourage safer portfolios, Congress resorted to regulating interest rates. For deposits payable on demand, no explicit interest was allowed. The ban on interest was also intended to discourage interbank deposits with correspondent banks, with the funds going instead to local borrowers. Small banks, however, continued to hold deposits with correspondent banks. Rather than paying interest, the correspondent banks offered various services free of charge.

The Federal Reserve Board set ceilings on the rates that member banks were permitted to pay on time and savings deposits. In 1935, the FDIC was empowered to do the same for all other insured banks. Regulation Q, issued by the Federal Reserve Board, established a ceiling of 3 percent as of November 1, 1933. The rate was well above what most banks paid.

Congressman Henry Bascom Steagall was responsible for the deposit insurance provisions of the Banking Act of 1933. For fifteen years he had battled for the reform, which he saw as benefiting community banking, as it allowed the banking public to have confidence in the safety of deposits made in local banks. Senator Arthur Hendrick Vandenberg pushed for deposit insurance to take effect immediately, but President Franklin D. Roosevelt was opposed. As a compromise, a temporary plan covering the first $2,500 in insured accounts went into effect on January 1, 1934. In the meantime, infusions of capital strengthened the banks that were permitted to reopen after Roosevelt's banking holiday from March 6 to March 13, 1933.

Between 1920 and 1933, thousands of minuscule small-town banks failed. The Banking Act of 1933 imposed a $50,000 minimum capital requirement to open a national bank; the minimum had been $25,000. Capital for each branch of a national bank had to at least match that required for a one-office bank in the same location. To prevent unhealthy competition resulting from bank proliferation, the Banking Act of 1935 later tightened the requirements for a bank to obtain a charter. The FDIC stood ready to deny insurance if excessive competition threatened.

Banks in the United States were overwhelmingly undiversified institutions doing business at a single location, and their fates were thus tied to the fortunes of local economies. To provide some banking services to localities in which banks had closed, states began to ease restrictions on branch banking in the early 1930's. The battle for permission to operate branches was fought hard in state legislatures and in Congress. Federally chartered national banks were authorized in 1927 to branch in the same community as their head offices if the state in which they were located did not prohibit branching. The Banking Act of 1933 permitted branches beyond the headquarters community, so that national banks could branch to the same extent as allowed for state banks. Interstate branches remained forbidden.

In 1922, the Federal Reserve Banks began to coordinate their purchases and sales of government securities (known as open market operations). The 1933 act placed open market operations under Federal Reserve Board regulation; the board could now disapprove policies recommended by the Federal Open Market Committee. Further, all relationships and transactions of the Federal Reserve Banks with foreign institutions were placed under control of the Federal Reserve Board. Both measures diminished the policy roles previously played by the twelve Federal Reserve Banks, particularly the powerful one in New York City.

The 1933 act also, for the first time, gave the Federal Reserve System some authority over bank holding companies that owned shares in member banks. A bank holding company could avoid this supervision if control over a member bank was exerted without the need to vote shares. Involvement of the Federal Reserve System with bank holding companies remained limited.

Exercise of authority over banking by individual states had led to a "competition in laxity" with federal regulators. Over the years, restrictions on national banks, under federal jurisdiction, had been eased in order to prevent them from switching to state charters and to encourage state banks to convert to national charters. Many states had weak or inadequate banking supervision. State banks failed at a much higher rate than national banks between 1920 and 1933.

Supporters of states' rights had succeeded in preventing a federal takeover of chartering, supervision, and regulation of all commercial banks. After the Banking Act of 1933, however, states had to share jurisdiction with the FDIC for nonmember banks covered by that agency's insurance. States retained the power to decide policy on branch banking. Some persisted in prohibiting all branches, but more broadened the territory in which branching was authorized. In no case was interstate branching permitted.

DEPOSIT INSURANCE

Deposit insurance, fiercely opposed by some bankers in 1933, became permanent with the Banking Act of 1935. Advocates hoped that deposit insurance would stimulate bank lending to the private sector as deposits increased. Bank deposits increased by more than 46 percent between 1934 and 1939, surpassing the record 1930 total by more than $2.6 billion. Total loans, however, failed to increase significantly, reflecting the weak recovery of business investment spending and the timidity of bank lending officers.

The FDIC had been organized in September, 1933. All member banks were required to join; solvent nonmember banks were also eligible. Banks paid an initial premium of 0.25 percent of insurable deposits. By the beginning of 1934, 87 percent of all commercial banks had joined the FDIC, and more than 96 percent of all deposits were covered. By the end of that year, 93 percent of commercial banks had joined, and 98 percent of deposits were covered. All but about 1 percent of applicant banks qualified for deposit insurance.

To remain insured, nonmember banks were expected to become member banks by mid-1936. This deadline was first extended and then abandoned in 1939. A majority of American banks continued to be nonmembers, enjoying the lower minimum capital and lower reserve requirements demanded by many state charters as opposed to the requirements imposed by the Federal Reserve Board.

The FDIC later proved successful in one of its goals, that of preventing a new wave of bank failures triggered by depositors' fears. Even as hundreds of banks were forced to close in the 1980's, depositors did not panic and rush to remove their funds.

Ceilings on interest rates did not hamper the gathering of deposits by banks until the 1950's. Thereafter, competition with other investment outlets that offered returns higher than those permitted under Regulation Q caused some hardships for banks. Interest rate regulations for time and savings deposits were eliminated in 1986.

The separation of commercial from investment banking called for in the Banking Act of 1933 had already begun before the act was passed. The two leading American banks, Chase National Bank and National City Bank, announced plans to eliminate their affiliates in March, 1933. The Morgan investment banking business, sharply reduced by the Depression, was continued by several partners who left to form Morgan, Stanley & Company. The historic name of J. P. Morgan & Company now belonged to a commercial bank that became Morgan Guaranty Trust Company in 1959. Other large investment banks chose to eliminate their deposit-taking activities.

The 1933 act began the process of diminishing the autonomy of the twelve Federal Reserve Banks and centralizing power in the Federal Reserve Board in Washington. The Banking Act of 1935 completed that shift. In many significant ways, however, the American banking system was unchanged by New Deal legislation. Major problems left unresolved involved the dual banking system of state and national banks, the division of responsibilities among federal agencies, and limited ability of banks to branch and thus to diversify their lending and deposit bases. The 1933 act also created some problems by failing to make deposit insurance premiums related to risk and by banning interest on demand deposits, making it more difficult for banks to get those deposits.

Benjamin J. Klebaner

SOURCES FOR FURTHER STUDY

Benston, George J. *The Separation of Commercial and Investment Banking: The Glass-Steagall Act Revisited and Reconsidered.* New York: Oxford University Press, 1990.

Burns, Helen M. *The American Banking Community and New Deal Banking Reforms, 1933-1935.* Westport, Conn.: Greenwood Press, 1974.

Chandler, Lester Vernon. *America's Greatest Depression, 1922-1941.* New York: Harper & Row, 1970.

_____. *American Monetary Policy, 1928-1941.* New York: Harper & Row, 1971.

Friedman, Milton, and Anna Jacobson Schwartz. *A Monetary History of the United States, 1867-1960.* Princeton, N.J.: Princeton University Press, 1963.

Kennedy, Susan Estabrook. *The Banking Crisis of 1933.* Lexington: The University Press of Kentucky, 1973.

Klebaner, Benjamin J. "Banking Reform in the New Deal Era." *Quarterly Review (Banca Nazionale de Lavoro)* 178, no. 9 (1991): 319-341.

Krooss, Herman Edward. *Documentary History of Banking and Currency in the United States.* 4 vols. New York: Chelsea House Publishers, 1969.

Studenski, Paul, and Herman Edward Krooss. *Financial History of the United States.* 2d ed. New York: McGraw-Hill, 1963.

Westerfield, Ray B. *Money, Credit, and Banking.* New York: Ronald Press, 1938.

SEE ALSO: National Bank Acts (1863-1864); Federal Reserve Act (1913); McFadden Act (1927); Hundred Days legislation (1933); Securities Exchange Act (1934); Banking Act of 1935 (1935).

NATIONAL INDUSTRIAL RECOVERY ACT

DATE: June 16, 1933
U.S. STATUTES AT LARGE: 48 Stat. 200
U.S. CODE: 40 § 401
CATEGORIES: Business, Commerce, and Trade

The act encouraged firms in industrial sectors to develop codes of fair competition to "do their part" for economic recovery during the Great Depression.

Between 1929 and 1933, the U.S. economy descended into its worst economic depression in history. By 1932, one-fourth of the nation's workers were unemployed. Drastic decline in farm prices reduced farm incomes and led to widespread mortgage foreclosures. Banks and other businesses failed by the thousands.

In response, the voters overwhelmingly defeated the efforts of President Herbert Hoover to win reelection and brought into the presidency Franklin D. Roosevelt. Roosevelt had a few specific campaign promises: He would do a better job of balancing the budget, but he favored direct transfer payments for the relief of the unemployed and others suffering hardship. He offered the public a New Deal without giving much detail.

After his inauguration, March 4, 1933, Roosevelt's administration began a whirlwind of activity that came to be known as the Hundred Days. A bank holiday was declared, and the dollar was taken off the gold standard. Representatives of business were called upon to help formulate a program for industrial recovery. From this emerged the National Industrial Recovery Act (NIRA), approved June 16, 1933. It was to be administered by a National Recovery Administration (NRA). Roosevelt quickly appointed General Hugh Johnson to head the NRA. The program began in an explosion of public relations. A dramatic symbol—the Blue Eagle—was adopted, and business firms were encouraged to qualify to display in their windows a blue eagle poster bearing the words "We Do Our Part."

PROVISIONS

The law encouraged firms in each individual trade and industry sector to join together to draw up a code of fair competition. The assumption was that intense competition was a cause of declining prices, wages, and incomes, and if the intensity of competition were reduced, firms could profit more, produce more, and pay more. Each code was to submitted to the NRA administrator and, if approved, would have the force of law. Codes were exempted from antitrust prosecution.

Many of the codes contained provisions intended to prevent price cutting and to curtail output. The first code issued was for cotton textiles. It limited machinery operation to two forty-hour shifts per week. It was soon followed by codes for shipbuilding and electrical manufacturing that forbade selling below specified minimum prices. Other codes forbade prices below "cost," where formulas were provided for determining cost. Often firms were required to file price changes so competitors would know about them, a provision intended to deter such changes. Many of the practices forbidden in the codes were genuinely undesirable: misrepresentation, design piracy, commercial bribery, deceptive advertising, false branding, imitation of trademarks or designs.

The NIRA also contained important labor provisions. If businesses were to get higher prices, workers were to get higher wages. Section 7 of the NIRA required that every code contain certain labor provisions. One was "that employees shall have the right to organize and bargain collectively through representatives of their own choosing. . . ." Employers were forbidden to interfere with worker decisions about joining a union. Codes were to provide standards for minimum wages and maximum hours of work. The majority of codes called for a forty-hour work week. Efforts to spread work by reducing hours were somewhat successful; in industries surveyed by the Labor Department, average hours fell from 43.3 to 37.8 per week between June and October, 1933, and the number employed increased by about 7 percent. Minimum-wage provisions generally applied to plant workers but not office workers. Most codes provided for a minimum wage of at least forty cents an hour. Each industry formulated its own wage and hour standards, under pressure from the NRA authorities and sometimes from labor unions. Many codes forbade employment of children less than sixteen years of age.

BUSINESS REACTS

Even before the codes were put into effect, business firms reacted favorably to the prospect of higher prices. A large increase in inventory purchases helped to stimulate the economy during the summer and autumn of 1933. However, problems and contradictions soon emerged. Many codes were dominated by large firms and were drawn to put small or new competitors at a disadvantage. Each industry was pleased by the prospect of gaining higher selling prices, but displeased by having to pay higher wages and higher prices for inputs. The inventory boom died out by the end of 1933. The NIRA did not end the desire of individual firms to gain more business by offering a lower price. Code enforcement was often slow and difficult.

By the beginning of 1934, NRA codes covered about 90 percent of the industrial labor force. Ultimately, more than 550 codes were adopted. The code approach was based on the false premise that the Depression was caused by overproduction and excessive competition. The real cause was the drastic decline in total spending for goods and services. Another section of the NIRA dealt more directly with this problem. It authorized the creation of a Public Works Administration, which came under the direction of Secretary of the Interior Harold Ickes, to undertake construction projects. Ickes was primarily concerned that projects be useful and that they be constructed efficiently. This often meant they were slow to get under way, and that they did not offer many jobs for which the unemployed could qualify. Between 1933 and 1941, the Public Works Administration spent about $2.5 billion; the highest number of workers employed on its projects was 740,000 in mid-1936. Other government programs, such as the Civil Works Administration and Works Progress Administration, embodied more of a make-work orientation and provided more jobs.

CRITICISMS AND COURT CASES
In 1934, a National Recovery Review Board, headed by lawyer Clarence Darrow, strongly criticized the NRA codes as helping large firms oppress smaller firms and consumers. Hugh Johnson was forced to resign from the NRA in October, 1934, under fire for heavy drinking and an undiplomatic personality. He was replaced by a five-man board. In May, 1935, the Supreme Court held the code sections of NIRA to be unconstitutional in *Schechter Poultry Corporation v. United States.* The Court ruled that the regulation of industry went beyond the scope of interstate commerce, and the delegation of authority by Congress to the president and NRA administrators was excessive.

Many of the elements of the NRA program were reenacted by Congress in separate pieces of legislation. These included the National Labor Relations Act of 1935; the Fair Labor Standards Act of 1938; regulatory legislation for coal, petroleum, motor transport, and airlines; and laws restricting false and misleading advertising and price discrimination. After momentarily weakening antitrust with NIRA, after 1937, the government shifted to vigorous enforcement, blaming business concentration and inflexible prices for the severity of the Depression.

ASSESSMENT
As a measure to stimulate recovery from the Depression, the NIRA was not very effective, except for the demand stimulation resulting from Public Works Administration activities. Raising prices and

wages would tend to reduce output and employment, unless something were done to increase demand. Most economists have been critical of the tendency in the codes to reduce competition and encourage collusion and monopolistic practices. Although consumers were nominally represented in the code-making process, their interests were not protected. However, NIRA began a radical transformation of the work environment by encouraging the spread of labor unions, a process that was continued even more strongly by the National Labor Relations Act of 1935. NIRA also contributed to the reduction of the standard workweek and the extent of child labor. Politically, the measure probably helped to reassure the public that something was being done, and that radical transformation of the political system was not needed.

Paul B. Trescott

SOURCES FOR FURTHER STUDY

Fine, Sidney. *The Automobile Under the Blue Eagle: Labor, Management and the Automobile Manufacturing Code.* Ann Arbor: University of Michigan Press, 1963.

Hawley, Ellis W. *The New Deal and the Problem of Monopoly.* Princeton, N.J.: Princeton University Press, 1966.

Johnson, Hugh S. *The Blue Eagle from Egg to Earth.* Garden City, N.Y.: Doubleday Doran, 1935.

Lyon, Leverett S., ed. *The National Recovery Administration: An Analysis and Appraisal.* Washington, D.C.: Brookings Institution, 1935.

Ohl, John Kennedy. *Hugh S. Johnson and the New Deal.* De Kalb: Northern Illinois University Press, 1985.

Roos, Charles F. *NRA Economic Planning.* Bloomington, Ind.: Principia Press, 1937.

Vile, John R. *Encyclopedia of Constitutional Amendments, Proposed Amendments, and Amending Issues, 1789-1995.* Santa Barbara, Calif: ABC-CLIO, 1996.

Wilcox, Clair, Herbert F. Froser, and Patrick Murphy Malin, eds. *America's Recovery Program.* New York: Oxford University Press, 1934.

SEE ALSO: Hundred Days legislation (1933); National Labor Relations Act (1935); Fair Labor Standards Act (1938).

Twenty-first Amendment

Date: Ratified and certified December 5, 1933
U.S. Statutes at Large: 47 Stat. 1625
Categories: Constitutional Law; Food and Drugs

> *This amendment repealed the Eighteenth Amendment, which had prohibited the manufacture, sale, or transportation of intoxicating beverages.*

The Twenty-first Amendment to the Constitution repealed the Eighteenth Amendment, ending the thirteen-year period from 1920 to 1933 known as the Prohibition Era. The Eighteenth Amendment, also known as the Prohibition amendment, prohibited the manufacture, sale, or transportation of intoxicating beverages.

The Supreme Court and Prohibition

During the Prohibition era, in cases such as *United States v. Lanza* (1922), *Carroll v. United States* (1925), *Olmstead v. United States* (1928), and *United States v. Sprague* (1931), the Supreme Court strengthened the means for enforcing and upholding the Eighteenth Amendment. These decisions made some Americans aware that the constitutional prohibition of alcoholic beverages would have far-reaching ramifications for legal rights and influenced them to support the ratification of the Twenty-first Amendment, repealing the Prohibition amendment.

In *Lanza*, the Court held that while the Eighteenth Amendment established the prohibition of alcoholic beverages as a national policy, both the state and federal governments possessed independent authority to punish Prohibition infractions. This Court ruling meant that Prohibition offenders could be indicted and punished twice for nearly every violation. In *Carroll*, the Court stated that because an automobile transporting liquor could depart before a warrant could be attained, officers having reasonable grounds could lawfully search it without a warrant. This decision extended the search and seizure powers of agents enforcing Prohibition and police officers dealing with automobiles. In *Olmstead*, the Court upheld the use of wiretapping by law enforcement agencies in enforcing the constitutional prohibition of alcoholic beverages as well as other laws. The Court ruled that wiretapping by law enforcement agencies was lawful search and seizure. In *Sprague,* the Court indicated that Congress has an apparent right to choose the procedure of ratification of an amendment to the constitution. It declared that because Congress submitted the ratification of the Eighteenth Amendment to state legislatures, the amendment had been legally sanctioned.

RATIFICATION OF REPEAL

The restrictions on legal rights created by these Prohibition-era Court decisions influenced some Americans to become active in organizations campaigning for the repeal of the Eighteenth Amendment. Such organizations included the Association Against the Prohibition Amendment and the Women's Organization for National Prohibition Reform.

Partly in response to this campaigning, in 1933 Congress, which had been given the choice of ratification methods by Sprague, proposed that the repeal of the Eighteenth Amendment be submitted to state conventions instead of state legislatures for a vote. Between April and November, 1933, thirty-seven states held elections on whether to retain or repeal the Eighteenth Amendment. Nearly twenty-one million Americans voted, and 73 percent favored repeal. On December 5, 1933, the Twenty-first Amendment was ratified. It was the first amendment to be ratified by voters rather than legislators.

Louis Gesualdi

SOURCES FOR FURTHER STUDY

Brown, Everett Somerville. *Ratification of the Twenty-first Amendment to the Constitution of the United States: State Convention Records and Laws.* Ann Arbor: University of Michigan Press, 1938.

Cashman, Sean Dennis. *Prohibition, the Lie of the Land.* New York: Free Press, 1981.

Kyvig, David E. *Repealing National Prohibition.* Chicago: University of Chicago Press, 1979.

Vile, John R. *A Companion to the United States Constitution and Its Amendments.* 3d ed. Westport, Conn.: Greenwood Press, 2001.

_____. *Encyclopedia of Constitutional Amendments, Proposed Amendments, and Amending Issues, 1789-1995.* Santa Barbara, Calif: ABC-CLIO, 1996.

SEE ALSO: Eighteenth Amendment (1919).

MIGRATORY BIRD HUNTING AND CONSERVATION STAMP ACT

ALSO KNOWN AS: Duck Stamp Act
DATE: March 16, 1934
U.S. STATUTES AT LARGE: 48 Stat. 452
U.S. CODE: 16 § 718
CATEGORIES: Animals; Environment and Conservation

Enactment of this act provided the first regular federal funding for waterfowl management in the United States.

On March 16, 1934, the U.S. Congress enacted the Migratory Bird Hunting and Conservation Stamp Act, often known as the Duck Stamp Act, to provide critical funds for wetlands and waterfowl conservation programs. Until this action, no stable funding source was available for this conservation work. As with many conservation programs, a long, twisting journey was taken over many years to enact this far-reaching legislation.

DECLINE OF WETLANDS AND WATERFOWL

Waterfowl populations declined sharply in number in the early 1900's. Extensive habitat loss caused by the long drought of the 1930's, overharvest by market hunting, and the Great Depression created both ecological and financial crises for resource-management programs. Water from prairie potholes, ponds, and marshes had disappeared, and with it the nesting and rearing habitat for waterfowl. Dust storms raged, and the Dust Bowl created a biological crisis. Waterfowl numbers in North America reached their lowest point in history. Many conservationists predicted the extinction of ducks and geese in the United States.

In January, 1934, President Franklin Roosevelt appointed a special waterfowl committee of Jay N. ("Ding") Darling, Thomas Beck, and Aldo Leopold to determine the needs of waterfowl management and outline a plan for saving this disappearing resource. They estimated that $50 million was needed for the purchase and restoration of wetlands for wildlife, with special emphasis on migratory waterfowl. Finding such an immense sum during the Depression was improbable.

FUNDING LOST HABITAT

The new director of the Bureau of Biological Survey (which would later be renamed the U.S. Fish and Wildlife Service), Darling revived the idea of a duck stamp as a funding measure for restoring lost waterfowl habitat. Congress had passed legislation in 1929 to buy land for waterfowl refuges, but it did not provide any stable funding provisions in the legislation. Without funds, waterfowl refuge was only a paper program.

Under Darling's lobbying, Congress passed the Migratory Bird Hunting and Conservation Stamp Act, which required all waterfowl hunters sixteen years of age and older to buy stamps, sign them, and paste them to the back of their state hunting license. Sold at local U.S. Post Offices, this stamp was required only for hunting ducks and geese, not for other migratory game birds. Darling, an astute political cartoonist and outstanding artist, designed the first duck stamp in 1934; it sold for one dollar. All funds from the sale of this stamp were to be used for waterfowl management and the acquisition of wetland habitat essential for restoring waterfowl numbers. The Migratory Bird Hunting and Conservation Stamp Act of 1934 was the first major federal statute to establish a special fund to be used exclusively for wildlife conservation purposes.

BEGINNINGS OF THE DUCK STAMP

The idea of issuing a federal waterfowl stamp to provide funds for the acquisition of public hunting grounds originated with George A. Lawyer, chief U.S. game warden, shortly after the end of World War I. Such a bill was debated several times in Congress but failed to pass four times between 1921 and 1926. Dr. William T. Hornaday led the formidable opposition against the Game Refuge-Public Shooting Grounds Bill. Hornaday believed that liberal bag limits and the use of semiautomatic shotguns was causing the slaughter of too many ducks and geese, and he argued that the creation of game refuges was simply a method of concentrating waterfowl for more killing by hunters. He called supporters of this bill "game hogs" and "butchers."

Senator Peter Norbeck reintroduced the Game Refuge-Public Shooting Grounds Bill in the opening days of the Seventieth Congress. After bitter debate, the federal licensing and public hunting grounds features were removed from it, and the Norbeck bill passed the Senate. Congressman August H. Andresen of Minnesota authored a new bill identical to the amended Norbeck bill on January 23, 1929. Without provision for congressional monies, this bill quickly passed the House. After eight years of disagreement and acrimonious charges, on February 8, 1929, the Norbeck-Andresen Act established a feasible waterfowl refuge law.

The idea of a federal hunting license for waterfowl, which died with the passage of the Norbeck-Andresen Act, sprang to life during the Great Depression and the Dust Bowl. In early 1927, drought, drainage of wetlands, and expanding hunting and poaching pressure caused waterfowl numbers to decline sharply. In the fall of 1929, drought-stricken populations of waterfowl began to plummet sharply. On December 31, 1929, the bag limit was reduced from twenty-five to fifteen ducks a day, but the waterfowl crash continued.

Frederick C. Walcott, a Connecticut senator and an avid duck hunter, viewed the waterfowl crash with alarm. His great desire for wildlife conservation led him to establish the Senate Special Committee on the Conservation of Wildlife Resources. As its first chairman, he proposed a greatly intensified waterfowl management program in 1931. The funding of this management effort revived the American Game Association's idea of a federal hunting stamp. On April 4, 1932, more than one hundred witnesses were heard by Walcott's committee. Most of the witnesses favored the hunting stamp proposal. Progress toward enactment of a duck stamp act was rapid, with the Migratory Bird Hunting and Conservation Stamp Act becoming law on March 16, 1934.

IMPACT AND LATER AMENDMENTS

Before the crash of waterfowl populations in the 1920's, the U.S. government had set aside about 744,000 acres of habitat for all wildlife. By 1942, almost three million acres had been set aside for the preservation of waterfowl alone. Much of the money for this land acquisition came from the Migratory Bird Hunting and Conservation Stamp Act of 1934. Over the years, increases in the duck stamp fee have been instituted to cover the acquisition and management of wildlife areas, although inadequate funding for acquisition of lands for wildlife, especially waterfowl, is a continuing problem for wildlife conservationists. In 1961, the Wetland Loan Act was enacted to supplement duck stamp dollars. Reauthorized in 1986 as the Emergency Wetlands Resources Act, it provided additional dollars for land acquisition. In 2001, the

Electronic Duck Stamp Act allowed for digital duck stamps.

Since the inception of the duck stamp, more than 3.5 million acres of waterfowl habitat have been preserved since the 1930's through the duck stamp program. Because of the success of the U.S. government in raising monies through the sale of duck stamps for waterfowl conservation, many states in the United States also issue stamps to fund their conservation needs. Stamps for upland game birds, trout, turkeys, and nongame animals raise several million dollars each year for important conservation activities. Such programs are thus legacies of a time when it seemed that waterfowl, one of the nation's priceless resources, might disappear forever from North America.

David L. Chesemore

SOURCES FOR FURTHER STUDY

Farley, John L. *Duck Stamps and Wildlife Refuges.* Circular 37. Washington, D.C.: U.S. Department of the Interior. Fish and Wildlife Service, 1959.

Gilmore, Jene C. *Art for Conservation: The Federal Duck Stamps.* Barre, Mass.: Barre, 1971.

Linduska, Joseph P. *Waterfowl Tomorrow.* Washington, D.C.: Government Printing Office, 1964.

McBride, David P. *The Federal Duck Stamps: A Complete Guide.* Piscataway, N.J.: Winchester Press, 1984.

SEE ALSO: Migratory Bird Act (1913); Migratory Bird Treaty Act (1918); Endangered Species Preservation Act (1966); Endangered Species Act (1973); Convention on the Conservation of Migratory Species of Wild Animals (1979).

TYDINGS-MCDUFFIE ACT

ALSO KNOWN AS: Philippines Commonwealth Independence Act
DATE: March 24, 1934
U.S. STATUTES AT LARGE: 48 Stat. 456
PUBLIC LAW: 73-127
CATEGORIES: Foreign Relations; Land Management

Promising Philippine independence from the United States by 1944, the act paved the way for expansion of U.S. economic interests in the islands.

On March 24, 1934, President Franklin D. Roosevelt signed into law the Philippines Commonwealth Independence Act, popularly known as the Tydings-McDuffie Act. The law promised independence to the Philippines by 1944, following a ten-year transition period of "commonwealth status." During that time, the islands were to be governed by their own national legislature and executive branches; policy-making power, however, would continue to remain in the United States. This commonwealth system was in place when the Philippines were invaded and occupied by the Japanese in 1942, an event that delayed Philippine independence for two years, until 1946.

THE HAWES-CUTTING-HARE ACT

Initial support for the Philippine legislation came from particular special interest groups both in the United States and in the Philippines. Striving for their own nationhood, many native Filipino lobbying groups pushed hard for the act's passage. A more economically based pressure came from American beet sugar producers, who sought to eliminate competition from island goods, and from trade union leaders, who wanted to prevent the influx of Filipino workers into the Hawaiian islands and the U.S. mainland. These groups had earlier lent similar support to the legislative predecessor of the Tydings-McDuffie Act, the Hawes-Cutting-Hare Act of 1932. The earlier act's attempt to curb competitive imports from the Philippines was rejected by the U.S. Senate in a close vote.

After the defeat of the Hawes-Cutting-Hare legislation, a new contingent of Filipino supporters of independence traveled to Washington, D.C., where they were joined by those groups of politically influential Americans who supported Philippine autonomy. Sergio Osmena led the Philippine delegation but his call for immediate independence was too drastic for many in the American support group. He was subsequently recalled to Manila. His replacement, Manuel Quezón took a less politically offensive position, emphasizing a gradualist approach to independence for the islands. Thus, he was able to enlist the support of American politicians who favored a more moderate approach to Philippine independence. The resulting coalition influenced the passage of the Tydings-McDuffie Act.

EFFECTS OF TYDINGS-McDUFFIE

Following enactment of the Tydings-McDuffie legislation, the Filipino delegation returned home to draft a constitution and to elect officials who would oversee the gradual transition to Philippine autonomy. Manuel Quezón and Sergio Osmena were elected president and vice president, respectively, of the new Philippines Commonwealth. Although steps were taken to create a Filipino-based political structure, most of the political decision-making authority still rested with the United States. Filipinos did, however, retain limited control over internal political affairs, but all foreign policy, defense, and monetary matters were defined and implemented in Washington. This political arrangement clearly benefited the United States at the expense of the Filipinos. The commonwealth was prohibited from legislating most of its own economic policies. In particular, legislation was passed which imposed duties on Philippine exports to America.

Under the new commonwealth system the cliental politics and economics of the old colonial structure were perfected. Key provisions of the Tydings-McDuffie Act and of its amendments saw to this. Increasingly, the Philippine presidency came to resemble the office of an American state governor. Quezón was accorded certain discretionary powers, but only where American interests were not affected. He could organize an army but could not deploy it without the consent of President Roosevelt. Travel to foreign lands and discussion of trade agreements with foreign officials could take place but Quezón was powerless to conclude any formal agreement. The enactment of any official Philippine trade agreements remained under the authority of the U.S. high commissioner of the Philippines. This position, strengthened by the provisions of the Tydings-McDuffie Act, protected the interests of the United States in all foreign relations and established official relationships between the Philippines and all other nations.

Looking after American interests abroad required the centralization of political authority in Manila. As a result, domestic policies were often delegated from the top level of Philippine government. It was under such an arrangement that President Quezón increasingly took advantage of his position. As long as his policy initiatives did not conflict with American interests, he wielded immense power, especially toward those who opposed his policies. Quezón often crushed his opposition with American blessings. The elimination of domestic competition greatly increased Quezón's confidence. He began to challenge some of the policies of American commonwealth administrators and even, at times, those of the high commissioner. Chastised at this level, he boldly began to take his conflicts to the American president. While he was successful in protesting the directives of the high commissioner on some occasions, his appeals to President Roosevelt most often produced results that reinforced American hegemony in the Philippines.

Under the structure authorized by the Tydings-McDuffie Act, the goal of true Philippine independence was increasingly circumvented. In the name of independence, American sovereignty over the Philippines continued. American suzerainty was magnified by a commonwealth political system that furthered American economic interests at the expense of the islands' competing in the world market. In the end, the Philippines became increasingly dependent on American economic interests. Commonwealth status destroyed that which the Philippines needed in order to compete economically on a global scale: revenue from the export of duty-free goods to the United States. Without trade revenues the Philippines became increasingly dependent on the United States for loans and investment, made, of course, with the understanding that United States interests came first. As the Philippine treasury emptied, the commonwealth thus became more indebted to its patron, the United States. The implementation of the Tydings-McDuffie Act both initiated and reinforced this condition.

The new relationship between the Philippines and the United States established by the Tydings-McDuffie Act produced a paradox: The closer the Philippines came to political independence from the United States, the more economically dependent upon America it became. In the end, the Tydings-McDuffie Act reinforced the idea that the only kind of independence that would be granted to the Filipinos was the kind that the United States could not grant.

Thomas J. Edward Walker,
Cynthia Gwynne Yaudes, and
Ruby L. Stoner

SOURCES FOR FURTHER STUDY
Constantino, Renato. *A History of the Philippines*. New York: Monthly Review Press, 1975.
Gallego, Manuel. *The Price of Philippine Independence Under the Tydings-McDuffie Act: An Anti-View of the So-Called Independence Law*. Manila: Barristers Book Company, 1939.
Grunder, Garel A., and William E. Lively. *The Philippines and the United States*. Norman: University of Oklahoma Press, 1951.
Hayden, John Ralston. *The Philippines: A Study in National Development*. New York: Macmillan, 1942.
Karnow, Stanley. *In Our Image: America's Empire in the Philippines*. New York: Random House, 1989.
Paredes, Ruby R., ed. *Philippine Colonial Democracy*. New Haven, Conn.: Yale University Press, 1988.

SEE ALSO: Treaty of Paris (1898).

ANTI-RACKETEERING ACT

ALSO KNOWN AS: Copeland Act
DATE: May 18, 1934
U.S. STATUTES AT LARGE: 48 Stat. 979
CATEGORIES: Business, Commerce, and Trade; Crimes and Criminal Procedure

This legislation protected trade and commerce from interference by criminal threats of violence or coercion; it was the first federal law to fight the control that organized crime held over local communities.

During the 1920's and 1930's, there was a significant increase in gangster activity and organized crime in the United States. Groups of criminals used bribery, extortion, threats, and violence to manipulate and control political officials, judges, and policemen and to harass local businesses. These groups were suspected of controlling gambling, prostitution, and the illegal sale of alcohol. Local authorities felt helpless in their fight to end criminally controlled rackets.

The 1934 Anti-Racketeering Act was proposed by Assistant Attorney General Joseph B. Keenan. Keenan, testifying before the

Senate Judiciary Subcommittee on March 2, 1934, asserted that federal authorities needed an antiracketeering law to help fight organized crime. Racketeers were debilitating legitimate businesses and communities. To fight back, local authorities needed assistance from the federal government. The Anti-Racketeering Act was one of six changes in the criminal justice code recommended by Keenan to aid the Department of Justice in its goal of putting every gangster, racketeer, and kidnapper out of business and into jail.

The Anti-Racketeering Act was one of several crime-fighting bills submitted to Congress by Senator Hy Ashurst of Arizona and Senator Royal Copeland of New York. Reflecting the recommendations made by Keenan, these bills aimed to reduce crime in the United States by increasing the powers of the federal government to assist local communities. The crime bills were vigorously supported by President Franklin D. Roosevelt. The House of Representatives quickly approved all six bills on May 5, 1934, and the Senate passed them on May 15. Numerous criminals were subsequently arrested and convicted under the Anti-Racketeering Act.

PROVISIONS AND IMPACT

Under the Anti-Racketeering Act, racketeering was defined as any act or threat of violence committed to divert or interfere with interstate commerce and any actual or intended attempts at extortion in connection with interstate commerce transactions. Racketeering included any acts or coercions used to force an individual or business to join or not to join any organization or to buy or not to buy goods. It included any acts of violence to individuals in connection with such activities. Those convicted of racketeering would receive a maximum of ninety-nine years in prison and a fine commensurate with the profits derived from racketeering transactions.

The Anti-Racketeering Act remained unchanged until 1946, when Congress passed the Hobbs Act. The Hobbs Act placed previously exempted illegal labor-union activity within the reach of federal prosecutors. In 1970, Congress passed the Racketeer Influenced and Corrupt Organizations Act (RICO), which increased penalties for those convicted of racketeering and permitted the seizure of assets acquired or used at the time of the criminal activity.

Leslie Stricker

SOURCES FOR FURTHER STUDY

Philcox, Norman W. *An Introduction to Organized Crime.* Springfield, Ill.: Charles C Thomas, 1978.

U.S. Department of Justice. Organized Crime and Racketeering Section. *Racketeer Influenced and Corrupt Organizations (RICO): A Manual for Federal Prosecutors.* 2d rev. ed. Washington, D.C.: Government Printing Office, 1988.

Wallance, Gregory J. "Criminal Justice: Outgunning the Mob." *American Bar Association Journal* 80 (March 1, 1994).

Welling, Sarah N., Pamela H. Bucy, and Sara Sun Beale. *Federal Criminal Law and Related Actions: Crimes, Forfeiture, the False Claims Act, and RICO.* Eagan, Minn.: West Group, 1998.

SEE ALSO: Interstate Commerce Act (1887); Hobbs Act (1946); Racketeer Influenced and Corrupt Organizations Act (1970).

SECURITIES EXCHANGE ACT

DATE: June 6, 1934
U.S. STATUTES AT LARGE: 48 Stat. 881
PUBLIC LAW: 73-291
U.S. CODE: 15 § 78a et seq.
CATEGORIES: Banking, Money, and Finance; Business, Commerce, and Trade; Government Procedure and Organization

The law created a quasi-judicial administrative body, the Securities and Exchange Commission, with broad powers to regulate the securities markets and protect the public interest.

The Securities Exchange Act of 1934 solidified the expanding role of the federal government in protecting the investing public. Passed in the aftermath of the greatest stock market collapse in history, this legislation established a new administrative agency with broad powers to ensure that many of the financial abuses and deceptive practices of the past would not recur.

Need to Protect Investors

Historically, as economic activity increases in volume, complexity, and sophistication, the corporation emerges as the dominant form of business organization. Corporate entities thrive because of the continued and expanding capital investment of people willing to accept the risks and rewards of ownership but unwilling or unable to actually participate in management of the business operation. Through the issuance of securities by corporations, ownership can be spread over a broad base of individuals, thus maximizing the potential for invested resources.

In order to facilitate this capital exchange process, organized marketplaces have developed throughout the world. These capital markets provide the mechanism for the corporate distribution of debt and equity securities as well as the subsequent transfer of these securities between individuals.

Because of the inherent separation of corporate management from ownership, current and potential investors operate under a distinct informational disadvantage. Capital contributors are at the mercy of claims made by the "insiders." Exploitation of unwary investors inevitably occurs, and securities markets merely serve to provide an organized forum within which to execute such schemes on a broad scale.

Early State Legislation

Government, concerned with ensuring an adequate supply of available capital in order to sustain economic growth, has a natural interest in protecting investors and maintaining public confidence in these securities markets. In the United States, attempts at regulation of securities were first made at the state level. In response to widespread fraudulent activities of stock promoters, Kansas enacted a statute in 1911 to protect the public interest. In the first year following enactment of this law, approximately fifteen hundred applications to sell securities in Kansas were filed. Only 14 percent were accepted, the rest being judged fraudulent (75 percent) or too highly speculative (11 percent).

Other legislatures followed Kansas's lead, and by 1913, twenty-two other states had passed laws similar in intent but widely varying in approach. These state securities laws are often called blue-sky laws, since the speculative schemes they attempted to foil often involved little more than selling "pieces of the sky," or worthless securities.

For various reasons, the individual state attempts to regulate securities markets were not very effective. Perhaps the greatest problem arose from the tactic of "interstate escape." Individuals or companies could continue deceptive and fraudulent practices merely by moving across state lines (physically or through the mails) to another jurisdiction where regulations were inadequate, poorly enforced, or perhaps even nonexistent. To limit such evasion, some form of federal intervention was needed.

THE ROARING 1920's
During the 1920's, there was a veritable explosion in securities market activity. Small investors entered the market in numbers larger than ever before. National brokerage firms doubled the number of their branch offices and reported phenomenal increases in business. Despite the vigorous trading and investing activity, the strength of the market was quickly eroding as a result of a number of prevailing traditions.

First, stock price manipulation was common. This was often executed by means of a manipulation pool, in which a syndicate of corporate officials and market operators join forces and, through a succession of equally matched buying and selling orders ("wash sales") among themselves, create the false impression of feverish activity, thus driving up the price of the stock. At the height of this artificial activity, the stock is sold, huge profits are reaped by the syndicate, and the stock price then subsequently plummets. As an example of the success of this gambit, a pool formed in March, 1929, to trade in Radio Corporation of America stock operated for only a seven-day period and netted a profit of almost $5 million.

The excessive use of credit to finance speculative stock transactions (that is, buying stocks "on margin") was another tradition that undermined the stability of the market. An investment as small as $100 could purchase $1,000 in securities (with a 10 percent margin), and there were no limits to the level of credit a broker could extend to a customer. This practice effectively lured potential capital away from productive economic investment and toward mere market speculation.

A third practice that hindered the efficient operation of the securities market relates to the misuse of corporate information by insiders. Corporate officials could withhold information, either positive or negative. By timing its release after they had already positioned themselves in the market, they could benefit from the price fluctuation when the news finally became public.

The weight of these traditions finally culminated in the stock market crash of October, 1929. This was a financial earthquake of dramatic proportions. The aggregate value of all stocks listed on the New York Stock Exchange (the largest capital market in the United States, handling 90 percent of all stock transactions on a dollar basis) declined from $89 billion before the crash to only $15 billion by 1932. The economic depression that rapidly deepened following the crash was the worst economic crisis in U.S. history.

SECURITIES ACT OF 1933

In March, 1932, the Senate Banking and Currency Committee was empowered to investigate the securities industry. This inquiry was continued and greatly expanded in scope after the election of Franklin D. Roosevelt as president in November, 1932. Roosevelt had been on record since his tenure as governor of New York as being highly critical of various stock market activities. The 1932 Democratic national platform on which he ran explicitly called for federal supervision of securities transactions.

Ferdinand Pecora served as legal counsel to this committee during its extensive investigations in 1933 and 1934. He compiled an impressive body of evidence concerning financial corruption and malpractice. Pecora personally elicited much of the damaging evidence from the most prestigious financial leaders of the time and was invaluable in documenting the need for securities regulation. For example, his investigation disclosed that of the $50 billion of new securities issued during the decade after World War I, half had proved to be worthless.

With the passage of the Securities Act in 1933 (signed into law on May 5, 1933, soon after Roosevelt's inauguration, the federal government finally entered the arena of securities regulation. This bill was championed in Congress by Representative Sam Rayburn of Texas and Senator Duncan Fletcher of Florida. The 1933 act was primarily a disclosure statute, concerned only with the initial distribution of a security. Although it was an important first step and forerunner to more ambitious efforts in securities regulation, this legislation failed to adequately address many of the practices in the capital market that contributed to the 1929 collapse.

Fletcher and Rayburn once again introduced bills in Congress, based in large part on drafts written by investigator Pecora. At the time, there was significant and widespread opposition to stock market regulation. Government interference, it was argued, would likely upset the delicate workings of Wall Street. Richard Whitney, president of the New York Stock Exchange (NYSE), was at the vanguard of this resistance. Whitney organized a well-financed protest campaign and mobilized forces to defeat the proposed legislation. Overt threats were even made to relocate the NYSE to Montreal, Canada, which offered a less obtrusive regulatory environment. Intense lobbying efforts did result in some modifications of the original bills, but finally, on June 6, 1934, Roosevelt signed the Securities Exchange Act.

PROVISIONS OF THE 1934 ACT

The major provisions of the Securities Exchange Act deal with three broad areas of regulation in an attempt to prevent the abuses previously cited and thereby protect the public interest: full and fair disclosure, supervision of capital market practices, and administration of credit requirements. This act requires that all national securities exchanges register with and be subject to the regulations of the Securities and Exchange Commission (SEC), an administrative agency with quasi-judicial powers that was created by this legislation. The immediate result was the closing of nine stock exchanges that could not meet the new requirements, including a one-man exchange operating out of an Indiana poolroom.

All corporations with securities listed on a national exchange must file detailed registration statements with the SEC and are required to disclose financial information on a periodic basis, in a form that meets standards. The SEC retains discretionary power over the form and detail of such disclosures. SEC also requires periodic audits of these firms by independent accountants.

This last requirement has had a dramatic impact on the growth and development of the accounting profession. Certified public accountants were effectively granted a franchise to audit corporations with publicly traded securities. There was a substantial cost involved in terms of increased risk exposure. By expressing an opinion on the veracity of financial statements filed with the SEC, the auditor becomes legally liable to third parties (including investors) who may subsequently be harmed by reliance on that information.

In the area of actual market practices, the SEC had immediate and far-reaching impact. Because of the relative informational advantage that market participants have over the public, the SEC now closely scrutinizes their activities. Exchanges, brokers, and dealers must all register with the SEC and file periodic disclosure reports. Corporate insiders are subject to especially strict rules designed to prevent unfair profit-taking. Certain stock market manipulation schemes (for example, wash sales) are prohibited. In fact, any fraudulent, manipulative, or deceptive securities dealings, whether specified by the act or not, are prohibited for all market participants. The penalties for infraction include fines, imprisonment, or both.

Finally, in the area of credit, the 1934 act authorizes the Federal Reserve System to administer the extension of margin credit in securities trading, with the SEC as ultimate enforcer. This important component of government economic and monetary policy was no longer to be left in the hands of individual brokers.

EARLY COMMISSIONS

The first commission was composed of a presidentially appointed five-member bipartisan panel that included Ferdinand Pecora. (Ironically, Pecora was passed over as chairman in favor of Joseph Kennedy, who the year before had participated in a pool syndicate operation.) Since its inception, the SEC has progressed through a number of different phases. The first decade of operation was an innovative period in which the permanent machinery and procedures necessary to carry out the functions and responsibilities of the SEC were established. This period was also marked by a concerted effort on the part of the early commissioners to promote the agency to both the public and the business community as a powerful partner in the quest for honest financial activity, not as a mere enforcement arm of the government.

It was during this early period that a philosophy of operation began to evolve. Rather than merely coercing compliance through enforcement actions, the SEC often adopted the policy of encouraging self-regulation within a framework of governmental constraints. By inspiring confidence in the laws that it administered, the SEC hoped to foster a heightened sense of social responsibility and ethics among the private sector, leading to development of self-monitoring systems.

This pragmatic approach was perhaps most evident in the area of establishing accounting and reporting standards. Although the SEC had been empowered to develop and maintain standards and principles of accounting practice, it generally deferred to the accounting profession. Such concession did not occur automatically. The SEC first had to satisfy itself that the private sector's system of establishing accounting and auditing standards had progressed to an acceptable level.

The next twenty-year period was characterized by very little significant legislation or innovation. Investor confidence in the capital markets was generally high, and the SEC routinely carried on the mission that had been developed. Revitalization of the SEC came in the early 1960's, after a rash of litigation related to the civil and criminal liability issues involved in inaccurate financial disclosures. Various amendments to legislation administered by the SEC followed. In the 1970's, major legislation was passed to combat corporate bribery and other illegal business practices.

During the 1980's, the SEC was guided by a doctrine of facilitation. Major efforts to expand full and fair disclosure and to streamline and standardize reporting requirements demonstrated the SEC's commitment to improving the efficiency of the flow of information and ultimately the flow of capital investment in the economy. A decade of unprecedented economic prosperity followed during the 1990's. Then, in 2001, with disclosures by companies such as Enron and Worldcom that revealed questionable accounting practices that had inflated these companies' appearance of profitability, the SEC came under scrutiny for what some perceived as inadequate oversight of corporate business practices. The SEC required that all chief executive officers and chief financial officers of major companies file sworn statements backing up the claims made in their reports to investors and made these statements available for public scrutiny on its Web site.

Jon R. Carpenter

SOURCES FOR FURTHER STUDY

Chatov, Robert. *Corporate Financial Reporting.* New York: Free Press, 1975.

De Bedts, Ralph F. *The New Deal's SEC.* New York: Columbia University Press, 1964.

Ellenberger, Jack S., and Ellen P. Mahar, comps. *Legislative History of the Securities Act of 1933 and Securities Exchange Act of 1934.* South Hackensack, N.J.: F. B. Rothman, 1973.

Pointer, Larry Gene, and Richard G. Schroeder. *An Introduction to the Securities and Exchange Commission.* Plano Texas: Business Publications, 1986.

Rappaport, Louis H. *SEC Accounting Practice and Procedure.* 3d ed. New York: Ronald Press, 1972.

Tyler, Poyntz, ed. *Securities, Exchanges, and the SEC.* New York: H. W. Wilson, 1965.

SEE ALSO: Payne-Aldrich Tariff Act (1909); Hundred Days legislation (1933); Banking Act of 1933 (1933); Banking Act of 1935 (1935).

NATIONAL FIREARMS ACT AND FEDERAL FIREARMS ACT

DATE: June 6, 1934 (NFA); June 30, 1938 (FFA)
U.S. STATUTES AT LARGE: 48 Stat. 1236 (NFA); 52 Stat. 1252 (FFA)
U.S. CODE: 26 § 5845 (NFA); 15 § 901 (FFA)
CATEGORIES: Crimes and Criminal Procedure; Tariffs and Taxation

The first federal statutes that restricted the keeping and bearing of arms, the 1934 and 1938 firearms acts represented the first significant federal involvement in taxing and controlling firearm possession and established the struggle between the federal government and the National Rifle Association.

The 1934 National Firearms Act required a license for the interstate transfer of machine guns, silencers, and short-barreled rifles and shotguns. The licensing procedure involved a two-hundred-dollar transfer tax and the use of a tax stamp. Although the law's initiator, Attorney General Homer Cummings, wanted the act to apply to all concealable firearms, records of congressional hearings show that it was concealable automatic weapons with which lawmakers were primarily concerned. As a compromise between the bill's advocates and opponents, handguns were removed from the law. Major opposition to the bill came from the National Rifle Association.

The 1938 Federal Firearms Act established a general licensing and record-keeping procedure for manufacturers and dealers shipping or receiving any firearms or ammunition across state lines. Restrictions included forbidding the interstate sale of guns by unlicensed dealers. The act prohibited the interstate sale of guns to fugitives and to people who had been convicted of violent crimes; also prohibited was transporting stolen firearms across state lines. These two acts were to be the only federal firearms legislation until the government again became interested in firearm legislation in the late 1960's.

Maria A. Hernandez

SOURCE FOR FURTHER STUDY
United States. Internal Revenue Service. *National Firearms Act and Federal Firearms Act.* Washington, D.C.: Government Printing Office, 1966.

SEE ALSO: Second Amendment (1789); Pittman-Robertson Wildlife Restoration Act (1937); Brady Handgun Violence Protection Act (1994); Violent Crime Control and Law Enforcement Act (1994).

INDIAN REORGANIZATION ACT

ALSO KNOWN AS: Wheeler-Howard Act
DATE: June 18, 1934
U.S. STATUTES AT LARGE: 48 Stat. 984
U.S. CODE: 25 § 461
CATEGORIES: Native Americans

One of the most important pieces of legislation affecting Native Americans reversed policies of forced assimilation and promoted tribal self-government.

The New Deal policy toward American Indians in the 1930's and early 1940's and its centerpiece, the Indian Reorganization Act, were a reaction to the controversies generated by previous federal policies toward American Indians. From the 1870's through the 1920's, tribal peoples were confined to government-controlled reservations and subjected to a policy aimed at bringing them into the dominant society's mainstream through forced assimilation. Government and church-run schools attempted to eradicate native languages and religion, customs and dress, tribalism and group loyalty, and replace them with Christian values, traditions, and institutions. To foster individualism and undermine tribalism, congressional legislation allotted the tribal communal domain to small individual holdings and opened surplus land for public sale.

This ambitious social experiment did not work as its original reform-minded advocates had intended. Under allotment, American Indians lost most of their lands to whites, while the educational experience undermined or destroyed indigenous peoples' heritage and culture without providing a viable substitute. The common results were demoralization, loss of identity, abject poverty, poor health, and defective education. These conditions, documented by independent studies, sparked a high-level, decade-long debate in the 1920's about American Indian policy. Congress, the Department of the Interior, and the authoritarian management style of the department's Bureau of Indian Affairs (BIA) came under sharp criticism.

JOHN COLLIER AND THE BIA

The political upheaval wrought by the Great Depression and the election of Franklin D. Roosevelt in 1932 provided reformers with an opportunity to reshape American Indian policy. In 1933, John Collier, a persistent critic of the BIA, became commissioner of Indian Affairs and directed the bureau until 1945.

Collier, a former social worker in New York City, had been introduced to the Pueblo cultures of the Southwest in 1920. Collier had experienced a native society that had maintained its communal and group traditions. Collier believed that he had discovered a

"Red Atlantis," whose communal life and harmonious relationship with the natural world contained lessons and hope for the regeneration of Western society through a cooperative commonwealth.

After taking office, Collier began to reverse past government policy by initiating the Indian New Deal through executive orders and lobbying activities. In January, 1934, he forbade interference with traditional Native Americans' religious practices, declared their culture equal to all others, and encouraged the revival of native languages. Next, Collier ended forced attendance at Christian religious exercises by American Indian children at boarding schools. The commissioner persuaded Congress to repeal espionage and gag rules that restricted free speech and other civil liberties on reservations. Collier also decreased BIA controls and interference with tribal courts and tribal law. Finally, he placed a moratorium on the further sale of tribal lands.

Collier then sought to implement his goals of American Indian cultural freedom and political self-determination through legislation. He and his associates drew up a forty-eight-page document containing four sections aimed at replacing the agency's authoritarian approach with a new bilateral relationship between the tribes and the federal government. Title I dealt with the restoration of tribal self-government and economic revitalization to make tribal society viable. Tribes would petition for home-rule elections, adopt constitutions, and charter a tax-exempt corporation to set up businesses, manage property, and borrow from a federal revolving loan program. Title II, which focused on education, promoted the study of American Indian civilization and traditional arts and crafts, provided scholarships, and appropriated funds for primary and secondary education. Title III, which concerned Indian lands, ended allotments, returned previously allotted lands to tribal ownership, and restored unsold surplus reservation lands to tribal control. The federal government also was authorized to provide tribes with funds to rebuild their lost land base. Title IV proposed setting up a federal Court of Indian Affairs that would have original jurisdiction in cases involving Native Americans. In Congress, Representative Edgar Howard of Nebraska and Senator Burton K. Wheeler of Montana agreed to sponsor this initial version of what was to become the Indian Reorganization Act (IRA).

The proposed legislation immediately encountered opposition from both Indian and non-Indian sources. Few American Indians were consulted when the proposal was drawn up, which gave rise to suspicion and concern about some provisions. Those Native Americans who were most affected by assimilation policies over the last half century saw the act's provisions as taking a step backward. Some who held private allotments were concerned about losing them. Tribal leaders who viewed their sovereignty as inherent and some groups that already had constitutions or intact traditional political structures argued that the proposed BIA constitutional guidelines provided no new rights and, in fact, restricted tribal sovereignty. BIA constitutions resembled U.S. governmental bodies rather than traditional forms of tribal government. Some clergy and missionaries denounced the promotion of traditional culture as anti-Christian and pagan. A growing conservative coalition in Congress did not share Collier's radically progressive views on the restoration of traditional tribal cultures and the establishment of politically independent tribal nations.

COMPROMISE

In the end, Collier had to compromise. Getting the legislation out of the congressional committee in which it was stalled required the strong support of both President Roosevelt and Secretary of the Interior Harold Ickes. In the bill's final version, which passed on June 18, 1934, Title II, concerning Native American culture, and Title IV, which provided for an American Indian court, were deleted. The amount of funding to assist the establishment of tribal governments was cut back significantly. Other modifications greatly reduced the number of tribal peoples to be covered under the act. Senator Wheeler insisted on subjecting tribal self-government to the approval of the secretary of the interior and excluded from the act American Indians who were not members of tribes, as well as those tribes located in Oklahoma and Alaska. Another amendment by Howard required that each tribe hold a referendum to accept or reject the IRA.

In referenda held between 1933 and 1945, 174 tribes accepted the act while 73 voted against ratification, including the largest American Indian nation, the Navajo. However, only 92 of the tribes that voted in favor adopted IRA constitutions, and 71 took the next step of incorporating for the purpose of obtaining federal economic development loans. American Indians living in Oklahoma and Alaska were placed under the IRA by legislation passed in 1936.

Collier reluctantly accepted these changes, emphasizing the breakthrough represented by those parts of his original proposal that were retained. The commissioner also attempted to implement many of his goals through administrative actions and orders. The failure of Congress to appropriate the full amounts authorized in the IRA, continuing opposition to some of Collier's goals, and the commissioner's own misjudgments and administrative shortcomings were some of the factors that prevented his dream of a Red Atlantis from becoming reality. In the decade following the New Deal era, federal American Indian policy again adopted an assimilationist and antitribal orientation.

Nevertheless, the IRA was a landmark in federal American Indian policy, with some noteworthy results. Many scholars consider it the single most important piece of federal American Indian legislation. Accomplishments of the IRA and the Indian New Deal included halting the disappearance of the tribal land base and restoring several million acres to various reservations. The act permitted many tribes to assume a degree of economic and political control over their affairs. The restoration of religious freedom and traditional ceremonies were also important measures. With few exceptions, those tribes that received government loans used them to improve economic conditions on reservations and made repayment. American Indians were given preference for positions in the BIA. Many tribes have taken advantage of IRA provisions to defend sovereignty and survive. Most important, the reversal of past policies awakened hope and pride in being American Indian.

David A. Crain

Sources for Further Study

Deloria, Vine, ed. *The Indian Reorganization Act: Congresses and Bills.* Norman: University of Oklahoma Press, 2002.

Fey, Harold E., and D'Arcy McNickle. *Indians and Other Americans: Two Ways of Life Meet.* Rev. ed. New York: Harper & Row, 1970.

Kelly, Lawrence C. "The Indian Reorganization Act: The Dream and the Reality." *Pacific Historical Review* 44 (August, 1975): 291-312.

Kelly, William H., ed. *Indian Affairs and the Indian Reorganization Act: The Twenty Year Record.* Tucson: University of Arizona Press, 1954.

Parman, Donald L. *The Navajos and the New Deal.* New Haven, Conn.: Yale University Press, 1976.

Philp, Kenneth R. *John Collier's Crusade for Indian Reform, 1920-1954.* Tucson: University of Arizona Press, 1977. administrator.

Taylor, Graham D. *The New Deal and American Indian Tribalism: The Administration of the Indian Reorganization Act, 1934-1945.* Lincoln: University of Nebraska Press, 1980.

SEE ALSO: Indian Appropriation Act (1871); General Allotment Act (1887); Indian Citizenship Act (1924); Termination Resolution (1953); Public Law 280 (1953).

COMMUNICATIONS ACT

DATE: June 19, 1934
U.S. STATUTES AT LARGE: 48 Stat. 1034
U.S. CODE: 47 § 151
CATEGORIES: Communications and Media

This law broadened the federal government's regulatory powers beyond radio broadcasting to encompass all areas of telecommunications.

Through passage of this law in 1934, Congress replaced the seven-year-old Federal Radio Commission with the Federal Communications Commission (FCC). The new law was predicated on the belief that the broadcast spectrum was a public resource that must be owned and retained by the people. This theory held that the broadcast industry must be regulated by the federal government to ensure that a diversity of viewpoints are aired. The act broadened the government's authority beyond radio, giving it the power to regulate all telecommunications.

REGULATION OR CENSORSHIP?

Section 326 of the Communications Act specifically prohibited censorship by stating that nothing in the law should "be understood or construed to give the commission the power of censorship" over radio broadcasting and that no regulations or conditions should be promulgated that would "interfere with the right of free speech by means of radio communication." Although the law forbade the FCC from forcing stations to air—or to stop airing—specific programs, the law simultaneously directed the commission to regulate broadcasting so that it would be "in the public interest." This directive gave the FCC the power to revoke, or not renew, broadcast licenses in cases of flagrant disregard of broadcasters' responsibility.

Under the act, the FCC could determine who should broadcast, on which wavelengths, with what power, and when. Since the FCC was authorized to grant broadcast licenses for limited numbers of years at a time, license renewal proceedings gave the FCC the power to influence station policies, ranging from their advertising techniques to the amounts of time they devoted to news and public service programming. However, the FCC rarely used this power to cancel or refuse renewal of licenses. Instead, it has typically used indirect pressure to influence the content of broadcasts.

EQUAL TIME RULE

There has been widespread disagreement on how far the FCC should go in forcing licensees to serve the public interest. Section 315 of the Communications Act required broadcasters providing news coverage of political campaigns to cover candidates of every party seeking the same political offices equally. Some people have argued that this "equal time rule" amounts to a form of reverse censorship that violates broadcasters' First Amendment rights.

In 1959 the equal time rule was tested when members of the FCC voted 4-3 that a Chicago television station had to offer a candidate twenty-two seconds on its news program in order to balance the time it had devoted to showing Mayor Richard Daly greeting a foreign official. Both men were candidates in the Chicago mayoral election. Congress responded by amending the law to exempt noncampaign news coverage of an incumbent.

The following year Congress temporarily suspended section 315 to allow television networks to broadcast the debates between presidential candidates John F. Kennedy and Richard M. Nixon without having to include third-party candidates. In 1975 the FCC made this exception a permanent rule by declaring that stations could carry debates among pairs of major party candidates without the participation of minor party candidates.

The equal time rule required that stations offering broadcast time outside of their regular news programs to political candidates must offer equal time to the candidates' opponents. However, the rule also permitted stations to cover news events in which candidates appear without having to offer equal time to their opponents. The equal time rule does not apply to appearances of candidates on regular "bona fide" newscasts, news interviews, and news documentaries in which candidates appear incidentally. The difficulty for broadcasters has lain in deciding what constitutes real news.

POLITICAL ADVERTISING

Section 315 of the Communications Act has been most often applied to situations involving political advertising. The equal time rule states that if a licensee permits a legally qualified candidate for public office to use its station, it also must "afford equal opportunity to all other such candidates for that office." Broadcast stations that sell advertising time to political candidates thus cannot refuse to sell equal numbers of spots in the same time periods—and at the same prices—to candidates of other parties seeking the same offices.

The FCC has refined its rules on political advertising in order fully to implement section 315's requirements. These guarantee access to broadcast advertising for all candidates for federal office, ensure equal broadcast advertising opportunities to rival candidates for public office, require the lowest-unit rate charges for political advertising, and forbid censorship of the content of political advertisements—even if such content violates other FCC regulations, such as those pertaining to indecent language or broadcasts.

FAIRNESS QUESTIONS

Some of the problems of adhering to the equal time principle in political news coverage disappeared after Congress's 1959 ruling. However, the root issue of ensuring "fairness" in access to the airwaves and in presenting various sides of controversial issues remained. The FCC's so-called fairness doctrine, which was enforced until 1985, was based on the argument that because the airwaves are public property the FCC should direct licensed broadcasters to operate "in the public interest, convenience, and necessity." The belief is that the public interest is best served when the airwaves are accessible to differing viewpoints.

The difficulty of attempting to legislate "fairness" led the FCC to abandon the fairness doctrine. Broadcasters had long argued that extreme efforts to include opposing viewpoints in coverage and interpretation of controversial issues led to less, rather than better, coverage of important social issues. They argued that if stations had to seek out other viewpoints to air on every issue they wished to address, they would tend to avoid covering controversial issues. Broadcasters argued that this likelihood was increased by the fear that groups or individuals dissatisfied with a station's coverage might have grounds to oppose the station's license at renewal time.

Cynics claimed that broadcasters protesting the fairness doctrine really wanted to be free from pressure from minorities, women, senior citizens, and others demanding balanced coverage. This led to an unusual alliance of advocates for minority causes and big business, who had long felt discriminated against by network coverage of national issues, particularly since the social unrest of the 1960's and the Watergate era of the early 1970's heightened mistrust of established authority. The commission sided with broadcasters, whose voices included leading journalists usually sympathetic to minority viewpoints. Walter Cronkite and Eric Severeid, for example, argued that average citizens have so many ways to obtain differing viewpoints on social issues that it was no longer necessary to require broadcasters to seek out diverse perspectives themselves.

Although the FCC concluded that the fairness doctrine did not serve the public interest, it left intact the general requirement that broadcasters present issue-responsive programming. When a station's license renewal is challenged, this issue-responsive programming can become a major ingredient in a its ability to show that it has operated in the public interest. Thus the obligation that broadcasters provide balanced coverage of important public issues remained even though details on how they should do this were deregulated.

THE FUTURE

The strongest argument against continuing the regulations imposed by the Communications Act of 1934 has been the erosion of a central part of the philosophical basis for which the law was originally enacted. The argument that the airwaves belong to the public was based largely on their presumed scarcity—the notion that because the number of broadcast frequencies is finite, the federal government had to ensure that radio and television broadcasting was not dominated by those with the most money and power. Since the act was passed, however, there has been a steady growth in the number of licensed frequencies in the United States. By the mid-1990's there were more than eleven thousand radio stations and more than fifteen hundred television stations. There has also been a great expansion of cable television. These and other technological advances have mitigated against the old scarcity argument.

The 1994 election of the first Republican-controlled Congress in the telemedia age prompted many advocates of deregulation to favor a major overhaul of the Communications Act of 1934. Although many deregulatory changes were instituted through the Telecommunications Act of 1996, the rules pertaining to equal time, political advertising, and balanced news coverage of controversial issues remained.

Gerard Donnelly

SOURCES FOR FURTHER STUDY

Edwards, Verne E., Jr. *Journalism in a Free Society.* Dubuque, Iowa: William C. Brown, 1970.

Emery, Edwin, and Michael Emery. *The Press and America: An Interpretive History of the Mass Media.* 5th ed. Englewood Cliffs, N.J.: Prentice-Hall, 1984.

Gelman, Morrie, "Seventy-five Years of Pioneers: A Personalized History of the Fifth Estate from Frank Conrad to Rupert Murdoch." *Broadcasting and Cable* 125, no. 45 (November 6, 1995).

Krasnow, Erwin G., and Lawrence D. Longley. *The Politics of Broadcast Regulation.* New York: St. Martin's Press, 1973.

Lichty, Lawrence W., and Malachi C. Topping. *American Broadcasting: A Source Book on the History of Radio and Television.* New York: Hastings House, 1975.

Stephens, Mitchell. *Broadcast News: Radio Journalism and an Introduction to Television.* New York: Holt, Rinehart and Winston, 1980.

SEE ALSO: Comstock Act (1873); Communications Act Amendments (1960); Public Broadcasting Act (1967); Communications Decency Act (1996).

FEDERAL CREDIT UNION ACT

DATE: June 26, 1934
U.S. STATUTES AT LARGE: 48 Stat. 1216
U.S. CODE: 12 § 1751
CATEGORIES: Banking, Money, and Finance

> *By establishing a federal credit union system, the act encouraged savings and made credit more available to people of limited means.*

A federal credit union is a nonprofit, member-owned cooperative organized to encourage its members to put money into savings and to use these accumulated savings to make loans to members. It also has the function of educating members on how to manage their own finances. The federal government, through the National Credit Union Administration (NCUA), charters credit unions as corporations as well as supervising and insuring them.

FEDERAL CREDIT UNIONS

In order to generate and maintain a feeling of mutual responsibility, members of a federal credit union must have a common bond of employment, association, or residence. The members, with one vote each, elect a volunteer board of directors from the membership at an annual meeting. The board has authority to determine the maximum limits on loans and the interest rates to be charged. Interest rates tend to be favorable in comparison to those offered by other lenders because of the lower labor costs in volunteer organizations, lower losses on defaulted loans, and lower marketing costs. In addition to an unpaid board of directors, credit unions have officers who are generally unpaid or receive nominal salaries. The ratio of delinquent to outstanding loans in the early 1990's stood at half that of federally insured commercial banks. Personal contact and personal credit judgments play a large role in keeping this ratio low. Two major marketing advantages are the bond of clients to the credit union through membership and the close proximity of clients, with the credit union often located at an employee's place of work.

Loans can be designed to meet the needs of individual members. Federal credit unions must comply with all federal consumer protection laws, such as the Truth in Lending Act (1980) and the Equal Credit Opportunity Act (1975). Deposits by members are in the form of shares in the credit union and are frequently made through payroll deductions. Each account as of the early 1990's was insured up to $100,000 by the NCUA. Profits from lending money and other sources may be distributed to the members as dividends.

ORIGIN OF CREDIT UNIONS
The development of credit unions resulted from the needs of lower income groups. Prior to the existence of credit unions, there were a limited number of outlets for small savings or loans. In 1948, the first credit union was organized in Belgium. At the same time in Germany, F. Hermann Schulze-Delitzsch organized cooperative credit societies and developed the principle that the funds to be loaned to members would come from the savings of members. By 1880, about three thousand cooperative credit societies had been organized in Germany.

Friedrich Wilhelm Raiffeisen also organized cooperative credit societies in Germany but put greater emphasis on unselfish service to the organization. By 1920, his model for the earliest credit unions was being used in most countries in the world.

The credit union movement spread to the North American continent with the help of Alphonse Desjardins, a legislative journalist who was studying economic conditions in Europe in the late 1890's. In 1900, Desjardins used ideas from the Schulze-Delitzsch and Raiffeisen financial cooperatives to establish the first cooperative bank, La Caisse Populaire (the people's bank), in the city of Levis in the province of Quebec, Canada.

Edward A. Filene, a wealthy Boston merchant and philanthropist, was influential in bringing credit unions to the United States. His interest in the subject resulted from extensive travel throughout the world. He convinced Pierre Jay, commissioner of banking for Massachusetts, to work toward establishing a cooperative credit society in that state. Jay asked Desjardins to assist in passing a credit union act in Massachusetts. The Massachusetts Credit Union Act, the first complete credit union act in the United States, was enacted in 1909. In the same year, in Manchester, New Hampshire, Desjardins helped to organize the first legally chartered cooperative credit society in the United States.

Growth in the credit union movement was slow during the decade after passage of the Massachusetts act. By 1919, however, Filene believed that there was a sufficient number of credit unions to justify an organized move toward national legislation. He organized the National Committee on People's Banks to spearhead this task. The development of credit unions was aided by favorable conditions during the 1920's. General prosperity and development of new consumer goods resulted in higher savings by workers and greater demand for consumer credit.

Three factors were necessary to expand the movement: legislation allowing the chartering (incorporation) of credit unions, education of the general public regarding the movement, and voluntary associations of credit unions at the state level to further expand the movement. To facilitate each of these, the Credit Union National Extension Bureau (which became the Credit Union National Association in 1934) was created and financed by Filene. He hired Roy F. Bergengren as manager and Thomas W. Doig as assistant manager. Bergengren had started as the managing director of the Massachusetts Credit Union Association in 1920. He used the extension bureau to promote enabling legislation authorizing credit unions and helped organize individual credit unions.

The Great Depression had a favorable impact on the movement. In 1932, Congress authorized credit unions in the District of Columbia and allowed them to borrow from the Reconstruction Finance Corporation. By 1934, thirty-eight states had enacted credit union laws and more than twenty-four hundred credit unions were in operation.

Bergengren became increasingly convinced that national legislation was necessary. He argued that a federal law would permit the organization of credit unions in states that had refused to pass such legislation; that there was some possibility that other states might repeal their credit union laws, as West Virginia had done in 1931;

that a federal statute would be useful as a basis of organization in those states that had weak or defective laws; and that federal legislation should be complete before credit unions formed a national association.

PASSAGE OF THE ACT

The culmination of the legislative efforts of the Credit Union National Extension Bureau came on June 26, 1934, when Congress enacted the Federal Credit Union Act. The act provided for the chartering, supervision, and examination of federal credit unions by the United States government. The writers of the act tried to incorporate the best ideas from state laws.

In the same year, Congress chose the Farm Credit Administration (FCA) to supervise credit unions because of its expertise in examining other types of financial cooperatives chartered by the U.S. government. Claude R. Orchard was appointed the first director of the Credit Union Section, FCA. More than eighty-seven hundred federal credit unions were chartered during the nineteen years he served as director. Also in 1934, Bergengren and Filene held a national meeting of credit union delegates that led to the development of the Credit Union National Association (CUNA).

IMPACT

The most important impact of the Federal Credit Union Act of 1934 was the confidence it inspired in the American public regarding credit unions. Involvement by the federal government played a major role in the growth of credit unions, from almost 2,500 credit unions when the act was passed to 3,372 by the end of 1935. In 1937, Congress passed legislation prohibiting the taxation of federal credit unions except on the basis of real or personal property. This legislation further supported growth in the number of entities, which approached 8,000 by 1939.

Individual credit unions were also growing at an impressive rate. By March, 1936, Armour and Company employee credit unions had more than 22,000 members, had $1.25 million in assets, and had made loans up to that date of almost $7 million. There were twenty-four credit unions among Sears, Roebuck and Company employees, with 7,982 members, and credit unions associated with the U.S. Steel Corporation had almost 23,000 members. A credit union served employees of the United States Senate. Another credit union at the studios of Twentieth Century-Fox had more than one thousand members.

Many employers considered a credit union to be an important fringe benefit, with the advantage of involving no necessary cost to them. Space for the credit union offices often was provided on the premises, perhaps at reduced cost. Payroll withholdings both for regular savings and for installment collection of loans was another common service by employers.

In 1935, CUNA's national board of directors agreed to establish the CUNA Mutual Insurance Society. The society provided only borrowers' protection insurance to credit unions at first, adding life insurance for officers and families associated with CUNA in August, 1936. At the same time, the society considered writing automobile insurance but took no action. By the end of 1936, 437 credit unions in thirty states were members of the society. A total of twenty-three thousand loans were insured, with a total coverage of $2,425,000. The reserves of the society for payment of claims amounted to $11,000. Deposit insurance did not begin until 1970.

SUBSEQUENT LEGISLATION

The Credit Union Modernization Act of 1977 and 1978 revised much of the Federal Credit Union Act of 1934. The new legislation extended loan maturities, expanded real estate and home improvement loans, authorized self-replenishing credit lines to borrowers, and standardized participation loans with other credit unions. It also made many other changes in the technical operation of credit unions that expanded lending and investment authority.

The Financial Institutions Reform Act of 1978, as part of the Modernization Act, established the Central Liquidity Facility as part of the National Credit Union Administration. This organization added safety to credit union lending by providing liquidity for emergency needs. It was not intended to provide permanent financing. This legislation also restructured the National Credit Union Administration and set up a new administration board with increased supervisory functions.

The Depository Institutions Deregulation and Monetary Control Act was passed in 1980. This law affected credit unions directly by increasing deposit insurance coverage. It affected them indirectly by legalizing share drafts for banks and savings and loans, increasing competition for the credit union industry, which already offered share drafts. The act also required that depository institutions maintain some level of reserves with the Federal Reserve System. Most credit unions did not maintain these reserves because the requirement was not implemented for any institution with deposits of less than $2 million. The Garn-St. Germain Act of 1982 suspended the monetary reserve requirement for the first $2 million in reservable accounts. This act also gave credit unions more flexibility and authority to handle their own affairs, including greater freedom in mortgage markets.

In general, all this legislation, combined with favorable regulatory changes, made credit unions more competitive with banks and savings and loans. The industry was permitted to use a greater variety of sources for both assets and liabilities, and a greater range of financial activities was allowed. The interest rates that credit unions could pay on savings and charge for loans were relatively free from government control. Finally, credit unions still enjoyed the political and economic benefits of being nonprofit organizations.

Richard Goedde

SOURCES FOR FURTHER STUDY
Bergengren, Roy F. *Crusade: The Fight for Economic Democracy in North America, 1921-1945.* New York: Exposition Press, 1952.
_____. *CUNA Emerges.* Madison, Wis.: Credit Union National Association, 1935.
Croteau, John T. *The Economics of the Credit Union.* Detroit: Wayne State University Press, 1963.
_____. *The Federal Credit Union Policy and Practice.* New York: Harper & Brothers, 1956.
Moody, J. Carroll, and Gilbert C. Fite. *The Credit Union Movement Origins and Development, 1850-1970.* Lincoln: University of Nebraska Press, 1850-1970.
Pugh, Olin S., and F. Gerry Ingram. *Credit Unions: A Movement Becomes an Industry.* Reston: Reston Publishing Company, 1984.
U.S. National Credit Union Administration. *Development of Federal Credit Unions.* Washington, D.C.: Author, 1972.

SEE ALSO: McFadden Act (1927); Consumer Credit Protection Act (1968); Truth in Lending Act (1968); Fair Credit Reporting Act (1970); Equal Credit Opportunity Act (1974).

TAYLOR GRAZING ACT

DATE: June 28, 1934
U.S. STATUTES AT LARGE: 48 Stat. 1269
U.S. CODE: 43 § 315
CATEGORIES: Agriculture; Animals; Environment and Conservation; Land Management; Natural Resources

In the early 1930's, with much of the federal land in the West suffering from overgrazing and drought, the Taylor Grazing Act imposed regulations on the use of the remaining public domain of the American West.

With the United States in the throes of the Great Depression, the public lands of the American West suffered from severe drought and overgrazing. As Congressman Edward Taylor of Colorado warned his colleagues, "We are rapidly permitting the creations of small Sahara Deserts in every one of the Western states today." Until 1934, western stockmen grazed animals on federal lands without the need of permission and regulation.

In the laissez-faire economic atmosphere of the late 1920's, President Herbert Hoover's Commission on the Conservation and Administration of the Public Domain had recommended that the remaining public domain be turned over to the states with the federal government retaining title to mineral lands. Soon the Depression intervened, however, and concerned westerners channeled their energies into working with federal bureaucrats to shape an acceptable plan for managing those millions of acres of federal lands outside the purveyance of the National Park Service, National Forest Service, and other federal agencies.

AN END TO HOMESTEADING

The plan was named after Taylor (a Colorado Democrat), whose home district in western Colorado contained a high percentage of federal land. If a veteran congressman such as Taylor could see the benefit of federal regulation, most westerners could also. Even old stockmen who had previously opposed the federal presence as a matter of principle gave grudging approval to Taylor's legislation.

The bill ended the free use of the public domain. Homesteading would no longer be permitted. Eighty million acres of western land would be given to a new federal agency, the U.S. Grazing Service, under the Department of the Interior. Local grazing districts were established, and policies would be set by the ranchers themselves. Users would pay a nominal fee to rent the land for ten-year periods, with a portion of the proceeds going to support conservation projects. The Taylor Grazing Act firmly upheld the economic status quo in the public-land West by ordering that "preference" be given in the issuance of grazing permits to "landowners engaged in the livestock business" and those living near or in the grazing district. In 1936 the act was amended, increasing the total acreage under its domain to 142 million acres.

CRITICISMS AND OUTFALLS

Because it was founded and administered by westerners during an era of economic duress, the implementation of the Taylor Grazing Act was relatively free of controversy, but several critics of its authority soon appeared. Senator Pat McCarran (a Nevada Democrat) tried to challenge the system of uniform grazing fees. In 1946 Wyoming Republican senator Edward V. Robertson harked back to the old Hoover Commission by calling for a "return" of all federal lands to the states, a strategy echoed in the late 1970's by the so-called Sagebrush Rebellion. McCarran and other western critics of the Grazing Service succeeded in trimming its budget during World War II and forcing its merger with the General Land Office in 1946. The new agency, the Bureau of Land Management, would administer the public domain in the years ahead.

Steven C. Schulte

SOURCES FOR FURTHER STUDY

Barnes, Will C. *The Story of the Range.* Washington, D.C.: Government Printing Office, 1926.

Foss, Phillip O. *Politics and Grass.* Seattle: University of Washington Press, 1960.

Hays, Samuel P. *Conservation and the Gospel of Efficiency.* Cambridge, Mass.: Harvard University Press, 1959.

Muhn, James, and Hanson R. Stuart. *Opportunity and Challenge: The Story of the BLM.* Washington, D.C.: U.S. Department of the Interior. Bureau of Land Management, 1988.

Peffer, E. Louise. *The Closing of the Public Domain.* Stanford, Calif.: Stanford University Press, 1951.

U.S. Congress. Senate. *The Western Range.* 74th Congress, 2d. session, 1936. Senate Document 199.

U.S. Department of the Interior. Bureau of Land Management. *Fifty Years of Public Land Management: 1934-1984.* Washington, D.C.: Author, 1984.

SEE ALSO: Homestead Act (1862); General Mining Act (1872); Reclamation Act (1902); National Park Service Organic Act (1916); Mineral Leasing Act (1920); Multiple Use-Sustained Yield Act (1960); Wilderness Act (1964); Forest and Rangeland Renewable Resources Planning Act (1974).

NATIONAL LABOR RELATIONS ACT

ALSO KNOWN AS: Wagner-Connery Act
DATE: July 5, 1935
U.S. STATUTES AT LARGE: 49 Stat. 449
U.S. CODE: 29 § 151
CATEGORIES: Labor and Employment

> *Through this law, the federal government accepted the right of labor to use collective bargaining, marking the birth of "big labor."*

A commonly repeated fallacy relative to the New Deal is that Franklin Delano Roosevelt, almost immediately after his inauguration in 1933, turned his back on the nation's business interests and instead cultivated and indulged those of labor. This misleading bit of fiction would have one believe that the president gave organized labor immense power in exchange for its support at the polls. The weakness of this interpretation becomes apparent when one studies the creation of what is described as the "Magna Carta of modern unionism." The National Labor Relations Act (Wagner-Connery Act), mainly the work of Senator Robert F. Wagner of New York. Its adoption must be credited more to Wagner's perseverance than to any support received from the president or his administration.

LABOR LEGISLATION

When the New Deal started, organized labor was in serious retreat. During the 1920's, a combination of general prosperity, vigorous business attacks, and weak leadership had seriously depleted the ranks of trade unions. The Depression was merely an additional burden. The union movement achieved a small victory on March 23, 1932, when Congress passed the Norris-La Guardia Act, which prohibited courts from granting management injunctions against union activities. The law, interpreted as disallowing employers from proscribing workers from becoming involved in union activities, had no teeth, however.

In 1933, the National Industrial Recovery Act (NIRA) included a provision requiring all industries submitting codes to the government to pledge themselves to the recognition of labor's right to collective bargaining. In practice, however, this section proved worthless, because of the promotion of company unions and the plurality of bargaining units in any one industry.

The main difficulty in reforming NIRA's labor policy was the attitude of the Roosevelt administration. General Hugh S. Johnson, administrator of the National Recovery Administration (NRA), looked upon strikes in a code industry as similar to treason. Both Johnson and Roosevelt believed that business recovery had first priority. The president hardly could be described as pro-union but rather as reflecting a paternalistic approach. He sympathized with the worker, but he apparently had no desire to use the federal government to build up the strength of unions.

Labor grew increasingly restive under this situation, and during 1934, a number of serious strikes broke out. Senator Wagner, a leading union supporter, recognized the ineffectiveness of the NIRA's labor provision and took steps to remedy this condition. he succeeded in establishing a National Labor Board to hear grievances of workers and was named by Johnson to head the body. However, this board had no power to execute its decisions. Wagner believed that the situation was critical, because in his mind, economic recovery and stability could come only when the U.S. worker shared extensively in the benefits of increased productivity. The only hope for the survival of capitalism, in his opinion, was a complete redistribution of wealth. Wagner was convinced that this redistribution would come about only when the worker had gained the power of collective bargaining, and that this level of trade unionism could develop only with the assistance of the federal government.

NATIONAL LABOR RELATIONS BOARD

In March, 1934, Wagner introduced a bill into Congress to prevent unfair labor practices and to put teeth into the labor provisions of the NIRA. The president, however, was not inclined to support such a measure. Instead, on June 29, 1934, he established the National Labor Relations Board to replace the NRA's National Labor Board. Lloyd K. Garrison, dean of the Wisconsin Law School, was appointed chairman. Designed to hear workers' grievances, the board depended upon the cooperation of the NRA and the Department of Justice for its effectiveness. By November, 1934, most people realized that the board was useless. Neither General Johnson nor his successor, Donald R. Richberg, indicated any intention of cooperating with the board. Recovery was still most important, and the administration theme was cooperation with business.

The congressional election of 1934 swept away the right wing of the Republican Party. With the failure of the temporary National Labor Relations Board, the American Federation of Labor, finally recognizing the importance of Wagner's efforts in Congress, began a gigantic lobbying campaign. Finally, the Supreme Court appeared to be no longer hostile to New Deal legislation.

PROVISIONS AND PASSAGE

Senator Wagner now moved to resubmit his original bill. With the support of both Francis Biddle and Garrison, and aided by the effective lobby of the American Federation of Labor, Wagner introduced a measure in the Senate in February, 1935. It had a number of important provisions. First, all workers employed in industries that were engaged in interstate commerce were to be granted the right to join a union of their own choice and to bargain collectively. Second, the union that won majority support in a secret ballot election was to be granted sole bargaining privileges in that industry. Third, employers would be required to reorganize this union and to bargain in good faith. Fourth, the existing National Labor Relations Board was to be reestablished as an independent agency with the power to conduct elections to determine bargaining units and to prevent certain unfair labor practices by means of subpoenas, cease and desist orders, and court action. Fifth, to implement provisions of the act, management was asked to engage in affirmative action, a new term that was understood to mean that the burden of voluntary compliance was on management, such as reinstating workers with back pay who had been discharged from engaging in union activity, now protected by the law. The term next appeared in the text of Executive Order 10925, which President John F. Kennedy issued in 1961, requiring contractors to desegregate voluntarily as a condition of doing business with the federal government.

The bill had a stormy but quick passage through Congress. A number of Southern senators attempted to persuade Roosevelt to intervene against the bill, but Wagner succeeded in keeping the White House neutral. Business interests insisted that the bill threatened U.S. recovery. Violent opposition also came from the American Communist Party. Despite this opposition and the lack of backing from the Roosevelt administration, the bill passed the Senate by a vote of 63 to 12.

Court Cases

One week later, on May 24, 1935, Roosevelt belatedly announced his support for the Wagner Bill. Three days after that, the Supreme Court declared the NIRA unconstitutional. It is still not clear why Roosevelt decided to come to the support of Wagner at that time. Perhaps he was impressed by the wide margin by which the bill passed the Senate. On June 27, 1935, with backing from the administration, the bill easily passed the House by voice vote, and on July 5, 1935, Roosevelt signed it. The Wagner Act meant that the federal government was now behind the drive for the unionization of U.S. labor. Coming at the same time that labor itself was undergoing the internal revolution that spawned the militant Congress of Industrial Organizations, the National Labor Relations Act symbolized the birth of "big labor."

Soon after the Wagner Act passed, a challenge appeared in federal court. In *National Labor Relations Board v. Jones & Laughlin Steel Corporation* (1937), parts of the act were declared unconstitutional. Guarantees in the National Labor Relations Act have been whittled down by two major amendments—the Labor-Management Relations Act (Taft-Hartley Act) of 1947 and the Labor-Management Reporting and Disclosure Act (Landrum-Griffin Act) of 1959.

With the decline in union membership in the late twentieth century, the heyday of the National Labor Relations Act seems in the distant past. Formed primarily to protect workers with limited educational backgrounds, whose employment alternatives were limited, the union movement since has been diminished because many workers have enough education to shift jobs, and work requiring less educational preparation either is being replaced by machines or is being exported by multinational corporations to less developed countries at significantly lower wages.

George Q. Flynn, updated by
Michael Haas

SOURCES FOR FURTHER STUDY
Bernstein, Irving. *The New Deal Collective Bargaining Policy.* Berkeley: University of California Press, 1950.
Derber, Milton, and Edwin Young, eds. *Labor and the New Deal.* Madison: University of Wisconsin Press, 1957.
Hardin, Patrick, ed. *The Developing Labor Law.* 3d ed. Chicago: Bureau of National Affairs, 1992.
Millis, Harry A., and Emily C. Brown. *From the Wagner Act to Taft-Hartley: A Study of National Labor Policy and Labor Relations.* Chicago: University of Chicago Press, 1950.
Smolen, Joseph S., ed. *The National Labor Relations Act: As Amended by the Taft-Hartley Act and the Landrum-Griffin Act.* Minneapolis: University of Minnesota, 1962.

SEE ALSO: Norris-La Guardia Act (1932); National Industrial Recovery Act (1933); Labor-Management Relations Act (1947).

SOCIAL SECURITY ACT

DATE: August 14, 1935
U.S. STATUTES AT LARGE: 49 Stat. 620
U.S. CODE: 42 § 301 et seq.
CATEGORIES: Health and Welfare

Among the most far-reaching laws of the twentieth century, the Social Security Act authorized the United States' first national program of economic protection during retirement, unemployment, and disability.

Although Social Security in the United States is most often associated with a program for older, retired persons, the creators of the 1935 legislation viewed old-age dependency in the larger context of major changes in the economy and in family structure. They tended to believe that if economic security could be assured to the oldest members of society, such security could also be made a reality for other citizens. The original legislation did not profess to solve deep structural problems of unemployment and poverty—it was designed to provide the first links in the safety net that would protect U.S. citizens from future economic disasters. From the beginning, social welfare programs reflected an uncertainty of purpose between adequacy—a concept that benefits should be based on the needs of the recipients, and equity—a notion that benefits should reflect contributions made by the participants.

PRECEDENTS AND RATIONALES

By the 1930's, most of the nations of Western Europe had enacted some kind of social insurance legislation providing for old-age care and unemployment compensation. For a number of reasons, however, the United States had lagged behind in such efforts. It was not until the administration of Franklin Delano Roosevelt that the United States adopted an effective social security measure. The general economic depression of the decade undoubtedly contributed to the momentum needed to pass social security legislation, for during the Great Depression, many people in the United States came to see economic insecurity as a social problem, not merely a matter of individual virtue and responsibility. By 1934, considerable support had developed for utopian schemes, such as that developed by Dr. Francis E. Townsend, whose Old-Age Revolving Pension Club was lobbying for a monthly grant of two hundred dollars for every citizen over sixty years of age.

There was nothing radical about a plan for old-age pensions. Both private pensions and veterans' benefits existed long before the New Deal. Partly because such plans proved inadequate during the Depression, the Democratic platform of 1932 called for public retirement pensions and for unemployment compensation. By the 1930's, almost half the states had some kind of old-age pension, but these were generally limited in scope. Only Wisconsin had a working unemployment compensation plan. In 1932, Senator Robert F. Wagner of New York and Representative David J. Lewis of Mary-

land introduced bills in Congress calling for a federal unemployment plan patterned after that of Wisconsin. The same year, Senator Clarence C. Dill of Washington and Representative William P.
Connery of Massachusetts introduced a bill providing for federal
grants to those states establishing old-age pensions.

FRANCES PERKINS

It was not until 1934 that President Roosevelt decided to take the
initiative in the field of social insurance legislation. He asked Congress to delay action on the existing bills while he appointed a special committee to look into all aspects of social security, with the
aim of presenting a comprehensive measure at the 1935 congressional session. In June, 1934, he established the Committee on Economic Security, with Secretary of Labor Frances Perkins as chair.
Perkins took a broad view of her job and aimed to bring U.S. social
insurance up to that of advanced European countries. She soon
discovered, however, that there were divergent opinions, especially on the subject of how unemployment compensation should
be handled. The debate centered on whether the compensation
should be strictly a national operation.

On one side of the question stood a group of Wisconsin social
workers, such as Paul Rauschenbush and his wife Elizabeth Brandeis Rauschenbush. They advocated a joint state-national plan that
would allow for greater experimentation and variety. They also
pointed out that a joint approach would be more likely to meet
constitutional objections. Others, such as Rexford G. Tugwell,
Abraham Epstein, former secretary of the American Association of
Old-Age Security, and Professor Paul Douglas of the University of
Chicago recommended a solely national system to avoid unequal
coverage and protect the highly mobile U.S. worker. Perkins sided
with the Wisconsin group, and the final recommendation of the
committee followed the decentralized approach: unemployment
compensation would be financed by a federal tax on total payrolls,
with 90 percent of the tax going to the states to implement the program. The report also advocated a contributory national program
of old-age pensions. Roosevelt accepted the committee's report.

PASSAGE, PROVISIONS, AND IMPACT

The Social Security bill was submitted to Congress in January,
1935, by Senator Wagner and Congressman Lewis. The air was

filled with warnings that the act would destroy individual responsibility and the principles of self-help, but it was passed in the Senate
by 76 votes to 6, and in the House by 371 votes to 33. On August 14,
1935, Roosevelt signed the measure.

Money to fund the old-age insurance plan was to come from a
tax to be levied on employees' wages and employers' payrolls. Benefits would be payable at sixty-five years of age. The unemployment
compensation provisions followed the recommendations of the
Perkins Committee. In addition, the federal government would extend grants to the states for the care of the destitute elderly not covered by Social Security, and provide aid on a matching basis to
states for the care of dependent mothers, children, and the blind,
and for public health services. A Social Security Board was set up to
administer the various provisions of the act.

While clearly innovative for its time, the Social Security Act was
considered inadequate by many of its planners. The idea that a
worker should pay one-half the cost of his own retirement stopped
far short of most of the European plans. As Tugwell pointed out in
1934, the worker would already be paying a disproportionate share
as a consumer, because the employer's payroll tax in the program
would immediately be passed on in the form of higher prices. Roosevelt defended the payroll tax by pointing to the political strength
it gave the program. Because workers contributed to the pension
fund, they built up equity in it. The sense that workers had earned
a right to future benefits would make it difficult, if not impossible,
for subsequent administrations to deny coverage or to dismantle
the program. A weak feature of the law was its limited scope: It omitted farmworkers and domestics from unemployment compensation
and contained no health insurance provisions of any kind. The law
also reflected the assumptions of its framers that men were the principal wage earners and that women were economically dependent.
Nevertheless, the act represented the beginning of a growing belief
that the federal government had a responsibility to ensure certain
benefits to its citizens. It provided a floor of basic economic protection and a greater level of uniformity of assistance among the states.

Long-Term Problems, Potential Solutions
By the end of the twentieth century, a number of problems in the
Social Security system demanded attention. Since the system be-
gan, a large workforce contributed payroll taxes to support pay-

ments to a relatively small number of retirees. As the large number of "baby boomers"—those born in the two decades following World War II—reached retirement age, however, the proportion of citizens eligible for benefits increased more rapidly than the workforce. Amendments to the Social Security Act passed in 1983 anticipated the situation and raised taxes to create a surplus of funds in the system, but the program was still foreseen to be depleted by the year 2030. Younger workers feared that the social security system would be bankrupt before they became eligible for benefits.

Although most politicians were reluctant to propose major changes in the popular program, several types of reforms were suggested, including privatization of the system by allowing workers to invest in their own retirement accounts, thereby abolishing the social security trust fund. Others advocated a series of more modest changes: diverting some of the payroll taxes into savings accounts, increasing payroll taxes in small increments, raising the retirement age, limiting cost-of-living adjustments, or a combination of these.

George Q. Flynn, updated by
Mary Welek Atwell

SOURCES FOR FURTHER STUDY

Achenbaum, W. Andrew. *Social Security: Visions and Revisions.* New York: Cambridge University Press, 1986.

Berkowitz, Edward D. *America's Welfare State: From Roosevelt to Reagan.* Baltimore: The Johns Hopkins University Press, 1991.

Haber, Carole, and Brian Gratton. *Old Age and the Search for Security: An American Social History.* Bloomington: Indiana University Press, 1993.

Louchheim, Katie, ed. *The Making of the New Deal: The Insiders Speak.* Cambridge, Mass.: Harvard University Press, 1983.

Miller, Dorothy C. *Women and Social Welfare: A Feminist Analysis.* New York: Praeger, 1990.

Perkins, Frances. *The Roosevelt I Knew.* New York: Viking Press, 1946.

SEE ALSO: Dependent Pension Act (1890); Sheppard-Towner Act (1921); World War Adjusted Compensation Act (1924); Hundred Days legislation (1933); Aid to Families with Dependent Children (1935); Personal Responsibility and Work Opportunity Reconciliation Act (1996).

AID TO FAMILIES WITH DEPENDENT CHILDREN

ALSO KNOWN AS: part of the Social Security Act
DATE: August 14, 1935
U.S. STATUTES AT LARGE: 49 Stat. 620
U.S. CODE: 42 § 301 et seq.
CATEGORIES: Children's Issues; Health and Welfare; Women's Issues

Aid to Families with Dependent Children was established to provide minimum income support to impoverished families, especially women and their children.

Originally titled Aid to Dependent Children (ADC), Aid to Families with Dependent Children (AFDC) was established in 1935 as one provision of the Social Security Act, a key piece of legislation during the New Deal era. The purpose of AFDC is to provide cash public assistance to needy families with children. It is a combined federal and state-administered program, with states defining the definition of "need" and the level of payments.

In 1993 approximately 5,050,000 families, or 9,598,000 children and 4,659,000 adults, received AFDC payments. The typical AFDC family included a mother and one child who remained on welfare for less than two years. The average monthly payment per family was $377, with payments varying greatly from state to state. In 1993 New England and some West Coast states granted the highest average benefits of more than $500 per month, while the eastern and western South Central states granted the lowest, with family benefits averaging slightly more than $160 per month. The state with the highest average monthly benefits was Alaska ($748), and the state with the lowest was Mississippi ($120).

ELIGIBILITY

States must comply with federal guidelines in order to qualify for financial grants. However, states were free to decide whom they would assist, how much assistance they would grant, and how assistance would be administered. In all states, adult recipients had to register for employment and training. Each state also computed a "needs standard," which took into account the cost of food, shelter,

647

utilities, clothing, health care, and other necessities. If families' needs exceed their income and assets, they may qualify for the program, but the federal government did not require that states provide the full amount of the difference between needs and income if they chose not to do so.

In many states, the standard of need was set below the official poverty level. Thousands of poor families were ineligible for benefits. In addition to demonstrating financial need, children receiving benefits generally had to be under the age of eighteen. Eligible families usually were headed by single mothers, but in some states the AFDC-UP program provided coverage for dual-parent families with unemployed fathers.

HISTORY

As a minimum income support system, ADC was modeled after mother's aid legislation passed by many states in the early 1900's, which established widow's pensions. These entitlements were designed to help working-class widows keep their children out of orphanages. When ADC was created in 1935, Congress's intention was to cushion poverty and to enable mothers to stay home with their children. Early relief was based on the assumption that only certain categories of people qualified. Those who did qualify were closely monitored in terms of need, resources, and sexual behavior. Unwed mothers were denied assistance.

The 1930's program was established in the face of great opposition from conservative business and government officials throughout the United States, who argued that government intervention on behalf of the poor would undermine their desire to work. Southern legislators also felt that generous assistance would erode the low-wage structure of employment. They were particularly opposed to ADC and other programs that provided aid for the poor. Fearing that federal officials would be more sympathetic, especially to impoverished African Americans, they fought to ensure local control over the administration of ADC.

REGIONAL DIFFERENCES

Despite fierce opposition, ADC provided cash to assist children who had been left without a parent because of disability, death, or continued absence. Because ADC was administered at the state and local levels, there were vast differences in payment levels. Regional differences in ideologies concerning the poor as well as differences in local economies resulted in unequal entitlements. For example, in 1939 Arkansas provided an average of $8.10 monthly, while Massachusetts provided $61.07.

HISTORY OF IMPLEMENTATION

For fifteen years ADC provided funds for dependent children only. It contained "man in the house" rules, which prohibited against benefits when a male resided in the household and discriminated against African American mothers and against unmarried women, who were thought unsuitable. In some states recipients were also expected to work low-wage jobs in return for their benefits.

In 1950, when the program was renamed AFDC, Congress passed a provision that included a caretaker grant to help pay for mothers' essential expenses. In 1964 the administration of President Lyndon B. Johnson launched the War on Poverty, increasing federal matching funds so that state and county welfare departments could accept more applicants. Throughout the late 1960's, as pressure from the National Welfare Rights Organization and the Civil Rights movement mounted, the Supreme Court continued to remove barriers to eligibility. Relief was expanded, and reform permitted states to extend aid to families with an unemployed father at home.

WELFARE REFORM

Despite expansion during the 1960's, politicians continued to fuel anti-welfare sentiment. By the 1980's the "privatization" initiatives of the administration of President Ronald Reagan reduced services in the public sector, resulting in a dramatic decrease in the number of poor families receiving aid. During the administration of President Bill Clinton, the Personal Responsibility and Work Opportunity Reconciliation Act of 1996 marked a commitment by the federal government to cut funding for AFDC further. This act was comparable to earlier battles over welfare control that pitted states against the federal government. With this act, states have more individual control over the nation's neediest citizens. With grants from the federal government, states will run their own welfare programs. To qualify for money, all states must comply with certain broad provisions, including a lifetime family benefit limit of five years. After receiving aid, recipients must also find work within two years. Other provisions include cuts in food stamps and aid to immigrants and disabled children.

The Personal Responsibility and Work Opportunity Reconciliation Act replaced AFDC with a program known as Temporary Assistance for Needy Families (TANF). This act represented a clear break with the New Deal policies begun in the 1930's. It was based on the assumption that the poor remain poor because they lack motivation to succeed and that government assistance encourages an unproductive life. It was argued that if aid is denied, poverty will be made more brutal and people will no longer choose to remain on welfare because they will have to work.

During the last two decades of the twentieth century, few people denied that the AFDC system needed to be moved forward and improved. As in earlier times, however, analysts disagreed about how to accomplish this. While some advocated minor changes, others sought to change the system completely or to abolish aid altogether. The 1990's initiatives were criticized for failing to address the root causes of poverty in the United States, for ignoring the work done by welfare mothers in the home, and for failing to acknowledge that half of all single mothers who spend any time on AFDC are also employed during that period.

Eleanor A. LaPointe

BIBLIOGRAPHY

Abramovitz, Mimi. *Regulating the Lives of Women: Social Welfare Policy from Colonial Times to the Present.* Boston: South End Press, 1988.

Cozic, Charles P., and Paul A. Winters, eds. *Welfare: Opposing Viewpoints.* San Diego: Greenhaven Press, 1997.

Feagin, Joe R. *Subordinating the Poor: Welfare and American Beliefs.* Englewood Cliffs, N.J.: Prentice Hall, 1975.

Gordon, Linda. *Pitied but Not Entitled: Single Mothers and the History of Welfare.* New York: Free Press, 1994.

Komisar, Lucy. *Down and Out in the USA: A History of Public Welfare.* Rev. ed. New York: Franklin Watts, 1977.

Quadagno, Jill S. *The Color of Welfare: How Racism Undermined the War on Poverty.* New York: Oxford University Press, 1994.

Rank, Mark Robert. *Living on the Edge: The Realities of Welfare in America.* New York: Columbia University Press, 1994.

Sidel, Ruth. *Women and Children Last: The Plight of Poor Women in Affluent America.* New York: Penguin, 1992.

Tarantino, Thomas Howard, and Dismas Becker, eds. *Welfare Mothers Speak Out: We Ain't Gonna Shuffle Anymore.* New York: W. W. Norton, 1972.

Teghtsoonian, Katherine. "Promises, Promises: 'Choices for Women' in Canadian and American Child Care Policy Debates." *Feminist Studies* 22 (Spring, 1996).

Trattner, Walter I. *From Poor Law to Welfare State: A History of Social Welfare in America.* 5th ed. New York: Free Press, 1994.

SEE ALSO: Sheppard-Towner Act (1921); Social Security Act (1935); Personal Responsibility and Work Opportunity Reconciliation Act (1996).

BANKING ACT OF 1935

DATE: August 23, 1935
U.S. STATUTES AT LARGE: 49 Stat. 684
PUBLIC LAW: 74-305
CATEGORIES: Banking, Money, and Finance

By centralizing monetary control, the Banking Act of 1935 assured businesspeople of a more stable and predictable economic environment and allowed long-range planning.

The Banking Act of 1935 reorganized control of the U.S. monetary system, centralizing power in the hands of the Board of Governors of the Federal Reserve System and the Federal Open Market Committee.

PRE-1935 CONDITIONS
Prior to the act, each of the twelve Federal Reserve Banks that had been established by the Federal Reserve Act of 1913 had been freer to pursue policies of their own choosing. This lack of central control had the potential to create chaotic business conditions. Businesspeople could not be sure what credit policies the Federal Reserve Banks would implement. As a result, an entrepreneur could

not predict confidently whether his or her customers would face an economic upturn and easy credit in upcoming months or instead be discouraged from purchasing because of an economic downturn that might be allowed or encouraged by the local Federal Reserve Bank. Furthermore, a business could unexpectedly find itself at a competitive disadvantage in relation to a rival in another city if Federal Reserve Banks differed in their monetary policies. These types of uncertainties made business planning and forecasting difficult.

The Federal Reserve Act of 1913 had represented a desire to put knowledge of the economy and its monetary system to work. Its passage marked the first systematic attempt to influence the U.S. economy through monetary policy (governmental control of the national money supply and credit conditions). A committee of experts with specialized knowledge not commonly held by politicians would guide monetary policy. Concern about how to balance potential control of the monetary system for political purposes against domination of it by private banking interests led to a splitting of power between private bankers and the presidentially appointed Federal Reserve Board.

The Federal Reserve Board could indirectly change interest rates charged by banks or change the amount of money available to lend, by recommending to the twelve Federal Reserve Banks that they change the interest rate on loans they made to banks or by recommending purchases or sales of government bonds and bills. The Federal Reserve Board made few recommendations of either type during its first twenty years. Instead, the chief executive officers, or "governors," of the twelve Reserve Banks took independent control of monetary policy through the Governors Conference. That group made its own policy choices, then offered them to the Federal Reserve Board for ratification. The Federal Reserve Act of 1913 did not provide for this conference; its unauthorized action was indicative of private banks' reluctance to yield to central control.

In addition, the individual Federal Reserve Banks were free to ignore recommendations of the Federal Reserve Board. The New York Reserve Bank in particular acted independently. Its governor, Benjamin Strong, also acted as a powerful leader among the officials who set monetary policy for the system as a whole. Strong's death in 1928 left the system without commanding leadership. Following the 1929 stock market crash, the New York Reserve Bank favored buying government bonds from banks to provide purchasing power to the economy. It acted on this policy, but Strong's successor was unable to persuade the rest of the Federal Reserve System to follow along. The Great Depression might have been far less severe if he had.

Between the stock market crash and the banking holiday declared by President Franklin D. Roosevelt in 1933, the Federal Reserve Banks operated essentially independently, according to the beliefs of their own boards of directors. The Federal Reserve Board was weak and divided in opinion. The Open Market Investment Committee (an authorized body that replaced the Governors Conference in 1923), with one member from each Federal Reserve Bank, was similarly powerless. Each bank's representative came to meetings with directions from the bank's board of directors, and those banks rarely were unified in their goals. The decentralized control in the period from 1929 to 1933 led to monetary policy that has been described as inept and possibly as worsening the Depression.

BANKING ACT OF 1933

The Banking Act of 1933 set up the Federal Open Market Committee (FOMC), as successor to the Open Market Investment Committee, to determine appropriate bond sales or purchases for the Federal Reserve System. The FOMC also had one member from each Reserve Bank. It instituted all policy actions, and the Federal Reserve Board had only the power to approve or disapprove. Reserve Banks remained free not to participate in any open market operations recommended by the FOMC.

System officials blamed inadequate powers, rather than misuse of powers, for their inability to stop the Depression's economic contraction and to prevent bank panics and failures. Furthermore, many system officials were willing to tolerate the bank failures, seeing them as proper punishment for poor management or excessive earlier speculation in financial markets. The failures were concentrated among smaller banks and those that were not members of the Federal Reserve System, so they were of relatively little interest to the larger banks with the most influence in the system. The larger banks, in fact, saw the failures as a way of shaking their small competitors out of the market.

THE 1935 ACT

In response to the behavior of the Federal Reserve System in the 1920's and early 1930's, Marriner Eccles, a banker and Treasury Department official, devised a plan to correct what he saw as flaws in the monetary control system. He and many others believed that better use of monetary policy could be a powerful tool to end the Depression. Some argued that improper use of monetary policy had exaggerated the economic downturn and that, therefore, less rather than more central control was indicated. Eccles, however, wanted to implement the powers of the Federal Reserve System more broadly and to establish conscious centralized control of the monetary system.

Eccles's proposals formed the basis for Title II of the Banking Act of 1935, which stirred strong debate in Congress. Senator Carter Glass, who had helped develop the Federal Reserve Act of 1913 and had coauthored the Glass-Steagall Act, particularly opposed changing the nature of the system. It was argued that a stronger Federal Reserve Board would become an arm of the political administration rather than provide independent judgment. These debates led to rewording the act to reduce control by the executive branch.

The act reorganized the central bodies of the Federal Reserve System. The Federal Reserve Board was renamed the Board of Governors of the Federal Reserve System, and the secretary of the treasury and comptroller of the currency were dropped from membership. Each of the board's seven members was to be appointed by the president, but their fourteen-year terms would overlap, so that no single presidential administration could appoint a majority. The FOMC was reconstituted to include all members of the Board of Governors and five presidents of Federal Reserve Banks. Those five positions would be filled by the twelve Reserve Bank presidents on a rotating basis. They were to give independent policy recommendations rather than be guided by their banks' boards of directors as in the past. Most important, each Reserve Bank was required to follow the policies recommended by the FOMC and not operate on its own.

The Board of Governors also gained the power to set reserve requirements, or the percentage of deposits that private banks in the system had to keep available to meet demands for withdrawals. The act left election of Reserve Bank presidents and vice presidents up to the banks' boards of directors but made those choices subject to approval by the Board of Governors. These main provisions of the Banking Act of 1935 took power from the individual Reserve Banks and centralized it within the Board of Governors and FOMC. Eccles, who had been made chair of the Federal Reserve Board late in November, 1934, was chosen to chair the new Board of Governors that replaced it.

IMPACT OF THE 1935 ACT

The most important impact of the Banking Act of 1935 was its message: In the future, there would be a centralized guiding hand behind U.S. monetary policy. Along with other New Deal reforms such as the establishment of the Federal Deposit Insurance Corporation (which the Banking Act of 1935 amended), the act helped to persuade the American business community that there would not be another Great Depression. Businesspeople could predict a more stable American economy in which the government promoted a steady course of growth, with neither excessive unemployment nor the opposite problem, high rates of inflation.

Businesspeople became relatively certain of being able to obtain bank credit for promising projects. Previously, they sometimes had faced bank loan officers who were unwilling to lend because they were uncertain about future national financial conditions and the availability of funds to their banks. Centralized and planned monetary control greatly reduced these uncertainties.

Although individual banks would still fail, depositors and borrowers could rely on the Federal Reserve System to prevent large-scale bank failures. Banks themselves could count on a steadier, more predictable monetary policy environment in which to conduct business. Centralization of power made it possible and profitable for businesses and especially financial speculators to monitor the FOMC and try to guess its policy decisions, which were kept secret for several weeks to avoid any disruptive effects on financial markets. A new job function of "Fed watcher" thus was created.

Formal centralization of control did not end debates concerning independence of the Federal Reserve System. Individual bankers still wanted influence within the system, and the Treasury Department was unwilling to relinquish control of the system completely. The Board of Governors agreed at first to cooperate with the Treasury by buying government bonds, as a means of keeping bond prices high to aid the financing of government operations. In 1936, the Board of Governors also exercised its new power to raise the required reserve rate. This acted to reduce the amount of money available to the financial system, more than offsetting the effects of bond purchases. The combined policy contributed to a minor recession in 1936 and 1937. Congress then proposed very specific guidelines for establishing monetary policy, leaving little room for discretion on the part of Federal Reserve System officials. The proposal was not made law, but system officials heeded the implicit warning to coordinate plans with other government agencies.

The Board of Governors and FOMC chose not to exercise their powers to any great degree during the 1930's, generally letting recovery from the Depression run its course. During World War II, the Reserve Banks agreed to cooperate with the Treasury's borrowing, buying Treasury bonds to maintain their price and keep interest rates low. As the war neared its end, however, the Treasury's desire to keep interest rates low conflicted with the FOMC's wish to restrain the growth of the money supply as a means of preventing inflation.

The Employment Act of 1946 stated that the government had a responsibility to use all of its tools in a coordinated fashion to maximize employment, production, and purchasing power. Implicitly, the act recognized that neither fiscal policy (use of government powers to tax and spend) nor monetary policy alone was powerful enough to control the U.S. economy. The FOMC continued to buy Treasury bond issues, but Federal Reserve System officials argued more strongly against the constraint that this cooperation imposed on their decisions. In March, 1951, an agreement was reached under which the FOMC was no longer responsible for supporting the price of Treasury bonds. That left the system without a clear and specific policy objective. The public had begun to believe in the power of monetary policy, so Federal Reserve System officials wanted to state clearly how that policy would be used.

An appropriate growth rate of the money supply was chosen as one objective. The FOMC would provide enough money to finance business expansion without causing inflation. The second objective was to vary credit conditions countercyclically, reducing credit availability during business expansions and allowing easier credit during contractions, as a means of offsetting business cycles. The

Board of Governors and the FOMC began to exercise their powers of central control in a manner basically independent of political or private business interests.

A. J. Sobczak

SOURCES FOR FURTHER STUDY
Broaddus, Alfred. *A Primer on the Fed.* Richmond, Va.: Federal Reserve Bank of Richmond, 1988.
Clifford, Albert Jerome. *The Independence of the Federal Reserve System.* Philadelphia: University of Pennsylvania Press, 1965.
Friedman, Milton, and Anna Jacobson Schwartz. *A Monetary History of the United States 1867-1960.* Princeton, N.J.: Princeton University Press, 1963.
Krooss, Herman E., ed. *Documentary History of Banking and Currency in the United States.* New York: Chelsea House, 1969.
Moore, Carl H. *The Federal Reserve System: A History of the First Seventy-five Years.* Jefferson, N.C.: McFarland, 1990.
Patman, Wright. *The Federal Reserve System: A Study Prepared for the Use of the Joint Economic Committee, Congress of the United States.* Washington, D.C.: Government Printing Office, 1976.
Saint-Phalle, Thibaut de. *The Federal Reserve An Intentional Mystery.* New York: Praeger, 1985.

SEE ALSO: Federal Reserve Act (1913); McFadden Act (1927); Banking Act of 1933 (1933); Employment Act (1946).

NEUTRALITY ACTS

DATE: August 31, 1935; February 29, 1936; May 1, 1937; November 4, 1939
U.S. STATUTES AT LARGE: 49 Stat. 1081 (1935); 49 Stat. 1153 (1936); 50 Stat. 121 (1937); 54 Stat. 4 (1939)
CATEGORIES: Foreign Relations

Strong isolationist sentiment during the 1930's prompted this legislation to prevent foreign entanglements.

Foreign policy was of secondary importance in the estimation of most people in the United States during the early 1930's, as the nation was preoccupied with the struggle to recover from the Great Depression. By 1935, however, a congressional movement had been initiated to formulate legislative safeguards that would prevent the United States from becoming involved in foreign entanglements. President Franklin D. Roosevelt and Secretary of State Cordell Hull supported such safeguards, so long as the chief executive retained discretionary power in their application. Ignoring the president's wishes, Congress passed a series of neutrality acts in 1935, 1936, 1937, and 1939, limiting presidential options. Although these acts demonstrated the strength of isolationist sentiment, they could not keep the United States out of a second world war.

NEED FOR NEUTRALITY

The neutrality acts stemmed, in large part, from a reevaluation of the reasons for the United States' entry into World War I. Noteworthy in this regard was Senator Gerald P. Nye, a North Dakota Republican, who chaired the committee investigating the munitions industry and seeking evidence of possible economic pressures leading to the nation's involvement in World War I. Supported by a vigorous peace lobby in 1934, Nye dramatically publicized the thesis that the United States had been duped into entering World War I to assist unscrupulous armaments producers and bankers, so-called merchants of death, who stood to profit financially by an Allied victory. This conclusion strengthened an existing feeling that some kind of neutrality legislation, which included an arms embargo, was needed to prevent such a catastrophe in the future.

In March, 1935, with public opinion staunchly against involvement in any future war, Roosevelt asked the Nye Committee to study the neutrality question and formulate appropriate legislation. Entrusted with this new task, Nye and his colleagues proposed several resolutions, one of which prohibited the export of arms and ammunition to all belligerents. Because Nye's resolutions did not give the president the authority to distinguish between aggressors and victims or to embargo the sale of arms to aggressors exclusively, Roosevelt had the Department of State draft legislation that did so. The State Department measure was lost when the Senate Foreign Relations Committee, dominated by two isolationist senators, William E. Borah of Idaho and Hiram W. Johnson of California, produced its own bill.

FIRST NEUTRALITY ACT

The Foreign Relations Committee measure, approved by both the Senate and the House, was to last six months. It provided for an impartial arms embargo of nations engaged in a conflict recognized by the president, prohibited U.S. ships from carrying war matériel to belligerents, and recommended that U.S. citizens be warned against traveling on belligerent ships. Roosevelt opposed the mandatory embargo and regretted that the act did not apply to non-munitions war materials. Nevertheless, he accepted the bill on August 31, fearing that a failure to do so would adversely affect domestic reforms then under consideration in Congress and believing that he could persuade the legislators to revise the act by the time it expired on February 29, 1936.

SECOND NEUTRALITY ACT

Unfortunately for Roosevelt, a State Department neutrality resolution of January 3, 1936, which gave the president discretionary authority to limit the sale of raw materials to belligerents, ran into serious opposition from Nye, Borah, Johnson, and other isolationists. With the expiration date of the 1935 measure fast approaching, Congress, in mid-February, passed a new act slightly more stringent than the first. Extending the basic provisions of the first act, the Second Neutrality Act also required the president to extend the arms embargo to any third party that became involved in a conflict and forbade loans by U.S. citizens to belligerents. Recognizing that there was no chance for the State Department measure and wary of creating an antiadministration issue in an election year, Roosevelt signed the Second Neutrality Act on February 29, 1936.

THIRD NEUTRALITY ACT

Like its predecessor, the Second Neutrality Act carried an expiration date: May 1, 1937. When Congress began to debate a new measure in early 1937, neither the wisdom of the basic principle of keeping the United States out of war nor the implementation of this goal through an arms embargo was questioned. As the nation emerged from the Depression, however, pressure mounted for some kind of compromise that would permit business as usual with Europe, even in wartime. Bernard M. Baruch, a noted financier, suggested that a practical solution would be a cash-and-carry formula. He reasoned that if U.S. businesses could sell goods, with the exception of arms, on the basis of immediate delivery and payment by the buyer, the risk of U.S. involvement in war would be minimized. Both Roosevelt and the advocates of strict neutrality favored the cash-and-carry plan, the president believing it would favor Great Britain, the European state controlling the sea. The new, permanent neutrality bill that emerged in April retained the mandatory embargo on arms, the ban on loans, and the prohibition on travel; but it gave the president discretion, until May 1, 1939, to place all belligerent trade except arms under the cash-and-carry formula. On May 1, the Third Neutrality Act, having passed both the House and the Senate, was signed by Roosevelt.

Two months later, in the first test of this act, the futility of legislating for unforeseen diplomatic contingencies was revealed. In July, 1937, without a declaration of war, Japan launched a full-scale attack against China. Adherence to the neutrality act would work to the advantage of the aggressor, Japan, whose powerful navy dominated the seas off the coast of China. Therefore, Roosevelt made no official recognition of the conflict, and the neutrality act was not implemented in East Asia.

In the months that followed, Roosevelt had little reason to suspect that isolationism was losing strength. Public reaction to his call for collective security, given in his Chicago "Quarantine Speech" of October 5, 1937, was mixed. The Ludlow Amendment, requiring a favorable national referendum before a declaration of war, was only narrowly defeated in the House on January 10, 1938. Alarm in the United States at the ominous trend of events in Europe and the Far East must be attributed to the nation's relaxation of its policy of strict neutrality. In March, 1938, Adolf Hitler's Germany annexed Austria and began to make demands on Czechoslovakia. Meanwhile, the Japanese extended their aggression in China.

FOURTH NEUTRALITY ACT

By the beginning of 1939, Roosevelt had concluded that the neutrality act of 1937 needed revision. On January 4, in his state of the union address, the president warned of increasing threats to peace and pointed out that U.S. neutrality laws could operate unfairly, giving aid to aggressors and denying it to victims. Although he knew that Congress would not agree to a discretionary arms embargo, Roosevelt hoped it might agree to modify the law allowing for the sale of arms on a cash-and-carry basis. While Germany and other aggressors would be eligible, the administration anticipated that Great Britain and France would benefit most, because of their control of the sea. In April, with the president's approval, Senator Key Pittman of Nevada introduced a resolution providing for the repeal of the arms embargo and the placing of all trade with belligerents on a cash-and-carry basis. Congress, under the influence of Borah, Johnson, and Nye, who were adamant in their opposition, rejected the proposal.

Congress's attitude toward a revision of the 1937 law changed after Germany's assault on Poland on September 1, 1939. Learning from discussions with a number of legislators that a repeal of the arms embargo might be possible, Roosevelt called Congress into special session on September 23. Reiterating his belief that the existing law aided aggression, the president requested that the sale of all goods, including arms, be placed on a cash-and-carry basis. By shrewdly courting Southern conservatives, dispensing patronage, and securing indefatigable public relations work by internationalists, the president succeeded in pushing his revision through Congress by a close vote. On November 4, 1939, Roosevelt signed the Fourth Neutrality Act, and the United States took its first step toward becoming the arsenal of democracy.

George Q. Flynn, updated by
Bruce J. DeHart

SOURCES FOR FURTHER STUDY

Cole, Wayne S. *Roosevelt and the Isolationists, 1932-1945.* Lincoln: University of Nebraska Press, 1983.

Dallek, Robert. *Franklin D. Roosevelt and American Foreign Policy, 1932-1945.* New York: Oxford University Press, 1995.

Davis, Kenneth S. *FDR: The New Deal Years, 1933-1937* and *FDR: Into the Storm, 1937-1940.* New York: Random House, 1986, 1993.

Divine, Robert A. *The Reluctant Belligerent: American Entry into World War II.* New York: John Wiley & Sons, 1965.

SEE ALSO: Ogdensburg Agreement (1940); Lend-Lease Act (1941).

ROBINSON-PATMAN ANTIDISCRIMINATION ACT

ALSO KNOWN AS: Robinson-Patman Price Discrimination Act
DATE: June 19, 1936
U.S. STATUTES AT LARGE: 49 Stat. 1526
U.S. CODE: 15 § 13
CATEGORIES: Business, Commerce, and Trade

> *The Robinson-Patman Antidiscrimination Act amended the Clayton Act of 1914 to make it more difficult for firms to charge different prices to different buyers, particularly if the buyers were businesses buying to resell.*

The Robinson-Patman Antidiscrimination Act was passed in order to strengthen the provisions of the Clayton Act (1914) with regard to price discrimination.

PRICE DISCRIMINATION

Price discrimination occurs when a seller charges different prices to different buyers for the same product or service when there are no comparable differences in the cost of serving the different customers. For example, barbershops and film theaters commonly charge children less than adults; electricity rates are often higher for residential customers than for businesses. Charging different prices to different buyers can often increase profits for the sellers, provided that the seller can separate the markets so favored buyers do not resell to the less favored ones, and provided that demand is significantly less sensitive to price in one market than in another.

During the notorious "trust movement" of the late nineteenth century, it was often asserted that aggressive and predatory firms such as John D. Rockefeller's Standard Oil Company used price discrimination as a means of harassing rivals. The big trust might offer its product for sale at a very low price in the area served by the smaller and weaker rival, thereby "persuading" the rival firm to enter into collusion with the trust or to sell out to it on favorable terms. At the same time, the trust might be selling at a much higher price in other localities, with the price limited by people's ability to buy cheaply in one area and ship for resale into an area with higher prices.

Because of the ill repute of price discrimination, it was explicitly outlawed by section 2 of the Clayton Act of 1914, in situations in which its effect "may be to substantially lessen competition or tend to create a monopoly in any line of commerce." If price differences reflected differences in grade, quality, quantity, costs of selling, or costs of transportation, they were not discriminatory. Furthermore, a discriminatory price offered "in good faith to meet competition" would not be illegal. The Federal Trade Commission (FTC), created in 1914, was given the principal responsibility for enforcing the act, responding mainly to complaints from injured parties. Not many cases were brought by the FTC, and its efforts to prevent price discrimination met with a number of rebuffs from the courts.

CHAIN STORES

Strong pressure to amend the Clayton Act reflected a shift in focus. During the 1920's, the United States economy experienced a large increase in the activity of chain stores such as the A&P grocery chain and mass marketers such as Sears Roebuck. Because of their size, these firms were often able to gain price concessions from their suppliers, price concessions that worked to the competitive disadvantage of smaller wholesalers and retailers trying to compete with such large operations as A&P or Sears. The FTC completed an exhaustive report on chain stores in 1934 and provided examples of the preferential treatment of large buyers. The FTC also issued a complaint against Goodyear Tire and Rubber Company alleging that unlawful price discrimination was involved in its contract to sell tires to Sears at cost plus 6 percent. The commission alleged that Sears was gaining an advantage of 29 to 40 percent over its retail competitors by this discriminatory pricing arrangement.

Political efforts to limit chain store activities were undertaken by independent wholesalers and retailers on a number of fronts. A number of states, for example, levied special taxes on chain stores. The lobbying efforts intensified when the depression following 1929 drove many small firms out of business. The legal counsel for the United States Wholesale Grocers Association drafted a bill to amend the price discrimination law to make it a stronger protection for smaller firms against mass distributors. Senator Joseph T.

Robinson of Arkansas and Representative Wright Patman of Texas introduced the bill in Congress, where it was commonly known as the "Anti-Chain-Store" Act. In Senate debate, Senator Marvel Mills Logan of Kentucky presented the major arguments for the bill.

AMENDING THE CLAYTON ACT

The Robinson-Patman Antidiscrimination Act was approved on June 19, 1936. The test criterion of illegal discrimination was broadened: Discrimination was now illegal if its effect might be "to injure, destroy, or prevent competition with any person who either grants or knowingly receives the benefit of such discrimination, or with customers of either of them." The thrust of this change was that price discrimination might be illegal if it simply caused injury to some competitor, even if the vigor of competition itself was not impaired and no monopoly was created. The law was also amended to justify quantity discounts only if they made "due allowance" for cost differences; thus firms accused of illegal price discrimination might be required to present data on the costs of handling orders and shipments of different sizes.

Whereas the Clayton Act permitted discriminatory pricing "to meet competition," the Robinson-Patman Antidiscrimination Act restricted this provision; firms could make price cuts "to meet the equally low price of a competitor" but presumably not to undercut that price. The FTC was given authority to set limits on quantity discounts if it found that "available purchasers in greater quantities are so few as to render differentials on account thereof unjustly discriminatory or promotive of monopoly." In other words, a price reduction might be illegal even if it could be shown to reflect proportionately lower costs, if it appeared to give monopoly power to one or two very large buyers, such as Sears or A&P. The FTC has never invoked such restrictions.

Large purchasers were often able to dispense with the services of brokers in dealing with suppliers. They would sometimes pressure their suppliers to give them price concessions in lieu of the brokerage charges those suppliers might have paid under different conditions. The 1936 law prohibited such brokerage allowances when no independent broker was involved. Special provisions such as promotional allowances, advertising allowances, and services or facilities provided by sellers were required to be available to all businesses that bought a company's products, on "proportionally equal" terms. If Coca-Cola Company, for example, were willing to subsidize Kroger's advertising of Coke, it had to make similar subsidies available to smaller retail firms, proportional perhaps to their purchases of Coke during the previous year.

ENFORCEMENT

Enforcement of the Robinson-Patman Antidiscrimination Act, like that of the original Clayton Act, was primarily through the FTC, which was authorized to issue orders to "cease and desist" when it found evidence of illegal price discrimination. These orders carried no direct penalty, and if the firms continued their violations, the FTC had to go to court to make its orders hold up. The 1936 law also provided that injured parties could sue for damages. Criminal prosecutions could be brought by the Justice Department, but this had not happened by 1990.

In the first twelve years following the Robinson-Patman Antidiscrimination Act, the FTC issued 186 cease-and-desist orders involving price discrimination. Of these, 104 were based on the prohibitions against paying brokerage allowances where no brokers' services were involved. Immediately after passage of the act, the A&P grocery chain began to insist that its suppliers provide price concessions equal to former brokerage allowances, those concessions now to take the form of quantity discounts. The FTC moved quickly to block this and was upheld in the courts. In some other brokerage allowance cases, prohibitions appear to have been directed unfairly against independent purchasing agencies and cooperative buying agencies serving small firms.

The next most frequent type of complaint concerned promotional allowances, subsidies and services made available to large buyers on a discriminatory basis. The FTC issued fifty-four such cease-and-desist orders up to the beginning of 1948. For example, Corn Products Refining Company was ordered to stop paying to advertise products of the Curtiss Candy Company, since it was not comparably advertising for smaller customers. The Elizabeth Arden cosmetics firm was ordered to stop its policy of supplying demonstrators to help its large retail customers sell its products, since smaller retailers were not offered similar opportunities.

The FTC also dealt with a number of cases involving quantity discounts. Firms offering discounts on individual orders sometimes successfully showed cost justifications, but price concessions based on cumulative orders over a sustained period were usually banned. Morton Salt, for example, was permitted to sell more cheaply for carload shipments than for less-than-carload shipments but not to offer further discounts based on the number of cases purchased over a twelve-month period.

Ironically, there have been very few cases of local price cutting such as those attributed to the old predatory trusts. Some such considerations were involved in a case involving the Utah Pie Company, a small local enterprise that lost significant sales in its home territory when major national firms made discriminatory price reductions for sales in Salt Lake City. The Supreme Court found the discrimination illegal in *Utah Pie Company v. Continental Baking Company* (1967) even though Utah Pie continued to be profitable during the price war.

The FTC was able to use the Robinson-Patman Antidiscrimination Act as the basis for an attack on systems of delivered pricing for certain heavy products such as steel, cement, and corn syrup. These involved the so-called "basing point" system, under which customers in a given locality would find all suppliers quoting identical delivered prices, regardless of how close the supplier might be. A seller shipping from a longer distance would realize a smaller net price after paying shipping charges. The pricing system was employed as a way for sellers to avoid direct price competition with one another. A series of cases in 1945 and 1948 found that such pricing systems violated the Robinson-Patman Antidiscrimination Act.

ASSESSMENT

The Robinson-Patman Antidiscrimination Act has not been well regarded by economists studying antitrust policy. Firms competing actively for business may often charge different prices to different customers, and such practices need not lead to oppressive monopoly. Wholesale and retail trade, on which much of the litigation has focused, is generally characterized by easy entry for new firms and absence of sizable economies of large-scale operation. Those characteristics make it unlikely that dangerous monopoly will arise. The A&P grocery chain, which was a primary target of the law, has faded into insignificance so apparently did not benefit greatly from any monopoly power. A large proportion of FTC orders relating to price discrimination have involved the food products industry, which is highly competitive. Critics of the law hold that it had the purpose and effect of reducing the vigor of competition. They argue that the test of illegality has often been whether some competitor was injured by a low price, rather than whether the vigor of competition itself was impaired. Competition potentially injures competitors but is desirable (according to economists) as a way of improving efficiency and securing high-quality products at low prices for consumers. Defenders of the law argue that large firms have strategic advantages that do not reflect superior quality or efficiency and that it is appropriate to counterbalance these. For example, large firms may be in a better position to lobby for preferential treatment by government units or to engage in costly lawsuits against smaller rivals. Only about 6 percent of the FTC complaints involving price discrimination issued between 1961 and 1974, however, involved firms with more than $100 million in annual sales. Many relatively small firms face the possibility of being cited for violations, and the law has given rise to a large and confusing body of litigation. The consensus among economists is that the Robinson-Patman Antidiscrimination Act is one of many well-intentioned pieces of economic micromanagement that has ended up generating more costs than benefits.

Paul B. Trescott

SOURCES FOR FURTHER STUDY

Adelman, Morris A. *A&P: A Study in Price-Cost Behavior and Public Policy.* Cambridge, Mass.: Harvard University Press, 1959.

Benson, Bruce L., and M. L. Greenhut. "Special Interests, Bureaucrats, and Antitrust: An Explanation of the Antitrust Paradox." In *Antitrust and Regulation,* edited by Ronald E. Grieson. Lexington, Mass.: Lexington Books, 1986.

Blackburn, John D., and Elliot I. Klayman. *The Legal Environment of Business,* edited by Martin H. Malin. 4th ed. Homewood, Ill.: Irwin, 1991.

Blair, Roger D., and David L. Kaserman. *Antitrust Economics.* Homewood, Ill.: Richard D. Irwin, 1985.

Dirlam, Joel B., and Alfred E. Kahn. *Fair Competition: The Law and Economics of Antitrust Policy.* Ithaca, N.Y.: Cornell University Press, 1954.

Kintner, Earl W., ed. *Federal Antitrust Laws and Related Statutes: A Legislative History.* 11 vols. Buffalo, N.Y.: William S. Hein, 1978, 1982-1985.

Patman, Wright. *Complete Guide to the Robinson-Patman Act.* Englewood Cliffs, N.J.: Prentice-Hall, 1963.

Purdy, Harry L., Martin L. Lindahl, and William A. Carter. *Corporate Concentration and Public Policy.* 2d ed. New York: Prentice-Hall, 1950.

Scherer, Frederic M. *Industrial Market Structure and Economic Performance.* 2d ed. Boston: Houghton Mifflin, 1980.

Seplaki, Les. *Antitrust and the Economics of the Market.* New York: Harcourt Brace Jovanovich, 1982.

See also: Clayton Antitrust Act (1914); Federal Trade Commission Act (1914); Miller-Tydings Fair Trade Act (1937).

OKLAHOMA WELFARE ACT

DATE: June 26, 1936
U.S. STATUTES AT LARGE: 49 Stat. 1967
U.S. CODE: 25 § 501
CATEGORIES: Native Americans

This act made provision for all Indian tribes, bands, or groups in Oklahoma to adopt a constitution allowing for self-government; the act also allowed the secretary of the interior to purchase land to be held in trust for all Oklahoma Indians, and allowed small groups of Indians to form a local cooperative association and receive interest-free loans from the Revolving Loan Fund for Indians.

A major reform of U.S. policy toward American Indians resulted in the Indian Reorganization Act (IRA, or Wheeler-Howard Act), enacted by Congress on June 18, 1934. With this act, further allotment of tribal lands to individual Indians was prohibited, purchase of additional lands for Indians by the secretary of the interior was authorized, and a fund (the Revolving Loan Fund for Indians) was established that could be used for tribal enterprises. The IRA allowed and encouraged the tribes or groups to adopt written constitutions allowing for self-government, gave Indians applying for positions in the Bureau of Indian Affairs preference over other applicants, and called for very strict conservation practices on Indian lands. Oklahoma, however, was excluded from the IRA because the IRA was essentially a system of reservation government, and it was deemed inappropriate for Oklahoma because, at the time of statehood, the Five Civilized Tribes had given up their autonomy.

In 1936, the benefits of the IRA were extended to Oklahoma by way of a separate statute, the Oklahoma Indian Welfare Act. This act authorized the secretary of the interior to purchase, at his discretion, good agricultural and grazing land, from within or without reservations, to hold in trust for the tribe, band, group, or individual Indian for whose benefit the land was acquired. Title to all lands was to be taken in the name of the United States and held by the United States. All land was exempt from any and all federal taxes, but the state of Oklahoma could levy and collect a gross production tax upon all oil and gas produced from the land. The secretary of the interior was responsible for overseeing the payment of these taxes to Oklahoma. Any tribe or band in the state of Oklahoma was given the right to organize for its common welfare and could adopt a constitution and bylaws; these had to follow the rules and regulations set forth by the secretary of the interior. Any ten or more Indians, as determined by the official tribe rolls, or Indian descendants of such enrolled members, in convenient proximity to each other, could be chartered as a local cooperative association for the following purposes: credit administration, production, marketing, consumers' protection, or land management. Funds from the Revolving Loan Fund for Indians could be used to provide interest-free loans to these groups.

Lynn M. Mason

Sources for Further Study

Deloria, Vine, ed. *The Indian Reorganization Act: Congresses and Bills.* Norman: University of Oklahoma Press, 2002.

Kelly, Lawrence C. "The Indian Reorganization Act: The Dream and the Reality." *Pacific Historical Review* 44 (August, 1975): 291-312.

Kelly, William H., ed. *Indian Affairs and the Indian Reorganization Act: The Twenty Year Record.* Tucson: University of Arizona Press, 1954.

Philp, Kenneth R. *John Collier's Crusade for Indian Reform, 1920-1954.* Tucson: University of Arizona Press, 1977.

Taylor, Graham D. *The New Deal and American Indian Tribalism: The Administration of the Indian Reorganization Act, 1934-1945.* Lincoln: University of Nebraska Press, 1980.

SEE ALSO: General Allotment Act (1887); Burke Act (1906); Indian Citizenship Act (1924); Indian Reorganization Act (1934).

RECIPROCAL TRADE ACT

DATE: November 11, 1936
CATEGORIES: Business, Commerce, and Trade; Foreign Relations; Treaties and Agreements

The treaty was the first reciprocal trade agreement between the United States and Canada since 1854.

A reciprocal trade agreement between two nations provides for both countries to reduce tariffs on trade goods. Such agreements between the United States and Canada date to 1854.

CANADIAN-U.S. TRADE AGREEMENTS: NINETEENTH CENTURY
British diplomats had begun negotiations with Washington two years earlier. They were unable to reach a conclusion at the time, however, because of a dispute over fishing rights off the eastern coast of Canada. Negotiations continued until the fisheries dispute was resolved and a reciprocity treaty was signed on June 6, 1854. This treaty allowed fishermen from the United States the right to catch fish in the Atlantic coastal fisheries off Newfoundland, which were then the richest fishing grounds in the world. British fishing boats were granted permission to operate in U.S. coastal waters off Maine. The agreement also created a list of free goods, such as timber, wheat, and corn, that both countries would not tax. Trade increased rapidly after ratification of this treaty.

In 1866, because of complaints from U.S. farmers, the United States repealed its part of the agreement. The Civil War had ended a year earlier, which enabled many veterans to resume farming; they protested loudly against free importation of Canadian grain, so reciprocity was ended. The Canadians wanted a new agreement, however, and in 1871 sent a delegation to Washington, D.C., to open trade talks. Nothing came of the talks, and the 1871 Treaty of Washington barely mentioned reciprocity.

EARLY TWENTIETH CENTURY

The issue was not raised again until 1911. Canada's finance minister, William S. Fielding, told the House of Commons that negotiations with the United States would begin immediately. The goal was to obtain as much free trade as possible, and Fielding suggested that once that was accomplished, the Canadian economy would flourish and unemployment would decline rapidly. A loud protest from workers and industrialists in Ontario indicated that many Canadians did not agree. These protesters argued that reciprocity and free trade would be a tremendous advantage for powerful industries in the United States, such as steel and textile companies, who would flood Canada with huge amounts of goods, driving Canadian industries into bankruptcy and costing thousands of jobs. Trade became the major issue in the election of that year. Conservatives denounced reciprocity in the campaign and won the election, bringing an end to discussions of free trade with the United States.

In 1924, both nations signed a treaty limiting halibut fishing off the coast of Washington and British Columbia, but reciprocity talks continued to falter. Republican administrations in the United States wanted only one thing from the Canadians, an agreement to construct the St. Lawrence Seaway linking the Great Lakes with the Atlantic Ocean. This massive project would make it easier to ship grain from the Midwest to Europe and, it was hoped, greatly improve the prosperity of farmers in the region. By 1932, it seemed as if negotiations on this project were about completed. President Herbert Hoover signed an agreement in July with the Canadians, but the Senate was unable to get the two-thirds majority required by the Constitution for ratification. The major opposition came from senators opposed to the seaway's projected high costs. The seaway would not be constructed for another twenty-five years.

ROOSEVELT ADMINISTRATION

Canadian-U.S. relations improved greatly after the inauguration of President Franklin Delano Roosevelt in 1933. He promoted a Good Neighbor Policy with all nations in the Western Hemisphere, which included support for reciprocal trade agreements. Talks with Canada began in 1934 but were not concluded until two years later. Roosevelt had signed the Reciprocal Trade Agreements Act of 1934, significantly lowering tariffs on many items. This bilateral agreement was not satisfactory, however, to the newly elected Liberal government of Prime Minister William Lyon Mackenzie King. King, a fervent advocate of reciprocal trade agreements, led a delegation to Washington to discuss such an agreement with representatives of the Department of State. Secretary of State Cordell Hull headed the U.S. negotiating team.

Hull favored reducing trade restrictions with as many nations as possible, but he faced considerable criticism for his position within his own Democratic Party and especially from conservatives in the Republican Party. He knew it would be difficult to win the two-thirds majority vote in the Senate for approval of any bill reducing tariffs. Many conservatives in both parties thought higher tariffs rather than lower presented the best opportunity for protecting jobs. The Great Depression, they argued, made it necessary for countries to protect themselves from competition from outside states by building a high tariff wall.

The U.S. secretary of state wanted Canada and the United States to reach an agreement quickly. This, he explained to the Canadians, would demonstrate to the rest of the world, especially the Europeans, that persons of goodwill could still sit down and negotiate peacefully. The Germans, Italians, and Japanese seemed to prefer war or economic suicide to any attempt to discuss seriously the mutual sacrifices required by reciprocal trade treaties. The United States and Canada could show world leaders an alternate course for resolving economic problems. Friendly nations had to show that talking still could produce results. The fact that the King government recently had signed a bilateral agreement with the German Nazis angered Hull, but he indicated that it would not stand in the way of the current discussions. It was hoped that reciprocal trade agreements could reduce conflict in the world and provide an alternative to cut-throat methods of bilateral trading, with each nation looking out only for its own narrow self-interest.

THE NEED FOR FREE TRADE

Hull believed that unless freer world trade was provided for, the nations of Europe and the Far East would face continued economic strife and chaos. Economic disaster would affect all countries and bring about an even worse financial collapse than the Great Depression. Only a broad program to remove excessive trade barriers, he told the Canadian delegation, could save the situation. The world needed a policy of equal treatment for all nations and a method to promote and protect fair trade methods and practices. If nations such as the United States and Canada refused to take the first steps in this direction, catastrophic consequences awaited the peoples of the world.

Such warnings of the terrible consequences of failure encouraged a quick end to negotiations. The final result, the Reciprocal Trade Act of 1936, produced far fewer reductions in trade barriers than had been gained in 1854, but it proved satisfactory to both sides. The United States agreed to admit limited amounts of cream, cattle, lumber, and potatoes with significantly reduced rates. In return, Canada accepted more manufactured goods from the United States. Liberals hoped that this trade would produce higher incomes for Canadian farmers, loggers, and ranchers. They also predicted it would reduce Canada's economic dependence on the United States. As it turned out, it made little difference. Both policies, the high tariffs favored by Conservatives in the 1920's and the Liberal support for freer trade, had the same result: They increased Canadian economic dependence on the United States.

From 1923 to 1935, the period of the highest tariffs on U.S. manufactured goods, the number of U.S.-owned factories and businesses in Canada increased from 524 to 816. U.S. goods were kept out, but corporations bought the factories or built new ones in Canada rather than pay the increased rates. As one Canadian economist expressed the situation, it made little difference whether Canadians were buried by U.S. exports or U.S. branch plants—they would lose control of their economy either way. The 1936 agreement remained in effect until 1947, when both nations signed a general agreement that superseded prior trade treaties.

Leslie V. Tischauser

SOURCES FOR FURTHER STUDY

Corbett, Percy E. *The Settlement of Canadian-American Disputes: A Critical Study of Meetings and Results.* New Haven: Conn.: Yale University Press, 1937.

McInnis, Edgar. *Canada: A Political and Social History.* Toronto: Holt, Rinehart and Winston, 1990.

U.S. Department of State. *British Dominions and Canada.* Vol. 1 in *Papers Relating to the Foreign Policy of the United States, 1936.* Washington, D.C.: Government Printing Office, 1951.

Welles, Sumner. *Seven Decisions That Shaped History.* New York: Harper, 1951.

SEE ALSO: Treaty of Washington (1871); Halibut Treaty (1924); Smoot-Hawley Tariff Act (1930); Good Neighbor Policy (1933); General Agreement on Tariffs and Trade of 1947 (1947).

MARIHUANA TAX ACT

DATE: August 2, 1937
U.S. STATUTES AT LARGE: 50 Stat. 551
PUBLIC LAW: 75-238
CATEGORIES: Agriculture; Food and Drugs; Tariffs and Taxation

The law created an occupational excise tax imposed on everyone involved with producing, processing, trading, or using the various products of the hemp plant.

With the Marihuana Tax Act, the federal government set out to suppress illicit uses of the hemp plant while not disrupting its industrial or medicinal uses. Harry J. Anslinger, commissioner of narcotics of the Federal Bureau of Narcotics of the U.S. Treasury Department, drafted the proposal for the Marihuana Tax Act. On April 14, 1937, Representative Robert L. Doughton (North Carolina) introduced the bill, which was designed to control the trade in marijuana and suppress illicit use of the substance. Anybody involved with handling the plant or its products was to obtain a license and register with the Internal Revenue Service. Taxes on the handling of marijuana would range from one to twenty-four dollars. In response to criticism from hemp producers, their tax was reduced from five dollars in the original bill to one dollar in the final act. Hemp producers believed that the higher tax would have forced small growers out of business.

Thomas Winter

SOURCE FOR FURTHER STUDY
Solomon, David, ed. *The Marihuana Papers.* New York: New American Library, 1968.

SEE ALSO: Pure Food and Drugs Act (1906); Opium Exclusion Act (1909); Harrison Narcotic Drug Act (1914); Food, Drug, and Cosmetic Act (1938); Comprehensive Drug Abuse Prevention and Control Act (1970); National Narcotics Act (1984).

MILLER-TYDINGS FAIR TRADE ACT

DATE: August 17, 1937
U.S. STATUTES AT LARGE: 50 Stat. 693
CATEGORIES: Business, Commerce, and Trade; Copyrights, Patents, and Trademarks

By allowing manufacturers to maintain minimum prices, the Miller-Tydings Act promised small retailers protection from chain-store competition, but adverse court decisions and changing economic circumstances diminished the impact of the law.

The Miller-Tydings Act of 1937 amended the Sherman Antitrust Act of 1890 so as to legalize retail price maintenance, thus allowing manufacturers to maintain minimum prices for the sale of their goods. Manufacturers used retail price maintenance to protect their goodwill, hoping that high prices would keep retailers from cutting services to customers. Independent retailers hoped that retail price maintenance would eliminate price competition from chain stores. Prior to the act, the courts had held retail price maintenance to be in violation of the Federal Trade Commission Act of 1914.

ANTI-CHAIN STORE MOVEMENT

The Miller-Tydings Act embodied the anti-chain store sentiment prevalent in the 1920's and 1930's. During the early twentieth century, independent retailers had confronted new types of competition as department stores appeared in large cities and mail-order houses began to sell goods throughout the nation. The rapid rise of chain stores in the 1920's further eroded the market share of small businesses. Chain stores attracted customers by offering prices lower than those of their single-store competitors. This form of mass marketing spread rapidly as the automobile connected small towns to larger urban markets. Chain stores sales continued to increase during the cost-conscious Depression years, and by 1935 the chains handled nearly one-fourth of all retail sales.

Independent retailers responded by sponsoring advertising campaigns encouraging Americans to "trade at home" and by boycotting those manufacturers that sold to chain stores. Ambitious politicians also seized upon anti-chain store sentiment to attract the votes of independent merchants and others critical of big business. The anti-chain store movement gained additional momentum in the South and West, where politicians played on the populist fear of "outside" corporations controlling local economies. This movement found expression in state laws that discriminated against chain stores. During the 1920's and 1930's, almost every state imposed punitive taxes upon chain stores.

THE DRIVE FOR FAIR TRADE

During the early twentieth century, organized merchants had tried to overcome the competitive advantage of mass marketers by urging manufacturers to fix minimum retail prices, a practice known as retail price maintenance or "fair trade." The Supreme Court, however, ruled against retail price fixing. Manufacturers and retailers interested in retail price maintenance then sought to secure the passage of laws legalizing fair trade. The American Fair Trade League (AFTL) and the National Association of Retail Druggists (NARD) led this drive for fair trade. The AFTL represented manufacturers of trademarked goods that wished to use fair trade as a means to protect their goodwill. By maintaining minimum prices, manufacturers hoped to attract those retailers interested in emphasizing quality and service rather than price. As chain stores increased their market share, however, many manufacturers sought higher sales volume and abandoned retail price maintenance.

The druggists hoped to increase their profit margins and reduce chain store competition. The NARD, widely considered to be one of the most powerful trade associations in the country, conducted intense, well-organized campaigns in support of fair trade legislation. In 1931, California enacted a fair trade law drafted by the NARD, and several other states quickly followed suit. In 1936, the Supreme Court upheld the constitutionality of these laws. Thereafter, fair trade advocates met with virtually no opposition on the state level. In 1937 alone, twenty-eight states passed fair trade laws, and by 1940, a total of forty-four had enacted some form of this legislation.

At the federal level, however, proponents of fair trade met resistance from within the executive and legislative branches of the government. The Federal Trade Commission had always opposed fair trade legislation on the grounds that it lessened competition and violated the spirit of antitrust legislation. Since 1914, Congress had also rejected bills aimed at legalizing retail price maintenance. Thus, the impact of state fair trade laws remained limited because products sold in interstate commerce, under federal law, could not be subject to fair trade agreements.

DRAFTING AND PASSAGE
Having failed to secure a national fair trade law, the proponents of retail price maintenance sought the passage of permissive legislation allowing states to settle the issue. In 1935, the NARD enhanced its influence by hiring Herbert Levy, a law partner of Senator Millard Tydings (Democrat from Maryland). Levy persuaded Tydings to sponsor a bill drafted by the NARD. Representative John E. Miller (Democrat from Arkansas) introduced a companion bill in the House of Representatives. Tydings's bill met with opposition from Representative Emanuel Celler (Democrat from New York), who feared it would reduce price competition. President Franklin D. Roosevelt also expressed his belief that the bill would increase the cost of living and slow recovery by removing purchasing power from the economy. Congressional supporters,

however, played on sentiments in favor of states' rights by emphasizing that the law merely gave the states the right to determine
their position on fair trade.

In July, 1937, Tydings hoped to avoid a presidential veto by at-
taching his bill as a rider to a bill granting appropriations to the
District of Columbia. Despite the opposition of consumer groups
and nearly all economists, Congress passed this legislation by an
overwhelming margin. President Roosevelt criticized the use of
this evasive tactic but signed the bill into law on August 17, 1937.

PROVISIONS AND IMPACT

By amending the Sherman Act, this law granted an antitrust exemption for retail price maintenance agreements. Manufacturers
of trademarked or brand-name goods could now prohibit retailers
from selling their product below a minimum price. Tydings neglected to incorporate a nonsigner clause that would make retail
price maintenance agreements binding on all merchants within a
state. This defect would later allow the Supreme Court effectively
to nullify the law. Although technically an antitrust law, the Miller-
Tydings Act did not authorize the Federal Trade Commission to
police resale price agreements; instead, Congress left it to manufacturers to enforce their own fair trade contracts.

The Miller-Tydings Act of 1937 expanded the marketing options
of manufacturers by allowing them to emphasize quality and service rather than price. The act also reflected congressional concern with the fate of small business. Along with other legislation
such as the Robinson-Patman Antidiscrimination Act of 1936
(which limited the quantity discounts available to chain stores),
this law aimed to reduce the competitive advantage of discounters.
Independent retailers hoped that the elimination of price competition would enable them to compete more successfully with mass
marketers.

The impact of the Miller-Tydings Act varied from trade to trade.
Retail price maintenance flourished in oligopolistic industries
with trade associations strong enough to enforce compliance with
fair trade agreements. Manufacturers found that they could maintain minimum prices on luxury goods that already sold at a high
profit margin. Thus, retail price maintenance spread most rapidly
in drugs, cosmetics, jewelry, alcoholic beverages, tobacco, books,
electrical appliances, cameras, and hardware. In 1950, the number

of manufacturers engaged in retail price maintenance peaked at approximately sixteen hundred.

Despite the success of retail price maintenance in these fields, less than 10 percent of all goods were sold under fair trade contracts. Several factors limited the appeal of retail price maintenance. First, manufacturers using this tactic still faced price competition from other manufacturers, so the minimum prices set could not be too high. In addition, mass marketers responded to retail price maintenance by adopting an increasing number of private brands, especially in the grocery trade. Discounters also offered rebates and accepted trade-ins as a way to evade retail price agreements. Many price cutters simply flouted the law, confident that manufacturers could not afford to enforce their fair trade contracts. Indeed, several leading consumer goods manufacturers, including General Electric and the Sheaffer Pen Company, initially pursued a policy of price maintenance but abandoned this marketing strategy because the costs of enforcement were too high. Other manufacturers paid lip service to fair trade while at the same time seeking high sales volume through chain stores.

THE DECLINE OF "FAIR TRADE"
The Miller-Tydings Act failed to satisfy the demands of independent retailers hungry for higher margins. Ironically, the high margins on fair trade products attracted mass marketers, thus intensifying competition. Although the price of fair trade products increased after passage of this act, the NARD and other trade associations still criticized manufacturers for setting their minimum prices too low. These associations also found it difficult to persuade many manufacturers to abandon volume sales and adopt fair trade. As a result, several of these organizations decided to engage in coercive practices prohibited by the Miller-Tydings Act. The act allowed manufacturers to voluntarily set minimum prices, but retailers could not legally conspire to force manufacturers into fair trade. Nevertheless, the NARD proceeded to boycott and blacklist manufacturers that did not maintain minimum prices.

The rise of new types of competition also limited the impact of fair trade. During the 1950's, discount chains spread rapidly, and department stores responded by carrying a greater number of private brands. R. H. Macy & Company, for example, carried more than fourteen hundred products under its own name. By 1954, fewer than nine hundred manufacturers sold fair trade products, and the number continued to dwindle through the end of the decade. In 1956, a Senate Small Business Committee survey of retailers revealed widespread pessimism about the future of retail price maintenance.

During the late 1930's and 1940's, the courts upheld the constitutionality of the Miller-Tydings Act, but this favorable treatment did not last into the 1950's. In 1951, the Supreme Court ruled that fair trade agreements could not be enforced against nonsigners in interstate commerce. Congress overrode the Court by passing the McGuire Act (1952), but the Court's strongly worded indictment of fair trade continued to influence the thinking of lower courts. Critical studies by economists and the Federal Trade Commission also fostered a judicial climate of opinion hostile to fair trade. During the 1950's and 1960's, state courts throughout the United States invalidated all or part of their fair trade laws, and by 1975 only eleven states had fair trade laws on the books.

REPEAL

The Miller-Tydings Act finally fell victim to the inflationary climate of the 1970's. In 1937, the sponsors of the act had hoped to raise prices in a deflationary period, but policymakers in the inflationary postwar years became more concerned with reducing prices. Economists estimated that fair trade raised the nation's cost of living by several billion dollars per year. In 1975, President Gerald Ford urged repeal of fair trade legislation as part of his WIN ("Whip Inflation Now") program. Senator Edward W. Brooke (Republican of Massachusetts) introduced legislation to repeal the Miller-Tydings Act. His bill gathered overwhelming support from both liberals and conservatives. The resulting Consumer Goods Pricing Act repealed the Miller-Tydings Act and ended the experiment with retail price maintenance.

Jonathan Bean

SOURCES FOR FURTHER STUDY

Blackford, Mansel G. *A History of Small Business in America.* New York: Twayne, 1991.

Bork, Robert H. *The Antitrust Paradox: A Policy at War with Itself.* New York: Basic Books, 1978.

Hawley, Ellis W. *The New Deal and the Problem of Monopoly: A Study in Economic Ambivalence.* Princeton, N.J.: Princeton University Press, 1966.

Kintner, Earl W., ed. *Federal Antitrust Laws and Related Statutes: A Legislative History.* 11 vols. Buffalo, N.Y.: William S. Hein, 1978, 1982-1985.

Palamountain, Joseph Cornwall, Jr. *The Politics of Distribution.* Cambridge, Mass.: Harvard University Press, 1955.

Strasser, Susan. *Satisfaction Guaranteed The Making of the American Mass Market.* New York: Pantheon Books, 1989.

Yamey, B. C., ed. *Resale Price Maintenance.* Chicago: Aldine, 1966.

SEE ALSO: Sherman Antitrust Act (1890); Clayton Antitrust Act (1914); Federal Trade Commission Act (1914); Robinson-Patman Antidiscrimination Act (1936).

PITTMAN-ROBERTSON WILDLIFE RESTORATION ACT

ALSO KNOWN AS: Federal Aid in Wildlife Act
DATE: September 2, 1937
U.S. STATUTES AT LARGE: 50 Stat. 917
U.S. CODE: 16 § 669 et seq.
CATEGORIES: Animals; Environment and Conservation; Tariffs and Taxation

The act authorized funding of state wildlife agencies through federal excise taxes on sporting guns and ammunition used in hunting.

On September 2, 1937, Franklin D. Roosevelt signed the Pittman-Robertson Act, which authorized the federal government to collect manufacturers' excise taxes on sporting guns and ammunition and to transfer the money to state wildlife agencies. This law originated through the cooperation of conservationists, primarily hunters, and manufacturers of sporting arms and ammunition. The revenues collected have been used to support wildlife management, including purchase of critical habitat, management of existing refuges, hunter training, and wildlife restoration. Many species whose survival had once been threatened have thereby been able to thrive. The law, also called the Federal Aid in Wildlife Act, was initiated by Carl Shoemaker, a conservationist, and was sponsored through Congress in less than three months by Senator Key Pittman and Representative A. Willis Robertson.

BACKGROUND

In the early years of the twentieth century, as sport hunting became increasingly popular and wildlife habitat and wildlife itself became increasingly scarce, leading conservationists tried to develop and fund a refuge system to benefit wildlife and sportsmen. Several laws were passed as a result. The Migratory Bird Conservation Act of 1929 set up a refuge system to be financed by congressional appropriations. In 1934, largely through the efforts of Jay Norwood "Ding" Darling as chief of the Bureau of Biological Survey, the Duck Stamp and Fish Wildlife Coordination Acts, which provided funding for wetland conservation, were passed.

With Darling, Shoemaker—as special investigator of the Senate Special Committee on Conservation and Wildlife Resources—helped to organize the first North American Wildlife Conference in 1936, which created the National Wildlife Federation. At the second North American Wildlife Conference in 1937, Shoemaker and others started to develop what would become the Pittman-Robertson law by modifying suggestions made by John B. Burnham and T. Gilbert Pearson in 1925. Burnham and Pearson had suggested that the 10 percent excise tax on sporting arms and ammunition be used to finance refuges instead of being considered part of general moneys, but the proposed financing did not go through because Congress repealed all excise taxes, although they were reinstated in 1932.

TAXING SPORTING GUNS

In 1937, Shoemaker suggested that the current 11 percent manufacturers' excise tax on sporting guns and ammunition be allocated to the states equitably. In order to apportion funding equitably and to balance the small populations of the Western states with the high populations of the East, his formula included the number of paid license holders as well as the area of the states. This approach would balance the Western states with their relatively small populations but large land area with the larger number of licensed hunters in the more populous, but smaller eastern states. The draft bill was supported by the Bureau of Biological Survey, state wildlife agencies, and conservation organizations. The firearms industry supported it as well after Shoemaker agreed to the suggestion of Charles L. Horn of the Federal Cartridge Company to lower the percentage of tax collections used for administrative costs by the Biological Survey from his proposed 10 percent to 8 percent.

Shoemaker enlisted the support of Senator Key Pittman of Nevada, chairman of the Special Committee on Wildlife, and Representative A. Willis Robertson of Virginia, chairman of the House Select Committee on Conservation of Wildlife Resources. Robertson had been a member of the Virginia Game and Inland Fisheries Commission and knew that state legislatures sometimes used funds from license receipts for state programs other than those of the wildlife agencies. He therefore added to Shoemaker's bill the prohibition of the diversion of funds for purposes other than the administration of the state fish and game department. The modified bill moved through the Senate very quickly. In the House, however, the Agriculture Committee, not the Wildlife Committee, had jurisdiction over the bill. In order to entice Representative Scott Lucas from Illinois, chairman of the Agriculture Committee, to move the bill through the House more quickly, Shoemaker encouraged Illinois women's groups and garden clubs to contact Lucas. The bill passed the House on August 17 and was signed by Franklin D. Roosevelt on September 2, 1937.

IMPLEMENTATION

Ira N. Gabrielson, chief of the Bureau of Biological Survey, and his assistant, Albert M. Day, implemented the Pittman-Robertson Act. Day determined that the funds were to be used for three types of state projects: to purchase land to rehabilitate wildlife, to develop and improve land's suitability for birds and mammals, and to research ways to solve problems of wildlife restoration. In order to ensure that management of state wildlife programs was performed by professionals and not political appointees, Gabrielson and Day also required that management personnel hired through Pittman-Robertson funds be trained and competent.

Despite excise tax revenues of around $3 million in 1938, Congress allocated only $1 million that first year and continued to refuse to allocate the funds to the state wildlife agencies until the 1950's. In 1939, the Bureau of Biological Survey was removed from the Department of Agriculture and placed in the Department of the Interior, where it was combined with the Bureau of Fisheries of the Department of Commerce. This new agency was called the Fish and Wildlife Service. In 1951, as part of the Appropriations Act, Congress agreed to transfer all the tax collections to the state wildlife agencies. In 1956, Congress agreed to release $13 million of back tax revenues. Thus excise tax revenues collected from hunters have been used to replenish wildlife and their habitat throughout the United States.

LONG-RANGE IMPACT

The Pittman-Robertson Act was enacted to reverse the decline of wildlife in the United States. Over the years, as its influence has grown, it has financed scientific research of particular species and their habitats, habitat restoration, hunter education, and wildlife research in general. As a result, the decline of many species has been reversed, habitat has been restored, and hunting accidents and fatalities in many states have declined. Among the species helped by the act are the wild turkey, white-tailed deer, the bighorn sheep, and the black bear, the prairie chicken, the mountain lion, the Canada goose, the pronghorn antelope, the elk, the caribou, the beaver, the sea otter, the gray and fox squirrels, the mule deer, the wood duck, the chukar partridge, the bobcat, and the ring-necked pheasant.

The law has also increased the professionalism of wildlife research and management by setting professional standards for management personnel as well as requiring that projects meet national standards. It also has served as a dependable source of money so that states may engage in long-term programs. It has provided professionals with a means of exchanging information to ensure that managers were aware of projects in different states. Funds have also been used to support cooperative programs with nongovernment organizations.

Margaret F. Boorstein

SOURCES FOR FURTHER STUDY
National Research Council of the National Academy of Sciences. *Land Use and Wildlife Resources.* Washington, D.C.: National Academy of Sciences, 1970.
Owen, A. L. Riesch. *Conservation Under F. D. R.* New York: Praeger, 1983.
_____. "Wildlife Aid from Gun Taxes." *Nature Magazine* 30 (December, 1937): 361-362.
Sheldon, H. P. "Game Restoration." *Country Life and the Sportsman* 74 (June, 1938): 28, 90.
U.S. Department of the Interior. Fish and Wildlife Service. *Restoring America's Wildlife: 1937-1987: The First Fifty Years of the Federal Aid in Wildlife Restoration (Pittman-Robertson) Act.* Washington, D.C.: Author, 1987.

SEE ALSO: Migratory Bird Act (1913); Migratory Bird Treaty Act (1918); Migratory Bird Hunting and Conservation Stamp Act (1934); Wilderness Act (1964); Animal Welfare Act (1966); Endangered Species Preservation Act (1966); Endangered Species Act (1973); Eastern Wilderness Act (1975).

WHEELER-LEA ACT

DATE: March 21, 1938
U.S. STATUTES AT LARGE: 52 Stat. 111
U.S. CODE: 15 § 41
CATEGORIES: Business, Commerce, and Trade

By adding jurisdiction over "unfair and deceptive acts or practices in commerce" to section 5 of the 1914 Federal Trade Commission Act, the Wheeler-Lea Act broadened the FTC's power over unfair competition.

The first decade of the twentieth century witnessed numerous investigations by the U.S. Department of Commerce into alleged monopolistic business practices in the farm equipment, petroleum, steel, and tobacco industries, among others. Two schools of thought had evolved concerning antimonopoly and antitrust legislation. One group believed that all trusts should be abolished, whereas the other group thought that Congress should instead establish mechanisms to regulate monopolistic practices. The latter thinking prevailed and led Congress to enact the Federal Trade Commission Act in 1914. The Federal Trade Commission (FTC) was activated the following year.

REGULATING ADVERTISING

Many analysts trace the origins of the Federal Trade Commission to the advertising industry association currently known as the American Advertising Federation (AAF). In 1905, several local advertising clubs (primarily in Chicago, Cincinnati, Cleveland, Detroit, Indianapolis, and St. Louis) formed what became the Associated Advertising Clubs of the World, with one of its goals being elimination of false and deceptive advertising practices common at the time. This association's 1912 truth-in-advertising campaign is generally credited as being the first, and its lobbying efforts eventually led to President Woodrow Wilson's recommendations in 1914 that the Federal Trade Commission be formed. The vigilance committees set up by member clubs in many cities also resulted in establishment of the Council of Better Business Bureaus.

The Federal Trade Commission Act focused on protecting competitors from unfair trade practices of other businesses. The act did not specifically define unfair competition, leaving that determination up to the FTC on a case-by-case basis. Legislators may not have intended the FTC to have strong punitive powers, but rather to serve as a barrier to protect weaker businesses from the predatory behavior of monopolies. The FTC grew to police the activities of business in general, not simply monopolistic practices, and developed strong punitive capabilities.

The power to regulate advertising was given to the FTC under section 5 of the 1914 act. The wording of this section originally prohibited only unfair methods of "competition." This led to a 1931 Supreme Court decision that held that the commission was without jurisdiction unless actual injury to competitors could be proved. The decision involved a questionable weight-reduction product that could have been dangerous for some consumers. The Court's decision seriously limited the FTC's power to intervene in cases in which consumers, but not competitors, were injured. Congress subsequently amended the FTC Act in 1938, thereby closing the loophole opened by this decision. This amending legislation is commonly known as the Wheeler-Lea Act.

THE AMENDMENT

At the federal level, the Wheeler-Lea Act gave the government its most important control over false and deceptive advertising. Section 5 of the Federal Trade Commission Act was amended to read, "Unfair methods of competition in commerce and unfair or deceptive acts or practices in commerce are hereby declared unlawful." The intent behind the Wheeler-Lea Act was twofold. First, Congress wanted to expand the FTC's jurisdiction over unfair competition by extending it into commerce as well as industry. Second, Congress intended to give the commission more power to regulate false and deceptive advertising of food, drugs, therapeutic devices, and cosmetics.

The first objective was accomplished by modifying section 5 as previously discussed. The second goal was reached through section 12(a) of the amended act, which made it illegal to disseminate false information concerning foods, drugs, therapeutic devices, or cosmetics for the purpose of inducing their purchase. No matter how incidental a marketer's behavior seems, the FTC has the authority to act if a false advertisement is sent through the U.S. mail or is concerned with commerce. False advertising that violates section 12(a) is by default unfair and deceptive under section 5.

The definition of false advertising in section 15 of the Wheeler-Lea Act was designed to be very inclusive. The intent to be false or deceptive was not specified as a necessary element; legislators wanted any materially misleading advertising to be subject to or cause for FTC action, regardless of the advertiser's intent. Media and advertising agencies were exempted from liability if they cooperated with the agency's investigation.

Aggrieved competitors who have, for example, been directly named in what they consider to be a false or deceptive comparative advertising campaign have several options for resolution of the problem. They can complain to industry arbitration organizations such as the Better Business Bureau's National Advertising Division (NAD) and appeal an NAD decision to the National Advertising Review Board (NARB). They can ask for assistance from the media in which the questionable ads are disseminated or take the issue directly to court under section 43(a) of the Lanham Act. They can resort to local and state regulatory bodies (such as the state attorney general) or file a complaint with the Federal Trade Commission. The commission is also capable of issuing its own complaint under section 5, even if no business or individual has lodged a complaint.

Advertisers usually consent to stop running advertisements disputed by the FTC. If the FTC believes that an advertisement is false or deceptive but the sponsor refuses to sign a consent decree and stop using the ad, the commission can issue a cease-and-desist order requiring the advertiser to stop running the questionable campaign. Under section 5, cease-and-desist orders become final in sixty days unless the advertiser requests a court review. If the advertiser requests a hearing, the cease-and-desist order cannot become final until an administrative law judge has reviewed the case. If the order is upheld by the judge, the sponsor can appeal to the full commission. Advertisers who violate final cease-and-desist orders are subject to substantial fines.

The FTC can seek court remedies under sections 13 and 14 of the amended act. These include injunctions to stop the campaign in question as well as fines or imprisonment for sponsors of the advertisement in severe cases that involve blatant intent to defraud or reckless endangerment of consumers. In some cases, even though the FTC believed that section 12 had been violated, the courts have disagreed with the commission and denied requests for injunctions to stop ad campaigns.

THE FTC'S MISSION

Largely because of the Wheeler-Lea Act, the core of the FTC's regulatory mission has become its efforts to end deceptive advertising, although antitrust concerns still influence FTC policy. The aggressiveness with which the FTC is able to carry out its mission depends heavily on the philosophy of the FTC chairperson as well as the presidential administration's relationship with business. There have been periods during which the agency was perceived as weak and ineffective, such as the late 1960's. With the Wheeler-Lea Act as a foundation, the FTC underwent major reorganizations and staffing changes during the 1970's, resulting in a more powerful and effective regulatory force. The Reagan administration sought to disarm the FTC during the 1980's, but during the administration of George H. W. Bush the agency aggressively addressed alcohol and tobacco advertising directed at underage persons.

In spite of these inconsistencies, the FTC developed into a more powerful regulator of advertising after the implementation of the Wheeler-Lea Act in 1938. Two areas in which this trend has become most apparent are the commission's requirement for substantiation of claims made in ads and its use of forced corrective advertising to help counter false advertising claims. Particularly since 1970, the FTC has asked that sponsors of numerous disputed claims offer proof that the claims they made are true. Product claims that are literally untrue (that is, cannot be proven in laboratory tests) are considered to be inherently deceptive. Claims are also judged according to how the average "rational" consumer will perceive them.

CONSUMER SURVEYS

The FTC often admits as evidence consumer survey results designed to determine the perceptions of average consumers to the claims in question. Thomas J. Maronick, formerly with the FTC Bureau of Consumer Protection, analyzed cases handled by the FTC from the 1960's through the 1980's. His analysis suggests that the FTC used the following guidelines in assessing consumer surveys designed to evaluate claims of deceptive advertising: the experience and competence of the marketing research firm or individual conducting the survey; whether the methodology is "generally accepted" and interviewers are properly trained to reduce respondent bias; the representativeness of the sample in relation to the appropriate group of consumers; and the use of control groups (consumers not exposed to the claims, subsequently used to compare with those who were exposed) to produce more valid research; the relationships between the attorneys involved and the researcher (close relationships were not viewed favorably); whether the study was conducted before the advertisement was challenged (if so, it was given more credibility); whether the study used leading questions (especially open-ended versus closed-ended questions) to suggest desired answers; and finally, whether the conditions under which the study was conducted represented a natural viewing state for consumers, such as their homes.

CORRECTIVE ADVERTISING

In a move considered to be much more drastic than requiring claim substantiation, the FTC also began to force sponsors of deceptive advertising to pay for corrective advertising disclaiming previously made false statements. In one of the first corrective advertising cases, the FTC required the makers of Listerine to include in a ten-million-dollar advertising campaign a disclaimer that the mouthwash did not kill germs that cause the common cold, as the brand had previously claimed. The commission thought that the false Listerine claim of common cold prevention was a major reason that consumers selected the brand, and that the corrective advertising campaign was the best method for eliminating misperceptions.

At first, sponsors were required to disclose that their original campaign had been ruled false and deceptive by the FTC. This generated criticism from those who thought that the requirement was beyond the FTC's scope of remedial authority. The FTC took heed and later only required sponsors to disclose that, contrary to what their previous advertising had stated, the claim in question was not true. In addition, the agency's original requirement that 25 percent of the advertisement's space or time be devoted to the corrective message was changed to 25 percent of advertising expenditures during the same time period that other advertisements were run.

The FTC's call for corrective advertising is probably the single most controversial activity ultimately derived from the expanded power given to the agency through the Wheeler-Lea Act. Had the language of the original act not been modified, the commission would not have obtained the authority to require sponsors to run corrective advertising for the sake of consumers who had acquired false information.

William T. Neese

SOURCES FOR FURTHER STUDY
Digges, Isaac W. *The Modern Law of Advertising and Marketing.* New York: Funk & Wagnalls, 1948.
Dillon, Tom. "What Is Deceptive Advertising?" *Journal of Advertising Research* 13, no. 10 (1973): 9-12.
Garon, Philip A., ed. *Advertising Law Anthology.* National Law Anthology Series 2. Washington, D.C.: International Library, 1974.
Kintner, Earl W. *A Primer on the Law of Deceptive Practices: A Guide for the Businessman.* New York: Macmillan, 1971.

_____, ed. *Federal Antitrust Laws and Related Statutes: A Legislative History.* 11 vols. Buffalo, N.Y.: William S. Hein, 1978, 1982-1985.

Maronick, Thomas J. "Copy Tests in FTC Deception Cases: Guidelines for Researchers." *Journal of Advertising Research* 31, no. 12 (1991): 9-17.

Muris, Timothy J., ed. *The Federal Trade Commission Since 1970 Economic Regulation and Bureaucratic Behavior.* New York: Cambridge University Press, 1981.

Russell, J. Thomas, and W. Ronald Lane. *Kleppner's Advertising Procedure.* 12th ed. Englewood Cliffs, N.J.: Prentice-Hall, 1993.

Ulanoff, Stanley M. *Advertising in America.* New York: Hastings House, 1977.

SEE ALSO: Interstate Commerce Act (1887); Sherman Antitrust Act (1890); Federal Trade Commission Act (1914); Clayton Antitrust Act (1914); Celler-Kefauver Act (1950); Truth in Lending Act (1968); Parens Patriae Act (1974); Antitrust Procedures and Penalties Act (1974).

FOREIGN AGENTS REGISTRATION ACT

DATE: June 8, 1938
U.S. STATUTES AT LARGE: 52 Stat. 631
U.S. CODE: 22 § 611
CATEGORIES: Communications and Media; Military and National Security; Speech and Expression

This federal law authorized the U.S. government to restrict importation of any foreign films and publications that it classified as "propaganda."

The 1938 Foreign Agents Registration Act (FARA) was designed to restrict distribution of foreign films and publications in the United States. It required that any film produced in a foreign country that could be considered political propaganda had to be so labeled. During the 1980's the law was given an expansive interpretation under the Reagan administration. In 1982 the Department of Justice sought to require three films produced by the National Film Board of Canada to be labeled as propaganda.

POLITICAL PROPAGANDA AND CENSORSHIP

Two of the Canadian films were about acid rain—a sensitive subject in U.S.-Canadian relations; the third, *If You Love This Planet* won an Academy Award. The Justice Department summarized the message of this film as: "Unless we shake off our indifference and work to prevent nuclear war, we stand a slim chance of surviving the twentieth century." The Justice Department ordered the Film Board of Canada to include a message with the films that the U.S. government did not necessarily approve of its content and that the films contained "political propaganda." Under U.S. law, the Film Board of Canada was also required to provide the Justice Department with the names of the persons and organizations in the United States who ordered the films.

CHALLENGES TO THE LAW'S CONSTITUTIONALITY

The following year, in Washington, D.C., and California respectively, the American Civil Liberties Union (ACLU) and California state senator Barry Keene—who had planned to sponsor showings of these Canadian films to support his own views—filed separate suits against the Justice Department, claiming that FARA was unconstitutional. The ACLU argued that labeling the Canadian films as propaganda might prejudice potential viewers and might even deter people from viewing the films at all, because the label "denigrates the films' messages." Furthermore, the ACLU argued that requiring a listing of the names of the exhibitors might injure exhibitors' reputations because they would be stigmatized as exhibitors of "un-American" or "unpatriotic materials." In 1984, in *Block v. Smith*, the U.S. District Court for the District of Columbia dismissed the ACLU suit, ruling that the term "political propaganda" did not in itself necessarily have negative connotations. An appeals court reversed part of this decision by holding that Block, the distributor of the Canadian films, had proven "concrete harm"; however, it simultaneously affirmed the lower court's ruling that the "propaganda" label was acceptable, and that Block must still report the names of the persons who ordered his films.

Meanwhile, California's Senator Keene, objecting to being labeled a disseminator of political propaganda, advanced similar arguments. The U.S. District Court in San Bernardino, California, enjoined application of FARA to the three Canadian films; this was affirmed at the appellate level. In 1987 the U.S. Supreme Court, in *Meese v. Keene*, held that the label of "political propaganda," when used in a "neutral and even-handed manner," is not intended as censorship, and "has no pejorative connotation." Writing for a 5-3 majority, Justice John Paul Stevens conceded there was "a risk that a partially informed audience might believe that a film that must be registered with the Department of Justice is suspect. But there is no evidence that this suspicion . . . has had the effect of government censorship." The Supreme Court thus upheld the decision to label the three Canadian films as "propaganda" under FARA.

Juliet Dee

Sources for Further Study

Pattison, Joseph E., and John L. Taylor, eds. *The Registration of Foreign Agents in the United States: A Practical and Legal Guide.* Washington, D.C.: District of Columbia Bar, 1981.

United States. General Accounting Office. *Foreign Agent Registration: Former Federal Officials Representing Foreign Interests Before the U.S. Government. Report to Congressional Requesters.* Washington, D.C.: Author, 1992.

SEE ALSO: First Amendment (1789); Sedition Act of 1798 (1798); Comstock Act (1873); Espionage Acts (1917-1918); Communications Act (1934); Communications Decency Act (1996).

NATURAL GAS ACT

DATE: June 21, 1938
U.S. STATUTES AT LARGE: 52 Stat. 821
U.S. CODE: 15 § 717
CATEGORIES: Business, Commerce, and Trade; Energy; Natural Resources

The Natural Gas Act mandated the Federal Power Commission to control gas prices in interstate commerce and to decide which pipelines may enter the interstate market.

On June 21, 1938, Congress passed the Natural Gas Act (NGA), and seven days later, President Franklin Roosevelt signed it into law. The NGA provided the Federal Power Commission (FPC) much discretion in determining "just and reasonable" rates for the sale of natural gas in interstate commerce. The findings of the commission were to be "conclusive" so long as "supported by substantial evidence," but these findings could be challenged in court. The regulation of prices was not to apply to local sales or to intrastate deliveries; the state public-service commissions would continue to regulate these services. The FPC was given additional powers to regulate interstate pipelines and to award certificates of public convenience and necessity, meaning that no new pipeline could enter the interstate market without FPC approval. The major purpose of the law was to protect consumers from excessive prices, while public safety and conservation of a scarce resource were secondary considerations.

EARLIER GAS REGULATIONS

Since the late nineteenth century, the federal government had been regulating interstate business that was monopolistic or "affected with a public interest." Until the late 1920's, however, natural gas was generally an intrastate business, and it had been regulated by the state public-service commissions since the turn of the century. The business changed as improvements in metals and welding made it possible for long seamless pipelines to cross state borders between areas of production and large urban centers in the North, and by 1936, thirty-five states had access to supplies of natural gas. The Supreme Court in *Missouri v. Kansas Natural Gas* (1924) interrupted the status quo by ruling that the states could no longer regulate the prices of natural gas transported from one state to another, because the Constitution gave Congress exclusive power to regulate interstate commerce.

After the Court's decision, those suspicious of the large energy companies wanted the Congress to "fill in the gap" in the regulation of natural gas. In 1928, the Senate instructed the Federal Trade Commission to investigate the matter, and the commission's one-hundred-volume study recommended federal regulation of both electricity and natural gas. With the support of this study, the New Deal Congress passed the Federal Power Act of 1935, which enlarged the scope of the FPC and authorized it to regulate electricity sold between states. The FPC had both quasi-legislative and quasi-judicial functions, so that it could formulate rules with the force of law and interpret these rules in specific cases, subject to appeals in the federal courts.

DRAFTING THE 1938 LAW

After the passage of the Federal Power Act, Representative Samuel Rayburn, one of the strongest proponents of New Deal regulations in the House, instructed legislative drafters to take the law and to use it as a model for similar legislation authorizing controls of natural gas sales. As Rayburn introduced the bill into the House, Burton Wheeler introduced the same bill into the Senate. Natural gas companies and state regulators, however, objected to some of the features of the Rayburn bill, and it failed to become law. The next year, Representative Clarence Lea, chairman of the appropriate commerce subcommittee, revised the bill with the assistance of Clyde Seavey, one of the members of the FPC. Lea introduced the new bill into the House that year, and although there was little opposition, there was not enough interest to get it to the floor for a vote.

Lea then turned to the natural gas companies for their views; after making some changes, he introduced the bill a second time in April, 1937. The companies had decided that regulation was in their interest. At this time, the companies' major problem was that oversupplies were driving down costs, and they were now happy to accept regulation in exchange for a guaranteed profit margin. In spite of a consensus in favor of regulation, the Senate was slower than the House to vote in favor of the bill, and the differences between the two chambers were not worked out until June 21, 1938.

AMBIGUITIES

Compared with many innovative laws of the New Deal, the NGA was considered rather unexceptional, and the press at the time almost ignored the issue. The NGA was vague and ambiguous in several key areas, and thus the implications of the law would evolve with judicial challenges.

The most uncertain portion of the NGA was the statement that FPC regulation would not extend to "the production and gathering of natural gas." It was clear that the FPC would not have authority over the physical production of gas. Since the term "production and gathering" was not defined, however, it was unclear whether the FPC was authorized to regulate the sale of gas in the fields if the gas was destined for the interstate markets, or whether FPC regulations would apply only after the gas had been sold. This particular ambiguity would be the most controversial aspect of the history of the NGA. Over the years, interpreting this and similar provisions of the NGA would give employment to a large number of lawyers.

COURT BATTLES

The first major court battle of the NGA had to do with the method that the FPC was to use in determining "just and reasonable" rates. When the act was passed, regulatory bodies generally were following the fair-value standard that a pro-business Supreme Court had articulated in its 1897 *Smythe v. Ames* decision. According to this standard, regulated businesses were entitled to a rate of return based on the value of their capital investment. Beginning in 1942, a more aggressive FPC changed its standard to one of production investment costs, which meant a lower rate of return for gas businesses. The issue was tested in court in *Federal Power Commission v. Hope Natural Gas* (1944), in which the Supreme Court supported the FPC's position and overruled the *Smythe* precedent. The Court enunciated the principle that government regulators were no longer required to use the investment-value standard, but they could use any reasonable method or formula.

A more long-standing controversy was whether the FPC was authorized to regulate the price charged for natural gas in the fields (at the wellheads). The issue was complex, because while large companies were involved in both the production and the transmission of natural gas, there were some four thousand independent producers who were not involved in interstate transmission. At first, the FPC did not regulate any sales in the fields, but in 1942, the FPC began to regulate the large companies that both produced gas and controlled pipelines. The FPC decided against the regulation of the independent producers, but in the surprising landmark case *Phillips Petroleum Co. v. Wisconsin* (1954), the Supreme Court ruled that the intent of Congress in 1938 had been to regulate the sale of natural gas in the fields when its destination was interstate commerce.

Since the *Phillips* decision required the FPC to regulate the sale of thousands of independents, the work of the FPC became much more extensive and complex. Lawyers and economists tended to look upon the *Phillips* decision as almost of equal importance to the NGA itself. Until 1960, the FPC made individual price determinations through a case-by-case approach. After a study pointed to the FPC as an example of the "breakdown of the administrative process," the commission changed to the area rate method, which was a determination of the reasonable requirements within each of twenty-three geographic regions. In the 1970's, the FPC changed to one standard rate to be used nationwide.

THE 1970'S "ENERGY CRISES"

Until about 1968, large supplies of natural gas kept prices low, but by 1972, the FPC acknowledged that there actually were shortages in parts of the country. Because oil and gas are often substituted for each other, the increase in oil prices after the embargo of 1973 had a great impact on the market for natural gas. By about 1975, gas prices in the intrastate markets were about twice as high as those in the interstate market, and it was becoming apparent that price regulations were contributing to gas shortages in the interstate market. The situation became critical in the cold winter of 1976 and 1977, when a lack of supplies forced four thousand manufacturing plants to close and resulted in 1,200,000 workers temporarily losing their jobs. Hundreds of schools had to close their doors in order to protect gas supplies for residential consumers.

President Jimmy Carter and his administration concluded that the only answer was to move to the deregulation of natural gas at the wellheads, and the result was the Natural Gas Policy Act (NGPA) of 1978. The NGPA was complex because it made a distinction among about twenty different categories of natural gas. The schedules provided that price controls for new gas and hard-to-get gas from deep wells would end by 1985, while the lifting of controls on old gas and gas in shallow wells would not end until 1987. President Ronald Reagan and his administration were committed to competitive markets, and they generally supported the principles of the NGPA of 1978. After the beginning of decontrols, prices did increase significantly by 1982, but adequate supplies ceased to be a problem. Thereafter, new discoveries of natural gas appeared to produce a satisfactory equilibrium and the public lost interest in the issue.

LEGACY

By the 1990's, the controversies of the Natural Gas Act of 1938 were a memory. Most economists tended to conclude that the NGPA of 1982 was a positive step, and few people wanted to return to the field regulations that began with the *Phillips* decision. It was not clear whether the Natural Gas Act had actually operated in the interest of the consumer, because evidence indicated that the realities of supply and demand had always influenced prices more than had price regulations.

With the growing concern for the environment, there was a new complexity about the implications of the term "conservation" in regard to the natural gas industry. Since the passage of the NGA in 1938, the justification for conserving natural gas had been to place a limit on how much gas was consumed so that supplies would last longer. Natural gas, however, is a clean-burning, environmentally friendly fuel, and efforts to decrease its use result in an increased use of other forms of energy that do more ecological damage. The limits of the obtainable reserves of this wonderful resource are as yet unknown.

Thomas T. Lewis

SOURCES FOR FURTHER STUDY

Baum, Robert. *The Federal Power Commission and State Utility Regulation.* Washington, D.C.: American Council on Public Affairs, 1942.

Bryer, Stephen, and Paul MacAvoy. *Energy Regulation by the Federal Power Commission.* Washington, D.C.: Brookings Institute, 1974.

DeVane, Dozier. "Highlights of Legislative History of the Federal Power Act of 1935 and the Natural Gas Act of 1938." *George Washington Law Review* 14 (December, 1945): 30-41.

Hawkins, Claud. *The Field Price Regulation of Natural Gas.* Tallahassee: Florida State University Press, 1969.

Kohlmeier, Louis, Jr. *The Regulators: Watchdog Agencies and the Public Interest.* New York: Harper & Row, 1969.

Sanders, M. Elizabeth. *The Regulation of Natural Gas: Policy and Politics, 1938-1978.* Philadelphia: Temple University Press, 1981.

Yale Law Journal. "Federal Price Control of Natural Gas Sold to Interstate Pipelines." 59 (1950): 1468-1515.

SEE ALSO: Interstate Commerce Act (1887); Federal Power Act (1920); Atomic Energy Act of 1954 (1954); Energy Policy and Conservation Act (1975); Department of Energy Organization Act (1977); Public Utility Regulatory Policies Act (1978).

FOOD, DRUG, AND COSMETIC ACT

ALSO KNOWN AS: Federal Food, Drug, and Cosmetic Act
DATE: June 24, 1938
U.S. STATUTES AT LARGE: 52 Stat. 1040
U.S. CODE: 21 § 301
CATEGORIES: Agriculture; Food and Drugs; Health and Welfare

Congress authorized the inspection of the food-manufacturing process by government officials and required that new food and drug products meet government-approved standards before being marketed.

Federal involvement in the regulation of foods, drugs, and cosmetics began with the Pure Food and Drugs Act of 1906. Safety in the food supply was the initial emphasis of that legislation, despite its full title: "An Act for preventing the manufacture, sale, or transportation of adulterated or misbranded or poisonous or deleterious foods, drugs, medicines, and liquors, for regulating traffic therein, and for other purposes."

THE PURE FOOD AND DRUG ACT

Beginning in the 1890's, pure-food bills were often submitted to Congress but were never passed. The public did not seem concerned about the problem. Harvey W. Wiley, chief of the division of chemistry in the Department of Agriculture, stimulated some interest with his famous "poison squad" experiments with several food additives, such as salicylic acid and formaldehyde, in 1902. Articles by muckrakers added to the growing interest, and Upton Sinclair's *The Jungle* (1906) dramatized the need for pure-food legislation.

The bill became law in June, 1906. The law made misrepresentation of a product illegal, but it did not require the manufacturer to inform the buyer of the contents of the product. If the manufacturer did list a product's ingredients, the government would monitor the accuracy of what was printed on the package.

Several cases involving the 1906 law reached the U.S. Supreme Court. Following the arguments of Justice Oliver Wendell Holmes, the Court agreed that the law required that labels relate accurately to contents. The Court, however, sided with the defendants that the government had no constitutional authority to determine false therapeutic claims where there was conflicting medical testimony. Congress could write laws, but it could not cross the boundary between fact and opinion.

The regulatory part of the Bureau of Chemistry became the Food, Drug, and Insecticide Administration in 1927 and, in 1931, the Food and Drug Administration (FDA). By then, the office had a budget of more than $1.5 million and five hundred employees. Still, the FDA was mainly concerned with pure food, not drugs. Ensuring accurate information was the primary function of the FDA. Given correct information, it was the inherent responsibility of the consumer to make decisions regarding personal health and well-being. The FDA was restrained by the Supreme Court from extending its control over the sale of drugs.

A NEED FOR NEW FOOD AND DRUGS LEGISLATION

Prior to the New Deal, there was little public support for government regulation of the marketplace. People wanted unrestrained freedom to buy their own food and medicine as they saw fit. The Great Depression, however, ushered in a liberal and sympathetic Congress, which cooperated in the New Deal activism by passing many of the bills sought by the Franklin Roosevelt administration.

In spite of this liberal political climate, there was not enough political interest in new food and drugs legislation until 1938, following another health catastrophe. Sulfanilamide had proved itself a wonder drug in the fight against infections. When the Massengill Company produced the drug in liquid form, however, it used diethylene glycol as a solvent. The result was toxic, and 107 people died as a result. The pharmaceutical company, which had not tested the drug for toxicity, was fined $26,100.

This tragedy provided the impetus to bring about the passage of the new law under the guidance of the respected director of the FDA, Walter Campbell, and Rexford Tugwell, the undersecretary of agriculture. The Food, Drug, and Cosmetic Act of 1938 passed the House without a dissenting vote, despite the sharp changes it brought in regulatory philosophy.

PROVISIONS AND A NEW PHILOSOPHY

New drugs would not be legally marketable until they were shown to be safe by tests acceptable to the FDA. The law authorized power of seizure and criminal sanctions and authorized the inspection of factories during the manufacturing process. The House report stated, "The bill is not intended to restrict in any way the availability of drugs for self-medication. On the contrary, it is intended to make self-medication safer and more effective." Within six months, however, the FDA was sharply curtailing the availability of drugs by requiring a doctor's prescription to purchase medicinal drugs that had hitherto been freely available.

This event changed the philosophy of the relationship between government regulators and consumers. The FDA would establish food standards, seek to control harmful foods, and require more informative labeling. Cosmetics and therapeutic devices came under government control for the first time, and the FDA began making factory inspections. The FDA had to be convinced of a new drug's safety before the drug could be marketed in the United States.

Determination of safety was made chiefly by the FDA's Office of New Drug Evaluation (ONDE), which consisted of six divisions, each in charge of specific drug categories. If a drug was approved after the involved process, the company was obligated to notify the FDA of any information it received that indicated unexpected adverse reactions. The FDA could then remove a drug from the market or require changes in labeling, such as adding a warning, listing an additional side effect, or removing an approved use. The FDA also would monitor the advertising used to promote the drug to ensure that the information given conformed to government requirements.

LONG-RANGE IMPACT

The 1938 Food, Drug, and Cosmetic Act was supplemented with other legislation, such as the Drug Amendments Act of 1962, but would remain the basic tool for ensuring pure foods, drugs, and cosmetics for years to come. Prior to 1938, American consumers could purchase from a pharmacist almost any nonnarcotic drug they thought they needed. In fact, as late as 1929 only about 25 percent of drug sales were ordered by prescriptions, and in most of those purchases the prescription was merely a convenience, not a requirement. Pharmacists were independent of the control of doctors, and consumers could use their own judgment in deciding the best choice in medicines. The responsibility was in the hands of each individual, not in the hands of the government or the medical profession. With the passage of the Food, Drug, and Cosmetic Act of 1938, there was a stunning difference in the availability of drugs to the consumer. The FDA in effect considered consumers incapable of making their own medicinal drug choices; rather, a professional guide to that decision-making process was deemed necessary.

Another effect of the 1938 law was a profound change in drug-related marketing and advertising. For example, doctors were soon inundated with advertisements and promotional schemes from pharmaceutical companies. Prior to 1938, manufacturers generally did not feel the need to advertise to doctors. The decision to buy was the consumer's and did not depend upon brokering by the medical profession or the government, a fact that was reflected in the advertising strategy.

LATER AMENDMENTS

Many laws since the 1938 act have amended or otherwise addressed the regulation of food and drugs in the United States, including, among others, the Pesticide Amendments of 1954, the Food Additives Amendment of 1958, the Color Additive Amendments of 1960, the Drug Amendments of 1962, the Medical Device Amendments of 1976, the Animal Drug Amendments of 1986, the Drug Price Competition and Patent Term Restoration Act of 1984, the Generic Animal Drug and Patent Term Restoration Act of 1988, the Prescription Drug Marketing Act of 1988, the Safe Medical Devices Act of 1990, the Nutrition Labeling and Education Act of 1990, the Prescription Drug User Fee Act of 1992, the Dietary

Supplement Health and Education Act of 1994, the Food Quality Protection Act of 1996, the Food and Drug Administration Modernization Act of 1997 (FDAMA).

Of these, two in particular are worth noting: The Dietary Supplement Health and Education Act of 1994 removed dietary supplements from the FDA's regulatory oversight. Previously, under the Food Additives Amendment of 1958, the FDA treated food supplements as foods and therefore evaluated the safety of such ingredients as stringently as it did other foods. The 1994 law amended the 1938 law, adding sections on supplements per se. Therefore dietary supplements were no longer subject to the premarket safety evaluations imposed on other new food ingredients (or new uses of old ingredients), although they still had to meet other safety requirements. The result was a flooding of the marketplace with a wide variety of supplements, from those medically acknowledged as healthful to others whose benefits were more questionable, and a degree of return to the pre-1938 consumer decisions about self-medication.

The other major law, the 1997 FDAMA, was the most far-reaching set of amendments since the 1938 law itself, provided for the fast-track review of medical devices, regulated advertising of unapproved uses of approved drugs and devices, and imposed rules for health claims for foods; it also reactivated the 1992 Prescription Drug User Fee Act. This sweeping set of revisions had an immediately visible impact in the sudden appearance of television advertisements for prescription drugs, since the law had relaxed restrictions on such commercials. The effect was a sevenfold increase between 1996 and 2002 on drug companies' advertising expenditures, as well as new pressures on physicians to prescribe drugs—for nasal congestion, gastrointestinal distress, hormone-related syndromes, and a variety of other conditions—to patients who had seen these drugs advertised on television with the recommendation that viewers "ask their doctor."

William H. Burnside, updated by
Christina J. Moose

SOURCES FOR FURTHER STUDY
Anderson, Oscar E. *The Health of a Nation: Harvey W. Wiley and the Fight for Pure Food.* Chicago: University of Chicago Press, 1958.

Hinich, Melvin J., and Richard Staelin. *Consumer Protection Legislation and the U.S. Food Industry.* New York: Pergamon Press, 1980.

Quirk, Paul J. "Food and Drug Administration." In *The Politics of Regulation,* edited by James Q. Wilson. New York: Basic Books, 1980.

Temin, Peter. *Taking Your Medicine: Drug Regulation in the United States.* Cambridge, Mass.: Harvard University Press, 1980.

Young, James Harvey. "Food and Drug Administration." In *Government Agencies,* edited by Donald R. Whitnah. Westport, Conn.: Greenwood Press, 1983.

SEE ALSO: Pure Food and Drugs Act (1906); Food Additives Amendment (1958); Hazardous Substances Labeling Act (1960); Wholesome Poultry Products Act (1968); Food Security Act (1985).

FAIR LABOR STANDARDS ACT

DATE: June 25, 1938
U.S. STATUTES AT LARGE: 52 Stat. 1060
U.S. CODE: 29 § 201
CATEGORIES: Children's Issues; Labor and Employment

This law established the federal minimum wage, created a compulsory overtime system, and prohibited most child labor.

Beginning with Massachusetts in 1912, seventeen U.S. states had adopted minimum-wage laws by 1923. For constitutional reasons, their coverage was limited to women (and perhaps children), excluding adult men. However, the Supreme Court ruled such laws unconstitutional in *Adkins v. Children's Hospital* (1923).

WAGE-HOUR MEASURES
The disastrous Great Depression that followed 1929 brought radical economic changes under President Franklin D. Roosevelt's New Deal. Drastic deflation had induced a substantial decline in wage rates and a great increase in unemployment. Presidents Her-

bert Hoover and Roosevelt both favored higher wages to try to increase workers' purchasing power. There was widespread support for measures to shorten hours of work, in order to spread the work around. Bills to reduce work hours were introduced into Congress in 1933 by Senator Hugo Black and Congressman William Connery. Secretary of Labor Frances Perkins favored efforts to support or raise wages by industry boards.

All of these ideas were reflected in the administration of the National Industrial Recovery Act (NIRA) of 1933. Each of the 585 codes of fair competition adopted under NIRA contained minimum-wage provisions; although varying from one industry to another, they generally were thirty cents per hour or more and applied to men as well as women. In about one-fourth of the codes, lower minimums were provided for women. However, the NIRA was ruled unconstitutional in 1935. A number of states enacted new minimums and were aided by a Supreme Court decision in 1937 that largely reversed the Adkins doctrine (*West Coast Hotel Co. v. Parrish*). Of the twenty-nine state laws in force by 1941, all but two applied only to women.

An administration wage-hour bill developed by Secretary Perkins was introduced in Congress in May, 1937. Traditional opposition by organized labor to minimum-wage legislation had been reduced by the formation of an independent Congress of Industrial Organizations (CIO) in 1935. The wage-hour bill, also sponsored by Senator Black and Congressman Connery, proposed a labor standards board to set industry-specific provisions relating to wages, hours, and child labor. A new bill in 1938 provided for more uniform statutory provisions, but with some discretionary authority to be lodged in the Wage-Hour Division of the Department of Labor.

WAGE PROVISIONS

As finally adopted, the Fair Labor Standards Act (FLSA) contained two types of minimum-wage provisions. In section 6, statutory minimum rates were set at twenty-five cents per hour for the first year, thirty cents per hour for the following six years, and forty cents per hour beginning in 1945. Sections 5 and 8 authorized the "wage-hour administrator" to establish industry wage committees that could recommend minimum hourly rates to be at least twenty-five cents in the first year and thirty cents thereafter, but not to exceed forty cents. The committees, composed of representatives of employers, workers, and government officials, would make recommendations to the administrator. Through 1940, such committees had made recommendations for a dozen industries, mainly involving clothing and textiles. However, the rapid rise in wages during World War II rendered them obsolete, and they were abolished in 1949.

The minimum-wage provisions applied generally to employees "engaged in commerce or in production of goods for commerce." Many sectors were exempted, notably agriculture and local retailing and service trades. Partial coverage applied to construction, wholesale trade, and agricultural processing. The administrator was empowered to permit subminimum wages for learners, apprentices, messengers, and workers with disabilities. No differentials were permitted between men and women. However, a large proportion of female workers were excluded by the exemption of trade and services.

Actions to enforce the law against employers paying low wages could be initiated either by the affected worker (or a union representing him or her) or by the government. Workers could sue employers for the amount they should have been paid and could collect damages of an equal amount, totaling to double damages. The Wage-Hour Division of the Department of Labor could initiate actions against employers, seeking either civil or criminal penalties.

It is estimated that in 1941, more than fourteen million workers were covered, about one-fourth of the labor force. An estimated 350,000 covered workers were paid less than the twenty-five-cent minimum in 1938 and about 900,000 received less than the thirty-cent minimum in 1939.

HOURS PROVISIONS

One goal of the law was to shorten the number of hours worked by individual workers, so that work could be spread more widely to help reduce unemployment. The law provided that employers had to pay one and a half times the basic hourly rate for hours worked by an individual in excess of forty-four per week in the first year, forty-two per week the second, and forty per week beginning in 1940. However, many categories of administrative and professional workers were excluded from these provisions. Industries with pronounced seasonal patterns of operation could obtain from the administrator permission to have individuals work as much as fifty-six hours per week and twelve hours per day for as much as fourteen weeks without paying overtime.

CHILD LABOR PROVISIONS

The law also brought to completion a long effort to secure federal legislation limiting child labor. Most states had some restrictions on the employment of children, particularly in night work or hazardous industries. A federal law in 1916 had prohibited shipment in interstate commerce of goods produced in violation of detailed child labor conditions regarding age, employment sector, and hours worked. The Supreme Court ruled this unconstitutional in 1918 (*Hammer v. Dagenhart*). Congress responded by reenacting similar provisions to be enforced by a tax, but this also was struck down by the Supreme Court (*Bailey v. Drexel Furniture*, 1922). Congress then passed a constitutional amendment authorizing federal regulation of child labor, but by 1941, only twenty-eight states had ratified it.

Encouraged by the changed tone of Supreme Court rulings in 1937, Congress enacted section 12 of the FLSA to forbid interstate shipment of goods produced using workers under sixteen years of age, with the exception of children working for their parents or working in sectors designated by the administrator as acceptable. Supreme Court approval came in *U.S. v. Darby Lumber Co.* (1941).

MINIMUM WAGE INCREASES

The inflation of the 1940's carried actual wages well above the minimum. Many workers benefited from the premium pay for overtime, as wartime prosperity increased employment and work hours. Congress raised the minimum wage in 1949 and numerous times thereafter, bringing the level to $4.35, beginning in 1989. In 1996, Congress voted to increase the level to $5.25. For most of its history to that time, the minimum wage was 40 to 50 percent of average wages. Large increases in coverage were mandated in 1961 and 1967. Coverage of private, nonfarm employment rose from about 61 percent in 1950 to 69 percent in 1961, 83 percent in 1967, and 86 percent in 1978. Most sectors with concentrated female employment were covered by then.

By 1977, coverage of domestic service reached 64 percent of workers, other services 74 percent, and retail trade 79 percent. State laws extended coverage still further. However, enforcement against small firms was loose, and employers of waitpersons were permitted to claim anticipated tips as part of their compliance. In addition, the mid-1980's saw a decline of an annual minimum-wage income to below the poverty level as defined by the U.S. government. In 1989, amendments to the FLSA eliminated minimum-wage and overtime exemptions for small businesses and raised the minimum wage to $3.80 per hour. The minimum wage went up to 4.25 per hour in 1991, $4.75 in 1996, and $5.15 in September of 1997. The basic minimum wage typically varies by age, type of occupation, and type of compensation.

ARGUMENTS PRO AND CON

Arguments in favor of increasing the minimum wage typically revolve around the expected increase in buying power among consumers and therefore a positive impact on economic growth. Other arguments in favor of increase point to social equity and the discrepancies between "minimum" and "living" wages, particularly the concern over the wage dipping below the poverty line.

Some economists believe that the statutory minimum wage tends to raise wage levels slightly but to decrease employment opportunities. The requirement to pay higher wages can drive some firms out of business, cause others to decrease output and employment, and encourage others to find labor-saving procedures. Wages in uncovered sectors can be reduced by workers displaced from the covered sector. Thus, women's wages may have been adversely affected prior to the late 1970's. Studies in the 1990's suggested impacts only on teenage workers of both genders.

Paul B. Trescott

SOURCES FOR FURTHER STUDY

Bernstein, Irving. *A Caring Society: The New Deal, the Worker, and the Great Depression.* Boston: Houghton Mifflin, 1985.
Card, David, and Alan B. Krueger. *Myth and Measurement: The New Economics of the Minimum Wage.* Princeton, N.J.: Princeton University Press, 1995.

Levin-Waldman, Oren M. *The Case of the Minimum Wage: Competing Policy Models.* Albany: State University of New York Press, 2001.

Norlund, Willis J. *The Quest for a Living Wage: The History of the Federal Minimum Wage Program.* Westport, Conn.: Greenwood Press, 1997.

Peterson, John M. *Minimum Wages: Measures and Industry Effects.* Washington, D.C.: American Enterprise institute, 1981.

Rottenberg, Simon, ed. *The Economics of Legal Minimum Wages.* Washington, D.C.: American Enterprise Institute, 1981.

SEE ALSO: National Industrial Recovery Act (1933); National Labor Relations Act (1935); Social Security Act (1935); Labor-Management Relations Act (1947); Occupational Safety and Health Act (1970).

HATCH ACT

ALSO KNOWN AS: Political Activities Act
DATE: August 2, 1939
U.S. STATUTES AT LARGE: 53 Stat. 1147
PUBLIC LAW: 76-252
CATEGORIES: Voting and Elections

This law restricted the political activities of federal employees by prohibiting them from using their official authority to affect an election or to engage in political management or campaigns.

The Hatch Act was enacted in response to a special Senate investigation showing that government officials had coerced federal workers to contribute to the reelection campaign of a U.S. senator in 1938. A second, and possibly more important reason for its passage was a fear that President Franklin D. Roosevelt would use the growing number of federal workers as a formidable political machine. In March of 1939, Senator Carl Hatch of New Mexico introduced legislation incorporating the recommendations of the special Senate committee prohibiting the involvement of federal employees in any political organization. They retained the right to vote and could privately express their political opinions. Political appointees and policy-making employees were not included in the act. By restricting the political activity of federal workers, the act addressed three objectives: It precluded the use of the federal workforce for political purposes; it prevented the bureaucracy from becoming a powerful political actor; and it reduced the influence of partisan politics in the hiring, promotion, and firing of federal employees. The Hatch Act was amended in 1993 to allow federal employees, acting as private citizens, to engage in any legal political activity while not on the job.

W. David Patton

SOURCES FOR FURTHER STUDY

Eccles, James R. *Hatch Act and the American Bureaucracy.* New York: Vantage Press, 1981.

Kohout, Martin D. "House Panel Proposes Revising Hatch Act." *PA Times* 10, no. 19 (October 23, 1987): 1.

Library of Congress. Congressional Research Service. *The Hatch Act Proscription Against Participation by State and Federal Employees in Political Management and Political Campaigns: A Legislative History.* Hein's Federal Legislative Histories Collection 055. Washington, D.C.: Author, 1975.

Linsley, Clyde. "Unhatched? Unions Want to Unhatch the Hatch Act and This Time May Succeed." *Government Executive* 19, no. 9 (September, 1987): 70-72.

Willen, Mark. "House Passes Bill Overhauling 1939 Hatch Act." *Congressional Quarterly Weekly Report* 45, no. 47 (November 21, 1987): 2885-2886.

Yadlosky, Elizabeth. *The Hatch Act Proscription Against Participation by State and Federal Employees in Political Management and Political Campaigns: A Legislative History.* Washington, D.C.: Congressional Research Service, 1973.

SEE ALSO: Hatch Act (1939); Federal Election Campaign Act (1972); Ethics in Government Act (1978); Twenty-seventh Amendment (1992); Bipartisan Campaign Reform Act (2002).

SMITH ACT

DATE: June 28, 1940
U.S. STATUTES AT LARGE: 54 Stat. 670-671
U.S. CODE: 18 § 2385
CATEGORIES: Crimes and Criminal Procedure; Speech and Expression

The Smith Act made it a crime to advocate, or to conspire to advocate, the violent overthrow of the government.

The Smith Act was a product of American anxieties during the late 1930's. As the world moved toward war, Americans grew more suspicious of foreigners and their ideologies. By 1939 opinion surveys revealed broad public support for new restrictions on aliens and for the hearings of the new House Committee on Un-American Activities, which had been created to investigate anti-American propaganda activities. Reflecting this suspicion, Congress considered forty different measures aimed at aliens and subversive propaganda. Representative Howard W. Smith of Virginia drew from several of those proposals to create an omnibus antiradical bill that he introduced in March, 1939.

Smith's bill contained new requirements for aliens, criminalized efforts to interfere with military recruitment and discipline, and sought to punish anyone advocating the violent overthrow of the government. The House of Representatives approved Smith's measure by a vote of 272 to 40 in late June, 1939, but Congress adjourned before the Senate could consider the bill. A year later the Senate passed a slightly modified version without a roll call vote, and on June 28, 1940, President Franklin D. Roosevelt signed the measure into law.

SEDITION CLAUSES

The most controversial provisions of the Smith Act were contained in its sedition sections, which made it unlawful knowingly to advocate, advise, or teach the violent overthrow of any government in the United States. The act also provided penalties of up to five years in jail and fines of up to ten thousand dollars for anyone who published, distributed or displayed printed materials advocating the violent overthrow of the government or who organized or who knowingly joined any society advocating such a goal. The measure also contained a conspiracy section that carried the same penalties for any person who conspired with anyone else to commit the aforementioned acts.

The Smith Act was aimed principally at the purveyors of subversive propaganda. Since existing law already prohibited conspiracies to overthrow the government, the Smith Act added only the element of advocacy. Earlier proposals in Congress had called for restrictions on propaganda stemming from Nazi and communist sources, and Smith drew heavily on these proposals in drafting his measure. His law was designed to eliminate one category of expression from the American marketplace of ideas.

ENFORCEMENT OF THE ACT

Under President Roosevelt, the Justice Department proved reluctant to enforce the advocacy sections of the Smith Act. In 1941 eighteen members of the Socialist Workers Party were convicted of violating the act's provisions outlawing attempts to promote disloyalty among the armed services, and in 1944 twenty-eight alleged pro-Nazis were indicted on similar charges. However, their case was dropped after the death of the trial judge.

After World War II the Cold War gave the Smith Act new life. Mounting frustrations over Soviet expansion abroad and growing public concerns over communist subversion at home convinced the Truman administration to use the Smith Act against American communists. In July, 1948, the Justice Department brought charges against eleven members of the central committee of the Communist Party of the United States (CPUSA). Lacking proof of direct incitement or actual revolutionary deeds by the accused, the federal prosecutors sought conviction under the conspiracy section of the act. Members of the party's central committee were charged with conspiring to teach and advocate the overthrow of the government and with conspiring to form the CPUSA to achieve those ends. The stormy nine-month trial ended in October, 1949, with a guilty verdict. Each defendant was fined ten thousand dollars and sentenced to five years in jail.

THE DENNIS CASE

In 1951 the U.S. Supreme Court affirmed, by a vote of 6 to 2, the constitutionality of the Smith Act in *Dennis v. United States.* Chief

Justice Fred M. Vinson's majority opinion paid homage to the American tradition of freedom of speech, noting that it rested on the "hypothesis that speech can rebut speech, propaganda will answer propaganda, free debate of ideas will result in the wisest governmental policies." However, Vinson went on to declare that free speech "must, on occasion, be subordinated to other values and considerations," in this case, to the right of the government to protect itself. In his effort to balance the value of free speech against the authority of the government, Vinson relied on the Court's long-standing "clear and present danger" test. Prior rulings using this test had suggested that before the government could limit speech, it had to establish the existence of a serious danger that was both obvious and imminent. But Vinson concluded that the words "clear and present" did not require the government to "wait until the putsch is about to be executed." Even though a communist coup was unlikely to succeed, the "gravity of the evil" was sufficient to justify this "invasion of free speech."

Vinson's opinion elicited two vigorous dissents. Justice William O. Douglas denied that American communists represented any "clear and present danger to the republic." To him, they were the "miserable merchants of unwanted ideas," whose conviction should be set aside. Justice Hugo Black went further. He noted that the members of the CPUSA had not been charged with overt acts against the government, or even with saying or writing anything subversive. Instead they were charged with conspiracy to form a political party that might use speech and other forms of communication to advocate certain ideas in the future. Black found their conviction "a virulent form of prior censorship of speech and press" that was forbidden by the First Amendment. He would have declared the Smith Act unconstitutional.

LATER PROSECUTIONS

With the Smith Act affirmed, the Department of Justice began prosecuting minor CPUSA leaders. By the spring of 1956, when the Supreme Court agreed to hear a second Smith Act case, 102 party functionaries had been convicted and twenty-eight other cases were still pending. In *Yates v. United States*, decided in June, 1957, the Court narrowed the implications of the *Dennis* ruling and made prosecution under the Smith Act more difficult. Justice John Marshall Harlan's majority opinion drew a distinction between advocacy of abstract doctrines, such as those contained in Marxist theory, and advocacy of illegal acts. Harlan concluded that the Smith Act had never been intended to prohibit advocacy and teaching of forcible overthrow as abstract principles, divorced from actions. Consequently, the government's prosecutions were flawed. Faced with this stricter standard, the Justice Department ceased all further actions under the advocacy section of the law. Charges were dropped, or the convictions reversed, in cases involving ninety CPUSA members. The Smith Act was dead. Nevertheless, the government's efforts to use the act to destroy the Communist Party had largely succeeded. By 1958 the party's leadership was in disarray and its membership had largely vanished.

Jerold L. Simmons

Sources for Further Study

Belknap, Michael R. *Cold War Political Justice: The Smith Act, the Communist Party, and American Civil Liberties.* Westport, Conn.: Greenwood Press, 1977.

Emerson, Thomas I., David Haber, and Norman Dorsen, eds. *Political and Civil Rights in the United States.* Boston: Little, Brown, 1967.

Steinberg, Peter. *The Great "Red Menace": United States Prosecution of American Communists, 1947-1952.* Westport, Conn.: Greenwood Press, 1984.

See also: First Amendment (1789); Sedition Act of 1798 (1798); Espionage Acts (1917-1918); Foreign Agents Registration Act (1938).

Ogdensburg Agreement

Date: August 16, 1940

Categories: Foreign Relations; Military and National Security; Treaties and Agreements

The United States and Canada came to an agreement on hemispheric defense.

After only slight hesitation, Canada had followed the mother country, Great Britain, in going to war against Germany in 1939. Canada's southern neighbor, the United States, was sympathetic to Great Britain and her allies but avowed to remain neutral.

The situation changed drastically after the Germans conquered France in June, 1940. The German armies seemed invincible, and there was a real threat that they might cross the English Channel and conquer Great Britain. The United States, realizing the gravity of the world situation, became more concerned about its security and that of the Western Hemisphere. The British prime minister, Winston Churchill, developed a contingency plan to have the royal family, in the event of a German takeover, flee Britain and take sanctuary in Canada. Clearly, the Atlantic Ocean was no longer a barrier to world conflict.

LEND-LEASE

Franklin D. Roosevelt, the president of the United States, was worried about both Western Hemisphere security and Great Britain's ability to stay in the war. He wanted to help Great Britain and prepare his own country for the war he knew it would one day enter, but he believed that the U.S. public was not ready for full-fledged participation. Roosevelt therefore conceived the lend-lease policy to address both issues. Under lend-lease, Great Britain would lease certain military bases in the Western Hemisphere (in Newfoundland, Bermuda, and elsewhere) to the United States for ninety-nine years. In return, the United States would lend surplus aircraft and other military equipment to Great Britain. Thus, the British military would be strengthened, and the United States would gain control of bases that would help it defend the Western Hemisphere against potential German aggression.

Canada was not consulted under this agreement. Although a close ally and associate of Great Britain, since the Statute of Westminster in 1931 Canada had been a sovereign nation. The Canadian prime minster, William Lyon Mackenzie King, had been slow to recognize the threat posed by Nazi Germany. King, indeed, was ambivalent about his country's entry into the European war until the very last moment. There were many political pressures on King not to enter the war, ranging from Francophones in Quebec, whose fierce opposition to Britain made them reluctant to enter the war even though their own mother country, France, was on the

British side, to isolationist farmers in the prairie provinces, who saw no apparent need to intervene in foreign disputes. Most Canadians, however, supported King when he decided to commit Canada to the war effort at the side of Great Britain.

CANADA IN THE WAR

Once engaged in the war, King shared the concerns of Roosevelt and Churchill regarding Western Hemisphere security and was heartened by the lend-lease agreement. Nevertheless, he was concerned about Canadian national sovereignty as affected by the accord, especially in the case of Newfoundland. Newfoundland's close geographical proximity to Canada put it in the natural Canadian sphere of influence. Newfoundland had been an independent, self-governing dominion for sixty years, until the 1930's, when, because of its inability to handle the economic depression of that era, it had been taken over by Great Britain. King and the majority of the Canadian public expected that one day Newfoundland would join the rest of Canada (as, in fact, it did in 1949). He thus was unwilling to accept the permanent transfer of bases in Newfoundland to U.S. sovereignty.

Roosevelt was friendly toward Canada and knew the country well from his summer visits to the Canadian island of Campobello. Recognizing King's concern over the situation, Roosevelt advised the Canadian leader that he would be reviewing troops in the town of Ogdensburg, located in northern New York State close to the Canadian border, on August 16. King decided that it would be to Canada's advantage for him to meet Roosevelt at Ogdensburg. In deference to Canadian public opinion, he made no public announcement of the visit, fearing that it would be seen as an act of submission or surrender to the United States.

KING AND ROOSEVELT MEET AT OGDENSBURG

King did his best to keep the meeting a secret. Even J. L. Ralston, the Canadian minister of defense, whose responsibilities were vitally concerned with the situation, learned of the meeting only through reading the next day's newspapers. On the morning of August 16, Roosevelt arrived in Ogdensburg, accompanied by the U.S. ambassador to Canada, J. Pierrepont Moffat. Roosevelt met King, and the two men together reviewed U.S. troops. Roosevelt and King then repaired to a railway carriage, where the substantive discussions were held.

The two men were very different. King was a mystic who regularly held séances in order to communicate with the spirit of his dead mother. Roosevelt, on the other hand, was regarded by many as the ultimate political opportunist, although his fierce commitment to democracy and liberalism never wavered. Nevertheless, the two men, who knew each other from previous meetings, had established a good working rapport, and they quickly reached a broad consensus.

THE CONTINENTAL SYSTEM

The centerpiece of this consensus was the so-called Continental System. The Continental System provided that Canada and the United States would regularly consult each other about military conditions. It also stipulated that the two countries would prepare themselves to mount a common defense of the Western Hemisphere. It even allowed for the possibility of temporary U.S. bases being established on Canadian soil. This was the aspect of the Continental System most disagreeable to Canadian nationalists. The U.S. bases, however, were only in the context of Canadian involvement in the lend-lease policy. Although King and Canada had not been involved in the formulation of this policy, Roosevelt's briefing apprised the Canadian prime minister of the lend-lease initiative, of which King wholeheartedly approved. King and Roosevelt also reached agreement on the status of Newfoundland. Roosevelt abjured any possible U.S. intent to control or annex Newfoundland permanently and stated that the future status of Newfoundland was up to the inhabitants of the island themselves, in consultation with the Canadian and British governments.

IMPACT ON CANADIAN-U.S. RELATIONS

The most important achievements of the Ogdensburg meeting were not in the precise terms hammered out between Roosevelt and King but in the general spirit of understanding and mutual support built between the two men. Canada and the United States had been friends for many years, but the two countries had never really been allies. The Ogdensburg Agreement prepared Canada and the United States for the alliance that would exist between them when the United States entered World War II in 1941 and that would continue through the postwar years.

The Ogdensburg Agreement also represented a shift on the part of Canadian military and defense policy from a primary orientation toward Great Britain to a similar orientation toward the United States. By 1940, Canadian independence had been fully achieved. Canada, large in area but small in population, would inevitably have to engage in cooperation and alliance with another, more powerful country. Canada previously had been wary of the United States, since the latter country was so much larger in population. The dominance of the United States on the North American continent had caused observers periodically to wonder if Canada might eventually be annexed by the United States. Although the Ogdensburg Agreement might have seemed to subordinate Canada to U.S. defense policy, it had the countervailing effect of firmly enshrining the interests of an independent Canada within a North American defense context. This reaffirmation of Canadian independence substantially assisted U.S.-Canadian cooperation after the United States entered the war. It also smoothed the way for eventual Canadian participation in two postwar defense alliances led by the United States: the North Atlantic Treaty Organization (NATO) and the North American Air Defense Pact (NORAD).

Predictably, King faced considerable outcry in the Canadian nationalist press once he returned to Ottawa and his meeting with Roosevelt was revealed to the public. However, his achievement in the Ogdensburg meeting was considerable, helping cement Allied cooperation in the long and determined struggle against Nazi Germany and its threat to democracy and freedom.

Nicholas Birns

Sources for Further Study

Gibson, Frederick, and Jonathan G. Rossie, eds. *The Road to Ogdensburg*. East Lansing: Michigan State University Press, 1993.

Kimball, W. F. *The Most Unsordid Act: Lend-Lease, 1939-1941*. Baltimore: The Johns Hopkins University Press, 1969.

Pickersgill, J. W. *The Mackenzie King Record*. Toronto: University of Toronto Press, 1960.

Stacey, C. P. *Arms, Men, and Governments: The War Policies of Canada, 1939-1945*. Ottawa: Queen's Printers, 1970.

Teatero, William. *Mackenzie King: Man of Mission.* Don Mills, Ont.: Nelson, 1979.

SEE ALSO: Monroe Doctrine (1823); Smoot-Hawley Tariff Act (1930); Good Neighbor Policy (1933); Neutrality Acts (1935-1939); Lend-Lease Act (1941); North Atlantic Treaty (1949).

LEND-LEASE ACT

DATE: March 11, 1941
U.S. STATUTES AT LARGE: 55 Stat. 31
U.S. CODE: 22 § 411
CATEGORIES: Foreign Relations; Military and National Security

> *The Lend-Lease Act enabled the United States to provide aid and support to Great Britain during World War II while maintaining official neutrality.*

Nazi Germany's invasion of Poland on September 1, 1939, plunged Europe into a second major war within twenty-five years—a war that would prove to be the worst in human history. As in the beginning of World War I, the United States hoped to remain neutral, although popular sentiment weighed heavily toward Great Britain and France. With memories of World War I still fresh in the minds of most Americans, isolationist views prevailed.

GROWTH OF NAZI GERMANY

For six years prior to Germany's move against Poland, the United States watched developments in Europe with concern. Adolf Hitler, whose Nazi Party governed Germany, made no attempt to conceal his intentions to break with the Treaty of Versailles, rearm Germany, and expand Nazi control throughout Europe. At the same time, Italy's Benito Mussolini advanced aggressively against Ethiopia, and Japan continued military operations in China.

Keenly aware of these developments, Congress in 1935 legislated the first in a series of neutrality laws. A six-month renewable

719

act, the legislation prohibited the United States from selling arms or transporting munitions to belligerent nations. When it was renewed, a ban against making loans to warring nations was included. Congress and the president believed such a foreign policy would prevent the United States from slipping into another European war, should one arise.

The following year, developments in Europe proved peace to be but an illusion. Hitler's forces moved unopposed into the Rhineland, a French territory. In 1937, Germany involved itself in the Spanish Civil War and sealed the Rome-Berlin alliance. The United States responded with the Neutrality Act of 1937, which retained the principal features of the 1935 act but, at Roosevelt's urging, allowed presidential discretion to sell military goods to belligerents on a "cash and carry" basis, provided the material was not transported on U.S. ships. The altered policy pleased manufacturers who wanted to profit while the nation remained officially neutral and apart from the European crisis. The new policy also pleased those in the United States who thought it essential to aid the country's traditional allies.

THE UNITED STATES ABANDONS NEUTRALITY

Germany's expansion continued, and in his state of the union address, on January 4, 1939, President Roosevelt announced his dismay over the course of European affairs and his dissatisfaction with existing neutrality laws. He believed that the 1937 act benefited Hitler more than it did France or Great Britain. If Hitler's enemies were unable to acquire sufficient material for defense, Germany would find the Western nations unable to halt Nazi aggression. Surely, the president hinted, the United States could devise methods short of war to aid British and French military defense preparations.

Early that summer, the British government made a direct appeal to Roosevelt for military supplies, and in June, the president suggested revision of the Neutrality Act of 1937 to broaden the cash-and-carry provision. Fearful that such a program of support for Great Britain would cast the United States in an image of cobelligerent, isolationists in Congress blocked Roosevelt's efforts. Germany's invasion of Poland on September 1, and the British-French declaration of war that followed, changed the congressional mood. By year's end, revisions to the 1937 act were sanctioned, making it easier for Britain to obtain needed supplies.

ARSENAL OF DEMOCRACY

France fell to the Nazis in June, 1940. Great Britain was the sole surviving power in Europe. Many thought that the United States should provide direct military aid to the British, the United States' front line against Germany. If Britain collapsed, the United States would become Hitler's next target. Others contended that the United States needed to strengthen its own defenses in preparation for Nazi actions in the Western Hemisphere. Roosevelt chose to follow both courses. He gained approval from Congress to appropriate funds for U.S. rearmament and for a peacetime compulsory military training law. In June, using executive authority, Roosevelt authorized the supply of outdated aircraft and rifles to Great Britain; in September, he arranged with Britain the exchange of fifty U.S. naval destroyers for leases of British naval bases.

Great Britain's financial reserves dwindled as autumn faded. In December, Prime Minister Winston Churchill informed Roosevelt that the cash-and-carry system needed modification. Roosevelt understood that Great Britain could not withstand further Nazi attacks without direct U.S. aid and that the United States' own security was largely dependent on British resistance to Hitler. In mid-December, Roosevelt conceived the idea of lend-lease: War goods would be provided Allied nations and either returned or paid for at war's end. In both a press conference and a radio "fireside chat," Roosevelt stated that the best defense for the United States was a strong Great Britain. Every step short of war should be taken to help the British Empire defend itself. Great Britain's inability to pay cash for U.S. supplies should not relegate the empire to Nazi conquest. To lend or lease the necessary goods would provide for Great Britain's immediate war needs and indirectly benefit the United States by making Great Britain the United States' front line of defense. Roosevelt presented an analogy to clarify the proposal: "Suppose my neighbor's home catches fire, and I have a length of garden hose four hundred or five hundred feet away. If he can take my garden hose and connect it up with his hydrant, I may help him to put out his fire." If the hose survived the fire, it would be returned. Should it be damaged, the neighbor would replace it. Military aid would be treated in the same way. The United States must become the "arsenal of democracy" and provide the goods necessary to halt Nazi expansion.

PASSAGE OF LEND-LEASE

To secure permission and funding to aid Great Britain, Roosevelt introduced into the House of Representatives the Lend-Lease bill. The bill generated intense debate. Opponents said the measure would move the United States from neutrality to the status of active nonbelligerent and risk war with Germany. They believed that it would be more logical to plan to build the United States' own defenses. Supporters argued that Hitler posed a real, direct threat to the United States, and that aiding Great Britain would make U.S. entry into the war less likely. Public opinion favored the president. Although 82 percent of Americans believed war was inevitable, nearly 80 percent opposed entry unless the nation were directly attacked.

After two months of congressional debate, the Lend-Lease Act was passed on March 11, 1941. It permitted the president to lend or lease war materiel to any nation whose defense was deemed critical to the United States, and it authorized an immediate appropriation of seven billion dollars for Great Britain. In June, following Germany's invasion of Russia, Roosevelt extended lend-lease to the Soviet Union. The Lend-Lease Act retained official U.S. neutrality, but the measure also placed the United States more squarely in opposition to Nazi Germany. In March, 1941, the United States teetered on the brink of war.

By war's end, in 1945, the United States had appropriated slightly more than fifty billion dollars under the lend-lease program. Great Britain received twenty-seven billion dollars of aid, the Soviet Union was provided ten billion dollars, and the remaining funds supplied goods to other Allied nations.

HISTORIAL ASSESSMENT

Roosevelt's contemporaries and postwar scholars have questioned the president's prewar direction of U.S. policy, particularly with regard to lend-lease. Some have argued that Roosevelt desperately wanted U.S. entry into the war long before Pearl Harbor but was restrained by popular opinion and political realities. Therefore, they argue, Roosevelt worked within the system to place the United States on an ever-advancing course toward war by molding public opinion, relaxing neutrality laws, and securing lend-lease. Others contend the president hoped to avoid intervention in Europe's war. Lend-lease thus was a practical method for the United States to aid the Allies while remaining a nonbelligerent. Regardless of Roosevelt's motives, Japan's attack on Pearl Harbor on December 7, 1941, sealed the United States' fate. War came to the United States.

Kenneth William Townsend

SOURCES FOR FURTHER STUDY

Dobson, Alan P. *U.S. Wartime Aid to Britain, 1940-1946.* New York: St. Martin's Press, 1986.

Herring, George C., Jr. *Aid to Russia, 1941-1946: Strategy, Diplomacy, the Origins of the Cold War.* New York: Columbia University Press, 1973.

Jones, Robert Huhn. *The Roads to Russia: United States Lend-Lease to the Soviet Union.* Norman: University of Oklahoma Press, 1969.

Kimball, Warren F. *The Most Unsordid Act: Lend-Lease, 1939-1941.* Baltimore: The Johns Hopkins University Press, 1969.

Langer, William L., and S. Everett Gleason. *The Undeclared War, 1940-1941.* Gloucester, Mass.: Peter Smith, 1968.

Van Tuyll, Hubert P. *Feeding the Bear: American Aid to the Soviet Union, 1941-1945.* New York: Greenwood Press, 1989.

SEE ALSO: Neutrality Acts (1935-1939); Ogdensburg Agreement (1940).

EXECUTIVE ORDER 8802

DATE: Issued June 25, 1941

CATEGORIES: African Americans; Civil Rights and Liberties; Military and National Security

A major step in the advancement of African American civil rights, this executive order prohibited discrimination in the military.

Ever since the Revolutionary War, the United States had experienced difficulty in bringing African Americans into its military. Although one of the victims of the Boston Massacre, Crispus Attucks, was an African American, and black soldiers were with George Washington when he made his famous 1776 Christmas crossing of the Delaware to attack the Hessians at Trenton and Princeton, it was not until the Civil War that African American troops were officially recruited into the United States Army.

Even then, however, a rigid policy of segregation was maintained. In the two wars that followed, the Spanish-American War and World War I, both the Army and Navy had black troops, but largely in supporting roles, and always as separate, segregated units. In addition, black troop strength was kept deliberately low, partly to avoid offending white soldiers and partly because the military establishment had a low opinion of the abilities of African American troops.

THE AGE OF JIM CROW

During the 1930's, however, under the presidency of Franklin Delano Roosevelt, these prejudiced attitudes began to change. Roosevelt's New Deal, which had been put into place to fight the ravages of the Great Depression, also addressed a number of social conditions, including civil rights. Although civil rights were never at the forefront of Roosevelt's agenda, his administration was more committed to them than any previous presidency had been, and his wife, the redoubtable Eleanor Roosevelt, was an especially strong and capable advocate for racial equality and justice. In addition, the shrewdly realistic president, who foresaw the coming struggle with Nazi Germany, realized that the U.S. military needed every capable citizen, of whatever color or background. The policy of "Jim Crowism," or rigid segregation of blacks and whites, remained largely in place, however.

SLOW PROGRESS

Correctly estimating the extent and depth of prejudice against African American participation in the military, especially in positions of responsibility, Roosevelt moved cautiously. He had been assistant secretary of the Navy under President Woodrow Wilson during World War I; now, Roosevelt prodded and encouraged the Navy high command to enlist additional African Americans and to place them in positions of greater responsibility than stewards or mess servers. Gradually and slowly, the Navy responded. A similar broadening took place in the Army in 1935, when the president insisted that African American medical officers and chaplains be called up from the reserves. On October 9, 1940, Roosevelt announced a revised racial policy for the armed forces; its intent was to bring more African Americans into the military and to place them in positions of trust and responsibility. At a slow but perceptible pace, the United States military was becoming more receptive to African Americans.

The progress was not sufficiently rapid for many African Americans, among them A. Philip Randolph, president of the Brotherhood of Sleeping Car Porters, one of the strongest and most effective African American unions in the country. Randolph, who well understood that black voters had become an essential part of the Democratic Party's electoral base, calculated that Roosevelt would need to respond to African American demands, especially as the 1940 presidential elections approached. Randolph's logic and timing were correct.

DESEGREGATING THE MILITARY

In 1940, Roosevelt ran for an unprecedented third term as president. Randolph, along with former Republican city councilman Grant Reynolds of New York City, began a campaign against the Jim Crow practices still prevalent in the United States military. Randolph and Reynolds also called for greater opportunities for African American workers in the rapidly growing defense industries, which had arisen as the United States rearmed against the threat from Nazi Germany and imperialist Japan. As the campaign intensified, Roosevelt faced a difficult situation that threatened his Southern, conservative support at the same time that it endangered his urban, liberal allies. When Randolph announced plans for a march on Washington, scheduled for July 1, 1941, Roosevelt knew he must act. His determination was steeled by the resolve of his wife Eleanor, who had long been a champion of equal rights for African Americans, and whose contacts with the black community were strong and deep.

On June 25, 1941, Roosevelt issued Executive Order 8802, which enunciated a broad policy of racial equality in the armed forces and the defense industry. The order was clear and sweeping in its intent:

> In offering the policy of full participation in the defense program by all persons regardless of color, race, creed, or national origin, and directing certain action in furtherance of said policy . . . all departments of the government, including the Armed Forces, shall lead the way in erasing discrimination over color or race.

President Roosevelt backed up the policy by establishing the Fair Employment Practices Commission, which was charged with monitoring and enforcing compliance among civilian contractors. It is estimated that Roosevelt's executive order, combined with the work of the commission, helped to bring fifty-three thousand African American civilians into defense industry jobs they otherwise would not have held.

SLOW PROGRESS

The timing of the policy was impeccable. Randolph and the other campaign leaders, satisfied that the Roosevelt administration was sincere in its commitment to civil rights, called off the march on Washington. Political conservatives, who otherwise might have challenged the president's order, had to admit that it would not be proper to expect African Americans to serve in the military without allowing them to hold responsible positions and achieve corresponding rank. Black voters responded enthusiastically to the Roosevelt reelection campaign, helping him to sweep to victory in the November balloting.

Inevitably, there were racial tensions and outbreaks of violence, especially in lower- and middle-class Northern neighborhoods. In 1943, for example, tension between black and white workers led to open violence at a park on Belle Isle near Detroit; in the end, federal troops had to be called in to restore order, and twenty-five African Americans and nine whites had been killed. Similar, if less bloody, events took place in other cities. Still, the transition to a more equitable situation continued in both civilian and military life.

However, the traditional segregation remained. During World War II, black units still were kept separate and apart from white troops, and generally reserved for support and logistical duties rather than combat. When the difficulties and emergencies of battle required it, African American units were brought into the fighting line; generally, they acquitted themselves well. By the end of the war, African Americans had distinguished themselves as ground soldiers, sailors, and pilots in both combat and noncombat situations. After the surrender of the Axis powers in 1945, there was a sense of inevitable change ahead for the United States military. The question of whether it would be a peaceful, productive change remained.

TRUMAN AND EXECUTIVE ORDER 9981

Harry S. Truman, who assumed the presidency in 1945 after the death of Franklin Roosevelt, was determined to make the change in a proper fashion. He assembled a special Civil Rights Committee which, on October 30, 1947, issued its report, *To Secure These Rights.* Clearly and unhesitatingly, the report called for the elimination of segregation in the United States military.

As the 1948 presidential elections approached, the issue of African Americans in the military affected the political atmosphere. Truman and the national Democratic Party, as heirs of the Roosevelt New Deal, had strong connections with the Civil Rights movement and its leaders; at the same time, much of the traditional Democratic strength was in the South, where civil rights issues were strongly opposed by the entrenched establishment. Southern politicians, such as Strom Thurmond of South Carolina, threatened to bolt the party if the Democrats adopted a strong civil rights platform at their convention; however, inspired by the passionate appeal of Mayor Hubert H. Humphrey of Minneapolis, the Democrats did indeed adopt a positive plank on civil rights. The Southerners stormed out, nominating Thurmond to run on the "Dixiecrat" ticket, and Truman went on to win a come-from-behind victory in November.

One element of that victory was his own Executive Order 9981, issued on July 26, 1948, just after the Democratic Party convention. Truman's order was similar to but stronger than Roosevelt's: It required equal opportunity in the armed forces of the United States, regardless of race, and called upon the military services to move immediately to implement the directive. The Air Force reacted promptly and soon achieved remarkable integration of black and white troops; the Navy and Marines were more hesitant in their acceptance. In the end, however, all branches of the armed forces responded, making them among the most egalitarian and equitable of U.S. institutions.

Michael Witkoski

SOURCES FOR FURTHER STUDY
Dalifiume, Richard. *Desegregation of the U.S. Armed Forces: Fighting on Two Fronts, 1939-1953.* Columbia: University of Missouri Press, 1969.
Nalty, Bernard C. *Strength for the Fight: A History of Black Americans in the Military.* New York: Free Press, 1986.
Stillman, Richard J. *Integration of the Negro in the U.S. Armed Forces.* New York: Frederick A. Praeger, 1968.
U.S. Department of Defense. Office of the Deputy Assistant Secretary of Defense for Civilian Personnel Policy/Equal Opportunity. *Black Americans in Defense of Our Nation.* Washington, D.C.: Government Printing Office, 1991.
Woodward, C. Vann. *The Strange Career of Jim Crow.* 2d rev. ed. New York: Oxford University Press, 1966.

SEE ALSO: Jim Crow laws (1880's-1954); Disfranchisement laws (1890); Civil Rights Act of 1957 (1957); Civil Rights Act of 1960 (1960); Civil Rights Act of 1964 (1964).

EMERGENCY PRICE CONTROL ACT

DATE: January 30, 1942
U.S. STATUTES AT LARGE: 56 Stat. 23
CATEGORIES: Business, Commerce, and Trade; Military and National Security

Adoption of the Emergency Price Control Act gave the Office of Price Administration the power to control prices of civilian goods and rents during World War II.

As the American military buildup in the face of the threat from the Axis Powers accelerated in the spring of 1940, the United States began to face shortages of critical materials. Shortages raised difficult and politically sensitive questions concerning the proportion of the nation's resources to reserve for civilian use and how to allocate the available supplies fairly. The problem was aggravated because government spending on defense was placing large amounts of cash into the hands of consumers. The United States spent an estimated $288 billion to fight World War II, compared to the $9 billion annual federal budget in 1940. Disposable personal income (income after taxes) rose from $92 billion to $151 billion during the war, while the supply of civilian goods and services (measured in constant dollars) increased only from $77.6 billion to $95.4 billion. With so much money pursuing a limited supply of goods, the government became concerned with preventing runaway inflation that could wreck the economy.

CONTROLLING INFLATION

The federal government followed a complex of strategies to keep inflation under control. Higher taxes imposed by the Revenue Act of 1942 soaked up part of the increased consumer purchasing power. Expanded sales of Series E government savings bonds to individuals similarly took out of circulation money that otherwise would have gone to purchase goods and services. Another weapon was the wage stabilization program administered by the National War Labor Board, which was established in January, 1942, to settle labor disputes in war industries. The Office of Price Administration, however, constituted the linchpin in the battle against inflation.

President Franklin D. Roosevelt established the Office of Price Administration and Civilian Supply (OPACS) by executive order on April 11, 1941. The OPACS was given a dual responsibility. It was to prevent inflationary price increases and to stimulate provision of the necessary supply of materials and commodities required for civilian use, in such a manner as not to conflict with military defense needs. Concurrently, it was to ensure the "equitable distribution" of that supply among competing civilian demands. Roosevelt appointed as OPACS administrator Leon Henderson, an economist who had risen from director of the Research and Planning Division of the National Recovery Administration to become one of the most influential New Deal leaders. In 1939, Roosevelt had appointed Henderson to the Securities and Exchange Commission. An outspoken champion of competition, opponent of monopoly, and defender of consumers, Henderson was temperamentally and ideologically at odds with the business executives who were brought to Washington, D.C., to mobilize the economy for the impending war. Roosevelt aggravated the situation by his typical practice of dividing responsibility and leaving blurred the lines of authority among different officials.

Henderson perceived a duty to act as spokesman for civilian needs. He accordingly came into bitter conflict with William S. Knudsen in the spring of 1941 over control of the priority system for the allocation of scarce materials. Knudsen, a former General Motors executive, as director-general of the Office of Production Management (OPM) was responsible for expanding military production. Roosevelt's establishment of the Supply Priorities and Allocations Board (SPAB) in August, 1941, under former Sears, Roebuck and Company executive Donald M. Nelson placed that control in the hands of those giving military demands top priority. With the establishment of the SPAB, the functions of the OPACS in the allocation of materials among competing civilian users was transferred to the OPM. The result was the administrative separation of price control from production control. The OPACS was renamed the Office of Price Administration (OPA).

A LAW FOR PRICE STABILIZATION
Rising prices accompanying the defense buildup shifted the focus of Henderson's attention to the problem of inflation. The OPA lacked effective power to halt the spiral of rising prices, and the inflation rate reached 2 percent per month by the end of 1941. Although Roosevelt asked Congress in July, 1941, for prompt action on price stabilization, the lawmakers dragged their feet until after Pearl Harbor. The Emergency Price Control Act, which Roosevelt signed into law on January 30, 1942, authorized the OPA to set maximum prices and to establish rent controls in areas in which defense activity had affected rent levels. Because Henderson thought some price increases to be necessary as incentives to expand production, he delayed acting under this new authority until late April. The OPA then issued its first General Maximum Price Regulation, requiring that sellers charge no more than the highest price charged in March, 1942. This move slowed down, but failed to halt, the rise in the cost of living.

The regulation worked satisfactorily for standardized articles but did not do so for products such as clothing, for which manufacturers and sellers could hide price increases through changes in style, quality, or packaging. The biggest loophole, however, was the provision that the congressional farm bloc wrote into the Emergency Price Control Act barring the imposition of price ceilings on farm products until their price reached 110 percent of "parity," a level that would put product prices where farmers believed they ought to be. With most farm products thus excluded from price controls, food prices increased 11 percent during 1942.

MILITARY VS. CIVILIAN NEEDS

The conflict over allocation of resources between military and civilian needs resurfaced in the so-called "feasibility" dispute that reached its climax in the fall of 1942. Henderson took the lead in attacking the armed services for exaggerating their supply needs at the expense of the civilian economy. The immediate dispute was resolved by a compromise whereby the military program was cut back through extending scheduled delivery dates farther into the future. The military won the larger battle. In October, 1942, Roosevelt established the Office of Economic Stabilization under James F. Byrnes, formerly a senator from South Carolina and Supreme Court justice, to take charge of wage and price stabilization.

Because of his political skills, his contacts in Congress, and Roosevelt's confidence, Byrnes was able to expand his control over all matters relating to the economy. That control was formalized by the creation in May, 1943, of the new Office of War Mobilization, which was to coordinate the activities of the different war agencies. With Byrnes in charge, the armed services had the upper hand when questions arose about military versus civilian needs. At the same time, the military services successfully resisted the imposition of OPA price ceilings on the purchase of military supplies. In the fall of 1942, Henderson had to agree to exempt "strictly military goods" from maximum price controls in return for a promise by the services to try to hold down prices and the profits of suppliers. Although this exemption did not apply to materials going into military end products, approximately two-thirds of the War Department's prime contracts were outside OPA control.

WAGE-SALARY FREEZES

The OPA was more successful in maintaining price ceilings on consumer goods. Faced with a continued rise in the cost of living resulting from exemption of most farm products from the Emergency Maximum Price Regulation, Roosevelt in September, 1942, warned Congress that unless the lawmakers voted to rectify the situation, he would act himself on the basis of his war powers. After a bitter struggle, Congress approved the Anti-Inflation Act of October, 1942, giving Roosevelt most of what he wanted. The legislation authorized the president to freeze wages and salaries, prices (including those of agricultural products), and rents at their levels on September 15. Roosevelt proceeded immediately to institute freezes.

The cost of living, however, continued to rise. By April, 1943, prices were on average 6.2 percent above the September 15 level, with food prices rising even more. The OPA came under increasing pressure from producer groups and their congressional allies to relax price controls, and from labor unions for higher wages. The turning point in the battle against inflation came on April 8, 1943, when Roosevelt ordered the economic stabilization agencies to "hold the line" against further price and wage increases. He followed this order with governmental seizure of coal mines to break a miners' strike for higher wages. The OPA simultaneously launched an aggressive campaign to roll back food prices. That campaign culminated in a 10 percent reduction in the retail prices of meat, coffee, and butter.

WARTIME RATIONING

Along with price and rent controls, the OPA adopted a system of rationing for particularly scarce commodities. The purposes of rationing were to combat inflation by preventing a bidding war for scarce goods, to ensure equitable distribution, and to give priority to military needs by restricting consumer demand. Rationing began at the end of December, 1941, with automobile tires as the first rationed good. A severe rubber shortage had resulted from the Japanese seizure of Southeast Asia. Rationing was extended to sugar, coffee, and gasoline in 1942. Rationing was instituted in 1943 for meats, fats and oils, butter, cheese, and processed foods. Shoes were added later. At the peak of rationing, the OPA administered thirteen rationing programs. Rationed goods still represented only one-seventh of total consumer expenditures.

There were two types of rationing. One—applied, for example, to gasoline and rubber tires—involved a priority system under which different quotas were allotted on the basis of need. Equal rations for all were the rule, with few exceptions. The second type of rationing, the point system, was a scheme whereby a whole family of items (such as meats, fish, cheese, and butter) was lumped together, with each item in the family given a point value. Consumers were allotted a certain number of points per month and were free to spend those points as wished. The OPA exercised control at the final stage of the distribution chain. Retailers would collect ration coupons or stamps from their customers and had to give them to their suppliers before they could get a new supply of the article. Administration at the consumer level was delegated to approximately fifty-six hundred local rationing boards. This arrangement had important political advantages, as the boards were made up of respected and influential members of the local community. The accompanying price was lack of uniformity across the country.

ADMINISTRATIVE INFIGHTING

From the first, the OPA was a center of political infighting. As was the norm under Roosevelt, rival bureaucrats maneuvered to expand their empires. Thus Henderson clashed with Secretary of the Interior Harold L. Ickes, the petroleum administrator, over gasoline rationing, and with War Food Administrator Chester C. Davis over food rationing. Patronage-hungry politicians strove to control appointments to OPA positions. A host of rival interests jockeyed for favored treatment. Henderson's vocal championship of consumers against pressure groups from business, agriculture, and labor antagonized producer groups and the conservative coalition of Southern Democrats and Republicans in Congress. In December, 1942, Henderson resigned, officially for reasons of health; he appears to have been pushed out by Roosevelt because he had become too much of a political liability. Roosevelt replaced Henderson as OPA administrator in January, 1943, with Prentiss M. Brown, a Democratic senator from Michigan who had just been defeated for reelection partly because of his support for agricultural price controls. Brown was succeeded in October, 1943, by former advertising executive Chester Bowles. In February, 1946, New Deal lawyer and Federal Communications Commission chairman Paul Porter became the last OPA administrator.

OPA: SUCCESSES, FAILURES, FINAL DAYS

The OPA did not work perfectly. There were numerous cases of evasion of price controls and rationing. Landlords in areas where housing was scarce, for example, often demanded an under-the-table payoff before renting an apartment. There was a large black market in such goods as coffee and soap. Because of the time and difficulties involved, the OPA rarely instituted criminal prosecutions of violators; its major enforcement tool was a court injunction to prevent further illegal sales. Mistakes in the handling of rationing were a major contributor to the OPA's unpopularity. The introduction of rationing for sugar and coffee was accompanied by what many thought was excessively restrictive and pointless bureaucracy and regulation. Even worse, the OPA had by 1944 issued food rationing coupons far in excess of available supplies. A survey in late fall showed that consumers had an average of 2.8 months of unused food coupons. When the temporarily successful German counterattack in the Battle of the Bulge at the end of 1944 threatened to further cut supplies, authorities canceled the unused coupons despite their previous pledge that no such action would be taken.

The OPA was largely successful in keeping consumer prices under control. Living costs had increased by almost two-thirds from 1914 to the end of World War I. In contrast, the cost of living rose only by approximately 28 percent from 1940 to the end of World War II. Most of that increase came before adoption of the Anti-Inflation Act of October, 1942. Living costs increased less than 2 percent during the last two years of the war. Perhaps most important, most Americans enjoyed a higher standard of living at the war's end than they had before it began.

The end of the war led to a bitter struggle over continuation of the OPA. The new president, Harry S. Truman, backed Bowles in his plan for a gradual relaxation of wartime controls over prices, wages, and scarce commodities to smooth the transition to a peacetime economy. On the day after the surrender of Japan, the OPA ended rationing of gasoline, fuel oil, and processed foods. By the end of 1945, only sugar remained under rationing. During late 1945 and early 1946, the OPA was able to control price increases, but inflationary pressures were gaining momentum. Consumers were buying in black markets, labor unions were pushing for wage hikes, and manufacturers and farmers had joined with Republican leaders in Congress to demand an end to all controls. A battle raged through the spring of 1946 over extension of the OPA. In late June, 1946, a conservative coalition of Republicans and Southern Democrats passed a price control bill extending the OPA for one year but drastically cutting its powers and commanding it to decontrol prices "as rapidly as possible." Instead of acquiescing, Truman vetoed the bill on June 29 and allowed price controls to expire on July 1.

Prices rose sharply, while shortages continued of meat, sugar, electrical appliances, housing, and automobiles. In late July, Congress approved a second bill extending price and rent controls for one year. Truman reluctantly accepted it, but the damage had been done. The new measure was even weaker and more confusing than the one that Truman had vetoed. Republican speakers and advertisements during the election campaign in the fall of 1946 made the confusion and failure in the price control program a major theme. One incident was particularly damaging to the Truman administration and the Democrats. When the OPA restored price ceilings on meat in August, 1946, farmers withdrew their cattle from the market to force a change in policy. While shoppers waited in vain for meat, Republicans seized on the shortage as a campaign issue. After the Republicans won control of both houses of Congress, Truman gave up the fight. He ended all wage and price controls, except those on rents, sugar, and rice, on November 9, 1946. The OPA began to wind up its affairs a month later.

John Braeman

SOURCES FOR FURTHER STUDY

Bowles, Chester. *Promises to Keep: My Years in Public Life, 1941-1969.* New York: Harper & Row, 1971.

Chandler, Lester V. *Inflation in the United States, 1940-1948.* New York: Harper & Brothers, 1951.

Chandler, Lester V., and Donald H. Wallace, eds. *Economic Mobilization and Stabilization: Selected Materials on the Economics of War and Defense.* New York: Henry Holt, 1951.

Harris, Seymour. *Price and Related Controls in the United States.* New York: McGraw-Hill, 1945.

Mansfield, Harvey C. *A Short History of OPA.* Washington, D.C.: Office of Temporary Controls, OPA, 1948.

Polenberg, Richard. *War and Society: The United States, 1941-1945.* Philadelphia: J.B. Lippincott, 1972. An excellent survey of all aspects of the American home front during World War II. Includes a brief but perceptive account of the struggle for economic stabilization.

Rockoff, Hugh. *Drastic Measures: A History of Wage and Price Controls in the United States.* Cambridge England: Cambridge University Press, 1984. A comprehensive history of efforts to control wages and prices. Compares the United States' experiences in World War I, World War II, and the Korean War.

Somers, Herman M. *Presidential Agency OWMR, the Office of War Mobilization and Reconversion.* Cambridge, Mass.: Harvard University Press, 1950. An excellent account of James F. Byrnes's coordination and direction of the wartime government management of the economy.

U.S. Bureau of the Budget. *The United States at War.* Washington, D.C.: Government Printing Office, 1946. This official history is a comprehensive survey of the wartime government management of the economy.

SEE ALSO: Neutrality Acts (1935-1939); Lend-Lease Act (1941); G.I. Bill (1944); Employment Act (1946).

IMMIGRATION ACT OF 1943

ALSO KNOWN AS: Magnuson Act
DATE: December 17, 1943
U.S. STATUTES AT LARGE: 57 Stat. 600
CATEGORIES: Asia or Asian Americans; Immigration

The Immigration Act of 1943 repealed Asian exclusion laws, opening the way for further immigration reforms.

The passage by Congress of the Immigration Act of 1943, also known as the Magnuson Act, and President Franklin D. Roosevelt's signing it into law ended the era of legal exclusion of Chinese immigrants to the United States and began an era during which sizable numbers of Chinese and other Asian immigrants came to the country. It helped bring about significant changes in race relations in the United States.

The first wave of Chinese immigrants came from the Pearl River delta region in southern China. They began coming to California in 1848 during the gold rush and continued to come to the western states as miners, railroad builders, farmers, fishermen, and factory workers. Most were men. Many came as contract laborers and intended to return to China. Anti-Chinese feelings, begun during the gold rush and expressed in mob actions and local discriminatory laws, culminated in the Chinese Exclusion Act of 1882, barring the immigration of Chinese laborers for ten years. The act was renewed in 1892, applied to Hawaii when those islands were annexed by the United States in 1898, and made permanent in 1904. Another bill, passed in 1924, made Asians ineligible for U.S. citizenship and disallowed Chinese wives of U.S. citizens to immigrate to the United States. As a result, the Chinese population in the United States declined from a peak of 107,475 in 1880 to 77,504 in 1940.

NEW ATTITUDES TOWARD CHINA

The passage of the Magnuson Act of 1943, which repealed the Chinese Exclusion Act of 1882, inaugurated profound changes in the status of ethnic Chinese who were citizens or residents of the United States. It made Chinese immigrants, many of whom had lived in the United States for years, eligible for citizenship. It also allotted a minuscule quota of 105 Chinese persons per year who could enter the United States as immigrants. The 1943 bill was a result of recognition of China's growing international status after 1928 under the Nationalist government and growing U.S. sympathy for China's heroic resistance to Japanese aggression after 1937. It also was intended to counter Japanese wartime propaganda aimed at discrediting the United States among Asians by portraying it as a racist nation.

World War II was a turning point for Chinese-U.S. relations. After Japan's attack on Pearl Harbor in December, 1941, China and the United States became allies against the Axis powers. Madame Chiang Kai-shek, wife of China's wartime leader, won widespread respect and sympathy for China during her visit to the United States; she was the second female foreign leader to address a joint session of Congress. In 1943, the United States and Great Britain also signed new equal treaties with China that ended a century of international inequality for China. These events and the contributions of Chinese Americans in the war favorably affected the position and status of Chinese Americans. The 1943 act also opened the door for other legislation that allowed more Chinese to immigrate to the United States. In the long run, these laws had a major impact on the formation of Chinese families in the United States.

RELATED LEGISLATION

The War Brides Act of 1945, for example, permitted foreign-born wives of U.S. soldiers to enter the United States and become naturalized. Approximately six thousand Chinese women entered the United States during the next several years as wives of U.S. servicemen. An amendment to this act, passed in 1946, put the Chinese wives and children of U.S. citizens outside the quota, resulting in the reunion of many separated families and allowing ten thousand Chinese, mostly wives, and also children of U.S. citizens of Chinese ethnicity, to enter the country during the next eight years. The Displaced Persons Act of 1948 granted permanent resident status, and eventually the right of citizenship, to 3,465 Chinese students, scholars, and others stranded in the United States by the widespread civil war that erupted between the Chinese Nationalists and Communists after the end of World War II. The Refugee Relief Act of 1953 allowed an additional 2,777 refugees to remain in the United States after the civil war ended in a Communist victory and the establishment of the People's Republic of China. Some Chinese students from the Republic of China on Taiwan, who came to study in the United States after 1950 and found employment and sponsors after the end of their studies, were also permitted to remain and were eligible for naturalization.

The four immigration acts passed between 1943 and 1953 can be viewed as a result of the alliance between the United States and the Republic of China in World War II and U.S. involvement in the Chinese civil war that followed. In a wider context, they were also the result of changing views on race and race relations that World War II and related events brought about. Finally, they heralded the Immigration and Nationality Act Amendments of 1965, which revolutionized U.S. immigration policy in ending racial quotas. Its most dramatic consequence was the significant increase of Asian immigrants in general, and Chinese immigrants in particular, into the United States.

THE NEW IMMIGRANTS

The new immigrants changed the makeup of Chinese American society and caused a change in the way the Chinese were perceived by the majority groups in the United States. Whereas most of the earlier immigrants tended to live in ghettoized Chinatowns, were poorly educated, and overwhelmingly worked in low-status jobs as laundrymen, miners, or railroad workers, the new immigrants were highly educated, cosmopolitan, and professional. They came from the middle class, traced their roots to all parts of China, had little difficulty acculturating and assimilating into the academic and professional milieu of peoples of European ethnicity in the United States, and tended not to live in Chinatowns. The latter group was mainly responsible for revolutionizing the way Chinese Americans were perceived in the United States.

Jiu-Hwa Lo Upshur

SOURCES FOR FURTHER STUDY

Chan, Sucheng, ed. *Entry Denied, Exclusion and the Chinese Community in America, 1882-1943*. Philadelphia: Temple University Press, 1991.

Chen, Jack. *The Chinese of America*. San Francisco: Harper & Row, 1980.

Min, Pyong Gap, ed. *Asian Americans Contemporary Trends and Issues*. Thousand Oaks, Calif.: Sage Publications, 1995.

Riggs, Fred W. *Pressure on Congress: A Study of the Repeal of Chinese Exclusion*. 1950. Reprint. Westport, Conn.: Greenwood Press, 1972.

Steiner, Stanley. *Fusang, the Chinese Who Built America*. New York: Harper & Row, 1979.

Sung, Betty Lee. *Mountain of Gold: The Story of the Chinese in America*. New York: I Company, 1967.

Tung, William L. *The Chinese in America, 1870-1973: Chronology and a Fact Book*. Dobbs Ferry, N.Y.: Oceana, 1974.

SEE ALSO: Page Law (1875); Chinese Exclusion Act (1882); Alien land laws (1913); Immigration Act of 1917 (1917); Immigration Act of 1921 (1921); Cable Act (1922); Immigration Act of 1924 (1924); War Brides Act (1945); Immigration and Nationality Act of 1952 (1952); Refugee Relief Act (1953); Immigration and Nationality Act Amendments of 1965 (1965).

G.I. BILL

ALSO KNOWN AS: Servicemen's Readjustment Act
DATE: June 22, 1944
U.S. STATUTES AT LARGE: 58 Stat. 284
PUBLIC LAW: 78-346
U.S. CODE: 38 § 694
CATEGORIES: Education; Health and Welfare

Federal subsidies for the education of veterans boosted reintegration of military personnel into the U.S. economy after World War II.

World War II had a twofold effect on education in the United States. In the short run, the existence of many colleges and universities was seriously jeopardized. Both students and faculty members were removed by the selective service draft and by patriotic volunteering. Small private colleges, often perilously close to financial ruin, were among the institutions most severely affected. In the long run, however, the war served as a tremendous impetus in convincing people that the national government had a role to play in assuring that all citizens were given an opportunity to pursue formal education to the limit of their natural ability.

The first tangible sign of this new concern was the passage in 1944 of the Serviceman's Readjustment Act, familiarly known as the G.I. Bill of Rights, which was concerned with the federal financing of educational opportunities for returning veterans. While this particular act undoubtedly was affected by wartime sentiments, the concept of federal responsibility in education soon enjoyed wide support.

THE NEED TO FUND MASSIVE EDUCATION

President Franklin D. Roosevelt and others began thinking about the interrupted education of many U.S. soldiers and sailors soon after the attack on Pearl Harbor in December, 1941. In 1942, a report entitled *Statement of Principles Relating to the Educational Problems of Returning Soldiers, Sailors, and Displaced War Industry Workers* was published by the Institute of Adult Education of Teachers College, Columbia University. The report emphasized the need for some sort of postwar vocational and educational program for veterans, financed by the national government. In July, 1942, Roosevelt discussed the matter with President George F. Zook and other officials of the American Council on Education. Convinced of the federal responsibility in this area, Roosevelt initiated a Conference on Postwar Readjustment of Civilian and Military Personnel, which in June, 1942, submitted a recommendation for action.

This "Demobilization and Reconversion" report indicated that the following action was needed: the development of a vocational training program for returning veterans; the establishment of special courses at regular colleges and universities for returnees; the financing of such educational services by the federal government; and the cooperation of local and state agencies with the federal government in the execution of this program. Roosevelt charged the War and Navy departments with establishing precise guidelines and recommendations for the implementation of these goals. The report that the War and Navy departments issued on October 27, 1943, became the basis for the G.I. Bill.

Roosevelt's legislative proposal to Congress was assisted by a number of factors. Of primary concern was the patriotic sentiment engendered by persons such as newspaper columnist Ernie Pyle, who insisted that the country owed its veterans something. The American Legion also lobbied in support of the bill. In addition, a number of government planners saw problems in the demobilization of an estimated fifteen million service people into the civilian economy.

It seemed reasonable to spread the returning veterans among educational institutions of many different kinds—vocational schools and especially colleges. Draft statistics that indicated that U.S. education had been failing significantly in the prewar years were another important factor. The selective service studies provided a unique opportunity to measure the educational progress of a vast segment of the American public. To the chagrin of professional educators, the government announced that more than 676,000 men were disqualified from military service because they lacked the minimum of four years of formal schooling. Furthermore, it became clear that U.S. education also had failed to produce enough qualified mathematicians, scientists, and foreign-language experts. The problems of too few schools, too few competent teachers, and too few course offerings all pointed to one conclusion in the eyes of many educators and politicians: Only a major injection of federal funds could enable U.S. education to meet the idealistic goals

741

established for it. The first hesitant steps in this direction were taken during World War II. On March 24, 1943, President Roosevelt signed into law the Vocational Rehabilitation Bill, which provided federal funds for the retraining and rehabilitation of disabled veterans and workers in the civilian defense industry. This was followed on June 22, 1944, by the Serviceman's Readjustment Act.

PROVISIONS AND IMPLICATIONS

Under the provisions of the G.I. Bill, veterans were defined as those individuals with more than ninety days of active service after September 16, 1940, who possessed an honorable discharge. These persons were to receive an opportunity to further their education on a full- or part-time basis at any approved educational or training institution of their selection. The course of study could range from graduate work to elementary courses and had to be completed within a four-year period. The university or college was free to pass on the veteran's eligibility to enroll in any of its programs, and normal standards were to be considered in force. The federal government would pay all tuition and fees required by the university. In addition, the veteran was entitled to a subsistence check each month. The amount of the check varied with the number of dependents and was increased to keep pace with inflation. By 1947, a veteran with one or more dependents was entitled to ninety dollars per month. A single veteran received sixty-five dollars per month. The act also provided money for new veterans' hospitals and guaranteed unemployment compensation of twenty dollars per week for a period of one year after separation. Finally, low-interest loans were made available to veterans interested in purchasing a home or farm or establishing a new business.

The implications of this act were tremendous. The national government was guaranteeing the educational opportunity of more than fifteen million citizens. The responsibility for this education was to be shared by the individual, the institution, and the national government. The flood of returnees soon swamped both public and private institutions in the United States. Schools that had been facing bankruptcy soon found themselves engaged in building programs. Special married-student dormitories sprang into existence to accommodate this new type of student. Altogether, the veterans caused a revolution in the techniques and status of U.S. higher education. At its crest in 1947, the flood of veterans represented more than one million students out of a total student population of two and one-half million. In 1952, a new G.I. Bill was passed for veterans of the Korean War; later, the Vietnam War became the occasion for a further extension.

A NEW TYPE OF STUDENT

The original G.I. Bill of 1944 brought a different type of student to college campuses. Some had had their education interrupted by the war. Others never had envisioned receiving a college education, because of the cost. Thus, the campuses swelled with so-called nontraditional students, that is, students older than the usual eighteen- to twenty-two-year-olds. Their maturity and experiences added markedly to the academic activity. The sheer numbers of students also strained the college facilities and the stamina of faculty and staff. Year-round programs, night classes, and academic counseling became necessary. Much to the dismay of conservative academics, the schools provided program acceleration and credit for experiential learning. Many of these changes became standard parts of the educational experience at most institutions of higher learning. Continuing education (adult learning) for either credit or educational enrichment became commonplace at both secondary and higher-education institutions. The G.I. Bill is also credited with providing African Americans with greater opportunities for higher education, as well as helping to improve the quality of education at traditionally African American institutions.

George Q. Flynn, updated by
Albert C. Jensen

SOURCES FOR FURTHER STUDY

Hyman, Harold M. *American Singularity: The 1787 Northwest Ordinance, the 1862 Homestead and Morrill Acts, and the 1944 G.I. Bill.* Athens: University of Georgia Press, 1986.

Kandel, Issac L. *The Impact of the War upon American Education.* Chapel Hill: University of North Carolina Press, 1948.

Kiester, Edwin, Jr. "Uncle Sam Wants You . . . to Go to College," *Smithsonian* 25 (November 1, 1994).

Montgomery, G. V. "The Montgomery G.I. Bill: Development, Implementation, and Impact." *Education Record* 75, no. 4 (Fall, 1994): 49-54.

Rose, Amy D. "Significant and Unintended Consequences: The G.I. Bill and Adult Education." *Education Record* 75, no. 4 (Fall, 1994): 47-48.

Tiedt, Sidney W. *The Role of the Federal Government in Education.* New York: Oxford University Press, 1966.

Wilson, Reginald. "G.I. Bill Expands Access for African Americans." *Education Record* 75, no. 4 (Fall, 1994): 32-39.

Zook, Jim. "As G.I. Bill Marks Its Fiftieth Year, Use of Educational Benefits Rises." *Chronicle of Higher Education* 40, no. 41 (June 15, 1994): A27.

SEE ALSO: Executive Order 8802 (1941); Employment Act (1946); National Defense Education Act (1958); Economic Opportunity Act (1964); Higher Education Act (1965).

BRETTON WOODS AGREEMENT

DATE: Concluded July 31, 1944
U.S. STATUTES AT LARGE: 82 Stat. 188
PUBLIC LAW: 90-349
U.S. CODE: 22 § 286
CATEGORIES: Banking, Money, and Finance; Foreign Relations; Treaties and Agreements

The Bretton Woods Agreement provided the basis for the postwar fixed exchange rate system and the establishment of the International Monetary Fund and the World Bank.

In July of 1944, about seven hundred delegates, representing forty-four countries, met at the first United Nations Monetary and Financial Conference, held at the Mount Washington Hotel in Bretton Woods, New Hampshire. The purpose of the conference was to develop an agreement to deal with the organization of the post-World War II international economy, more specifically the promotion of exchange rate stability and the restoration of international trade.

THE BRETTON WOODS CONFERENCE

In a message he read in the conference's keynote speech, President Franklin D. Roosevelt warned the delegates of the importance and necessity of cooperating in peacetime as they had in war. He expressed his utmost confidence in their ability to work out their differences. He indicated further that this conference marked the beginning of a broad effort to bring about international cooperation with the aim of developing a sound, dynamic, expanding world economy, with rising living standards for all, in the postwar period.

The conference ran from July 1 to July 22, 1944. The immediate purpose of the conference was the development of a stabilization fund and a vehicle to finance postwar reconstruction. The agreements made were not binding on any of the nations at the conference. They were to be referred to the various national governments, which could either accept or reject them.

Secretary of the Treasury Henry J. Morgenthau, Jr., headed the U.S. delegation and was elected president of the conference. Harry Dexter White acted as his monetary adviser and developed the American proposals. The British team was headed by John Maynard Keynes, an adviser to the British Treasury who developed a proposal that was far more visionary and radical than the American proposal.

The Bretton Woods conference produced the basis for the two major post-World War II international financial institutions, the International Monetary Fund and the International Bank for Reconstruction and Development, more commonly known as the World Bank. Both of these institutions were formally established on December 27, 1945, when the representatives of thirty nations met in Washington, D.C., for a signing ceremony. By the end of 1946, membership had reached thirty-five nations.

INTERNATIONAL MONETARY FUND

The function of the International Monetary Fund was to promote stability in the exchange rates of currencies and to assist nations suffering from short-term balance of payments problems, or imbalances in their imports and exports or financial transactions with the rest of the world. The function of the World Bank was to finance postwar reconstruction and economic development in less developed nations.

The basic goals of the International Monetary Fund—the promotion of exchange rate stability and assistance with balance of payments deficits—were aimed at rectifying problems created by common practices that restricted trade during the 1930's. Many nations during that period used deficits in their balance of payments as a rationale for restricting trade. The manipulation of currency values was a common practice.

The underlying purpose of both institutions was to foster international cooperation in the restoration of international trade and the development of a healthy world economy. The level of cooperation of the Allied nations during World War II was unprecedented, and the spirit of international cooperation prevailing at the end of World War II was different from the economic nationalism and political chaos that prevailed during the 1930's. The lesson had been learned: Extreme economic nationalism and political chaos in the prewar period were major reasons for the war.

THE BRETTON WOODS SYSTEM

The exchange rate system envisioned by this agreement, known as the Bretton Woods System, was an exchange rate regime of stable but adjustable foreign exchange parities. Essentially it was a compromise between the fixed exchange rates of the nineteenth century gold standard and floating exchange rates. The system was often characterized as an "adjustable peg." Day-to-day fluctuations in the prices of currencies, measured in terms of other currencies of gold, were to be limited to a band of 1 percent above or below the agreed-upon price, or par value. Each nation was responsible for limiting the fluctuations of the value of its currency. The narrow band of fluctuations around the par value was similar to that which prevailed under the nineteenth century gold standard, with the important exception that the Bretton Woods System specifically provided for periodic changes in exchange rates. The Bretton Woods System was a compromise in another important sense. It was an attempt to capture the automatic adjustment process under the gold standard while removing some of the harshness of this process by allowing a discretionary change in exchange rates in the face of a "fundamental disequilibrium" in a nation's balance of payments.

The Bretton Woods System provided two basic mechanisms of adjustment: inflating (deflating) the domestic economy for nations with surpluses (deficits) in their balance of payments, or altering the par value of a nation's currency. The latter course of action, changing a currency par value, was only to be used when the nation suffered from a "fundamental disequilibrium" in its balance of payments. Deficits and surpluses continuing over some period of time were supposed to be equally undesirable. In practice, however, more pressure for adjustment was placed on the deficit nations, the result of mercantilistic bias, which looked down upon net importers of goods.

Essentially, adjustment under the Bretton Woods System was a zero-sum game. Any devaluation was matched by a revaluation. The existence of persistent surpluses made it more difficult for deficit nations to adjust. Even though nations' tolerance for unemployment and inflation vary over time and from nation to nation, at any point in time, it is probably more difficult from the perspective of domestic politics for a deficit nation to deflate its economy than it is for a surplus nation to inflate its economy. Deflating a nation's economy usually means more unemployment, slower growth, and reduced profits, each of which represents a political disaster for a modern democracy. Consequently, deflation of the domestic economy by nations with deficits in their balance of payments was rarely accomplished.

The alternative mechanism of adjustment was a change in the par value of the currency of a nation facing a "fundamental disequilibrium" in its balance of payments. More pressure to adjust was placed, once again, on the deficit nations. Consequently, this mechanism became currency devaluations for those nations suffering from persistent deficits in their balance of payments. Many nations could not or would not embrace this policy for either domestic or international political reasons. The "adjustable peg" seemed to move only in one direction, if it moved at all, and that direction was downward, with devaluations of currencies.

In practice, the compromise between fixed and adjustable exchange rates did not work. There was a tendency to delay adjustment. When the inevitable adjustment came, it was large and disruptive. A fundamental shortcoming of the Bretton Woods System was the failure to provide for an orderly addition to international liquidity—a central source for borrowing—needed to support growth in world trade.

THE U.S. DOLLAR AND THE SMITHSONIAN AGREEMENT

The United States took on the role of supplying additional liquidity to the world by running balance of payment deficits on a continuous basis. The U.S. dollar rapidly became the world's major vehicle for payment and reserve currency, or currency used to support the value of the domestic currency. Through these continuous balance of payments deficits, U.S. dollars sent abroad to buy goods and services and for investment purposes did not return. The rest of the world used additional U.S. dollar holdings for monetary reserves and to supplement world liquidity.

Deficits in the United States balance of payments became chronic and persistent, leading to a weakening of the U.S. dollar. Monetary crises followed, and confidence in the dollar waned. The ability of the U.S. Treasury to convert U.S. dollars into gold became questionable as these balance of payments deficits grew, and eventually the Bretton Woods System collapsed.

In 1971, an unprecedented deficit in the U.S. balance of payments developed as a result of a flight from the U.S. dollar and a substantial trade deficit. President Richard M. Nixon suspended the convertibility of the U.S. dollar into gold and imposed a 10 percent surtax on all imports. These actions had the effect of a unilateral devaluation of the U.S. dollar, pulling out the linchpin from the Bretton Woods System.

An attempt was made to rescue the Bretton Woods System at the Smithsonian Conference, convened in Washington, D.C., on December 18, 1971. The U.S. dollar, which was clearly overvalued at the time, was devalued by about 8 percent through an increase in the price of gold from $35 to $38 per ounce. The band in which a currency's value could fluctuate around the par value also was widened, from 1 percent to 2.25 percent above or below par.

What the Smithsonian Agreement proposed to do, ironically, was to introduce stability through adjustable rates. This "reform," in fact, attempted to implement the very essence of what the Bretton Woods System was supposed to be, short-term fixed exchange rates with periodic adjustability and long-term stability. On its very first test, in June of 1972, the reformed regime established only six months earlier began to collapse. By the second quarter of 1973, floating exchange rates, with the values of currencies determined by daily transactions in free markets, were a reality, and the Bretton Woods System had passed into history.

HISTORIAL ASSESSMENT

The Bretton Woods era encompassed not only the most rapid and widely distributed period of world economic growth in history but also a period of notable economic stability, including price stability. Conventional wisdom among economists at one time seems to have been that the rules and strictures of the Bretton Woods System played little or no role in the impressive world economic growth of the period. Economists are beginning to question this conventional wisdom as they reexamine the Bretton Woods era. The growth of both gross domestic product and international trade slowed significantly after 1973. A growing number of economists attribute this slower growth to the increased volatility of exchange rates that prevailed after the collapse of the Bretton Woods System. The stable, fixed foreign exchange rates of the Bretton Woods System acted to reduce both the risks and the costs of international trade and investment, encouraging more of these activities.

Daniel C. Falkowski

SOURCES FOR FURTHER STUDY

Bilson, John F. O. "Macroeconomic Stability and Flexible Rates." *American Economic Review* 75, no. 5 (1985): 62-67.

Murphy, Carter J. "Reflections on the Exchange Rate System." *American Economic Review* 75, no. 5 (1985): 68-73.

Scammell, W. M. *International Monetary Policy: Bretton Woods and After.* New York: John Wiley & Sons, 1975.

Solomon, Robert. *The International Monetary System: 1945-1981.* New York: Harper & Row, 1982.

Williamson, John. "On the System in Bretton Woods." *American Economic Review* 75, no. 5 (1985): 74-79.

Yeager, Leland B. *International Monetary, Relations Theory, History and Policy.* 2d ed. New York: Harper & Row, 1976.

SEE ALSO: Smoot-Hawley Tariff Act (1930); Reciprocal Trade Act (1936); Miller-Tydings Fair Trade Act (1937); General Agreement on Tariffs and Trade of 1947 (1947).

Yalta Conference agreements

Date: Concluded February 4-11, 1945
Categories: Foreign Relations; Treaties and Agreements

At the end of World War II, the leaders of the "Big Three" powers—the United States, Great Britain, and the Soviet Union—met in Yalta to determine the future of Germany, the future of Poland, and the nature of a world organization to replace the discredited League of Nations.

In February, 1945, the armies of the Soviet Union moved rapidly toward Berlin with the Nazis in full retreat. In the West, British and U.S. forces, commanded by General Dwight D. Eisenhower, prepared to invade Germany. The unconditional surrender of Germany was expected in a matter of weeks. In the Far East, U.S. forces moved steadily from island to island across the Pacific toward a final invasion of the Japanese home islands. The possibility of using an atomic bomb to end the war remained questionable. Military experts did not believe the bomb could be made ready before the end of the year.

With the defeats of Germany and Japan a certainty, the Big Three Allied leaders—Prime Minister Winston Churchill of Great Britain, Communist Party secretary Joseph Stalin of the Soviet Union, and President Franklin D. Roosevelt of the United States—met to plan the postwar world. It was the last time the three would see one another, for Roosevelt died on April 12, 1945, just two months after the conference ended and less than a month before Germany surrendered. At Stalin's request, the Allies gathered at Livadia Palace (once a summer home of Czar Nicholas II) at Yalta on the Crimean Peninsula of the Black Sea. The conference lasted from February 4 to February 11, 1945.

POSTWAR EUROPE

Yalta represented the height of Allied cooperation. The Big Three spoke happily of the end of the fighting, but conflicting aims and conflicting personalities led to compromises in the spirit of cooperation that failed to satisfy any of them. Four major issues were discussed, and in spite of much talk of cooperation, no comprehensive settlement proved possible. The future of Germany, the future of Poland, the nature of a world organization to replace the discredited League of Nations, and the Soviet Union's formal entrance into the war against Japan were all highly controversial issues that needed to be settled by the Big Three.

Upon the defeat of Germany, Stalin wanted to divide that country into permanent zones of occupation; and he wanted reparations in kind (food and industry) to compensate for the nearly twenty million Russian dead and the Nazi destruction of one thousand Russian towns and cities. Stalin demanded a harsh policy to prevent Germany from ever making war again. Churchill agreed to divide Germany, but not permanently. He insisted that a healthy Europe depended upon a prosperous Germany. Roosevelt's position was somewhere between these two views. Stalin's reparations demands were incorporated into the conference's final protocol, and the three powers called for Germany's "dismemberment" into occupation zones during the period following surrender. A U.S. proposal granting France the status of an occupying power gained Stalin's reluctant approval. The details of Allied occupation policy, however, as well as the precise amount of reparations, were deferred to a later meeting.

In addition to a neutralized Germany, Stalin wanted the security of a friendly Polish government. He sought boundaries giving Russia territory from eastern Poland, while compensating the Poles with part of eastern Germany. The Soviet Union recognized the provisional Polish government in Warsaw (the so-called Lublin Poles), but both Great Britain and the United States insisted that the Polish government-in-exile in London also participate in the political rebuilding of Poland after the war. The Big Three agreed on a formula calling for the reorganization of the Lublin government with open elections, worded in such a way that both sides could see their respective interests maintained. The question of Poland's postwar boundaries also found a compromise solution. Ignoring the protests of the London Poles, the Big Three set the Curzon Line as the basis for Poland's eastern border, thereby sanctioning Russian reacquisition of areas lost in the fighting during the Russian Civil War of 1918-1921. As compensation, the Poles would receive substantial accessions of territory in the north and west, but the precise delineation of the new German frontier was left to the peace conference.

THE UNITED NATIONS

Primarily at U.S. insistence, discussion of a world organization to maintain the postwar peace enjoyed a high priority at Yalta. The Big Three planned an international conference to be held in San Francisco in April, at which the United Nations would be formed. Stalin, Roosevelt, and Churchill reached agreements on several points concerning membership and voting in the new body. Churchill resented U.S. proposals for United Nations trusteeships of colonial territories, which the British prime minister interpreted as an attempt by Roosevelt to dismantle the British Empire. Stalin exploited the disagreement over trusteeships between the Western Allies to gain Churchill's support for his own plan to have two Soviet republics recognized as independent voting members of the new United Nations. The atomic bomb was still a somewhat vague conception at Yalta, and so it was assumed that the Soviets would be needed to defeat Japan. Stalin promised that in return for Russian territory ceded to Japan under Russia's czarist imperial government, he would declare war on Japan within three months of Germany's surrender. The agreement on the Far East was not made public in February, 1945.

The agreements at Yalta could have become the basis for an amicable peace, for the spirit of the conference was one of hope and trust. In the spring and summer, however, charges of bad faith and double-dealing began to replace the spirit of compromise. Serious disagreements that heralded the Cold War to come were soon in evidence, and within a short time, the good will that marked the Yalta Conference had vanished.

Burton Kaufman, updated by
William Allison

SOURCES FOR FURTHER STUDY

Buhite, Russell D. *Decisions at Yalta: An Appraisal of Summit Diplomacy.* Wilmington, Del.: Scholarly Resources, 1986.

Clemens, Diane Shaver. *Yalta.* New York: Oxford University Press, 1970.

Gardner, Lloyd C. *Spheres of Influence: The Great Powers Partition Europe, from Munich to Yalta.* Chicago: Ivan R. Dee, 1991.

Snell, John L., ed. *The Meaning of Yalta: Big Three Diplomacy and the New Balance of Power.* Baton Rouge: Louisiana State University Press, 1956.

Theoharis, Athan G. *The Yalta Myths: An Issue in U.S. Politics, 1945-1955.* Columbia: University of Missouri Press, 1970.

SEE ALSO: Treaty of Versailles (1919); Kellogg-Briand Pact (1928); Good Neighbor Policy (1933); Bretton Woods Agreement (1944); Truman Doctrine (1947); General Agreement on Tariffs and Trade of 1947 (1947); Inter-American Treaty of Reciprocal Assistance (1948); North Atlantic Treaty (1949); Tripartite Security Treaty (1952); U.S.-Japanese Treaty (1952).

WAR BRIDES ACT

DATE: December 28, 1945
U.S. STATUTES AT LARGE: 59 Stat. 659
U.S. CODE: 8 § 232
CATEGORIES: Asia or Asian Americans; Immigration; Women's Issues

The War Brides Act relaxed immigration regulations to allow foreign-born spouses and children of U.S. military personnel to settle in the United States.

Between 1939 and 1946, more than sixteen million U.S. servicemen, primarily single and between eighteen and thirty years of age, were deployed to war theaters in foreign lands. Although the U.S. government discouraged servicemen from marrying—believing the single soldier, without distractions, would be of more value to the war effort—one million marriages to foreign nationals occurred during and shortly after the war. Aware of the potential for these liaisons, the U.S. War Department had issued a regulation requiring personnel on duty in any foreign country or possession of the United States to notify their commanding officer of any intention to marry at least two months in advance. Enacted in June, 1942, the regulation demanded strict adherence, and the waiting period was waived rarely, with a possible exception for the pregnancy of the bride-to-be. Usually, permission to marry was granted; however, certain couples, for example U.S.-German, U.S.-Japanese, and those of different races, either encountered longer waiting periods or were denied permission completely.

PASSAGE OF THE ACT

Many of those couples who had been granted permission and had married were separated for two to three years. In October, 1945, the Married Women's Association picketed for transport to allow their families to reunite. Evidently, the three thousand members' voices were heard; on December 28, 1945, the Seventy-ninth Congress passed an act to expedite the admission to the United States of alien spouses and alien minor children of U.S. citizens who had served in or were honorably discharged from the armed forces during World War II. These spouses had to meet the criteria for admission under the current immigration laws, including a thorough medical examination, and the application had to be filed within three years of the date of the act.

THE WAR BRIDE SHIPS

Following passage of the War Brides Act, thirty vessels, primarily hospital ships and army troopships, were selected to transport the women, children, and a few men ("male war brides") to the United States. Even the *Queen Elizabeth* and the *Queen Mary* were recruited for the task, because of their capacity to carry large groups of people. Transportation requests were prioritized by the military as follows: dependents of personnel above the fourth enlisted grade, dependents of personnel already placed on orders to the United States, wives of prisoners of war, wives of men wounded in action, and wives of men hospitalized in the United States. At the bottom of the priority pool were fiancées and spouses in interracial marriages.

Before debarking, the spouse (usually a woman) had to present her passport and visa, her sworn affidavit from her husband that he could and would support her upon arrival, two copies of her birth certificate, two copies of any police record she might have, any military discharge papers she might have, and a railroad ticket to her destination from New York. The families who saw them off knew they might never see their children and grandchildren again.

The American Red Cross was officially requested by the War Department to function as a clearinghouse for the brides, and many Red Cross volunteers served as "trainers" for the women in how to become American wives. Since many did not speak English, the

Red Cross also offered classes to aid in practical communication skills.

On January 26, 1946, the first war bride ship, the SS *Argentina*, left Southampton, England, with 452 brides, 173 children, and 1 groom on board. Lauded as the "Pilgrim Mothers" voyage or the "Diaper Run," the voyage was highly publicized. Many of the brides, upon arriving in the United States on February 4, were greeted by the U.S. press.

In Germany and Japan, permission to marry had not easily been attained and often was not granted at all. The ban on marriage to Germans was lifted on December 11, 1946, with twenty-five hundred applications submitted by the end of the year; in Japan, the ban lingered much longer.

During the first months of occupation during the war, approximately one-half million U.S. soldiers had been stationed in or near Yokohama. Many young women, fearing for their lives, hid from these "barbarians," but since the U.S. military was often the only source of employment, the women were forced to venture out. The country was in a cultural flux, resulting from economic deprivation, matriarchal predominance and female enfranchisement, and the abjuration of divinity by Emperor Hirohito. As the U.S. soldiers and Japanese women worked together, romantic relationships often developed, and because official permission to marry could not be obtained, many such couples were wed in secret in traditional Japanese ceremonies.

Although as many as one hundred thousand Japanese brides were deserted, others sought immigration to the United States. However, one proviso of the War Brides Act was that émigrés could not be excluded under any other provision of immigration law. The Oriental Exclusion Act of 1924 was still in place, and although Public Law 199 had overridden the act to allow Chinese immigration, the Japanese were still excluded. Many were not allowed admission to the United States until July, 1947, when President Harry Truman signed the Soldier Brides Act, a thirty-day reprieve on race inadmissibility.

LIFE IN AMERICA

In many cases, life for the war brides in the United States was not what they had expected. Many were treated poorly by isolationists who placed personal blame on all foreigners for U.S. involvement in the war. Because of the influx of soldiers returning to the civilian population, available housing and jobs were limited. Often the brides found themselves in the middle of a family-run farm, with some as sharecroppers. Frequently, when adjustment to civilian life was difficult for the former military man, he would rejoin his outfit, leaving the bride behind with his family—strangers who were sometimes hostile to the foreigner in their midst. Many of the marriages made in haste soured just as quickly through homesickness, promises unkept, or abuse. War brides who were unhappy or abused often stayed in their marriages, however, from fear of losing their children or of being deported.

Marriage did not confer automatic citizenship on foreign brides. They were required to pass exams to be naturalized, and many were still incapable of communicating in any but their native tongue. Public assistance was unavailable for these women.

Within one year of the mass exodus from Europe and Asia, one out of three of the war marriages had ended in divorce, and it was predicted that by 1950, the statistics would be two out of three. This prediction proved incorrect, however. Many of the war brides not only preserved their marriages but also became valuable members of their communities and contributors to American culture. In April, 1985, several hundred of these women, men, and children journeyed to Long Beach, California, for a reunion, appropriately held aboard the dry-docked *Queen Mary.*

Joyce Duncan

SOURCES FOR FURTHER STUDY

Hibbert, Joyce. *The War Brides.* Toronto: PMA Books, 1978.
Kubat, Daniel, et al. *The Politics of Migration Policies.* New York: Center for Migration Studies, 1979.
Michener, James. *Sayonara.* New York: Ballantine, 1954.
Moravia, Alberto. *Two Women.* New York: Playboy, 1981.
Shukert, Elfrieda Berthiaume, and Barbara Smith Scibetta. *War Brides of World War II.* Novato, Calif.: Presidio Press, 1988.

SEE ALSO: Cable Act (1922); Immigration Act of 1924 (1924); Immigration Act of 1943 (1943); Immigration and Nationality Act of 1952 (1952); Refugee Relief Act (1953); Immigration and Nationality Act Amendments of 1965 (1965); Immigration Reform and Control Act of 1986 (1986); Amerasian Homecoming Act (1987).

EMPLOYMENT ACT

ALSO KNOWN AS: Murray Act
DATE: February 20, 1946
U.S. STATUTES AT LARGE: 60 Stat. 23
PUBLIC LAW: 79-304
U.S. CODE: 15 § 1021
CATEGORIES: Labor and Employment

Congress passed this legislation to stimulate the economy following World War II, creating agencies in Congress and the executive branch to focus on problems of depression and inflation.

During the last months of World War II (1941-1945), people in the United States looked ahead anxiously to the nation's postwar economy. Their gravest worry was the possibility of a catastrophic depression. When the war ended, the nation would face the immediate task of demobilizing eleven million members of the armed forces and reconverting the economy to a peacetime basis. As soon as possible, a war-weary nation hoped to scrap price controls and rationing, cut taxes, and turn industry back to the production of consumer goods, such as automobiles. Still, the memory lingered of the Great Depression of the 1930's, with its mass unemployment, farm foreclosures, bank failures, and idle factories. Perhaps the sudden end of wartime spending would again plunge the nation back into depression. By early 1945, many economists were predicting eight to ten million unemployed when the returning troops were released from service. However, the levels of production, income, and employment reached during the war had given the United States a taste of a full-production economy. After the sacrifices of war, people were determined to settle for nothing less. In 1944, the Democratic platform pledged to guarantee full employment after the war, and the Republicans made virtually the same promise.

PASSAGE OF THE ACT

Only a month after the atomic bombs had been dropped over Hiroshima and Nagasaki, as hostilities ceased, the new president, Harry S. Truman, urged the passage of full-employment legislation then pending before Congress. The outcome was the Employment Act of 1946. On January 22, 1945, Senator James E. Murray had introduced a full-employment bill. The bill asserted that "all Americans able to work and seeking work have the right to useful, remunerative, regular, and full-time employment. . . ." Furthermore, it was the government's responsibility "to provide such a volume of Federal investment and expenditure as may be needed to assure continuing full employment. . . ." The president was directed to present a forecast of aggregate demand for goods and services throughout the economy, compare it with the level needed for full employment, and recommend changes in federal spending to remedy any shortfall or excess.

Murray's Full Employment Bill passed the Senate (with amendments) on September 28, 1945, by a vote of 71 to 10, and was endorsed by President Truman. Over the next year, however, the Murray bill underwent a drastic metamorphosis. Congressional conservatives cut out any federal guarantee of the right to a job or of full employment. They also reduced the force of the government's commitment to forecasting and eliminated specific mention of public works and other kinds of compensatory spending. The ultimate result was the Employment Act, signed into law by President Truman February 20, 1946.

TWO MAIN PROVISIONS

The final law contained two main provisions. The first committed the government "to promote maximum employment, production, and purchasing power." In practice, this strange wording came to be seen as a mandate to avoid significant depression or inflation. Second, two agencies were established to carry out the commitment. Congress set up a Council of Economic Advisors (CEA), consisting of three economists, to assist the president in drawing up an annual report on the state of the economy. In Congress, a Joint Committee on the Economic Report (later renamed the Joint Economic Committee—JEC) was to review the president's report and make recommendations of its own. President Truman soon appointed Edwin Nourse, Leon Keyserling, and John D. Clark as the first Council of Economic Advisors.

KEYNESIAN ECONOMIC THEORY

The Employment Act was a statutory expression of what the United States had learned during the Great Depression and World War II.

The act's spiritual father was British economist John Maynard Keynes. In 1936, Keynes had published his landmark work *The General Theory of Employment, Interest, and Money.* Keynes did not endorse fashionable proposals for nationalization or economic planning of specific industries. Rather, he argued that government could help a free market to work well if it used monetary and fiscal measures to help stabilize the aggregate demand for goods and services. A nation, Keynes argued, could actually pull itself out of a depression if the government stimulated the economy through deficit spending for public works and other purposes. As supporting evidence, many people pointed to the rapidity with which the U.S. economy was restored to full employment when federal defense spending skyrocketed from 1940 on. The ambitious provisions of the original Full Employment Bill assumed that government economists could accurately forecast undesirable declines or increases in aggregate demand, and that government could easily offset these with fiscal measures, such as spending increases or tax-rate changes. Well-founded skepticism about both of these propositions lay behind the scaling down of the bill's scope.

From the end of World War II through the end of the twentieth century, every president has used the philosophy and machinery of the Employment Act to keep the economy from falling into a dangerous boom-and-bust cycle. In the immediate postwar years, Truman faced a confusing economic situation that was just the reverse of what experts had predicted—shortages instead of surplus and inflation instead of depression and deflation. These problems became acute during the Korean War, and both the CEA and the JEC contributed significantly to research on managing the economy under renewed war conditions. Their influence helped persuade Congress to increase tax rates so that the war did not lead to large federal deficits.

THE COUNCIL OF ECONOMIC ADVISORS

Experience soon demonstrated some problems inherent in the workings of the Employment Act. The first chairman, Edwin Nourse, visualized the CEA as a relatively nonpolitical body reflecting the technical expertise of professional economists. Realistically, however, the CEA had no clientele or constituency of its own, and therefore no real political power, except in relation to the president; therefore, CEA members have been chosen for conformity with the outlook of the president. This has meant that the likelihood that the CEA will shape the president's economic views is not great. A second issue arises because the Federal Reserve System, which has potentially a large influence on demand management policies, is relatively independent of the president and therefore of the CEA.

The CEA has involved many prominent professional economists, such as James Tobin, Herbert Stein, Walter Heller, Martin Feldstein, and Alan Blinder. The agency has produced significant research and commentary, but has not been a major policy influence. Nor has the JEC, which does not initiate legislation in its own right.

SUBSEQUENT LEGISLATION

In 1978, the Employment Act was significantly extended by the Full Employment and Balanced Growth Act (Humphrey-Hawkins Act), which established nonbinding targets of 4 percent for unemployment and 3 percent for inflation, to be achieved by 1983. The unemployment target generally was recognized as unrealistic. Good economic performance in the 1980's and 1990's usually involved getting unemployment below 6 percent. However, the inflation target was eventually fulfilled in the early 1990's. The Humphrey-Hawkins Act directly addressed the issue of Federal Reserve Board policy, instructing the Federal Reserve to report directly to Congress concerning the relationship between its policy targets and the goals articulated by the act.

Donald Holley, updated by
Paul B. Trescott

SOURCES FOR FURTHER STUDY

Bailey, Stephen K. *Congress Makes a Law: The Story Behind the Employment Act of 1946.* New York: Columbia University Press, 1950.

Canterbury, E. Ray. *The President's Council of Economic Advisors: A Study of Its Functions and Its Influence on the Chief Executive's Decisions.* New York: Exposition Press, 1961.

Carlson, Keith M. "Federal Fiscal Policy Since the Employment Act of 1946." *Review (Federal Reserve Bank of St. Louis)* 69, no. 10 (December, 1987): 14-25.

Colm, Gerhard, ed. *The Employment Act, Past and Future: A Tenth Anniversary Symposium.* Special Report by the NPA Board of Trustees and Standing Committees 41. Washington, D.C.: National Planning Association, 1956.

DeLong, J. Bradford. *Keynesianism, Pennsylvania Avenue Style: Some Economic Consequences of the Employment Act of 1946.* Cambridge, Mass.: National Bureau of Economic Research, 1996.

Flash, Edward S. *Economic Advice and Presidential Leadership: The Council of Economic Advisors.* New York: Columbia University Press, 1965.

Nourse, Edwin G. *Economics in the Public Service: Administrative Aspects of the Employment Act.* New York: Harcourt, Brace and World, 1953.

Stein, Herbert. *The Fiscal Revolution in America.* Chicago: University of Chicago Press, 1969.

SEE ALSO: Banking Act of 1935 (1935); G.I. Bill (1944); Federal Tort Claims Act (1946); Labor-Management Relations Act (1947); Landrum-Griffin Act (1959); Equal Pay Act (1963); Economic Opportunity Act (1964); Age Discrimination in Employment Act (1967); Equal Employment Opportunity Act (1972); Comprehensive Employment Training Act (1973); Employee Retirement Income Security Act (1974); Age Discrimination Act (1975).

HOBBS ACT

ALSO KNOWN AS: Anti-Racketeering Act of 1946
DATE: July 3, 1946
U.S. STATUTES AT LARGE: 60 Stat. 420
U.S. CODE: 18 § 1951
CATEGORIES: Business, Commerce, and Trade; Crimes and Criminal Procedure; Labor and Employment

This act made it unlawful to interfere with interstate commerce by robbery or extortion and reined labor unions' ability to enforce the interests of their constituencies within the boundaries of the law.

The bill that became the Hobbs Act (or Anti-Racketeering Act of 1946) was introduced by Congressman Carl Hobbs from Alabama on January 3, 1945, in response to a 1942 Supreme Court decision in favor of Local 807 of the Teamsters Union of New York. The Court decision had essentially nullified the Anti-Racketeering Act of 1934, and the purpose of the Hobbs Act was to put new antiracketeering legislation on the books by amending the 1934 act. Title I, section 2 of the Hobbs Act stated that it was a felony to obstruct, delay, or affect interstate commerce "in any way or degree" through robbery or extortion. To make the act effective, it redefined the key terms "commerce," "robbery," and "extortion."

Debate over the bill centered on its effect on workers and organized labor. Supporters of the bill argued that it protected farmers from harassment by the Teamsters Union and pointed out that Title II of the bill upheld previous laws guaranteeing labor's rights. Foes of the bill nevertheless questioned whether the bill was merely an antiracketeering measure or was also intended to be antilabor. They pointed out that the Hobbs Act would make it difficult for a union to picket a company effectively during a strike.

Thomas Winter

SOURCES FOR FURTHER STUDY

Philcox, Norman W. *An Introduction to Organized Crime.* Springfield, Ill.: Charles C Thomas, 1978. An overview of RICO and its applications

Wallance, Gregory J. "Criminal Justice: Outgunning the Mob." *American Bar Association Journal* 80 (March 1, 1994).

Welling, Sarah N., Pamela H. Bucy, and Sara Sun Beale. *Federal Criminal Law and Related Actions: Crimes, Forfeiture, the False Claims Act, and Rico.* Eagan, Minn.: West Group, 1998.

SEE ALSO: Anti-Racketeering Act (1934); Organized Crime Control Act (1970); Racketeer Influenced and Corrupt Organizations Act (1970).

FEDERAL TORT CLAIMS ACT

DATE: August 2, 1946
U.S. STATUTES AT LARGE: 60 Stat. 842
PUBLIC LAW: 15 § 41
CATEGORIES: Civil Rights and Liberties

> *The statute enabled private citizens to sue the government when a federal employee harms a third party or private property by committing an intentional tort or by negligence. The Supreme Court later barred military personnel from suing the federal government for injuries suffered while performing their jobs.*

The Federal Tort Claims Act was passed in 1946 to protect third parties injured by the actions of federal government employees. If a federal employee, acting within the scope of his or her employment, injures a third party, then the federal government can be held liable for the employee's actions. Historically, the federal government was protected by the doctrine of sovereign immunity, which prevented a lawsuit's being filed against a government authority without the government's consent. The 1946 act limits the protection of the doctrine and allows third parties to seek compensation.

However, when the lawsuit arises out of injury to military personnel acting within the scope of their service, the Supreme Court held that the government cannot be sued under the act. Vietnam veterans exposed to the herbicide Agent Orange filed a class action suit against the federal government and the herbicide's manufacturers. In one case, *In re "Agent Orange" Product Liability Litigation* (1980), the manufacturers reached a pretrial settlement with several of the veterans and their families. The suit against the federal government was dismissed by the lower court, and the Court refused to hear the appeals by the veterans. The Court continued to maintain that the act does not extend to suits filed by military personnel. In *Hercules v. United States* (1996), the Court stated that this exclusion is still viable.

Additionally, the Court refuses to impose liability when a private business contracting with the federal government attempts to hold the government responsible for negligent acts performed by the business. The injured third party can seek compensation from the business but not from the government.

However, when the federal government is liable, the Court has enforced the provisions of the act. In *Molzof v. United States* (1992), a veteran suffered irreversible brain damage because of negligence at a Veterans Administration hospital. The lower court granted damages under the act but refused to award damages for future medical expenses and for loss of enjoyment of life. The lower court held that awarding such damages would be providing punitive damages, which the act expressly prohibits; the act prohibits awarding damages solely for the purpose of punishing the government for its actions. The Court reversed the decision, finding that although the award of such damages may have a punitive effect, it should be considered compensatory.

Patricia Jackson

SOURCE FOR FURTHER STUDY
Ball, Howard. "The U.S. Supreme Court's Glossing of the Federal Tort Claims Act: Statutory Construction and Veterans' Tort." *The Western Political Quarterly* 41, no. 3 (September, 1988): 529-552.

SEE ALSO: Eleventh Amendment (1798).

TRUMAN DOCTRINE

DATE: Issued March 12, 1947
CATEGORIES: Foreign Relations

Following World War II, the president articulated the cornerstone of forty years of subsequent U.S. foreign policy.

Soon after the conclusion of World War II, the United States was faced with the necessity of finding a new approach to the problem of peaceful stabilization in international affairs. Franklin D. Roosevelt's concept of a postwar peace based on cooperation between the United States and the Soviet Union proved to be ineffective.

The Soviet army occupied most of Eastern and Central Europe, and it was made clear that the Soviet Union would not tolerate independent regimes there. Despite the agreements made at the Yalta Conference, Joseph Stalin, the Soviet dictator, unilaterally imposed communist regimes on Poland, Hungary, Bulgaria, Czechoslovakia, and Romania. The protests of the United States and Great Britain did not alter this policy of Soviet control. Furthermore, the Soviet government attempted to expand into areas where it had no military control, including Greece, Turkey, and Iran.

Beginnings of the Cold War

In confronting these emergencies, the United States at first tried ad hoc measures which, although essentially successful in achieving their immediate objectives, failed to establish policy guidelines for the postwar world. In Iran, the Soviet Union refused to withdraw its occupation forces and made demands through diplomatic channels for exclusive oil and mineral rights. The United States and Great Britain joined in a strong protest, which implied the threat of Western military assistance to counter Soviet pressure. In March, 1946, Soviet troops began a complete withdrawal, and the Iranian government succeeded in stabilizing its rule. In the case of Turkey, the Soviet Union sent several diplomatic notes in 1945 and 1946 that demanded the cession of border territory and a joint administration of the Dardanelles. These demands were to be ratified in a treaty that also would provide for the leasing of navy and army bases in the Dardanelles to the Soviets to implement joint control. Following a second Soviet note, the United States sent a strong naval fleet into the Mediterranean, the first U.S. warships to be sent into those waters during peacetime since 1803. A week later, Great Britain joined the United States in rejecting Soviet demands on Turkey. Meanwhile, in Greece, only extensive British military and economic aid prevented a complete collapse of the war-torn country and a *coup d'état* by communist guerrillas.

Following extensive domestic debate, the United States formally abandoned its traditional peacetime isolationist approach to world affairs and adopted a long-range policy intended to deal with Soviet expansionism. One position in the debate was dramatized by Winston Churchill, the former prime minister of Great Britain, in a speech at Fulton, Missouri, in early 1946. There, with President Truman on the platform, Churchill characterized the Soviet

Union as an expansionist state that would react only to a strong counterforce. Soviet expansion, Churchill believed, could be prevented only by a collaboration between the United States and Great Britain to preserve the independence of Europe and to prevent the extension of what came to be called the Iron Curtain. A contrasting attitude was expressed by Secretary of Commerce Henry A. Wallace, who declared that only American-Soviet cooperation could prevent another war. He pointed out that the Soviet desire for control of areas on its borders was understandable and reasonable, and that the United States had long acted to secure its own hemispheric security.

Substantial segments of U.S. public opinion supported either Churchill or Wallace. However, the State Department sought a middle ground. Rejecting both the Soviet-expansion position of Churchill and the sphere-of-influence concept of Wallace, Secretary of State James F. Byrnes urged the Soviet Union to adopt a more cooperative diplomatic policy. The United States, he said, should pursue a policy of firmness and patience and wait for the Soviets to see the reasonableness of negotiation. It appeared to many, including President Truman, that the United States was the one that was always being reasonable, not the Soviet Union. By 1947, the administration had adopted the position that the revolutionary postulates of the Soviet regime made traditional diplomacy impossible.

TRUMAN ARTICULATES HIS POLICY

The first step in the development of the new policy toward the Soviet Union appeared in response to the continuing Soviet threat to Greece and Turkey. In February, 1947, Great Britain informed the State Department that His Majesty's Government could no longer continue to support the regime in Greece. Great Britain, like all Western Europe, was suffering from grave economic problems. As the British Empire retreated, the United States stepped forward. Within the next few weeks, President Truman decided that the independence of Greece and the recovery of Europe were crucial for the security of the United States. On March 12, 1947, the president appeared before a joint session of Congress and presented what became known as the Truman Doctrine. He outlined the desperate situation in both Greece and Turkey and called upon the American people to "help free peoples to maintain their free institutions and their national integrity against aggressive movements that seek to impose upon them totalitarian regimes." Most important, he pointed out, was the fact that such totalitarian aggression was a direct threat to the security of the United States. In response, Congress appropriated four hundred million dollars for economic aid to both Greece and Turkey. Additionally, the president was authorized to dispatch civilian and military advisers to help both nations defend their sovereignty.

THE MARSHALL PLAN

The next step in this new policy was to bring the same consideration to bear upon Western Europe, an even more critical area. There is debate over the degree to which the Marshall Plan was motivated by the desire to contain Soviet influence in Western Europe; nevertheless, to proponents of this new internationalism in U.S. foreign policy, it clearly seemed axiomatic that if aid to Greece and Turkey could be justified because of their strategic importance, the United States must aid other European countries where the situation was equally desperate. Great Britain was suffering from the wartime destruction of its factories and the loss of its capability to export manufactured goods. Germany was in ruins and virtually incapable of feeding its population. In France and Italy, the Communist Party had wide support within the industrial laboring class and was working by both overt and covert means for a radical change in the government of both countries. A further difficulty was that the winter of 1946-1947 was the most severe experienced by Europeans for generations.

From a military viewpoint, new weaponry made it essential that European control of the Atlantic gateways be in friendly hands. In terms of trained technicians, industrial capacity, and raw materials, Western Europe was a potential giant worth keeping in the U.S. camp. These factors led to an announcement by the new secretary of state, George C. Marshall, at Harvard University in June, 1947, of what came to be known as the Marshall Plan. Assuming that the European countries could develop a cooperative approach to their economic problems, the United States, said Marshall, would assist in their recovery. Congress eventually authorized a grant of seventeen billion dollars to the Organization for European Economic Cooperation over a four-year period. A total of about twelve billion dollars was actually spent. Although aid was offered to all European nations, including the Soviet Union, the Soviet-dominated areas were not permitted to cooperate because that would have meant revealing Soviet economic secrets and sacrificing Soviet economic control. Success of the Marshall Plan emerged quickly; in 1952, Europe exceeded its prewar production figures by some 200 percent.

KENNAN AND CONTAINMENT

A discussion of the theory behind the policy embodied in the Truman Doctrine and the Marshall Plan appeared in an unsigned article on the subject of containment in the July, 1947, issue of *Foreign Affairs*. The author, it was later disclosed, was George F. Kennan, a high-ranking member of the State Department. Kennan's essay proposed that the antagonism that existed between the United States and the Soviet Union was merely the logical extension of certain basic Soviet assumptions. The United States, Kennan maintained, could count on Soviet hostility because the rhetoric of the Bolshevik Revolution demanded war against capitalist states. World War II had submerged this antagonism only temporarily. "These characteristics of Soviet policy," he wrote, "like the postulates from which they flow, are basic to the internal nature of Soviet power, and will be with us . . . until the nature of Soviet power is changed."

The immediate question, Kennan insisted, was how the United States should counter this new ideological crusade and power drive that threatened to engulf Europe. In Kennan's view, the United States should adopt a policy of "long-term, patient, but firm and vigilant containment." To counter the Soviet policy, the United States should adopt a long-range course of diplomacy toward the Soviet Union and pursue it consistently. This containment, or the counterapplication of force wherever Soviet expansion threatened, had a negative aspect, because it put a tremendous burden on U.S. consistency and steadfastness. On the positive side, through containment, the United States could help to work changes within the Soviet system and help modify the revolutionary zeal of the regime. If expansionist dynamics were constantly frustrated, Kennan reasoned, the forces must be expended within the system itself, and this would mean some modification of totalitarian control.

Although many persons in the United States remained vocally critical of it, containment became the official Cold War policy of the United States until the Soviet Union began its public collapse in the summer of 1991. In the words of former national security adviser and secretary of state Henry Kissinger, history has shown that "Kennan came closest, and earliest, in his predicting of the fate that would befall Soviet power."

George Q. Flynn, updated by
Joseph R. Rudolph, Jr.

SOURCES FOR FURTHER STUDY

Acheson, Dean. *Present at the Creation: My Years in the State Department.* New York: Norton, 1969.

Jones, Howard. *"A New Kind of War": America's Global Strategy and the Truman Doctrine in Greece.* New York: Oxford University Press, 1989.

Jones, Joseph M. *The Fifteen Weeks (February 21-June 5, 1947).* New York: Viking Press, 1955.

Lieberman, Sanford R., et al., eds. *The Soviet Empire Reconsidered.* Boulder, Colo.: Westview Press, 1994.

McGhee, George Crews. *The U.S.-Turkish-NATO Middle East Connection: How the Truman Doctrine Contained the Soviets in the Middle East.* New York: St. Martin's Press, 1990.

Rees, David. *The Age of Containment: The Cold War, 1945-1965.* New York: St. Martin's Press, 1967.

SEE ALSO: Bretton Woods Agreement (1944); Yalta Conference agreements (1945); National Security Act (1947); Eisenhower Doctrine (1957).

LABOR-MANAGEMENT RELATIONS ACT

ALSO KNOWN AS: Taft-Hartley Act
DATE: June 23, 1947
U.S. STATUTES AT LARGE: 61 Stat. 136
U.S. CODE: 29 § 141
CATEGORIES: Business, Commerce, and Trade; Labor and Employment

By specifically limiting unions' powers, this legislation addressed the public perception of excessive union power in the workplace and was hotly contested by pro-labor constituencies.

In the decade between passage of the National Labor Relations Act (NLRA, also called the Wagner Act) and the end of World War II, union membership tripled. By 1947, there were approximately fifteen million union members in the United States. In 1935, the NLRA had recognized the right of workers to organize and act collectively.

World War II was a period of labor-management harmony. The National War Labor Board, on which both labor and management were represented, controlled wage increases and minimized work stoppages and strikes in the national interest. With the end of the war in 1945, however, overtime pay ended and real income fell with rising inflation. As a result, union leaders came under pressure from the rank and file to secure wage increases which would help restore purchasing power.

In 1945-1946, hours lost to work stoppages and strikes hit a historic high. Employers and the public perceived a growing imbalance in labor-management relations, as unions seemed to be abusing their new-found powers. With the election of a Republican Congress in 1946, legislators were prompt in framing a bill that substantially amended the Wagner Act.

The intent of the Labor-Management Relations Act was to "rein in" the unions in the general public interest. The bill outlawed the "closed shop," which required union membership as a precondition of employment. It also enabled individual states to pass "right to work" legislation allowing a worker not to join a union, even though it represents him. The law itemized a list of "unfair labor practices" that included jurisdictional strikes between worker-competing unions, excessive union initiation fees, refusal to bargain in good faith with employers, and "featherbedding," or forcing employers to hire unessential workers. The act required unions to file financial reports with the Department of Labor and forbade coercion of workers regarding their rights to join or not join a union. It also declared that striking a third party to force that employer to cease doing business with the primary employer—a tactic known as a secondary boycott—is illegal.

The most important aspect of the Taft-Hartley Act was the

eighty-day "cooling off" period, which the president, having declared a national emergency, can seek via court injunction. During this period, labor returns to work while union and management continue to seek an agreement.

Labor railed against the enactment of the Labor-Management Relations Act, calling it a suppression of the labor movement by a malevolent Congress. Membership in unions continued to grow until 1954. The eighty-day cooling off clause was invoked seventeen times by Presidents Harry Truman and Dwight Eisenhower. The reality of a harsher environment for the labor movement was supplemental in the uniting of the American Federation of Labor (AFL) and the Congress of Industrial Organizations (CIO) in 1953.

In October, 2002, a lockout by the managers of the West Coast ports resulted in a work stoppage that deadlocked when managers and dock workers could not agree on workers' participation in the inevitable job restructuring that would follow from the introduction of new technologies in inventory-taking and similar tasks. After two weeks during which incoming goods, including products such as produce and meat, piled up in the Los Angeles, San Francisco, and Seattle ports, President George W. Bush invoked the Taft-Hartley Act to impose the eighty-day cooling-off period. This was only the thirty-fifth time the law had been invoked during a lockout (imposed by managers) as opposed to a strike.

John A. Sondey, updated by
Christina J. Moose

SOURCES FOR FURTHER STUDY

Lee, R. Alton. *Truman and Taft-Hartley: A Question of Mandate*. Westport, Conn.: Greenwood Press, 1980.

Sloan, Irving J., ed. and comp. *The Labor-Management Relations Act of 1947*. Dobbs Ferry, N.Y.: Oceana, 1984.

Smolen, Joseph S., ed. *The National Labor Relations Act: As Amended by the Taft-Hartley Act and the Landrum-Griffin Act*. Minneapolis: University of Minnesota, 1962.

SEE ALSO: Norris-La Guardia Act (1932); National Labor Relations Act (1935); Fair Labor Standards Act (1938); Communist Control Act (1954); Jencks Act (1957); Landrum-Griffin Act (1959).

PRESIDENTIAL SUCCESSION ACT

DATE: July 18, 1947
U.S. STATUTES AT LARGE: 61 Stat. 380
U.S. CODE: 3 § 19
CATEGORIES: Government Procedure and Organization

This amendment corrected weaknesses in the line of presidential succession as outlined in the original Constitution.

The Constitution empowers the Congress to designate which officer shall act as president in case of vacancy of both the president and vice president. The first presidential succession law was written in 1792, making the president pro tempore of the Senate, followed by the Speaker of the House, successors to the president and vice president of the United States.

Concerns about presidential succession grew, however, as a series of events highlighted weaknesses in the current provisions. The possibility of the president pro tempore acting with self-interest was accentuated by the impeachment of President Andrew Johnson in 1868. In addition, if both high posts became vacant during a recess of Congress, there would be neither a Speaker of the House nor a president pro tempore of the Senate to fill the vacancy. Furthermore, party politics made the possibility of a successor of an opposing party an unworkable solution. As a result, the Presidential Succession Act of 1886 designated the secretary of state to exercise presidential power in case both the president and vice president were unable to serve.

The 1886 provisions were in effect at the time that Harry Truman ascended to the White House upon the death of President Franklin Roosevelt. Truman suggested to Congress and eventually secured what were considered more democratic provisions of succession.

The 1947 provisions state that in the case of death, resignation, removal, incapacitation, or failure to qualify the president and vice president, the Speaker of the House of Representatives, upon resigning as Speaker, will act as president. If the Speaker is unable to serve or there is no Speaker, the president pro tempore of the Senate, upon resigning as president pro tempore, shall act as president. Under these circumstances, a person serving utilizes the current presidential power, except when (1) the service is due to the lack of qualifying of the president or vice president, in which case the individual serves only until one of them qualifies, or (2) the service is due to the inability of the president or vice president, in which case the individual serves only until the inability is removed. If there are no presiding legislative officers or those officers lack the qualifications to act as president, Cabinet members in order of their succession will serve, beginning with the secretary of state. The power to act as president exists only until a presiding legislative officer is qualified.

There is ongoing criticism of the Presidential Succession Act. The primary question is that the two presiding legislative officials in the line of succession are not constitutionally designated "officials" and therefore cannot meet the mandate established in Article II for president. Another criticism is that the act declares that someone is president rather than that he or she is to assume those duties only temporarily as acting president. Amendments have been proposed that would alter the current provisions, particularly eliminating the president pro tempore from the line of succession, since the post is largely ceremonial. As Cabinet departments have been created and eliminated, Congress has passed corresponding amendments to the Presidential Succession Act to reflect the change.

Priscilla H. Zotti

SOURCES FOR FURTHER STUDY

Manning, John F. "Not Proved: Some Lingering Questions About Legislative Succession to the Presidency." *Stanford Law Review* 48, no. 141 (1995).

Silva, Ruth C. "The Presidential Succession Act of 1947." *Michigan Law Review* 47, no. 451 (1949).

SEE ALSO: U.S. Constitution: Provisions (1787); Twelfth Amendment (1804); Electoral Count Act (1887); Twentieth Amendment (1933); Twenty-second Amendment (1951); Twenty-fifth Amendment (1967).

NATIONAL SECURITY ACT

DATE: July 26, 1947
U.S. STATUTES AT LARGE: 61 Stat. 496
U.S. CODE: 50 § 401
CATEGORIES: Military and National Security

A new U.S. defense policy avoids costly duplication of effort and allows for flexibility in times of national emergency.

As steps were taken to strengthen the U.S. commitment to European security by means of the Truman Doctrine and the Marshall Plan, it became increasingly clear that measures were needed at home to increase the efficiency of the United States military establishment. A major impetus to the reorganization of the U.S. defense system had come from the obvious weaknesses revealed during World War II. One prime example of such weaknesses was the military disaster at Pearl Harbor. The war also had revealed numerous cases of duplication of effort among the various services. Another new factor that needed to be considered was that Cold War diplomacy required close collaboration between military and diplomatic elements, a condition that had hardly existed during the war. Therefore, many officials, including President Harry S. Truman, thought that the need for a more efficient system of defense was obvious.

DISPUTES AMONG THE THREE SERVICE BRANCHES

On July 26, 1947, the Truman administration accomplished one of its more outstanding contributions, the passage of the National Security Act, but reaching an agreement on the exact details of the reorganization and centralization of the military establishment had not been an easy task. As early as 1945, President Truman had submitted a plan for reorganization to Congress, but it took two years to settle the differences of opinion among the three branches of the armed forces. The Navy was especially reluctant to sacrifice its independence to what it feared would be a defense establishment dominated by the Army. In particular, the Navy feared that the new system might mean the abolishment of the Marines, or at least their transferral to the Army. Another sensitive area of dispute centered on the Navy's newly acquired air capability. Having become firmly convinced of the value of aircraft carriers during World War II, the Navy wanted to expand its air arm, which would include the construction of super-carriers able to accommodate the newly designed jet planes. Many admirals feared that an Army-dominated defense system might mean an emphasis of land-based, long-distance bombers. During 1946 and 1947, President Truman worked to bring together the Army, represented by Secretary of War Robert P. Patterson, and the Navy, represented by Secretary of the Navy James V. Forrestal. In this campaign, Truman was assisted especially by Forrestal, who, although entirely sympathetic to the Navy's point of view, did work for a reasonable compromise.

A New Defense Structure

As a result of these meetings, agreements were reached that culminated in the National Security Act of 1947. The act created a Department of Defense (called the National Military Establishment until 1949) with a secretary holding cabinet rank. The Department of the Army, the Department of the Navy, and a new Department of the Air Force were made into separate subcabinet agencies in the Department of Defense. The act also gave legal recognition to the Joint Chiefs of Staff, with a rotating chairman. Each of the three services would be represented on this committee, which was to be responsible for providing close military coordination, preparing defense plans, and making strategy recommendations to another new agency, the National Security Council, which was to be chaired by the president of the United States. The other members of the National Security Council were to include the vice president, the secretary of state, the secretary of defense, the secretaries of the three services, and the chairman of the board of another new agency, the National Security Resources Board. The president could designate additional persons to serve on the Security Council; under Truman, the council had twenty members. Critics labeled the council "Mr. Truman's Politburo," because it attempted to blend diplomatic and military considerations at the highest level of national interest. Finally, the act created the Central Intelligence Agency as an independent source of security information.

More Interservice Rivalry

This impressive reorganization plan had barely gotten under way when serious problems arose. In some instances, these problems were merely carryovers from the traditional competition between the Army and the Navy; the new system did little to eliminate interservice rivalry, despite the outstanding work of Forrestal as first secretary of defense. Some opponents pointed out that the new system merely created one more contending party, the Air Force. The three services soon were engaged in conducting separate, elaborate publicity and congressional lobbying campaigns to gain increased shares of money for defense purposes. The Navy championed the merits of its super-carrier program, while the Air Force pointed to the new B-36 bomber as the best defense investment. Secretary Forrestal tried to mediate this struggle, but the issues seemed to be beyond the capacity of any one person to control. In failing health, the secretary resigned on March 3, 1949. Although interservice rivalry still existed, Forrestal had reported prior to his resignation that the new defense system had already saved the U.S. taxpayer more than $56 million.

The new secretary of defense appointed by President Truman was Louis A. Johnson of West Virginia, who approached his job with a pugnacious attitude that may have been a result of his lack of administrative experience at a comparably high level of government employment. He soon plunged into the interservice rivalry by favoring the Air Force. The building of new naval aircraft carriers was suspended, and considerable amounts of money went into expanding the strength of the Air Force. Although this executive policy saved money, some critics claimed that it weakened national defense. The State Department joined in the growing criticism of Johnson because it resented the new secretary's unilateral approach to national security. Apparently it was not long before Truman had reason to regret his appointment of Johnson, and in September, 1950, he turned to General George C. Marshall, former secretary of state, to take over the Department of Defense. The simultaneous appointment of Marshall's service colleague, General Omar N. Bradley, as chairman of the Joint Chiefs of Staff helped to make operations smoother within the Defense Department.

THE BATTLE OF THE PENTAGON

Equally important were congressional modifications of the original system. In 1949, the Hoover Commission, appointed by President Truman to investigate government administration and efficiency, reported that changes were needed in the Department of Defense. In August, 1949, a new bill was passed that gave the secretary of defense more power in dealing with the individual services. In July, 1958, the "Battle of the Pentagon" was further resolved with the passage of the Defense Department Reorganization Act.

The full implications of the new diplomatic and military structures created by the National Security Act became evident during the administration of Richard Nixon. Nixon's national security adviser and secretary of state, Henry A. Kissinger, established the supremacy of those two positions over the rest of the foreign-policy-making apparatus. Although efforts were made to decentralize foreign-policy decision making after Kissinger's departure, his legacy continued into subsequent administrations. The overall result of the National Security Act was to create a U.S. foreign-policy-making system that fit the country's new and unprecedented role as a global superpower. The demise of the Cold War at the end of the 1980's helped to spur a reexamination of that system, including the budgetary priority accorded the Department of Defense and the powers and effectiveness of the Central Intelligence Agency.

George Q. Flynn, updated by
Steve D. Boilard

SOURCES FOR FURTHER STUDY

Destler, I. M. "National Security Advice to U.S. Presidents: Some Lessons from Thirty Years." *World Politics* 29, no. 2 (January, 1977): 143-176.

Hoxie, R. Gordon. "James V. Forrestal and the National Security Act of 1947." In *Command Decision and the Presidency: A Study in National Security Policy and Organization.* New York: Readers Digest Press, 1977.

Leffler, Melvyn P. *A Preponderance of Power: National Security, the Truman Administration, and the Cold War.* Stanford, Calif.: Stanford University Press, 1992.

Rosati, Jerel A. "Presidential Management and the NSC Process." In *Politics of United States Foreign Policy.* Fort Worth, Tex.: Harcourt Brace Jovanovich, 1993.

Theoharis, Athan G., ed. *The Truman Presidency: The Origins of the Imperial Presidency and the National Security State.* Stanfordville, N.Y.: Earl M. Coleman Enterprises, 1979.

SEE ALSO: National Defense Act (1916); North Atlantic Treaty (1949); Internal Security Act (1950); War Powers Resolution (1973); USA Patriot Act (2001).

INTER-AMERICAN TREATY OF RECIPROCAL ASSISTANCE

ALSO KNOWN AS: Rio Treaty
DATE: Signed September 2, 1947; U.S. ratification December 19, 1947; in force December 2, 1948
CATEGORIES: Foreign Relations; Treaties and Agreements

A defensive alliance of Western Hemisphere nations, this agreement was a move toward a multilateral approach to the Monroe Doctrine and the most important inter-American agreement in its day.

As World War II approached, hemispheric defense became a matter of concern. The reality of war heightened these feelings and led to the creation of a security mechanism for dealing with a perceived threat to the Americas. From February 21 to March 6, 1945, the Inter-American Conference on War and Peace met in Mexico City and adopted the Act of Chapultepec, which endorsed joint action in repelling any aggression against an American state. Because the agreement was primarily a wartime measure, new conditions of the early postwar era, notably the onset of the Cold War, underscored a need to update the Chapultepec act with a permanent pact.

A COLD WAR ALLIANCE

Foreign ministers of the American republics met from August 15 to September 2, 1947, in Rio de Janeiro. The result was the Inter-American Treaty of Reciprocal Assistance, commonly known as the Rio Treaty. The agreement was a move toward a multilateral approach to the Monroe Doctrine and the most important inter-American agreement up to that time. Signed by participants on September 2, 1947, the Rio Treaty took force on December 12,

1948, in accord with Treaty Article 22, which required ratification by two-thirds of the signatory states.

The treaty's key statement, found in Article 3, states that "an armed attack by any State against an American State shall be considered an attack against all of the American states. . . ." Consultations on matters to which the treaty refers are to be carried out through meetings of foreign ministers of the signatory American republics. This provision was later inserted in the Charter of the Organization of American States (OAS). Finally, efforts were made to coordinate the Rio Treaty with the United Nations Charter, which allowed this type of regional defense organization. Therefore, the U.N. Security Council is recognized as a higher authority.

USE OF THE TREATY

Since the treaty took force in December, 1948, it has been invoked approximately twenty times. One notable occasion was the 1962 Cuban Missile Crisis, when the OAS council authorized use of force for first time under the treaty to halt shipments of military equipment to Cuba from the Soviet bloc. In 1982, OAS members sided with Argentina against Britain in the Falklands War while the United States abstained. On September 19, 2001, the treaty was again invoked in response to the September 11, 2001, terrorist attacks on New York's World Trade Center towers and the Pentagon in Washington, D.C. Under the treaty, force cannot be used against a member state without unanimous consent. However, other measures may be approved by a two-thirds majority.

The Rio Treaty may be seen as a facet of Pan-Americanism, the movement toward economic, military, political, and social cooperation in the Western Hemisphere. The U.S. State Department has described the treaty as "a pillar of collective hemispheric . . . defense architecture." Most, although not all, OAS members are parties to the Rio Treaty. It should also be noted that this pact served as a model for an alliance founded in 1949, the North Atlantic Treaty Organization.

David A. Crain

SOURCES FOR FURTHER STUDY

A Decade of American Foreign Policy: Basic Documents, 1941-1949. Washington, D.C.: Government Printing Office, 1985.

Inman, Samuel G. *Inter-American Conferences, 1826-1954: History and Problems*. St. Louis: Washington University Press, 1965.

SEE ALSO: Monroe Doctrine (1823); Platt Amendment (1903); Good Neighbor Policy (1933); North Atlantic Treaty (1949).

GENERAL AGREEMENT ON TARIFFS AND TRADE OF 1947

DATE: Signed October 30, 1947
CATEGORIES: Agriculture; Business, Commerce, and Trade; Foreign Relations; Tariffs and Taxation; Treaties and Agreements

The General Agreement on Tariffs and Trade set basic rules under which open and nondiscriminatory trade can take place.

On October 30, 1947, representatives of twenty-three countries, meeting in Geneva, Switzerland, signed the General Agreement on Tariffs and Trade (GATT) to reduce trade barriers among signatory nations. GATT was an attempt to combat the rise of worldwide protectionism that had preceded World War II. By providing a set of rules for open and nondiscriminatory trade and a mechanism to implement these rules, GATT sought to create an institutional framework within which international trade could be conducted as stably and predictably as possible.

THE DEPRESSION YEARS

When the Great Depression set in, Congress passed the highly protective Smoot-Hawley Tariff Act in 1930, raising average tariff rates on imports almost 60 percent. Great Britain passed the Import Duties Act in 1932, abandoning its traditional free trade policy. Other countries responded with restrictive import policies in self-defense. The result was a downward spiral in international trade, with the volume of trade in manufactured goods declining by 40 percent by the end of 1932.

The U.S. view on international trade began to change after the Democratic victory in the presidential election in 1932. The new secretary of state, Cordell Hull, strongly favored U.S. leadership in arresting the worldwide protectionist wave. He was convinced that the elimination of trade barriers was the best means of reversing the downward spiral in international trade, which would in turn allow higher standards of living for all countries and promote lasting peace. After several years of his intensive lobbying, the Reciprocal Trade Agreements Act (RTA Act), an amendment of the Smoot-Hawley Act, was passed in 1934. The RTA Act empowered the president, for a period of three years, to initiate trade agreements on the basis of reciprocal tariff reductions. Reductions of U.S. tariffs were limited to 50 percent. The RTA Act was extended several times. The United States concluded agreements with twenty-nine countries on the basis of most-favored-nation treatment before the outbreak of World War II. The idea of negotiating reciprocal tariff reductions, embodied in the RTA Act, was the conceptual basis for GATT.

BRETTON WOODS
Soon after the United States entered World War II, the Allied nations, particularly the United States and Great Britain, started discussion on postwar trade and monetary issues. The discussion led to the Bretton Woods Conference in July, 1944, at Bretton Woods, New Hampshire. This conference established the charters of the International Monetary Fund and the International Bank for Reconstruction and Development (commonly known as the World Bank) to deal with international monetary issues. It also recognized the need for a comparable institution focusing on trade to complement the monetary institutions.

THE INTERNATIONAL TRADE ORGANIZATION
Negotiations on the form and functions of an International Trade Organization (ITO) were first held on a bilateral basis between the United States and Great Britain. The United States pressed for nondiscrimination, whereby no country is favored over others, Great Britain insisted on continuation of its Imperial Preference, under which British goods receive preferential access to the markets of its former colonies and vice versa. A compromise was reached, and the results of those bilateral negotiations were pub-

lished in November, 1945, in the Proposals for Expansion of World Trade and Employment. The United States expanded those proposals into a draft charter for the ITO in 1946. The charter was amended in successive conferences from 1946 to 1948 in London, New York, Geneva, and Havana. The final version of the ITO charter, known as the Havana Charter, was drawn up in Havana on March 4, 1948. The charter, which represented a series of agreements among fifty-three countries, never came into effect because most countries, including the United States, failed to ratify it.

THE BIRTH OF GATT
At the same time that the United States published the proposals, it invited several countries to participate in negotiations to reduce tariffs and other trade barriers on the basis of principles laid out in the proposals. The United States proposed to embody all individual treaties into a multilateral treaty. GATT was thus drawn up as a general framework for rights and obligations of tariff reductions for twenty-three participating nations. GATT came into being before the Havana Conference but in accordance with the draft charter for the ITO that was currently under discussion. It was originally envisaged as the first of a number of agreements that were to be negotiated under the auspices of the ITO. It was supposed to be a provisional agency that would go out of existence once the ITO was established. The power and the bureaucratic size of the proposed ITO faced strong opposition in the U.S. Congress. Consequently, the Havana Charter was not put before the U.S. Senate for ratification for fear of its defeat. When it was clear that the United States would not ratify the Havana Charter, GATT became by default the underpinning of an international institution, assuming part of the commercial policy role that had been assigned to the ITO.

PROVISIONS OF GATT
Technically speaking, GATT is not an organization of which countries become members but a treaty among contracting parties. As a multilateral agreement, GATT has no binding authority over its signatories. When countries agree to GATT, they are expected to commit to three fundamental principles: nondiscrimination, as embodied in the most-favored-nation clause (all countries should be treated equally); a general prohibition of export subsidies (ex-

cept for agriculture) and import quotas, from which developing countries are exempted; and a requirement that any new tariff be offset by a reduction in other tariffs.

The agreement itself was without precedent. No agreement had ever been completed before GATT that included more countries, covered more trade, involved more extensive actions, or represented a wider consensus on commercial policy. It provided a promising contrast to the record of failures to liberalize trade that had characterized the years between the two world wars.

Among the twenty-three participating countries, 123 bilateral negotiations occurred. The United States was a party to 22 of them, and the remaining 101 took place among the other members of the group. The signatory nations accounted for more than three-fourths of world trade, and negotiations covered two-thirds of trade among member nations. Tariff was reduced on about fifty thousand items, accounting for about half of world trade. Average tariff rates were cut by about one-third in the United States. By 1950, average tariffs on dutiable imports into the United States had fallen by about 75 percent as compared to Smoot-Hawley levels.

Assessment and Later Agreements

GATT is a remarkable success story of an international organization. Over the years, it has provided the framework for an open trade system and a set of rules for nondiscrimination and settlement of international trade disputes. From 1947 to 1979, seven "rounds" of trade negotiations were completed under GATT auspices: in 1947 (Geneva), 1949 (Annecy, France), 1951 (Torquay, the United Kingdom), 1956 (Geneva), 1960-1961 (Geneva, the "Dillion Round"), 1962-1967 (Geneva, the "Kennedy Round"), and 1973-1979 (Tokyo). An eighth session began in 1986 (the "Uruguay Round") and ended in December, 1993. The tariff reductions in rounds two through five were minimal. The volumes of trade covered by the fourth and fifth rounds were only $2.5 and $4.9 billion. The Kennedy Round and the Tokyo Round resulted in significant economic benefits to all major trading nations.

Significant progress toward free trade among market economy (nonsocialist) countries in manufactured and semimanufactured goods was accomplished in the Kennedy Round. The value of trade covered in these negotiations among forty-eight countries was $40 billion. Duties were cut on average by 35 percent spreading over the broadest set of products (sixty thousand) to date, with some cuts made on almost 80 percent of all dutiable imports. By the conclusion of this round, the weighted average tariff rate of the United States was 8.3 percent, that of the original six European Economic Community (EEC) countries was 8.3 percent, that of the United Kingdom was 10.2 percent, and that of Japan was 10.9 percent. Post-Kennedy Round tariffs in industrial countries averaged 8.7 percent. For the first time, an agreement was reached to resolve conflicts over nontariff barriers, particularly elimination of import quotas on almost all nonagricultural products. In some cases, tariffs were completely eliminated, as for tropical food products from developing countries. Developing countries played a minor role in negotiations and were not subject to significant tariff reductions.

The Tokyo Round was negotiated by ninety-nine countries and covered $155 billion in trade. The average tariff cut was about 34 percent. By the conclusion of this round, the weighted average tariff rates on finished and semifinished manufactures of the United States was 4.9 percent, that of EEC countries was 6.0 percent, and that of Japan was 5.4 percent. Post-Tokyo Round tariffs among industrial countries stood at an average of 4.7 percent. The Tokyo Round negotiations resulted in the first comprehensive agreement on reducing nontariff barriers such as quotas. The Tokyo Round failed to reach an agreement on a safeguard code and on eliminating heavy restrictions on trade on agricultural products.

The most complex and ambitious round, the Uruguay Round, was launched by ninety countries on September 20, 1986, in Punta del Este, Uruguay. Originally scheduled to be completed by the end of 1990, the Uruguay Round was aimed at the further liberalization and expansion of trade. It sought to extend GATT principles to new sectors (agriculture, services), improve their application to old sectors (textiles, garments), reexamine old issues (safeguard protections), and embrace new issues such as intellectual property, with discussion of copyrights, computer software, and patent protection. By early 1993, no agreement had been reached because of disputes between the European Community and the United States regarding agricultural subsidies. Various compromises resulted in an agreement in December.

Baban Hasnat

SOURCES FOR FURTHER STUDY

Bhagwati, Jagdish. *The World Trading System at Risk.* Princeton, N.J.: Princeton University Press, 1991.

Dam, Kenneth W. *The GATT Law and International Economic Organization.* Chicago: University of Chicago Press, 1970.

Gardner, Richard N. *Sterling-Dollar Diplomacy The Origins and the Prospects of Our International Economic Order.* Expanded ed. New York: McGraw-Hill, 1969.

Jackson, John H. *Restructuring the GATT System.* New York: Council on Foreign Relations Press, 1990.

_____. *The World Trading System Law and Policy of International Economic Relations.* Cambridge, Mass.: MIT Press, 1989.

Kock, Karin. *International Trade Policy and the Gatt 1947-1967.* Stockholm, Sweden: Almqvist & Wiksell, 1969.

Tussie, Diana. *The Less Developed Countries and the World Trading System: A Challenge to the GATT.* New York: St. Martin's Press, 1987.

Wilcox, Clair. *A Charter for World Trade.* New York: Macmillan, 1949.

SEE ALSO: Smoot-Hawley Tariff Act (1930); Good Neighbor Policy (1933); Miller-Tydings Fair Trade Act (1937); Bretton Woods Agreement (1944); North American Free Trade Agreement (1993); General Agreement on Tariffs and Trade of 1994 (1994).

WATER POLLUTION CONTROL ACT

DATE: June 30, 1948
U.S. STATUTES AT LARGE: 62 Stat. 1155
PUBLIC LAW: 80-845
U.S. CODE: 33 § 1251
CATEGORIES: Environment and Conservation; Natural Resources

The Water Pollution Control Act extended the reach of the federal government by establishing cooperative arrangements with the states for grants, research, and technical assistance.

On June 30, 1948, President Harry S. Truman signed the Water Pollution Control Act (WPCA). The act addressed the nation's water-quality problems by attempting to establish a cooperative relationship between the federal and state governments. It resulted from decades of debate over the appropriate role of the national government in what was long considered a state concern. Amended several times by Congress, the 1948 legislation was the model for future federal clean-water statutes.

PRIOR LEGISLATION AND POLICY
Prior to 1948, Congress had considered nearly one hundred measures dealing with water pollution but had passed only three. The Refuse Act (1886) prohibited dumping of refuse that obstructed navigation in New York Harbor. The Rivers and Harbors Act (1899) broadened the refuse regulations to any navigable water in the United States. The Oil Pollution Act (1924) prohibited discharging petroleum in coastal waters. Aside from these three regulations, the federal government offered research and technical assistance to the states through the Public Health Service, the U.S. Geological Survey, the Army Corps of Engineers, and the Bureau of Mines.

The management of pollution in the first half of the twentieth century was considered a state responsibility. Most states had created health departments to act on water-quality issues, especially as they related to waterborne diseases such as typhoid that produce high death rates. Local governments had made meaningful progress in supplying potable water supplies. Population growth and the expansion of manufacturing, however, inundated the nation's waters with sewage and industrial wastes.

THE NEED FOR NATIONAL REGULATION
In the twentieth century, water-quality problems became so acute and difficult to manage that state governments put pressure on Congress to provide additional assistance. The problem was especially severe in rivers that flowed through several states. Congressional action resulted in increased research support that tended to illustrate the magnitude of the problem, increase public concern, and clarify the need for federal involvement.

Water Pollution in the United States (1934), the most meaningful survey during the period, was undertaken by the National Resources Committee to inform Congress and President Franklin D. Roosevelt of the status of the nation's rivers and to offer recommendations. The committee, chaired by the renowned sanitary engineer Abel Wolman, compiled its report using the science and technical skills of some of the leading engineering and sanitation experts in the United States. Produced with the assistance of the U.S. Public Health Service, the Army Corps of Engineers, and representatives from the states and industry, the report recognized stream pollution as a growing threat to the nation. It focused on dangers for the populated Northeast, where rivers were drinking sources as well as sinks for domestic and industrial wastes. The advisory committee's recommendation recognized the role of the federal government as a cooperative party to the states, and made recommendations that would enlarge the national government's role. Many of these recommendations are found in the 1948 legislation.

In 1935, Senator Augustine Lonergan of Connecticut, encouraged by conservation groups such as the Izaak Walton League of America, the General Federation of Women's Clubs, and state governments, proposed federal water-pollution control legislation. After a series of debates and revisions, a bill was passed in 1939, only to be vetoed by President Roosevelt because of technical errors relating to grant allocations. In 1940, Congress considered a revised bill, but it died, and Congress then became distracted by the demands of World War II.

PASSAGE AND PROVISIONS

The Water Pollution Control Act of 1948, sponsored by senators Alben Barkley of Kentucky and Robert A. Taft of Ohio, authorized federal grants to state and municipal governments and interstate agencies to help finance engineering studies and construction of water-treatment works. The act provided $1 million a year for the studies (limited to $20,000 each or one-third of actual cost), $1 million a year for examination of industrial waste problems, and $22 million a year for treatment-plant construction loans (limited to $250,000 each or one-third estimated cost), with total expenditures of $216 million over eight years.

The WPCA authorized the Public Health Service to enhance its existing research functions and produce extensive programs with the states and interstate agencies to seek solutions to all aspects of water pollution, to support uniform water standards, and to promulgate interstate agreements. The Division of Water Pollution Control, created as a department of the Public Health Service, was designated to administer the legislation. It established ten field units in the United States, with a base of operations and main research facility, the Robert A. Taft Sanitary Engineering Center, in Cincinnati, Ohio.

The act provided for federal enforcement, but only at state request. With the WPCA, Congress attempted to promote state and federal cooperation—a sharing of responsibility. The states maintained control but received technical and financial assistance.

IMPLEMENTATION AND IMPACT

Conflicts within Congress and the White House over funding, authority of the federal government, and reluctance by some states that feared federal domination and defended "states' rights" restrained the full implementation of the WPCA. Because of budget and political constraints, the construction-loan program was never funded. Only about $11 million was appropriated, mostly devoted to Public Health Services projects. Thus, although the WPCA proved ineffective in providing meaningful solutions to the nation's pollution problems, it opened the door for greater federal involvement in the decades ahead. Amendments to the WPCA in 1956, 1961, 1965, and 1966 expanded federal participation.

As a matter of public-policy philosophy, Congress justified the act by stating that the nation's health and welfare depended on water-pollution control. Although the WPCA established in Congress some jurisdiction over pollution control in the nation's waters, it reaffirmed the states' primary responsibility and authority. With subsequent amendments, this authority would shift toward a national policy.

The significance of the Water Pollution Control Act was in expanding the existing research and technical role of the federal government and, at the same time, establishing a rationale for future expansion and domination of water-quality issues. Though the act itself had little immediate impact, it constituted a shift in responsibility away from the states to the national government. Funding for water-treatment and sewage facilities became entwined with state acceptance of federally approved water standards, research techniques, and statutes.

Congress expanded the role of the U.S. Public Health Service to facilitate the gathering of information. As the research revealed the extent of harm done, and as the states realized that many of these problems were beyond their control, pressure mounted on Congress to broaden its responsibility. Thus federalism, centralization, and science transformed water-control legislation during an era when regulatory authority shifted from the states to the national government. The WPCA represents a crucial point in that shift.

The broadening of federal authority in 1948 also established a rationale for closer examination of another environmental problem—air pollution. Four months after the WPCA passage, Donora, Pennsylvania, experienced a heavy smog that killed twenty people and sickened 43 percent of the population. The Donora event prompted an investigation by the U.S. Public Health Service and led to the passage of the Air Pollution Control Act (1955), which was approximately modeled on the WPCA.

Nicholas A. Casner

SOURCES FOR FURTHER STUDY

Davies, J. Clarence, and Barbara S. Davies. *The Politics of Pollution.* Indianapolis: Bobbs-Merrill, 1975.

Dworsky, Leonard B. "Analysis of Federal Water Pollution Control Legislation, 1948-1966." *Journal of the American Water Works Association* 59 (June, 1967): 651-668.

_____. *Conservation in the United States: Documentary History—Pollution.* Edgemont, Pa.: Chelsea House, 1971.

Melosi, Martin V. *Pollution and Reform in American Cities, 1870-1930.* Austin: University of Texas Press, 1980.

Murphy, Earl Finbar. *Water Purity: A Study in Legal Control of Natural Resources.* Madison: University of Wisconsin Press, 1961.

Tarr, Joel A. "The Search for the Ultimate Sink: Urban Air, Land, and Water Pollution in Historical Perspective." *Records of the Historical Society of Washington, D.C.* 51 (1984): 1-29.

U.S. Congress. House, National Resource Committee. *Water Pollution in the United States.* Third Report of the Special Advisory Committee. House Document No. 155. Washington, D.C.: Government Printing Office, 1939.

U.S. Treasury Department. *Stream Pollution: A Digest of Judicial Decisions and Compilation of Legislation Relating to the Subject.* Public Health Service Bulletin No. 87. Washington, D.C.: Government Printing Office, 1918.

SEE ALSO: Oil Pollution Act of 1924 (1924); Air Pollution Control Act (1955); Water Pollution Control Act Amendments of 1956 (1956); Water Resources Research Act (1964); Clean Water Act and Amendments (1965); Wild and Scenic Rivers Act and National Trails System Act (1968); Water Pollution Control Act Amendments of 1972 (1972); Safe Drinking Water Act (1974); Toxic Substances Control Act (1976); Oil Pollution Act of 1990 (1990).

GENOCIDE TREATY

ALSO KNOWN AS: Convention on the Prevention and Punishment of the Crime of Genocide

DATE: Signed December 12, 1948; in force 1951; U.S. ratification November 23, 1988

CATEGORIES: Foreign Relations; Treaties and Agreements

Although it took the United States four decades to ratify the treaty, this international agreement made genocide an international crime during both war and peace.

Horrified by the extermination of six million Jews during World War II, Polish professor of international law Raphael Lemkin coined the term "genocide," which combined the Greek word for race or nation, *genos*, with the Latin-derived root for killing, *cide*. After the Nuremberg Trials revealed the extent of Nazi atrocities, human rights lawyers in the United Nations hoped that a treaty would prevent, or at least minimize, such acts in the future.

The Convention on the Prevention and Punishment of the Crime of Genocide, receiving U.N. endorsement in 1948 and entering into force in 1951, recognized genocide as a crime under international law in times of either war or peace. The treaty defined genocide as any of five acts: (1) killing members of a particular "national, ethnic, racial, or religious group," (2) causing them "serious bodily or mental harm," (3) deliberately creating conditions calculated to bring about a group's full or partial destruction, (4) imposing measures to prevent births in a group, and (5) forcibly removing children from a group.

Those nations ratifying the treaty have the obligation of enforcing its provisions with appropriate legislation. Any party to the treaty has the right to call on U.N. bodies to take action suppressing or preventing genocidal acts. Prosecution for genocidal acts may be conducted by either domestic or international courts. Disagreements between governments about applications of the treaty are to be arbitrated by the International Court of Justice.

Although President Harry S. Truman signed the treaty in 1948, the U.S. Senate did not ratify it until forty years later. Even then, the Senate specified a number of "reservations" and "understandings" for its enforcement. The most significant reservation was that no dispute in which the United States was a party could be submitted to the International Court of Justice without U.S. consent. The most noteworthy understanding was that the treaty would require no action prohibited by the U.S. Constitution as interpreted by the United States. These conditions mean that the U.S. government reserves the right to decide whether and how the treaty might be applied to itself. Other countries have adopted similar restrictions.

Despite numerous instances of genocide, the punishment of violators by international courts did not take place until the 1990's, when the United Nations authorized prosecutions for crimes against humanity in Rwanda and the former Yugoslavia. In 1998, a Rwandan mayor was the first person to be convicted of genocide, and the conviction of a Bosnian Serb was handed down in 2001.

A more important step toward enforcement of the Genocide Treaty was the establishment of an International Criminal Court (ICC) with jurisdiction over cases of genocide and other crimes against humanity. When it entered into force in July, 2002, the effectiveness of the ICC was uncertain, because loopholes allowed countries to shield their citizens from ICC prosecution for war crimes and because several countries, including the United States, refused to ratify the ICC treaty.

Thomas T. Lewis

SOURCES FOR FURTHER STUDY
Ball, Howard. *Prosecuting War Crimes and Genocide: The Twentieth-Century Experience.* Lawrence: University Press of Kansas, 1999.

LeBlanc, Lawrence. *The United States and the Genocide Convention.* Durham, N.C.: Duke University Press, 1991.

Power, Samantha. *A Problem from Hell: America and the Age of Genocide.* New York: Basic Books, 2002.

SEE ALSO: Geneva Protocol (1925); Kellogg-Briand Pact (1928); Yalta Conference agreements (1945).

NORTH ATLANTIC TREATY

DATE: Signed April 4, 1949
CATEGORIES: Foreign Relations; Military and National Security; Treaties and Agreements

Twelve democracies, including the United States and Canada, established an association for mutual defense against the Soviet Union.

On April 4, 1949, the United States and eleven other nations (Belgium, Canada, Denmark, France, Great Britain, Iceland, Italy, Luxembourg, the Netherlands, Norway, and Portugal) signed a treaty of alliance establishing the North Atlantic Treaty Organization (NATO), committing the signatories to the principle of common security on a regional basis. By joining, the United States under President Harry S. Truman took a precedent-shattering step; it had never before concluded a military alliance in peacetime with any European state. Participation in NATO meant that the United States had modified one of its oldest principles, which stemmed from the advice of George Washington and Thomas Jefferson: to avoid entangling alliances.

COLD WAR POLICIES

The genesis for such an alliance emerged from the Truman administration's containment policy, with the fundamental objective of opposing Soviet expansionist efforts in Europe after World War II. The United States had committed itself in the 1947 Truman Doctrine to assisting European nations facing civil war or external threats from the Soviet Union. The United States extended military and economic aid to Greece and Turkey that year (April 23) to counter Soviet ambitions in the region, as those countries were too weak to be self-sustaining.

Also in 1947, Secretary of State George Marshall proposed the more ambitious European Recovery Program. Economic aid through this costly effort, often called the Marshall Plan, greatly assisted the European economy after the program began in 1948. There was widespread belief in the United States, however, that Europe's full economic and psychological recovery would not be possible until Europeans believed themselves safe from the threat of the Red Army. Thus, military security was essential for continued economic recovery.

Several major events in 1948 revealed the widening Cold War in Europe. A communist *coup d'état* in Czechoslovakia, the Soviet blockade of Berlin (lasting into 1949), and other Soviet actions convinced the Truman administration of the need for more extensive, long-term U.S. involvement in Europe. Despite appeals from European leaders for the creation of a common front, however, Truman was not sufficiently confident of public and congressional support to move directly toward an alliance. In June, 1948, the Senate approved the Vandenberg Resolution by a vote of 64 to 4, which declared support for U.S. participation in regional arrangements for "continuous and effective self-help and mutual aid." This pronouncement was interpreted by some as an attempt to limit presidential power in foreign affairs rather than as a sincere expression of support for collective security. Only after the presidential election of 1948 and cautious discussions with the principal European nations did the Truman administration act to move the United States away from its traditional isolationism.

LOOKING FOR SECURITY IN EUROPE

In March, 1948, five European nations—Great Britain, France, Belgium, the Netherlands, and Luxembourg—signed the Brussels Pact, a fifty-year defensive alliance. Its terms obligated the signatories to come to the aid of any member attacked by an aggressor. The Brussels Pact nations invited the United States to participate, but there were numerous obstacles to concerted action at that time, even though the Vandenberg Resolution showed U.S. interest in a mutual security system. In January, 1949, more positive support was expressed in Truman's inaugural address, which promised that the United States would contribute to the defense of friendly nations.

The United States began negotiations with a number of European states, with the aim of creating a cooperative system of military security against the presumed Soviet threat to Western Europe. These discussions were criticized by some people in the United States and especially by communist authorities in Moscow. They accused the United States of undercutting the United Nations and jeopardizing world peace by forming a bloc of states for aggressive purposes. The United States answered this accusation by pointing out that Article 51 of the U.N. Charter allowed for regional defense pacts, and that the proposed alliance clearly was defensive in character.

Dean Acheson, who succeeded Marshall as secretary of state in early 1949, believed that the United States should look to military and diplomatic arrangements to meet the communist challenge rather than rely upon the institutional procedures of the United Nations, which could be blocked by a Soviet veto. Negotiations achieved the desired objective of an expanded association of democratic states. In ceremonies in Washington, D.C., on April 4, 1949, the North Atlantic Treaty was signed by representatives of twelve nations—Belgium, Canada, Denmark, France, Iceland, Italy, Luxembourg, the Netherlands, Norway, Portugal, the United States, and the United Kingdom. They reaffirmed their support of the United Nations, vowed to cooperate in the maintenance of the stability and well-being of the North Atlantic region, and promised to work together for collective defense and the preservation of peace and general security.

TREATY PROVISIONS

Although the pact bound its members to settle international disputes by peaceful means, Article 5 stated that "the Parties agree that an armed attack against one or more of them in Europe or North America shall be considered an attack against them all." Any attack would be met by armed force, if necessary. Each member state was permitted to adopt its own response to aggression after consultation with its allies. The treaty provided for the establishment of the NATO council, on which each of the signatory states was to be represented. The council created a defense committee and other departments to develop measures for the nations' common defense. No signatory was committed absolutely to go to war, but the treaty was a powerful moral commitment to aid members threatened by aggression. The treaty was to be in effect for at least twenty years, and could be renewed.

Senate hearings on the North Atlantic Treaty, while not endangering its chances of ratification by the United States, resulted in sometimes bitter debate concerning the wisdom of U.S. involvement. Prominent national political figures, such as Senator Robert Taft, warned against the United States assuming major long-term responsibilities. These discussions revealed that the Truman administration could not anticipate all the military implications of the new alliance. Nevertheless, on July 21, 1949, the Senate approved the North Atlantic Treaty by a vote of 82 to 13. Eleven of the thirteen who voted "no" were Republicans, but both Republicans and Democrats supported the treaty. By late August, following ratification by member governments, the North Atlantic Treaty Organization officially went into effect. The next two years saw the creation of the alliance's administrative structure and the planning for military cooperation under the NATO system.

LONG-RANGE SIGNIFICANCE

The adoption of the pact demonstrated the signatories' willingness to make military commitments for their common security. Although NATO was never used in actual combat with the Soviet Union, its formation illustrated the unity of spirit and dedication of its Western democracies. Members who entered NATO later included Greece and Turkey (1952), West Germany (1955), and Spain (1981). NATO succeeded in fulfilling its primary purpose of creating a viable military counterweight to Soviet power.

With the collapse of communist systems in the states of Eastern Europe in 1989, followed by the disintegration of the Soviet Union in 1991, the relevance and functions of NATO had to be considered. Despite the apparent ending of the Cold War, all member governments agreed that the organization still served the primary objective of promoting stability within Europe, even as new problems (such as the Yugoslav civil war) appeared on the horizon. Several East European states formerly associated with the Soviet Union applied during the 1990's for NATO membership, fearful of the possibility of a resurgence of Russian expansionism. Moscow initially opposed those overtures, providing renewed credibility of the need for this defensive alliance system to exist against potential Russian aggression in the twenty-first century. Ironically, only a decade later, Russia and the United States had formed a closer relationship in response to terrorist actions in the late 1990's and culminating in terrorist attacks on U.S. soil in September, 2001. The deaths of more than three thousand citizens from scores of nations when terrorist flew passenger jets into the World Trade Center towers and the Pentagon forced world nations to reassess old alliances.

Theodore A. Wilson, updated by
Taylor Stults

SOURCES FOR FURTHER STUDY

Acheson, Dean. *Present at the Creation: My Years in the State Department.* New York: W. W. Norton, 1969.

Feis, Herbert. *From Trust to Terror: The Onset of the Cold War, 1945-1950.* New York: W. W. Norton, 1970.

Kaplan, Lawrence S. *NATO and the United States: The Enduring Alliance.* New York: Twayne, 1988.

Rose, Clive. *Campaigns Against Western Defence: NATO's Adversaries and Critics.* New York: St. Martin's Press, 1985.

Sherwen, Nicholas, ed. *NATO's Anxious Birth: The Prophetic Vision of the 1940's.* New York: St. Martin's Press, 1985.

Truman, Harry. *Memoirs: Years of Trial and Hope, 1946-1952.* Garden City, N.Y.: Doubleday, 1956.

Vandenberg, Arthur H. *The Private Papers of Senator Vandenberg.* Boston: Houghton Mifflin, 1952.

SEE ALSO: Monroe Doctrine (1823); Neutrality Acts (1935-1939); Lend-Lease Act (1941); Bretton Woods Agreement (1944); Yalta Conference agreements (1945); Truman Doctrine (1947); Eisenhower Doctrine (1957); Nuclear Test Ban Treaty (1963); Nuclear Nonproliferation Treaty (1968); SALT I Treaty (1972); SALT II Treaty (1979); INF Treaty (1987); START II Treaty (1993); U.S.-Russia Arms Agreement (2002).

NAVAJO-HOPI REHABILITATION ACT

DATE: April 19, 1950
U.S. STATUTES AT LARGE: 64 Stat. 44
PUBLIC LAW: 81-474
U.S. CODE: 25 § 631
CATEGORIES: Native Americans

In an attempt to improve conditions in one of the most impoverished areas of the United States, this act funded the construction of roads, schools, and other developments on the Navajo and Hopi reservations.

The Navajo-Hopi Long Range Rehabilitation Act of 1950 was passed by Congress to construct basic facilities on the Navajo and Hopi reservations. Passed in response to more than twenty years of deteriorating economic conditions on the Navajo Reservation, the act authorized funding for school construction, roads, and other projects.

In the 1930's the federal government had initiated a range-management program on the Navajo and Hopi reservations. Central to the program was reducing the amount of livestock on the range. This devastated the Navajo sheep-based pastoral economy. The full effects of stock reduction were partially obscured during World War II, when thousands of Navajos joined the service or worked in war-related industries. When these people returned home, however, livestock regulations and insufficient resources prevented a renewal of the pastoral economy. Unusually harsh winters added to the distress and drew national attention to the impoverished conditions among the more than sixty thousand Navajos residing in Navajo country.

Reservation schools could accommodate only about 25 percent of the student-age population. All-weather roads were practically nonexistent on the reservations. Inadequate roads contributed to health, education, and economic problems. Infant mortality was high and school enrollments low. After passing minor emergency relief measures, Congress considered a more comprehensive approach. A 1949 bill to fund improvements on the Navajo and Hopi reservations, reflecting a resurgent congressional interest in limiting tribal sovereignty, also included a provision that extended the jurisdiction of state law over the two reservations. Citing this provision, President Harry Truman vetoed the bill.

In 1950 the president signed the Navajo Rehabilitation Act, which emerged from Congress without the offending jurisdictional provision. This version also provided expanded opportunities for Hopi participation in projects. The act appropriated $88,570,000. The largest portion, $25 million, was for school construction, followed by $20 million for roads and $19 million for rangelands and irrigation projects. Lesser amounts were appropriated for health and water facilities, industrial development, and other projects. More than $9 million was allocated for relocating and resettling individuals away from the two reservations. There were also provisions for loans and leases. Finally, one provision (ignored for more than thirty years) authorized the Navajo tribe to adopt a tribal constitution. In 1958, Public Law 85-740 provided an additional $20 million to complete road construction. By 1962, more than 80 percent of the total appropriation had been expended, including nearly all the dollars targeted for roads and schools.

The major benefit of the act was the substantial improvement in roads and schools on the reservation. All-weather roads have provided greater access to job locations and markets. School attendance increased dramatically through the 1950's and 1960's, as did the overall educational attainment of the population.

Eric Henderson

SOURCE FOR FURTHER STUDY
Parman, Donald L. *The Navajos and the New Deal.* New Haven, Conn.: Yale University Press, 1976.

SEE ALSO: Navajo-Hopi Land Settlement Act (1974).

INTERNAL SECURITY ACT

ALSO KNOWN AS: McCarran Act
DATE: September 23, 1950
U.S. STATUTES AT LARGE: 64 Stat. 987
U.S. CODE: 50 § 831
CATEGORIES: Civil Rights and Liberties; Military and National Security

This statute, which established the Subversive Activities Control Board, aimed at stopping communist subversion in the United States, calling for the registration of all known communist organizations and individuals in the United States.

The Internal Security Act, sponsored by Senator Patrick A. McCarran of Nevada, attacked the alleged communist threat. It created a Subversive Activities Control Board that could, with approval of the U.S. attorney general, order an organization that it found to be communist to register with the Justice Department and submit information concerning its membership, activities, and finances. Furthermore, the act prohibited known communists from being employed by the federal government, denied them the right to use U.S. passports, and made it a felony for anyone to attempt to establish a totalitarian dictatorship in the United States. Another provision arranged for emergency arrest and detention of any person likely to commit espionage or sabotage.

President Harry S. Truman vetoed the act on the grounds that it violated the Bill of Rights, but his veto was overridden by an 89 percent majority vote. McCarran's newly formed Senate Internal Security Subcommittee worked closely with the Federal Bureau of Investigation and conducted hearings for the next twenty-seven years in an attempt to enforce the act. In *Communist Party v. Subversive Activities Control Board* (1961), the Supreme Court upheld the legality of registration but would not rule on the constitutionality of the 1950 act until it was enforced. In *Albertson v. Subversive Activities Control Board* (1965), the Supreme Court ruled that registration, which could have negative repercussions, was self-incrimination and therefore violated the Fifth Amendment. In 1968 Congress

amended the 1950 act to eliminate the self-registration requirements, and the act's provisions were dismantled piece by piece during the 1970's.

Alvin K. Benson

SOURCE FOR FURTHER STUDY
Library of Congress. Legislative Reference Service. *Internal Security
Act of 1950, as Amended, and Communist Control Act of 1954.* 91st
Congress, 1st session. Washington, D.C.: Government Printing
Office, 1969.

SEE ALSO: Fifth Amendment (1789); Espionage Acts (1917-1918);
Smith Act (1940); Communist Control Act (1954).

CELLER-KEFAUVER ACT

DATE: December 29, 1950
U.S. STATUTES AT LARGE: 64 Stat. 1125
CATEGORIES: Business, Commerce, and Trade

> *By prohibiting certain types of mergers between firms in the same in-
> dustry, the Celler-Kefauver Act led companies to form conglomerates
> made up of companies in unrelated industries.*

The Celler-Kefauver Act of 1950 amended the Clayton Act by closing a loophole that had allowed companies to avoid antitrust suits
by acquiring the assets (rather than the stock) of another company.
Government enforcement of the Celler-Kefauver Act encouraged
companies to seek growth through a strategy of diversification.
Thus, the Celler-Kefauver Act contributed to the conglomerate
movement of the 1960's.

THE CLAYTON ACT
The roots of the Celler-Kefauver Act can be traced to passage of the
Clayton Antitrust Act in 1914. Section 2 of this law prohibited busi-
ness firms from acquiring the stock of another company if the re-

sulting merger lessened competition. The Clayton Act, however, made no mention of mergers based on the purchase of another company's assets. During the 1920's, American companies took advantage of this loophole to form mergers based on the acquisition of assets. The Federal Trade Commission (FTC) prosecuted the companies involved in these mergers but, in 1926, the Supreme Court ruled that the Clayton Act did not apply to acquisition of corporate assets. The Court's interpretation made the Clayton Act an ineffective weapon against monopoly.

In 1927, the FTC asked Congress to amend the Clayton Act to close the loophole, but during this prosperous decade Congress lost interest in strict enforcement of the antitrust laws. During the late 1920's and early 1930's, the government downplayed antitrust policy as President Herbert Hoover encouraged corporations to cooperate in a wide range of activities. President Franklin D. Roosevelt granted antitrust exemptions to those companies cooperating with the National Recovery Administration (1933-1935). NRA officials hoped that cooperation in the form of mergers and price controls would lift the nation out of the Great Depression.

During the late 1930's, Roosevelt reversed direction and attempted to silence his critics in big business by supporting a renewed antitrust campaign led by Thurman Arnold, head of the Justice Department's Antitrust Division. Roosevelt also called for the creation of a Temporary National Economic Committee (TNEC) to study the effects of monopoly on the American economy. In its final report, in 1941, the TNEC recommended passage of legislation designed to close the asset loophole. Along with officials in the FTC and the Justice Department, the members of the TNEC formed an activist community committed to strengthening the nation's antimonopoly legislation. Although World War II brought a temporary halt to their activity, this antitrust community pledged to resume its antimonopoly crusade once the war ended.

RENEWED CALLS FOR ANTITRUST MEASURES

Several factors sparked a renewed interest in antitrust enforcement in the immediate postwar period. First, a growing number of observers worried that the wartime placement of military contracts with big business had increased the overall level of economic concentration. In December, 1946, the House Small Business Committee's Subcommittee on Monopoly (chaired by Estes Kefauver, a liberal Democrat from Tennessee) issued a report concluding that big business had benefited disporportionately from the wartime boom. The Kefauver report criticized the lackluster wartime performance of the government's antitrust agencies and called for an amendment to the Clayton Act that would close the asset loophole. Meanwhile, the FTC tried to justify its existence by securing passage of stronger antitrust legislation. The FTC described the weak merger movement of the late 1940's as a grave threat to competition. The FTC enjoyed the support of President Harry S. Truman, a longtime advocate of antitrust enforcement. During his presidency, Truman appointed ardent antitrusters to the FTC and secured additional appropriations for the enforcement of antitrust legislation.

At the conclusion of World War II, congressional antitrusters introduced a flurry of bills designed to strengthen the Clayton Antitrust Act. In 1945, Senator Joseph O'Mahoney (Democrat of Wyoming) and Representative Kefauver introduced legislation that would close the asset loophole. Their bills remained in committee, however, and for the next several years they failed in efforts to push their legislation through a Republican-controlled Congress. In 1948, the Democrats secured control of both houses of Congress, thus increasing the likelihood that a major piece of antitrust legislation would become law. During the presidential campaign, Truman had supported legislation to close the assets loophole. He interpreted his victory in the election as a mandate to go forward with strict enforcement of the antitrust law. In 1949, Truman encouraged the chairman of the House Judiciary Committee, Emanuel Celler (Democrat of New York) to go forward with an investigation of monopolies. Celler used his committee hearings as a forum to promote his bill to amend the Clayton Act. As a newly elected senator, Estes Kefauver introduced a companion bill in the Senate. The Celler-Kefauver bills prohibited companies from acquiring the assets of other companies if the resulting mergers substantially lessened competition.

FEARS OF BIG BUSINESS

Celler and Kefauver broke with antitrust tradition by emphasizing the alleged evils of bigness per se. In the past, the government had been concerned with the intent behind mergers and their actual effect on competition. The Supreme Court had established a "rule of reason" to govern antitrust cases. According to the Court, antitrust law applied only to unreasonable restraints upon trade. Celler and Kefauver believed that bigness automatically reduced efficiency, dampened innovation, and diminished opportunities for small business. They also argued that big business had given rise to big labor and big government. Ultimately, big business threatened the foundations of American democracy, since an all-powerful state would be required to regulate the nation's monopolies. Celler and Kefauver resorted to Cold War rhetoric, arguing that their legislation would prevent the emergence of a totalitarian state.

PASSAGE, PROVISIONS, AND WEAK ENFORCEMENT

The business press feared that the legislation would radically restructure the American economy. Critics of the legislation, led by the United States Chamber of Commerce, believed that existing antitrust laws could prevent the development of monopolies. These opponents also criticized the FTC for exaggerating the extent of the postwar merger movement and for failing to show that mergers actually had lessened competition. Republican conservatives, however, failed to block passage of this legislation. On August 15, the House passed Celler's bill (H.R. 2734) by a vote of 223 to 92. The Senate subsequently passed Kefauver's bill and, on December 29, 1950, President Truman signed it into law.

The Celler-Kefauver Act of 1950 sent a message to the business community that the federal government would closely examine the effects of any mergers between companies in the same industry. The act also gave the nation's antitrust agencies a powerful new weapon in their campaign against monopoly. The act did not apply, however, to mergers between companies in unrelated industries. Consequently, numerous articles appeared in the business press encouraging companies to seek growth through diversification.

Despite its active role in the passage of the Celler-Kefauver Act, the Truman administration failed to enforce the law, in large part because the government reduced its antitrust activity in order to secure the cooperation of business during the Korean War. A budget-conscious Congress also reduced funding for the antitrust agencies. Corporate executives nevertheless remained cautious about acquiring competitors, and the number of mergers dropped off in the early 1950's.

THE 1950'S AND 1960'S: STRICT ENFORCEMENT

Under the administration of President Dwight D. Eisenhower (1953-1961), the Justice Department and the FTC responded to renewed merger activity by acting more aggressively in their prosecution of antitrust cases. In 1955, the attorney general's National Committee to Study the Antitrust Laws issued a report calling for stricter enforcement of antitrust legislation. The report also outlined the government's interpretation of the Celler-Kefauver Act. According to the committee, the government need not prove that a company had intended to lessen competition by acquiring a rival; instead, the government could simply use market share as a measure of competition in an industry. The committee's report did not address the question of conglomerate mergers.

The FTC and the Justice Department followed the guidelines set forth by the attorney general's committee. During the Eisenhower administration, the two agencies prosecuted more than fifty cases involving alleged violations of the Celler-Kefauver Act. In one important case, brought against the Pillsbury Company, the FTC ruled that the Celler-Kefauver Act allowed the agency to prohibit mergers that lessened competition in regional or local, as opposed to national, markets. The government also brought cases against a number of the nation's largest companies, including Bethlehem Steel, Lever Brothers, Crown Zellerbach, Minute Maid, and Anheuser-Busch. Nearly all of these cases involved mergers within the same industry.

President John F. Kennedy's attorney general continued to charge many companies with violations of the Celler-Kefauver Act. The U.S. Supreme Court approved of the government's strict enforcement of the law. In the landmark *Brown Shoe* case (1962), the Court ruled that the government could halt a merger if there was a chance that it might lessen competition in any region of the country. During the 1960's, the Court continued to consider mergers a threat to competition and, between 1962 and 1970, the nation's highest court decided in favor of the government in all but one of the merger cases.

The hostile environment led companies to avoid mergers within the same industry. Corporate executives began to pursue a strategy of diversification, forming mergers with companies in unrelated fields. Government enforcement of the Celler-Kefauver Act thus indirectly facilitated the massive conglomerate movement of the

1950's and 1960's. In 1969, President Richard Nixon's attorney general brought antitrust suits against several conglomerates. These companies eventually settled out of court, but the suits brought against them led many businesspeople to fear prosecution, and the merger movement finally slowed.

A NEW MERGER MOVEMENT
In the early 1970's, the Supreme Court under Chief Justice Warren Burger began deciding against the government in antitrust cases. During this same period, economists and legal scholars also attacked the long-held assumption that mergers necessarily resulted in lessened competition. Led by Robert H. Bork, these scholars argued that mergers often increased efficiency and lowered costs. These critics of the Celler-Kefauver Act preferred to rely upon the market to police mergers. This intellectual climate of opinion influenced policymakers, and the government stopped enforcing the Celler-Kefauver Act. With the threat of government prosecution diminished, the United States witnessed yet another merger movement in the late 1970's and the 1980's.

Jonathan Bean

SOURCES FOR FURTHER STUDY
Bork, Robert H. "The Crash of Merger Policy: The Brown Shoe Decision." In *The Antitrust Paradox: A Policy at War with Itself.* New York: Basic Books, 1978.
Celler, Emanuel. *You Never Leave Brooklyn: The Autobiography of Emanuel Celler.* New York: J. Day, 1953.
Fligstein, Neil. *The Transformation of Corporation Control.* Cambridge, Mass.: Harvard Universtiy Press, 1990.
Fontenay, Charles L. *Estes Kefauver: A Biography.* Knoxville: University of Tennessee Press, 1980.
Kintner, Earl W., ed. *Federal Antitrust Laws and Related Statutes: A Legislative History.* 11 vols. Buffalo, N.Y.: William S. Hein, 1978, 1982-1985.
Kovaleff, Theodore Philip. *Business and Government During the Eisenhower Administration: A Study of the Antitrust Policy of the Antitrust Division of the Justice Department.* Athens: Ohio University Press, 1980.

SEE ALSO: Interstate Commerce Act (1887); Sherman Antitrust Act (1890); Federal Trade Commission Act (1914); Clayton Antitrust Act (1914); Wheeler-Lea Act (1938); Truth in Lending Act (1968); Parens Patriae Act (1974); Antitrust Procedures and Penalties Act (1974).

TWENTY-SECOND AMENDMENT

DATE: Ratified February 27, 1951; certified March 1, 1951
U.S. STATUTES AT LARGE: 61 Stat. 959
CATEGORIES: Constitutional Law; Government Procedure and Organization

Shortly after Franklin Roosevelt's unprecedented fourth term as president, the Twenty-second Amendment was adopted to establish presidential term limits.

The office of the presidency was the most original political office created by the Framers of the Constitution. George Washington, for whom the office was created, largely set its parameters by his actions. By practice, he established the custom of an informal two-term limit on the presidency. With the possible exception of Ulysses S. Grant, who favored a third nonconsecutive term for himself in 1880, and Theodore Roosevelt's 1912 Bull Moose campaign for another term, the tradition was upheld until Franklin D. Roosevelt was elected to a third term in 1940 and a fourth term in 1944. The unprecedented fourth term was in large part a result of the nation's involvement in World War II. However, the two-term tradition had not just been broken, it had been shattered, and a predictable backlash occurred after Roosevelt's death in 1945.

Presidential term limits had been rejected at the Constitutional Convention in 1787. Similarly, some 270 such resolutions introduced in the Congress prior to 1947 were also rejected. However, immediately after Republicans captured both chambers of Congress in the 1946 election, a term-limit resolution passed quickly the following year. Republicans supported it overwhelmingly; Democrats, except for Southerners, opposed it. Despite its quick passage in the Congress, ratification of the amendment by the states was much slower. Even though Republican-controlled states ratified the amendment easily in 1947 and most southern states concurred soon afterward, ratification by three-fourths of the states took until February 27, 1951. As a result of the Twenty-second Amendment, a president is limited to serving two full terms, or no more than ten years in the case of a vice president who replaces a president.

The Twenty-second Amendment, the first amendment to the U.S. Constitution to limit voter suffrage, was driven by partisan vengeance fueled by Franklin Roosevelt's unprecedented multiple terms of office. Subsequent presidents Harry Truman, Dwight Eisenhower, and Ronald Reagan considered the amendment undemocratic and urged repeal without success. Nonetheless, with the shift in the balance of power during the twentieth century from the legislative to the executive branch, the American public seems comfortable with retaining this added constitutional check on presidential power, even if it effectively makes a second-term president a "lame duck."

William D. Pederson

SOURCES FOR FURTHER STUDY

Bernstein, Richard B. *Amending America: If We Love the Constitution So Much, Why Do We Keep Trying to Change It?* New York: Random House, 1993.

Grimes, Alan P. *Democracy and the Amendments to the Constitution.* Lexington, Mass.: Lexington Books, 1978.

Reagan, Ronald W., Joseph M. Bessette, and Bruce Buchanan. *Restoring the Presidency: Reconsidering the Twenty-second Amendment.* Washington, D.C.: National Legal Center for the Public Interest, 1990.

Vile, John R. *Encyclopedia of Constitutional Amendments, Proposed Amendments, and Amending Issues, 1789-1995.* Santa Barbara, Calif: ABC-CLIO, 1996.

SEE ALSO: U.S. Constitution: Provisions (1787); Twelfth Amendment (1804); Presidential Succession Act (1947); Twenty-fifth Amendment (1967).

TRIPARTITE SECURITY TREATY

ALSO KNOWN AS: Anzus Treaty
DATE: Signed September 1, 1951; in force April 29, 1952
CATEGORIES: Foreign Relations; Military and National Security;
Treaties and Agreements

This treaty, signed a few years after World War II, was designed to
send a signal to China and the Soviet Union that Western-oriented
countries were determined to stop new aggressive moves in the Pacific.

Immediately after World War II, Australia pressed for a regional security arrangement, but the United States demurred. Soon, several
events gave greater urgency to the idea. In 1949, communists won
the civil war in China. In February, 1950, the Sino-Soviet Treaty of
Friendship and Mutual Assistance was signed, and in June, 1950,
North Korea's army entered South Korea. Australia and New Zealand were the first countries to join the United States in sending
troops for the United Nations (U.N.) Command in Korea.

John Foster Dulles, foreign policy adviser to the U.S. secretary of
state, believed that a power vacuum existed because demilitarized
Japan was still under Allied occupation, so communist countries
were moving to fill the void. Accordingly, he considered a peace
treaty with Japan to be a top priority. Australia and New Zealand,
however, said that they would be interested in signing a Japanese
peace treaty only if they were included in a formal defensive arrangement involving the United States. Dulles then went to Canberra in February, 1951, to meet Australian external affairs minister Percy Spender and New Zealand minister for foreign affairs
Frederick Doidge in order to discuss proposals for a defensive arrangement among the three countries. Promising military aid to
both countries, Dulles then prepared a draft treaty, which was
signed during the first day of the Japanese peace conference in San
Francisco.

The treaty came into force exactly one day after the Japanese
Peace Treaty went into effect. The aim was to send a signal to
Beijing and Moscow that Western-oriented countries were determined to stop new aggressive moves in the Pacific. To avoid the impression that the treaty dealt with the entire Pacific area, the acro-

nym "Anzus" (referring to Australia, New Zealand, and the United States) was accepted in August, 1952, at the inaugural meeting of the Council, the principal organ established by the treaty.

Articles IV-V, which as of 2002 had never been utilized, provide that armed attacks "on the metropolitan territory of any of the Parties, or on the island territories under its jurisdiction in the Pacific" should be reported immediately to the U.N. Security Council. Until the Security Council acts, Anzus countries are authorized to coordinate their own actions to meet aggression, but there is no guarantee that the countries will come to one another's aid in response to such attacks.

In 1962 the "treaty area" was clarified to include the many Pacific island territories then under the jurisdiction of the Anzus powers. Today, only the Tokelau Islands, under New Zealand rule, appear to be covered.

In late 1984, New Zealand's newly elected prime minister David Lange announced that no American naval ships could dock in New Zealand unless advance assurances were given that no nuclear weapons were on board. Washington then refused to meet any New Zealand representative and canceled the next scheduled Council meeting; the Anzus Council ceased to exist. Australia and the United States have continued to cooperate within the framework of the treaty, holding meetings known as "Ausmins," though the tripartite treaty is technically still in force.

Michael Haas

SOURCES FOR FURTHER STUDY

Bercovitch, Jacob, ed. *Anzus in Crisis: Alliance Management in International Affairs.* New York: St. Martin's Press, 1988.
Holdich, Roger, et al., eds. *The Anzus Treaty 1951.* Canberra, Australia: Department of Foreign Affairs and Trade, 2001.

SEE ALSO: U.S.-Japanese Treaty (1951).

U.S.-JAPANESE TREATY

DATE: Signed September 8, 1951; in force April 28, 1952
CATEGORIES: Asia or Asian Americans; Foreign Relations; Military
and National Security; Treaties and Agreements

*In this post-World War II treaty, the United States agreed to assume
primary responsibility for the conventional defense of a disarmed Japan and an exclusive role in providing nuclear deterrence.*

After Japan surrendered in August, 1945, to end World War II, the
Allied powers set up a military occupation to restructure the country so that militaristic ventures would never again emerge and Japan could regain economic prosperity. Nevertheless, unexpected
developments soon changed the balance of power in Asia. Communist forces triumphed in China in 1949. The Sino-Soviet Treaty of
Friendship and Mutual Assistance was concluded in February,
1950, and the Korean peninsula was engulfed in war from June,
1950.

Some observers argued that there was a power vacuum in Asia,
so communist countries were seeking to fill the void. Accordingly,
the United States convened a peace conference in San Francisco,
resulting in a treaty signed by forty-eight countries (excluding the
Soviet Union) on September 8, 1951, which served to end the
Allied occupation. That same day, Japan and the United States
signed a bilateral "mutual assistance" treaty, something permitted
by the peace treaty.

The U.S.-Japanese security treaty was one-sided, not "mutual."
The American-drafted Japanese constitution left a pacifist and disarmed country, so the United States agreed in the treaty to assume
primary responsibility for Japan's conventional defense and an exclusive role in providing nuclear deterrence. Tokyo was not asked
to assist in defending the United States. Japan agreed to assist in responding to conventional attacks on its territory, so the National
Police Reserve was upgraded to the Self-Defense Force, ultimately
to consist of 275,000 persons, to which the United States pledged
in 1954 to provide economic assistance. Article I provided that
U.S. Army, Navy, and Air Force personnel could be stationed at

U.S.-operated bases throughout the country. Article II banned that right to any third country.

In 1960, the security treaty was renegotiated, replacing the earlier document, to provide Japan a firmer guarantee of American support in case of attack. Thus, Japan was later called a full-fledged "ally" of the United States, although the basic relationship remained unchanged.

Japan, in short, was a military protectorate of the United States, an "unsinkable aircraft carrier." Between 1951 and 2002, the United States spent more than $1 trillion on Japan's defense, thereby enabling Japan to spend government funds to boost its economy. In the 1950's Prime Minister Shigeru Yoshida, accordingly, articulated principles of a foreign policy that have guided policy ever since. Through the Yoshida Doctrine, Japan agreed that reliance on the American security guarantee meant abandoning an independent role in international security matters, slowly developing the capabilities of the Self-Defense Force, pursuing national and later regional economic prosperity, and advancing Japan's interests abroad by nonmilitary means.

As the twenty-first century dawned, the premises for the treaty had eroded. The Cold War was over, and although nuclear threats from China and North Korea remained, they seemed likely to target Japan only because of the presence of the American military. Japan had the resources to defend itself, and Japanese press reports of misconduct by American soldiers in Japan exposed the unpopularity of what some observers perceived as continued military occupation.

Michael Haas

Sources for Further Study

Osius, Ted. *The U.S.-Japan Security Alliance: Why It Matters and How to Strengthen It.* Westport, Conn.: Praeger, 2002.

Satoh, Yukio. *The Evolution of Japanese Security Policy.* London: International Institute for Strategic Studies, 1982.

See also: Truman Doctrine (1947); Tripartite Security Treaty (1951); Eisenhower Doctrine (1957).

IMMIGRATION AND NATIONALITY ACT OF 1952

ALSO KNOWN AS: McCarran-Walter Act
DATE: June 27, 1952
U.S. STATUTES AT LARGE: 66 Stat. 166
PUBLIC LAW: 82-414
U.S. CODE: 8 § 1101
CATEGORIES: Asia or Asian Americans; Immigration

The Immigration and Nationality Act of 1952 removed restrictions on Asian immigration.

In the early 1950's, as it had periodically throughout the twentieth century, immigration again became the subject of intense national debate, and a movement arose to reform immigration law. At the time, there were more than two hundred federal laws dealing with immigration, with little coordination among them.

REFORM EFFORTS

The movement toward immigration reform actually began in 1947, with a U.S. Senate committee investigation on immigration laws, resulting in a voluminous report in 1950 and a proposed bill. The ensuing debate was divided between those who wanted to abandon the quota system and increase the numbers of immigrants admitted and those who hoped to shape immigration law to enforce the status quo. Leaders of the latter camp were the architects of the Immigration and Nationality Act of 1952: Patrick McCarran, senator from Nevada, Francis Walter, congressman from Pennsylvania, and Richard Arens, staff director of the Senate Subcommittee to Investigate Immigration and Naturalization. McCarran was the author of the Internal Security Act of 1951, which provided for registration of communist organizations and the internment of communists during national emergencies. Walter was an immigration specialist who had backed legislation to admit Europeans from camps for displaced persons. Arens had been staff director for the House Committee on Un-American Activities. Each looked upon immigration control as an extension of his work to defend the United States against foreign and domestic enemies.

McCarran was most outspoken in defending the concept of restrictions on the basis of national origin, stating in the Senate:

There are hard-core indigestible blocs who have not become integrated into the American way of life, but who, on the contrary, are its deadly enemy. . . . this Nation is the last hope of western civilization; and if this oasis of the world shall be overrun, perverted, contaminated, or destroyed, then the last flickering light of humanity will be extinguished.

Arens branded critics of the proposed act as communists, misguided liberals enraptured by communist propaganda, apologists for specific immigrant groups, or "professional vote solicitors who fawn on nationality groups, appealing to them not as Americans but as hyphenated Americans." Among the bill's critics, however, were Harry S. Truman, the U.S. president in 1952, and Hubert H. Humphrey, senator from Minnesota and future Democratic presidential nominee. One liberal senator, Herbert Lehman, attacked the national origins provisions of the existing immigration code as a racist measure that smacked of the ethnic purity policies of the recently defeated German Nazis. Truman vetoed the bill, but his veto was overridden, 278 to 113 in the House, and 57 to 26 in the Senate.

PROVISIONS OF THE ACT

In several areas, the 1952 law made no significant changes: Quotas for European immigrants were little changed, no quotas were instituted for immigrants from North and South American countries, and the issue of illegal immigration was given scant attention. There were significant changes in some areas, however: reversal of the ban on Asian immigration, extension of naturalization to persons regardless of race or sex, and the first provision for refugees as a special class of immigrants.

The Asiatic Barred Zone, established in 1917, was eliminated by providing for twenty-five hundred entries from the area—a minuscule number for the region, but the first recognition of Asian immigration rights in decades. This small concession for Asians was offset partially by the fact that anyone whose ancestry was at least half Asian would be counted under the quota for the Asian country of ancestry, even if the person was a resident of another country. This provision, which was unlike the system of counting quotas for

European countries, was specifically and openly designed to prevent Asians living in North and South American countries, which had no quota restrictions, from flooding into the United States.

The Immigration and Nationality Act of 1952, or McCarran-Walter Act, also ensured for the first time that the "right of a person to become a naturalized citizen of the United States shall not be denied or abridged because of race or sex." The provision of not denying citizenship based on sex addressed the issue of women who had lost their U.S. citizenship by marrying foreign men of certain categories; men who had married women from those categories had never lost their citizenship.

The issue of refugees was a new concern resulting from World War II. More than seven million persons had lost their homelands in the aftermath of the war, as a result of the conquering and reorganization of countries primarily in Eastern Europe. The 1952 act did not present a comprehensive solution to the problem of refugees but did give the attorney general special power, subject to congressional overview, to admit refugees into the United States under a special status. Although this was expected to be a seldom-used provision of the law, regular upheavals throughout the world later made it an important avenue of immigration into the United States.

Finally, the Immigration and Nationality Act also included stringent security procedures designed to prevent communist subversives from infiltrating the United States through immigration. Some of these harsh measures were specifically mentioned by Truman in his veto message, but the anticommunist Cold War climate made such measures hard to defeat.

CRITICISM OF THE ACT
Over the objections of Congress, President Truman appointed a special commission to examine immigration in September, 1952. After hearings in several cities, it issued the report *Whom Shall We Welcome?*, which was critical of the McCarran-Walter Act. Some liberal Democrats attempted to make the 1952 presidential election a forum on immigration policy, but without success. Dwight D. Eisenhower, the victorious Republican nominee for president, made few specific statements on immigration policy during the campaign. After his election, however, he proposed a special provision for allowing almost a quarter of a million refugees from commu-

nism to immigrate to the United States over a two-year period, couching his proposal in terms of humanitarianism and foreign policy. The resulting Refugee Relief Act of 1953 allowed the admission of 214,000 refugees, but only if they had assurance of jobs and housing or were close relatives of U.S. citizens and could pass extensive screening procedures designed to deter subversives. Several similar exceptions in the following years managed to undercut the McCarran-Walter Act, which its many critics had been unable to overturn outright.

Irene Struthers

SOURCES FOR FURTHER STUDY

Dimmitt, Marius A. *The Enactment of the McCarran-Walter Act of 1952.* Ph.D. dissertation. Lawrence: University Press of Kansas, 1971.

LeMay, Michael C. *From Open Door to Dutch Door: An Analysis of U.S. Immigration Policy Since 1820.* New York: Praeger, 1987.

_____, ed. *The Gatekeepers: Comparative Immigration Policy.* New York: Praeger, 1989.

Reimers, David M. "Recent Immigration Policy: An Analysis." In *The Gateway: U.S. Immigration Issues and Policies,* edited by Barry R. Chiswick. Washington, D.C.: American Enterprise Institute for Public Policy Research, 1982.

SEE ALSO: Chinese Exclusion Act (1882); Gentlemen's Agreement (1907); Alien land laws (1913); Immigration Act of 1917 (1917); Immigration Act of 1921 (1921); Cable Act (1922); Immigration Act of 1924 (1924); Immigration Act of 1943 (1943); War Brides Act (1945); Refugee Relief Act (1953); Immigration and Nationality Act Amendments of 1965 (1965).

TERMINATION RESOLUTION

DATE: Issued August 1, 1953
CATEGORIES: Native Americans

Congress ended its policy of special treatment of Native Americans.

Termination was viewed by its advocates as freeing American Indians from special laws and regulations, making them equal to other citizens, and by opponents as precipitously withdrawing federal responsibility and programs. The term used for the federal policy came to be applied to the people themselves: "terminated" tribes. Termination actions included repealing laws setting American Indians apart, ending Bureau of Indian Affairs (BIA) services by transferring them to other federal agencies or to the states, and terminating recognition of the sovereign status of specific tribes.

Termination, many have observed, did not deviate from the norm of federal policy. Its emphasis on breaking up American Indian land holdings is often compared to the General Allotment Act of 1887 (the Dawes Act). The latter required the allocation of a certain number of acres to each person and, during its forty-seven years in force, reduced tribal lands by nearly ninety-one million acres.

PROS AND CONS

In public debate, opponents of termination argued that the United States had a special obligation to American Indians because they had been conquered and deprived of their customary way of life. All people in the United States, opponents said, have the right to be different and to live in the groupings they prefer. Any changes in federal supervision of American Indians should be implemented slowly and with the involvement of the affected tribes; rather than dissolving tribal communities, federal policy should continue meeting tribes' special needs until those needs no longer exist. Opponents also pointed to American Indian culture, tribal lands, and tribal government—their form of community—as their source of strength.

Advocates of termination asserted that all U.S. citizens should be similar, and there should be no communities with special legal rights. Dissolving separate American Indian communities would expedite the integration of these people into the mainstream. American Indians, according to Senator Arthur V. Wakens, would be freed from wardship or federal restrictions and would become self-reliant, with no diminution of their tribal culture. Wakens saw termination as liberation of American Indians and compared it to the Emancipation Proclamation. Non-natives objected to the Indian Reorganization Act (IRA) of 1934, the prior federal policy, and were swayed toward termination by a variety of arguments: American Indian communal property ownership and their form of government resembled communism; the IRA's promotion of American Indian traditions amounted to condoning heathenism; developers wanted tribal lands made available; and Congress perceived that the resignation of Indian Commissioner John Collier (the IRA's chief advocate) and severe BIA budget cuts had diminished its effectiveness, necessitating a stepped-up program of assimilation.

ZIMMERMAN'S FORMULA

After Collier's resignation, Senator William Langer asked Acting Commissioner William Zimmerman for a formula for evaluating tribal readiness for termination. On February 8, 1947, Zimmerman presented, in a congressional hearing, three categories of tribes—those who could be terminated immediately, those who could function with little federal supervision within ten years, and those who needed more than ten years to prepare. He discussed the four criteria used in his lists and presented three specimen termination bills. This testimony was embraced by termination supporters and, Zimmerman believed, frequently misquoted.

In 1950, Dillon Myer, a staunch advocate of immediate termination, became Commissioner of Indian Affairs. Although he claimed to be streamlining the BIA, it seemed to some that he was moving to dissolve both the bureau and all IRA programs. Myer was asked to write a legislative proposal for expeditious termination of federal supervision of American Indians. The result was House Concurrent Resolution 108 (August 1, 1953), which passed with little debate. The resolution directed Congress to make American Indians subject to the same laws, privileges, and responsibilities as other citizens; to end their wardship status; and to free specific tribes from federal control as soon as possible. Once the named tribes were terminated, the BIA offices serving them would be abolished.

PL 83-280 (August 15, 1953) also advanced termination. It transferred to the states, without tribal consent, jurisdiction over civil and criminal offenses on reservations in California, Minnesota, Nebraska, Oregon, and Wisconsin. It provided that, by legislative action, any other state could assume similar jurisdiction.

TERMINATION BILLS OF 1954-1962

A rush of termination bills was introduced in 1954. As problems with the termination process became known and the membership of congressional committees changed (after 1956), legislation slowed. These acts caused several changes: Tribal lands were either appraised or put under a corporation's management; the federal government no longer protected the land for the tribe; state legislative and judicial authority replaced tribal government; tribe members no longer received a state tax exemption; and tribes lost the benefits of special federal health, education, and other social programs.

Fifteen termination acts were passed between 1954 and 1962, affecting 110 tribes or bands in eight states: the Menominee, Klamath, Western Oregon (sixty-one tribes and bands), Alabama-Coushatta, Mixed-Blood Ute, Southern Paiute, Lower Lake Rancheria, Wyandotte, Peoria, Ottawa, Coyote Valley Ranch, California Rancheria (37 rancherias), Catawba, and Ponca.

Termination of the Menominee of Wisconsin received the most attention. The tribe was specifically targeted in House Concurrent Resolution 108, and their termination act was passed on June 17, 1954. They appeared to be the healthiest tribe economically, as a result of their lumbering and forestry operations, but were not as ready for termination as they seemed. In 1951, the Menominee won a fifteen-year legal battle against the federal government, awarding them $8.5 million in damages for mismanagement of their tribal forest. They could not obtain the award, however, until Congress passed an act appropriating it. The tribe asked that part of the money be released—amounting to fifteen hundred dollars per capita. Senator Wakens's Subcommittee on Indian Affairs told the tribe that if they could manage fifteen hundred dollars per person, they were ready for freedom from federal wardship. Termination, he suggested, was inevitable, and the tribe would not receive the money unless they moved to accept a termination amendment to the per-capita payment bill. The election was not a true tribal referendum, as only 174 members voted; many of these later said that they had not understood what they were voting for.

Final termination of the Menominee did not go into effect until 1961. The tribe had to decide how to set up municipalities, establish a tax system, provide law and order, and sell their tribal assets. There were complications concerning the payment of estimated taxes on Menominee forests. Federal officials saw the tribe's reluctance as procrastination. State agencies could provide only limited assistance, because the tribe was still under federal control.

As a result of these experiences and others, both American Indians and non-Indians became critical of termination. BIA expenditures spiraled in the late 1950's. Many terminated tribe members felt uncomfortable living in the mainstream and often were not accepted socially by non-Indians. Relocated Indians often suffered poverty in the cities and often became dependent on social programs. Some terminated tribes later applied for federal recognition. During its short span (the last act was passed in 1962), termination affected 13,263 of a total population of 400,000, or 3 percent of the federally recognized American Indians. The acts withdrew 1,365,801 acres of trust land, or 3 percent of the approximately 43,000,000 acres held in 1953. The end of federal endorsement of the termination policy was seen in 1969, when President Richard Nixon, in a message to Congress, called for promotion of self-determination and the strengthening of American Indian autonomy without threatening community.

Glenn Ellen Starr

SOURCES FOR FURTHER STUDY

Fixico, Donald L. *Termination and Relocation: Federal Indian Policy, 1945-1960.* Albuquerque: University of New Mexico Press, 1986.

La Farge, Oliver. "Termination of Federal Supervision: Disintegration and the American Indians." *Annals of the American Academy of Political and Social Science* 311 (May, 1957): 41-46.

Philip, Kenneth R. *Termination Revisited: American Indians on the Trail to Self-Determination, 1933-1953.* Lincoln: University of Nebraska Press, 2002.

Prucha, Francis Paul. *The Great Father: The United States Government and the American Indian.* Vol. 2. Lincoln: University of Nebraska Press, 1984.

St. Germain, Jill. *Indian Treaty-Making Policy in the United States and Canada, 1867-1877.* Lincoln: University of Nebraska Press, 2001.

Stefon, Frederick J. "The Irony of Termination: 1943-1958." *The Indian Historian* 11, no. 3 (Summer, 1978): 3-14.

Walch, Michael C. "Terminating the Indian Termination Policy." *Stanford Law Review* 35, no. 6 (July, 1983): 1181-1215.

SEE ALSO: General Allotment Act (1887); Burke Act (1906); Indian Citizenship Act (1924); Indian Reorganization Act (1934); Public Law 280 (1953).

REFUGEE RELIEF ACT

DATE: August 7, 1953
U.S. STATUTES AT LARGE: 67 Stat. 400
PUBLIC LAW: 83-203
CATEGORIES: Asia or Asian Americans; Immigration

The act created a means of admitting into the United States those displaced persons outside the national quota system requiring admission on an emergency basis.

The events of World War II and its immediate aftermath left millions of people displaced from their homelands. Included among those who had been made homeless by the destruction were Jewish survivors of the Nazi-perpetrated Holocaust and increasing numbers of political refugees who fled their homelands as communist governments took control in Eastern Europe. In the United States, from the close of World War II well into the 1950's, a debate raged about how restrictive or generous U.S. immigration and asylum law should be in view of the nation's own interests and the larger humanitarian imperatives.

QUOTAS AND WAR REFUGEES
Since 1924, U.S. immigration law had been based on a quota system, which was viewed as highly discriminatory against various countries and peoples. Under the pressures of war, however, Congress had allowed temporary immigration to help labor-starved industry. With China as one of the main U.S. allies in the Pacific war, Congress revoked the ban on Chinese immigration in 1943; in 1945, it approved the War Brides Act, which permitted the entry of the alien spouses and children of members of the U.S. armed forces. President Harry S. Truman approved the admission of about forty thousand wartime refugees after the war and urged Congress to adopt less restrictive legislation that would permit the resettlement of larger numbers of displaced persons (DPs).

Congress felt pressure to act, not only from the president but also from private charitable agencies that sought to liberalize admission policies in favor of DPs in Europe and elsewhere. Two Jewish aid agencies, the American Council on Judaism (ACJ) and the

American Jewish Committee (AJC), joined forces with numerous Christian and other non-Jewish agencies to form the Citizens' Committee on Displaced Persons. This new group was headed by Earl G. Harrison and included on its board of directors many prominent U.S. citizens, among them Eleanor Roosevelt. The committee heavily lobbied the predominantly restrictionist Congress and supported legislation calling for the admission of 400,000 DPs. A long and rancorous debate followed, which produced a substantially watered-down bill known as the Displaced Persons Act of 1948. This act permitted 202,000 admission slots for DPs in Europe who feared to return to communist-held countries. While retaining the immigration quotas of previous years, the act allowed countries to borrow against future years' quotas to accommodate DPs with immediate needs. It only permitted entry of people displaced prior to April 21, 1947, in the Allied occupied zones of Germany and Austria who were registered with the International Refugee Organization (IRO) and who were not communists. It required that the DPs be guaranteed employment by U.S. charitable agencies or other sponsors, and it gave preference to DPs with professional skills. While criticizing its discriminatory features, Truman signed the legislation, which also established the Displaced Persons Commission.

Efforts by the Citizens' Committee on Displaced Persons and others to liberalize the Displaced Persons Act continued, as events in Europe and the deepening of the Cold War led to a climate more supportive of DP resettlement. Although delayed by Senator Patrick A. McCarran of Nevada, amendments eventually passed by Congress expanded the numbers of admission slots to 341,000 and relaxed the cutoff dates for eligibility and entry into the United States. When the Displaced Persons Act expired on December 31, 1951, President Truman relied on the regular immigration quotas and on the U.S. Escapee Program, established under the authority of the 1951 Mutual Security Act, to provide asylum in the United States to political refugees from communism. Truman also established a Commission on Immigration and Naturalization, which held hearings that demonstrated considerable support for liberalized admission of refugees from communism. Even as the 1952 Immigration and Nationality Act, sponsored by Senator McCarran (and often called the McCarran-Walter Act), reemphasized the restrictive quota system for regular immigration, consensus was building to place emergency refugee admissions outside the regular immigration quota system. The Refugee Relief Act of 1953, also sometimes referred to as the Church bill because of the strong support it received from religious refugee assistance agencies, was the result of this ongoing debate about how to restructure U.S. immigration and refugee policy.

BEYOND QUOTAS

The Refugee Relief Act of 1953 made 209,000 special immigrant visas available to refugees and other special categories of persons. These were not tied in any way to the regular immigration quotas for countries under the 1952 Immigration and Nationality Act. This was seen as a major reform by private humanitarian organizations. In the years that followed, the 1958 act enabled the emergency entry of refugees from communism. President Dwight D. Eisenhower, for example, invoked the act just before it was to expire, to provide emergency resettlement opportunities for Hungarian refugees in the waning months of 1956. Eisenhower also took advantage of his parole power, as acknowledged in the 1952 Immigration and Nationality Act and earlier immigration legislation, to provide asylum opportunities for Hungarian refugees. The United States eventually accepted more than thirty-two thousand Hungarians. Thus, through the provisions of the Refugee Relief Act of 1953, subsequent ad hoc emergency refugee legislation, and the Immigration and Nationality Act of 1952, the U.S. government coped with refugee admissions until 1980, when Congress passed the more comprehensive and progressive Migration and Refugee Act.

IMPACT AND ASSESSMENT

The Refugee Relief Act of 1953 was one brief but essential mechanism by which the U.S. government sought to fulfill humanitarian and political objectives relating to refugees. It represented an improvement on the Displaced Persons Act, although that much-maligned piece of legislation eventually led to the resettlement of about four hundred thousand persons to the United States, by far the single largest number of European refugees resettled by any country in the immediate postwar era. The Refugee Relief Act of 1953 also represented a bridge to later legislation, such as the Migration and Refugee Act of 1980, by treating emergency refugee admission outside the context of regular immigration quotas. It also represented the mistaken belief in the early 1950's that refugee situations were temporary and amendable to ad hoc solutions.

Still, the United States and other Western nations during the early 1950's established the groundwork for more stable legal and institutional mechanisms for dealing with refugee situations. The United States supported the creation of the United Nations Relief and Rehabilitation Administration in 1943 and the IRO in 1947 to cope with the needs of displaced persons and refugees in postwar Europe. Both were viewed as temporary agencies, as were the United Nations High Commissioner for Refugees (UNHCR) and the Intergovernmental Committee for European Migration (ICEM), which began operations in 1952. In time, however, these bodies developed into permanent features of the international humanitarian landscape with the support of later U.S. administrations.

The building of both legal and institutional mechanisms for coping with humanitarian problems was often highly controversial, heavily steeped in political motivation, and shortsighted. As measured in the huge numbers of persons assisted and protected over the years, however, the efforts are viewed by many as precious if difficult ones, of which the Displaced Persons Act of 1948 and the Refugee Relief Act of 1953 were imperfect but necessary components.

Robert F. Gorman

Sources for Further Study

Carlin, James L. *The Refugee Connection: A Lifetime of Running a Lifeline.* New York: Macmillan, 1989.

Fuchs, Lawrence H. "Immigration, Pluralism, and Public Policy: The Challenge of the Pluribus to the Unum." In *U.S. Immigration and Refugee Policy: Global and Domestic Issues,* edited by Mary M. Kritz. Lexington, Mass.: D. C. Heath, 1982.

Loescher, Gil, and John A. Scanlan. *Calculated Kindness: Refugees and America's Half-Open Door, 1945 to Present.* New York: Free Press, 1986.

Nichols, J. Bruce. *The Uneasy Alliance: Religion, Refugee Work, and U.S. Foreign Policy.* Oxford, England: Oxford University Press, 1989.

Sanders, Ronald. *Shores of Refuge: A Hundred Years of Jewish Immigration.* New York: Schocken Books, 1988.
Zucker, Norman L., and Naomi Flink Zucker. *The Guarded Gate: The Reality of American Refugee Policy.* New York: Harcourt Brace Jovanovich, 1987.

SEE ALSO: Immigration Act of 1924 (1924); Immigration Act of 1943 (1943); War Brides Act (1945); Immigration and Nationality Act of 1952 (1952); Amerasian Homecoming Act (1987).

PUBLIC LAW 280

DATE: August 15, 1953
U.S. STATUTES AT LARGE: 67 Stat. 588
PUBLIC LAW: 83-280
U.S. CODE: 18 § 1161-1162, 25 § 1321-1322, 28 § 1360
CATEGORIES: Native Americans

This law limited tribal sovereignty by allowing courts in some states to have jurisdiction over Indian reservations.

During the early 1950's, federal Indian policy returned to the goal of promoting the assimilation of Indians into American society. Tribes were considered to be major barriers to this end, and a number of policies were developed to reduce their influence. One of these measures was Public Law 280, which sought to place tribal Indians under the jurisdiction of the laws of the states in which they resided. This marked a significant change in the legal status of Native Americans, for while Indians had long been subject to federal law, they had usually been considered to be subject to their own tribal courts when on reservations. Like other measures of the 1950's, Public Law 280 sought to undermine those aspects of Indians' legal status that set them apart from other Americans.

PROVISIONS
Passed by Congress in August, 1953, Public Law 280 authorized state courts to assume civil and criminal jurisdiction of all Indian lands in the states of California, Minnesota, Nebraska, Oregon,

and Wisconsin. (Three reservations were excluded by name in the act.) Furthermore, other states were allowed to extend jurisdiction over reservations if they desired by making the necessary changes in their laws or constitutions. A few limits were placed on state powers: States could not levy property taxes on reservations or exercise jurisdiction with regard to Indian water rights. By 1968 nine additional states had extended jurisdiction over Indian lands within their borders.

NATIVE AMERICAN RESPONSE

Public Law 280 was very unpopular with American Indians, who saw it as a drastic limitation on the tribal right of self-government that had been enacted without their consent. (President Dwight D. Eisenhower had objected to the lack of a provision for tribal consent but had signed the act when Congress refused to amend it.)

Indian resentment of the act helped to persuade Congress to amend its provisions in the changed atmosphere of later years. The Indian Civil Rights Act of 1968 included provisions (known collectively as the Indian Bill of Rights) that were intended to safeguard Native American rights. One section altered Public Law 280 to require Indian consent before future extensions of state jurisdiction. States were also allowed to return jurisdiction to tribes. Public Law 280 was further limited in its impact by the Indian Child Welfare Act (1978), which gave tribal courts exclusive jurisdiction over child custody cases on reservations.

Though initially seen as a major threat to tribal self-government, modification of Public Law 280 lessened its potential for restricting tribal authority. Some states found that they preferred to avoid the expense involved in extending legal jurisdiction, while some tribes found it useful to ask the states to provide law and order. By the late twentieth century, the law was being used in a somewhat more cooperative manner that took Indian opinions into account.

William C. Lowe

SOURCES FOR FURTHER STUDY

Ackerman, David M. *Background Report on Public Law 280. Prepared at the Request of Henry M. Jackson, Chairman, Committee on Interior and Insular Affairs, United States Senate.* 94th Congress, 1st session. Washington, D.C.: Government Printing Office, 1975.

Goldberg-Ambrose, Carole, and Timothy Carr Seward. *Planting Tail Feathers: Tribal Survival and Public Law 280.* Los Angeles: American Indian Studies Center, University of California, 1997.

SEE ALSO: Termination Resolution (1953); Indian Civil Rights Act (1968); Indian Child Welfare Act (1978).

COMMUNIST CONTROL ACT

DATE: August 24, 1954
U.S. STATUTES AT LARGE: 68 Stat. 775
PUBLIC LAW: 83-637
U.S. CODE: 50 § 841-844
CATEGORIES: Civil Rights and Liberties

> *This legislation, by outlawing the Communist Party, made it more difficult for Communist organizations to operate in the United States and imposed legal, political, and economic penalties on party members.*

In the 1940's and 1950's Congress passed three major pieces of legislation designed to limit and then eliminate the Communist Party of the United States. The Smith Act of 1940 made it a criminal offense willfully to advocate the overthrow of the government of the United States or any state by force or violence or to organize any association which promoted such an overthrow. The 1950 Internal Security Act required Communist-action organizations and Communist-front organizations to register and provide for public inspection membership lists, their sources of funding and expenditures, and listings of all printing presses and duplicating machines. Members of organizations that failed to register were required to register, and members were subject to comprehensive restrictions and criminal sanctions.

Finally, in 1954 Congress passed the Communist Control Act. This legislation, by outlawing the Communist Party, made it more difficult for Communist organizations to operate in the United

States. The Communist Party lost all its legal rights, including its right to sue in court, to make contracts, to publish newspapers, and to conduct other activities that all legal organizations were entitled to conduct. Labor organizations found to be Communist-controlled were to be stripped of their rights under the Taft-Hartley law (the Labor-Management Relations Act of 1947). They could not get their names on a ballot to win or protect representation rights, and they could not bring complaints against employers.

While the act did not make Communist Party membership a crime, it did impose legal, political, and economic penalties on party members. For example, party members were required to register with the Justice Department under the terms of the Internal Security Act if not already registered by the party itself. Failure to do so could result in fines up to $10,000 and prison terms as long as five years. Once registered, the Communist Party member was prohibited from government employment, from working in a defense plant, and from obtaining a passport.

There were several legal challenges to the Communist Control Act. In 1954, section 3 of the act was upheld in a New Jersey court case, *Salwen v. Rees*, as the basis for denying a candidate the right to appear on the ballot under the Communist Party label. In 1957, New York denied the claim of a Communist Party member to unemployment insurance and suspended the registration of the Communist Party as an employer. The New York courts reversed the denial of the individual's claim but upheld the suspension of the party as an employer. The U.S. Supreme Court reversed the decision in 1961 in *Communist Party vs. Catherwood*, concerning the party suspension; however, it did not rule on broader constitutional issues.

The Communist Control Act raised constitutional questions under the First Amendment, the Fifth Amendment, and the ban against bills of attainder; however, the Justice Department did not push for a general test of its provisions in court. By the early 1960's, the legislative acts passed in the 1940's and 1950's were, in general, constitutionally rejected.

William V. Moore

SOURCES FOR FURTHER STUDY
Emerson, Thomas I., David Haber, and Norman Dorsen. *Political and Civil Rights in the United States*. Boston: Little, Brown, 1967.
Library of Congress. Legislative Reference Service. *Internal Security Act of 1950, as Amended, and Communist Control Act of 1954*. 91st Congress, 1st session. Washington, D.C.: Government Printing Office, 1969.

SEE ALSO: Espionage Acts (1917-1918); Smith Act (1940); Labor-Management Relations Act (1947); Internal Security Act (1950); Jencks Act (1957).

ATOMIC ENERGY ACT OF 1954

DATE: August 30, 1954
U.S. STATUTES AT LARGE: 68 Stat. 921
PUBLIC LAW: 102-486
U.S. CODE: 42 § 2011
CATEGORIES: Energy; Natural Resources

President Dwight D. Eisenhower signed into law a bill designed to promote the peacetime uses of nuclear energy.

The Atomic Energy Act of 1946 provided for the establishment of a civilian group, the Atomic Energy Commission (AEC), whose specified tasks included not only stewardship of all fissionable materials but also the exercise of broad controls over every aspect, military as well as civilian, of atomic energy development in the United States. As custodian and delegated promoter of the peaceful atom, however, the AEC was handicapped, since much information on nuclear technology was classified and therefore unavailable to private industry. Since the formation of a civilian nuclear industry was deemed highly desirable by all parties, including the president, Congress, and private industry, the revised Atomic Energy Act of 1954 was specifically designed to grant the right to private corporations to own and operate nuclear power plants. The AEC became both licenser and regulator.

ATOMIC ENERGY

The first actual generation of electricity from a nuclear reactor took place in 1953 at a national laboratory in Idaho and promised a welcome gift of nuclear power for peacetime uses for an increasingly energy-dependent industrial society, especially in light of the steady depletion of the world's conventional energy supplies. However, the by-products of the fissioning process are highly radioactive chemical elements whose potential for harm to living organisms has been well documented. There was concern not only about the possibility for the accidental release of these substances but also about the issue of the ultimate disposal of the highly radioactive residues of the spent fuels.

In a speech, called "Atoms for Peace," delivered to the General Assembly of the United Nations in December, 1953, President Eisenhower gave impetus to the movement toward civilian atomic energy development. By proposing the establishment of an international commission that would supervise a stockpile of fissionable materials contributed by U.N. members, Eisenhower was taking the first step in a plan that could help to relieve worldwide tensions concerning nuclear energy and its attendant problems. His speech concluded with the pledge that the United States would ensure that "the miraculous inventiveness of man shall not be dedicated to his death, but consecrated to his life." While the hope offered in that speech was welcomed enthusiastically by an audience nevertheless concerned about the potential for disaster, it took three years before the International Atomic Energy Agency was founded, and its subsequent functions turned more on standards for radiation protection than on the dissemination of knowledge about power production. As a direct consequence of Eisenhower's faith in the potential of the atom, however, the government passed an amendment to the Atomic Energy Act of 1946.

THE 1954 ACT

Under the revised act of 1954, the federal government would license private industry to construct and operate domestic nuclear power plants. At the same time, while limiting the AEC's direct involvement in the manufacture and distribution of nuclear power, it was hoped that the private sector would be encouraged to take it on. People believed that private industry would be more efficient in managing the development of this new and important industry. The AEC would, however, subsidize research in the field of nuclear power so that private industry would be free of the burdensome costs that further development would entail.

One key provision of the act was the requirement that public hearings be held in each case where a construction permit was sought. It was expected that the AEC would reach agreement with the potential permittee on the details of the plans, so that the public hearing would not simply provide a forum for those who believed that the dangers of nuclear power outweighed any advantages it might bring. Under the rules, however, any person or group to challenge an application on grounds of safety was to be denied access to any AEC files that might reveal concerns about safety. In 1973, the National Science Foundation characterized these procedures as a charade whose sole purpose was to advance quickly the establishment of the nuclear power industry in the United States.

DEBATES OVER NUCLEAR POWER

In the climate of the times, there was widespread controversy about nuclear power issues. Many of the principal scientists who had been involved in the Manhattan Project, which developed the first atomic bomb, including the head of the group, J. Robert Oppenheimer, had considerable doubts about the prognosis for domestic uses. Others, such as presidential science adviser and discoverer of the fissionable element plutonium Glenn Seaborg, foresaw a future in which cheap atomic power would provide inexhaustible quantities of electricity sufficient to power the world's needs indefinitely. AEC chairman and investment banker Lewis L. Strauss was equally optimistic when he asserted that the promise of nuclear power was such that it would soon prove to be "too cheap to meter."

The establishment by act of Congress of a plan in which the AEC would become the promoter, custodian, and administrator for the domestic nuclear power industry posed a number of challenges. The first private company to oversee a civilian project was the Westinghouse Electric Corporation. Westinghouse collaborated with a Pittsburgh utility company in the construction of a pressurized water reactor, similar in type to the one under way for the U.S. Navy.

NUCLEAR SUBMARINES

Under the supervision of Admiral Hyman Rickover, the Navy project entailed the construction of the world's first nuclear-powered submarine. At that time, conventional power sources for submarines were of two kinds: diesel engines for surface use, since they required air intake and exhaust, and batteries for underwater travel. Rickover's plan was to construct a small, powerful nuclear reactor that would meet a submarine's energy needs under any conditions. Working from a company-sponsored laboratory on a project that remained under his close supervision, Rickover was able to oversee an effective working relationship among the Navy, private industry, and the AEC. After solving many practical engineering problems, the project finally succeeded in launching the USS *Nautilus*, the world's first nuclear-powered vessel. That event spurred the enthusiasm of nuclear power's supporters, since it demonstrated the feasibility of a cooperative project of the kind envisioned by the 1954 act.

NUCLEAR POWER PLANTS

In the years immediately following the building of the *Nautilus*, several companies and consortia became actively engaged in the planning process for new nuclear power plants. Concerns emerged, however, about where to build them. Remote locations were unacceptable to the private utilities, who preferred to have their operations closer to the power grids that they would supply. The first generation of nuclear power reactors therefore were placed in close proximity to large urban areas. Within a span of twenty-five years, eighteen functioning plants were built in the United States, and in the next five years the total exceeded fifty. Many more were in the planning stage.

   Increasing concerns about the potential for a nuclear accident that might result in the release of radioactive particles began to slow the building process. The public's concern continued to grow, in spite of the assurances contained in an AEC-sponsored report, the Brookhaven Report, which placed the casualty rate in a "maximum credible accident" at a vanishingly low level. The report also stated, however, that potential contamination of the surrounding land might extend as far as fifteen miles from the plant site and could cover extremely large land areas, with consequent loss of life and property perhaps reaching billions of dollars in value. These continuing fears, together with doubts expressed by groups of professionals such as the Union of Concerned Scientists, helped to slow the exploitation of nuclear power.

THE WINDSCALE ACCIDENT

Then, in October, 1957, a reactor in Great Britain, Windscale, designed to create nuclear fuels, suffered a severe accident resulting in widespread contamination of nearly four hundred square miles of the surrounding area, necessitating the government's seizure of all crops growing within it. One prominent scientist concluded that, following the complete failure of the reactor's containment vessel, more fission products were released into the atmosphere than had been set free in the weapon exploded over Hiroshima, Japan, in 1945.

CLEAN AIR ACT

In 1963, the National Environmental Policy Act, also known as the Clean Air Act, coupled with widening public concerns about atmospheric contaminants that had become the principal focus of the Nuclear Test Ban Treaty of the same year, gave rise to increased pressures to contain the growth of the nuclear power industry. In addition, the Clean Air Act required that assessments be made of the total impact of any proposed plant, including a cost-benefit analysis encompassing all aspects that might affect the local community. By the mid-1970's, these additional constraints, together with escalating costs that resulted from consequent delays, effectively served to bring to a halt any new construction.

THREE MILE ISLAND AND CHERNOBYL

The catastrophic accident at Three Mile Island, unit 2, located near Harrisburg, Pennsylvania, on March 28, 1979, provided compelling evidence of the fragility and potential lethality of nuclear power plants in the United States. Working in a critical area of the plant with the main reactor generating close to full capacity, a maintenance crew accidentally closed off one of the reactor's sources of coolant. In spite of the mechanisms that were in place to prevent damage and hazard from such an occurrence, a pressure-relief valve stuck in the open position, causing the main-reactor coolant to escape. Control room personnel had no warning of the problem and further compounded it by shutting off the pumps that controlled emergency cooling water. Thus, the reactor core began to overheat, coming within what was estimated to be thirty minutes of a complete meltdown—a potential catastrophe of the first magnitude.

Such an accident did in fact occur in April, 1986, when the first acknowledged case of a reactor meltdown was reported at the Chernobyl nuclear complex in the Soviet Union. The resulting cloud of radioactive debris was swept up into the atmosphere and dispersed not only over the Soviet Union, but also over a significant area of Northern Europe. Approximately one million times more radiation was released into the atmosphere than was released during the Three Mile Island incident.

LEGACY OF THE AEA

While there are still more than one hundred active nuclear power stations in the United States—about one-quarter of the worldwide total—the dream envisioned in the act of 1954, that the peaceful capture of the power of the atom would provide a virtually endless, free source of energy, was not achieved in the twentieth century. At the beginning of the twenty-first century, ongoing controversies about the disposal of nuclear wastes, fears of terrorist attacks on the U.S. mainland, and a presidential administration that did not seem to prioritize alternatives to petrochemical forms of energy suggested that a safe nuclear "utopia" was not within sight.

David G. Fenton

SOURCES FOR FURTHER STUDY

Balogh, Brian. *Chain Reaction*. Cambridge, England: Cambridge University Press, 1991.

Cohen, Bernard L. *The Nuclear Energy Option*. New York: Plenum Press, 1990.

Ford, Daniel. *The Cult of the Atom*. New York: Simon & Schuster, 1982.

Losee, Madeleine, comp. *Legislative History of the U.S. Atomic Energy Act of 1954, Publi Law 703, 83rd Congress*. 3 vols. Buffalo, N.Y.: William S. Hein, 1955.

Robinson, Marilynne. *Mother Country*. New York: Farrar, Straus & Giroux, 1989.

Wolfson, Richard. *Nuclear Choices*. Cambridge, Mass.: MIT Press, 1991.

SEE ALSO: Price-Anderson Act (1957); Nuclear Test Ban Treaty (1963); Clean Air Act (1963); Nuclear Nonproliferation Treaty (1968); Low-Level Radioactive Waste Policy Act (1980); Superfund Act (1980); Nuclear Waste Policy Act (1983).

FORMOSA RESOLUTION

DATE: January 29, 1955
U.S. STATUTES AT LARGE: 69 Stat. 7
CATEGORIES: Asia or Asian Americans; Foreign Relations

Passage of a joint resolution affirmed presidential power to defend Taiwan and demonstrated the willingness of the United States to wage an active Cold War.

In 1949, as the communists took over mainland China at the end of the Chinese civil war, Chiang Kai-shek, president of the Republic of China, or Nationalist China, withdrew with part of his government and army to the island of Formosa and the nearby Pescadores Islands. Formosa, a Portuguese name meaning "beautiful," was still used in the 1950's to describe the island in the West; as Asian nomenclature began to replace colonial-era names, the island's Chinese name, Taiwan, was used exclusively and the name Formosa passed into history. Formosa and the Pescadores had been held by the Japanese from 1895 until their return to China in 1945, at the end of World War II. Chiang claimed that his was still the legitimate government of China and announced his intention to return to the mainland and to power. His troops also held other islands off the China coast, notably Quemoy, a short distance from the port of Amoy; Matsu, off Foochow; and the Tachens, located about two hundred miles to the north of Matsu.

THE CONFLICT OVER FORMOSA (TAIWAN)

Both Chiang and the Chinese communists held that Formosa was a province of China, and Quemoy and Matsu were part of the mainland province of Fukien. Though Quemoy and Matsu were small, both sides saw them as stepping-stones. In Chiang's view, they were strategic for a return to the mainland; to the communists, they were a step toward the inclusion of Formosa in their regime. The islands were staging points for occasional raids on the mainland and came under air attack from the communists.

The United States had supported Chiang in the civil war and recognized his regime as the legitimate government for all China. The Korean War (1950-1953), and the Chinese communist role in it, strengthened U.S. antipathy toward the communists. Military and economic aid went to Formosa, and the Seventh Fleet patrolled the Formosa Strait to prevent invasion. Chiang increased the armament and garrisons on Quemoy and Matsu against the advice of many individuals in the U.S. military establishment. The mainland regime placed even larger forces on the shore facing the islands. In August and September, 1954, the communists began a bombardment of the islands, killing two U.S. military advisers.

Throughout the autumn, debate over policy continued, both within the United States and between the United States and its allies. Some of the Joint Chiefs of Staff and some members of Congress (such as Senator William F. Knowland of California) were willing to encourage Chiang in a return to the mainland and to give U.S. support to his forces on Quemoy and Matsu. This policy was popularly known as "unleashing Chiang Kai-shek." Others saw in such steps either continued defeat for Chiang or involvement in a major Asian war (World War III in some predictions), or both. Secretary of State John Foster Dulles viewed the question of Formosa and the offshore islands within the context of the Cold War, then at its height. To him, the maintenance of a strong Nationalist presence off the coast of mainland China would keep the Chinese communist regime off balance, while offering some hope to those who wanted it overthrown.

A Mutual Defense Treaty

As a result of these debates within the government, a somewhat more definite policy toward Nationalist China began to emerge. On December 2, 1954, the United States and Nationalist China concluded a mutual defense treaty. No specific mention was made in the treaty about offshore islands, however. Consequently, a month later, the Chinese communists launched bombardment and air attacks on these islands. On January 24, 1955, as the attacks continued, President Dwight D. Eisenhower sent a special message to Congress in which he asked for authority to use the armed forces of the United States to protect Formosa, the Pescadores, and what he vaguely referred to as certain "closely related localities." This authority, like the mutual defense treaty, would not commit the United States in advance to the defense of the offshore islands, nor would it limit United States action in advance.

President Eisenhower pointed out that the measure was not a constitutional necessity; he already had the requisite authority both as commander in chief and under the terms of the mutual security treaty already signed but not as yet ratified by the Senate. He wanted a demonstration of the unity of the United States and its resolve, while making thoroughly clear the authority of the president. In communist China, Premier Zhou Enlai called the message a war message.

The Resolution Passes Congress

The message went to the new Eighty-fourth Congress, which had Democratic majority in both houses. In response, the chairmen of the respective committees, Democrats Walter George in the Senate and James P. Richards in the House, introduced the joint resolution that became known as the Formosa Resolution. The resolution took as its premise the vital interest of the United States in peace in the western Pacific and the danger to peace from communist attacks in the area. It took note of the statement of mutual interest in the treaty submitted to the Senate. It therefore resolved:

> That the President of the United States . . . is authorized to employ the Armed Forces of the United States as he deems necessary for the specific purpose of securing and protecting Formosa and the Pescadores against armed attack, this authority to include the securing and protection of such related positions and territories of that area now in friendly hands and the taking of such other measures as he judges to be required or appropriate in assuring the defense of Formosa and the Pescadores.

There was strong bipartisan support among U.S. politicians for aggressive anticommunist positions. The House passed the resolution on January 25, 1955, by a vote of 410 to 3. In the Senate committee, an amendment to turn Formosa and the Pescadores over to the authority of the United Nations, and giving authorization to the president only until the United Nations acted, was defeated. Another amendment to limit the authority to Formosa and the Pescadores also lost. A similar amendment to draw a line back of Quemoy and Matsu, limiting the president's authority to Formosa and the Pescadores, was introduced on the Senate floor by Senator Herbert Lehman of New York. It was defeated 74 to 13. The Senate passed the resolution 85 to 3, on January 28, 1955, and President Eisenhower signed it the next day.

IMMEDIATE IMPACT

The mutual security treaty with Nationalist China was ratified in February. Efforts to persuade Chiang Kai-shek to reduce his forces on Quemoy and Matsu and make them mere outposts failed. That same month, however, Chiang did evacuate the Tachen Islands, which the communists promptly occupied. Communist Premier Zhou Enlai, in an attempt to strike a conciliatory note, told the Afro-Asian Conference meeting in Bandung, Indonesia, in April, that his country did not want war with the United States. He further expressed his willingness to negotiate on Far Eastern issues, including that of Formosa. As a result, by May, without formal statement or agreement, there was an effective cease-fire in the Formosa Straits.

In the wake of the passage of the Formosa Resolution and the ratification of the mutual defense treaty with Nationalist China, President Eisenhower addressed a letter to British prime minister Winston Churchill on February 9, 1955, in which he set forth his ideas on the importance of defending Formosa and the offshore islands. The United States depended on an island (Formosa) and a peninsula (Korea) as its defense line in Southeast Asia. The loss of Formosa would be a serious break in that line. The weakening of Chiang Kai-shek's forces could mean the loss of Formosa. The denial of their expectation to return to mainland China would be destructive of their morale. Therefore, it was important to the United States not only to aid in the defense of Formosa but also not to accept, or seem to accept, the loss of the offshore islands, which were of strategic importance in launching a return to the mainland. These ideas helped set the posture of U.S. policy in the Far East for some time to come.

HISTORICAL PERSPECTIVE

Judgments of the Formosa Resolution at the time of its passage and in historical perspective must depend greatly on attitudes toward the larger question of policy toward China. The overwhelming vote in Congress in favor of the Formosa Resolution may be taken as clear evidence of opinion there, and presumably of opinion throughout the country, that communist expansion must be resisted, but the United States ought not be involved in further war. From another, but related, perspective, the Formosa Resolution was a reflection of the Cold War mentality that saw no possibility for diplomatic recognition of the communist regime on the Chinese mainland.

Even after this Cold War mentality had waned, the legacy of the Formosa Resolution ensured that the United States maintained residual ties with the nationalist regime in Taiwan even after it afforded diplomatic recognition to mainland China in 1979. As U.S.-China tensions began to increase in the mid-1990's, the consensus among U.S. policymakers was that something should be done if China were to invade Taiwan. Thus, the impact of the Formosa Resolution was not confined to its immediate aftermath.

George J. Fleming, updated by
Nicholas Birns

SOURCES FOR FURTHER STUDY

Bueler, William M. *U.S. China Policy and the Problem of Taiwan*. Boulder: Colorado Associated University Press, 1971.

Copper, John Franklin. *China Diplomacy: The Washington-Taipei-Beijing Triangle*. Boulder, Colo.: Westview Press, 1992.

Eisenhower, Dwight D. *Mandate for Change, 1953-1956*. Garden City, N.Y.: Doubleday, 1963.

Hickey, Dennis Van Vranken. *United States-Taiwan Security Ties: From Cold War to Beyond Containment*. Westport, Conn.: Praeger, 1994.

Hsieh, Chiao Chiao. *Strategy for Survival: The Foreign Policy and External Relations of the Republic of China on Taiwan, 1949-1979*. London: Sherwood Press, 1985.

SEE ALSO: Treaty of Wang Hiya (1844); Burlingame Treaty (1868); Tripartite Security Treaty (1952); U.S.-Japanese Treaty (1952); Eisenhower Doctrine (1957); Tonkin Gulf Resolution (1964); War Powers Resolution (1973); Taiwan Relations Act (1979).

AIR POLLUTION CONTROL ACT

DATE: July 14, 1955
U.S. STATUTES AT LARGE: 69 Stat. 322
PUBLIC LAW: 84-159
CATEGORIES: Environment and Conservation; Natural Resources

Congress passed the first U.S. legislation to help control and prevent air pollution.

On July 14, 1955, the U.S. Congress enacted the first federal legislation to control air pollution, the Air Pollution Control Act. The objectives of this act included protecting national air resources so as to promote public health and welfare, providing technical and financial assistance to state and local governments by the federal government for air pollution prevention and control programs, initiating a national research program to prevent and control air pollution, and assisting in the development and operation of air pollution control programs. This act recognized that, although sources of air pollution were local problems, federal assistance was necessary to develop cooperative air pollution control programs between state and local governments. In 1955, it was necessary to identify pollution sources, analyze effects of air pollution, and initiate effective legislation and enforcement by government regulatory agencies.

AIR POLLUTION CRISES

Enactment of the Air Pollution Control Act was in response to serious health-threatening crises that occurred in the years preceding 1955. These air pollution crises were the result of increasing urban and industrial development in the United States. In 1860, the United States was a nation of 31.5 million people, 20 percent of whom lived in urban areas. By 1900, the urban population in the United States had risen to more than 30 million, 40 percent of the total population. The trend of increasing urban population coincided with rapid industrial development and its production of smoke and sulfur dioxide. Industrial development spawned development of the chemical industry, which increased the amount and type of pollutants emitted from factory stacks. Industrial activities in the United States increased to meet military needs during World

War II; however, this caused increased air pollution, which was especially critical in cities such as Los Angeles, California.

In February, 1945, Los Angeles created the position of director of air pollution control to enforce laws pertaining to control of air pollution, to solicit public cooperation through education, and to obtain technical support to carry out the director's duties. In 1947, Los Angeles County, which included forty-five separate cities, was designated as an Air Pollution Control District by the California state legislature. This allowed for enforcement of laws and a permit system within the district. Dr. Louis C. McCabe was the initial director of the Air Pollution Control District.

Between 1947 and 1955, several incidents occurred that directed attention to the serious effects of air pollution. One of the most critical events occurred in October, 1948, at Donora, Pennsylvania, a suburb twenty-five miles south of Pittsburgh. Atmospheric conditions were such that a stable air mass settled for several days over Western Pennsylvania and Eastern Ohio. A temperature inversion and fog trapped pollutants, primarily from the zinc works at the American Steel and Wire Company, and created a heavy smog. After four days, twenty people were dead and nearly six thousand had become ill with symptoms of gasping and chest pains. Hospitals were filled to capacity. This incident made it clear that air pollution was a health hazard that demanded attention.

Problems at Donora were followed by similar episodes of dangerous smog in London, England, during December, 1952. More than four thousand people died as the result of air filled with soot, smoke, and factory emissions. In the following months, more than eight thousand people died of respiratory-related causes that were blamed on the December smog. During October, 1954, a heavy smog that hung over Los Angeles for nine consecutive days resulted in widespread eye irritation. The smog was blamed on excessive motor-vehicle exhaust; in response, police set up roadblocks to check vehicles for excessive emissions of fumes.

THE NEED FOR FEDERAL ACTION

These serious air pollution events ignited efforts by Congress to establish the first air pollution control legislation. Senators Thomas Kuchel of California and Homer Capehart of Indiana wrote an important letter to President Dwight D. Eisenhower on August 5, 1954, that implored the president to establish an interdepartmental committee of federal agencies from health, housing, agriculture, transportation, economy, industry, and research to control smog. This letter was referred to Oveta Culp Hobby, secretary of health, education, and welfare. Hobby responded with a statement of her support for the proposed committee, and she began soliciting representatives from the Departments of Agriculture, the Interior, Commerce, and Defense, in addition to the Atomic Energy Commission and the National Science Foundation.

Another important letter from Kuchel to Eisenhower was written on October 21, 1954. In his letter, Kuchel called the president's attention to the current serious smog emergency in Los Angeles and outlined his ideas on how the U.S. Public Health Service, Bureau of Standards, and Bureau of Mines could contribute their energies to avert a national health problem related to air pollution.

As a consequence of such activism, the Interdepartment Ad Hoc Committee on Community Air Pollution was formed and met initially on November 16, 1954. The committee discussed prospective legislation and the principles upon which it would be based. A report, "The Federal Role in Community Air Pollution Problems," was produced by the committee in April, 1955. Work by this committee resulted in meetings between key federal officials and congressional personnel, which concluded in a bill (S. 928) sponsored by Senator Kuchel to amend the Water Pollution Control Act in order to provide for air pollution control.

In late April, 1955, Secretary Hobby answered a request for comments on bill S. 928 with a letter to Senator Dennis Chavez, chairman of the Senate Committee on Public Works. Hobby justified a five-year duration of work and appropriations from this bill, from July 1, 1955, to June 30, 1960, of $5 million per year. The bill called for an Air Pollution Control Advisory Board that Hobby believed could be better fulfilled by using the ad hoc committee already organized. Bill S. 928 received exclusively favorable testimony for enactment during hearings held by the Senate Committee on Public Works. On July 14, 1955, bill S. 928 was enacted as Public Law 159 and was known as the Air Pollution Control Act of 1955.

A NEW PUBLIC ATTITUDE
In the two years following enactment of the Air Pollution Control Act of 1955, significant changes took place in response to air pollution. These were summarized during an address on the review of

progress made under the Air Pollution Control Act of 1955 by U.S. surgeon general Leroy Burneyk to the National Conference on Air Pollution in November, 1958. Across the United States, people became aware that air pollution was indeed a problem that demanded attention. Clean air could no longer be taken for granted. Eleven states passed initial laws or strengthened existing laws regarding air pollution control. Statewide air pollution control statutes were developed for Oregon, Washington, Delaware, New York, and Florida to maintain reasonable air purity. A National Air Sampling Network expanded to include 181 cities and fifty-one non-urban environments where airborne solid particles and liquid droplet concentrations were monitored. Gas sampling was identified as a necessary and important addition to the network. Research collaboration on air pollution control and on the health effects of specific pollutants increased dramatically. The Public Health Service worked with the Bureau of Mines and the U.S. Weather Bureau to analyze air pollution from motor vehicles. Education on air pollution control increased.

SUBSEQUENT LEGISLATION
Over the years immediately following 1958, evidence of the first air pollution legislation resulted in additional emphasis through amendments to the 1955 act and through new legislation. The Air Pollution Control Act of 1955 was amended in 1959 to extend appropriations for four additional years, through June, 1964. Congress mandated cooperation between federal agencies and the Department of Health, Education, and Welfare for air pollution prevention and control. Another amendment in 1960 included a required report from the surgeon general to Congress with respect to the growing problem of pollution from motor-vehicle exhaust. The 1962 amendment to the Air Pollution Control Act of 1955 extended appropriations an additional two years through June, 1966. This amendment required permanent studies on the air pollution discharged from motor vehicles.

During 1963, the Air Pollution Control Act was replaced by the Clean Air Act of 1963. This new act directed that new training programs and research commence, new financial grants to states and municipalities be made, and federal intervention stop interstate air pollution. More explicit authority for air pollution control was given to the Department of Health, Education, and Welfare. By

1963, most local governments were in favor of and had instituted air pollution control laws. Since then, the act has been amended many times.

In 1970, the U.S. Environmental Protection Agency (EPA) was founded by President Richard M. Nixon. Its purpose was to monitor and enforce environmental laws, including laws on air pollution. In 1993, the EPA reported a decline in the levels of six major air pollutants from 1982 to 1991. The EPA attributed this successful control to federal restrictions in the Clean Air Act and to favorable weather patterns. Oil companies agreed in 1992 to provide cleaner-burning gasoline to the U.S. cities with poorest air quality by 1995.

The Automobile

There are problems resulting from air pollution that remain to be solved. Many cities in the United States still fail to meet air quality standards mandated by the Clean Air Act and its amendments. There are enough airborne poisons to deliver several pounds of poisons to every U.S. citizen. The main cause of air pollution remains the motor vehicle, which was identified as a problem as early as 1955. Although individual automobiles are producing less pollution than they were in 1970, there were significantly more automobiles on the road by the end of the century, and many of these were fuel-inefficient gas-guzzlers, despite both federal and state emissions regulations.

Aside from air quality, the emissions from these vehicles are directly related to such serious and daunting environmental problems as global warming, climate change, increases in frequency and intensity of storm activity, and acid rain. Acid rain, a precipitation containing high levels of sulfuric or nitric acids, has steadily become a more serious contaminant, damaging vegetation, drinking water, and aquatic life and even damaging buildings and monuments. Air pollution from automobiles and sulfur-burning industrial plants are the main sources of such acidic pollution. The Clean Air Act of 1990 was the first legislation that attempted to regulate emissions that cause acid rain. Acid rain is especially difficult to control with restrictions, because pollution sources are frequently in one state while the rain falls in a different state; the problem thus requires federal intervention.

Garrett L. Van Wicklen

SOURCES FOR FURTHER STUDY

Chanlett, E. T. "Our Air Environment in the Workplace and the Community." In *Environmental Protection*. New York: McGraw-Hill, 1973.

Degler, Stanley E., and Sandra C. Bloom. *Federal Pollution Control Programs: Water, Air and Solid Wastes*. Washington, D.C.: BNA Books, 1969.

Dworsky, Leonard B., comp. *Pollution*. New York: Chelsea House, 1971.

Tomany, J. P. "Air Pollution Control Regulations." In *Air Pollution: The Emissions, the Regulations, and the Controls*. New York: American Elsevier, 1975.

Wark, K., and Cecil F. Warner. "Federal Legislation and Regulatory Trends." In *Air Pollution: Its Origins and Control*. New York: IEP, 1976.

SEE ALSO: Clean Air Act (1963); Motor Vehicle Air Pollution Control Act (1965); Clean Air Act Amendments of 1970 (1970); National Environmental Policy Act (1970); Clean Air Act Amendments of 1977 (1977); Alternative Motor Fuels Act (1988); Clean Air Act Amendments of 1990 (1990).

WATER POLLUTION CONTROL ACT AMENDMENTS OF 1956

DATE: July 9, 1956
U.S. STATUTES AT LARGE: 70 Stat. 498
PUBLIC LAW: 84-660
U.S. CODE: 33 § 1251
CATEGORIES: Environment and Conservation; Natural Resources

The Water Pollution Control Act of 1956 amended the 1948 Water Pollution Control Act, increasing federal funds for pollution-control programs and water-treatment plants as well as strengthening federal powers.

The U.S. Congress passed the amended Water Pollution Control Act on June 27, 1956, three days before the 1948 version of the act was due to expire, and President Dwight D. Eisenhower signed it into law on July 9, 1956. It was thought that the act would enable the nation to produce the huge quantities of clean, fresh water needed by the ever-increasing national population and its giant industrial complex.

EARLY LEGISLATION

Federal legislation concerning water-pollution control first began with the limited Rivers and Harbors Act of 1899, which was administered by the secretary of the Army and which protected navigation by prohibiting discharge of most refuse into U.S. waters. That law was followed in 1912 by the first federal legislation on health-related aspects of water pollution, the Public Health Service Act; this important act mandated the investigation of the relationship between water pollution and human health. In 1924, the Oil Pollution Act, also administered by the secretary of the Army, attempted to diminish the discharge into U.S. waters of petroleum "that endangers ocean life, as well as our harbors and recreational facilities." These three acts defined the early federal role in exploring problems associated with the regulation of water quality.

PROVISIONS OF THE 1956 LAW

Over the years, the federal government acquired strong regulatory and enforcement powers, beginning with the five-year Water Pollution Control Act of 1948, which was extended until 1956 (Public Laws 80-845 and 82-579) and then in 1956 replaced with Public Law 84-660. The responsibility of administering Public Law 84-660 was vested in the surgeon general of the Public Health Service, who was under the supervision and direction of the secretary of health, education, and welfare.

Public Law 84-660 addressed some of the shortcomings of the 1948 act. The new law eliminated a provision in the 1948 act that allowed states to override federal authority in certain cases. In addition, the 1956 legislation addressed the fact that funds authorized by the earlier act for the construction of water-treatment plants had not been made available as expected.

Governmental efforts to deal with water pollution have focused mainly on visible natural bodies of water such as rivers and lakes, where pollutants include myriad substances found in farm runoff, municipal sewage, and industrial effluents. These substances include inorganic chemicals such as salts and agricultural fertilizers, organic chemicals dumped in the course of food processing, insecticides and other pesticides, by-products vented in chemical company effluents, and radioisotopes.

The provisions of Public Law 84-660 included the authorization of $500 million in matching funds over ten years for the construction of community water-treatment facilities. Funding was limited to $250,000 or 30 percent of the total cost of a project (whichever was less), and half of all funds was allocated for communities with populations of 125,000 or fewer. Some funds were allocated for research on water pollution, its treatment, and its control, to be carried out at universities and other nongovernmental agencies.

The surgeon general was made responsible for overseeing state preparations of comprehensive water-pollution control programs and research projects. It was hoped that more uniform laws concerning the prevention, handling, and control of water pollution would result. The federal government planned to spend $3 million annually between 1957 and 1961 for state aid, with allocations made on the basis of state population, the extent of the pollution observed, and the extent of the need envisioned. The federal contributions were not to exceed two-thirds of the total costs for any program, and all projects needed the approval of the surgeon general.

The act also established a nine-member Water Pollution Control Board, to be named by the president, and specified procedures for the surgeon general to initiate antipollution measures in states where pollution was occurring. If, after a conference called by the surgeon general, a state did not within six months comply with recommendations for cleanup, the secretary of health, education, and welfare was authorized to call a public hearing and issue further recommendations. The state would then be given a further six months in which to take action; if it did not do so, the U.S. attorney general could override the state and initiate a federal suit.

SOURCES OF WATER POLLUTION

A major reason for the Water Pollution Control Act was the ever-growing demand for fresh, clean water, a demand that required the cleanup of interstate waters at as many points as possible. In 1955, the Public Health Service observed that since 1935 the amount of dumped municipal waste had risen by 10 percent and that of industrial waste had almost doubled. In 1956, the service estimated that municipalities and industry would each need to spend $500 million or more annually for ten years to maintain an adequate supply of clean water. It was further estimated that municipal expenditure would be nearly equally divided among replacing worn-out water-treatment facilities, meeting increasing water demands, and completing construction of new water-treatment plants. Such a forecast made the need for the new Water Pollution Control Act clear.

The two main sources of water pollution in the United States are industry and municipalities. The development and passage of the Water Pollution Control Act of 1956 helped to reduce both types of pollution. A problem associated with the act was that its main enforcement tools—the conferences called by the surgeon general— relied heavily, like those of the preceding law, upon negotiated agreements, state agency pressures, and the force of local public opinion. On the other hand, the "reasonable" time period for a state's compliance had been codified not to exceed six months.

RESPONSE AND SUBSEQUENT LEGISLATION

The responses to the Water Pollution Control Act ranged from appreciation, as expressed by the American Municipal Association, which believed that extensive federal aid was essential in solving the water-pollution problem, to disappointment that the federal government was not doing enough and that the law's provisions were too limited. Industrial organizations such as the National Association of Manufacturers, which argued that state and local controls were sufficient to deal with pollution problems, strongly disliked the idea of strengthened federal control. The manufacturers' association asserted that it was inappropriate for state and local funds to be enhanced by federal contributions. Business interests therefore generally opposed federal controls, proposing that more would be accomplished by cooperation than by compulsion.

Between 1956 and 1965, water pollution continued to be a serious problem. In part, this was because many municipalities and industrial corporations failed to comply with the law in their handling of wastes. State and federal action under the Water Pollution Control Act of 1956 was not tough enough, and this action was limited to interstate waters. The Public Health Service, too, reacted slowly and leniently, initiating action on only seven of 125 interstate rivers that had been reported to be polluted. As a result, various private and public interest groups believed that further legislative action was needed for effective intervention. From 1965 on, a number of water quality acts were passed to strengthen protection of U.S. water resources and establish a national policy for the prevention, control, and abatement of water pollution. Stronger policies for enforcement of federal decisions were also eventually developed.

Yet to come was realization by corporate executives that informed public opinion could make or break their companies. In light of the general public's relative ignorance of environmental issues in the 1950's, there was substantial resistance to water cleanup by many companies. Not all industry was insensitive to the issue, however; in fact, many companies rallied sensibly to demands for pollution cleanup. Nevertheless, more complete compliance would later be found to require greatly enhanced federal enforcement, the creation of a much sterner control agency than the Public Health Service, and the development of a concerned and well-informed public.

Sanford S. Singer

SOURCES FOR FURTHER STUDY

Business Week. "Billions to Clean Up the Rivers." April 24, 1965, 50-58.

_____. "New Weapons Against Pollution." August 13, 1955, 136-137.

Farb, Peter. "Let's Clean Up All Our Polluted Rivers." *Reader's Digest,* October, 1957, 133-137.

Lapedes, Daniel N., et al., eds. *McGraw-Hill Encyclopedia of Environmental Science.* New York: McGraw-Hill, 1974.

Miller, G. Tyler, Jr., and David G. Lygre. *Chemistry: A Contemporary Approach.* 3d ed. Belmont, Calif.: Wadsworth, 1987.

Stein, Murray. "Legislation on Water Pollution Control." *Public Health Reports* 79 (August 8, 1964): 699-706.

SEE ALSO: Oil Pollution Act of 1924 (1924); Air Pollution Control Act (1955); Water Resources Research Act (1964); Clean Water Act and Amendments (1965); Wild and Scenic Rivers Act and National

Trails System Act (1968); Water Pollution Control Act Amendments of 1972 (1972); Safe Drinking Water Act (1974); Toxic Substances Control Act (1976); Oil Pollution Act of 1990 (1990).

EISENHOWER DOCTRINE

DATE: Issued January 5, 1957
CATEGORIES: Foreign Relations

A bipartisan foreign policy initiative articulated the U.S. effort to combat "international communism" in the Middle East.

In the aftermath of the Suez crisis of October, 1956, which created a power vacuum in the Middle East as a result of Great Britain's and France's invasion of Egypt, the United States reconsidered its position and policies in the Middle East. Acting through the United Nations, and for once in agreement with the Soviet Union, the United States had brought about the withdrawal of British and French forces from Egypt. The entire episode seemed not only to have weakened Western unity but also to have strengthened the position of the Soviet Union in the Arab countries and that of Gamal Abdel Nasser, the Egyptian president, as the leading spokesman of Arab nationalist feeling. Nasser envisioned himself to be the "voice of the Arabs," and his resisting the West and allying himself increasingly with the Soviet Union caused the United States to fear instability in the oil-rich and strategically located region. The Eisenhower administration saw a vacuum in the Middle East, which it feared would be filled by Soviet influence. President Dwight D. Eisenhower, therefore, offered a statement of policy, which became known as the Eisenhower Doctrine.

THE DOCTRINE
Issued as a message to Congress on January 5, 1957, after consultation with congressional leaders and with Dag Hammarskjöld, the secretary general of the United Nations, the doctrine proposed that the United States fill the vacuum with economic and military aid. Eisenhower asked the new Eighty-fifth Congress to appropri-

ate four hundred million dollars for two years for economic and military assistance to the nations of the Middle East, and to authorize the use of U.S. forces upon the request of any nation in the region threatened by communist aggression. Eisenhower appointed James P. Richards, the recently retired Democratic chair of the House Foreign Affairs Committee, to be his personal envoy to the Middle East. Richards's mission was clear: He was to explain the evils of international communism, solicit support from the region's leaders, and dispense aid to countries that publicly announced their loyalty to the West. Besides the provision of assistance, one purpose of the presidential request to Congress was to give the Soviet Union warning of U.S. intentions to prevent Soviet expansion in the Middle East and to make clear and public the national support for those intentions.

In some respects, the Eisenhower Doctrine followed the precedents of the Truman Doctrine of 1947 and the Formosa Resolution passed by Congress in 1955. It differed, however, from the Truman Doctrine in its application to a particular area; the Truman Doctrine, although occasioned by problems of Greece and Turkey, was a promise of U.S. support for any peoples resisting aggression. Moreover, neither earlier proposal carried the proviso that armed forces be sent only on the request of the other nation.

The House resolution on behalf of the president's request, introduced the same day, was approved by the Foreign Affairs Committee by a vote of 24 to 2 on January 24, and by the entire House on January 31 by a vote of 355 to 61. Senate action was slower. In debates in early March, Senator Richard Russell of Georgia proposed an amendment that would have deleted the military and economic assistance, but the amendment lost. A proposal by Senator J. William Fulbright of Arkansas for a white paper from the State Department detailing U.S. relations with the region also failed. The Senate passed the resolution, with some limiting changes, on March 5, by a vote of 72 to 19; the House accepted the Senate version on March 7, by 350 to 60; the president signed it on March 9, 1957.

REACTION

The announcement of the doctrine met mixed reactions. The votes in the Congress were probably indicative of general support; they are notable because the Democratic Party had majorities in both houses. The public trust in President Eisenhower, so recently reelected, was one factor; the general mood of the Cold War was another. Additionally, the selection of Richards to go to the Middle East as the administration's chief envoy helped solidify bipartisan support for the initiative.

Reactions abroad were less favorable. Denunciations from Moscow and Peking were expected. Prime Minister Jawaharlal Nehru of India thought the dangers of aggression were exaggerated and believed that the interests of peace were not forwarded by the U.S. action. The Arab states, led by Egypt, also reacted unfavorably. A mission led by Richards in the spring of 1957 did not even visit Egypt, Syria, or Jordan. Lebanon, Israel, Iraq, and Iran endorsed the policy, but other Middle Eastern countries, such as Libya, were lukewarm. Richards was briefly held hostage in Yemen when he refused to award that country enough economic assistance to persuade the small nation to oppose agents of international communism. Lebanon's history and situation explain both its acceptance and its later application of the Eisenhower Doctrine to that country.

CRISES IN LEBANON AND IRAQ

Alone among the Arab countries, which were overwhelmingly Muslim, Lebanon had a large Christian population; in the absence of accurate statistics, estimates place it near a majority. The ties to Rome of the majority of these (Maronites and other Catholics of non-Latin rites), the U.S. Protestant missionary and educational effort since the early nineteenth century, and the experience of French rule or mandate, gave Lebanon a view of the West and a relation to it different from that of the other Arab nations. Independent Lebanon had developed political and social traditions of its own to deal with religious differences. The most notable example was the tradition that the president be a Christian, the prime minister a Muslim. Under the surface, however, religious and regional hostilities were often bitter.

These international strains were increased and intensified by Arab feeling inflamed against Israel and by Nasserism—the extreme Arab movement toward unity and belligerence intimately associated with Egypt's leader. The immediate occasion of trouble in Lebanon was the possibility that President Camille Chamoun intended to have his term extended, contrary to the Lebanese constitution. Opposition forces organized against this move—some religious, some political opponents of Chamoun, some supported by

Syrian and Egyptian interests. Civil strife on this issue broke out in May, 1958.

Just as this turmoil in Lebanon seemed to be subsiding, an unexpected crisis erupted in Iraq. On July 14, 1958, a bloody revolution overthrew the pro-Western Iraqi government. President Chamoun appealed to the United States out of fear that the coup in Iraq was the result of a Soviet-Nasserite plot that would soon be reenacted in Lebanon. On July 15, on the orders of President Eisenhower, units of the Sixth Fleet landed U.S. Marines in Lebanon to preserve order. With the aid of Robert McClintock, the United States ambassador, the U.S. troops were kept in positions where they did not affect the local political situation. Robert Murphy, U.S. deputy undersecretary of state and an experienced diplomat, worked with the differing Lebanese forces to achieve settlement.

Whatever ambition he had entertained, Chamoun now gave up any intention of another term. With some difficulty, the negotiators persuaded General Fuad Shehab to accept the Lebanese presidency, to which he was elected by Lebanon's parliament on July 31. As commander of the army, Shehab had tried to maintain an impartial position, and he was one of the few people acceptable to almost all factions.

The exercise of the Eisenhower Doctrine thus resulted in accommodation. The Marines were withdrawn on October 25, 1958. This diplomatic effort represents the United States' Cold War approach to foreign policy. Egypt's coziness with the Soviet Union and Nasser's nationalistic rhetoric alarmed the United States and led to Richards's mission and the United States' later presence in Lebanon.

George J. Fleming, updated by
Joseph Edward Lee

SOURCES FOR FURTHER STUDY

Ambrose, Stephen. *Eisenhower.* New York: Simon & Schuster, 1984.

Hooper, Townshend. *The Devil and John Foster Dulles.* Boston: Little, Brown, 1973.

Nutting, Anthony. *Nasser.* New York: Random House, 1972.

Paterson, Thomas G., et al. *American Foreign Policy: A History.* Lexington, Mass.: McGraw-Hill, 1977.

SEE ALSO: Truman Doctrine (1947); Formosa Resolution (1955).

PRICE-ANDERSON ACT

DATE: August 16, 1957
U.S. STATUTES AT LARGE: 71 Stat. 576
PUBLIC LAW: 85-256
CATEGORIES: Energy; Environment and Conservation

> *Congress passed the Price-Anderson Act to limit how much money private producers of nuclear power would have to pay for damages caused by a catastrophic nuclear accident.*

On July 1 and August 16, 1957, the U.S. House of Representatives and the U.S. Senate passed, with little controversy or discussion, the Price-Anderson Act, which amended the 1954 Atomic Energy Act. The bill required builders of nuclear reactors to maintain a limited amount of private insurance, about $65 million, while the government would provide the remainder of the insurance, up to a maximum of $500 million for damages from any single accident, at no cost to the nuclear power industry.

ENCOURAGING NUCLEAR ENERGY

The amendment's purpose was to encourage the power industry to invest in nuclear plants at a time when private companies had not yet built such a plant. Nuclear plants cost too much, industry leaders explained, and a major cost was insurance in case of an incident. Power producers cited a 1957 Atomic Energy Commission (AEC) report estimating that, in a worst-case accident in a plant near a major city, the radioactive release of a core meltdown would immediately kill 3,400 people, cause serious injury to 43,000, and destroy about $7 billion in property in a region covering 150,000 square miles. Fear of such an accident and the costs involved prevented any company from constructing a nuclear power plant.

Congress hoped the Price-Anderson Act would help promote the growth of a private nuclear power industry by requiring the government to assume the insurance costs and the costs of any civilian damages. From 1945, when the government had begun studying uses of atomic power for peaceful purposes, the major research and experiments had been done in government laboratories. The Atomic Energy Act of 1946 mandated that control, production, and ownership of nuclear energy should be under the control of the Atomic Energy Commission. Beginning in 1948, the commission authorized a special program to develop a reactor for the production of electricity, but not until 1951 was any electricity produced, and then only a very small amount. Production of electricity from nuclear reaction proved to be very expensive and failed to convince any private electric company that nuclear energy was the wave of the future.

COLD WAR POWER RACE

In 1954, President Dwight D. Eisenhower asked Congress to create a program that would help beat the Soviets in the atomic power race. The president had first proposed "atoms for peace" in a speech to the United Nations the previous year. He asked Congress to set aside the 1946 law restricting nuclear development to Atomic Energy Commission projects and pressed for private development of nuclear energy plants. Congress debated the proposal vigorously and bitterly for several weeks. Advocates of public ownership of power plants argued that, since the federal government had already spent billions of dollars on research, it should not simply give away the information it had gathered to private companies without some control over prices these producers would charge for their product. The Eisenhower administration opposed any government controls.

The dispute ended in a victory for private power interests. Congress rejected arguments that, since taxpayers had paid for all development costs, they should benefit from low-cost government-owned power plants. The private companies, represented by the Edison Electric Institute, explained that it would be better for electricity to be marketed through private companies at commercially competitive rates. Cheap government prices would destroy the whole industry. The final bill met the demands of the industry by forbidding the AEC to produce or sell atomic power. The only regulation would come from the Federal Power Commission, but it could regulate rates only on electricity sold across state lines. The AEC was required to issue licenses for any nuclear plant that could demonstrate a "practical value for industrial or commercial purposes." Still, there was no interest among the private firms. Even after the addition of the Price-Anderson amendment in 1957, private electric companies believed that costs for building were too high.

In 1958, the AEC announced a five-year plan for construction of the nation's first nuclear-generating plant at Shippingport, Pennsylvania. After its construction, the plant was operated by the privately owned Duquesne Light Company. By 1964, only thirteen plants were in operation nationwide, and they sold less than 1 percent of the total electrical production in the United States. Congress then authorized the AEC to provide research and development work for all proposed plants, waived charges for leasing nuclear fuels from the AEC, and helped pay for construction costs. Only then did the industry begin to participate on a wider scale, though it still needed and received government assistance for its insurance obligations.

SAFETY CONCERNS AND THE RASMUSSEN REPORT

Congress created a new program for insurance coverage, however, that made the producers pay more than they had been required to pay under the 1957 law. Under provisions adopted in 1965, electric companies licensed to build nuclear plants by the AEC would have to carry as much insurance as was available through private sources, a figure Congress estimated to be about $60 million per facility. After the maximum of this insurance had been purchased, the government would provide extra coverage limited to the difference between that amount and $560 million. When this bill became law, that difference stood at about $500 million, but as more private insurance became available, it was expected that federal obligations would decline. Most experts still agreed that the possibility of any nuclear accident was very small, so that the government had little reason to fear financial obligation.

Concern over the safety of nuclear plants led to hearings by the Joint Energy Committee in 1973 and 1974. The committee heard AEC officials testify that nuclear reactors were safer than any other means of generating power. Consumer advocate Ralph Nader then took the stand and called nuclear power a dangerous form of "technological suicide." Antinuclear testimony also came from a scientist affiliated with the Union of Concerned Scientists. He cited a recent radioactive leak of 115,000 gallons of wastewater at the Hanford, Washington, plant as a sign of growing danger, and he predicted a major accident in the future. The danger was so great, he believed, that all nuclear construction had to be stopped immediately. A committee member who had worked at Hanford, however, labeled such fears irresponsible and advised his colleagues to ignore such fear-mongering. These comments reassured the other senators and congresspeople, and they concluded that a major accident was highly unlikely.

In order to reassure doubters, the joint committee established a committee of experts, headed by Norman C. Rasmussen, dean of the engineering department at the Massachusetts Institute of Technology, to study in more detail the risks of nuclear reactors. That report was to be completed by the end of 1974. While waiting for the report, Congress debated the insurance program once again. By this time, private insurance had been increased to nearly $110 million; the government's obligation had declined since 1965. The law still limited the total amount of disaster insurance that would be available in case of an accident to $560 million. Critics of this limit pointed out that three dozen new plants had been built since the limit had been established, and two hundred more were being planned. Each new plant increased the probability of a disaster, and it was believed that one serious accident could result in $7 billion in damages. Defenders of the lower limit pointed out that the government had actually never paid any claims under the Price-Anderson Act, there had been no major accidents, and many scientists believed there never would be a serious accident. After a lengthy debate in the Senate and the House, Congress voted for a five-year extension of the insurance program, with a provision allowing cancellation of the provisions if the Rasmussen Report concluded that reactors were unstable and dangerous.

Because of the latter provision, President Gerald Ford vetoed the bill, arguing that it took away his executive power. He would not sign legislation extending the insurance program if Congress insisted that it alone could cancel that program after publication of the Rasmussen Report. When Congress passed the same legislation in 1975 without the offending provision, the president quickly signed it into law. A few weeks later, Professor Rasmussen presented his report, *Reactor Safety Study,* to Congress. He concluded that the consequences of an accident were much smaller than were previously believed. The $560 million limit could adequately cover any "credible accident which might occur." The risk of an accident was nothing to be concerned about. A disaster at a nuclear plant, the study announced, was as likely as a meteorite crashing into a city, and the chances of such an event occurring were about one every million years. With such reassurance, there seemed to be little to fear and little to lose from an expanded government-sponsored insurance program. Republican John Anderson from Illinois argued that, without such financing, the private power industry would be put out of business because of high insurance costs. The House easily defeated an amendment seeking to eliminate the $560 million limit. The final bill extended coverage to 1987 and kept in place the liability law.

THREE MILE ISLAND AND CHERNOBYL

The nuclear power industry suffered a major shock on March 28, 1979, when the Three Mile Island reactor in Pennsylvania nearly melted down. The cost of decontaminating the reactor alone reached more than $1 billion. Still, Congress took no action to expand insurance coverage at that time. Fearing that increasing coverage would set a precedent for future bailouts, Congress responded by telling the owners of Three Mile Island that they would have to pay their own damages by raising their customers' rates.

The House and Senate did not take up the issue of insurance again until 1986. After considering several proposals to increase the $560 million ceiling, the House voted to set the limit paid to victims of a nuclear accident at $6.5 billion. The Senate disagreed, however, and on August 23, adopted a $2.4 billion limit. Two days later, a major nuclear accident occurred at Chernobyl in the Soviet Union. This incident, perhaps the worst disaster in the history of peaceful nuclear energy production, contributed to the adoption of higher limits by the Senate Energy Committee.

The final bill did not come before the full Congress for debate until late in 1987. It raised the total insurance available for any single disaster to nearly $7 billion. The major debate involved who would pay for this increased coverage and who should be held responsible for accidents caused by deliberate violations of safety rules. The House Energy Committee rejected an amendment that would make power companies responsible for accidents caused by negligence or safety violations. Republicans in the Senate and House opposed all amendments that sought to increase the electric industry's responsibility for paying for accident insurance. Senator Howard Metzenbaum, a Democrat from Ohio, led an effort to make private producers pay a penalty of at least $100 million after an accident caused by their negligence. Industry spokespeople opposed this measure and won a major victory when the Senate set more lenient penalties for safety violations. The Senate mandated a maximum fine of $100,000 per day for knowingly violating government safety rules. The top criminal penalties for deliberately breaking such rules were set at two years in prison and a $25,000 fine, no matter how much damage was caused. Even these penalties were left up to the discretion of the secretary of energy and could be appealed in court.

The final bill with the weakened penalties reached the president's desk on August 5, 1988. It extended the provisions of the Price-Anderson Act for fifteen more years but increased the total amount of government-financed insurance to $7 billion. If damages exceeded that amount, the president was required to send Congress a plan to find other sources of revenue to compensate victims of the nuclear accident. With these provisions, President Ronald Reagan signed the bill into law on August 20, and the private nuclear power industry was again insured against most damage claims, even if private producers had caused the accident by violations of safety rules. The federal government would thus continue to pay for damages caused by the private nuclear power industry.

Leslie V. Tischauser

SOURCES FOR FURTHER STUDY

Browne, Corinne, and Robert Munroe. *Time Bomb: Understanding the Threat of Nuclear Power.* New York: William Morrow, 1981.

Fuller, John G. *We Almost Lost Detroit.* New York: Reader's Digest Press, 1975.

Martin, Daniel. *Three Mile Island: Prologue or Epilogue?* Cambridge, Mass.: Ballinger, 1980.

Pringle, Peter, and James Spigelman. *The Nuclear Barons.* New York: Holt, Rinehart and Winston, 1981.

Williams, Robert C., and Philip L. Cantelon, eds. *The American Atom.* Philadelphia: University of Pennsylvania Press, 1984.

SEE ALSO: Atomic Energy Act of 1954 (1954); Low-Level Radioactive Waste Policy Act (1980); Superfund Act (1980); Nuclear Waste Policy Act (1983).

NIAGARA POWER ACT

ALSO KNOWN AS: Niagara Redevelopment Act
DATE: August 21, 1957
U.S. STATUTES AT LARGE: 71 Stat. 401
U.S. CODE: 16 § 836
PUBLIC LAW: 85-159
CATEGORIES: Energy; Natural Resources

The act allowed the New York Power Authority to build a dam at Niagara Falls, New York, and develop hydroelectric power for fifty years, providing low-cost energy to thousands of businesses and residents in the western New York area.

In 1881, the first hydroelectric power generating station was built on the Niagara River. The electricity that was produced powered the machinery of local mills and lit up village streets. During 1896, some of the electricity from Niagara Falls was transmitted to Buffalo, New York, about twenty-six miles away. Eventually, many hydropower plants were built along the Niagara River. An agreement between Canada and the United States in 1950 made more of the river's water available for the production of electricity. On June 7, 1956, a massive landslide partially destroyed the largest hydropower station along the river. With numerous manufacturing jobs threatened by the loss of low-cost electrical power in the region, a heated debate developed over the power-generating rights along the Niagara River.

On August 21, 1957, Congress passed the Niagara Power Act, allowing the New York Power Authority (NYPA) to build a dam at Niagara Falls, New York. It granted the NYPA a fifty-year federal license to develop the hydroelectric power potential of the Niagara River that fell under the jurisdiction of the United States. Under the direction of Robert Moses, the "Master Builder" of New York, the NYPA began construction of a hydropower plant about 4.5 miles downstream from the falls in March, 1958. The $532 million Niagara project was completed in January, 1961. By 1963, the 2.4-million-kilowatt facility was the second largest hydroelectric generating plant in the United States. Only the Grand Coulee Dam on the Columbia River produced more hydropower.

The Niagara complex consists of two main plants: the Robert Moses Niagara Power Plant (thirteen turbines) and the Lewiston Pump-Generating Plant (twelve pump-turbines). During times when the demand for electricity is low, the Lewiston turbines operate as pumps that transport water up to the plant's reservoir. When there is a high demand for electricity, these turbines act as generators. Combined with the power output of the Moses plant, the generated electricity is then doubled.

Since it began production, the Niagara Power Project has consistently met its federal mandate to supply low-cost electricity to the residents and businesses of western New York. The power generated by this complex costs about 60 percent less than the U.S. average rate for electricity. The facility has stimulated the economy of New York by providing thousands of jobs. The NYPA license for operating the Niagara complex will expire on August 21, 2007. As a result, the NYPA filed a formal request with the Federal Energy Regulatory Commission (FERC) in March, 2002, allowing for public participation in the Niagara relicensing process. The proposal was approved by the FERC on July 15, 2002. In seeking its new license, the NYPA plans to solicit the participation and financial support of interested groups and individuals.

Alvin K. Benson

SOURCES FOR FURTHER STUDY

Berton, Pierre. *Niagara: A History of the Falls.* Toronto: McClelland & Stewart, 1992.
Greenhill, Ralph, and Thomas D. Mahoney. *Niagara.* Toronto: University of Toronto Press, 1969.
McKinsey, Elizabeth R. *Niagara Falls: Icon of the American Sublime.* New York: Cambridge University Press, 1985.

SEE ALSO: Federal Power Act (1920).

JENCKS ACT

DATE: September 2, 1957
U.S. STATUTES AT LARGE: 71 Stat. 595
PUBLIC LAW: 85-269
U.S. CODE: 18 § 3500
CATEGORIES: Civil Rights and Liberties; Crimes and Criminal Procedure

> *This law provides that, in any federal criminal prosecution, no statement or report in the possession of the government "which was made by a Government witness or a prospective Government witness (other than the defendant) to an agent of the Government shall be the subject of subpoena, discovery, or inspection unless said witness has testified on direct examination in the trial of the case."*

A 1957 decision by the U.S. Supreme Court involved access by defendants to government files bearing on their trial. On the basis of statements by two paid informants of the Federal Bureau of Investigation (FBI), the government prosecuted Clinton Jencks, a labor union official, for failing to state that he was a member of the Communist Party. Jencks requested that the FBI reports be handed over to the trial judge for examination to determine whether they had value in impeaching the statements of the two informants. This request was refused.

On June 3, 1957, the Supreme Court went beyond Jencks's request by ordering the government to produce for Jencks's personal inspection all FBI reports "touching the events and activities" at issue in the trial (*Jencks v. United States*, 353 U.S. 657 [1957]). For the Court, Justice William Brennan held that since the testimony of the informants was crucial, its impeachment was of the utmost importance to the defendant. Brennan observed that unless the witness himself admits conflict between his reports and his court testimony, the defendant cannot prove it without inspecting the reports.

The reports that the government was ordered to produce would have to go first to the accused, and only after that to the judge to determine admissibility. In their concurrences, Justices Harold Burton and John Harlan disagreed with this part of the decision, contending that Jencks was only entitled to have the records submitted to the trial judge. Justice Tom Clark dissented, asserting that

> unless the Congress changes the rule announced by the Court today, those intelligence agencies of our Government engaged in law enforcement may as well close up shop for the Court has opened their files to the criminal and thus afforded him a Roman holiday for rummaging through confidential information as well as vital national secrets.

Congress took up this cry in its attacks on the decision.

Both houses of Congress quickly passed the Jencks Bill with huge majorities, and the bill became law on September 2, 1957. The statute provides that in any federal criminal prosecution, no statement or report in the possession of the government "which was made by a Government witness or a prospective Government witness (other than the defendant) to an agent of the Government shall be the subject of subpoena, discovery, or inspection unless said witness has testified on direct examination in the trial of the case." If a witness testifies, statements may be delivered to the defendant for examination and used unless the government claims that the statement contains irrelevant matter, in which case the statement shall be inspected by the court in private. The judge then may exclude irrelevant portions of the statement before submitting it to the defendant.

Under the *Jencks* decision implemented by the Jencks Act, when the government used informants in communist prosecutions, it had to be willing to have their relevant reports to the FBI made available to the defense. If the government thought it was important to have communists in jail, this was part of the price it had to pay. The Court affirmed the principle that all Americans, including communists, are entitled to due process of law before they go to jail.

Theodore M. Vestal

SOURCES FOR FURTHER STUDY

Murphy, Walter F. *Congress and the Court.* Chicago: University of Chicago Press, 1962.

Pritchett, C. Herman. *Congress Versus the Supreme Court: 1957-1960.* Minneapolis: University of Minnesota Press, 1961.
Vestal, Theodore M. *The Eisenhower Court and Civil Liberties.* Westport, Conn.: Praeger, 2002.

SEE ALSO: Labor-Management Relations Act (1947); Internal Security Act (1950); Communist Control Act (1954).

CIVIL RIGHTS ACT OF 1957

DATE: September 9, 1957
U.S. STATUTES AT LARGE: 71 Stat. 637
PUBLIC LAW: 85-315
U.S. CODE: 42 § 1971
CATEGORIES: African Americans; Civil Rights and Liberties; Voting and Elections

The first civil rights legislation in three-quarters of a century created the Civil Rights Commission to investigate civil rights violations and made harassment of those attempting to vote a federal crime.

During the mid-1950's, the Civil Rights movement gathered momentum as it challenged racial segregation and discrimination in many areas of American life. One area where progress proved slow was voting rights. Intimidation and irregular registration procedures limited electoral participation by African Americans. By 1957, support for legislation to protect voting rights was growing among Northern Republicans and Democrats in Congress. Yet Congress had not passed a civil rights bill since 1875, and there was strong southern opposition to any change in the status quo. It was, however, Senator Lyndon B. Johnson of Texas, the Senate majority leader, who took the lead. Not known at this point in his career as an advocate of civil rights, Johnson used his considerable legislative ability to shepherd the new bill through Congress. It passed just as the Little Rock school integration crisis was breaking.

The bill had several major provisions. It created a new body, the Civil Rights Commission, to investigate complaints of violations of civil rights. It raised the Civil Rights Section of the Department of Justice to the status of a division, to be headed by an assistant attorney general. It also made it a federal crime to harass those attempting to vote and allowed the attorney general to initiate proceedings against those violating the law.

The law's short-term effects were modest. Though the number of African American voters did grow, many impediments to voting remained, especially in the rural South. Many criticized the act's weak enforcement procedures: The Civil Rights Commission could gather information and investigate complaints, but it could take no action to protect those trying to vote. Not until passage of the Voting Rights Act of 1965 would effective machinery for ensuring voting rights be established.

On the other hand, in the early 1960's, the administration of President John F. Kennedy did use the act's provisions (which were strengthened by the 1960 Civil Rights Act) to proceed against some of the worst cases of harassment. Also the act broke a psychological barrier by putting the first national civil rights law in eighty-two years on the books. It also highlighted the importance of voting rights to the overall civil rights struggle.

William C. Lowe

SOURCES FOR FURTHER STUDY

Belknap, Michael R., ed. *Civil Rights, the White House, and the Justice Department, 1945-1968: Securing the Enactment of Civil Rights Legislation.* Vol. 13, *Civil Rights Act of 1964.* New York: Garland, 1991.

Casper, Jonathan D. *Lawyers Before the Warren Court: Civil Liberties and Civil Rights, 1957-66.* Urbana: University of Illinois Press, 1972.

Ware, Gilbert. *The National Association for the Advancement of Colored People and the Civil Rights Act of 1957.* 1 35mm reel. Film Thesis, Princeton University. Ann Arbor, Mich.: University Microfilms International, 1962.

SEE ALSO: Civil Rights Act of 1960 (1960); Twenty-fourth Amendment (1964); Twenty-sixth Amendment (1971); Voting Rights Act of 1965 (1965); Voting Rights Act of 1975 (1975).

NATIONAL DEFENSE EDUCATION ACT

DATE: September 2, 1958
U.S. STATUTES AT LARGE: 72 Stat. 1583
PUBLIC LAW: 85-864
U.S. CODE: 20 § 426
CATEGORIES: Education; Health and Welfare

The first omnibus education bill represented a great leap forward in the size and scope of federal activity in higher education, providing for student loans and fellowships.

The National Defense Education Act (NDEA) passed by a Democratic Congress during President Dwight D. Eisenhower's Republican administration in 1958 (the act being shepherded through the legislature by Senators Carl Elliott, Democrat of Alabama, and Majority Leader Lyndon B. Johnson, Democrat of Texas) was a landmark in federal higher education policy. The NDEA was in response to the Soviets' launch of Sputnik 1, which shocked American into a reevaluation of the state of education in the United States. The act forged a partnership between the government and colleges and universities to regain international leadership in graduate programs not only in science and math but also in foreign languages and area studies.

PROVISIONS

Title IV of the act provided college loans at low interest to students. President Eisenhower proposed a grants program, and the Democratic Congress rejoined that a loan program was preferred with students paying their own way. Title VI and its subsequent amendments supported fellowships in international fields and created Foreign Language and Area Studies (FLAS) programs. Administered by HEW, the NDEA provided the most direct assistance to universities for continuing work in international studies. Although it was conceived as a temporary, emergency program aimed at producing scientific manpower, it became a permanent and broader program well before its initial four-year authorization expired.

The NDEA represented a great leap forward in the size and scope of federal activity in higher education. It was also the first omnibus education bill, combining a variety of loosely related titles that could have been separate bills. The act was launched with excellence as the objective and standard.

In 1980, most of the provisions of the NDEA were encompassed in amendments to the Higher Education Act of 1965 and eventually were administered by the Department of Education. NDEA loans became National Direct Education Loans and, after amendments in the 1990's, Federal Direct Student Loans. Substantial numbers of student and parent borrowers have benefited from the program since its inception.

IMPACT

Since 1958, federal contribution through Title VII to colleges and universities has been a catalyst that has provided the prestige, the margin of excellence, and the drawing power for other funding. NDEA grants have assisted in funding some one hundred campus-based graduate centers, most of which focus on geographic area studies. The has also provided about thirty thousand grants to graduate students, most of whom would go on to teach in colleges and universities. There also have been more than two hundred awards to advance undergraduate international education at a variety of institutions. These accomplishments have come about with a very modest investment of federal funds. Federal support (in constant dollars) for international studies reached a high point in the late 1960's, when funding of the NDEA was at its apex. Federal funding for international education has been passed most successfully when brigaded with practical and strategic concerns such as national defense.

NDEA centers constitute an unprecedented national pool of competence in language and area teaching and research. The United States is instructing more students and producing more research concerning the lands and peoples of Asia, Africa, Latin America, and Eastern and Central Europe than is any other nation, but the area approach is limited in scope to basically a small portion of U.S. education, primarily at the graduate level in humanities and social science disciplines.

Theodore M. Vestal

SOURCES FOR FURTHER STUDY

Clowse, Barbara B. *Brainpower for the Cold War: The Sputnik Crisis and National Defense Education Act of 1958.* Westport, Conn.: Greenwood Press, 1981.

Lindquist, Clarence B. *NDEA Fellowships for College Teaching, 1958-68: Title IV, NDEA of 1958.* Washington, D.C.: U.S. Department of Heath, Education, and Welfare, 1971.

Vestal, Theodore M. *International Education: Its History and Promise for Today.* Westport, Conn.: Praeger, 1994.

SEE ALSO: G.I. Bill (1944); Higher Education Act (1965).

FOOD ADDITIVES AMENDMENT

ALSO KNOWN AS: Delaney Amendment
DATE: September 6, 1958
U.S. STATUTES AT LARGE: 72 Stat. 1784
PUBLIC LAW: 85-929
CATEGORIES: Food and Drugs

Following extensive debate about the long-term impact of food additives on public health, this amendment to the 1938 Food, Drug, and Cosmetic Act required safety clearance for food additives.

The use of chemical additives in food products as flavoring, as preservatives, or as part of packaging grew rapidly during the 1940's. The long-term impact of these chemicals on public health, however, remained largely unknown. This period also witnessed a substantial increase in the agricultural use of commercial pesticides such as DDT; again, it was unclear whether the pesticides used in production of raw agricultural goods caused any harm.

Given the enormous public health implications of these issues, the U.S. House of Representatives formed a select committee to investigate the use of chemicals in foods in June, 1950. Until March, 1952, this committee (also known as the Delaney Committee, headed by James J. Delaney, representative from New York) held extensive hearings on the impact of chemical additives and pesticides in products intended for human consumption. Findings from these hearings were published later in four volumes focused on fertilizers, cosmetics, food, and fluoridation. The volume devoted to food recommended that chemicals intended to be used with foods should be tested carefully before such use to ensure safety. Although this recommendation was not acted upon by Congress immediately, it provided a basis for the Food Additives Amendment of 1958.

CHEMICAL FOOD ADDITIVES

Chemical food additives can perform a wide variety of functions. Depending on the specific food product considered, additives serve to increase the acidity or alkalinity levels, preserve or age, increase or decrease water retention characteristics, enhance color or flavor appeal, and prevent spattering of cooking fats. Preservatives have been used widely to avoid or minimize the growth of microbes in foods over time. Antimycotic agents such as acetic acid and calcium propionate are employed to fight the growth of mold and other bacteria in bread; similarly, benzoic acid inhibits bacterial growth in pickles and fruit juices. Sulfur dioxide is a popular preservative for dried fruits. Antioxidants are often used in lard, crackers, and soup bases. Another class of additives, called sequestrants, is used to retain the color, flavor, or texture of many products. Emulsifiers (such as lecithin, monoglycerides, diglycerides, and dioctyl sodium sulfosucinate) are added to food products to improve their texture or other physical characteristics: for example, enhancing the whipping attribute in frozen desserts or facilitating the dissolution of hot chocolate in cold milk. Finally, other chemicals known as stabilizers, thickeners, buffers, and neutralizers are added to food products for a variety of purposes.

The Food, Drug, and Cosmetic Act, enacted in 1938, prohibited the presence of harmful or poisonous substances in food products. This provision was largely ineffective in practice because it did not require premarket clearance of food additives; it mandated premarket clearance only for new drugs and coal tar dyes. The Food and Drug Administration (FDA) had to bear the burden of proof to show that a given chemical food additive was harmful after it had been introduced in a product. Establishing such proof was difficult and time consuming. A major flaw in the regulatory framework during the 1950's was that as long as such proof was not established, even suspect food additives could be used legally in products available to the public.

PROVISIONS OF THE AMENDMENT

The Delaney Amendment of 1958 corrected this flaw by mandating premarket clearance of chemical additives that were not generally recognized as safe (GRAS). That is, if qualified scientists and experts believed that a given substance could be added safely to food products, the substance could be classified under the GRAS category and thereby exempted from the premarket clearance requirement. The inclusion of a new food additive under GRAS could be justified on the basis of scientific data; for food additives already in use before January 1, 1958, such justification could stem from prior safe-use experience in food products.

The Delaney Amendment mandated the submission to the FDA of certain details concerning any new food additive—the formula depicting its chemical composition, a description of proposed usage characteristics, the procedure used for its manufacture, and the manner in which its presence in food products could be detected accurately at the expected levels of use. In addition, the prospective user of the new additive was required to furnish evidence that the additive accomplished the intended effects on food and that the degree of additive usage was not higher than necessary to achieve these effects. More important, the user had to provide data documenting the safety of the proposed food additive. This evidence took the form of studies in which varying amounts of the additive were included in the intakes of at least two species of animals. Finally, even if the FDA approved the usage of a newly proposed food additive, it could limit the additive's usage by specifying tolerances. Tolerances are commonly determined through animal feeding tests. These tests of an additive may show, for example, that a 1 percent residue of the chemical has no adverse effect. A pharmacologist in charge then may arbitrarily divide by one hundred and say that 0.01 percent is safe for humans. Tolerances rest on the tenuous assumption that small doses of poisonous chemicals are harmless even if ingested over a long period of time; therefore, it is possible that tolerances lend acceptability to additives that are inherently dangerous to public health.

DEBATES OVER ANTICANCER AND GRANDFATHER CLAUSES

During the congressional hearings on the Delaney Amendment, two issues caused significant debate. The first controversy centered on the "Delaney anticancer clause," which declared that no food additive could be considered safe if it was found to induce cancer in humans or animals. This clause was opposed by several experts and even by the FDA, on the grounds that it was not in line with scientific judgment. For example, several individuals called into question the wisdom of banning the limited human consumption of food additives merely because they induced cancer in some animals. Others thought that it was inappropriate to focus on a specific disease (cancer) while establishing legislative standards. These objectives notwithstanding, the Delaney anticancer clause was incorporated into the 1958 amendment as signed into law.

The second issue involved sustained lobbying efforts by the food and chemical industries for the inclusion of a "grandfather clause," a provision specifically exempting all chemical additives in use at that time from the mandatory testing requirement. Delaney strongly objected to this plea because the grandfather clause would render almost 150 chemical additives automatically acceptable without any rigorous scientific evidence on their safety. Although industry representatives argued that the food additives in use qualified for exemption because of their past record of safety during prolonged use, it was unclear what constituted an acceptable definition of prolonged use for each additive. Some chemical food additives may require as long as twenty years before their cumulative health impact can be assessed. Furthermore, several chemical additives had been declared as unsafe only after they were used in food products for several years. For example, Anton Julius Carson, a medical expert from the University of Chicago, had testified before the Delaney Committee about the harmful effects of hydrofluoric acid and mineral oil, food additives that had been added routinely to beer and popcorn, respectively, for several years. Delaney also questioned the value of mandating public protection against new food additives through elaborate testing when "old" additives that were untested for safety were permitted in food products consumed by the public.

The grandfather clause was not incorporated into the 1958 amendment despite sustained efforts from the food and chemical industries. These industries, however, won other notable concessions. First, through a series of legislative measures, Congress gave the industry substantial time (until December, 1965) to finish safety evaluations of specific chemicals already in use. Second, the amendment did not incorporate the FDA viewpoint that chemical food additives should not only be harmless to humans but also must possess some functional value; the motivation was to discourage the use of additives that, while not considered unsafe, did not serve any useful purpose to consumers.

Both Delaney and George P. Larrick, the FDA commissioner, vehemently argued for the functional value provision. Larrick defined functional value as stemming from any characteristic of the food additive that directly benefited consumers by enhancing convenience or indirectly benefited consumers during the process of product distribution. Further, he provided several examples in which chemical additives had been added to food products only because it was profitable or convenient for the industry to do so, and not because they served any consumer interest: the use of boric acid to preserve codfish and whole eggs in an attempt to conceal poor manufacturing or storage practices; the reliance on fluorine chemicals in alcoholic beverages such as wine and beer to curb fermentation, a result better accomplished through pasteurization; the inclusion of monochloracetic acid in carbonated beverages as a substitute for proper sanitation practices; and the addition of salicylates in shrimp sauce to inhibit decomposition processes triggered by poor manufacturing or holding practices. Larrick argued in vain that the safe but unnecessary use of chemical additives should not be a prerogative of the food industry.

The 1958 amendment played a major role in promoting long-term public health primarily because of two features. It extended the premarket clearance requirement to food additives and prohibited the addition to foods of any chemicals shown to be animal carcinogens (substances that cause cancer in animals).

IMPACT

To appreciate the impact of the Food Additives Amendment, it is useful to study its interpretation and enforcement over the years. The anticancer clause applies to both direct and indirect food additives. The latter comprise chemicals that migrate into food from food packaging material. In addition, more than one hundred drugs used in food-producing animals are subject to the clause.

Three important practical issues arise from the clause. First, although it appears to categorically prohibit the addition of carcinogenic chemicals to foods, there appears to be considerable leeway in deciding whether a substance is carcinogenic. As one example, there was an intense debate as to whether saccharin is carcinogenic. Other fairly common additives are the subject of the same question. Second, a proviso in the clause specifically exempts carcinogenic food and animal drugs that are added to the feed of food-producing animals. That is, if chemical additives in animal feed do not harm the animal and do not leave any residue on the edible parts of the animal (intended for human consumption), such additives are exempt from the scope of the clause. Finally, no chemical food additive is strictly free from all carcinogens. Certain carcinogens such as lead and halogenated compounds contaminate all chemicals, including food additives, at minute levels. Moreover, subsequent to the 1958 amendment, it has become technologically feasible to analyze chemical substances at extremely low trace levels, measurable in parts per million or parts per billion.

For these reasons, the FDA developed a constituent policy in March, 1982, that states that a food additive can include carcinogens as long as the degree of risk associated with the extent of the carcinogenic presence is acceptably low. This is in keeping with the spirit of the 1958 amendment, although it is a reversal of the letter of the Delaney clause. In defining what constitutes an acceptably low standard, the FDA has used an upper limit of one case of cancer following the exposure of a million people to a food additive.

SUBSEQUENT LEGISLATION

In the early 1980's, several bills introduced in Congress contained language that called for revisions of the Delaney clause to avoid the ban of a carcinogenic additive if scientific evidence suggests that the human risks involved under intended conditions of use are negligible. None of the bills passed. However, in 1994 Congress passed the Dietary Supplement Health and Education Act, which effectively amended the 1958 law.

Prior to the 1994, food additives in dietery supplements (traditionally, vitamin and mineral preparations) were evaluated for safety. The 1994 law redefined "dietary supplement" to include substances such as ginseng, garlic, fish oils, psyllium, enzymes, glandulars, and combinations of these substances. Furthermore, the 1994 law contained provisions that then applied only to these dietary supplements and their ingredients. The effect of the new law was to make ingredients used in dietary supplements no longer subject to the premarket safety evaluations required of other new food ingredients or old food ingredients used for new purposes. They still, however, needed to meet the requirements of other safety provisions.

Siva Balasubramanian

SOURCES FOR FURTHER STUDY

Flamm, W. G. "Food-Borne Carcinogens." In *Chemical Safety Regulation and Compliance*, edited by Freddy Homburger and Judith K. Marquis. Basel, Switzerland: S. Karger, 1985.

Kleinfeld, Vincent A., and Alan H. Kaplan. *Federal Food, Drug, and Cosmetic Act Judicial and Adminstrative Record 1961-1964.* Chicago: Commerce Clearing House, 1965.

Kokoski, C. J. "Regulatory Food Additive Toxicology." In *Chemical Safety Regulation and Compliance*, edited by Freddy Homburger and Judith K. Marquis. Basel, Switzerland: S. Karger, 1985. Basel Switzerland: S. Karger, 1985.

Mooney, Booth. *The Hidden Assassins.* Chicago: Follett, 1966.

Skinner, K. "Scientific Change and the Evolution of Regulation." In *Chemical Safety Regulation and Compliance*, edited by Freddy Homburger and Judith K. Marquis. Basel, Switzerland: S. Karger, 1985.

U.S. Congress. House. Committee on Interstate and Foreign Commerce. Subcommittee on Public Health and Environment. *A Brief Legislative History of the Food, Drug, and Cosmetic Act.* Washington, D.C.: Government Printing Office, 1974.

SEE ALSO: Pure Food and Drugs Act (1906); Food, Drug, and Cosmetic Act (1938).

LANDRUM-GRIFFIN ACT

ALSO KNOWN AS: Labor-Management Reporting and Disclosure Act
DATE: September 14, 1959
U.S. STATUTES AT LARGE: 73 Stat. 519
PUBLIC LAW: 86-257
CATEGORIES: Crimes and Criminal Procedure; Labor and Employment

This law served as a bill of rights for union members and a curb on union misconduct, cracking down on criminal activity in unions and restoring lost rights of union members.

The Landrum-Griffin Act had its genesis in the hearings of the McClellan Committee from 1957 to 1959, which focused on crime within the labor movement. The Landrum-Griffin Act amended the National Labor Relations Act (or Wagner Act, 1935) and included a bill of rights for union members. It made explicit union members' right to assemble, speak out, vote, and attend meetings. The bill also required both national unions and local affiliates to file annual financial disclosure statements as a matter of public record.

The Landrum-Griffin Act limited the instances in which a national union could place a local under trusteeship. In some cases, the McClellan Committee had found, a trusteeship proviso had been misused by the national in order to obtain access to local funds or to silence dissent. The bill also required national and local unions to schedule regular elections. The Landrum-Griffin Act sought to close loopholes in the 1947 Labor-Management Relations Act (Taft-Hartley Act). It tightened restrictions on secondary boycotts, outlawed "hot cargo" agreements, and limited organizational and recognition picketing.

John A. Sondey

SOURCES FOR FURTHER STUDY

Bellace, Janice R. *The Landrum-Griffin Act: Twenty Years of Federal Protection of Union Members' Rights.* Philadelphia: Industrial Research Unit, Wharton School, University of Pennsylvania, 1979.

McLaughlin, Doris B., and Anita L. Schoomaker, eds. *The Landrum-Griffin Act and Union Democracy.* Ann Arbor: University of Michigan Press, 1979.

Smolen, Joseph S., ed. *The National Labor Relations Act: As Amended by the Taft-Hartley Act and the Landrum-Griffin Act.* Minneapolis: University of Minnesota, 1962.

See also: National Labor Relations Act (1935); Labor-Management Relations Act (1947).

CIVIL RIGHTS ACT OF 1960

Date: Passed May 6, 1960; first invoked May 9, 1960
U.S. Statutes at Large: 74 Stat. 90
Public law: 86-449
U.S. Code: 42 § 1971
Categories: African Americans; Civil Rights and Liberties; Voting and Elections

Additional protections for voting rights presaged a stronger Voting Rights Act five years later.

The Fifteenth Amendment to the Constitution, passed in 1870, was designed to protect the right of African Americans to vote. The amendment simply says: "The right of citizens of the United States to vote shall not be denied or abridged by the United States or by any State on account of race, color, or previous condition of servitude." Officials in the Southern states, however, found numerous ways to disfranchise black voters without violating the Fifteenth Amendment, such as the literacy test, poll tax, grandfather clause, and white primary. As a result of these voting barriers, most African Americans were eliminated as voters, in spite of what the Fifteenth Amendment was designed to do.

ENFORCING THE FIFTEENTH AMENDMENT
The civil rights bills of the late 1950's and the 1960's were designed to make the Fifteenth Amendment enforceable. Since the end of

Reconstruction, Congress had passed only one civil rights bill, in 1957. The 1957 law sought to empower the federal government to protect voting rights by seeking injunctions against voting rights violations. In reality, the 1957 law was so weak that only a few suits were brought by the Department of Justice against the illegal practices of voting officials. The 1957 Civil Rights Act established the U.S. Commission on Civil Rights, which was given the authority to investigate civil rights abuses. The commission could draw national attention to civil rights problems and recommend legislation to Congress, but it had no enforcement powers.

African Americans and civil rights supporters realized that something substantial was needed to protect black voting rights.

In 1959, President Dwight D. Eisenhower introduced a seven-point civil rights program. Three parts of the bill dealt with education and school desegregation, the most significant provision being the attempt to make it a crime to interfere with court-ordered desegregation. The bill requested a two-year extension of the Civil Rights Commission and contained several other provisions to combat economic discrimination. The only section of the law that involved voting rights was the provision that states must preserve voting records for three years. This provision was needed to prove whether there was a pattern or practice of discrimination in voting.

FLAWS OF THE BILL

Conspicuously missing from the Eisenhower bill was a request that Congress authorize the attorney general to bring civil proceedings to protect voting rights. This provision, known as Title III, had been the heart of the administration's 1957 Civil Rights Act. Title III would have allowed the federal government to prevent interference with civil rights instead of only being able to punish such interference after the fact. Intense Southern opposition to Title III forced the administration to abandon the provision in the 1957 Civil Rights Act, as Eisenhower believed that Congress was not ready to incorporate Title III in the administration's new bill.

The House judiciary subcommittee, comprising mostly Northern civil rights supporters, strengthened the Eisenhower bill and restored Title III. The full Judiciary Committee, containing many Southern opponents of civil rights, quickly gutted most of the stronger sections passed by the subcommittee. The weakened bill was passed by the Judiciary Committee and forwarded to the important Rules Committee. The Rules Committee, chaired by Howard Smith, a Virginia segregationist, did not act on the bill until civil rights supporters threatened to discharge the bill from the Rules Committee's jurisdiction. The Democratic Study Group, a newly formed organization consisting of liberal Democrats, led the movement to free the bill from the Rules Committee. The Rules Committee finally sent the civil rights bill to the floor of the House for consideration by the entire House.

A FIGHT IN CONGRESS

Southern Democrats led much of the opposition to the bill. Opponents contended that the bill went too far in protecting voting rights and encroached on the rights of states to control the election process. Representative William Colmer, a Democrat from Mississippi, said that "even in the darkest days of Reconstruction, the Congress never went as far as the proponents of this legislation, in this 1960 election year, propose to go." After defeating numerous Southern amendments to weaken an already weak bill, the House voted 311 to 109 to approve the civil rights bill and send it to the Senate.

The United States Senate has often been the burial ground of civil rights laws, especially during the 1940's, 1950's, and 1960's. This was primarily the result of two factors. First, Southern Democrats, by virtue of their seniority, controlled many key committees, including the Judiciary Committee, to which civil rights legislation, by jurisdiction, must be referred. Second, Southern senators were skillful in the use of legislative tactics, such as the filibuster, to kill legislation.

The Eisenhower bill was sent to the Senate Judiciary Committee, chaired by Democratic senator James Eastland of Mississippi. Eastland, a staunch segregationist, refused to act on the bill. Only as a result of a parliamentary maneuver undertaken by Majority Leader Lyndon B. Johnson and Minority Leader Everett Dirksen was the bill brought to the floor of the Senate for debate.

Southern senators, led by Democrat Richard Russell of Georgia, organized a filibuster. All Southern senators participated in the filibuster, with the exception of the two senators from Tennessee and the two senators from Texas. Supporters of the civil rights bill attempted to end the lengthy filibuster by invoking cloture, which required two-thirds of the Senate to vote to stop the filibuster. When the cloture vote took place, only forty-two of the one hundred senators voted to stop the filibuster. The civil rights supporters not only failed to get the two-thirds vote required but also failed to muster a simple majority.

A Weak Instrument

The defeat of cloture meant that the Southern Democratic senators had won and could dictate the terms of the final bill. The final, watered-down version of the bill contained little that would protect the voting rights of African Americans. The most significant provision authorized federal judges to appoint federal referees to assist African Americans in registering and voting if a pattern or practice of discrimination was found. The Senate passed the weakened bill by seventy-one to eighteen, and President Eisenhower signed the bill into law on May 6, 1960. The fact that only two other individuals were present when Eisenhower signed the bill into law testifies to its legislative insignificance.

Perhaps the weakness of the 1960 Civil Rights Act was its main legacy. The law proved to be unable to cope with many problems confronting African Americans in the South. Many blacks who attempted to register or vote lost their jobs, were subjected to violence, or were victimized by double standards or outright fraud on the part of voting officials. The impotence of the 1960 Civil Rights Act to deal with these issues, combined with the lack of progress in increasing the number of African American voters in the South, forced Congress to pass the powerful Voting Rights Act in 1965. This legislation would forever transform the political landscape of the South, and its consequences have continued to be felt.

Darryl Paulson

Sources for Further Study

Abernathy, Charles F. *Civil Rights and Constitutional Litigation: Cases and Materials.* 2d ed. St. Paul, Minn.: West, 1992.

Belknap, Michael R., ed. *Civil Rights, the White House, and the Justice Department, 1945-1968: Securing the Enactment of Civil Rights Legislation.* Vol. 13, *Civil Rights Act of 1964.* New York: Garland, 1991.

Berman, Daniel M. *A Bill Becomes a Law: Congress Enacts Civil Rights Legislation.* New York: Macmillan, 1966.

Black, Earl, and Merle Black. *The Vital South: How Presidents Are Elected.* Cambridge, Mass.: Harvard University Press, 1992.

Casper, Jonathan D. *Lawyers Before the Warren Court: Civil Liberties and Civil Rights, 1957-66.* Urbana: University of Illinois Press, 1972.

Grofman, Bernard, ed. *Legacies of the 1964 Civil Rights Act.* Charlottesville: University Press of Virginia, 2000.

Lawson, Steven F. *In Pursuit of Power: Southern Blacks and Electoral Politics, 1965-1982.* New York: Columbia University Press, 1985.

Loevy, Robert D. *To End All Segregation: The Politics of the Passage of the Civil Rights Act of 1964.* Lanham, Md.: University Press of America, 1990.

Tate, Katherine. *From Protest to Politics: The New Black Voters in American Elections.* Cambridge, Mass.: Harvard University Press, 1994.

Whalen, Charles, and Barbara Whalen. *The Longest Debate: A Legislative History of the 1964 Civil Rights Act.* Washington, D.C.: Seven Locks Press, 1985.

SEE ALSO: Jim Crow laws (1880's-1954); Disfranchisement laws (1890); Civil Rights Act of 1957 (1957); Twenty-fourth Amendment (1964); Twenty-sixth Amendment (1971); Voting Rights Act of 1965 (1965); Voting Rights Act of 1975 (1975).

MULTIPLE USE-SUSTAINED YIELD ACT

DATE: June 12, 1960
U.S. STATUTES AT LARGE: 74 Stat. 215
PUBLIC LAW: 86-517
U.S. CODE: 16 § 528
CATEGORIES: Agriculture; Animals; Environment and Conservation; Land Management; Natural Resources

Congress passed this act to codify a history of tradition and policy of the U.S. Department of Agriculture and the Forest Service.

When the Organic Act was passed in 1897, mandating the protection of timber and water resources for forest reserves, it remained the only significant legislation concerning national forest management for sixty-three years. Despite the constraints imposed by the act, the Forest Service did not restrict national forest-management practices to timber and water; range, wildlife, recreation, and minerals also were considered viable uses. Although improvements in timber-growing and logging methods had emerged, national forest management before World War II was oriented toward fire protection for the maintenance of forest reserves.

TAPPING PUBLIC LANDS FOR TIMBER

During the war, national forests contributed a significant proportion of the six billion board feet of timber harvested for American military purposes. Wood, was required for housing, ships, wharves, airplanes, trucks, crates, paper products, and explosives, among other items, and the chief of the Army Corps of Engineers Materials and Equipment Section maintained that because lumber was vital to the war effort, the lumber industry was "the most important industry in the country." Congress, convinced of timber's importance and believing that it would foster economic stability in logging communities dependent on federal sales, passed the Sustained-Yield Forest Management Act in 1944, authorizing the secretaries of agriculture and the interior to set aside federal forest lands for timber sales that otherwise would not be allowed. The Forest Service, heretofore unaccustomed to commercial silviculture (to avoid competition with struggling private timber companies), consequently reoriented operations toward production forestry.

After the war, Forest Service Chief Lyle Watts sought a reappraisal of U.S. forestry and advocated nationwide logging regulation. The country's timber supply was diminishing at a rate of 18.6 billion board feet a year, largely as a result of the civilian demand for lumber for home building and demands in reconstructing postwar Europe. Supply problems were compounded by poor timber management on private lands. Throughout the postwar years, however, controversy over regulation erupted between private and public forestry concerns. With the appointment of Richard E. McArdle as forest service chief in 1952, the debate eased when cooperation among private and public interests, not regulation, became viewed as a more feasible means of serving the public good.

NEED FOR A NEW FOREST MANAGEMENT POLICY

Although forests were principally considered reserves held by the Forest Service to be tapped when private supplies were depleted, the pace of logging on federal lands quickened after the war and into the 1950's because a large proportion of private lands were exhausted of timber, and the need for a national inventory of timber resources became more apparent. The Forest Service, pressured to alter its management policies, proposed a major plan, and *Timber Resources for America's Future* was released in 1958, detailing forestry projection and timber demands until the year 2000. The report indicated that surplus forest land in the United States no longer existed, and for wood shortages to be avoided, timber lands must be used optimally.

For decades, Forest Service propaganda had fashioned the image of the forest ranger who protected the forests from rapacious lumbermen. When a strong dollar and affordable transportation enabled the American public to venture into the national forests after the war to hike, fish, and camp, they were dismayed to see logging activity and felt deceived by the Forest Service's public relations campaign; consequently, the American public and special interest groups demanded protection of recreation areas.

In the meantime, as recreational use of national forests was escalating in addition to other demands such as mining and grazing, McArdle sought to bring a balance among these diverse and often conflicting activities by implementing the National Forest Development Program in 1959. The program called for a forty-year plan designed to accommodate the needs of multiple-use groups that relied on national forests. Only with federal legislation, however, could such a plan be effective. By 1960, fifty-three bills suggesting multiple-use and sustained-yield management had been introduced in Congress, and on June 12, 1960, President Dwight D. Eisenhower signed the Multiple Use-Sustained Yield Act (MUSYA), which had been passed by Congress four days earlier.

PROVISIONS OF THE ACT

MUSYA stated that "the national forests are established and shall be administered for outdoor recreation, range, timber, watershed, and wildlife and fish purposes." Although the Forest Service had engaged in multiple use throughout its history, the passage of MUSYA marked a highlight in U.S. forestry because multiple use became law. The law defined multiple use as the management of all the various renewable surface resources of the combination that will best meet the needs of the American people; making the most judicious use of the land for some or all of these resources or related services over areas large enough to provide sufficient latitude for periodic adjustments in use to conform to changing needs and conditions; that some land will be used less than all of the various resources, each with the other, without impairment of the productivity of the land, with consideration being given to the relative values of the various resources, and not necessarily the combination of uses that will give the greatest dollar return or the greatest unit output. Thus, economic profit would not be considered to be a constraint in all national forest management activities.

REACTION AND IMPACT
Because much of the country's forest land had been harvested without reforestation, a timber shortage was perceived by many conservationists to be imminent, and the concept of sustained yield was included in the legislation. More than a decade passed, however, before sustained yield became a significant issue. Sustained yield refers to a concept that restricts periodic harvest (annually or every few years) to no more than the ultimate timber growth in the same period. If harvest exceeds growth, timber inventory is reduced. Thus, sustained yield is a notion that suggests maintaining in perpetuity the same quantity of the national forests' timber.

The Forest Service maintained that all specified uses—outdoor recreation, range, timber, watershed, and wildlife and fish purposes—were accorded equal status under the new law, but scholars Samuel Dana and Sally Fairfax have noted that "the agency strained to have recreation mentioned first when the multiple uses were listed," in order to establish priorities. Although the agency claimed that the list was purely alphabetical, the Forest Service was concerned with losing land to the National Park Service, particularly lands designated for recreation use. Their diligent support of MUSYA was believed to be partially a response to that concern. With MUSYA's passage, the Forest Service was considered a legitimate steward of federal recreation lands, and that concern was alleviated.

Livestock ranchers also were pleased with the bill's passage. Although national forests had served their interests since the nineteenth century, only with MUSYA were they elevated to equality with other interest groups. In contrast, user groups devoted to timber and water resources reluctantly accepted their demotion to a status equal with that of other interest groups.

It was this lack of prioritization that elicited criticism of the bill because, although Congress passed MUSYA nearly unanimously, the act was not without controversy. The Sierra Club failed to support it because MUSYA lacked statutory management standards, and the club's executive director, David Brower, fought to ensure protection for recreational use, particularly wilderness recreation. Furthermore, the Sierra Club argued that foresters, predisposed to timber production, were not qualified to make value decisions concerning acreage that was to remain unmanaged. Only because a statement was incorporated into the act designating wilderness as consistent with MUSYA's provisions did the Sierra Club not actively oppose it.

SIERRA CLUB CAMPAIGN

Despite the truce inaugurated between the Sierra Club and the Forest Service concerning MUSYA, the club mounted a campaign in opposition to multiple use after the bill's passage, belying McArdle's prediction that MUSYA "undoubtedly will be looked upon in years to come as the basic charter for the administration of national forests." Public controversy erupted at the Fifth World Forestry Congress in late summer, 1960, when pamphlets opposing multiple use were distributed at the conference by the Sierra Club. During the 1960's, the environmental movement gained strength, and the Forest Service was challenged. After decades of public disinterest, the Forest Service was perceived to be an enemy of the environment.

The Sierra Club was not alone in demonstrating a lack of confidence in the government's multiple-use agenda. Along with other special-interest groups, the Wilderness Society lobbied intensively for federal wilderness sanctions, which resulted in the Wilderness Act of 1964. Although mining interests were allowed to continue their activities for twenty years after its passage, this legislation was significant because it showed how powerful recreational users were becoming—a potency that increased throughout the 1960's and 1970's.

During this time, recreationists and environmental-action groups were disturbed by the increased timber sales in national forests as well as by the visual blight resulting from clear-cutting. The need for development of U.S. forest policy was recognized when the public achieved this greater ecological awareness. This served as an impetus for post-MUSYA legislation relating to forest planning, which included the National Environmental Policy Act (NEPA) of 1969 and the Endangered Species Act (ESA) of 1973.

SUBSEQUENT LEGISLATION

Congress was prompted to enact new forest legislation partly because of a sharp rise in timber prices in 1969. In 1972, Senator Hubert Humphrey, a longtime wilderness advocate, presented legislation for greater congressional control in national forest management. In 1974, the Forest Service issued the Environmental Program for the Future, a prospectus on national forest management for the next ten years. Information provided by this project enabled Congress to develop the Forest and Rangeland Renewable Resources Planning Act (RPA), which was signed by President Gerald Ford on August 17, 1974. The Forest and Rangeland Renewable Resources Planning Act authorized the preparation of national forest decennial management plans, which included an assessment of projected renewable resources supply and demand, a renewable resources inventory, an outline of Forest Service obligations and programs, and forest management policies. RPA also required the Forest Service to investigate alternatives for meeting U.S. forest resource requirements. Critics have claimed that RPA "was an answer to a bureaucrat's prayer" because it generated much paperwork and enabled the Forest Service to develop "impossibly expensive" forest management plans. Congress responded by maintaining the agency's budget at reasonable levels, thus restricting the realization of true multiple-use plans.

Subsequent negotiations between Congress and the Forest Service, with intensive lobbying from environmental action groups and the timber industry, led to the National Forest Management Act (NFMA) of 1976, compromise legislation that amended RPA. Whereas RPA directed the secretary of agriculture to formulate national forest management plans, it did not indicate precisely what the plans were to include nor how the plans were to be prepared. The National Forest Management Act offered direction in these areas, particularly regarding timber removal, but also proposing guidance on a number of environmental issues such as species diversity and marginal lands. For example, NFMA mandated stricter regulation of clear-cutting, however throughout the 1980's, the Forest Service continued to rely on clear-cutting, which resulted in significant public opposition. Clear-cutting also fell into disfavor among many Forest Service foresters and by 1992, the agency adopted a policy of avoiding clear-cutting as a timber harvest method whenever possible.

Michael S. DeVivo

SOURCES FOR FURTHER STUDY

Cubbage, Frederic W., Jay O'Laughlin, and Charles S. Bullock. *Forest Resource Policy*. New York: John Wiley & Sons, 1993.

Dana, Samuel T., and Sally K. Fairfax. *Forest and Range Policy: Its Development in the United States*. New York: McGraw-Hill, 1980.

Ellefson, Paul V. *Forest Resources Policy: Process, Participants, and Programs*. New York: McGraw-Hill, 1992.

O'Toole, Randall. *Reforming the Forest Service*. Washington, D.C.: Island Press, 1988.

Robbins, William G. *American Forestry*. Lincoln: University of Nebraska Press, 1985.

Steen, Harold K. *The U.S. Forest Service: A History*. Seattle: University of Washington Press, 1976.

U.S. Department of Agriculture. *Timber Resources for America's Future*. Forest Resource Report 14. Washington, D.C.: Government Printing Office, 1958.

SEE ALSO: Taylor Grazing Act (1934); Pittman-Robertson Wildlife Restoration Act (1937); Wilderness Act (1964); Endangered Species Preservation Act (1966); Wild and Scenic Rivers Act and National Trails System Act (1968); National Environmental Policy Act (1970); Endangered Species Act (1973); Forest and Rangeland Renewable Resources Planning Act (1974); Eastern Wilderness Act (1975); National Forest Management Act (1976).

HAZARDOUS SUBSTANCES LABELING ACT

DATE: July 12, 1960
U.S. STATUTES AT LARGE: 74 Stat. 362
PUBLIC LAW: 86-613
CATEGORIES: Business, Commerce, and Trade; Environment and Conservation; Food and Drugs; Health and Welfare

The act required hazardous and potentially dangerous substances packaged for home use to have warning labels.

The Hazardous Substances Labeling Act authorized the Department of Health, Education, and Welfare to require labeling on packaged household substances that were toxic, corrosive, flammable, irritating, strongly sensitizing, or pressure-generating. Such substances had not been covered by previous legislation, including the 1938 Food, Drug, and Cosmetic Act and its amendments and the 1947 Federal Insecticide, Fungicide, and Rodenticide Act. The HSLA was the first legislation in a decade-long push to regulate consumer protection that included, in 1966, major amendments to the act itself. These amendments drastically expanded the scope of the HSLA and changed its name to the Hazardous Substances Act.

EARLIER LEGISLATION

Throughout most of U.S. history, evaluating product safety had been the buyer's responsibility, not the government's. In a largely agrarian society, in which most household products were made either at home or locally, such an approach was, for the most part, workable. At the beginning of the twentieth century, however, as American society became more industrialized and urban, and as previously unknown chemical additives and preservatives were being developed and more widely used, the approach became problematic. In part because of public reaction to Upton Sinclair's *The Jungle* (1906) and scandals involving the food industry and dangerous drugs and chemicals, the federal government began, for the first time, to assume limited responsibility for protecting the public from dangerous foods, drugs, and other products. Major legislation passed before World War II included the Biologics Control Act of 1902, the Pure Food and Drugs Act of 1906, the Meat Inspection Act of 1906, the Insecticide Act of 1910, and the Federal Food, Drug, and Cosmetic Act of 1938 (FDCA).

After World War II, a number of factors combined to cause legislators to question the adequacy of these laws. Perhaps most important were the countless new chemical compounds and atomic substances discovered by wartime researchers. Legislation current at the time could not begin to regulate these potentially dangerous materials. Further developments underscoring the need to evaluate existing product safety included a large increase in processed foods, several health scares involving chemicals and drugs, and an awareness, after years of experience with the legislation in force, of gaps and weaknesses in existing controls. Immediate action resulted in the Federal Insecticide, Fungicide, and Rodenticide Act of 1947 and a number of amendments to the FDCA.

PASSAGE AND PROVISIONS

In 1950, Congress convened the House Select Committee to Investigate the Use of Chemicals in Foods and Cosmetics. Headed by the Democrat James J. Delaney of New York, the committee issued its findings and recommendations in 1952. These recommendations, combined with cancer scares of the 1950's, contributed to public awareness of dangerous products and created an environment sympathetic to additional protective legislation.

Introduced to Congress on March 5, 1959, the HSLA supplemented the Caustic Poison Act of 1927, which had required warning labels on only twelve hazardous substances. By 1960, however, an estimated three hundred thousand common household products existed that contained dangerous substances but did not require such labels. In the face of Senate committee estimates that five thousand children were dying yearly after ingesting unmarked household products, the bill received strong backing from many influential organizations, including the American Medical Association, the Manufacturing Chemists' Association, and the Public Health Service. The Senate passed the bill on March 28, 1960, and the House passed an amended version on June 24, 1960. After approving the House amendments on June 24, 1960, the Senate forwarded the bill to President Eisenhower for his signature.

The law, which was administered by the Food and Drug Administration (FDA) under the auspices of the Department of Health, Education, and Welfare, banned from interstate commerce all unlabeled household products it defined as hazardous. It further required that prominent warning labels on all such hazardous products include the following: the name of the manufacturer; the common name of each toxic component; the signal word "danger" on products defined as flammable, corrosive, or highly toxic, and the word "warning" or "caution" as signals on all other hazardous materials; a specific descriptive warning such as "flammable," or "causes burns"; the word "poison" on all highly toxic substances; first-aid and storage and handling instructions; and the statement "keep out of reach of children." Although the law became effective immediately, manufacturers had until February, 1961, to comply. After that date, products not adequately labeled could be declared "misbranded" and were liable to seizure. Penalties for manufacturers who failed to comply included up to $3,000 in fines and prison terms of up to one year.

REACTION

Critics pointed out that the law did not provide for a centralized agency to test products to determine if they were hazardous, nor were manufacturers required to submit products and their accompanying labels to the FDA before marketing them. This oversight, they warned, would allow unscrupulous or underinformed manufacturers to sell dangerous products to the unsuspecting public. Only if the FDA learned of the product after it was on the market and then proved it was dangerous enough to be covered by the HSLA, could it move to force the manufacturer to add proper labeling or withdraw the product. Furthermore, no matter how dangerous a product was, a substance covered by the HSLA could not be banned from the market if it was properly labeled. Despite these weaknesses, most consumer protection advocates applauded the HSLA as a step in the right direction and used it as a springboard for more comprehensive legislation.

In his 1964 consumer interest message, President Lyndon B. Johnson claimed that consumer rights should include the right to safety, information, and choice, as well as the right to be heard. Johnson believed that these rights should be established by legislation and protected by the courts. He was not alone in these beliefs.

In part because of precedents set by legislation such as the HSLA and in part because of consumer demand, lawmakers were becoming advocates for the consumer. Government officials dedicated to consumer protection included Estes Kefauver, who chaired the Senate Antitrust and Monopoly subcommittee; Arthur Flemming, secretary of the Department of Health, Education, and Welfare, who championed consumer rights; and senators Philip Hart, Paul Douglas, Gaylord Nelson, and Warren Magnuson, and congressman Kenneth Roberts, all of whom sponsored some version of consumer-protection legislation, ranging from truth in lending to tire safety.

President Johnson continued to champion consumer rights in a second message delivered on March 21, 1966. Several of his recommendations addressed the weaknesses of the HSLA. Johnson called for legislation that would broaden the HSLA to include all hazardous substances, ban household substances so dangerous that warning labels would not provide adequate safeguards, and forbid sale of hazardous toys and other dangerous items marketed for children. Johnson also endorsed legislation that would require warning labels on pressurized containers, decrease amounts of children's aspirin in packages intended for home use, and mandate safety caps on certain patent drugs.

FURTHER LEGISLATION
Largely in response to the president's message, Congress enacted the Child Protection Act, which amended the HSLA in a number of ways. The bill, which was signed into law in November, 1966, included many of the president's recommendations. It amended the 1960 HSLA by allowing the FDA to ban from interstate commerce substances that it deemed so dangerous that, despite the presence of a warning label, public health and safety could not be protected. The amendments also expanded coverage of the law by requiring that unpackaged hazardous substances have warning labels attached in some way to the article in question and by redefining items covered to include toys or other articles intended for children. Upon passage, the new law (Public Law 89-756) became the Hazardous Substances Act (HSA); the word "labeling" was deleted to reflect the revised law's broader scope.

While the new law addressed many of the weaknesses exposed by critics of the HSLA, it excluded President Johnson's recommendations dealing with children's aspirin, safety caps on drugs, and pressurized cans. The drug industry, strongly opposed to these requests, had asked Congress for time to deal voluntarily with the problems they posed. In November, 1966, the same month the Hazardous Substances Act became law, the FDA reached an agreement with drug-industry representatives on the children's aspirin question. Beginning June 1, 1967, packages of children's aspirin intended for home use could contain no more than thirty-six tablets, and each individual tablet was limited to 1.25 grains of aspirin. This agreement was not part of the amendments to the HSLA, but it was reached largely because of the precedent the 1960 law had set and the pressure it and similar laws had brought to bear on the drug industry.

Because of the HSLA, the HSA, the aspirin-packaging agreement, and subsequent related legislation (including the 1973 requirement that all drugs and medications have childproof packaging), consumer prices rose in response to the more stringent packaging requirements. The legislation did, however, save lives. After 1960, for example, poisoning deaths among children under five years of age decreased dramatically. In 1960, the year the HSLA was passed, 2.2 children per 100,000 had died from poisoning in the United States. By 1988, that rate had dropped to 0.2 per 100,000. Banning dangerous toys such as those with small parts that could cause choking or suffocation also helped prevent injury and death among children.

Consumer legislation passed in the 1960's and 1970's formed the bedrock of consumer protection in the United States. Beginning with the HSLA in 1960, this legislation included the Fair Packaging and Labeling Act of 1966, the Poison Prevention Packaging Act of 1970, the Consumer Product Safety Act of 1972, and the Consumer Product Warranty Act of 1975. In 1972, as a result of the focus on consumer issues, Congress established the Consumer Product Safety Commission. Made up of five members appointed by the president and confirmed by the Senate, the commission was charged with protecting the public from potentially dangerous products. Such legislation, combined with strong public sentiment in its favor, helped keep consumerism a strong force in U.S. politics.

Jane M. Gilliland

Sources for Further Study

Asch, Peter. *Consumer Safety Regulation: Putting a Price on Life and Limb.* New York: Oxford University Press, 1988.

Congressional Quarterly, Inc. *Congress and the Nation.* Washington, D.C.: Author, 1965.

Evans, Joel R., ed. *Consumerism in the United States.* New York: Praeger, 1980.

Morganstern, Stanley. *Legal Protection for the Consumer.* Dobbs Ferry, N.Y.: Oceana, 1978.

Pertschuk, Michael. *Revolt Against Regulation: The Rise and Pause of the Consumer Movement.* Berkeley: University of California Press, 1982.

See also: Pure Food and Drugs Act (1906); Food, Drug, and Cosmetic Act (1938); Food Additives Amendment (1958); Kefauver-Harris Amendment (1962); Cigarette Warning Label Act (1966); Wholesome Poultry Products Act (1968); Child Protection and Toy Safety Act (1969); Child product safety laws (1970's); Lead-Based Paint Poisoning Prevention Act (1971); Consumer Product Safety Act (1972); Food Security Act (1985).

Communications Act Amendments

Date: September 13, 1960
U.S. Statutes at Large: 74 Stat. 889
Public law: 86-752
Categories: Communications and Media; Crimes and Criminal Procedure

This law outlawed the practice of "payola," or payments to disc jockeys from record manufacturers in exchange for broadcasting certain records.

A key provision in the Communications Act Amendments of 1960 (S. 1898) rendered illegal a prevalent practice in the radio broadcasting industry. Few listeners were aware that some record companies directly or indirectly paid disc jockeys for favoring certain records during radio broadcasts. This practice was called "payola."

The law against payola practices came about as a result of an extensive series of congressional hearings inspired by an inquiry into the rigging of television quiz shows. That inquiry shed some light on the prevalence of payola practices. In particular, during November, 1959, the Special Subcommittee on Legislative Oversight of the Congressional Committee on Interstate and Foreign Commerce learned from Max Hess, owner of a department store in Allentown, Pennsylvania, about several payments made in exchange for plugs about the store and its products in radio and television broadcasts. The congressional committee soon discovered that this form of bribery and other closely related forms were common, especially in the recorded music industry. Record producers regularly gave cash or products to disc jockeys in exchange for playing certain records on the air.

CONGRESSIONAL HEARINGS
Congressional hearings on payola began in 1960. Several disc jockeys who testified admitted having received money from various recording companies but claimed or implied that the payments were not in exchange for playing specific records during radio broadcasts. For example, David Maynard, a disc jockey for station WBZ in Boston, acknowledged having received more than $6,800 during the period from 1957 to 1959. He claimed that the payments were for his services in promoting records at "record hops" (dance events at which records were played) that were not broadcast. Similarly, Joseph Finan, formerly a disc jockey for station KYW in Cleveland, testified that he was regularly paid by record companies but that payments were not made in exchange for a commitment to broadcast specific records from these companies. Finan stressed that most radio stations received large numbers of records each week and that most disc jockeys found it impractical to listen to all these records. Such lack of attention could be a barrier to the sales potential of any specific record, since the amount of broadcast "exposure" on radio stations was believed to be a crucial determinant of sales success. Several companies therefore were willing to pay disc jockeys to listen to their records. The implication was that disc jockeys were asked only to give the records a fair hearing, not necessarily to broadcast them.

Other testimony, by record distributors, suggested that payola payments were fairly common in the record industry. Common justifications for payments to disc jockeys emerged from these hearings. First, disc jockeys often spent their time outside work listening to records at the request of distributors. Second, disc jockeys were often perceived as experts in evaluating records and in identifying those with promising sales potential, an expertise that individuals in the record industry apparently considered to be valuable. Third, because disc jockeys were often popular personalities, they could be employed to successfully promote specific records at nonbroadcast events such as record hops. Fourth, interested parties in the record industry (manufacturers, distributors, and promoters of records) often believed that payola was an acceptable means of establishing and maintaining business goodwill.

Also testifying were Earl W. Kintner, chairman of the Federal Trade Commission (FTC), and John C. Doerfer, chairman of the Federal Communications Commission (FCC). Kintner reiterated the FTC view that the nondisclosure of payola payments during broadcasts constituted a deceptive act under section 5 of the Federal Trade Commission Act, because radio audiences were wrongly led to believe that the records broadcast were chosen objectively for their merit or popularity. Further, he stated that the FTC had initiated or docketed several payola cases, and he offered insights into payola practices. First, although the principal form of payola payments was cash or check, sometimes they were "in kind" in the form of gifts such as jewelry, automobiles, or clothing. Second, payola was sometimes linked to "washout" practices in the recording industry; that is, payments made by disc jockeys to other artists who appeared during record hops or radio programs would be reimbursed by record companies. Third, record manufacturers in some cases arranged for disc jockeys to own an interest in their companies or the record labels they distributed. Several illustrations of this emerged during the testimony of Dick Clark, a disc jockey whom earlier testimonies had identified as seriously involved in payola practices. Payola also took the form of a record manufacturer or distributor assuming the mortgage payments for a disc jockey's home. Finally, Kintner suggested that one source of payola was free records furnished to distributors by record manufacturers. The distributors in some cases sold the free records at list prices and used the proceeds to finance payola payments. Kintner also shed light on a related set of practices called "plugola," which involved plugging products on television programs in return for surreptitious payments. This practice of "sneaked-in" advertising was similar to payola in that it involved deception in the broadcasting industry, as payments were made surreptitiously, without public knowledge.

In later testimony, Doerfer mentioned that the FCC had conducted a survey of more than five thousand broadcast licensees. He indicated that legitimate record industry practices potentially related to payola fell into four categories: supplying free records to broadcast stations (more than half of the licensees surveyed acknowledged receiving such free records); promoting record hops; providing junkets in exchange for exposure of records during broadcasts, or providing transportation to performers on broadcast programs in exchange for product plugs; and donating prizes to be awarded to listeners in exchange for plugs for the donor. Doerfer noted that the law prevalent at that time failed to allow direct jurisdiction of the FCC over the employees of a broadcast station in regard to payola practices. To remedy this, the FCC recommended an amendment to the law that would impose a criminal penalty for payola. Other recommendations included developing new rules to prohibit broadcasts of rigged quiz and other contest programs, checking for evidence of payola before renewing or transferring broadcast licenses, and requiring licensees to institute procedures designed to prevent payola among their employees.

PASSAGE AND PROVISIONS

Following the congressional hearings, the subcommittee chaired by Oren Harris presented a report recommending more legislative control to deter payola in the broadcasting field. The House version of the amended bill that followed held that the Communications Act of 1934 focused the responsibility for sponsorship identification exclusively on broadcasting licensees. Because the licensees frequently delegated the responsibilities for programming to employees, there was a need to extend the responsibility for sponsorship identification to broadcast station personnel. The bill suggested penalties for violations of the new rules. The FCC was authorized to suspend licenses for ten days, in addition to imposing a fine of one thousand dollars per day indefinitely for intentional violations. The suggested penalties were modified later. As signed into law on September 13, 1960, the Communications Act Amendments provided maximum penalties of ten thousand dollars and one year of imprisonment for violations regarding sponsorship identification.

IMPACT ON BROADCASTING AND RECORD INDUSTRIES

The congressional hearings on payola had a substantial impact on the broadcasting and record industries. Many broadcast stations were unaware of the nature and prevalence of payola practices. Several disc jockeys were fired for having accepted payola in the past. Some stations started exercising considerable control over the list of records that any disc jockey could choose for broadcast. A few stations even required that disc jockeys sign legal statements that they would desist from payola practices in the future. Disc jockeys who refused to sign these statements, among them Alan Freed, were fired.

The newly amended law prohibiting payola had a salutary effect. One isolated payola case did emerge following an investigation in 1976. In 1985, there was a new round of payola charges, focusing on independent promoters employed by record manufacturers. The promoters were accused of payola practices with respect to several Top 40 stations. In an effort to settle this controversy, six major record firms suspended several independent promoters in 1986. In 1988, the Justice Department investigated payola allegations, with payments to disc jockeys taking the form of cocaine and cash. In 1989, a federal grand jury in Los Angeles returned a fifty-seven-count indictment against record promoters Joseph Isgro, Raymond Anderson, and Jeffrey Monka. Reacting to these indictments, FCC Chairman Alfred Sikes stated that if the combination of drugs and payola was shown to exist among broadcast licensees, an intolerable consequence could be the violation of public trust in broadcasting. He emphasized that the FCC would maintain a vigilant posture in this regard.

These developments provoked House Telecommunications Subcommittee member Jack Fields to write to the FCC expressing fear about the resurgence of payola practices. In response, the FCC unanimously voted to warn broadcasters about provisions of the Communications Act that outlaw payola. In a statement, the FCC highlighted several aspects of current law. First, section 507 of the Communications Act prohibited any offer or acceptance of payment in consideration for broadcasts without the knowledge of the broadcast licensee; violations could be punished by up to a year in jail and up to ten thousand dollars in fines. Second, section 317 of the Communications Act required the disclosure of payments received in exchange for any broadcast. Violators of this provision could face fines and revocation of broadcast licenses. Finally, section 317 required broadcast licensees to exercise diligence to prevent payola.

Siva Balasubramanian

Sources for Further Study

Biagi, Shirley. *Media/Impact: An Introduction to Mass Media.* Belmont, Calif.: Wadsworth, 1988.

Grover, Ronald. "Here's a Not-So-Golden Oldie: Payola." *Business Week* 8, no. 15 (1989): 90.

U.S. Congress. House. Committee on Interstate and Foreign Commerce. *Responsibilities of Broadcasting Licensees and Station Personnel.* Washington, D.C.: Government Printing Office, 1960.

_____. *Songplugging and the Airwaves: A Functional Outline of the Popular Music Business.* Washington, D.C.: Government Printing Office, 1960.

Weinberg, Meyer. *TV in America: The Morality of Hard Cash.* New York: Ballantine Books, 1962.

See also: Communications Act (1934).

Twenty-third Amendment

Date: Ratified March 29, 1961; certified April 3, 1961
U.S. Statutes at Large: 74 Stat. 1057
Categories: Civil Rights and Liberties; Constitutional Law; Voting and Elections

Thus the Twenty-third Amendment became the first and only means by which residents of the District of Columbia could participate in national elections.

The District of Columbia was created in 1800, encompassing land contributed by the states of Maryland and Virginia. Residents of the District, however, were effectively disfranchised, because the Constitution provided for the electoral process for the president and Congress to take place only in states. As early as 1883, an amendment was proposed in Congress to grant the District representation in the electoral college. More than a dozen proposals were introduced between 1915 and 1923 to do the same, but they did not pass.

In 1959, Senator Estes Kefauver proposed an amendment to provide for the emergency functioning of Congress by granting state governors the right to fill mass vacancies. After the Senate Judiciary Committee approved this proposal, it went to the floor of the Senate, where Senator Spessard Holland of Florida proposed an amendment to abolish the poll tax and New York senator Kenneth B. Keating introduced an amendment to give the District of Columbia the right to select presidential electors as well as the right to representation in the U.S. House of Representatives. All three proposals were passed by the Senate and sent to the House.

In the House, the chair of the Judiciary Committee, Emanuel Celler of New York, modified the Kefauver-Holland-Keating proposal because he believed that the three-part Senate amendment would not pass in either the Judiciary Committee or the full House of Representatives. Celler proposed a narrower substitute, H.J. Res. 757, which granted the District of Columbia three electoral votes, no more than the number of the least populous state, even though the population of the District was greater than that of thirteen states. While there was opposition to the amendment from some Southerners and some Republicans, the proposal passed each house by the necessary two-thirds vote on June 16, 1960.

In order for the amendment to be ratified, three-fourths of the state legislatures had to approve the proposal. This was accomplished on March 29, 1961, when Kansas became the thirty-eighth state to ratify the amendment. The ratification process took only 286 days. Of the forty states to which the amendment had been submitted, only Arkansas rejected it. The only southern state that had ratified it was Tennessee. Once the amendment was ratified, Congress passed legislation establishing local voting laws defining age and residency requirements for the District. In 1964, residents of the District of Columbia voted in the presidential election for the first time.

In 1978, Congress proposed a new constitutional amendment that would have given the District representation in both houses of Congress; however, only ten states ratified this amendment within its seven-year time limit. Thus the Twenty-third Amendment remains the only means by which District residents can participate in national elections.

William V. Moore

SOURCES FOR FURTHER STUDY

Palmer, Kris E. *Constitutional Amendments 1789 to the Present*. Detroit: Gale Group, 2000.

Vile, John R. *A Companion to the United States Constitution and Its Amendments*. 3d ed. Westport, Conn.: Greenwood Press, 2001.

_____. *Encyclopedia of Constitutional Amendments, Proposed Amendments, and Amending Issues, 1789-1995*. Santa Barbara, Calif: ABC-CLIO, 1996.

Vose, Clement E. "When District of Columbia Representation Collides with the Constitutional Amendment Institution." *Publius* 9, no. 1 (Winter, 1979): 105-126.

SEE ALSO: Direct democracy laws (1913); Voting Rights Act of 1965 (1965); Voting Rights Act of 1975 (1975).

ANTARCTIC TREATY

DATE: Ratified June 23, 1961
CATEGORIES: Foreign Relations; Treaties and Agreements

The 1961 Antarctic Treaty is an international agreement in which signatory nations have agreed to set aside the Antarctic region for scientific and peaceful pursuits.

Antarctica, the large body of land and ice that surrounds the South Pole, is among the earth's most unique and wild places. The only continent with no indigenous human population, Antarctica exceeds 12 million square kilometers (5 million square miles) in size, almost 1.5 times larger than the continental United States. An ice layer averaging more than 1.6 kilometers (1 mile) in thickness covers approximately 95 percent of the land area. Although very few terrestrial species are found on the continent, the surrounding waters are rich in marine life and support large populations of marine mammals, birds, fish, and smaller creatures, some of which are found nowhere else on earth. Antarctica and its surrounding waters play a key but not yet fully understood role in the planet's weather and climate cycles.

In the early twentieth century seven nations asserted territorial claims on Antarctica, which persisted unresolved for decades. International scientific cooperation among twelve countries during the 1957 International Geophysical Year (IGY) led to the establishment of sixty research stations on the continent. As the IGY drew to a close, the scientific community argued that Antarctica should remain open for continuing scientific investigation and should be unfettered by national rivalries over territory.

TREATY PROVISIONS

This led to the negotiation of the Antarctic Treaty, which entered into force in 1961. Article 1 of the Antarctic Treaty requires that Antarctica be used only for peaceful purposes, and prohibits weapons testing on the continent. Article 2 establishes the freedom of scientific investigation in the Antarctic. Article 3 provides for the free international exchange of personnel and scientific results. Article 4 states that the treaty does not recognize or establish territorial claims, and provides that no new claims shall be made while the treaty is in force. Article 5 prohibits nuclear explosions or the dispersal of radioactive waste in Antarctica. Article 6 defines the region covered as all land and ice shelves below sixty degrees south latitude, but excludes the high seas from coverage. Article 7 provides that observers from all signatory nations shall have free access for inspection of all stations and equipment in the Antarctic. Other provisions of the treaty require periodic meetings of the signatory nations to exchange information and discuss treaty objectives, including the preservation and conservation of living resources in the Antarctic.

Initially, twelve nations signed and became consultative parties, agreeing to hold regular consultative meetings to discuss implementation of the treaty. Fifteen countries have since been granted consultative party status. Seventeen additional nations have acceded to the treaty but are not full parties and participate as observers only. The Antarctic Treaty was also the first major arms control agreement among the nuclear weapons states and provided a model for several subsequent agreements, including the 1963 Nuclear Test Ban Treaty (1963). The treaty specifically prohibits nuclear test explosions in Antarctica.

Consultative meetings have resulted in more than 150 implementation recommendations to national governments and have led to two additional treaties: the 1978 Convention for the Conservation of Antarctic Seals and the 1982 Convention on the Conservation of Antarctic Marine Living Resources (CCAMLR), which addresses fishery management. An unusual feature of the latter is that the applicable territory is defined by ecosystem criteria rather than by political boundaries. The Antarctic Treaty, related agreements, and recommendations form what is known as the Antarctic Treaty System.

Mineral Resources and Environmental Issues

Mineral discoveries in the 1970's led some nations and private companies to contemplate plans to exploit mineral resources. Environmental advocates and the scientific community, sharing a concern about potential impacts, led a long fight to prevent such activities. In 1991 the historic Antarctic Environmental Protocol was finally adopted, which banned mineral and oil exploration for a minimum of fifty years. Annexes to the protocol contain legally binding provisions regarding environmental assessments, protection of indigenous plants and animals, waste disposal, marine pollution, and designation of protected areas. The protocol entered into force in January, 1998, after ratification by all consultative parties.

Environmental issues that still posed challenges to the protection of Antarctica in the late 1990's included threats of overexploitation of Antarctic fisheries, impacts of expanding tourism, and the need for an agreement among the treaty parties regarding liability for environmental damages.

In 1977 environmental organizations interested in Antarctica formed the Antarctic and Southern Ocean Coalition (ASOC), which by 1998 included 230 member organizations from fifty countries. The ASOC has been accorded status as an expert observer to

the Antarctic Treaty System and represents member group interests. Environmentalists who have endorsed the concept of Antarctica as a "world park" lobbied for and strongly support the environmental protocol.

Phillip Greenberg

SOURCES FOR FURTHER STUDY
Auburn, F. M. *Antarctic Law and Politics.* Bloomington: Indiana Uni-
versity Press, 1982.
Daniels, P. C. "The Antarctic Treaty." *Science and Public Affairs* 26
(December, 1970): 11-15.
Parsons, Sir Anthony. *Antarctica: The Next Decade.* New York: Cam-
bridge University Press, 1987.
Shapley, Deborah. *The Seventh Continent: Antarctica in a Resource Age.*
Washington, D.C.: Resources for the Future, 1985.

SEE ALSO: Outer Space Treaty (1967); Seabed Treaty (1972); Convention on International Trade in Endangered Species (1975);
Convention on Long-Range Transboundary Air Pollution (1979);
Convention on the Conservation of Migratory Species of Wild Animals (1979); Law of the Sea Treaty (1982).

HOUSING ACT

DATE: June 30, 1961
U.S. STATUTES AT LARGE: 75 Stat. 149
PUBLIC LAW: 87-70
CATEGORIES: Health and Welfare; Housing

> *The Housing Act's objective was to facilitate "a decent home and suit-
able living environment for every American family." It and subsequent housing laws established public housing, slum clearance, urban renewal, and fair housing programs and policies.*

President John F. Kennedy inherited from his predecessors a legacy of federal involvement in the housing market. The Housing Act
of 1934, part of Franklin D. Roosevelt's New Deal, was the corner-

stone of all federal housing programs because it established the Federal Housing Administration (FHA) and federal mortgage insurance for single-family and multifamily homes. Two additional laws—the Housing Acts of 1937 and 1949—created the basic framework of low-rent public housing, slum clearance, and urban renewal, and the Servicemen's Readjustment Act of 1944, known as the G.I. Bill of Rights, guaranteed home mortgage loans for veterans.

The construction of homes for Americans able to afford private housing benefited from federal involvement. Pent-up demand generated during the Great Depression and World War II drove housing starts to record levels by the end of the 1940's. Despite the Korean War (1950-1953), which produced temporary shortages of building materials, housing starts averaged 1.5 million per year during the 1950's. In contrast, federal performance in the field of public housing and urban renewal was relatively feeble. Although the Housing Act of 1949 had proclaimed the ambitious goal "of a decent home and suitable living environment for every American family," public housing and urban renewal efforts had fallen far short of that objective.

When he took office in January, 1961, President Kennedy made a new housing law part of his legislative agenda. The result was the Housing Act, which attempted to enhance and supplement the private housing market. Among other provisions, the Housing Act reduced down payments for FHA mortgage loans and extended the loan period to thirty-five years, furnished federal aid for repair of dilapidated housing in urban areas, and increased funds for low-cost veterans mortgages. The most controversial section of the 1961 law was that creating a costly below-market-rate FHA insurance program for subsidized middle-income rental housing.

Praising the 1961 law as "a giant step toward better cities and improved housing," Kennedy appointed Robert C. Weaver, an impressively credentialed African American, to take charge of federal housing policy as head of the Housing and Home Finance Agency. The president also urged Congress to create a cabinet-level department to deal with the problems of America's cities. He failed, however, to overcome Republican and conservative Democratic opposition to his urban affairs bill. Blocked by the conservative coalition, Kennedy, on November 20, 1962, issued Executive Order 11063 on Equal Opportunity in Housing, which prohibited racial discrimination in new housing built with federal assistance. The executive order, though limited in scope and widely ignored by builders and lenders, marked the beginnings of federal fair housing policy. It fulfilled a promise that Kennedy had made during the 1960 election campaign to wipe out discrimination in federal housing programs with "a stroke of the pen."

Richard N. Chapman

SOURCES FOR FURTHER STUDY

Bratt, Rachel G., Chester Hartman, and Ann Meyerson, eds. *Critical Perspectives on Housing*. Philadelphia: Temple University Press, 1986.

Mason, Joseph B. *History of Housing in the U.S., 1930-1980*.

Mayer, Martin. *The Builders: Houses, People, Neighborhoods, Governments, Money*. New York: Norton, 1978.

Weicher, John C. *Housing: Federal Policies and Programs*. Washington, D.C. : American Enterprise Institute for Public Policy Research, 1980.

Wolman, Harold. *The Politics of Federal Housing*. New York, Dodd, Mead, 1971.

SEE ALSO: Hundred Days legislation (1933); Housing Act (1961); Housing and Urban Development Act (1965); Fair Housing Act (1968).

KEFAUVER-HARRIS AMENDMENT

DATE: October 10, 1962
U.S. STATUTES AT LARGE: 76 Stat. 788
PUBLIC LAW: 87-781
CATEGORIES: Business, Commerce, and Trade; Food and Drugs; Health and Welfare

As a result of public outcry over the effects of the drug thalidomide, the Kefauver-Harris Amendment gave the Food and Drug Administration new powers to regulate drug testing, marketing, and advertising.

The passage in 1962 of a major addition to the Food, Drug, and Cosmetic Act of 1938, the Kefauver-Harris Amendment, broadened the powers of the Food and Drug Administration (FDA) to license new drugs and to oversee their marketing and manufacture. The leading sponsor of the bill, Senator Estes Kefauver, had campaigned in Congress for several years for tighter regulations on American pharmaceutical producers. His efforts were given a high profile and a sense of urgency when, in 1962, controversy about the devastating effects on unborn children of the sedative thalidomide became public knowledge. Under great public pressure, Congress (which earlier had seemed ready to block drug reforms or to allow only mild new regulatory measures) passed and President John F. Kennedy signed the Kefauver bill, mandating stricter controls over new drugs by federal authorities.

THE THALIDOMIDE TRAGEDY

The development and worldwide marketing of the drug thalidomide was directed by a German company, Chemie Grünenthal. Grünenthal was one of several firms in Western Europe that flourished as a result of an "antibiotics boom" after World War II. Grünenthal had been in the pharmaceutical industry for a relatively short time. Like several other antibiotics manufacturers at the time, it did not begin as a chemical producer, as had the older drug manufacturers, but instead had its roots in brewing and distilling.

Grünenthal tested thalidomide on humans in West Germany, offering it to physicians and collecting data from them about the drug's effects. As a part of its communications with physicians participating in trials from 1955 through 1957, Grünenthal emphasized its belief that the drug was a nontoxic, barbiturate-free (thus nonaddictive) substance, suitable for widespread use as a sleep-inducing medication, even by children and pregnant women. The results Grünenthal gathered from human trials were mixed, yet the company pursued what it regarded as an extremely lucrative market, with assurances that the drug was completely safe—an almost unprecedented claim for a sedative. Grünenthal began offering thalidomide as an over-the-counter drug (but one that it encouraged physicians to recommend) under a variety of trade names, such as Distaval in Australia.

The parent company worked through several subsidiaries and licensees (such as Distillers Company Biochemicals Limited of Britain, or DCBL), but it controlled almost every aspect of the drug's distribution and advertising in dozens of countries. At least one company (Smith, Kline, and French Pharmaceuticals) that Grünenthal approached in the mid-1950's as a possible licensee for the United States market conducted its own tests of thalidomide. Because its testing found thalidomide to be ineffective in inducing sleep in animals, Smith, Kline and French declined to join with Grünenthal. It was not until the late 1950's that another American drug producer, Richardson-Merrell, decided to link with Grünenthal. It embarked on the process of gaining FDA approval for thalidomide. By 1959, thalidomide had become a great success in Europe for Grünenthal, with sales of tens of thousands of packets per month. By then, however, the company also was receiving a number of complaints from pharmacists and physicians about the drug's side effects, which ranged from sleeplessness to dizziness and constipation. Such effects mirrored reports from the earlier clinical trials.

After 1959, as it sought FDA approval for the drug, Richardson-Merrell followed the practice of other Grünenthal licensees such as DCBL of relying on Grünenthal's data from its human trials in West Germany when it informed U.S. physicians of the potential effects of thalidomide. Human testing in the United States, through clinical trials on consenting patients, was a necessary step in securing FDA approval for any drug newly marketed in America. Richardson-Merrell considered thalidomide a potential goldmine, which it would market in the United States under the name Kevadon. The company sent samples of thalidomide to more than twelve hundred physicians for widespread experimental use in more than twenty thousand patients of all ages. Patients received the drug in containers that most often were unlabeled except for dosage instructions. No previous drug in the United States had ever been distributed to more than two hundred physicians, nor had any experimental drug been administered to more than five thousand patients.

As it conducted human testing, Richardson-Merrell carried out its own animal tests of thalidomide. Although it did not test the drug on pregnant animals, the company implied to physicians participating in the trials that thalidomide could be prescribed safely to pregnant women and to children, in spite of the fact that

Grünenthal had little evidence that the drug would not permeate the placenta. Comparatively few pregnant women in the United States took thalidomide as a part of the trials. Such was not the case, however, in other parts of the world. Physicians in the largest women's hospital in Sydney, Australia, administered thalidomide as a sedative for pregnant women at about the same time as human trials in the United States began.

What at first seemed a routine application for FDA approval for Richardson-Merrell to market Kevadon in the United States proved upon closer scrutiny by one FDA official to be anything but usual. Frances Kelsey, a pharmacologist and new FDA medical officer, came across the Kevadon application. As Kelsey reviewed Richardson-Merrell's request, she raised questions about the company's animal-testing procedures, its unsophisticated descriptions of thalidomide's chemical properties, the absence of follow-up in the human trials, an emphasis on sales rather than testing in the literature distributed to physicians, and the company's failure to disclose to the FDA certain side effects that Kelsey had seen under discussion in European medical journals.

Deformed Infants and Drug Recalls

In the summer of 1961, physicians and public health authorities in both West Germany and Australia sounded an alarm in the medical community about thalidomide's potentially grave effects on early fetal development. Physicians had noted a significant jump in the number of babies born with a previously rare set of physical deformities, particularly the absence of normal limbs and their replacement by flipperlike appendages, a condition known as phocomelia. Widukind Lenz, a pediatrician who headed Hamburg's Children's Clinic, pushed for an investigation by public authorities into the possible link between the babies' birth defects and their mothers' taking of Contergan (the West German trade name for thalidomide) during pregnancy. Confronted with the results of that inquiry, Grünenthal agreed to remove thalidomide from West German markets in November, 1961, and from any other markets shortly afterward. DCBL recalled thalidomide within weeks, and Richardson-Merrell withdrew its own FDA application in March, 1962. The distribution of thalidomide had been so widespread, however, and its application (even in clinical trials in the United States) so poorly monitored by drug companies that no one—

physicians, companies, or patients—could be certain to whom thalidomide had been given. Concern about thalidomide led to the quick passage of the Kefauver-Harris Amendment.

KEFAUVER CURBS DRUG INDUSTRY

Senator Estes Kefauver, a respected congressional figure and leader within the Democratic Party since his vice-presidential bid in 1956, long had envisioned reform of the pharmaceutical industry in the United States. Kefauver had been instrumental in hearings on drug development and marketing as chair of the Senate Subcommittee on Antitrust and Monopoly. He had heard testimony since 1959 that convinced him of the need for curbs on advertising by drug companies, stricter federal regulations on drug pricing, and more authority for the FDA to test drugs prior to their approval.

Kefauver faced potent opposition from senatorial colleagues known to have close ties to pharmaceutical manufacturers when he sponsored legislation to achieve his goals, through an amendment to the 1938 Food, Drug, and Cosmetic Act, which had given the FDA many of its powers. Kefauver's case was bolstered by the testimony of several convincing witnesses before his and other committees. These witnesses included Helen Taussig, a doctor at Johns Hopkins Hospital who had observed the devastating effects of thalidomide in Europe and noted that marketing of the drug was continuing in less developed countries. A Kefauver proposal for drug industry reform and regulation was before Congress when the scope of the worldwide thalidomide tragedy and the story of Kelsey's timely intervention at the FDA were made public in national newspapers on July 15, 1962.

The public furor was immediate. Americans believed themselves to have had a narrow escape and called for action by Congress to prevent disasters on the scale of the thalidomide tragedy in other countries. In West Germany, more than five thousand children had been born with thalidomide-induced deformities; Great Britain, Australia, Canada, and Japan each had several hundred victims. In other nations, reporting procedures were so flawed that the number of babies affected could not be determined. Thorny issues were raised in the United States by even the limited exposure of the public to thalidomide. When the few pregnant women in America who had taken the drug just prior to its effects being publicized tried to obtain abortions, they faced strict state regulations on abortions. In many other areas of the world where thalidomide had been distributed, abortions in cases of fetal deformity were easier to obtain.

Kefauver suddenly found himself with substantial support in Congress for his proposals, which were much more stringent than the Kennedy administration had recommended only months earlier. Editorial praise for the Kefauver-Harris bill was overwhelming and Kefauver himself was pleased with the measure. The law was described as a great victory for consumers and a victory for the kind of administrative oversight of drug manufacturers that the FDA could provide.

PROVISIONS OF THE AMENDMENT

The new law stated that FDA approval for drugs new to the United States was to be given only after pharmaceutical manufacturers had demonstrated the safety and effectiveness of the substances. Companies could not rely on the trials of drugs by foreign associates or parent companies; trials had to be performed in the United States. Federal authorities were granted greater scope to inspect plants where drugs were made. The FDA gained increased ability to withdraw from the market drugs that it deemed to be an immediate hazard. The bill mandated not only extensive animal testing, but also well-monitored human clinical trials. The FDA application process was lengthened, drug companies had to supply physicians with much more extensive information about side effects of medication, and generic names had to be clearly visible on drug product labels.

The Kefauver-Harris Amendment did not provide for tracking of the effects of drugs once FDA approval was gained. Plans for following drugs after initial approval were developed in Great Britain after the thalidomide tragedy there. Drug surveillance was recommended by the World Health Organization as well. The bid did not approach the comprehensive reforms in West Germany after its thalidomide experience. There, insurance laws provided for compensation from the state if state licensing or monitoring failed and patients were harmed by drugs.

The comprehensive nature of other nations' responses to the thalidomide tragedy was related to the much higher number of birth defects caused by the drug in those nations, where it was sold openly. In Great Britain, the episode changed the nation's responses to drug testing and monitoring and altered longstanding British legal traditions. An investigative newspaper series on protracted litigation against DCBL was censored by British courts for interfering with the fair trial of the cases brought by thalidomide victims. In an important decision by the European Court of Human Rights, Great Britain's contempt-of-court law (which seemed to forbid such "pretrial" publicity in spite of the fact that the litigation was at least ten years old) was ruled to be an unacceptable limitation on free speech.

Elisabeth A. Cawthon

Sources for Further Study

European Court of Human Rights. *The Sunday Times Case.* Strasbourg, France: Greffe de la Cœur, Conseil de l'Europe, 1979.

Gorman, Joseph Bruce. *Estes Kefauver: A Political Biography.* New York: Oxford University Press, 1971.

Knightley, Phillip. *Suffer the Children: The Story of Thalidomide.* New York: Viking Press, 1979.

Mintz, Morton. *The Therapeutic Nightmare.* Boston: Houghton Mifflin, 1972.

Roskies, Ethel. *Abnormality and Normality: The Mothering of Thalidomide Children.* Ithaca, N.Y.: Cornell University Press, 1965.

See also: Pure Food and Drugs Act (1906); Food, Drug, and Cosmetic Act (1938); Food Additives Amendment (1958).

EQUAL PAY ACT

Date: June 10, 1963
U.S. Statutes at Large: 77 Stat. 56
Public law: 88-38
U.S. Code: 29 § 201 et seq.
Categories: Labor and Employment; Women's Issues

The act barred the practice of paying women less than men for doing the same job under equal conditions and inaugurated a series of court decisions that increasingly guaranteed women equal pay in employment.

The Equal Pay Act of 1963—the first federal legislation designed to promote equal employment opportunity for women—began its development as a national policy during the Kennedy administration. On December 14, 1961, President John F. Kennedy signed Executive Order 10980, establishing the President's Commission on the Status of Women (PCSW). From 1961 to 1963, the PCSW investigated women's position in U.S. society and drew up an agenda of reforms. Kennedy delegated responsibility for women's affairs to Esther Peterson, a labor unionist who supported labor legislation and opposed the Equal Rights Amendment. Peterson's appointment as director of the Women's Bureau and assistant secretary of the Department of Labor in charge of women's affairs made her the highest-ranking woman in the administration. At Peterson's bidding, Kennedy appointed former first lady Eleanor Roosevelt as chair of the PCSW. The PCSW legitimized discussion of government policy for women, and at its first meeting it endorsed equal pay legislation. Securing passage of the Equal Pay Act (EPA), however, fell primarily to Peterson.

EARLIER EQUAL PAY LAWS
Previously, the Women's Bureau had secured clauses requiring equal pay in some of the regulatory orders issued by the War Labor Boards during World Wars I and II, and in various National Recovery Administration codes during the New Deal in the 1930's. The first federal legislation relating specifically to equal pay was introduced in 1945, in partial acknowledgment of women's contribution to the war effort. In 1946, the Women's Equal Pay Bill passed the Senate, but it failed in the House. In 1952, the Women's Bureau brought together a coalition of women's organizations, trade unions, employer associations, and civic groups to organize the National Committee for Equal Pay, which lobbied for a bill. By 1953, only fifteen states had passed equal pay laws, nine having done so after 1946. Although equal pay bills were introduced in every session of Congress, no hearing had been held since 1950. A study of 510 union contracts in 1956 showed that 195 (38 percent) had

equal pay clauses. By 1962, twenty states had enacted equal pay laws, virtually all in the North.

PROVISIONS AND IMPACT

The Equal Pay Act of 1963 was the first legislative recognition of federal responsibility toward working women. It required employers subject to the Fair Labor Standards Act of 1938 (FLSA) to pay equal wages for equal work, regardless of the sex of the worker. The bill was similar to equal pay proposals that had come before Congress to no avail since 1945. Peterson's strategy for passing an equal pay bill involved gathering data proving a need for the bill and refuting arguments against it, then using that information to educate Congress. She had persuaded Secretary of Labor Arthur Goldberg to approve a bill prohibiting wage differentials because of sex, which was introduced early in 1962. An employer in commerce would be forbidden to "discriminate . . . on the basis of sex by paying wages to any employee at a rate less than the rate he pays to any employee of the opposite sex for work of comparable character on jobs the performance of which requires comparable skills." There was one exception: unequal wages paid "pursuant to a seniority or merit increase system which does not discriminate on the basis of sex."

The bill raised the question of whether the principle of nondiscrimination would apply to "equal" work or to "comparable" work, and its coverage concerned many businesses and manufacturers engaged in interstate or foreign commerce, or which produced goods for commerce. The act was amended, however: "Comparable" was changed to "equal," and "equal work" was defined as jobs of "equal skill, effort, and responsibility and . . . performed under similar working conditions." In effect, the courts came to interpret the law to mean virtually identical work. For example, a female social worker who could show that she was paid less for the same work done by a male social worker could win a case under the Equal Pay Act. However, if she were paid less than a male legal aid lawyer whose job was rated equally with hers in their employer's job evaluation plan, she would have no recourse.

Most of the opposition to the bill came from business and manufacturing interests. They argued that federal legislation was unnecessary, since market forces, backed by state equal pay laws, were already correcting inequities in pay. Another, contradictory, argument was that women had to be paid less because their higher turnover and absentee rates made them more costly to employ. By extension, opponents argued, an equal pay law might cause employers to cease hiring women altogether, or force employers to segregate jobs still further so that men and women would not be doing the same work.

The legislative history of the EPA was a steady retreat from the Department of Labor positions on comparable work and coverage. The first major concession occurred in the House Committee on Labor, which limited coverage by exempting employers with fewer than twenty-five employees. On the House floor, equal work replaced the comparable work standard. Coverage was further limited to single plants or establishments, making it legal for a firm with several plants to pay a higher rate to a man in plant A than to a woman in plant B doing the same work. The Senate insisted that EPA be part of FLSA, accept the same coverage (exempting women in agriculture, hotels, restaurants, laundries, smaller retail establishments, and administrative and managerial positions), and combine enforcement in the Wage and Hour Division of the Labor Department.

In the end, the House bill resembled the Senate's version. Representative Charles Goodell (Republican, New York) had proposed making the Equal Pay Act an amendment to the FLSA. Representative Edith Green (Democrat, Oregon), who sat on the House Committee on Education and Labor, which held hearings on the bill, incorporated Goodell's idea into her own bill. Senator Pat McNamara (Democrat, Michigan) presented a similar bill to the Senate. On May 23, 1963, the House adopted its own bill, and on May 28, the Senate went along. Kennedy signed the bill on June 10.

Richard K. Caputo

SOURCES FOR FURTHER STUDY

Bergmann, Barbara R. *The Economic Emergence of Women.* New York: Basic Books, 1985.

Bernstein, Irving. *Promises Kept: John F. Kennedy's New Frontier.* New York: Oxford University Press, 1991.

Caputo, Richard K. *Welfare and Freedom American Style II: The Role of the Federal Government, 1941-1980.* Vol. 2. *Federal Responses to People in Need.* Lanham, Md.: University Press of America, 1994.

Evans, Sara M., and Barbara J. Nelson. *Wage Justice: Comparable Worth and the Paradox of Technocratic Reform.* Chicago: University of Chicago Press, 1989.

Fogel, Walter. *The Equal Pay Act: Implications for Comparable Worth* (1984).

Graham, Hugh Davis. *The Civil Rights Era: Origins and Development of National Policy, 1960-1972.* New York: Oxford University Press, 1990.

Murphy, Thomas E. "Female Wage Discrimination: A Study of the Equal Pay Act, 1963-1970." *Cincinnati Law Review* 39 (Fall, 1970): 615-649.

United States. Congress. House. Committee on Education and Labor. *Legislative History of the Equal Pay Act of 1963 (Amending Section Six of the Fair Labor Standards Act of 1938, as Amended).* 88th Congress, 1st session. Washington, D.C.: General Printing Office. 1963.

Zelman, Patricia G. *Women, Work, and National Policy: The Kennedy-Johnson Years.* Ann Arbor, Mich.: UMI Research Press, 1982.

SEE ALSO: Equal Rights Amendment (1923); Title VII of the Civil Rights Act of 1964 (1964); Pregnancy Discrimination Act (1978); Women in Apprenticeship and Nontraditional Occupations Act (1992).

NUCLEAR TEST BAN TREATY

DATE: Senate ratified September 24, 1963
CATEGORIES: Foreign Relations; Treaties and Agreements

The Nuclear Test Ban Treaty was a major step in prohibiting the testing of nuclear weapons.

The story of the 1963 Nuclear Test Ban Treaty has its origins in the last year of World War II. On July 16, 1945, the United States exploded an atomic bomb, at Alamogordo, New Mexico. On August 6 and 9, the United States dropped the only atomic bombs ever used in wartime—on the Japanese cities of Hiroshima and Nagasaki. The end of the war came very shortly thereafter, but so did the realization that the United States had developed the most dreadful weapon ever devised by humans. Thus, from the end of World War II, people and governments began to seek a way to outlaw or control this newly developed power.

COLD WAR TENSIONS

Contributing greatly to the urgency of these efforts was the development of a so-called Cold War, an ideological struggle for power and influence that aligned the Soviet Union against its former wartime allies in the West, which were led by the United States. Although the Cold War was not a physical conflict, it was dangerous because of the possibility that the tension, hostility, suspicion, and fears that it generated could evolve into a shooting war. If that occurred and nuclear weapons were used, it would, some contended, destroy civilization.

Despite strenuous efforts, particularly by the United States government and its allies, nothing in the area of nuclear arms control was achieved for several years. During that period, nuclear weapons were developed further, becoming more sophisticated and destructive. The need for controls became more and more urgent.

EARLY PROPOSALS

The initial proposals for controlling nuclear energy came from the United States, Canada, and Great Britain. On November 15, 1945, a Three Power Declaration called on the United Nations to establish a commission to deal with issues of atomic energy. The following month, foreign ministers from the United States, Great Britain, and the Soviet Union met in Moscow and endorsed the creation of a United Nations Atomic Energy Commission.

On June 14, 1946, the United States delegation presented to the first meeting of the U.N. Atomic Energy Commission the Baruch Plan, named after its drafter, Bernard Baruch. The Baruch Plan called for the creation of an International Atomic Development Authority that would supervise all atomic development and see to it that the manufacture of all atomic weapons would cease and that all existing bombs would be disposed of. Soviet rejection of this proposal became clear a few days later, when Deputy Foreign Minister Andrei Gromyko offered an alternative proposal that called for a voluntary commitment to destroy existing bombs and not produce any others. The Soviet proposal called for control to come after disarmament, while the U.S. delegation proposed that controls be established first. This fundamental difference would complicate all subsequent negotiations for disarmament and arms control.

For several years thereafter, discussions continued in various United Nations committees and subcommittees without any agreement being recorded. A deadlock between the U.S. and Soviet positions constantly blocked progress. In September, 1949, the Soviet Union joined the United States as a nuclear power, by successfully exploding an atomic bomb. Following this, no significant new proposals in the area of nuclear arms control emerged for several years. Instead, each side reacted to the other's advances in nuclear technology. In October, 1952, the British exploded their first bomb; in November of the same year, the United States successfully tested its first hydrogen bomb; and in August, 1953, the Soviet Union exploded its first hydrogen bomb. While work proceeded on the peaceful uses of atomic energy, the United States and the Soviet Union embarked on a nuclear arms race that continued virtually without interruption for years, even after the two superpowers had achieved a capacity for overkill.

The pressure of world opinion to find some way to reduce the threat of nuclear conflict mounted. On March 1, 1954, a U.S. nuclear test conducted in Bikini Atoll in the Pacific Ocean produced worldwide reaction, because of the extent of the radioactive fallout. Protests came from the Japanese government and others. On April 2, the prime minister of India, Jawaharlal Nehru, proposed a halt to further nuclear testing. In the U.N. General Assembly, Burma soon called for an end to all further testing. A year later, in the General Assembly, both India and the Soviet Union proposed a test ban without supervision or inspection, on the grounds that no significant testing could go on undetected anyway. The Western powers balked, arguing against any proposal that did not entail effective inspection and verification. No agreements were concluded.

THE GENEVA MEETINGS

The year 1955 brought some relaxation in the relations between the United States and the Soviet Union, partly because of the so-called Spirit of Geneva that emerged from the Geneva Summit Conference in July of that year. This spirit did not produce any immediate progress in disarmament or arms control, but it did improve the atmosphere in which negotiations could proceed. In April, 1958, Soviet Premier Nikita Khrushchev wrote to President Dwight D. Eisenhower that the Soviet Union had decided unilaterally to halt its testing, and he called on the Western powers to do the same. Testing continued by both sides until October, but the Soviets, the United States, and Great Britain agreed to begin a new round of meetings in Geneva on October 31, 1958, aimed at a nuclear test ban treaty. Testing would be suspended for the next year. This voluntary moratorium on testing went into effect on November 3, 1958, and lasted until broken by the Soviet Union in September, 1961. In the meantime, France had joined the nuclear circle by exploding a bomb on February 13, 1960.

The Geneva meetings, properly called the Conference on the Discontinuance of Nuclear Weapon Tests, began on schedule at the end of October, 1958, and lasted for several years. In March, 1962, the work of the conference was transferred to a subcommittee of the Eighteen Nation Disarmament Conference. At first, there was some real progress, and agreement on a number of articles of a draft treaty was achieved. In May, 1960, following the much-publicized U-2 incident, the proposed Paris Summit Conference collapsed, and East-West tensions mounted again. The Soviet position hardened: The Soviets insisted that a test ban be considered as part of a larger treaty for general and complete disarmament. That relations had deteriorated drastically was evidenced by the Soviet announcement on August 30, 1961, that the Soviets intended to resume nuclear testing, which they did two days later. The United States and Great Britain responded on September 3 with a proposal for a ban on all atmospheric testing without international supervision; when no positive reply came from the Soviet Union, the United States resumed underground tests. On October 30, the Soviet Union exploded the largest bomb ever tested. Immediately, there were new outcries in the United Nations demanding an end to nuclear testing. The General Assembly adopted two resolutions to this effect, including one submitted by the United States and Great Britain.

EIGHTEEN NATION DISARMAMENT CONFERENCE

The next major push for a test ban came from the Eighteen Nation Disarmament Conference in March, 1962. At that time, a joint resolution from the eight nonaligned nations in attendance proposed a test ban agreement to be supervised by an international committee of experts that could conduct on-site investigations of unusual seismic disturbances at the invitation of the nation on whose territory the event occurred. The Soviet Union accepted the resolution as a basis for further discussion, but the Western powers accepted it as only one of the bases of discussion. The resolution was, in the Western view, too vague as to whether the on-site inspections would be mandatory or optional.

The issue of international inspection and verification continued to stand in the way of agreement between the Soviet Union and the United States. However, efforts to find a common ground did not cease. In August, the United States and Great Britain submitted jointly two proposals to the Test Ban Sub-Committee of the Eighteen Nation Disarmament Conference. One provided for a comprehensive test ban with an unspecified quota of on-site inspections; the other provided for a partial test ban with underground testing not included and with no international control of verification required. The Soviet delegation, while informally expressing interest, officially rejected both proposals. The potential for continued negotiations lifted hopes for an eventual agreement, but such hopes were shattered by the Cuban Missile Crisis in October.

KENNEDY AND KHRUSHCHEV

The Cuban crisis marked another turning point in Soviet-U.S. relations. For the first time, the prospect of a nuclear confrontation became very real and frightening. As a result, talks between U.S. and Soviet negotiators resumed, and the leaders of the Soviet Union and the United States, Premier Khrushchev and President John F. Kennedy, became increasingly involved in the formulation of policies and strategy. Kennedy was especially anxious to persuade the Soviets of the United States' sincere desire to reach some kind of agreement that would both ease the tensions and curtail the dangers from radioactive contamination of the environment. Discussion through the winter months of 1962-1963 indicated clearly that the principal obstacle to agreement was the issue of on-site inspection of unexplained seismic disturbances. Parts of the Soviet Union experience numerous earthquakes each year, which produce seismic effects similar to those of low-yield underground nuclear tests. The United States, therefore, insisted that a comprehensive test ban treaty must permit at least eight to ten on-site inspections to verify the causes of such occurrences. The most that the Soviet Council of Ministers would agree to was three inspections a year. By the spring of 1963, it appeared that another impasse had been reached.

President Kennedy was determined, however, not to miss any opportunity for agreement, and there were indications that Khrushchev was not averse to some kind of compromise. Consequently, on April 24, 1963, Kennedy and British prime minister Harold Macmillan issued a public appeal to Khrushchev to resume negotiations for a test ban treaty, to be conducted in Moscow by high-level representatives of the three powers. By June 9, Khrushchev had sent word to Washington, D.C., and London of his willingness to host the resumed talks in the Soviet capital. The following day, when Kennedy delivered the commencement address at American University, he not only announced the resumption of talks in Moscow but also declared that the United States had decided, as a sign of its sincere concern for peace, to bring to a halt its nuclear testing in the atmosphere. Such tests, he declared, would never be resumed unless other powers continued their own testing.

Kennedy's speech had the desired effect on Khrushchev. On July 2, in a speech delivered in East Berlin, Khrushchev responded by announcing that the Soviet Union was ready to agree to a limited or partial test ban treaty. On July 15, 1963, a U.S. delegation led by Averell Harriman, a British delegation led by Lord Laisham, and a Soviet delegation led by Foreign Minister Andrei Gromyko sat down in Moscow. In the next ten days, they hammered out the final treaty, which they initialed on July 25. On August 5, the Treaty Banning Nuclear Weapon Tests in the Atmosphere, in Outer Space, and Under Water was formally signed in Moscow by U.S. secretary of state Dean Rusk, British foreign secretary Alec Douglas-Home, and Gromyko. On September 24, by a vote of 80 to 19, it was ratified by the U.S. Senate.

PROVISIONS

The treaty as finally signed was concise and clearly stated, consisting of only five articles. The first article contained the statement of intent—that the signatories agreed to cease all nuclear testing in the atmosphere, in outer space, and under water, and also underground, in the event that such tests caused radioactive debris to fall outside the territory of the testing nation. The second article concerned the procedure for amending the treaty; the third invited the adherence of other nations; the fourth defined the treaty's duration as unlimited; and the fifth pertained to the depositing of the treaty, in both English and Russian, with the governments concerned.

Kennedy and Khrushchev each considered this treaty a significant achievement that could pave the way for other agreements and contribute to a reduction in international tension. It was hoped that the Western powers could persuade France to sign the treaty, while the Soviet Union urged the Chinese Communists to adhere as well. Such hopes were unfulfilled: The French were determined to develop their nuclear capacity independently, and the Chinese were soon to become the fifth nuclear power, by exploding an atomic bomb on October, 1964. However, more than a hundred other nations subsequently added their pledges to those of the United States, Great Britain, and the Soviet Union. A major first step had been taken toward creating a more peaceful world, as the treaty demonstrated that confrontation need not be the prevailing characteristic of East-West relations. Subsequently, both China and France acceded to the treaty.

LATER EFFORTS

Negotiations continued throughout the Cold War to end underground nuclear tests, which were permitted under the original treaty. A step in that direction was made on July 3, 1974, when Richard Nixon and Leonid Brezhnev signed the Threshold Test Ban Treaty in Moscow. This treaty prohibited nuclear weapons tests that had a yield exceeding 150 kilotons.

Serious efforts to prohibit all nuclear weapons tests had to await the end of the Cold War, in 1990. In December, 1994, the U.N. General Assembly resolved that adoption of a Comprehensive Nuclear Test Ban Treaty should be a priority objective. The issues that had to be resolved were whether to permit a limited number of underground tests, what methods of verification would be used, and whether the International Atomic Energy Agency should be the implementing organization. These issues were debated by the Conference on Disarmament, a thirty-eight-member disarmament body created by the United Nations.

Tyler Deierhoi, updated by
Joseph L. Nogee

SOURCES FOR FURTHER STUDY

Bloomfield, Lincoln P., W. C. Clemens, Jr., and Franklyn Griffiths. *Khrushchev and the Arms Race: Soviet Interests in Arms Control and Disarmament, 1954-1964*. Boston: MIT Press, 1966.

Bundy, McGeorge. *Danger and Survival, Choices About the Bomb in the First Fifty Years*. New York: Random House, 1988.

Carnesale, Albert, and Richard N. Haass, eds. *Superpower Arms Control, Setting the Record Straight*. Cambridge, Mass.: Ballinger, 1987.

Dean, Arthur H. *Test Ban and Disarmament: The Path of Negotiations*. New York: Harper & Row, 1966.

Epstein, William. *The Last Chance: Nuclear Proliferation and Arms Control*. New York: Free Press, 1976.

Graham, Thomas. *Disarmament Sketches: Three Decades of Arms Control and International Law*. Seattle: University of Washington Press, 2001.

Lepper, Mary Milling. *Foreign Policy Formulation*. Columbus, Ohio: Charles E. Merrill, 1971.

Mandelbaum, Michael, ed. *The Other Side of the Table: The Soviet Approach to Arms Control*. New York: Council on Foreign Relations Press, 1990.

Ranger, Robin. *Arms and Politics 1958-1978: Arms Control in a Changing Political Context*. Toronto, Canada: Gage, 1979.

Seaborg, Glenn T. *Kennedy, Khrushchev, and the Test Ban*. Berkeley: University of California Press, 1981.

SEE ALSO: Outer Space Treaty (1967); Nuclear Nonproliferation Treaty (1968); SALT I Treaty (1972); SALT II Treaty (1979); INF Treaty (1987); START II Treaty (1993).

MENTAL RETARDATION FACILITIES AND COMMUNITY MENTAL HEALTH CENTERS CONSTRUCTION ACT

DATE: October 31, 1963
U.S. STATUTES AT LARGE: 77 Stat. 282
PUBLIC LAW: 88-164
CATEGORIES: Disability Issues; Health and Welfare

This legislation extended grants to aid for construction of facilities for research on and treatment of the mentally ill and retarded.

Relatively little attention was given to the problems and needs of the mentally ill until the 1960's. During that time, there were an estimated 5.4 million people in the United States who were mentally ill in varying degrees.

SOCIAL CONDITIONS OF THE MENTALLY ILL

Developmentally disabled individuals for many years were not assured the basic rights afforded nondisabled people. Mentally ill people were relegated to the status of second-class citizens, and therefore few services were provided to aid in improving their daily lives. Children who were mentally ill were assigned to "special" schools because they were identified as being unable to learn. Their only hope was that they could be "trained," rather than educated, to become functioning adults. They were also presumed to need teaching in morals and ethics, since this was not considered inherent in their natural abilities. Many special schools were located far from children's homes, thus removing them from concerned family and friends.

Usually, the mentally ill and retarded adults were involuntarily placed in institutions, where they could be hidden from public view. These institutions on the whole had very poor conditions. Most were overcrowded, unsanitary, and extremely unpleasant. There was little in the way of education or training for the residents. School programs designed to teach turned into rote exercises administered by drill masters; the training programs, which focused on farm and garden activities and laundry and kitchen skills, became unpaid institutional maintenance assignments instead of programs teaching skills to help patients integrate into the community. Many residents of these institutions spent their days on a variety of drugs intended to calm them and keep them from causing trouble. Some states spent as little as two dollars per person per day on the care of the mentally ill; the average was only four dollars. Charges of mistreatment and neglect of the residents of these institutions became more and more frequent.

Part of the problem was that the specific causes of mental illness and retardation were unknown. Often, the mentally ill were neglected because their illnesses were misunderstood and clouded by superstitions and irrational fears. Developmentally disabled people were stereotyped as unstable, temperamental, and morally deficient. Further, because mental illness was an inherent defect, it was thought that medicine probably would not help its victims. The only "cure" was to perform surgery.

RESEARCH AND RECOGNITION OF THE MENTALLY ILL

During the 1950's and 1960's, the plight of the mentally ill in the United States began to get more recognition. As more scientific research was completed in the area of mental illness, people began to realize that mental disease was often the result of chemical imbalances rather than of uncontrollable factors. As more of the causes of mental illness began to come to light, the population of needy people received more attention. It was recognized that, in many ways, these people simply needed more help than others throughout their entire lives. Their needs included special education, health maintenance, legal protection, daily care, and sometimes community services. It was also recognized that their needs, to a great extent, depended on age and degree of mental illness. Individual states began to recognize the needs of this special population. For example, New York passed the first state-county mental health law, which provided state financing to county programs. The law's goal was to spend as much money outside state hospitals as inside.

The federal government also began to get involved. President Dwight D. Eisenhower signed the Mental Health Study Act of 1955, through which the federal government provided $0.25 million, to be matched in private funds, to invest in a national study. The study was set up to investigate the human and economic problems associated with mental illness, to assess current methods for dealing with them, and to recommend improvements and new programs. The final report was given to then-President John F. Kennedy.

Kennedy recognized that the problems of mentally ill Americans were a "most urgent need in the area of health improvement." He appointed a special panel to study the mentally retarded. The panel found, among other things, that only a small percentage of the mentally ill people in the United States were so severely afflicted that they required constant care or supervision. This finding and specific recommendations formed the primary basis of Kennedy's message to Congress, which in turn formed the basis of the Community Mental Health Centers Construction Act.

On February 5, 1963, Kennedy gave a speech to Congress on mental illness and mental retardation. In it, he called for a "bold new approach" to the problem by federal, state, and local governments. In the message, he requested that federal funds be transmitted to states so that they could detect, treat, and rehabilitate those identified as mentally ill. He said he wanted to get away from simply institutionalizing those who were mentally ill, a practice that was a burden on both the government and the individual families involved. Kennedy recommended that a matching-grant program be instituted to allow states to build community health centers. He requested federal grants for maternity and child health services to combat the problem of mental retardation. He supported special education programs for retarded children and increased teacher training, including improved vocational training. Finally, Kennedy supported federally financed research into the causes and prevention of mental illnesses.

After the message of February 5, hearings were held in the Senate on two separate bills directly relating to the recommendations proposed by Kennedy. Such a law had tremendous support in both the House and the Senate. Supporters believed that the concept of community health centers could lead to the treatment of many mental patients in their homes and decrease the populations of state mental hospitals. A bill was passed, and on October 31, 1963, Kennedy signed it into law. A few weeks later, he was assassinated, and Lyndon Johnson became president.

PROVISIONS
The Mental Retardation Facilities and Community Mental Health Centers Construction Act authorized construction of research cen-

ters. Between 1965 and 1967, $27 million was expended to establish twelve centers. A Mental Retardation Branch and the National Institute of Child Health and Human Development were developed to administer the research centers' policies. University Affiliated Facilities, or UAFs, were built as part of the act. Between 1965 and 1971, $38.5 million was allocated to eighteen UAF sites.

A Community Facilities Construction Program was also part of the act. This helped individual states build specially designed facilities for the diagnosis, treatment, education, training, and personal care of mentally ill people. The program received $90.2 million between 1965 and 1970. The centers were small, centrally located buildings that provided a wide range of psychiatric programs. These included inpatient and outpatient facilities, day and night care services, emergency services, precare, aftercare follow up, rehabilitation clinics, halfway houses, and foster care. There were facilities for training and research and for the evaluation of programs.

These programs were located within communities, thereby increasing the availability of psychiatric services to community residents. In this way, mental illness could be detected and treated before hospitalization was necessary. If hospitalization became necessary, separation from family and community would be minimized.

IMPACT

The Johnson administration continued to fund research programs associated with the new law. Money was allocated for many research grants to qualified personnel to investigate the causes and treatments of mental illness. Other groups also became involved in seeking appropriate solutions to the issues surrounding mental health. For example, the American Medical Association held a series of conferences to seek ways to speed up the attack on mental illness.

Mental health institutions changed as well. They began to include private institutions with cottages containing social rooms, classrooms, extensive playgrounds, and arts and crafts centers built to meet current recommended standards in the field. The goal was to encourage students to participate actively in the community. The goal no longer was to hide these people from society, but rather to prepare those with mental illness to lead productive lives with little help from others, if possible.

On a broader level, the law changed the way Americans thought about and treated mentally ill people. Until this attention was given, most Americans were uninformed about the problems the mentally ill faced. The act helped remove a large number of mentally ill persons from institutions and helped to integrate them into society, where they were no longer a financial burden on their families or the nation.

Nancy E. Marion

SOURCES FOR FURTHER STUDY

Birenbaum, Arnold, and Herbert J. Cohen. *Community Services for the Mentally Retarded*. Totowa, N.J.: Rowman & Allanheld, 1985.

Crissey, Marie S., and Marvin Rosen. *Institutions for the Mentally Retarded*. Austin, Tex.: PRO-ED, 1986.

Evans, Daryl P. *The Lives of Mentally Retarded People*. Boulder, Colo.: Westview Press, 1983.

Krishef, Curtis H. *An Introduction to Mental Retardation*. Springfield, Ill.: Charles C. Thomas, 1983.

Ludlow, Barbara L., Ann P. Turnbull, and Ruth Luckasson. *Transitions to Adult Life for People with Mental Retardation: Principles and Practices*. Baltimore: Paul H. Brookes, 1988.

Stroud, Marion, and Evelyn Sutton. *Expanding Options for Older Adults with Developmental Disabilities*. Baltimore: Paul H. Brookes, 1988.

Summers, J. A. *The Right to Grow Up*. Baltimore: Paul H. Brookes, 1986.

SEE ALSO: Architectural Barriers Act (1968); Family Planning Services and Population Research Act (1970); Child Abuse Prevention and Treatment Act (1974); Age Discrimination Act (1975); McKinney Homeless Assistance Act (1987); Americans with Disabilities Act (1990).

CLEAN AIR ACT

ALSO KNOWN AS: National Environmental Policy Act
DATE: December 17, 1963
U.S. STATUTES AT LARGE: 77 Stat. 392
PUBLIC LAW: 88-206
U.S. CODE: 42 § 7401
CATEGORIES: Environment and Conservation; Natural Resources

The Clean Air Act was the first law to grant the federal government enforcement authority to regulate air pollution.

The 1963 Clean Air Act (CAA) and its 1965 amendments attempted to improve air quality in the United States through federal support of air pollution research and aid to the states in establishing air pollution control agencies.

PROVISIONS

The 1970 CAA provided for national air quality standards by specifying maximum permissible ambient air concentrations for pollutants deemed harmful to human health and the environment. The deadline for the enforcement of the primary standards was set for 1982, but the deadline was extended; significant enforcement had yet to occur in the mid-1990's. The CAA also provided that the Environmental Protection Agency (EPA), established in 1970, was to set pollution standards for new plants and that states were to create state implementation plans for enforcement. The country was divided into 247 Air Quality Control Regions for enforcement purposes. Finally, the CAA mandated pollution standards for automobiles and trucks with specified deadlines for achievement; Congress, however, has repeatedly waived the deadlines.

IMPACT AND SUBSEQUENT LEGISLATION

The 1970 CAA and the 1977 amendments were successful in reducing several ambient air pollutants, most notably carbon monoxide, lead, and suspended particulates. However, ozone, nitrogen dioxide, volatile organic compounds, and sulfur dioxide would remain at high levels in many areas.

The 1990 amendments to the CAA are so far-ranging as to constitute a rewriting of the act. The 1990 amendments display an awareness of developing problems such as acid deposition and stratospheric ozone (Titles IV and VI). Title I provided a new enforcement scheme with specific categories for cities (Los Angeles is in a category by itself) for reaching pollution standards for ozone, carbon monoxide, and particulates, with a twenty-year deadline for compliance. Title II provided specific standards for mobile source pollution with deadlines for compliance. Title III established emission limits for hazardous or toxic air pollutants with numerous deadlines for enforcement. An innovative aspect of Title IV was the establishment of a process of emissions trading whereby the most polluting utilities could acquire the excess pollution capacity of less polluting utilities. The goal was to reduce progressively the total amount of sulfur dioxide emitted in the United States through the operation of market forces.

The CAA has been explicitly directed toward improving human health. Implicit in the CAA is a concern for the environment and the impact of air pollution on natural resources. Efforts to deal with acid deposition, for example, display a concern with the impact of sulfur dioxide on water and forest products. The implementation of automobile emission standards has had a positive effect on oil consumption.

The overall thrust of the Clean Air Act has been "technology-forcing"; in other words, industries are being forced to develop improved technologies to meet mandated standards. The results of this approach have been mixed in urban areas. Some improvement in air quality has certainly occurred. Nonetheless, costs are escalating for full achievement of the various standards of the CAA. As of 1995 only Vermont, Iowa, South Dakota, North Dakota, Wyoming, and Hawaii were in full compliance with federal standards.

John M. Theilmann

SOURCES FOR FURTHER STUDY
Davies, J. Clarence, III. *The Politics of Pollution.* New York: Pegasus, 1970.
Godish, Thad. *Air Quality.* 2d ed. Chelsea, Mich.: Lewis, 1991.
Havighurst, Clark C. *Air Pollution Control.* Dobbs Ferry, N.Y.: Oceana, 1969.
Hurley, William D. *Environmental Legislation.* Springfield, Ill.: Thomas Books, 1971.

Miller, E. Willard, and Ruby M. Miller. *Environmental Hazards: Air Pollution.* Santa Barbara, Calif.: ABC-CLIO, 1989.
Switzer, Jacqueline Vaughn. *Environmental Politics: Domestic and Global Dimensions.* New York: St. Martin's Press, 1994.

SEE ALSO: Air Pollution Control Act (1955); National Environmental Policy Act (1970); Clean Air Act Amendments of 1970 (1970); Clean Air Act Amendments of 1977 (1977); Alternative Motor Fuels Act (1988); Clean Air Act Amendments of 1990 (1990).

TWENTY-FOURTH AMENDMENT

DATE: Ratified January 23, 1964; certified February 4, 1964
U.S. STATUTES AT LARGE: 76 Stat. 1259
CATEGORIES: African Americans; Civil Rights and Liberties; Constitutional Law; Voting and Elections

Although the incidence of poll taxes was declining by the time of its enactment, the Twenty-fourth Amendment banned such taxes in primaries and federal elections and gave Congress power to enforce the amendment through legislation.

The Twenty-fourth Amendment, which eliminated the poll tax as a qualification for voting in federal elections, reads as follows:

Section 1. The right of citizens of the United States to vote in any primary or other election for President or Vice President, for electors for President or Vice President, or for Senator or Representative in Congress, shall not be denied or abridged by the United States or any State by reason of failure to pay any poll tax or other tax.

Section 2. The Congress shall have power to enforce this article by appropriate legislation.

Poll taxes, taxes that had to be paid before a person could vote, had been used to disenfranchise African Americans in the South since the mid-1800's. In *Breedlove v. Suttles* (1937), the Supreme

Court upheld a Georgia poll tax despite a challenge based on the equal protection and privileges and immunities clauses of the Fourteenth Amendment.

Through the enactment of the Twenty-fourth Amendment in 1964, Congress prohibited the use of poll taxes in federal elections. Virginia passed a statute that sought to circumvent the new amendment by offering voters the choice of either paying the tax or filing a certificate of residence six months before the election; however, the Court struck down this law in *Harman v. Forssenius* (1965) because it penalized those who chose to exercise a right already guaranteed by the amendment.

In *Harper v. Virginia State Board of Elections* (1966), the Court outlawed the poll tax as a voting requirement in state and local elections. Justice Hugo L. Black, the only remaining member of the Court that had rendered the 1937 decision, dissented.

Robert P. Ellis

SOURCE FOR FURTHER STUDY

Vile, John R. *Encyclopedia of Constitutional Amendments, Proposed Amendments, and Amending Issues, 1789-1995.* Santa Barbara, Calif: ABC-CLIO, 1996.

SEE ALSO: Black Codes of 1865 (1865); Civil Rights Act of 1866 (1866); Fifteenth Amendment (1870); Jim Crow laws (1880's-1954); Disfranchisement laws (1890); Voting Rights Act of 1965 (1965).

EXECUTIVE ORDER 11141

DATE: Issued February 12, 1964
CATEGORIES: Aging Issues; Civil Rights and Liberties

This executive order established the first formal federal prohibition on certain kinds of age discrimination and set the political and legal stage for further governmental support for equal opportunity for aging persons.

In March, 1963, as part of the struggle to achieve civil rights legislation, President John F. Kennedy issued a memorandum reaffirming the federal government's policy of hiring and promoting employees on the basis of merit alone and assuring that older people are not discriminated against on the basis of age.

After President Kennedy's death, President Lyndon B. Johnson continued the civil rights struggle. On February 12, 1964, just three months after becoming president, Johnson issued Executive Order 11141, *Declaring a Public Policy Against Discrimination on the Basis of Age*. The order prohibited age discrimination in employment by federal contractors and subcontractors. Firms performing contract work for the United States government were prohibited from discriminating in hiring, promoting, or discharging employees on the basis of age unless pursuant to a statutory requirement or retirement plan.

Although limited in scope to federal contractors (at that time there was no statutory authority for a more extensive order) President Johnson's order was significant because it ensured that the moral and political power of the government would work against age discrimination. There was an immense amount of federal contracting, and many older people were promoted, hired, or retained in their jobs longer than they would have been without the order. Many remained employed on projects other than those contracted by the federal government. The order and its associated regulations also provided Congress with a model for dealing with age discrimination when civil rights acts were later passed. Age discrimination prohibitions were later applied to all public and private employment that the federal government had the power to reach.

Robert Jacobs

SOURCES FOR FURTHER STUDY

Gregory, Raymond F. *Age Discrimination in the American Workplace: Old at a Young Age*. New Brunswick, N.J.: Rutgers University Press, 2001.

Hushbeck, Judith C. *Old and Obsolete: Age Discrimination and the American Worker, 1860-1920*. New York: Garland, 1989.

Kalet, Joseph E. *Age Discrimination in Employment Law*. Washington, D.C.: BNA Books, 1990.

O'Meara, Daniel P. *Protecting the Growing Number of Older Workers: The Age Discrimination in Employment Act.* Philadelphia: University of Pennsylvania, Center for Human Resources, 1989.

Segrave, Kerry. *Age Discrimination by Employers.* Jefferson, N.C.: McFarland Press, 2002.

SEE ALSO: Older Americans Act (1965); Age Discrimination in Employment Act (1967); Age Discrimination Act (1975); Older Workers Benefit Protection Act (1990).

U.S.-Soviet Consular Treaty

DATE: Signed June 1, 1964; Senate ratified March 16, 1967
CATEGORIES: Foreign Relations; Treaties and Agreements

Developed to allow for foreign consulates in the Soviet Union and the United States, this treaty was one of the first to work toward normalization of diplomatic relations between the two superpowers.

The 1967 U.S.-Soviet Consular Treaty represents one of the first major diplomatic efforts between the two superpowers in the Cold War era.

PROVISIONS

The treaty is divided into thirty separate articles that stipulate the conditions of establishing a foreign mission and the permissible functions each mission is allowed to undertake in the host nation. Of particular note are Articles 4 and 29, specifying that all diplomatic officers and staff are provided diplomatic immunity and that designated consuls are permitted to travel freely within their respective geographic regions. The treaty also specifies that the head consulate official be charged with protecting the rights and interests, including any commercial interests, of foreign nationals residing in the host country. The treaty goes on to state that the consulate is also designated to offer necessary diplomatic services, such as passport management, child custody issues and documentation of marriages, births, and deaths of its citizens.

RATIFICATION

The original treaty was signed on June 1, 1964, by the U.S. ambassador to the Soviet Union, Foy D. Kohler, and the Soviet minister of foreign affairs, Andrei Gromyko. The agreement was presented to the U.S. Senate for ratification in 1967. This three-year delay in presenting the treaty to the American legislative body was motivated partly by the 1964 presidential election and partly by the desire for most incumbents to illustrate an anti-Soviet stance in an attempt to gain popular support from the electorate.

The treaty was introduced to the Senate in the spring of 1967, despite continued opposition from conservative Republicans. Several senators viewed the treaty as too moderate toward the Soviet Union and hoped for an agreement that would take a firm stance against the Soviet Union and the continuing expansion of the Soviet sphere of influence. Several senators attempted to amend the treaty with a provision condemning the Soviets for their position and disapproving foreign involvement in Vietnam. Federal Bureau of Investigation head J. Edgar Hoover also opposed the treaty, believing that it would present new opportunities for Soviet espionage in the United States. Additional issues regarding diplomatic immunity for all Soviet consular officials and their diplomatic staffs were considered problematic for the U.S. Department of Justice.

Eventually, opposition to the treaty was withdrawn at the request of the Johnson administration, which actively lobbied for the treaty's ratification. On March 16, 1967, the Soviet-U.S. Consular Treaty was ratified by the United States Senate on a vote of 66 to 28, three more than the two-thirds majority required for ratification. The Soviet Union, in turn, ratified the agreement the following year on April 26, 1968. The treaty has since been modified to include consulates of the Russian Federation and the Commonwealth of Independent States.

Robert Mitchell

SOURCES FOR FURTHER STUDY

Stebbins, Richard P. *The United States in World Affairs, 1967.* New York: Simon and Schuster, 1967.

United States Treaties and Other International Agreements. Washington, D.C.: Government Printing Office, 1968.

SEE ALSO: Nuclear Test Ban Treaty (1963); Nuclear Nonproliferation Treaty (1968); Seabed Treaty (1972); SALT I Treaty (1972); SALT II Treaty (1979); Law of the Sea Treaty (1982); INF Treaty (1987); START II Treaty (1993); U.S.-Russia Arms Agreement (2002).

CIVIL RIGHTS ACT OF 1964

DATE: July 2, 1964
U.S. STATUTES AT LARGE: 78 Stat. 241
PUBLIC LAW: 88-352
U.S. CODE: 42 § 1971
CATEGORIES: African Americans; Civil Rights and Liberties

The Civil Rights Act of 1964 outlawed the exclusion of African Americans from hotels, theaters, restaurants, and other public accommodations; barred federal funds to any activity that involved racial discrimination; warranted the Justice Department to initiate school desegregation suits; and forbade racial discrimination in employment and union membership policies.

The road to the passage of the Civil Rights Act of 1964 was long and tortuous. Its passage was largely in response to protests and demonstrations initiated by civil rights activists and African American leaders.

In the 1950's, African Americans had mobilized a social movement, which spanned several decades, to eradicate the social injustices they faced throughout the United States. The mass effort to end legal segregation in public accommodations in the South had been sparked by Rosa Parks, an African American woman who, in 1955, had disobeyed the law by refusing to relinquish her seat to a white man on a crowded bus in Montgomery, Alabama. The subsequent Montgomery bus boycott heralded a new Civil Rights movement, which ended the Jim Crow laws that had forbidden African Americans from using the same public accommodations—transportation, hotels, restaurants, schools, and other public facilities—along with whites. Leaders such as Malcolm X—who encouraged African Americans to challenge unfair practices and laws by teaching black nationalism and racial pride—also played a major role in the passage of the 1964 Civil Rights Act.

PROPOSAL AND PASSAGE

The legislation that became the Civil Rights Act of 1964 was originally proposed by President John F. Kennedy on June 19, 1963, following a confrontation with Alabama governor George Wallace over the admission of black students to the University of Alabama. Kennedy declared that the bill should be passed "not merely for reasons of economic efficiency, world diplomacy and domestic tranquility—but above all because it is right." Kennedy would not see the bill's passage; he was assassinated on November 22 of that year.

The act was forcefully advocated by his successor, President Lyndon B. Johnson. Passage was facilitated both by pressure from civil rights advocates and by segregationist responses to those pressures. Events that helped rouse the public to support civil rights included the March on Washington in August, 1963, the bombing of black churches, the "battle of Oxford" that ensued when James Meredith sought to enter the University of Mississippi, the mistreatment of freedom marchers and freedom riders, and the murder in Mississippi of three civil rights workers.

Passage of the act came only after senators voted to end a filibuster on June 19, 1964, exactly one year after Kennedy had proposed the bill. Republican senator Everett Dirksen, the Senate minority leader, shared credit for passage of the act. Traditionally an opponent of civil rights legislation, Dirksen implored Republicans to support the bill as "an idea whose time has come."

PROVISIONS

Unlike the first two civil rights acts of the modern period—those of 1957 and 1960, which were limited principally to ensuring the right to vote—the 1964 act attacked segregation on a broad front. The final bill was stronger than Kennedy's proposal to Congress. Its main provisions are found in the first seven of the act's ten titles. Title I, concerned with voting, was intended to create more effective enforcement of the right to vote in federal elections without consideration of color or race. It expedites the procedure for settling voting rights suits and mandates that uniform standards be applied to all individuals seeking to register and vote. To diminish the discriminatory use of literacy and comprehension tests, it equates completion of the sixth grade with literacy. Finally, it empowers the U.S. attorney general to bring suit if there is a "pattern or practice" of voting discrimination.

Title II forbids discrimination on the basis of race, color, religion, or national origin in places of public accommodation. Privately owned or operated facilities, such as country clubs, are exempted from the Title II prohibition.

Title III deals with public facilities such as municipally owned or state-owned or operated hospitals, libraries, and parks. It authorizes the attorney general to bring a civil suit to order desegregation of any such facility whenever the attorney general receives a written complaint of discrimination from an individual or individuals unable to take the necessary legal actions themselves.

Title IV's concern is public education. Its main provision authorizes the U.S. Office of Education to organize training institutes to prepare school personnel to deal with desegregation; to assist school districts, states, and other political subdivisions in implementing school desegregation plans; and to offer financial assistance to school boards to facilitate their hiring of specialists for in-service training.

Title V reauthorized the U.S. Commission on Civil Rights, created by the Civil Rights Act of 1957, for four years and gave it the additional responsibilities of serving as a national clearinghouse for civil rights information and investigating allegations of fraud in voting.

Under Title VI, any federal body that offers contracts, grants, or loans is required to bar discrimination on the grounds of race, color, or national origin from programs it supports financially.

Title VII established a federal right to equal opportunity in employment and created the Equal Employment Opportunity Commission (EEOC) to assist in implementing this right. Under Title VII, employers, employment agencies, and labor unions are required to treat all persons without regard to their color, race, religion, sex, or national origin. Equality or nondiscrimination was mandated in all phases of employment, including hiring, firing, promotion, job assignments, and apprenticeship and training. Gender was inserted into the bill at the insistence of Senator James Eastland, a Democrat from Mississippi, in the vain hope that its inclusion would weaken support for the entire bill.

The final three sections of the act confer no rights. They provide structures within which federal authorities are to operate while mitigating possible conflicts with communities under pressure to comply with other provisions of the act.

ASSESSMENT

The act, at the time revolutionary in its coverage, would neverthe-less encounter obstacles to its effectiveness. These limitations in-cluded the large caseloads of enforcement agencies, such as the Equal Employment Opportunity Commission, delaying timely in-vestigations; the great length of time required to litigate cases; dif-ficulty in retaining attorneys; the high costs of litigation; problems in identifying coworkers willing to be witnesses; and reverse dis-crimination lawsuits arguing that employer policies to ensure the civil rights of protected classes violate the civil rights of others. Many of these conditions would hinder the effectiveness of the 1964 Civil Rights Act, its provisions, and enforcement agencies. Thus, although the 1964 Civil Rights Act has remained the founda-tion of a series of civil rights acts passed since the 1960's, the goal of equal opportunity for all citizens of the United States has contin-ued to be a worthwhile and necessary pursuit.

Doris F. Pierce and K. Sue Jewell
("Proposal and Passage," "Assessment"),
Ashton Wesley Welch
("Provisions")

SOURCES FOR FURTHER STUDY

Abraham, Henry J. *Freedom and the Court: Civil Rights and Liberties in the United States.* New York: Oxford University Press, 1967.

Belknap, Michael R., ed. *Civil Rights Act of 1964.* Vol. 13 in *Civil Rights, the White House, and the Justice Department, 1945-1968: Se-curing the Enactment of Civil Rights Legislation.* New York: Garland, 1991.

Bell, Derrick. *Faces at the Bottom of the Well: The Permanence of Racism.* New York: Basic Books, 1992.

_____. *Race, Racism, and American Law.* 2d ed. Boston: Little, Brown, 1977.

Bullock, Charles S., III, and Charles M. Lamb. *Implementation of Civil Rights Policy.* Monterey, Calif.: Brooks-Cole, 1984.

Celada, Raymond J. *Desegregation of Public Schools: Legislative History of Title IV of the Civil Rights Act of 1964.* Washington, D.C.: Library of Congress, Legislative Reference Service, 1967.

Graham, Hugh Davis. *The Civil Rights Era: Origins and Development of National Policy, 1960-1972.* New York: Oxford University Press, 1990.

Grofman, Bernard, ed. *Legacies of the 1964 Civil Rights Act.* Charlottesville: University Press of Virginia, 2000.

Harvey, James C. *Black Civil Rights During the Johnson Administration.* Jackson: University and College Press of Mississippi, 1973.

Loevy, Robert D. *To End All Segregation: The Politics of the Passage of the Civil Rights Act of 1964.* Lanham, Md.: University Press of America, 1990.

_____, ed. *The Civil Rights Act of 1964: The Passage of the Law That Ended Racial Segregation.* Albany: State University of New York Press, 1997.

Watson, Denton L. *Lion in the Lobby: Clarence Mitchell, Jr.'s Struggle for the Passage of Civil Rights Legislation.* New York: Morrow, 1990.

Whalen, Charles, and Barbara Whalen. *The Longest Debate: A Legislative History of the 1964 Civil Rights Act.* Washington, D.C.: Seven Locks Press, 1985.

SEE ALSO: Thirteenth Amendment (1865); Civil Rights Act of 1866 (1866); Fourteenth Amendment (1868); Fifteenth Amendment (1870); Civil Rights Act of 1957 (1957); Civil Rights Act of 1960 (1960); Title VII of the Civil Rights Act of 1964 (1964); Twenty-fourth Amendment (1964); Voting Rights Act of 1965 (1965); Civil Rights Act of 1968 (1968); Fair Housing Act (1968); Voting Rights Act of 1975 (1975); Civil Rights Act of 1991 (1991).

TITLE VII OF THE CIVIL RIGHTS ACT OF 1964

DATE: July 2, 1964
U.S. STATUTES AT LARGE: 78 Stat. 241
PUBLIC LAW: 88-352
U.S. CODE: 42 § 3045

CATEGORIES: Civil Rights and Liberties; Labor and Employment; Women's Issues

This legislation was one of the first attempts to address the issue of employment discrimination based on gender.

Title VII of the Civil Rights Act of 1964 prohibits discrimination based on race, color, religion, national origin, or sex in all terms, conditions, or privileges of employment. Originally, the Civil Rights Act was geared toward easing racial discrimination. The inclusion of the sex prohibition was tacked onto the bill by a Southern member of Congress to make a joke of the bill, divide its supporters, and ultimately lead to its defeat. The enactment of this major piece of antidiscrimination legislation is interesting because no organized women's group spoke on its behalf, although Democrat Martha W. Griffiths and other women legislators solidly supported its passage. It was decided that the best strategy to ensure the success of the initiative was to downplay the gender issue, and the strategy worked.

Title VII included an important exception: Discrimination based on sex, religion, or national origin (but not race) is permissible if it is a "bona fide occupational qualification reasonably necessary to the normal operation of that particular business enterprise." To enforce the act's provisions, the Equal Employment Opportunity Commission (EEOC) was established. From the beginning, EEOC officials refused to take the sex provision seriously. It was the EEOC's nonenforcement of the act that served as the catalyst for the formation of the National Organization for Women (NOW) in 1966.

Susan Grover

SOURCE FOR FURTHER STUDY
U.S. National Labor Relations Board. *Titles VII and XI of Civil Rights Act of 1964 and the Equal Employment Opportunity Act of 1972.* Buffalo, N.Y.: William S. Hein, 1978.

SEE ALSO: Equal Rights Amendment (1923); Equal Pay Act (1963); Civil Rights Act of 1964 (1964); Pregnancy Discrimination Act (1978); Women in Apprenticeship and Nontraditional Occupations Act (1992).

WATER RESOURCES RESEARCH ACT

DATE: July 17, 1964
U.S. STATUTES AT LARGE: 78 Stat. 329
PUBLIC LAW: 88-379
U.S. CODE: 42 § 1961
CATEGORIES: Environment and Conservation; Natural Resources

Responding to a number of studies on the uncertainty about the future availability of unpolluted water, Congress authorized federal support of water research in every state.

The Water Resources Research Act was one of several laws passed by Congress in the mid-1960's in response to growing concern about the availability of adequate water supplies for the nation. The passage of these laws marked the culmination of a legislative process that had begun with several reports: a report in 1961 by the Senate Select Subcommittee on Water Resources, chaired by Senator Robert S. Kerr, which had addressed the need for a comprehensive program on water research; a report by the National Academy of Sciences (NSA) that identified priority areas for future research; and a report issued in February, 1963, by the Task Group on Coordinated Water Resources Research of the Federal Council for Science and Technology, which suggested that research centers be set up at universities in different parts of the country to conduct research and provide training for scientists and engineers. This latter report drew an obvious parallel between centers for water-resources research and the agricultural experiment stations that had been set up under the Hatch Act at the nation's land-grant institutions, which were generally credited with having increased agricultural productivity.

PROVISIONS
As passed by Congress and signed into law, the Water Resources Research Act provided for the establishment of water-resource research centers in each of the states and in Puerto Rico. A federal Office of Water Resources Research was to guide and support the state centers. The act further provided three different types of funding: an annual allocation that would eventually reach $100,000 to each state's water-resources research center; additional funds to

match state contributions for water-resources research, rising from $1 million to $5 million over a five-year period; and additional funds to support water-resources research by other universities, private foundations, companies, individuals, or other government agencies. To implement the act, Congress authorized allocations of $75,000 to each of fourteen state water-resources research centers in October, 1964. The centers were to be located at the land-grant institutions in each state. In May, 1965, Congress provided funding of $52,000 to the remaining thirty-seven centers. By the end of the 1965 federal fiscal year on September 30, centers in all fifty states and Puerto Rico had received funds. That first year, funds were used to support 316 different water-research projects.

RELATED LEGISLATION

The Water Resources Research Act was only one of several laws enacted at about that time to protect the nation's water supply. In July, 1965, Congress passed the Water Resources Planning Act, which established a Water Resources Council, consisting of the heads of a number of major federal agencies, to conduct a continuing study of the nation's water needs. The act also gave the president authority to appoint commissions as needed to oversee the development of certain river basins. The National Water Commission Act of 1968 provided $5 million for a National Water Commission, which was allowed a five-year period to conduct a comprehensive examination of water-resource problems throughout the nation and to recommend appropriate management and conservation practices. The report of this commission led to the passage of the Water Pollution Control Act Amendments of 1972.

In 1971, Congress created the Office of Saline Water and, in 1974, combined it with the Office of Water Resources Research to form the Office of Water Research and Technology. The new office was assigned additional responsibilities under the Water Research and Conversion Act of 1977 and the Water Research and Development Act of 1978. In 1982, the functions of the Office of Water Research and Technology, including oversight of the water-resource research centers, were transferred to the U.S. Geological Survey.

IMPACT

Compared to other developments in water-resources research at the time, the Water Resources Research Act of 1964 could be viewed as an attempt to add impetus to an ongoing process and to broaden participation in water-resources research to every state in the nation. The Universities Council on Water Resources was established at about the same time and was expected to play a significant role in the initiation of the water-resources research centers. A new scientific journal, *Water Resources Research*, was inaugurated in the same year by the American Geophysical Union. The United Nations Economic Scientific and Cultural Organization (UNESCO) declared an International Hydrological Decade, which began in 1965. Water resources gained in stature as an academic discipline as a result of the Water Resource Research Act and other initiatives.

The vast program of water-resources research envisioned in the reports leading up to the passage of the Water Resources Research Act was never fully realized. Subsequent sessions of Congress failed to authorize the required funds, and the nation's attention was diverted to the rising cost of energy and the Vietnam conflict. The water-resources research centers nevertheless continued to operate and to provide leadership for university efforts to develop research and educational programs.

Donald R. Franceschetti

SOURCES FOR FURTHER STUDY

Black, Peter E. *Conservation of Water and Related Land Resources.* 2d ed. Totowa, N.J.: Rowman & Littlefield, 1987.

Hirshleifer, Jack, James C. DeHaven, and Jerome W. Milliman. *Water Supply: Economics, Technology, and Policy.* Chicago: University of Chicago Press, 1960.

Hufschmidt, Maynard M. "The Harvard Program: A Summing Up." In *Water Research,* edited by Allen V. Kneese and Stephen C. Smith. Baltimore: The Johns Hopkins University Press, 1966.

Kneese, Allen V. "Introduction: New Directions in Water Resources Research." In *Water Research,* edited by Allen V. Kneese and Stephen C. Smith. Baltimore: The Johns Hopkins University Press, 1966.

Renne, Roland R. "A Co-operative Water Research Program and the Nation's Future." In *Water Research,* edited by Allen V. Kneese and Stephen C. Smith. Baltimore: The Johns Hopkins University Press, 1966.

Schwartz, A. Truman, et al. *Chemistry in Context: Applying Chemistry to Society.* Dubuque, Iowa: William C. Brown, 1994.

Smith, Stephen C., and Emery N. Castle. *Economics and Public Policy in Water Resource Development.* Ames: Iowa State University Press, 1994.

SEE ALSO: Water Pollution Control Act (1948); Water Pollution Control Act Amendments of 1956 (1956); Clean Water Act and Amendments (1965); Water Pollution Control Act Amendments of 1972 (1972); Safe Drinking Water Act (1974).

TONKIN GULF RESOLUTION

ALSO KNOWN AS: Southeast Asia Resolution
DATE: August 10, 1964
U.S. STATUTES AT LARGE: 78 Stat. 384
PUBLIC LAW: 88-408
CATEGORIES: Asia or Asian Americans; Foreign Relations; Military and National Security

This resolution authorized the president "to take all necessary steps, including the use of armed force, to assist any member or protocol state of the Southeast Asia Collective Defense Treaty requesting assistance in defense of its freedom," effectively launching U.S. participation in the Vietnam War.

During the 1950's, the United States became increasingly committed to the independence and survival of the Republic of South Vietnam, which was engaged in a struggle with the communist Democratic Republic of Vietnam (North Vietnam). When Lyndon B. Johnson became president of the United States, the instability of the government of South Vietnam led to an increasing role for American advisers. By 1964, administration officials believed that only direct American involvement in the war, including air strikes and possibly ground troops, could save South Vietnam.

Noting that the Constitution gave Congress the authority to declare war, the Johnson administration sought congressional support for military action against North Vietnam that would not entail the political controversy that a formal declaration of war might entail. Johnson wanted a congressional resolution similar to that given President Dwight D. Eisenhower in 1955 authorizing him to use force if necessary during a crisis with Communist China. Aides to Johnson crafted the resolution in the spring of 1964, but congressional support for the resolution was noticeably lacking.

The opportunity Johnson sought came on the night of August 3, 1964, in the Gulf of Tonkin, off the coast of North Vietnam. North Vietnamese torpedo boats unsuccessfully attacked the USS *Maddox* in what the United States considered international waters. Although doubts appeared almost immediately regarding a possible second attack the following night, Johnson used the two alleged attacks to rally support for the resolution, which both houses of Congress approved on August 10.

Citing the alleged attacks of American vessels in international waters, the resolution authorized the president "to take all necessary measures to repel any armed attack against the forces of the United States and to prevent further aggression." The resolution further authorized the president "to take all necessary steps, including the use of armed force, to assist any member or protocol state of the Southeast Asia Collective Defense Treaty requesting assistance in defense of its freedom." The president could decide when the peace of the region allowed him to terminate the resolution.

The Tonkin Gulf Resolution served as the de facto declaration of war by the United States against North Vietnam in that it gave congressional permission for the president to use military force against it. With the resolution, Johnson had solid bipartisan congressional support for waging war in Southeast Asia.

Senator Wayne Morse (Democrat of Oregon), one of only two senators who voted against the resolution, introduced repealing legislation but was soundly defeated on March 1, 1966. The Tonkin Gulf Resolution remained in force until Johnson repudiated it on August 18, 1967. Congress repealed the resolution on December 31, 1970, although American ground troops remained in Vietnam until 1973.

Barry M. Stentiford

943

SOURCES FOR FURTHER STUDY
Galloway, John. *The Gulf of Tonkin Resolution.* Teaneck, N.J.: Fairleigh Dickinson University Press, 1970.
Moise, Edwin E. *Tonkin Gulf and the Escalation of the Vietnam War.* Chapel Hill: University of North Carolina Press, 1996.
Siff, Ezra Y., and Anthony B. Herbert. *Why the Senate Slept: The Gulf of Tonkin Resolution and the Beginning of America's Vietnam War.* Westport, Conn.: Praeger, 1999.

SEE ALSO: Formosa Resolution (1955); War Powers Resolution (1973).

ECONOMIC OPPORTUNITY ACT

DATE: August 20, 1964
U.S. STATUTES AT LARGE: 78 Stat. 508
PUBLIC LAW: 88-452
U.S. CODE: 42 § 2701
CATEGORIES: Education; Health and Welfare; Labor and Employment

> *This law, part of President Lyndon B. Johnson's War on Poverty, was designed to combat poverty in the United States by mobilizing human and financial resources.*

The Economic Opportunity Act (EOA) of 1964 was the result of various proposals and ideas that dated back to the social welfare initiatives of the New Deal in the 1930's. The EOA established the Office of Economic Opportunity (OEO) in the executive office of the president, which launched several programs in the War on Poverty, a domestic "war" that was necessary, according to President Lyndon B. Johnson, "so as to eliminate the paradox of poverty in the midst of plenty."

FOCUS ON OPPORTUNITY
The various programs had, as their feature value, a focus on opportunity. The EOA's declaration of purpose, in part, is to provide "the opportunity for education and training, the opportunity to work,

and the opportunity to live in decency and dignity." The EOA provided the funds for vocational training, created the Job Corps to train youths in conservation camps and urban centers and the Head Start program to help preschoolers from low-income families, encouraged Community Action Programs, extended loans to small-business owners willing to hire the unemployed, gave grants to farmers, set up a work-study program for college students, and established Volunteers in Service to America (VISTA), the domestic counterpart of the popular Peace Corps created by President John F. Kennedy.

New Deal Roots

President Johnson's dream of the Great Society and his attitude that government should use its powers for great accomplishments came, in part, from his political mentor, President Franklin D. Roosevelt. Like Roosevelt's New Deal legislation and Kennedy's New Frontier plans and policies, Johnson's vision included the hope of socially and politically engineering a better country for everyone. The concept and rationale of the many programs created by the EOA were quite controversial during their formative stages. Eventually, as with almost any piece of legislation, what finally got enacted reflected compromises and trade-offs among the various lobbies, administrative agencies, and congressional power blocs. Possibly the most controversial program established by the EOA was the Job Corps. It was one of the first government efforts directed at the problem of hard-core, unemployable youth.

The EOA was supported by New Deal Democrats (including Senator Hubert Humphrey, who later became Johnson's vice president) who envisioned a transformation of poverty-stricken individuals into well-adjusted, motivated, and upwardly mobile people. The act was opposed primarily by conservative Republicans who were against government intervention in domestic affairs, especially where it concerned social welfare legislation, and were concerned about the high costs of running these programs. Johnson was successful in passing the EOA partly because of the favorable pro-Democrat atmosphere created after Kennedy's assassination.

Programs

The programs enacted by the EOA under the auspices of the OEO ranged from well-known programs such as Head Start and the Job

Corps to less well known projects such as Senior Opportunities and Services, Legal Services, and Community Economic Development. All had the goal of helping the poor break the cycle of poverty and advance to live a better, fuller, more productive life. Some of the programs, such as Head Start, are generally regarded as successful; others remain controversial or have vanished. However, between 1964 and 1969, poverty rates decreased from 19 percent to 12 percent of the population.

The OEO was abolished by the Head Start, Economic Opportunity, and Community Partnership Act of 1975, which created the Community Services Administration. The EOA was repealed except for titles VIII and X by the Omnibus Budget Reconciliation Act of 1981.

Joseph E. Bauer

SOURCES FOR FURTHER STUDY

Johnson, Lyndon B. *The Vantage Point: Perspectives of the Presidency, 1963-1969*. New York, Holt, Rinehart and Winston 1971.

United States. *Public Papers of the Presidents of the United States: Lyndon B. Johnson*. 10 vols. Washington, D.C.: Government Printing Office, 1965-1970.

SEE ALSO: Hundred Days legislation (1933); Social Security Act (1935); Aid to Families with Dependent Children (1935); Housing and Urban Development Act (1965); Medicare and Medicaid Amendments (1965); Older Americans Act (1965); Executive Orders 11246 and 11375 (1965, 1967); Age Discrimination in Employment Act (1967); Fair Housing Act (1968).

INTEREST EQUALIZATION TAX ACT

DATE: September 2, 1964
U.S. STATUTES AT LARGE: 78 Stat. 843
PUBLIC LAW: 88-563
CATEGORIES: Business, Commerce, and Trade; Tariffs and Taxation

The act closed U.S. capital markets to foreign borrowing in response to a balance of payments deficit.

President Lyndon B. Johnson signed the Interest Equalization Tax into law on September 2, 1964. This legislation was a response to a continuous deficit in the Official Reserve Transactions Account of the United States' balance of payments and to a drain on U.S. gold reserves. The Official Reserve Transactions Account was a summary account used at the time to measure the overall impact of the balance of payments, a measure of the balance between money sent abroad and money brought into the country. The Interest Equalization Tax was retroactive to July 19, 1963, the date that President John F. Kennedy requested that Congress act on this matter. The tax was the first in a series of actions undertaken by the U.S. government to restrict the outflow of funds from the United States.

TEMPORARY PROVISION, LONG-TERM TRADE PROBLEM

The Senate Finance Committee approved the Interest Equalization Tax by a vote of 11 to 5, with Senate Minority Leader Everett Dirksen (Republican of Illinois) voting with the Democratic majority. Senator Jacob Javits (Republican of New York) had unsuccessfully attempted to substitute a voluntary capital issues committee for the legislation. Secretary of the Treasury Douglas Dillon characterized the legislation as temporary, noting that it would expire at the end of the following year, 1965. The administration, moreover, would not seek to extend the law, according to Dillon.

The Interest Equalization Tax was characterized as temporary for two reasons. First, policymakers did not appreciate the fundamental, significant structural changes that were taking place in the world economy. The large trade surplus (exports exceeding imports) that the United States enjoyed in the first decade after World War II was fading rapidly. The balance of payments problem, they perceived, was a transitory problem needing only a temporary solution. Second, one of the strongest arguments against the enactment of the tax was offered by Wall Street analysts. The long-term cost of restricting capital markets, they argued, would be too great. The New York financial markets, considered to be the center of world finance after supplanting the London markets following World War II, would be in danger of losing their heavily international flavor if the tax stayed in place too long.

During the 1950-1959 period, the deficit in the Official Reserve Transactions Account of the United States' balance of payments averaged $0.9 billion. That average figure increased to $1.7 billion in the 1958-1968 period. By 1962, when the balance of payments deficit problem was beginning to be recognized and acknowledged, the United States still held the largest supply of monetary gold in the world, even though its gold reserves had been shrinking since 1959 at a compound annual rate of 6.5 percent per year. United States monetary gold reserves stood at $16.4 billion, of which only $4.6 billion were "free reserves," the rest required by law to be held to back Federal Reserve notes and reserve deposits from members of the Federal Reserve System. In 1962, U.S. gold reserves stood at their lowest level since 1939.

ECONOMIC CONTEXT

To put the situation into perspective, the United States accumulated balance of payments deficits totaling approximately $24 billion between 1950 and 1961. Gold conversions (redemptions of dollars in exchange for gold) had accounted for almost one-third of this total and represented a loss of about one-third of the United States' monetary gold reserves. In June of 1967, foreign U.S. dollar claims against the United States stood at 226 percent of the total U.S. holdings of gold reserves. The deficits in the Official Reserve Transactions Account of the U.S. balance of payments were met by an outflow of U.S. monetary gold reserves and an increase in short-term liabilities to foreign holders of U.S. dollars. These short-term liabilities could be used to finance a run on the dollar whenever confidence in the dollar waned.

Under the Bretton Woods system, the international monetary system that operated from 1944 to 1972, the U.S. dollar and the British pound sterling were "reserve currencies." Nations subscribing to the system could keep their monetary reserves, which were used in international financial transactions, in the form of a reserve currency or gold. After the 1967 devaluation of the British pound sterling, the U.S. dollar became the world's premier reserve currency and vehicle for international transactions.

The value of the U.S. dollar under the Bretton Woods system was defined in terms of gold. One ounce of monetary gold was equal to $35.00. All other nations defined the par value of their currency in terms of the U.S. dollar, and thus in terms of gold. The Bretton

Woods system required that the United States run a continuous balance of payments deficit in order to supply the world with liquidity and monetary reserves. At some point, however, the U.S. balance of payments deficit became a problem.

The U.S. government looked to the U.S. capital markets, used to finance the international activities of foreign corporations and the foreign subsidiaries of U.S. multinational corporations, as one place to begin to stem the outflow of dollars. That outflow caused or at least allowed the balance of payments deficit. Dollars sent abroad eventually found their way back as a claim on the U.S. gold stock. Government officials feared that those claims would be realized. The U.S. stock of gold was insufficient to meet all the claims.

The Interest Equalization Tax was enacted to increase the interest rate in U.S. capital markets. At the time, interest rates in most foreign capital markets were at least 1 percent higher than the prevailing rate on comparable securities in the U.S. capital markets. Higher interest rates would increase the cost of borrowing and make U.S. capital markets less attractive. Foreigners would therefore borrow less and take fewer dollars out of the United States.

The Interest Equalization Tax effectively closed U.S. capital markets to foreign corporations and the foreign subsidiaries of U.S. multinational corporations. The legislation exempted international agencies, such as the World Bank and the Interamerican Development Bank, and foreign governments in developing nations. Foreign stocks sold in the United States would be taxed at a rate of 15 percent of their purchase price, while foreign bonds would be taxed at a rate ranging from 2.75 percent of their purchase price, for securities maturing in less than three years, up to 15 percent of their purchase price, for securities maturing in twenty-eight and a half years or more.

IMPACT

On its very first test, the Interest Equalization Tax worked perfectly. In September of 1963, the city of Oslo, Norway, offered $15 million in bonds paying an interest rate of 5.6 percent. The Interest Equalization Tax effectively reduced this rate to 4.9 percent for U.S. citizens. This relatively low rate proved unattractive to U.S. investors, and most of these securities were purchased by Europeans.

Because the Interest Equalization Tax was expected to be retroactive if passed, uncertainty over whether the tax would be passed created an atmosphere that acted to dramatically reduce the volume of foreign securities issued in U.S. capital markets. The total volume of foreign issues sold in U.S. markets in all of 1962 was $1.2 billion. In the first half of 1963, before the Interest Equalization Tax was proposed, the total volume was $1.3 billion. In the second half of 1963, the volume of foreign securities sold in U.S. capital markets fell to $315 million.

The U.S. dollar had a unique role and responsibility under the Bretton Woods system. To the extent that other nations were willing to hold additional U.S. dollars as monetary reserves and that their citizens were willing to hold additional U.S. dollar assets as investments, the United States could continue to run a deficit in its balance of payments with impunity and collect a seigniorage, consuming and investing more than it produced. This consumption and investment would be financed by the creation of additional U.S. dollars. At some point, the U.S. balance of payments deficits became chronic and persistent. These deficits developed very rapidly after the de facto convertibility of the major European currencies was achieved. When the deficits began, policymakers and those concerned with the international monetary system were still focusing on the U.S. dollar shortage, the idea that there was a long-term, fundamental imbalance in the international payments system in favor of the United States. Very suddenly and to the surprise of many, a dollar glut developed. The U.S. balance of payments deficits developed because the outflow of U.S. dollars was too large for the rest of the world to absorb as additional monetary reserves and increased dollar asset holdings.

These deficits were caused by several factors: rapid growth in the United States' overseas military expenditures, an increased flow of private overseas investment, extensive use of the U.S. capital markets to raise financing for projects undertaken by foreign subsidiaries of domestic international corporations as well as by foreign corporations, and an increase in official foreign aid grants. Surpluses on the balance of trade account, a measure of the balance between imports and exports of goods, did not grow fast enough to offset the increased overseas military expenditures, the flow of private investment, the use of the U.S. capital markets as a source of international finance, and official foreign aid grants.

A critical factor in the development of the U.S. balance of payments deficit was the failure of the U.S. trade surplus to grow. Had this surplus grown more rapidly than it did, the deficit problem might never have developed. The growth of the trade surplus would have absorbed some of the redundant dollars that were finding their way back to the United States to claim U.S. monetary gold reserves. Solving the dollar shortage would have required larger and larger U.S. balance of payments deficits. A permanent dollar shortage would have meant, had it actually existed, much slower economic growth, a worse allocation of world resources, and a slowing of the trend toward international economic and financial integration in the post-World War II period. A dollar glut, on the other hand, would prove to be much more dangerous. It would ultimately result in the collapse of the fixed exchange rate system established by the Bretton Woods Agreement, under which currencies were traded for each other at known, fixed rates of exchange. A dollar glut would make the fixed price of dollars appear too high, and other countries would become unwilling to hold them, trading them for gold.

The ability of foreign holders of U.S. dollars to convert their dollar holdings into gold was a central element of the Bretton Woods system and essential to support the claim that the U.S. dollar was "as good as gold." The U.S. Treasury's ability to convert U.S. dollars into gold became more and more problematic as the nation's balance of payments deficits grew. Monetary crises followed, confidence in the dollar waned, and eventually the Bretton Woods system collapsed.

The U.S. dollar played a unique role in the Bretton Woods system. When the U.S. dollar became overvalued relative to other major currencies of the world, the United States government could not unilaterally devalue the U.S. dollar. Because the dollar acted as a reserve currency, it could not be devalued. This was the price the United States paid for the special role of the U.S. dollar and the seigniorage collected when nations would freely accept dollars.

The Interest Equalization Tax did not solve the U.S. balance of payments problem, essentially because the world economy was undergoing significant structural changes and the balance of payments problem faced by the United States was misperceived as temporary in nature. By the late 1950's, the huge trade surpluses that the United States had enjoyed in the early postwar period were shrinking, both absolutely and relatively. The Interest Equalization Tax, moreover, only focused on one element of the problem, the use of U.S. capital markets as a source of international finance.

The closing of the U.S. capital markets to foreign borrowers was not a full solution to the United States' balance of payments problem. The Interest Equalization Tax was the first in a series of unsuccessful actions undertaken by the U.S. government to attempt to solve problems that would ultimately result in the collapse of the Bretton Woods system of fixed exchange rates.

Daniel C. Falkowski

SOURCES FOR FURTHER STUDY
Kindleberger, Charles P. *International Economics.* 4th ed. Homewood, Ill.: Richard D. Irwin, 1968.
Scammell, W. M. *International Monetary Policy: Bretton Woods and After.* New York: John Wiley & Sons, 1975.
Solomon, Robert. *The International Monetary System 1945-1981.* New York: Harper & Row, 1982.
U.S. Congress. Vol. 78 of *Statutes at Large.* Washington, D.C.: Government Printing Office, 1964.
Yeager, Leland B. *International Monetary Relations: Theory, History, and Policy.* 2d ed. New York: Harper & Row, 1976.

SEE ALSO: Bretton Woods Agreement (1944); General Agreement on Tariffs and Trade of 1947 (1947).

NATIONAL ARTS AND CULTURAL DEVELOPMENT ACT

DATE: September 3, 1964
U.S. STATUTES AT LARGE: 78 Stat. 905
CATEGORIES: Education; Health and Welfare; Speech and Expression

In 1965, Congress elected to support the arts by creating the National Foundation on the Arts and Humanities, which subsumed the National Endowment for the Humanities and the National Endowment for the Arts. These endowments could provide grants to states, nonprofit organizations, and individuals to promote the arts and humanities.

In 1948, leaders of twelve national arts organizations formed the Committee on Government and Art to secure federal support for the arts. They investigated the feasibility of federal support, but legislative commitment was minimal. In 1955, Senator Nelson A. Rockefeller, a proponent of the cause, supported an arts bill that passed in the Senate but failed in the House. In 1960, Rockefeller helped form the New York State Council on the Arts, and the same year Michigan created a state arts agency.

In 1960, presidential candidate John F. Kennedy supported an advisory committee on art. He endorsed the development of an advisory council in 1962 and appointed August Heckscher consultant on the arts. Heckscher wrote a report outlining why and how the federal government should support the arts and helped increase governmental and popular support for an arts bill. In 1963, Kennedy issued an executive order creating an arts commission. Kennedy considered Michael Straight for chair of the commission, but scandal erupted when Straight admitted to knowledge of Soviet espionage activities. Kennedy selected Richard Goodwin as commission chair but was assassinated before he could announce his selection. President Lyndon B. Johnson appointed Roger Stevens adviser for the bill in 1964. The National Arts and Cultural Development Act of 1964 passed in the House and Senate and was approved by Johnson, who named Stevens chair. The bill established a national council of the arts and a national arts foundation, and in 1965, the National Foundation on the Arts and Humanities was created. Although the 1964 act authorized annual appropriations of ten million dollars and a five-million-dollar treasury fund, authorized monies did not match the appropriation and the foundation received only half that amount.

IMPACT

Although the establishment of the National Foundation on the Arts and Humanities sent a positive message—that the federal government would support the arts—many other issues still had to be addressed. For example, the financial backing provisions were weak and the foundation's responsibilities were greater than it could conceivably accomplish. In addition, the act allowed money to be allotted to a variety of causes including the visual arts, theater, music, architecture, museums, and art education, but the foundation had the difficult task of deciding who would get how much. In

1969, President Richard M. Nixon asked Congress to double the appropriations of the endowments, which helped the foundation meet more of its goals.

Throughout the 1970's, the foundation's monetary allotment increased. Improvements in the system, such as establishing a panel to judge requests for money and setting specific goals and criteria, helped the foundation function. Since the 1960's, questions have arisen regarding whether the federal government should support the arts, how anyone can determine the value of one kind of art over another, and whether welfare or the public interest should take priority.

Andrea Donovan

SOURCE FOR FURTHER STUDY
Larson, Gary O. *The Reluctant Patron: The United States Government and the Arts.* Philadelphia: University of Pennsylvania Press, 1983.

SEE ALSO: Foreign Agents Registration Act (1938); Public Broadcasting Act (1967).

WILDERNESS ACT

DATE: September 3, 1964
U.S. STATUTES AT LARGE: 78 Stat. 890
PUBLIC LAW: 88-577
U.S. CODE: 16 § 1131 et seq.
CATEGORIES: Agriculture; Environment and Conservation; Land Management; Natural Resources

This act created the National Wilderness Preservation System, designated its first components, provided management direction for designated areas, and established a procedure by which new areas might be added to the system over time.

The first national parks, national forests, national monuments, and national wildlife refuges were all established prior to World

War I. Each set aside substantial areas of federal lands for conservation purposes, but those purposes differed from one system to the next. National forests emphasized scientific management of forest resources for economic purposes, national parks the preservation of scenic wonders and accommodation of tourists, national monuments the preservation of archaeological resources, and wildlife refuges the preservation of habitat for game species. Each of these systems contained significant de facto wilderness, but it was poorly protected and, after World War II, increasingly threatened by development.

Fearing for the wilderness that remained, conservation organizations, led by Howard Zahniser of the Wilderness Society, proposed legislation to establish a National Wilderness Preservation System. The proposed system was to be composed of undeveloped federal lands already managed for conservation purposes. Areas designated as wilderness were to remain within their respective conservation systems, but managing agencies would be required to preserve the wilderness character of areas under their jurisdiction. Efforts to pass a wilderness bill spanned a decade, but the essential elements of this proposal were enacted in 1964.

The Wilderness Act defined wilderness as "an area of undeveloped Federal land retaining its primeval character and influence, without permanent improvements or human habitation, which is protected and managed so as to preserve its natural conditions." The act prohibited roads, structures, commercial activity, and motor use, but significant exceptions were made to benefit mining, grazing, and reclamation users of national forest lands. The Wilderness Act designated wilderness areas comprising 3.7 million hectares, selecting from lands that had already been classified as wilderness by the Forest Service, and it directed the secretary of agriculture and secretary of the interior to survey undeveloped areas of the national forest, national park, and national wildlife refuge systems and to propose additional wilderness areas for designation by Congress.

Wilderness designation remains controversial, especially on national forest lands where protecting the wilderness resource means forgoing the economic benefits of timber harvest and most mining and water resource development. In the national parks these economic uses are generally prohibited regardless of wilderness status. Despite the controversy, the amount of wilderness protected continues to grow. The Federal Land Policy and Management Act of 1976 added Bureau of Land Management lands to those that are to be considered for wilderness designation. In 1980 the Alaska National Interest Lands Conservation Act more than doubled the area designated as wilderness, adding 22 million hectares. In 1997 the total area of federal land protected as wilderness exceeded 40 million hectares, and an additional 8 to 20 million hectares were expected to be added eventually.

Craig W. Allin

SOURCES FOR FURTHER STUDY
Allin, Craig W. *The Politics of Wilderness Preservation.* Westport, Conn.: Greenwood Press, 1982.
Frome, Michael. *Battle for the Wilderness.* New York: Praeger, 1974.
Hendee, John C., et al. *Wilderness Management.* Washington, D.C.: U.S. Forest Service, 1978.
Irland, Lloyd C. *Wilderness Economics and Policy.* Lexington, Mass.: Lexington Books, 1979.
Nash, Roderick. *Wilderness and the American Mind.* 3d ed. New Haven, Conn.: Yale University Press, 1986.

SEE ALSO: National Park Service Organic Act (1916); Multiple Use-Sustained Yield Act (1960); Wild and Scenic Rivers Act and National Trails System Act (1968); National Environmental Policy Act (1970); Eastern Wilderness Act (1975); National Forest Management Act (1976); Alaska National Interest Lands Conservation Act (1980).

OLDER AMERICANS ACT

DATE: July 14, 1965
U.S. STATUTES AT LARGE: 79 Stat. 219
PUBLIC LAW: 89-73
U.S. CODE: 42 § 3001
CATEGORIES: Aging Issues; Health and Welfare

This law provided funds for services for needy persons aged sixty and over, supplementing Social Security benefits.

Prior to 1965, research indicated that many senior citizens in the United States lacked adequate retirement income, health care, affordable housing, gainful employment, and meaningful civil, cultural, and recreational opportunities. In addition, as persons grew older, they were spending increasing percentages of their fixed incomes on medical care. Accordingly, as a part of President Lyndon B. Johnson's Great Society programs, Congress passed the Older Americans Act on July 14, 1965. Several amendments have been made to the act, including the Age Discrimination Act of 1975.

The act created the Administration on Aging (AoA), headed by a commissioner of aging within the Department of Health, Education, and Welfare. The Advisory Committee on Older Americans, consisting of the commissioner and fifteen people with relevant experience, was also established to provide expertise in designing new programs. In 1978, AoA was transferred to the new Department of Health and Human Services. Acting on recommendations of the 1992 White House Conference on Aging, Congress in 1993 amended the act by upgrading the commissioner to assistant secretary for aging; in addition, the Advisory Committee on Older Americans became the Federal Council on Aging.

The AoA provides grants to states. To obtain funds, each state must designate a state unit on aging (SUA), which must design a program to utilize the funds. SUAs then identify area agencies throughout each state, which form advisory councils to develop the area plan, hold hearings, represent older people, and review and comment on community programs. SUAs by law must have a full-time ombudsman to handle complaints. The AoA awards two types of grants: for research and development projects (which make needs assessments, develop new approaches—including clinics to provide legal assistance to poorer senior citizens and multipurpose activity centers—develop new methods to coordinate programs and services, and evaluate the various programs) and for training projects for personnel to run the programs.

Each state receives at least 1 percent of the total funding, and American Samoa, Guam, and the Virgin Islands each receive 0.5 percent. The remaining 49.5 percent is allocated on the basis of the relative size of the state's population. No more than 10 percent of each state's allotment can support SUA administrative expenses. The AoA also provides consultants, technical assistance, training personnel, research, and informational materials to the states. Priority program recipients are those who are homebound because of disability or illness. Meals-on-wheels services provide hot meals directly to their homes, and they are eligible for in-home support services, including home health aides. Low-income minorities are especially targeted.

Programs operating under the act have been criticized largely because, although the quality of services is much better in some states than others, the AoA has neither developed nor enforced minimum standards. In 1991, Congress held up renewal of the act while it developed a means test to ensure that only needy older persons would take advantage.

Michael Haas

SOURCES FOR FURTHER STUDY

Lee, Jik-Joen. *Development, Delivery, and Utilization of Services Under the Older Americans Act: A Perspective of Asian-American Elderly.* New York: Garland Publishing, 1992.

O'Shaughnessy, Carol. *Older Americans Act: Brief History of Legislation and Funding.* Washington, D.C.: Congressional Research Service, 1993.

United States. Senate. Subcommittee on Aging of the Committee on Human Resources. *Older Americans Amendment of 1975 (A Compilation of Public Law 94-135, Accompanying Reports, and Related Acts).* Washington, D.C.: Government Printing Office, 1978.

SEE ALSO: Executive Order 11141 (1964); Medicare and Medicaid Amendments (1965); Age Discrimination in Employment Act (1967); Age Discrimination Act (1975); Older Workers Benefit Protection Act (1990).

MEDICARE AND MEDICAID AMENDMENTS

DATE: July 30, 1965
U.S. STATUTES AT LARGE: 79 Stat. 286
PUBLIC LAW: 89-97
U.S. CODE: 42 § 1395 et seq.
CATEGORIES: Aging Issues; Health and Welfare

The passage of the Medicare and Medicaid amendments to the Social Security Act opened medical care to the elderly and the indigent.

The notion of governmental funding for the medical needs of United States citizens was not new in the 1960's. The road to Medicare and Medicaid began during the Depression, when President Franklin D. Roosevelt's New Deal administration set up programs to help those unable to provide for themselves. The Great Society administration of Lyndon B. Johnson finally saw passage of governmental medical insurance for the elderly and poor.

Private medical insurance had been available to consumers since the 1930's, when the nonprofit Blue Cross and Blue Shield programs began. During World War II, the War Stabilization Board exempted "fringe benefits," including health care and insurance, from its ban on wage increases. This gave employers an opportunity to place more value on their employees' work without violating the ban on pay increases and resulted in a dramatic increase in the number of Americans covered by medical insurance. Coverage, however, was largely limited to those in an employer or union plan and left the retired elderly and unemployed without coverage.

AN AGING POPULATION

Postwar medical advances made health care more expensive. Advances in technology made for medical miracles but came at a cost. In 1945, President Harry S. Truman recognized the financial burden of medical care on the elderly and called for the American Medical Association (AMA) and other groups to look into funding alternatives.

The 1950's brought more attention to the medical needs of the poor and elderly, as health care costs more than doubled during the decade. A program sponsored by Senator Robert Kerr (Democrat of Oklahoma) and Congressman Wilbur Mills (Democrat of Arkansas) that set up federal-state sharing of medical expenses for the "medically needy" helped lessen the cost burden. The program set up a vendor payments system whereby state agencies made direct payments to physicians and other medical providers. Aime Forand (Republican of Rhode Island) proposed a plan in 1959 that would provide hospitalization coverage for Social Security recipients and be funded through an additional Social Security tax.

By 1960, more than 17.5 million Americans had reached the age of sixty-five, and the proportion of elderly Americans was growing. Improved technologies had resulted in better medical care, which in turn meant longer lives. Studies showed that 15 percent of the average elderly person's income was spent on medical care, and concerns arose that this income (in most cases fixed) could not keep in step with rising medical costs. That same year, Health, Education, and Welfare Secretary Arthur Flemming proposed plans for medical insurance, using the term "medicare" for the first time. A year later, congressmen Cecil King and Clinton Anderson introduced an official proposal for a medicare plan. This program was similar to the Forand legislation but added an annual deductible and coverage of retirees from the railroads.

MEDICAL OPPOSITION

Opposition to this proposal came from an unexpected source, the AMA. The organization lobbied heavily against governmental involvement in the medical industry, fearing a loss of control over patient care. Doctors' groups publicly stated their intention not to treat patients under the program and spread fears within the American public of socialized medicine. The AMA's alternative solution was a program called "Eldercare," introduced in the House of Representatives by some Republican members. This state-administered private health insurance plan would be funded by a premium based on the purchaser's income, with federal subsidies for the needy. The plan soon died, after Republican Party leadership did not lend support.

Committee hearings reached gridlock on the issue. The King-Anderson proposal was tabled so that Congress could concentrate on tax and civil rights legislation during 1963 and 1964. The 1964 election reopened the door for health insurance. President Lyndon Johnson called for immediate attention to the issue of medical care for the elderly and the poor. In addition, the election put Democratic majorities into both the Senate and the House of Representatives. The AMA realized that some type of insurance plan was coming, and in 1965, James Appel, the president of the AMA, called for a compromise and encouraged doctors to participate in shaping new regulations governing health care.

PASSAGE AND PROVISIONS: MEDICARE
The Eighty-ninth Congress passed the Medicare and Medicaid bills in 1965 as amendments to the Social Security Act. Signed by President Johnson at the Harry S. Truman Library in Independence, Missouri, on July 30, 1965, the new programs went into effect on July 1, 1966. The first Medicare cards were given to former president Harry S. Truman and his wife.

Administered by the Department of Health, Education, and Welfare (HEW) and the Social Security Administration, Title XVIII of the Social Security Act (Health Insurance for the Aged), or Medicare, was divided into two programs. Part A, hospitalization, was an automatic program for those aged sixty-five and over and eligible for Social Security or railroad retirement benefits. People under the age of sixty-five could receive Medicare if they had been receiving Social Security for more two years as a result of a disability. The program was funded through a percentage of the Social Security taxes paid by all workers. It provided for sixty days of hospital care with a $40 deductible to be paid by the patient and an additional thirty days of coverage at a cost to the patient of $10 per day. Other provisions included one hundred days of nursing home care for treatment of certain medical conditions, with a $5 charge for each day after the first twenty, and up to one hundred home health-care visits after a hospitalization. The program did not cover long-term nursing home costs. Payments to medical providers were based on "usual, customary, and reasonable" charges.

The second program, Part B, had been an add-on amendment to the King-Anderson proposal in 1965. It offered medical benefits based on a voluntary enrollment; more than 90 percent of those eligible enrolled in the program. Enrollees had a monthly premium deducted from their Social Security payments ($3 per month in early years) which was then matched by the federal government from the general treasury. Once an annual $50 deductible was met, the plan paid for 80 percent of physicians' fees and supplies and an additional one hundred home nursing visits beyond those covered under Part A.

MEDICAID

A second amendment, Title XIX, Grants to States for Medical Assistance Programs, set up Medicaid. Medicaid was a cooperative program with responsibility shared by state and federal governments. Consolidating the Kerr-Mills programs to include the poor regardless of age, Medicaid increased annual federal grants to the states and called for additional medical care and screening for children in impoverished families. The program required states to cover all persons receiving cash assistance, although criteria for assistance and funding levels were to be determined on a state-by-state basis. Generally, those receiving Aid to Families with Dependent Children (AFDC) or public assistance were eligible. Medicaid also set limits on the amounts to be paid for various services. In 1966, California became the first state to establish a program, called Medi-Cal. New York followed in the same year. By 1968, forty-eight states had started Medicaid programs.

IMPACT ON PATIENTS AND THE MEDICAL PROFESSION

Both critics and proponents of the medical care programs hoped for better health care for elderly and poor Americans as a result of the passage of Medicare and Medicaid. Whether that goal was achieved depends on one's perspective. The almost 19.5 million elderly people who enrolled in the program during 1968 alone received more care, but that care came at an additional cost. Costs for prescription drugs and medical appliances such as walkers and braces, in addition to deductibles, kept medical costs at 15 percent or more of an elderly person's income. Medicaid recipients, especially children, received basic health care, but millions of small children still went without immunizations. Despite these problems, Medicare and Medicaid helped to encourage patients to play more active roles in their own health care. Patients began to question doctors about their options concerning treatment and providers. Patients and their families became a powerful consumer base as the medical industry became more of a business, with hospitals advertising to compete for patients in the early 1980's.

The Medicare and Medicaid programs underwent several revisions and amendments. Early changes brought about an extension in hospitalization from 90 to 120 days (1967) and gave certain patients with chronic kidney disease Medicare coverage (1972). Early Medicaid changes involved restrictions on funding and placed payments on a scale based on the Consumer Price Index (1970).

As costs increased, the federal government sought to control payments. In 1972, limits were placed on "reasonable costs," but it was not until the 1980's that major changes were made in the Medicare program. Beginning in 1983, Congress implemented the concept of Diagnosis Related Groups. This revision sought to level discrepancies between geographical areas by setting flat-fee payments for certain medical conditions instead of paying a percentage of fees and costs. Six years later, in 1989, Congress further limited funds paid by Medicare when it decreased payments to specialists by 11 percent while increasing payments to primary care physicians by 20 percent, effective in 1992. In addition, a Resource-Based Relative Value Scale was implemented in an attempt to balance unequal charges. The same year, a cap was placed on Medicare patient charges. For 1992, doctors could charge 20 percent more than Medicare covered; for 1993, the figure was 15 percent.

GAPS, LOOPHOLES, AND SUPPLEMENTAL INSURANCE

Despite numerous revisions and amendments, the Medicare and Medicaid programs retained several loopholes and gaps that raised costs either to the government or to consumers. Medicare did not cover long-term nursing home care or prescription drugs unless they were given in a hospital. The Medicaid program covered long-term care, but only once a patient was eligible for the program. This meant that elderly persons virtually were forced to deplete their life savings to qualify for Medicaid-covered nursing home care. Several books and lecture series appeared to help elderly persons and their families learn to "hide" assets in order to keep them from going toward medical costs. Another alternative was the growing popularity of home health agencies, which Medicare did cover. These agencies provided home nurse visits for those still able to care for themselves at a basic level.

To help combat the shortcomings of Medicare, private insurance companies developed supplemental policies. These "Medigap" plans helped with costs of prescription drugs as well as deductibles and charges above what was covered by Medicare. For example, a doctor visit might cost $40, even though Medicare set the prevailing charge for the area at $35. Once the deductible was met, Medicare would then pay 80 percent of the prevailing charge, or $28. If the doctor did not accept assignment (Medicare payment accepted as payment in full), the patient would then be responsible for the remaining $12. Supplemental policies often paid 80 percent of the remaining balance.

RISING COSTS

Congressional investigations into Medicare problems resulted in the Medicare Catastrophic Coverage Act of 1988, which attempted to close the gap between actual and covered costs through expanding benefits. The program increased coverage of hospital benefits, added coverage for prescription drugs, and put a limit on out-of-pocket expenses. The plan was designed to be financed by an increased premium and a surtax on the incomes of wealthier Social Security recipients, Complaints flooded into Washington that the elderly, whom the act meant to help, were actually hurt by increased costs. Public opposition became so strong that the act was repealed in 1989.

Medicaid was not without its own problems. To be eligible, a person had to be receiving cash assistance. In most states, these programs left out men and women without children. Most recipients of aid under Medicaid were children, and a high proportion of expenditures went for nursing home care for the elderly. Medicaid also placed a tremendous burden on states' budgets, with a 583 percent increase in spending in the first ten years of the program.

The state programs sought to decrease this burden through spending limits on a variety of medical areas, including drugs and physicians' fees. New payment limits often fell so far below the prevailing charges in an area that some doctors refused to participate in the program, resulting in a reduction of primary care physicians. Those who did participate under the Medicaid and Medicare programs often found themselves forced to increase charges to other patients to make up for the low payments from those covered by Medicare and Medicaid, creating a cycle of increased costs.

The rising costs of medical care fueled a constant debate over funding. States found themselves overburdened by the costs of

Medicaid programs, and both Medicaid and Medicare placed ever-increasing strains on federal funds. Five years into the programs, expenditures on Medicare had increased by 300 percent and those on Medicaid by 400 percent. By 1975, annual U.S. medical costs had reached $133 billion; by 1984, a billion dollars a day were spent on health care. By 1993, medical care costs were more than $700 billion a year and represented more than 12 percent of federal spending.

Administrative costs were often blamed for the rising costs, but a study conducted during the 1980's estimated administrative costs for Medicare and Medicaid at 3 to 5 percent of total costs, while private insurance plans had administrative costs ranging from 14 to 24 percent of the total bill. One administrative area that did promote problems was billing, in particular overcharging by hospitals and doctors. Numerous doctors and hospitals faced fraud charges for padding the bills of patients in order to make up the difference between program payments and actual costs or to make up for those patients who could not pay.

Funding the Medicare and Medicaid programs has been a struggle since their passage. The initial plans for funding proved unable to keep up with growing costs. More Americans were reaching the eligibility age for Medicare, and economic problems resulted in dramatic increases in the number of people receiving state assistance and Medicaid. Even so, many Americans were left with no medical coverage. The programs had opened medical coverage to more Americans and transformed the medical profession, but to remain effective they needed to keep pace with rising medical costs by finding new sources of funding.

Jennifer Davis

SOURCES FOR FURTHER STUDY

Budish, Armond D. *Avoiding the Medicaid Trap: How to Beat the Catastrophic Costs of Nursing Home Care.* Rev. ed. New York: Henry Holt, 1989.

Enthoven, Alain C. *Health Plan The Only Practical Solution to the Soaring Cost of Medical Care.* Reading, Mass.: Addison-Wesley, 1980.

Feingold, Eugene, ed. *Medicare Policy and Politics.* San Francisco: Chandler, 1966.

Grannemann, Thomas W., and Mark V. Pauly. *Controlling Medicaid Costs Federalism, Competition, and Choice.* Washington, D.C.: American Enterprise Institute for Public Policy Research, 1983.
Witkin, Erwin. *The Impact of Medicare.* Springfield, Ill.: Charles C. Thomas, 1971.

SEE ALSO: Sheppard-Towner Act (1921); Social Security Act (1935); Aid to Families with Dependent Children (1935); Older Americans Act (1965).

HIGHWAY BEAUTIFICATION ACT

DATE: August, 1965
U.S. STATUTES AT LARGE: 79 Stat. 1028
PUBLIC LAW: 89-285
CATEGORIES: Environment and Conservation

The act banned billboards within 660 feet of interstate or primary highways except in industrial or commercial areas.

In August of 1965, the Highway Beautification Act was passed into law, largely as a result of the persistence of President Lyndon B. Johnson, Lady Bird Johnson, and Laurance Spelman Rockefeller. Phillip Tocker, chairman of the Outdoor Advertising Association of America (OAAA), supported the bill as long as commercial and industrial zones were exempt and if people who were no longer allowed to rent land for billboards were compensated. The act stated that all signs within 660 feet of interstate and primary highways were banned, except for official direction signs and on-premise advertising. Commercial and industrial areas were exempt. States that did not enforce removal of all offending signs by 1970 could lose up to 20 percent of their federal highway funds.

Before the Highway Beautification Act of 1965 was passed, there was only one federal law specifically concerning billboards. It was passed in 1958 and stated that a bonus would be given to any state that controlled billboards within 660 feet of the federal interstate highway system. Only seven states qualified for bonuses: Kentucky, New York, Maine, New Hampshire, Ohio, Wisconsin, and Virginia.

THE MOVEMENT AGAINST BILLBOARDS

The billboard industry had grown so rapidly that in most cities there were more billboards than it was possible for a driver, or perhaps even a passenger, to read. The movement against billboards started in citizens' roadside councils and garden clubs throughout the United States. These groups disliked billboards for two reasons. First, they thought billboards were ugly and blocked out landscape. Second, there were numerous reports linking increased numbers of accidents to prevalence of billboards. Some studies showed that there were three times as many accidents in areas with billboards as compared to similar areas without billboards. Billboard opponents reasoned that drivers were distracted by the advertisements. A growing interest in removing billboards initiated the Highway Beautification Act.

In May of 1965, President Johnson held a conference at the White House to discuss the bill. Mrs. Cyril Fox, chair of the Pennsylvania Roadside Council and a representative of various roadside councils and garden clubs, attended this meeting. The bill that she and most beautification activists wanted to pass prohibited billboards within one thousand feet of interstate and primary highways, with no exempt areas. Her version of the bill also addressed other areas, including junkyards, landscaped areas, and scenic roads. New junkyards would be prohibited within one thousand feet of interstate and primary highways, and existing junkyards would either be removed or be screened by a fence of shrubbery within five years. States were to use 3 percent of their federal highway aid for landscaping and beautifying roadsides. States also would have to use one-third of their federal highway aid for secondary roads and access roads to recreational and scenic areas.

Phillip Tocker was invited to this May conference. His suggestions outraged the beautification activists. He would support the bill only if the distance restriction were changed to 660 feet, commercial and industrial areas were exempt, and the federal government would compensate for losses. Mrs. Cyril Fox, the roadside councils, and the garden clubs were displeased not only with Tocker but also with Laurance Rockefeller and his staff. The roadside councils and the garden clubs believed that since they had been fighting for years against billboards, they should have a more powerful position, the one that Rockefeller and his staff were fulfilling. At the end of the conference, Tocker's version of the bill was read to President Johnson. Fox, the roadside councils, and the garden clubs were disillusioned. After that conference, they no longer supported the bill, which they thought did not solve the problem. This lack of support made it difficult to pass the bill.

PASSAGE AND PROVISIONS

President Johnson's advisers were convinced that the bill had no chance of passing unless it exempted commercial and industrial areas, largely because of the influence of the OAAA. The OAAA was a strong organization with six hundred companies throughout the nation as members. They accounted for nearly 90 percent of all standardized outdoor advertising.

Even after the compromises made at the White House conference in May the bill was held up in Congress. Some supporters thought that it would be best to wait until 1966 and try to get a stronger bill passed. In August, President Johnson sent out an urgent message that he wanted the bill passed that year.

The bill that eventually passed had even more compromises than the one read to President Johnson in May. The Treasury Department was to compensate billboard owners and farmers who had rented out their land for billboards if their business was affected by the new law. The federal government would pay three-fourths the cost of the bill, with states paying the remaining one-fourth. Junkyards were exempt from screening or removal in commercial and industrial areas. The bill also authorized the use of federal funds for landscaping roadsides and for building scenic and recreational areas. These funds could be used for landscaping in right-of-way areas, work that states were supposed to be doing. The areas of commercial and industrial exemptions would be determined by the states, with the approval of the secretary of commerce. Secretary of Commerce John Connor assured Congress that a state's decision would rarely be overturned.

Although the bill that was passed was not nearly as strong as the original proposal, its passage proved difficult. Even though 83 percent of existing billboards were located in exempt areas and more could be added in those areas, the potential loss of even 15 percent of a $200 million a year industry caused opposition to the bill.

DECLINE OF OUTDOOR ADVERTISING

The Highway Beautification Act did not have a major direct effect on the decline of billboards. The first removal of a billboard as a result of the law did not occur until April 27, 1971. The main reason that offending billboards were not removed sooner was that the law stated that the owner of the billboard must be compensated. Because the federal government did not authorize a significant amount of funds until 1970, the states could not afford to compensate billboard owners. Many offending billboards existed long after the law passed. Some states even inquired if they could remove offending billboards and then compensate owners later, when federal funds came through. The answer was no, since the law clearly stated that there must be compensation for every billboard removed.

The OAAA thought that it had preserved the heart of its business through the compromises in the bill. Only 15 percent of its business would be cut, and the cuts would not take their full effect for five years. Losses would be compensated by the government. In addition, advertisers could put up larger signs beyond the restricted 660 feet, thus reaching essentially the same audience, and they could put up more signs on exempt roads.

Even with these opportunities, billboard use steadily declined after 1965. There are several reasons for the decline in billboard advertising. First, billboard advertising was not as effective as most other advertising media, particularly television advertising. Second, many cities were inundated with billboards. Many people became immune to them and stopped reading them. Some cities also enforced sign laws that were more strict than the federal law. Finally, beautification activists encouraged boycotts on products and services advertised on billboards. Such efforts did not make an enormous difference, but they did have some effect.

Dan Kennedy

SOURCES FOR FURTHER STUDY

Califano, Joseph E., Jr. *The Triumph and Tragedy of Lyndon Johnson.* New York: Simon & Schuster, 1991.

Drew, Elizabeth Brenner. "Lady Bird's Beauty Bill." *The Atlantic Monthly* 216 (December, 1965): 68-72.

Gotfryd, Bernard. "Signs of the Times." *Newsweek* 65 (March 8, 1965): 89-90.

Gould, Lewis. *Lady Bird Johnson and the Environment.* Lawrence: University Press of Kansas, 1988.

The New Republic. "Beauty and the Billboards." 154 (April 23, 1966): 8-9.

Newsweek. "The Sign Busters." 77 (June 7, 1971): 116-117.

Pell, Robert. "Escalating Ugliness." *America* 122 (June 12, 1965): 848-849.

SEE ALSO: Aircraft Noise Abatement Act (1968); Wild and Scenic Rivers Act and National Trails System Act (1968); National Environmental Policy Act (1970); Noise Control Act (1972).

VOTING RIGHTS ACT OF 1965

DATE: August 6, 1965
U.S. STATUTES AT LARGE: 79 Stat. 445
PUBLIC LAW: 89-110
U.S. CODE: 42 § 1971
CATEGORIES: African Americans; Civil Rights and Liberties; Voting and Elections

This statute permitted the federal government to expand its power and authority in order to increase black voter registration and participation in states where African Americans had been subject to discrimination.

At the turn of the twentieth century, southern states adopted numerous devices designed to disenfranchise African Americans and poor whites. The most common device was the literacy test, which required prospective voters to read, write, and interpret any part of the U.S. Constitution or state constitution. The inclusion of an interpretation requirement meant that registrars could reject literate African Americans by deeming their interpretations incorrect. Other devices included the white primary, which excluded

African Americans from voting in the Democratic Party primary, and poll taxes, which excluded many poor people, both black and white.

VOTER REGISTRATION AND THE CIVIL RIGHTS MOVEMENT

Because of these devices, only about 3 percent of African Americans were registered to vote in the South in 1940. By 1956 the percentage had increased to 25 percent of the black voting-age population. In contrast, 60 percent of the white voting-age population was registered. Efforts by African Americans to register intensified during the Civil Rights movement, and by November, 1964, approximately 43 percent of voting-age blacks in the South were registered. This registration, however, was uneven. In the Deep South, especially in the rural areas, black registration was significantly lower. For example, the average black registration rate in Alabama, Georgia, Louisiana, and South Carolina was approximately 22 percent while in Mississippi the figure was less than 7 percent.

Efforts to increase the registration of African Americans in the southern states involved a variety of organizations, including the Voter Education Project of the Southern Regional Council, the Congress of Racial Equality (CORE), the Student Nonviolent Coordinating Committee (SNCC), and the Southern Christian Leadership Conference (SCLC). The most important campaign occurred in Selma, Alabama, in 1965. In the fall of 1964 only 335 out of more than 15,000 African Americans of voting age were registered in Dallas County, Alabama. In Dallas County, registration was allowed only two days a month. Applicants had to fill in more than fifty blanks on a form, write a part of the Constitution from dictation, read four parts of the Constitution and answer four questions about what they had read, answer four questions on the working of government, and swear loyalty to both the state of Alabama and the United States.

Following several months of demonstrations and efforts, civil rights activists held a march from Selma to Montgomery, Alabama. State troopers and sheriff's posse men attacked marchers when they attempted to cross the Edmund Pettus Bridge in Selma, and approximately one hundred marchers were injured. National outrage over the attacks led to approval of the Voting Rights Act in August, 1965, by a vote of 328 to 74 in the House of Representatives and by a 79 to 18 vote in the Senate. On August 6, 1965, President

Lyndon B. Johnson signed the bill into law, referring to it as "one of the most monumental laws in the entire history of American freedom."

PROVISIONS

Upon the request of President Johnson, Attorney General Nicholas Katzenbach designed an exceptionally strong act. Its purpose was to enforce section 2 of the Fifteenth Amendment, which prohibited states or political subdivisions from applying a voter prerequisite to deny or abridge on account of race or color the right of any citizen of the United States to vote. The previous Civil Rights Acts passed in 1957, 1960, and 1964 contained provisions designed to end voter discrimination; however, their impact was limited because they required a case-by-case approach in seeking remedies. In addition, these acts did not allow the federal government to intervene on behalf of those subject to discrimination.

The 1965 Voting Rights Act included several provisions designed to overcome the shortcomings of the previous acts. First, section 4 of the act included a formula that targeted areas where discrimination was greatest and where federal government intervention in voter registration could be of the most help. The targeted areas were those that required a literacy test or similar test for registration prior to November 1, 1964, and where fewer than 50 percent of the eligible voters were either registered to vote or had actually voted in the 1964 presidential election. This provision affected the entire states of Alabama, Alaska, Georgia, Louisiana, Mississippi, South Carolina, and Virginia as well as twenty-six counties in North Carolina and one county in Arizona. In these areas, the Voting Rights Act eliminated for five years the use of literacy tests and other such devices as a prerequisite for registration. On August 7, 1965, Attorney General Katzenbach suspended the tests in these places. Later, in 1965 and 1966, additional counties in North Carolina and Arizona as well as one county each in Hawaii and Idaho were also targeted.

Section 5 of the act included a preclearance provision that required state and local governments covered by the triggering formula to submit any proposed changes in voting laws or practices that had not been in force on November 1, 1964, to the Justice Department or the federal district court in Washington, D.C. This was designed to prevent these governments from developing new techniques designed to limit African American participation in voting.

Under provisions in sections 6 and 7 of the act, the attorney general could send federal voter examiners in to gather names of eligible voters and present them to local officials, who were required to register them. Under section 8 of the law, the attorney general could also send observers or poll watchers to oversee elections to ensure that African Americans were permitted to vote and their votes were counted. During the first ten years of the act, examiners were sent to approximately sixty counties in the South, most of which were in Mississippi or Alabama. An estimated 15 percent of the African Americans who registered in this period were registered by these examiners. The federal government also assigned more than 6,500 poll watchers during the same period.

Section 3 gave the courts the authority to send federal registrars and poll watchers to locales outside covered jurisdictions if the attorney general or private parties brought suits. Section 10 instructed the attorney general to challenge the constitutionality of the poll tax as a prerequisite for voting in state and local elections. Section 11 prohibited anyone "acting under color of law" from preventing qualified voters from voting or intimidating, threatening, or coercing voters; it also prohibited voting fraud in federal elections. Section 12 stipulated punishment for violation of someone's voting rights. Finally, section 14 provided a detailed definition of voting.

COURT CASES

South Carolina sued to test the legality of the Voting Rights Act of 1965. In *South Carolina v. Katzenbach* (1966), the Supreme Court unanimously upheld the major provisions of the law. In its decision, the Court recognized that the act represented an uncommon extension of federal power; however, it justified these powers by noting that exceptional conditions could justify legislative measures that might otherwise be deemed inappropriate.

Other court cases followed concerning provisions of the act. *Harper v. Virginia State Board of Elections* (1966), the Court declared the poll tax for state and local elections unconstitutional. This overturned the court's 1937 decision in *Breedlove v. Suttles*, which stated that a poll tax did not violate the Constitution.

Although African American registration increased significantly, some southern locales used a variety of more subtle techniques to limit the impact of black voters. These included withholding information from black voters, failing to provide assistance to illiterate voters, purging voting rolls, disqualifying voters on technical grounds, requiring separate registration for different types of elections, moving polling places, and failing to provide adequate voting facilities in black precincts. Efforts were also made to dilute the impact of African American voters, which resulted in more court cases.

In *Allen v. Board of Elections* (1969), the Court examined the issue of dilution of black voters in Mississippi when the state moved from single-member districts to at-large elections. The Court held that the Voting Rights Act gave a broad interpretation to the right to vote and stated that voting included all actions necessary to make a vote effective. This greatly increased the importance of section 5 of the Voting Rights Act and resulted in many more challenges to proposed changes in election procedures in covered jurisdictions. For example, between 1965 and 1969 the Justice Department objected to only six proposed changes. By the end of 1989, 2,335 changes had been objected to under section 5.

In *White v. Regester* (1973), the Court unanimously agreed that multimember districts in the Texas counties of Bexar and Dallas were unconstitutional based on the totality of the circumstances, which included the cultural and economic realities of African Americans and Mexicans as well as the multimember districts. In general, this decision resulted in multimember districts being replaced by single-member districts.

In 1980, however, in *Mobile v. Bolden*, the Court held that the Fifteenth Amendment applied only to access to the ballot, not vote dilution, and that the Fourteenth and Fifteenth Amendments required a showing of purpose to discriminate. This decision was a setback for voting rights. However, in 1986 the Court gave explicit guidelines for dilution in *Thornburg v. Gingles*. In this North Carolina case, the Court provided a three-part test for determining if multimember districts resulted in dilution: The minority group had to be sufficiently large and geographically compact to constitute a majority in at least one single-member district; the minority group had to tend to vote as a bloc; and the majority group had to vote sufficiently as a bloc to enable it to normally defeat the minority's preferred candidate.

INCREASED REGISTRATION

Overall, despite manipulation and court challenges, the Voting Rights Act had a significant impact on the South. Within one month of its passage, more than 27,000 new African American voters were registered by federal examiners in Alabama, Louisiana, and Mississippi alone. By 1968 black registration in the South increased from 2 million to 3.3 million. In the seven states originally covered by the act, African American registration increased from 29.3 percent in March, 1965, to 56.6 percent by 1972. By 1988 black registration in the eleven states of the South stood at 63.7 percent; in the five Deep South states, it was 65.2 percent. Increased registration made African Americans important actors in the political process in many parts of the South and resulted in a significant rise in the number of black elected officials. In 1968 there were only 248 black elected officials in the South, but this number rose to 2,601 in 1982 and to 4,924 in 1993.

The Voting Rights Act was renewed several times following its original passage. Each time it was expanded, and it is now applicable to the entire United States. Some of the major additions to the act included extending the franchise to eighteen-year-olds, adding bilingual provisions that required voting information and ballots to be printed not only in English but also in other languages appropriate for local citizens, and creating a provision for minority access and influence districts. Therefore, the Voting Rights Act not only increased the federal government's role in voting but also resulted in significant increases in participation in the political process.

William V. Moore

SOURCES FOR FURTHER STUDY

Davidson, Chandler, ed. *Minority Vote Dilution.* Washington, D.C.: Howard University Press, 1984.

Elliott, Ward E. *The Rise of Guardian Democracy: The Supreme Court's Role in Voting Rights Disputes, 1845-1969.* Cambridge, Mass.: Howard University Press, 1974.

Garrow, David J. *Protest at Selma: Martin Luther King, Jr., and the Voting Rights Act of 1965.* New Haven, Conn.: Yale University Press, 1978.

Grofman, Bernard, and Chandler Davidson, eds. *Controversies in Minority Voting: The Voting Rights Act in Perspective.* Washington, D.C.: Brookings Institution, 1992.

Hanus, Jerome J. *The Voting Rights Act of 1965, as Amended: History, Effects, and Alternatives.* Washington, D.C.: Government Printing Office, 1976.

SEE ALSO: Black Codes of 1865 (1865); Civil Rights Act of 1866 (1866); Fifteenth Amendment (1870); Jim Crow laws (1880's-1954); Disfranchisement laws (1890); Civil Rights Act of 1957 (1957); Civil Rights Act of 1960 (1960); Twenty-fourth Amendment (1964); Civil Rights Act of 1964 (1964); Voting Rights Act of 1975 (1975); Twenty-sixth Amendment (1971).

HOUSING AND URBAN DEVELOPMENT ACT

DATE: September 9, 1965
U.S. STATUTES AT LARGE: 79 Stat. 670
PUBLIC LAW: 89-174
U.S. CODE: 42 § 3536
CATEGORIES: Health and Welfare; Housing

Part of the Johnson administration's Great Society program, this law created a cabinet-level department of urban affairs, the Department of Housing and Urban Development, to aid in securing decent housing for American citizens.

Following the assassination of President John F. Kennedy, President Lyndon B. Johnson capitalized on the nation's sombre mood and urged Congress to adopt Kennedy's legislative agenda as a memorial to the slain president. Johnson's landslide victory in the 1964 presidential election increased Democratic majorities in Congress and made possible a deluge of Great Society legislation, including the Housing and Urban Development Act of 1965.

PROVISIONS

As Kennedy had earlier proposed, the new law created a cabinet-level department of urban affairs, the Department of Housing and Urban Development (HUD). The core of the new cabinet department was the Housing and Home Finance Agency, which included the Federal Housing Administration, Urban Renewal Administration, and Public Housing Administration. Johnson chose Weaver to fill the secretary of HUD position, making Weaver the first African American cabinet officer in U.S. history.

In calling for passage of the Housing and Urban Development Act of 1965, Johnson had declared that "the ultimate goal in our free enterprise system must be a decent home for every American family." Like most other Great Society programs, the law failed to achieve Johnson's purpose, but it did create new "leased housing" and rent-supplement plans to assist the poor. Other features of the 1965 housing act included FHA loans without down payments for veterans, lower down payments on other FHA mortgage loans, and low-interest loans for rural housing.

The following year, Congress passed the Model Cities Act of 1966. To improve the quality of urban life, the federal government funded comprehensive model cities projects that included construction of low- and middle-income housing. Soon, however, the model cities program bogged down in squabbling between federal and local agencies. It had scant effect on urban housing.

Undismayed by the troubles afflicting model cities, in 1968, Johnson submitted another sweeping bill to Congress. The Housing and Urban Development Act of 1968, called the most ambitious housing program in U.S. history, was designed to eradicate substandard housing within ten years through the construction of twenty-six million new homes and apartments. The law extended interest-rate subsidy and rent-supplement programs to increase the construction and repair of low-rent housing and to expand home ownership by low-income Americans. It also created the Government National Mortgage Association to purchase mortgage loans written at below-market rates and allowed the privatization of the Federal National Mortgage Association, formed during the 1930's by the Federal Housing Administration to provide a secondary market for home mortgage loans. Finally, the housing law of 1968 contrived an assortment of other programs, including "new communities," neighborhood development, housing rehabilitation, and "national housing partnerships" intended to facilitate the investment of corporate money in low-income housing in blighted urban areas.

IMPACT

Taken together, the various provisions of the Housing and Urban Development Act of 1968 constituted a heightened federal commitment to public housing. The effects of the 1968 law would not be felt until after President Richard M. Nixon took office in 1969. Despite abuses and scandals that plagued the public housing program, by 1972, 1.3 million low- and moderate-income housing units had been completed. Although the 1968 housing act did not lift many Americans out of poverty, it did allow some moderate-income families to become home owners. Additionally, as was the case with earlier housing legislation dating back to the 1930's, the 1968 law provided not only profits for lenders, developers, and builders but also jobs for workers.

Civil rights legislation also affected housing in the United States during the 1960's. The Civil Rights Act of 1964 moved in the direction of fair housing policy by prohibiting racial discrimination in federally subsidized housing programs. The private, nonfederally assisted housing market remained largely untouched, and in January, 1966, President Johnson urged Congress to adopt a fair housing law to eliminate racial discrimination. Following the assassination of Martin Luther King, Jr., Congress in April, 1968, adopted the Civil Rights Act of 1968, which included Title VIII, a fair housing statute that outlawed racial discrimination in virtually all public and private housing.

SUBSEQUENT EVENTS

The 1960's were a decade of strong housing growth, with more than fourteen million homes constructed. Of those homes, 97.5 percent were produced by the private sector. That astonishing statistic furnished ammunition for critics of public housing who complained that federal housing policy continued to be skewed in favor of the affluent, especially by the federal income tax deduction for home mortgage interest, which was much more advantageous for the wealthy. Critics claimed that federal policy had aided lenders, developers, and builders in their profit-making endeavors and had promoted suburbanization for the largely white middle and upper classes, while public housing programs for the poor remained underfunded and wholly inadequate. According to leftist critics, urban renewal meant removal of slum housing and displacement of racial minorities without replacement of the housing units that were demolished.

Conservative critics were equally harsh in their evaluation of Great Society housing laws and programs. In the conservative view, public housing and urban renewal were expensive and wasteful, ran contrary to the logic of the private marketplace, and probably made conditions in urban areas worse instead of better. Conservatives concluded that the federal government should cease its messy, meddlesome intervention and allow the private market to function. In January, 1973, partly in response to the conservative critique and alarmed about multiplying scandals, President Nixon suspended all federally subsidized public housing programs. The public housing and urban renewal programs of the 1960's, enacted with such great expectations, proved disappointing in operation and, for many Americans, had come to symbolize the failure of the Great Society.

Richard N. Chapman

SOURCES FOR FURTHER STUDY

Bratt, Rachel G., Chester Hartman, and Ann Meyerson, eds. *Critical Perspectives on Housing.* Philadelphia: Temple University Press, 1986.

Mason, Joseph B. *History of Housing in the U.S., 1930-1980.* Houston, Tex.: Gulf Publishing, 1982.

Mayer, Martin. *The Builders: Houses, People, Neighborhoods, Governments, Money.* New York: Norton, 1978.

Weicher, John C. *Housing: Federal Policies and Programs.* Washington, D.C.: American Enterprise Institute for Public Policy Research, 1980.

Wolman, Harold. *The Politics of Federal Housing.* New York, Dodd, Mead, 1971.

SEE ALSO: Housing Act (1961); Civil Rights Act of 1964 (1964); Civil Rights Act of 1968 (1968); Fair Housing Act (1968).

EXECUTIVE ORDERS 11246 AND 11375

DATE: Issued September 24, 1965; October 13, 1967
CATEGORIES: African Americans; Civil Rights and Liberties; Labor
and Employment; Women's Issues

*These executive orders broadened the scope of affirmative action be-
yond racial desegregation to a wide range of employment issues.*

In issuing Executive Order 8802 in 1941, Franklin D. Roosevelt was
the first in a line of presidents who charged federal contractors not
to discriminate against employees on the basis of race, creed, or
color. In 1961, John F. Kennedy's Executive Order 10925, the first
to use the term "affirmative action," was understood as a requirement for Southern contractors to desegregate.

After Congress outlawed employment discrimination in Title
VII of the Civil Rights Act of 1964, Lyndon Johnson issued Executive Order 11246, on September 24, 1965, to supersede 10925.
Part 1 of the order dealt with nondiscrimination in federal government employment. The main innovation was in part 2, in which
contractors doing business with the federal government were required to root out employment discrimination, in advance of complaints based on race, creed, color, or national origin, by changing
personnel policies, practices, and procedures in regard to such
matters as hiring, promotion, transfer, recruitment, layoff, rates
of pay, and selection for training. The secretary of labor was to
enforce the order, and the U.S. Department of Labor's Office of
Federal Contract Compliance Programs became the monitoring
agency for 11246.

On October 13, 1967, Johnson amended 11246 with Executive
Order 11375 to add gender to the list of protected classes. The record reveals that white women have gained more from 11246, as
amended by 11375, than have members of minority groups.

Michael Haas

SOURCES FOR FURTHER STUDY
Bullock, Charles S., III, and Charles M. Lamb. *Implementation of
Civil Rights Policy.* Monterey, Calif.: Brooks-Cole, 1984.

Graham, Hugh Davis. *The Civil Rights Era: Origins and Development of National Policy, 1960-1972.* New York: Oxford University Press, 1990.

Loevy, Robert D. *To End All Segregation: The Politics of the Passage of the Civil Rights Act of 1964.* Lanham, Md.: University Press of America, 1990.

_____, ed. *The Civil Rights Act of 1964: The Passage of the Law That Ended Racial Segregation.* Albany: State University of New York Press, 1997.

SEE ALSO: Equal Pay Act (1963); Economic Opportunity Act (1964); Title VII of the Civil Rights Act (1964); Equal Employment Opportunity Act (1972).

CLEAN WATER ACT AND AMENDMENTS

ALSO KNOWN AS: Water Pollution Control Act
DATE: Original act passed October 2, 1965
U.S. STATUTES AT LARGE: 79 Stat. 903 (1965 act)
PUBLIC LAW: 89-234 (1965 act)
CATEGORIES: Environment and Conservation; Natural Resources

The legislation now called the Clean Water Act was largely shaped by the 1972 amendments to the original act of 1965 and was strengthened by later amendments. The Environmental Protection Agency, in cooperation with other federal, state, and local agencies, administers the numerous programs established by the legislation.

Before the mid-1960's, the regulation of water pollution was mostly left up to the states. The earliest federal law was the Rivers and Harbors Act of 1899, which prohibited the dumping of debris into navigable waters. Although the purpose of the law was to protect interstate navigation, it became an instrument for regulating water quality sixty years after its passage. The Oil Pollution Act of 1924 prohibited the discharge of oil into interstate waterways, with criminal sanctions for violations. The first Federal Water Pollution Control Act, (FWPCA), passed in 1948, authorized the preparation of federal pollution abatement plans, which the states could either accept or reject, and provided some financial assistance for state projects. Although the FWPCA was amended in 1956 and 1961, it still contained no effective mechanisms for the federal enforcement of standards.

Provisions

By this period, however, many Americans were recognizing water pollution as a national problem that required a national solution. The Clean Water Act of 1965 introduced the policy of minimum water quality standards that could be enforced in federal courts. The standards applied regardless of whether discharges could be proven to harm human health. The act also significantly increased federal funds for sewage plant construction. A 1966 amendment required the reporting of discharges into waterways, with civil penalties for failure to comply. Amendments in 1970 established federal licensing for the discharge of pollutants into navigable rivers and provided plans and funding for the detection and removal of oil spills.

1972 Amendments

Congress and President Richard Nixon agreed that existing programs were ineffective in controlling water pollution, and the resulting 1972 amendments established the basic framework for the Clean Water Act. The centerpiece of the landmark amendments was the national pollutant discharge elimination system (NPDES), which utilized the command-and-control methods earlier enacted in the Clean Air Act (1963). The premise of the legislation was that polluting surface water is an unlawful activity, except for those exemptions specifically allowed in the act. The announced goal was to eliminate all pollutants discharged into U.S. surface waters by 1985.

In addition to standards of quality for ambient water, the amendments also included technology-based standards. Industrial dischargers were given until 1977 to make use of the "best practicable technology" in that industry, and the standard was be increased to the "best technology available" by 1982. The 1972 act also included stringent limitations on the release of toxic chemicals judged harmful to human health. For members of Congress, the most popular part of the act was the grant program for the construction of publicly owned treatment works (POTWs).

The Environmental Protection Agency (EPA), created just two years earlier, was assigned the primary responsibility of regulating and enforcing the legislation. The agency could issue five-year permits for the discharge of pollutants, and any discharge without a license or contrary to the terms of a license was punishable by either civil or criminal sanctions. When faced with a discharge of oil or other hazardous substances, the EPA could go to court and seek a penalty of up to $50,000 per violation and up to $250,000 in the case of willful misconduct. In addition, a discharger might be assessed the costs of removal, up to $50 million. Because of the technical complexity of the law, the EPA for many years relied more on civil penalties than criminal prosecutions.

The 1972 amendments prohibit the discharge of dredged or fill materials into navigable waters unless authorized by a permit issued by the Army Corps of Engineers. Based on the literal wording of the statute, the corps at first regulated only actually, potentially, and historically navigable waters. In 1975, however, the corps revised its regulations to include jurisdiction over all coastal and freshwater wetlands, provided they were inundated often enough to support vegetation adapted for saturated soils. The Supreme Court endorsed the corp's broad construction of the law.

1977 AMENDMENTS

The Clean Water Act amendments of 1977, giving the legislation its present name, focused on a large variety of technical issues. They required industry to use the best available technology to remove toxic pollutants within six years. For conventional pollutants, businesses could seek a waiver from the technology requirements if the removal of the pollutant was not worth the cost. The act further required an environmental impact statement for any federal project involving wetlands, and it extended liability for oil-spill cleanups from 12 miles to 200 miles offshore.

1987 AMENDMENTS

The amendments of 1987, entitled the Water Quality Act, were passed over President Ronald Reagan's veto. In addition to increasing the powers of the EPA, the act significantly raised the criminal penalties for acts of pollution. Individuals who knowingly discharge certain dangerous pollutants can receive a fine of up to $250,000 and imprisonment for up to fifteen years. The maximum prison term for making false statements or tampering with monitoring equipment was increased from six months to two years. The most controversial part of the act was authorization of $18 billion for the construction of wastewater treatment plants. In 1990 Congress further amended the Clean Water Act with the Oil Pollution Act, which strengthened cleanup requirements and penalties for discharges.

RELATED LEGISLATION
In addition to the Clean Water Act, several closely related federal laws also deal with water pollution. In 1972 Congress passed the Marine Protection, Research, and Sanctuaries Act to regulate ocean dumping, and an amendment of 1988 prohibited ocean dumping of all wastes other than dredge spoil. The Safe Drinking Water Act (1974) authorized the EPA to regulate contaminants in tap water as well as injections into underground sources of drinking water. Amendments of 1986 required the EPA to regulate eighty-three contaminants within three years and authorized the EPA to issue new administrative orders and take enforcement action.

IMPACT
Some of the worst instances of water pollution have been curtailed in the years since the Clean Water Act was overhauled in 1972, even though the act has manifestly failed to achieve its stated goals. It is probably inevitable that economic prosperity and population growth will mean that water in the United States will never be completely free of pollutants. Since 1972, nevertheless, the American public has become increasingly intolerant of dirty and unhealthful water, and Congress, reflecting public sentiment, has continued to strengthen the Clean Water Act.

Thomas T. Lewis

SOURCES FOR FURTHER STUDY
Adler, Robert, and Jessica Landman. *The Clean Water Act Twenty Years Later,* Washington, D.C.: Island Press, 1993.
Vanderver, Timothy, Jr., *Environmental Law Handbook.* Washington, D.C.: Bureau of National Affairs, 1994.

SEE ALSO: Oil Pollution Act of 1924 (1924); Water Pollution Control Act (1948); Water Pollution Control Act Amendments of 1956 (1956); Water Resources Research Act (1964); Water Pollution Control Act Amendments of 1972 (1972); Safe Drinking Water Act (1974); Oil Pollution Act of 1990 (1990).

IMMIGRATION AND NATIONALITY ACT AMENDMENTS OF 1965

DATE: October 3, 1965
U.S. STATUTES AT LARGE: 79 Stat. 911
PUBLIC LAW: 89-236
U.S. CODE: 8 § 1101
CATEGORIES: Asia or Asian Americans; Immigration; Latinos

The Immigration and Nationality Act Amendments of 1965 removed restrictions on non-European immigration, significantly altering the ethnic makeup of U.S. immigrants.

The Immigration and Nationality Act of 1952 codified legislation that had developed haphazardly over the past century. Although it liberalized some areas, it was discriminatory in that quotas were allotted according to national origins. This resulted in western and northern European nations receiving no less than 85 percent of the total allotment. The Immigration and Nationality Act of 1965 allowed non-Europeans to enter the United States on an equal basis with Europeans. Before the 1965 legislation, U.S. immigration policies favored northern and western Europeans.

REFORM BEGINS
With the election of John F. Kennedy in 1960, circumstances for meaningful immigration reform came into being: Kennedy believed that immigration was a source of national strength, the Civil Rights movement had promoted an ideology to eliminate racist policies, and the U.S. position during the Cold War necessitated that immigration policies be just. Thus, Kennedy had Abba Schwartz,

an expert on refugee and immigration matters, develop a plan to revise immigration policy.

In July of 1963, Kennedy sent his proposal for immigration reform to Congress. His recommendations had three major provisions: the quota system should be phased out over a five-year period; no natives of any one country should receive more than 10 percent of the newly authorized quota numbers; and a seven-person immigration board should be set up to advise the president. Kennedy also advocated that family reunification remain a priority; the Asiatic Barred Zone be eliminated; and nonquota status be granted to residents of Jamaica and Trinidad and Tobago, as it was to other Western Hemisphere residents. Last, the preference structure was to be altered to liberalize requirements for skilled people.

After the assassination of President Kennedy, President Lyndon B. Johnson took up the cause of immigration. Although immigration was not a major issue during the 1964 campaign, both sides had courted diverse ethnic communities, whose will now had to be considered. The Democratic Party's landslide victory gave Johnson a strong mandate for his Great Society programs, of which immigration reform was a component. Secretary of State Dean Rusk argued the need for immigration reform to bolster U.S. foreign policy. Rusk, Attorney General Robert F. Kennedy, and others criticized the current system for being discriminatory and argued that the proposed changes would be economically advantageous to the United States. Senator Edward "Ted" Kennedy held hearings and concluded that "all recognized the unworkability of the national origins quota system."

Outside Congress, ethnic, voluntary, and religious organizations lobbied and provided testimony before Congress. They echoed the administration's arguments about discrimination. A few Southerners in Congress argued that the national origins concept was not discriminatory—it was a mirror reflecting the U.S. population, so those who would best assimilate into U.S. society would enter. However, the focus of the congressional debate was on how to alter the national origins system, not on whether it should be changed. The most disputed provisions concerned whether emphasis should be on needed skills, family reunification, or limits set on Western Hemisphere immigration. Family unification prevailed.

PROVISIONS

The new law replaced the national origins system with hemispheric caps, 170,000 from the Old World and 120,000 from the New. Spouses, unmarried minor children, and parents of U.S. citizens were exempt from numerical quotas. Preferences were granted first to unmarried adult children of U.S. citizens (20 percent); next, to spouses and unmarried adult children of permanent resident aliens (20 percent). Professionals, scientists, and artists of exceptional ability were awarded third preference (10 percent) but required certification from the U.S. Department of Labor. Married children of U.S. citizens had fourth preference (10 percent). Next were those brothers and sisters of U.S. citizens who were older than twenty-one years of age (24 percent), followed by skilled and unskilled workers in occupations for which labor was in short supply (10 percent). Refugees from communist or communist-dominated countries or the Middle East were seventh (6 percent). Nonpreference status was assigned to anyone not eligible under any of the above categories; there have been more preference applicants than can be accommodated, so nonpreference status has not been used.

UNINTENDED CONSEQUENCES

The law had unexpected consequences. The framers of the legislation expected that the Old World slots would be filled by Europeans. They assumed that family reunification would favor Europeans, because they dominated the U.S. population. However, those from Europe who wanted to come were in the lower preference categories, while well-trained Asians had been coming to the United States since 1943 and were well qualified for preference positions. Once they, or anyone else, became a permanent resident, a whole group of people became eligible to enter the country under the third preference category. After a five-year wait—the residential requirement for citizenship—more persons became eligible under the second preference category. As a result, many individual immigrants were directly or indirectly responsible for twenty-five to fifty additional new immigrants.

The law set forth a global ceiling of 290,000, but actual totals ranged from 398,089 in 1977 to 904,292 in 1993. Refugees and those exempt from numerical limitations were the two major categories that caused these variations. The refugee count had varied according to situations such as that of the "boat people" from Cuba in 1981. In 1991, refugees and asylees totaled 139,079; in 1993, they totaled 127,343. Persons in nonpreference categories increased from 113,083 in 1976 to 255,059 in 1993. Total immigration for 1991 was 827,167 and for 1993 was 904,292—well above the global ceiling.

The Immigration and Nationality Act of 1965 enabled some of the most able medical, scientific, engineering, skilled, and other professional talent to enter the United States. The medical profession illustrates this trend. In the ten years after the enactment of the 1965 act, seventy-five thousand foreign physicians entered the United States. By 1974, immigrant physicians made up one-fifth of the total number of physicians and one-third of the interns and residents in the United States. Each immigrant doctor represented more than a million dollars in education costs. In addition, they often took positions in the inner-city and rural areas, which prevented the collapse of the delivery of medical services to those locations.

Arthur W. Helweg

SOURCES FOR FURTHER STUDY

Daniels, Roger. *Coming to America: A History of Immigration and Ethnicity in American Life.* New York: HarperCollins, 1990.

Glazer, Nathan, ed. *Clamor at the Gates: The New American Immigration.* San Francisco: ICS Press, 1985.

_____. *Ethnic Dilemmas 1964-1982.* Cambridge, Mass.: Harvard University Press, 1983.

Helweg, Arthur W., and Usha M. Helweg. *An Immigrant Success Story: East Indians in America.* Philadelphia: University of Pennsylvania Press, 1990.

Papademetriou, Demetrios G., and Mark J. Miller, eds. *The Unavoidable Issue: U.S. Immigration Policy in the 1980's.* Philadelphia: Institute for the Study of Human Issues, 1983.

Reimers, David M. *Still the Golden Door: The Third World Comes to America.* 2d ed. New York: Columbia University Press, 1992.

SEE ALSO: Immigration Act of 1917 (1917); Immigration Act of 1921 (1921); Immigration Act of 1924 (1924); Immigration Act of 1943 (1943); War Brides Act (1945); Immigration and Nationality Act of 1952 (1952); Refugee Relief Act (1953); Immigration Reform and Control Act of 1986 (1986); Immigration Act of 1990 (1990).

MOTOR VEHICLE AIR POLLUTION CONTROL ACT

DATE: October 20, 1965
U.S. STATUTES AT LARGE: 79 Stat. 992
PUBLIC LAW: 89-272
CATEGORIES: Environment and Conservation; Transportation

The act, an early effort to control automobile emissions, addressed both air pollution and solid waste.

The Motor Vehicle Air Pollution and Control Act was one in a series of pollution-control acts that included the Clean Air Act of 1965 and the Clean Air Amendment of 1977. The act complemented a series of regulations, ranging from safety standards to fuel-efficiency standards that changed the face of the American automobile industry. The effort to clean up air affected by automobile emissions involved an after-the-fact strategy that relied on the establishment of government standards and a mandate to force industry to meet those standards.

PROVISIONS

In 1965, two essentially separate pieces of legislation, one dealing with air pollution and a second dealing with solid waste material, were merged and passed by the U.S. Congress as the Vehicle Air Pollution and Control Act. The act, principally an effort to control air pollution caused by automotive exhaust, also authorized a national research program to dispose of solid waste. The new law authorized the secretary of health, education, and welfare to establish standards that limited the amount of carbon monoxide, hydrocarbons, or other air pollutants emitted from gasoline or diesel fuels in automobiles, trucks, and buses.

Specifically, that section of the law only affected new motor vehicles or engines and prohibited the domestic sale, manufacture for domestic sale, or importation of any vehicle not in conformity with the limits. Fines of up to $1,000 per automobile or per engine could be levied against manufacturers who did not comply. Manufacturers had to submit sample vehicles to the HEW secretary, who

989

oversaw tests for compliance. Other sections of the legislation made provisions for action against U.S. companies by foreign nations for air pollution. Finally, a provision of the act authorized funds for federal research to reduce emissions of sulfur oxide from heating plants and electric power plants. Elements of the solid waste disposal act initiated federal research into waste disposal, established authority over disposal problems, defined solid waste, and authorized grants for surveys and for education or training of individuals to deal with solid waste.

BACKGROUND

In 1964, the Senate Public Works Committee Special Subcommittee on Air and Water Pollution released a report entitled "Steps Toward Cleaner Air." It recommended legislation to deal with automobile exhaust, including minimum national standards for limiting exhaust emissions, similar limits for diesel exhaust, grants for solid waste disposal, and establishment of a technical committee to investigate ways to reduce sulfur oxide. The full committee estimated that approximately 82.5 million automobiles, trucks, and buses in the United States emitted more than 14 million tons of hydrocarbons, 4 million tons of nitrogen oxides, and 75 million tons of carbon dioxide per year. Concluding that automobile emissions "constitute a major proportion of the community air pollution problem in all large cities" and that the technological skills and equipment needed to reduce pollution had passed the research stage, the committee found no reason to delay more serious control measures. Various pollution tax schemes were considered but were not put into effect.

IMPACT

The overall effectiveness of the measures, however, remains a matter of debate. Regression analyses of particulate and sulfur emissions by industry have indicated that regulations had little impact on usage levels or pollutant outputs. Environmental activists have maintained that such studies merely show that the results of the legislation had not been fully realized at the time of the studies. Yet studies comparing emission levels for states in compliance with Environmental Protection Agency (EPA) regulations with those not in compliance revealed no difference in the levels of emissions.

Furthermore, in developing regulations, the federal government often simply followed the lead of states such as California, which had already established emissions limitations effective with the 1968 automobile model year.

Certainly, there were successes directly attributable to the Clean Air Act. From 1967 to 1976, hydrocarbon emissions in the San Francisco area were reduced 25 percent, and daily observed oxidant levels fell by a comparable amount. Carbon monoxide levels in New York dropped more quickly than projected. Moreover, a major effect of the legislation was to expand the role of the federal government in supervising and mandating air quality improvement. Amendments to the Clean Air Act of 1977, for example, required the federal government to provide information to states to control motor-vehicle emissions, and the imposition of catalytic converters in 1974 shifted the nation away from the use of leaded gasoline.

Larry Schweikart

SOURCES FOR FURTHER STUDY

Bruce-Briggs, B. *The War Against the Automobile.* New York: E. P. Dutton, 1977.

Esposito, John C., and Larry Silverman. *Vanishing Air: The Ralph Nader Study Group Report on Air Pollution.* New York: Grossman, 1970.

MacAvoy, Paul. *Industry Regulation and the Performance of the American Economy.* New York: W. W. Norton, 1992.

Nader, Ralph. *Unsafe at Any Speed: The Designed-in Dangers of the American Automobile.* New York: Grossman, 1965.

Rae, John B. *The American Automobile Industry.* Boston: G. K. Hall, 1984.

SEE ALSO: Air Pollution Control Act (1955); Clean Air Act (1963); Clean Air Act Amendments of 1970 (1970); Clean Air Act Amendments of 1977 (1977); Alternative Motor Fuels Act (1988); Clean Air Act Amendments of 1990 (1990).

SOLID WASTE DISPOSAL ACT

DATE: October 20, 1965
U.S. STATUTES AT LARGE: 79 Stat. 997
PUBLIC LAW: 89-272
U.S. CODE: 42 § 3251
CATEGORIES: Environment and Conservation; Natural Resources

The act marked the first federal attempt to address inadequate solid waste disposal methods.

The Solid Waste Disposal Act, which was passed on October 20, 1965, was the first federal law on solid waste management. In its opening statement, the act noted "an ever mounting increase" in discarded materials from population and economic growth—an increase that, coupled with the concentration of population in metropolitan areas, was creating serious financial, management, intergovernmental, and technical problems in the disposal of solid waste. Although the responsibility for solid waste disposal lay with state and local governments, the matter was of national concern.

PREVIOUS GARBAGE MANAGEMENT

At the time the Solid Waste Disposal Act was passed, the methods of dealing with garbage had not evolved much since early in the century, when local governments had assumed the responsibility for collecting and disposing of garbage. Collection methods had improved somewhat with the development of compression technology, which led to such innovations as the packer truck and the transfer station. Disposal methods had remained largely land-based and tended to use open dumps, which were coming into conflict with evolving pollution-reduction programs. The incinerators in use at the time were a mixture of plain-burner and waste-to-energy facilities; they too were beginning to be affected by pollution initiatives.

Only a small amount of garbage was being recycled through source separation, but that approach was being reevaluated as compaction and other procedures, which were easier to implement, became more widespread. In a time of economic prosperity, it was easier to start with new materials than bother with source-separated ones.

A major survey conducted by the Public Health Service found that the existing system of collecting and disposing of solid waste in the United States was primarily administered by local governments. Collection was usually weekly and under the authority of the local government. Land-based ground disposal, which was less expensive than other options, was still the more common method. Incineration was used in the disposal of paper, food, and yard waste.

The survey also revealed that 94 percent of land-disposal systems and 75 percent of incinerators were inadequate. Incinerators, though they reduced the volume of waste, produced air pollution. The land sites were not sanitary landfills but dumps, where materials were left exposed and could lead to serious environmental and health problems. Nearly 90 percent of the dumps did not cover the materials daily; three-quarters were judged to be unsightly, and those that burned materials to reduce the volume thereby released air pollution. The survey indicated that what was needed were sanitary landfills that were covered with earth daily and where no burning would occur; unsightliness and odors, as well as insects and vermin, would thus be minimized.

PROVISIONS OF THE ACT
The act recommended that the federal government provide financial and technical assistance to local agencies for the solution of solid waste problems. The new law also set goals for the reduction of unsalvaged materials and for the implementation of proper and economical solid waste disposal practices. The research and development program included conservation of natural resources and reduction of waste.

The act also urged the cooperation of various governmental units in this effort. The secretary of health, education, and welfare was to be allowed as much as $20 million to use in such efforts, and smaller amounts were allotted for the secretary of the interior. In its legislative history of the act, the Public Works Committee reported that a slightly smaller amount of money was actually expended. In 1967, when $14 million had been authorized and $12.4 million requested and appropriated by Congress, $12.3 million was actually expended. Later, such underexpenditures became common.

The act funded the gathering of basic information, scientific research, and demonstration projects. A publication summarizing the projects between 1965 and 1970 indicated the early focus on information gathering. There were many small grants on training and research, which ranged from a health-hazard study to a model code and even a mathematical model of waste flows. Of this group of forty-five expenditures, a few involved basic science, but most were geared to applications. A small number of moderately funded projects studied the disposal management in specific industries; some specific technical projects received larger grants. Often, the research results and grant reports were later published by the Environmental Protection Agency (EPA), thus guaranteeing wide, inexpensive circulation subsidized by the taxpayers. This was ideal for disseminating the information and implementing changes. More important, such basic information was the foundation for later initiatives at the local government level.

IMPACT

After passage of the 1965 act, new disposal systems were financed by users and local governments. Improved higher-compaction trucks were added to the collection system, and all waste, even that which had formerly been source-separated, began to be collected together, compacted, and taken to central, rural sites, where it was covered with earth at the end of each day. The development of these sanitary landfills came relatively quickly; often swamp lands were reclaimed for the purpose. Source separation and centralized recycling efforts became obsolete. These developments changed everyday life in the United States.

Nancy R. Bain

SOURCES FOR FURTHER STUDY

Melosi, Martin V. *Garbage in the Cities: Refuse, Reform, and the Environment, 1880-1980.* College Station: Texas A&M University Press, 1981.

Packard, Vance. *The Waste Makers.* New York: David McKay, 1960.

Rathje, William, and Cullen Murphy. *Rubbish! The Archaeology of Garbage.* New York: HarperCollins, 1992.

Small, William E. *Third Pollution: The National Problem of Solid Waste Disposal.* New York: Praeger, 1971.

Udall, Stewart L. *The Quiet Crisis.* New York: Holt, Rinehart and Winston, 1963.

SEE ALSO: Hazardous Substances Labeling Act (1960); Resource Recovery Act (1970); Toxic Substances Control Act (1976); Low-Level Radioactive Waste Policy Act (1980); Pollution Prevention Act (1990).

HIGHER EDUCATION ACT

DATE: November 8, 1965
U.S. STATUTES AT LARGE: 79 Stat. 1219
PUBLIC LAW: 89-329
U.S. CODE: 20 § 1001
CATEGORIES: Education

> *This landmark legislation greatly increased the federal role in higher education as a keystone to the Great Society and War on Poverty programs.*

In 1960, the federal government supported about 9 percent of U.S. higher education funding, mostly through the G.I. Bill, the National Defense Education Act of 1958 (NDEA), and various social security programs. One billion dollars went to support land-grant universities, veterans, science education, libraries, and college housing in 1961. That year, President John F. Kennedy introduced a bill to support $2.8 billion in faculty loans and $892 million in merit- and need-based loans to students at four-year institutions; it was defeated.

By 1965, the climate had changed. Both President Lyndon B. Johnson (a former teacher) and the heavily Democratic Congress considered education key to their antipoverty and Great Society programs. The bill passed the House by 368 to 22 and the Senate by 79 to 3. Johnson signed the Higher Education Act at his old college in San Marcos, Texas, on November 9, 1965, to "strengthen the educational resources of our colleges and universities and to provide financial assistance for students in post-secondary and higher education."

PROVISIONS

The act's fifty-two pages are divided into eight titles. The first title allotted $25 million to establish "urban land-grant" programs of community service, including continuing education. The second appropriated $50 million for building up library and media collections and training specialists. Title III set aside $55 million to help "developing institutions"—largely southern African American schools—that were "struggling for survival and are isolated from the main currents of academic life." Potential faculty were to be encouraged with special fellowships, and "cooperative" partnerships with stronger northern schools were also envisaged.

Title IV was revolutionary in its restructuring of federal aid to students. NDEA needs-tested loans were extended and complemented by an additional $70 million in aid to schools for Educational Opportunity Grants to undergraduates "of exceptional financial need," insurance for $700 million in commercial loans (to be doubled two years hence), and $129 million for work-study programs, an extension of the Economic Opportunity Act of 1964.

Title V sought to improve the preparation of teachers and established the National Teacher Corps, an analog to President Kennedy's Peace Corps, "to strengthen the educational opportunities available to children in areas having concentrations of low-income families." Experienced teachers and inexperienced teacher-interns were to be enrolled and sent to these areas to augment teaching staffs. The title also approved $40 million for forty-five hundred fellowships to support training for school teachers. Title VI authorized $40 million for classroom televisions and training of media specialists. Title VII expanded the funding of the Higher Education Facilities Act of 1963, while Title VIII prohibited "federal control of education."

IMPACT

General aid increased tenfold between 1964 and 1971, and by 1970, two million students, or one in four, were receiving federal aid. The triad of grants, loans, and work-study—all enormously expanded—formed the basis for federal aid to students. Though they had played an insignificant role in 1965, education lobbyists soon became a powerful force behind the ever-increasing flow of funds, and Congress eagerly took over where the president had left off. Through rules for student funding, the federal government could now gain compliance with antidiscrimination policies, even from private schools. The 1968 amendments added six new programs—including aid to "disadvantaged students" and the Law School Clinical Experience Program—and appropriations of $2.46 billion, more than twice the amount Johnson requested.

Joseph P. Byrne

SOURCE FOR FURTHER STUDY
Graham, Hugh Davis. *The Uncertain Triumph: Federal Education Policy in the Kennedy and Johnson Years.* Graham. Chapel Hill: University of North Carolina Press, 1984.

SEE ALSO: G.I. Bill (1944); National Defense Education Act (1958); Economic Opportunity Act (1964); Higher Education Act (1965); Title IX of the Education Amendments of 1972 (1972); Indian Education Acts (1972, 1978); Women's Educational Equity Act (1978); Perkins Act (1990).

CIGARETTE WARNING LABEL ACT

ALSO KNOWN AS: Federal Cigarette Labeling and Advertising Act
DATE: January 1, 1966
U.S. STATUTES AT LARGE: 79 Stat. 282
PUBLIC LAW: 89-92
U.S. CODE: 15 § 1331
CATEGORIES: Business, Commerce, and Trade; Food and Drugs; Health and Welfare

This law required health warning labels on cigarette packages.

From the time it emerged as the economic salvation of the Virginia colony in the early seventeenth century until the latter half of the twentieth century, tobacco prompted arguments over the possibility of harmful health effects and its capacity to addict its users. Because of the popularity of tobacco generally, and cigarettes specifically, little governmental action was proposed to limit smoking

997

until the middle of the 1960's. At that time, a broad coalition capitalized upon a landmark governmental report and succeeded in passing the first piece of legislation designed to decrease the use of tobacco products by making smokers aware of the potential health risks they faced.

THE LINK BETWEEN SMOKING AND HEALTH

By the beginning of the 1960's, the rate of cigarette consumption among all Americans over eighteen years of age had hit its peak. In 1963, the average American smoked 4,345 cigarettes. At about this time, an increase in the number of cases of several serious diseases, most particularly lung cancer, was reported by statisticians. In March, 1962, Senator Maurine B. Neuberger (Democrat of Oregon) introduced legislation calling for the formation of a presidential commission to study the relationship between smoking and health. In June of that year, U.S. Surgeon General Luther L. Terry announced the formation of a group of experts who would study the existing scientific literature to determine whether a link did, in fact, exist between tobacco and various health problems. In fairness to those who supported smoking, one-half of the panel did smoke, and the Tobacco Institute, the industry's umbrella organization, was allowed to veto any committee members it found objectionable.

In spite of the balance of the committee, its conclusions were unanimous and striking. In a two-volume report that was released on a Saturday (when the stock markets were closed, so that the potential for a negative reaction against the stocks of the tobacco companies would be limited), the Surgeon General's Advisory Committee concluded that cigarette smoking constituted a health hazard of proportions significant enough to warrant direct governmental action. The reaction to the report by various groups reflected their varied attitudes toward smoking in general. The Tobacco Institute disputed the existence of any causal link between smoking and cancer, while the American Cancer Society declared that the reduction of cigarette smoking represented the greatest possibility for the prevention of cancer, other serious illnesses, and premature death. In the House of Representatives, thirty-one separate bills were introduced in response to the report. Most of them called for further study of the supposed link between smoking and ill health.

THE WARNING LABEL DEBATE

While Congress considered its next step, the Federal Trade Commission (FTC) prepared new regulations and scheduled public hearings on the proposal to require all cigarette packages to carry a specific health warning. By January, 1965, the FTC had two separate warnings under consideration:

> Caution: Cigarette smoking is a health hazard: The Surgeon General's Advisory Committee on Smoking and Health has found that cigarette smoking contributes substantially to mortality from certain specific diseases and to the overall death rate.

and a more direct one:

> Caution: Cigarette smoking is dangerous to health. It may cause death from cancer and other diseases.

Prior to the announcement of the FTC's plan to require the warning labels, the tobacco industry prepared its own strategy to minimize the negative impact of any governmental action. The most important aspect of the plan was the employment of Earle C. Clements as a registered lobbyist on behalf of the industry. In addition to all of his contacts as a former Senate majority whip in the late 1950's, Clements had been one of Lyndon Johnson's most trusted aides while both served in the Senate. Clements developed the successful strategy that the tobacco interests pursued to limit the damage to their business.

Realizing that a warning label was unavoidable, Clements urged the corporate leaders of the six major cigarette manufacturers to ask Congress for legislation requiring labels, rather than allow the FTC to control the issue. Clements's logic rested on the knowledge that the tobacco interests could lobby for the least intrusive labeling requirements possible by dealing with an elected body, Congress, rather than an appointed one, the FTC.

STRONGER MEASURES

Clements's plans directly conflicted with the proposals of Senator Neuberger, whose husband had died of cancer. A devoted opponent of smoking, she had carried on her husband's crusade against the tobacco companies after his death, when she was elected to fill his unexpired Senate term. She proposed a strict warning on cigarette package labels in addition to a requirement that all cigarette advertising carry the health warning. She also suggested barring advertising of cigarettes and other tobacco products from radio and television.

The battle between these two positions was fought principally in the Senate Commerce Committee, where Warren Magnuson worked to achieve the most fair bill possible. Although not as devoted to the antismoking cause as Maurine Neuberger, Magnuson was committed to reducing the number of tobacco-related deaths in the United States. The Commerce Committee first debated the possibility of a total ban on the advertisement of cigarettes and other tobacco-related products. After a long fight, the Senate committee settled on a four-year moratorium on any actions by the FTC to ban advertising. Although this disappointed many health advocates, the tobacco interests had been pushing hard for a moratorium in perpetuity.

THE FINAL WORDING

The Commerce Committee then turned its attention to the wording, size, and other specific requirements for the package warning. After much debate, the compromise called for a statement that read:

> Caution: Cigarette Smoking may be Hazardous to Your Health.

After minimal debate, the full Senate approved the bill by a vote of 72 to 5 in July, 1965. Attention then turned to the White House and the question of how President Johnson would respond to the bill. A former three-pack-a-day smoker before a severe heart attack forced him to give up the practice, Johnson understood the hazards of smoking as well as the difficulty many experienced when they tried to quit the habit. Although there was a small movement within his administration to veto the bill because the warning was not as explicit as it could have been, Johnson signed Senate Bill 559 into law on July 27, 1965. As Public Law 89-92, it took effect on January 1, 1966.

IMPACT OF THE LABELING LAW

The consequences of the first cigarette labeling law were many and far-reaching. On one hand, the bill represented another in a long string of victories for the tobacco companies. The warning on the packages was significantly less severe than it could have been, given the findings in the Surgeon General's Advisory Committee report. A complete medical consensus did not exist, however, on the connection between smoking and illness. The prestigious American Medical Association did not endorse the conclusions of the original report, and many members of Congress used that lack of an endorsement to bolster their calls for further study of the problem.

Over time, the FTC's and Neuberger's original recommendations became law. One of the clauses of Public Law 89-92, included as a result of the Senate Commerce Committee's deliberations, was the requirement that both the FTC and the Department of Health, Education, and Welfare submit annual reports to Congress evaluating the effectiveness of the law and the current nature of cigarette advertising. These reports discussed current themes in print, radio, and television ads such as brand loyalty and never failed to mention that any negative aspects of smoking or tobacco addiction were absent from the ads.

As the four-year moratorium on action against cigarette advertising passed, the FTC and then Congress held hearings on tougher warning labels, the inclusion of these new warnings in all print advertising, and a total ban on any radio or television advertising. On April 1, 1970, President Richard M. Nixon signed the Public Health Cigarette Smoking Act, which barred television and radio ads for cigarettes. Cigarette advertising appeared in the electronic media for the final time on January 1, 1971.

Perhaps the most important aspect of Public Law 89-92 was that its evolution marked the first time that cigarette manufacturers acknowledged that a relationship between smoking and ill health did exist. In spite of its protests to the contrary, the Tobacco Institute's lobbying for the passage of this bill signified an acceptance of the validity of the growing medical evidence documenting the link. As time has passed, the bulk of this evidence has increased. Each time the surgeon general releases a report examining the relationship between smoking and health, the conclusion becomes less ambiguous. These later reports have become the basis for more recent legislation restricting smoking in public facilities and have lent considerable support to the nonsmokers' rights and antismoking movements in the United States and elsewhere.

E. A. Reed

SOURCES FOR FURTHER STUDY
Diehl, Harold S. *Tobacco and Your Health: The Smoking Controversy.* New York: McGraw-Hill, 1969.
Drew, Elizabeth B. "The Quiet Victory of the Cigarette Lobby: How It Found the Best Filter Yet—Congress." *Atlantic Monthly* 216 (September, 1965): 75-79.
Patterson, James T. "Smoking and Cancer." In *The Dread Disease: Cancer and Modern American Culture.* Cambridge: Harvard University Press, 1987.
Price, David E. "The Commerce Committee in Action." In *Who Makes the Laws? Creativity and Power in Senate Committees.* Cambridge, Mass.: Schenkman, 1972.
Troyer, Ronald J., and Gerald E. Markle. *Cigarettes: The Battle over Smoking.* New Brunswick, N.J.: Rutgers University Press, 1983.

SEE ALSO: Public Health Cigarette Smoking Act (1970).

FREEDOM OF INFORMATION ACT

DATE: July 4, 1966
U.S. STATUTES AT LARGE: 80 Stat. 250
PUBLIC LAW: 89-487
U.S. CODE: 5 § 552
CATEGORIES: Civil Rights and Liberties

The act reversed long-standing government policies and practices regarding public access to information by establishing the right of access to government information and agency records as essential to a free and open society.

The Freedom of Information Act (FOIA) grew out of many years of reform effort. Its original passage in 1966 was the result of a ten-year congressional campaign, in which media representatives played a leading role. It was drafted as a revision of the public information section of the Administrative Procedures Act (1946), which contained such expansive exceptions that most agencies could effectively avoid disclosing to the public almost anything they wished. Until FOIA went into effect in 1967, public access to federal government records and documents was governed by a "need to know" policy. Persons requesting information had to demonstrate why it should be made available.

Before 1966, the old Administrative Procedures Act (APA) permitted individual government agencies not to disclose any functions that the agencies themselves claimed either should be kept secret in the public interest, or were matters relating solely to their internal management. The APA mandated that all agency records be made available to persons who were properly and directly concerned, except information censored for good cause. Once an agency censored information, citizens had no right of appeal.

PROVISIONS AND PURPOSE

FOIA was enacted to give the public increased access to federal government records. On the day that President Lyndon B. Johnson signed it into law, he declared that the principle upon which the legislation was based was that "a democracy works best when people have all the information that the security of the Nation permits." FOIA's purpose was to establish a general philosophy of full agency disclosure—except in clearly delineated cases—and to provide legal procedures by which citizens and the press could obtain information wrongfully withheld. It was believed that full public disclosure would further democracy by enabling better informed citizens to scrutinize government actions and thereby discourage corruption and waste.

FOIA's original wording granted the public access only to government paper "files." In 1974 the law was amended to apply to "records"—a term that the courts have interpreted to apply to a much broader range of material, making it more difficult for agencies to censor entire files. "Records" include not only the papers constituting files, but also films—including X rays—and computer media. Other physical objects, however, such as the rifle believed to have been used to kill President John F. Kennedy, are not considered records, principally because they are not reproducible.

FEDERAL AGENCIES SUBJECT TO FOIA

Government entities are considered to be "agencies" when they have authority to perform specific government functions. FOIA itself defines as agencies all government bodies other than those directly connected to the U.S. Congress, federal courts, the governments of U.S. territories and possessions, and the District of Columbia. The law specifically includes all federal executive and military departments, government-controlled corporations, federal government corporations, and other establishments in the executive branch of the federal government, including the Executive Office of the President, and independent regulatory agencies. (State and municipal government bodies are not subject to FOIA.)

EXEMPTIONS TO FOIA

The law lists nine categories of government records that federal agencies need not disclose to the public. These exemptions recognize the fact that censorship of some types of information may be necessary to safeguard certain legitimate government and private interests. However, agencies claiming any of these exemptions bear the burden of showing that the information should be protected under the law.

The first exemption covers information relating to national defense and foreign policy. An executive order must be issued to classify and protect this information pursuant to established standards and procedures, including submission of affidavits showing how the release of such information might damage national security. However, the language of this exemption does not provide any substantive standard for withholding information. A specific executive order must be reviewed to give the exemption meaning. In 1982, Executive Order 12356 was issued; as amended, it lists ten categories of information to be considered for classification. These include information on military plans, weapons, or operations; the capabilities and vulnerabilities of systems, installations, projects, or plans relating to the national security; information on foreign governments; intelligence-gathering activities; foreign relations; scientific, technological, or economic matters relating to national security; federal programs for safeguarding nuclear materials and facilities; cryptology; confidential sources; and any information relating to national security that the president or other officials determine should be protected from unauthorized disclosure.

Some national security information, even when it falls within one or more of these categories, may nevertheless not be classified. The key question is whether disclosure—by itself or in the context of other information—can reasonably be expected to damage national security. Information cannot be classified simply for the purpose of concealing violations of the law, inefficiency, or administrative errors; to prevent embarrassment to a person, organization, or agency; to restrain competition; or to delay release of information not requiring protection in the interest of national security. Further, basic scientific research not clearly related to national security is not classifiable.

Executive Order 12356 provides that information should be declassified or downgraded as soon as national security considerations permit. Further, if the director of the Information Security Oversight Office determines that any information is classified in violation of this executive order, the director may mandate declassification. The director's decisions are appealable to the National Security Council, with the information remaining classified pending appeal.

OTHER EXEMPTIONS

The second exemption concerns records relating solely to the internal personnel rules and practices of an agency. Its purpose is to relieve government agencies of the burden of assembling and maintaining for public review records in which the public is unlikely to be interested. It also covers internal agency procedures, such as instructions to investigators, inspectors, and auditors, disclosure of which could damage agency operations.

The third exemption incorporates by reference various federal information nondisclosure statutes and precludes disclosure of certain information protected by other statutes. Nondisclosure is authorized when other statutes either prohibit disclosure outright, or confer to an agency discretionary power to withhold material, while providing guidelines for exercising such discretion or specifying the types of material to which discretion applies. Citizens wishing to examine agency documents that are withheld under the terms of this exemption can legally appeal to have them released under the terms of the Federal Rules of Civil Procedure.

The fourth exemption protects confidential business information. Its purpose is to protect the interests of persons, corporations, and other entities who disclose trade secrets and other confidential information to government agencies and to protect the government. Two tests have been defined to determine whether information can be classified as confidential business information. The so-called "competitive advantage test" asks whether release of the information in question is likely to cause substantial competitive injury to the entity that provided it. The "chilling effect test" questions how much the agency needs the information, and whether voluntary cooperation is required for the agency to obtain the information and whether its disclosure will impair the government's ability to collect similar information in the future. Any information that qualifies under any of these tests is exempted.

The fifth exemption encompasses the executive branch's inter-agency or intra-agency memoranda or letters, if they are deliberative, consultative, or within the attorney-client or attorney work product privileges. This exemption from public disclosure allows for full, frank, and uninhibited written exchange of ideas and opinions among government policymakers and advisers. Such writings may be censored if their disclosure would discourage intra-agency discussion and thereby impede the ability of an agency to perform its functions.

The sixth exemption prevents disclosure of information that would constitute a clearly unwarranted invasion of personal privacy. Examples of such information might include personal medical records. However, this exemption does not apply in cases in which it is judged that public need for release of the information outweighs any possible injury to a person's privacy.

The seventh exemption protects certain investigatory records compiled for law enforcement purposes. To qualify for this exemption it must be shown that release of such records might interfere with enforcement proceedings; deprive someone of his or her right to a fair trial or impartial adjudication; constitute an unwarranted invasion of personal privacy; disclose the identities of confidential sources, including state, local, or foreign agencies or authorities, or private institutions that have furnished information confidentially; disclose techniques, procedures, or guidelines for law enforcement investigations or prosecutions, and thereby possibly assist someone to circumvent the law; or endanger someone's life or physical safety.

The eighth exemption protects from disclosure reports prepared by or for agencies that regulate or supervise financial institutions. Its purpose is to enhance the security and integrity of financial institutions. Government reports on financial institutions often contain frank evaluations of institutions such as banks; indiscriminate disclosure of such information might, for example, lead to a harmful rush on a bank.

The final exemption allows nondisclosure of ecological and geophysical information and data concerning wells, including maps. Geological explorations by private oil companies were not previously protected by the trade secrets provisions of disclosure laws. It was believed that disclosure of seismic reports and other exploratory findings generated by oil companies could provide speculators unfair advantage over those companies which incurred the exploration costs.

FOIA's enumerated exemptions are not mandatory bars to disclosure. An agency may, at its own discretion, voluntarily disclose exempt information as it deems fit. However, when an agency elects to release exempt materials, it may limit access to such information to certain individuals.

RELEASE OF PARTIALLY EXEMPT INFORMATION

FOIA also addresses requests for information some parts of which are exempt and other parts are not. In such instances the agencies must release "segregable portions" that remain after the material that is exempt from release has been deleted. An agency must release any remaining material that is at all intelligible after deletions have been made. If there are any doubts about the intelligibility or responsiveness of the remaining nonexempt material, those doubts are to be resolved in favor of release.

HOW THE PUBLIC RECEIVES DOCUMENTS

FOIA requests must typically be in writing; agencies often provide prepared forms for this purpose. Submission of written requests trigger the running of set time limits for agencies to respond. Agencies are only required to act on requests that "reasonably describe" identifiable nonexempt records. Although one test is whether requested records can be located with reasonable efforts, the size of a request alone cannot be the measure of whether it reasonably describes an identifiable record. In contrast, a request for "all" information pertaining to a certain type of record would not be sufficiently descriptive to meet the requirement.

The government cannot consider the interests of parties requesting information before determining whether to release or censor it. Courts have consistently held that a requester's needs, purposes, or motivation do not affect the requester's right to inspect agency records.

RECOURSE FOR AGENCY NONCOMPLIANCE

Any agency denial of a request—for any reason—for information can be appealed under FOIA. The most common reason for appeals has been the failure of agencies to respond to requests within the law's statutory time limits. Agencies commonly deny requests by citing backlogs of requests, and inadequate staffing to perform record searches. Public requests can be frustrated by long delays and expense incurred while denials are appealed. Furthermore, even if an appeal is granted and a court directs an agency to comply with the request, the agency can assert—for the first time—that the requested records are exempt. This will start the appeal process all over again.

EFFECT OF FOIA

As drafted, FOIA has been generally regarded as a substantial improvement over the APA. In practice, however, FOIA has often proved to be an inadequate means by which to obtain government information. The law's enumerated exemptions afford government agencies many ways in which to censor documents, in whole or in part. Many cases have been reported wherein citizens have filed FOIA requests and not received their denial letters until five years after the original filing. Many court battles have been fought to determine whether certain government entities are even subject to FOIA. Each time that a court has ruled a government entity to be an agency subject to FOIA, the agency has been ordered to draft guidelines for preserving and releasing its records. Through such court battles, citizens have been granted additional rights to obtain government documents pursuant to FOIA. Furthermore, FOIA has allowed certain plaintiffs in civil court cases against the United States government, or its agencies, to obtain documents implicating the U.S. government or its agencies, which has lead to judgments or settlements against the U.S. government which could not have been obtained before the enactment of FOIA.

David R. Sobel

SOURCES FOR FURTHER STUDY

Adler, Allan. *Using the Freedom of Information Act: A Step by Step Guide.* Washington, D.C.: American Civil Liberties Union Foundation, 1990.

Holsinger, Ralph L. *Media Law.* 2d ed. New York: McGraw-Hill, 1991.

Marwick, Christine M. *Your Right to Government Information.* New York: Bantam, 1985.

Tedford, Thomas L. *Freedom of Speech in the United States.* 2d ed. New York: McGraw-Hill, 1993.

U.S. Congress. House. *Citizen's Guide to the Freedom of Information Act.* Chicago: Commerce Clearing House, 1987.

U.S. Congress. House. Committee on Government Operations. Foreign Operations and Government Information Subcommittee. *U.S. Government Information Policies and Practices: Administration and Operation of the Freedom of Information Act (Part Four). Hearings Before a Subcommittee of the Committee on Government Operations, House of Representatives.* 92d Congress. Washington, D.C.: Government Printing Office, 1972.

U.S. Department of Justice. Attorney General's Advocacy Institute. *The Freedom of Information Act for Attorneys and Access Professionals.* Washington, D.C.: Government Printing Office, 1989.

U.S. General Services Administration. *Your Right to Federal Records: Questions and Answers on the Freedom of Information Act and the Privacy Act.* Washington, D.C.: Government Printing Office, 1984.

Weaver, Maureen, ed. *The Freedom of Information Act: Why It's Important and How to Use It.* Washington, D.C.: Campaign for Political Rights, in cooperation with the Center for National Security Studies, 1982.

SEE ALSO: Privacy Act (1974); Privacy Protection Act (1980).

ANIMAL WELFARE ACT

DATE: August 24, 1966
U.S. STATUTES AT LARGE: 80 Stat. 350
PUBLIC LAW: 89-544
U.S. CODE: 7 § 2131-2155

CATEGORIES: Agriculture; Animals; Business, Commerce, and Trade; Environment and Conservation

The Animal Welfare Act represents the first U.S. statute on the use of animals in research.

Over the years, research using animals has resulted in substantial and undeniable benefits to humans. Once some people recognized that animals have a capacity to feel pain comparable to their own, however, the practice began to be questioned on ethical, moral, and philosophical grounds. As a result of the development of the pharmaceutical and petrochemical industries in the 1930's, there was a dramatic increase of research using animals. At that time, animals also began to be used more in the testing of non-medical products, such as cosmetics, and in weapons and space research. Eventually, a reaction began, and a spate of animal-welfare acts were introduced and debated in both houses of Congress between 1960 and 1966.

INHUMANE TREATMENT

Two events had raised public awareness of the need for some protection for animals: the fate of a missing pet dog suspected of having been stolen by a dealer, and a photo essay in *Life* magazine that depicted the inhumane treatment of dogs by dealers. The fate of the pet was never ascertained, but the fact that it had been impossible for the family and public officials to investigate the dealer convinced people that legislation was needed. The first step was taken when congressmen Warren Magnuson and Joseph Y. Resnick introduced a bill to regulate trade in dogs.

The Animal Welfare Act of 1966 grew out of the ensuing six-year debate in Congress, which focused on many of the issues of using animals for teaching and research, in exhibitions, and as pets. Much of the credit for the act's passage went to a grassroots effort led by Christine Stevens, an activist and founder of the Animal Welfare Institute. Stevens was given special recognition in the congressional record of the Eighty-ninth Congress for her contribution.

PROVISIONS FOR SOME ANIMALS

The 1966 act regulated the sale, transport, and handling of dogs, cats, monkeys, guinea pigs, hamsters, and rabbits. The secretary of agriculture was made responsible for establishing standards for humane treatment and transportation of those animals, but no specific standards were set in the act itself, nor did it include provisions for enforcing the regulations. The legislation had other serious weaknesses: It did not empower the Department of Agriculture to interfere in research designs or specific experiments; it addressed only the supply and care of animals, not the kind of procedures to which they were subjected; it covered only those institutions that receive federal funding; and it did not extend to rats and mice, which account for nearly 80 percent of all laboratory animals.

AMENDMENTS AND OTHER LEGISLATION

The debate over animal use continued after the Animal Welfare Act of 1966, and a number of amendments were added to the 1966 bill that significantly strengthened its provisions. The first amendment, in 1970, directed the secretary of agriculture to set standards for treatment and transportation of research animals and charged the Department of Agriculture with inspecting all official animal facilities and removing or humanely destroying suffering animals. A 1976 amendment mandated additional protection for animals being transported and tried to ensure humane care and treatment of animals; the amendment also prohibited the sale or use of stolen animals.

Between 1979 and 1982, the Ninety-sixth and Ninety-seventh Congresses debated a Research Modernization Act, which proposed reallocating 30 to 50 percent of all federal research funds that involved animals in order to establish an institute for the development of alternatives to animal testing. This debate was fueled by a widespread public letter-writing campaign, as a result of which public hearings were held in the House of Representatives. The Research Modernization Act was not passed, but debate over a subsequent bill, introduced in 1982, eventually led to a strong 1985 amendment to the 1966 Animal Welfare Act.

The 1985 amendment directed researchers to use specific standards of humane treatment and to design experiments so as to minimize pain and distress. Institutions that carry out animal research were required to establish a committee (one member of which had to be from outside the institution) to review research procedures and inspect facilities; these committees were responsible for filing reports with the Department of Agriculture and federal funding agencies.

A related statute, the Health Research Extension Act of 1985, directed the secretary of health and human services, through the National Institutes of Health (NIH), to establish guidelines at NIH-funded facilities for the care and treatment of research animals and the training of laboratory personnel in the humane treatment of animals. The director of the NIH was empowered to revoke grants to institutions that failed to meet the provisions outlined in the act. A separate piece of legislation, the Consumer Products Safe Testing Act of 1989, specifically prohibited the use of LD toxicity testing on live animals for determining product safety. In LD testing, animals were treated with increasing concentrations of a potentially toxic substance in order to determine the amount needed to kill 50 percent of the animals within fourteen days. Such testing was found to be inaccurate, misleading, and unnecessary. The act also mandated that each federal department or agency head review requirements or recommendations for the use of any type of animal toxicity tests for premarket evaluation of a product; departments and agencies were directed to order nonanimal toxicity testing whenever that would be as valid as using live animals. Federal departments and agencies were told to review their toxicity testing regulations at least every two years.

The 1990 amendment to the Animal Welfare Act authorized the secretary of agriculture to investigate anyone suspected of violating provisions of the act and gave the secretary authority to direct the attorney general to issue temporary restraining orders or injunctions for the protection of animals.

ANIMAL RIGHTS MOVEMENT

Even as amendments were added, the debate over animal use continued, driven by activists who believed the use of vertebrate animals in research to be unnecessary and often to involve excessive animal suffering resulting from improper techniques and inadequate standards of humane treatment. The animal rights movement gained strength throughout the 1980's as groups began to work together toward common goals. Academic debate on the moral status of animals helped legitimize the movement. Militancy also increased: Some activists believed they were justified in vandalizing research laboratories and "liberating" research animals. Scientists themselves became increasingly willing to criticize aspects of animal research. This willingness was in part the result of public sentiment, which convinced the scientific community that additional regulations were not only inevitable but also necessary to defuse some of the criticism.

The number of animals used for research decreased significantly after the 1970's as a result, at least in part, of scientists developing alternative research methods such as physical and chemical analytic techniques, use of biologically active products, and computer modeling and mathematical analysis. Systems using microorganisms were found to be effective substitutes for animals in the testing of cancer-causing chemicals. Cell-culture techniques carried out in vitro (in a test tube or laboratory flask) almost entirely replaced the controversial Draize rabbit eye-irritation toxicity text, which had been used for determining the safety of cosmetics. In some cases, human clinical and epidemiological studies were implemented directly following in vitro tests. Moreover, as a result of heightened public scrutiny, scientists who continued to experiment on animals refined their techniques to reduce stress and pain to the animals.

The series of amendments and related legislation strengthened the Animal Welfare Act of 1966 but did not end the debate between animal rights proponents and scientific communities over the use of animals for research. In June, 1994, the U.S. district court of appeals in Washington, D.C., overturned a 1992 district court order that had charged the Department of Agriculture with monitoring the treatment at universities of research rats, mice, and birds, none of which were covered by the 1966 act or its amendments. In July, 1994, a 1991 court order was overturned that had mandated exercise for research dogs and provisions for the psychological well-being of nonhuman primates. Both rulings were made on the basis that the individuals and groups who had brought the suits had no legal standing to challenge existing regulations. That convinced animal-welfare advocates that the way to strengthen the Animal Welfare Act further was not through the courts but through Congress.

Linda E. Fisher

SOURCES FOR FURTHER STUDY
Fox, Michael Allen. *The Case for Animal Experimentation.* Berkeley: University of California Press, 1986.
Friedman, Ruth. *Animal Experimentation and Animal Rights.* Oryx Science Bibliographies 9. Phoenix, Ariz.: Oryx Press, 1987.
Garner, Robert. *Animals, Politics, and Morality.* Manchester, England: Manchester University Press, 1993.
Moss, Thomas H. "The Modern Politics of Laboratory Animal Use." *BioScience* 34 (November, 1984): 621-625.
Rowan, Andrew N. *Of Mice, Models, and Men: A Critical Evaluation of Animal Research.* Albany: State University of New York Press, 1984.

SEE ALSO: Endangered Species Preservation Act (1966); Endangered Species Act (1973); Convention on International Trade in Endangered Species (1975); Convention on the Conservation of Migratory Species of Wild Animals (1979).

NATIONAL TRAFFIC AND MOTOR VEHICLE SAFETY ACT

DATE: September 9, 1966
U.S. STATUTES AT LARGE: 80 Stat. 730
PUBLIC LAW: 89-563
U.S. CODE: 49 § 30101-30169
CATEGORIES: Business, Commerce, and Trade; Health and Welfare; Transportation

Spurred by activist Ralph Nader, this act for the first time mandated vehicle safety standards.

On September 9, 1966, President Lyndon Johnson approved the National Traffic and Motor Vehicle Safety Act. The legislation marked the first time the federal government acted to regulate the automobile industry. It required the federal government to develop a program to reduce the number of deaths and injuries caused by auto accidents. Prior to this legislation, the federal government allowed the automobile industry to regulate itself. The lack of government regulation was leading to a large number of deaths and injuries caused by car accidents, a fact brought to the public's attention by consumer advocate Ralph Nader in his 1965 book *Unsafe at Any Speed.* The act passed unanimously in both the House of Representatives and the Senate.

SAFETY PROVISIONS AND RESPONSE

The new law led to the creation of a federal agency, the National Highway Traffic Safety Administration (NHTSA), which was given the task of developing standards for vehicle safety. The standards were to be based on the standards established in the mid-1960's for cars purchased by the federal government. These twenty-six standards included seat belts, backup lights, impact-absorbing steering columns, front-seat headrests, interior padding (especially on the dashboard), rearview mirrors, four-way flashers or hazard lights to signal a disabled or stopped vehicle, and rear-window defogging devices. The standards were to take effect on all 1968 model vehicles.

Although the early standards developed by the NHTSA were minor modifications of those established by the federal government for its own cars, the automobile industry opposed them at every step in the rule-making process. Supporters of increased automobile safety, including Nader, criticized the new agency for not issuing stricter standards. The federal court system usually sided with the automobile manufacturers. In one of the first rulings on automobile safety standards, a federal appeals court decided that the agency could not use findings from crash tests using dummies to support a standard requiring passive restraints. Because of legal challenges, the agency worked fourteen years, until 1984, to issue a standard requiring air bags in American automobiles.

AMENDMENTS

In 1974, Congress amended the act to give the NHTSA the power to enforce recall decisions on defective vehicles. If an equipment failure led to a safety risk in a significant number of vehicles, the agency could order the manufacturer to issue a recall notice and fix the defect in consumers' vehicles. The federal courts allowed the agency to keep this power.

Congress enacted another significant amendment in 2000. This amendment, the Transportation Recall Enhancement, Accountability, and Documentation (TREAD) Act, was in response to a large number of accidents involving Ford vehicles with Firestone tires. Ford and Firestone were accused of not informing the government and the public of the problems with tire treads separating, which had caused drivers to lose control of their vehicles. The TREAD act strengthened the defect notification process by requiring car and tire manufacturers to disclose problems with the reporting of a safety recall conducted in a foreign country.

John David Rausch, Jr.

SOURCES FOR FURTHER STUDY
Hansen, Brian. "Auto Safety." *CQ Researcher,* October 26, 2001.
Mashaw, Jerry L., and David L. Harfst. *The Struggle for Auto Safety.* Cambridge, Mass.: Harvard University Press, 1990.

SEE ALSO: Motor Vehicle Theft Act (1919); Motor Vehicle Air Pollution Control Act (1965); Child product safety laws (1970's); Consumer Product Safety Act (1972); Motor Vehicle Theft Law Enforcement Act (1984); Alternative Motor Fuels Act (1988).

ENDANGERED SPECIES PRESERVATION ACT

DATE: October 15, 1966
U.S. STATUTES AT LARGE: 80 Stat. 926
PUBLIC LAW: 89-669
CATEGORIES: Animals; Environment and Conservation; Natural Resources

The law was designed for the conservation, protection, restoration, and propagation of native species of wildlife threatened with extinction.

The Endangered Species Preservation Act in 1966 was the first legislation in the United States specifically concerned with the protection and conservation of species threatened with extinction. It was the culmination of a long history of wildlife management and wildlife protection legislation, the earliest of which had been passed in the colonial period.

EARLY LEGISLATION AND OVERSIGHT

In 1900, however, the federal government took its first cautious step toward national regulation of wildlife with the Lacey Act. Using the federal government's constitutional authority to regulate interstate commerce, the Lacey Act prohibited the interstate transportation of any wild bird or mammal killed in violation of state law. The act also authorized the government to preserve, distribute, introduce, and restore wild bird populations where and when necessary. This was in response to the decline of birds such as the passenger pigeon, which became extinct in 1914, and the Carolina parakeet, which became extinct in 1918.

Another step was taken in 1918 with the passage of the Migratory Bird Treaty Act. Based on the government's authority to enter into treaties with other nations, the act ratified a treaty between the United States and Great Britain (on behalf of Canada) that determined federal authority for the custody and protection of migratory birds. The role of the federal government in protecting wildlife continued to expand through many subsequent laws, but none of them addressed the problem of species with seriously declining populations.

Early federal wildlife protection efforts emanated from the Department of Agriculture and Department of Commerce until, in 1939, wildlife management and protection was transferred to the Department of the Interior.

In 1964, the Bureau of Sport Fisheries and Wildlife, which was part of the Department of the Interior, inaugurated the Committee on Rare and Endangered Wildlife Species, which issued the first federal list of rare and endangered species, identifying sixty-three vertebrate species. The Land and Water Conservation Fund Act of that year authorized the department to purchase habitat for the preservation of species threatened with extinction. Congress refused to fund these programs without clarification of the department's legislative authority, so the legislation had negligible impact.

PASSAGE AND PROVISIONS

In 1965, the staff of the Department of the Interior drafted legislation for a comprehensive program to protect, conserve, and restore wild populations of endangered species. The resulting bills, one in the House of Representatives and one in the Senate, were uncontroversial and passed easily, because almost everyone supported the concept, the scope of the legislation seemed limited, and no one realized the eventual impact. Among the seven conservation bills President Johnson signed into law in 1966 was the Endangered Species Preservation Act, the first significant measure to conserve wildlife species in danger of extinction.

Previous acts had provided various kinds of protection for wildlife; the Endangered Species Preservation Act specifically protected species in danger of becoming extinct. The act represented further expansion of federal authority; this was, in fact, the only aspect of the law to undergo debate, because some considered it to conflict with states' rights over wildlife. The consensus was, however, that the act addressed an area of wildlife management that game-oriented state agencies had been neglecting. Because of heightened environmental awareness on the part of both the public and Congress, the Department of the Interior was able to get the endangered species program funded and implemented.

The most significant effect of the 1966 act was the bridge it provided between the pre-1966 acts regarding federal wildlife management and post-1966 acts concerning endangered species. Before 1966, most wildlife management legislation was passed and enforced by state wildlife agencies, which concentrated on game species—mostly mammals, birds, and fish. The state agencies were funded primarily by state revenues from hunting and fishing licenses, and by the Pittman-Robertson and the Dingell-Johnson acts, which imposed federal excise taxes on hunting and fishing equipment. State wildlife management basically benefited hunters and fishers, while federal legislation before 1966 was cautious and primarily concerned with agricultural pests and species of commercial interest.

The 1966 act was also a significant first step in extending existing federal wildlife management authority to the protection of endangered species, and it prepared the way for the Endangered Species Conservation Act of 1969 and the Endangered Species Act of 1973, which was the most comprehensive endangered species legislation of its time anywhere in the world. The 1966 act provided for the conservation, protection, restoration, and propagation of selected species of native wildlife threatened with extinction. The primary method for accomplishing this was habitat acquisition, which was authorized and funded through the existing Land and Water Conservation Fund Act of 1964, among other laws. The 1966 act also encouraged federal agencies to assist the Department of the Interior in protecting endangered wildlife.

The determination that a species was threatened with extinction was made by the secretary of the interior on the basis of a set of vague criteria. Although the 1966 act did not define wildlife, it did prohibit the removal or possession of protected fish, birds, mammals, other wild vertebrates and invertebrates, nests, and eggs. Only about seventy-eight species were defined as endangered, most of them large, popular species that could be easily protected by the existing park and refuge system.

IMPACT
There was little immediate impact beyond the public exposure of the endangered species issue. Moreover, given the quickly maturing conservation movement of the late 1960's, it soon became apparent that the 1966 act had serious limitations. Only native species were covered—there was no protection for foreign species—and in practice only birds and mammals were seriously considered. Enforcement of prohibitions against the taking of protected animals was weak and pertained only to federal lands, nor did the act restrict interstate commerce. The habitat protection effort, too, was weak, because once land was acquired for or designated as a protected habitat, the act had no provisions for actual protection beyond calling for cooperation with other federal agencies.

The short-term effect of the 1966 act was therefore minimal, but its long-term importance was demonstrated by the passage of the more authoritative 1969 and the even stronger 1973 endangered species acts. Several other acts and treaties also came into force, including the Marine Mammal Protection Act, Animal Welfare Act, African Elephant Conservation Act, Wild Free-Roaming Horses and Burros Act, Convention on International Trade in Endangered Species of Wild Fauna and Flora (CITES), Convention on Nature Protection and Wildlife Preservation in the Western Hemisphere, and Convention on the Conservation of Migratory Species of Wild Animals.

The 1966 act also gave impetus to the concept of listing and thereby increasing public awareness of endangered species. In contrast to the seventy-eight species listed in 1966, by the year 2000 there were well over one thousand species listed as either endangered or threatened, with more being considered for inclusion.

Vernon N. Kisling, Jr.

SOURCES FOR FURTHER STUDY
Bean, Michael J. *The Evolution of National Wildlife Law.* Rev. ed. New York: Praeger, 1983.
Clepper, Henry, ed. *Origins of American Conservation.* New York: Ronald Press, 1966.
Littel, Richard. *Endangered and Other Protected Species: Federal Law and Regulation.* Washington, D.C.: Bureau of National Affairs, 1992.
Lund, Thomas A. *American Wildlife Law.* Berkeley: University of California Press, 1980.
U.S. Congress. Senate. Committee on Environmental and Public Works. *A Legislative History of the Endangered Species Act of 1973, as Amended in 1976, 1977, 1978, 1979, and 1980.* Washington, D.C.: Government Printing Office, 1982.
Yaffee, Steven L. *Prohibitive Policy: Implementing the Federal Endangered Species Act.* Cambridge, Mass.: MIT Press, 1982.

SEE ALSO: Migratory Bird Act (1913); Migratory Bird Treaty Act (1918); Migratory Bird Hunting and Conservation Stamp Act (1934); Pittman-Robertson Wildlife Restoration Act (1937); Animal Welfare Act (1966); Marine Mammal Protection Act (1972); Endangered Species Act (1973); Convention on International Trade in Endangered Species (1975); Convention on the Conservation of Migratory Species of Wild Animals (1979).

TWENTY-FIFTH AMENDMENT

DATE: Ratified February 23, 1967
CATEGORIES: Constitutional Law; Government Procedure and Organization

The Twenty-fifth Amendment provides clear procedures for fulfilling the duties of the presidency should the president be unable to discharge the duties of the office, or in the event of the death, removal from office, or resignation of the president. It also provides for the prompt filling of the office of vice president should a vacancy occur.

The Twenty-fifth Amendment was formally signed and proclaimed by President Lyndon B. Johnson in a White House ceremony on February 23, 1967. The four-section amendment specifically addresses issues related to presidential disability and succession. These concerns date back to the forming of the nation and would come to a head during the Watergate scandal that forced President Richard M. Nixon from office.

EARLIER CASES OF PRESIDENTIAL DEATH WHILE IN OFFICE

The first succession law was signed by President George Washington in 1792, declaring that the vice president would succeed the president, followed by the president pro tempore of the Senate, and then the Speaker of the House. On June 19, 1886, the succession law was revised, in part because of concerns raised when Chester A. Arthur ascended to the office of president following the assassination of James Garfield. No president pro tempore or Speaker was in office at the time. This law put the secretary of state in line behind the vice president, followed by cabinet heads.

Following the death of Franklin D. Roosevelt in office, President Harry S. Truman questioned the fitness of unelected cabinet members to hold the office. A bill placing the Speaker and the president pro tempore in line after the vice president was challenged. The Supreme Court's decision in *Lamar v. United States* (1916) and the Constitution were used to declare the proposal's legality. The legislation was passed into law on July 18, 1947. The assassination of President John F. Kennedy in 1963 rekindled the succession debate, as the Speaker of the House was quite elderly.

APPLICATIONS OF THE AMENDMENT

Six years after ratification, the amendment would be tested. Spiro Agnew resigned the vice presidency amid legal difficulties, and Gerald R. Ford assumed the office in 1973. Shortly thereafter, the Court ordered President Nixon to turn over audiotapes as possible evidence in the Watergate hearings. He announced his resignation on August 8, 1974, and Ford assumed the presidency the next day. Using the provisions of the Twenty-fifth Amendment, Nelson A.

Rockefeller was later confirmed to the office of vice president. The application of the Twenty-fifth Amendment therefore resulted in two unelected officials holding the highest offices in the nation.

The disability provisions were employed by Ronald Reagan and subsequent presidents. The amendment ensures that the duties of the presidency will continually be carried out in a timely manner.

Kathleen Schongar

SOURCES FOR FURTHER STUDY

Feerick, John D. *The Twenty-fifth Amendment.* New York: Fordham University Press, 1976.

Vile, John R. *A Companion to the United States Constitution and Its Amendments.* 3d ed. Westport, Conn.: Greenwood Press, 2001.

_____. *Encyclopedia of Constitutional Amendments, Proposed Amendments, and Amending Issues, 1789-1995.* Santa Barbara, Calif: ABC-CLIO, 1996.

SEE ALSO: U.S. Constitution: Provisions (1787); Twelfth Amendment (1804); Electoral Count Act (1887); Presidential Succession Act (1947); Twenty-second Amendment (1951).

OUTER SPACE TREATY

DATE: Ratified April 25, 1967; in force October 10, 1967
CATEGORIES: Environment and Conservation; Foreign Relations; Natural Resources; Treaties and Agreements

This agreement, made at the height of the Cold War, mandated the peaceful use of outer space by all nations.

After the end of World War II, the Cold War between the United States and the Union of Soviet Socialist Republics, or Soviet Union, was the principal global rivalry. Throughout the next few decades this rivalry took many forms. The development of rockets, with the related goals of space exploration and development of weapons delivery systems, constituted a prime area of competition. With the launching of Sputnik 1 in October, 1957, the "space race"—which had been under way for a decade—was apparent to everyone.

From 1959 to 1963, the number of outer-space-related proposals made by the United States and the Soviet Union greatly increased. The United States' proposals tended to focus on banning the placement of weapons of mass destruction in orbit around Earth, while the Soviet Union sought a comprehensive disarmament treaty, which would include provisions for outer space.

In September, 1963, the Soviet Union stated that a separate treaty regarding outer space would be acceptable. This statement was quickly followed by a general statement of agreement by the United States. During October, 1963, the General Assembly of the United Nations passed a resolution supporting the statements made by both countries. However, not until 1966 were substantive proposals for a treaty were put forward by the United States and the Soviet Union. The United States' proposal dealt only with the area close to Earth, while the Soviet proposal dealt with all of outer space. The United States accepted the broader vision for cooperation, and by the end of the year agreement on the details of the treaty had been reached. Since 1967, about 120 national governments have acted on it in some official manner.

As an arms control agreement, there were two major points. The first was that no nuclear weapons, or other weapons of mass destruction, could be placed in orbit around Earth or stationed elsewhere in outer space. The second (Article IV) was agreement that the "Moon and other celestial bodies shall be used by all States Parties to the Treaty exclusively for peaceful purposes." Military bases, maneuvers, and weapons testing were also prohibited in outer space, although members of the military can participate in peaceful exploration. These broad provisions mean that any national rivalries should not extend militarily into outer space. However, the treaty contains no provisions for verification of compliance, with the exception that all facilities located on the Moon or another celestial body shall be open to visits by members of other countries.

Other major provisions include a statement that the Moon and other celestial bodies cannot be claimed as the property of any nation. While each nation is responsible for the activities it or its citizens undertake, exploration and the related scientific study is to be undertaken for the good of all people. To facilitate this exploration, there are provisions to assist astronauts who are in trouble or who make an emergency landing outside their home country.

Donald A. Watt

SOURCES FOR FURTHER STUDY
McCain, Morris. *Understanding Arms Control: The Options.* New York: W. W. Norton, 1989.
Wainhouse, David W., et al. *Arms Control Agreements: Designs for Verification and Organization.* Baltimore: The Johns Hopkins University Press, 1968.

SEE ALSO: North Atlantic Treaty (1949); Eisenhower Doctrine (1957); Nuclear Test Ban Treaty (1963); U.S.-Soviet Consular Treaty (1967); Nuclear Nonproliferation Treaty (1968); Seabed Treaty (1972); SALT I Treaty (1972); SALT II Treaty (1979); Law of the Sea Treaty (1982); INF Treaty (1987); START II Treaty (1993).

PUBLIC BROADCASTING ACT

DATE: November 7, 1967
U.S. STATUTES AT LARGE: 81 Stat. 365
PUBLIC LAW: 90-129
U.S. CODE: 47 § 390
CATEGORIES: Communications and Media; Speech and Expression

This law was designed to develop public broadcasting, although its content restrictions limited public broadcasting's expressive freedom.

The Public Broadcasting Act of 1967 has been credited with helping what had been known as educational radio and television evolve into a mature source of news, entertainment, and education. However, because some legislators were concerned that federal involvement in broadcasting might lead to an "Orwellian" government network used for propaganda purposes, the law also included two important content restrictions.

Section 399 prevented public broadcasters from editorializing or supporting political candidates. Although it allowed individual commentators to express opinions, this section constrained station managements from broadcasting their own opinions. Some congressional advocates of the provision contended that it would help insulate stations from political pressure to support particular issues or candidates. Other supporters acknowledged that they had been the targets of commercial press editorials in the past and welcomed the ability to restrain public broadcasting from editorializing. More than a decade later a consortium of groups challenged the constitutionality of section 399. In 1984 the U.S. Supreme Court voted 5-4 to overturn the provision as a violation of public broadcasters' First Amendment rights in *Federal Communications Commission v. League of Women Voters.* The Court's majority opinion stated that the value of editorial contributions to the marketplace of ideas outweighed any harm that public broadcasters might suffer if their editorials angered politicians.

Another restrictive provision of the Public Broadcasting Act required all programs or series funded by the Corporation for Public Broadcasting (CPB)—which had been created by the act to channel federal dollars to public stations—to maintain objectivity and balance. Demanding such balance was viewed as a means of ensuring that public stations would not serve as propaganda voices for those supporting one side of controversial issues. In 1975 the Federal Communications Commission (FCC), responding to a complaint over two allegedly biased public television programs, held that it could enforce no stronger requirement than the fairness doctrine—an FCC regulation calling for balanced coverage of issues over a station's overall programming. The U.S. Court of Appeals for the District of Columbia upheld that decision, ruling that requiring the FCC to demand balance within individual programs or series would threaten broadcasters' expressive freedom. That case did not end congressional attempts to mandate greater objectivity within public broadcasting.

In 1992 Congress attached an amendment to the CPB funding bill, requiring the CPB to ensure that public television programming was balanced and objective, and to report annually to Congress on its progress toward achieving such balance. Congress's action illustrates the Public Broadcasting Act's greatest threat to public broadcasters' freedom of speech: its failure to provide for any source of dedicated federal funding. Requiring public broadcasters to depend on congressional appropriations for a significant part of their operating budgets meant that legislators unhappy with public broadcasting programming could manifest their displeasure by reducing the system's funding. This power was exemplified in 1972 when President Richard M. Nixon, angered by what he perceived as public television's liberal bias, vetoed CPB's appropriations bill.

Howard M. Kleiman

SOURCES FOR FURTHER STUDY

Emery, Edwin, and Michael Emery. *The Press and America: An Interpretive History of the Mass Media.* 5th ed. Englewood Cliffs, N.J.: Prentice-Hall, 1984.

Krasnow, Erwin G., and Lawrence D. Longley. *The Politics of Broadcast Regulation.* New York: St. Martin's Press, 1973.

Lichty, Lawrence W., and Malachi C. Topping. *American Broadcasting: A Source Book on the History of Radio and Television.* New York: Hastings House, 1975.

SEE ALSO: First Amendment (1789); Communications Act (1934); Communications Act Amendments (1960); Communications Decency Act (1996); Internet Tax Freedom Act (1998).

AGE DISCRIMINATION IN EMPLOYMENT ACT

DATE: December 15, 1967
U.S. STATUTES AT LARGE: 81 Stat. 602
PUBLIC LAW: 90-202
U.S. CODE: 29 § 621
CATEGORIES: Aging Issues; Civil Rights and Liberties; Health and Welfare; Labor and Employment

The Age Discrimination in Employment Act (ADEA) promotes employment of older persons based on their ability rather than age, prohibits arbitrary age discrimination in employment, and helps employers and employees to resolve problems arising from the effects of age on employment.

The enactment of the ADEA by Congress was deemed necessary to protect the civil rights of workers between the ages of forty and sixty-five, many of whom who found themselves disadvantaged in retaining employment or in regaining employment following displacement from a job. The law prohibits age discrimination, or ageism, in hiring, discharge, pay, promotion, and other terms and conditions of employment. Through the ADEA, Congress intended to bar employers from setting arbitrary age limits that disregarded workers' potential for job performance. Congress recognized that the incidence of unemployment—especially long-term unemployment with resultant deterioration of skill, morale, and employer acceptability—was high among older workers and that the existence of arbitrary age discrimination in industries burdened commerce and impeded the flow of goods.

The U.S. secretary of labor administers and enforces the ADEA through the Equal Employment Opportunity Commission. The act applies to employers with more than twenty employees, to employment agencies, and to unions. The ADEA's protections apply to both employees and applicants for a job. Most states have enacted laws parallel to the federal law.

The ADEA provides for exceptions. Any action that may otherwise be unlawful under the ADEA is legal if age is related to a bona fide occupational qualification that is reasonably necessary for the normal operation of the particular business. In some jobs, an employee must meet certain physical qualifications that an older person cannot satisfy; for example, public safety concerns may validly affect age-related employment decisions regarding the piloting of aircraft, fire fighting, or law enforcement, whereas valid commercial considerations may affect hiring decisions regarding the modeling of clothes for teenagers. The law stipulates that an employer is not required to hire anyone who is unqualified to do a job, regardless of age, and that it is legal to discharge an older employee for good cause.

Employees or applicants may agree to waive their rights under the ADEA. For a waiver to be considered voluntary and valid, minimum standards must be met. The waiver must be in writing and be understandable, it must specifically refer to ADEA rights, it may not waive rights or claims that may arise in the future, it must be in exchange for valuable consideration, it must advise the individual in writing to consult an attorney before signing the waiver, and it must provide the individual at least twenty-one days to consider the agreement and at least seven days to revoke it after signing it.

In 1978, an amendment of the ADEA extended protection to employees up to seventy years of age. On October 7, 1998, President Bill Clinton signed the Higher Education Amendments of 1998, which allowed colleges and universities to offer age-based early retirement programs to tenured college and university faculty without violating the ADEA. Thus, tenured faculty may be offered "supplemental benefits upon voluntary retirement that are reduced or eliminated on the basis of age," as long as the benefits are in addition to any retirement or severance benefits generally offered to tenured faculty.

Manjit S. Kang

Sources for Further Study

Gregory, Raymond F. *Age Discrimination in the American Workplace: Old at a Young Age.* New Brunswick, N.J.: Rutgers University Press, 2001.

Hushbeck, Judith C. *Old and Obsolete: Age Discrimination and the American Worker, 1860-1920.* New York: Garland, 1989.

Kalet, Joseph E. *Age Discrimination in Employment Law.* Washington, D.C.: BNA Books, 1990.

O'Meara, Daniel P. *Protecting the Growing Number of Older Workers: The Age Discrimination in Employment Act.* Philadelphia: University of Pennsylvania, Center for Human Resources, 1989.

Segrave, Kerry. *Age Discrimination by Employers.* Jefferson, N.C.: McFarland Press, 2002.

See also: Executive Order 11141 (1964); National Arts and Cultural Development Act (1964); Medicare and Medicaid Amendments (1965); Older Americans Act (1965); Age Discrimination in Employment Act (1967); Age Discrimination Act (1975); Older Workers Benefit Protection Act (1990).

BILINGUAL EDUCATION ACT

DATE: January 2, 1968
U.S. STATUTES AT LARGE: Older Workers Benefit Protection Act
(1990)81 Stat. 816
PUBLIC LAW: 89-10
U.S. CODE: 20 § 7401
CATEGORIES: Asia or Asian Americans; Education; Latinos

The act sought to prevent economic and social discrimination against students with limited English proficiency by increasing the students' English-language skills while maintaining their access to learning through their native language.

Bilingual education was thrust into the forefront of public attention in the 1960's, when Dade County, Florida, announced a successful experiment with a bilingual program for newly arrived Cuban refugees, most of whom were non-English proficient (NEP) or limited-English proficient (LEP). Citing Title VI of the Civil Rights Act of 1964, which prohibits discrimination in school districts receiving federal funds, Mexican American advocacy groups supported the concept of bilingual instruction as a programmatic remedy for unequal educational attainments by Mexican Americans. The advocacy groups argued that without the ability to speak English, Mexican Americans could participate in neither the economic nor the political mainstream of the country.

PASSAGE OF THE BILL

Responding to pressure from his constituents, Texas senator Ralph W. Yarborough championed the cause of bilingual education by introducing a bill in early 1967 that sought to assist schools with a high percentage of low-income Latinos. In the House of Representatives, the bill ultimately gained forty-nine cosponsors, notably George E. Brown, Jr., and Edward R. Roybal of California and James H. Scheuer of New York. As the bill received bipartisan support, attention broadened to consider the plight of LEP/NEP students of American Indian, Asian, French Canadian, French Creole, and Portuguese ancestries. During the debate, statistics were presented showing that 11 percent of U.S. residents had a mother tongue other than English, and 3 million school-age children spoke a language other than English, 1.75 million of whom spoke Spanish.

Public hearings on the proposed legislation were held in Los Angeles, New York City, and three cities in Texas (Corpus Christi, Edinburg, and San Antonio). In addition to Hispanic advocacy groups, support for the bill came from the National Education Association. Since professional educators had no consensus on which teaching strategy worked best in boosting achievement levels for LEP and NEP students, they lobbied Congress to provide funding for research.

Congress passed the Bilingual Education Act of 1968 as an amendment to the Elementary and Secondary Education Act of 1965, and $400 million was authorized to be spent for research from 1968 to 1973, although much less actually was appropriated. Funds were to be used to remedy LEP/NEP problems in languages other than English spoken by a substantial number of students.

SUBSEQUENT DEVELOPMENTS
On January 21, 1974, the Supreme Court ruled in *Lau v. Nichols* that failure to use special methods to enable language-minority students to enter mainstream English classes was impermissible. The court, however, refused to rule on what pedagogical method would be best for mainstreaming LEP and NEP students into English-only classes, leaving the choice of method to local school districts.

Subsequent to *Lau*, Congress held hearings to assess the impact, which was determined to affect five million schoolchildren. One result was the Equal Educational Opportunities Act in 1974, a provision of which requires "appropriate action to overcome language barriers that impede equal participation." A second statute was the Bilingual Education Act of 1974, which provided federal funds to finance efforts at compliance with *Lau* for all affected students, not just for low-income students. In 1978, when the law was extended, objections to experiments in bilingual education mounted, and Congress restricted funding to educational projects in which no more than 40 percent of the students were native English speakers.

Several alternative methods of language instruction were studied. Submersion, which entailed placing LEP/NEP students into English-only classes on a sink-or-swim basis, was the method outlawed by *Lau*. Teaching English to Students of Other Languages (TESOL) was designed to remove LEP/NEP students from the mainstream to take special instruction in English. Immersion involved employing bilingual instructors who could teach in either language. Transitional bilingual education, the most popular program, involved fast-track English instruction aimed at rapid mainstreaming. Bilingual maintenance programs were designed to enable LEP/NEP students to retain language proficiency in the native language while learning English. Bilingual/bicultural programs went beyond bilingual maintenance to provide instruction in aspects of both the root and U.S. cultures. Culturally pluralistic programs, as adopted later at Texas border towns, were designed to integrate LEP/NEP and English-speaking students into multilingual/multicultural classrooms, so that both majority and minority children could learn together.

When objective studies demonstrated that the various bilingual instructional programs did not improve achievement levels for Mexican Americans, Congress passed new legislation, providing funds for capacity building, that is, to train teachers from language minority groups and to develop instructional materials for use in the classroom. The first such law, the Bilingual Education Amendments of 1981, was followed by the Bilingual Education Improvement Act of 1983 and the Bilingual Education Acts of 1984 and 1988.

During the eight years that Ronald Reagan was president, civil rights compliance reviews on language and other forms of educational discrimination decreased by 90 percent. In 1991, after Congress held hearings on the matter, the U.S. Department of Education's Office for Civil Rights set equal educational opportunities for national-origin minority and Native American students as its top priority. Although the battle to recognize Spanish and other languages as legitimate languages of instruction succeeded in the 1960's and 1970's, efforts to abolish bilingual education gained momentum in the 1980's and 1990's. In the late 1990's, Californians passed an initiative ending bilingual education in the schools.

Michael Haas

Sources for Further Study

Bull, Barry L., Royal T. Fruehling, and Virgie Chattergy. *The Ethics of Multicultural and Bilingual Education.* New York: Columbia University Press, 1992.

Crawford, James. *Language Loyalties: A Source Book on the Official English Controversy.* Chicago : University of Chicago Press, 1992.
Leibowitz, Arnold. *The Bilingual Education Act: A Legislative Analysis.* Rosslyn, Va.: InterAmerica Research Associates, National Clearinghouse for Bilingual Education, 1980.
Moran, Rachel F. "Of Democracy, Devaluation, and Bilingual Education." *Creighton Law Review* 26 (February, 1993): 255-319.
Porter, Rosalie P. *Forked Tongue: The Politics of Bilingual Education.* New York: Basic Books, 1990.
Rossell, Christine H., and J. Michael Ross. "The Social Science Evidence on Bilingual Education." *Journal of Law & Education* 15 (Fall, 1986): 385-419.
Wagner, Stephen T. "The Historical Background of Bilingualism and Biculturalism in the United States." In *The New Bilingualism: An American Dilemma,* edited by Martin Ridge. Los Angeles: University of Southern California Press, 1981.

SEE ALSO: Equal Employment Opportunity Act (1972); Education for All Handicapped Children Act (1975); Indian Education Acts (1972, 1978).

CIVIL RIGHTS ACT OF 1968

DATE: April 11, 1968
U.S. STATUTES AT LARGE: 82 Stat. 81
PUBLIC LAW: 90-284
U.S. CODE: 25 § 1301
CATEGORIES: African Americans; Civil Rights and Liberties; Housing

The Civil Rights Act of 1968 banned racial discrimination in the sale or rental of most types of housing; it also extended most of the protections of the Bill of Rights to Native Americans.

After 1965, the Civil Rights movement devoted increasing attention to conditions in the North. It found much segregation there, a condition that was rooted in residential patterns rather than in Jim Crow laws. The prevalence of segregated housing determined the composition of schools and other aspects of urban life. Martin Luther King, Jr.'s Chicago campaign in 1966 focused national attention on the housing issue. His lack of success showed that white resistance to opening neighborhoods to minority residents was strong and would be difficult to overcome. Urban riots in northern and western cities provoked a "white backlash," as many northern whites ceased their support for further civil rights reform. In 1966 and 1967, President Lyndon B. Johnson tried and failed to persuade Congress to pass civil rights bills outlawing discrimination in housing.

PASSING THE ACT

In 1968, liberal Democrats in the Senate brought forward a new civil rights bill containing a fair housing provision. Heavy lobbying by Clarence Mitchell, of the National Association for the Advancement of Colored People (NAACP), helped to marshal a majority of senators in support of the bill. As with earlier civil rights measures, southern senators attempted to talk the bill to death with a filibuster. However, in return for some relatively minor modifications in the bill, the leader of the Republican minority, Senator Everett Dirksen of Illinois, agreed to support an attempt to cut off the filibuster. This succeeded, and the bill passed the Senate on March 11, 1968.

In the House of Representatives, passage was far from sure. The assassination of Martin Luther King, Jr., on April 4, however, shocked the country and dramatically altered the political landscape. Support for the bill grew; it passed easily and was signed by President Johnson on April 11.

FAIR HOUSING

The main thrust of the 1968 Civil Rights Act was to outlaw discrimination on the basis of race, religion, or national origin in the sale and rental of most forms of housing in the United States, as well as in the advertising, listing, and financing of housing. Exempted from the act's coverage were single-family houses not listed with real estate agents and small apartment buildings lived in by the owner. (About a month after the act became law, the Supreme Court ruled, in the case of *Jones v. Alfred H. Mayer Company*, that the Civil Rights Act of 1866 prohibited racial discrimination in housing and other property transactions.) Two other provisions of the act also grew out of the racial turmoil of the 1960's. One enumerated specific civil rights whose violations were punishable under federal law. Another sought to make the act more acceptable to the growing number of Americans concerned about urban riots by specifying stiff penalties for inciting or engaging in riots.

As a housing measure, the act proved disappointing. Its enforcement provisions were weak. Those with complaints of discrimination were directed to file them with the Department of Housing and Urban Development (HUD), which would then attempt to negotiate a voluntary settlement. If this failed, complainants would have to file their own lawsuits; the federal government would intervene only in cases where there was a clear pattern of past discrimination. In addition, white resentment at attempts to integrate neighborhoods remained high. Banks often found ways to avoid the law's provisions, making it difficult for many African American families to secure necessary financing. By the late twentieth century, it was clear that the act had not ended the country's dominant pattern of racial segregation in housing.

INDIAN BILL OF RIGHTS

The Civil Rights Act of 1968 contained another provision unrelated to concerns over fair housing: the Indian Bill of Rights, also known as the Indian Civil Rights Act. This was grounded in the fact that Indians on reservations, as members of tribal communities, were not considered to be covered by the Bill of Rights. In 1896, the Supreme Court had ruled, in the case of *Talton v. Mayes*, that the Bill of Rights did not apply to Indian tribes or to their courts. In 1961, Senator Sam Ervin, a North Carolina Democrat, was surprised to discover the fact. Over the next several years, he held hearings on the subject. In 1968, he was able to amend the civil rights bill moving through the Senate to include coverage of Indian rights.

The Indian Bill of Rights extended a variety of constitutional protections to Native Americans with regard to the authority of their tribal governments. Among these were freedom of speech and religion, as well as protections for those suspected or accused of crimes. In fact, all or part of the First, Fourth, Fifth, Six, and Eighth Amendments were held to apply to reservation Indians, as was the Fourteenth Amendment's guarantee of due process. Some parts of the Bill of Rights were not included, however; the First

Amendment's ban of religious establishments was not included, in deference to tribal customs, nor were the Second Amendment's right to bear arms or the Third's prohibition against the quartering of troops. Most important to most Indians was a provision that required tribal permission before states could further extend jurisdiction over tribal land.

William C. Lowe

SOURCES FOR FURTHER STUDY
Johnson, Lyndon B. *The Vantage Point: Perspectives of the Presidency 1963-1969.* New York: Holt, Rinehart and Winston, 1971.
Kushner, James A. *Fair Housing: Discrimination in Real Estate, Community Development, and Revitalization.* New York: McGraw-Hill, 1983.
Nieman, Donald G. *Promises to Keep: African-Americans and the Constitutional Order, 1776 to the Present.* New York: Oxford University Press, 1991.
Smolla, Rodney A., and Chester James Antieau. *Federal Civil Rights Acts* 2 vols. 3rd ed. Deerfield, Ill.: Clark Boardman Callaghan, 1994.
Wunder, John R. *"Retained by the People": A History of the American Indians and the Bill of Rights.* New York: Oxford University Press, 1994.

SEE ALSO: Civil Rights Act of 1866 (1866); Fourteenth Amendment (1868); Housing Act (1961); Civil Rights Act of 1964 (1964); Title VII of the Civil Rights Act of 1964 (1964); Housing and Urban Development Act (1965); Fair Housing Act (1968); Indian Civil Rights Act (1968).

FAIR HOUSING ACT

ALSO KNOWN AS: Part of the Civil Rights Act of 1968
DATE: April 11, 1968
U.S. STATUTES AT LARGE: 82 Stat. 81
PUBLIC LAW: 90-284
U.S. CODE: 42 § 3601
CATEGORIES: African Americans; Civil Rights and Liberties; Health and Welfare; Housing

The act prohibited discrimination in housing, helping to break racial enclaves in residential neighborhoods and promoting upward mobility for minorities.

The Civil Rights Act of 1866 provided that all citizens should have the same rights "to inherit, purchase, lease, sell, hold, and convey real and personal property," but the law was never enforced. Instead, such federal agencies as the Farmers Home Administration, the Federal Housing Administration, and the Veterans Administration financially supported segregated housing until 1962, when President John F. Kennedy issued Executive Order 11063 to stop the practice.

California passed a general nondiscrimination law in 1959 and an explicit fair housing law in 1963. In 1964, voters enacted Proposition 14, an initiative to repeal the 1963 statute and the applicability of the 1959 law to housing. When a landlord in Santa Ana refused to rent to an African American in 1963, the latter sued, thus challenging Proposition 14. The California Supreme Court, which heard the case in 1966, ruled that Proposition 14 was contrary to the Fourteenth Amendment to the U.S. Constitution, because it was not neutral on the matter of housing discrimination; instead, based on the context in which it was adopted, Proposition 14 served to legitimate and promote discrimination. On appeal, the U.S. Supreme Court let the California Supreme Court decision stand in *Reitman v. Mulkey* (1967).

JOHNSON'S EFFORTS

President Lyndon B. Johnson had hoped to include housing discrimination as a provision in the comprehensive Civil Rights Act of 1964, but he demurred when southern senators threatened to block the nomination of Robert Weaver as the first African American cabinet appointee. After 1964, southern members of Congress were adamantly opposed to any expansion of civil rights. Although Johnson urged passage of a federal law against housing discrimination in requests to Congress in 1966 and 1967, there was no mention of the idea during his State of the Union address in 1968. Liberal members of Congress pressed the issue regardless, and southern senators responded by threatening a filibuster. This threat emboldened Senators Edward W. Brooke and Walter F. Mondale, a moderate Republican and a liberal Democrat, respectively, to cosponsor fair housing legislation, but they needed the support of conservative midwestern Republicans to break a filibuster. Illinois Republican senator Everett Dirksen arranged a compromise whereby housing discrimination would be declared illegal, but federal enforcement power would be minimal.

In the wake of *Reitman v. Mulkey,* the assassination of Martin Luther King, Jr., on April 4, 1968, and subsequent urban riots, Congress established fair housing as a national priority on April 10 by adopting Titles VIII and IX of the Civil Rights Act of 1968, also known as the Fair Housing Act or Open Housing Act. Signed by Johnson on the following day, the law originally prohibited discrimination in housing on the basis of race, color, religion, or national origin. In 1974, an amendment expanded the coverage to include sex (gender) discrimination; in 1988, the law was extended to protect persons with disabilities and families with children younger than eighteen years of age.

TITLE VIII PROVISIONS

Title VIII prohibits discrimination in the sale or rental of dwellings, in the financing of housing, in advertising, in the use of a multiple listing service, and in practices that "otherwise make unavailable or deny" housing, a phrase that some courts have interpreted to outlaw exclusionary zoning, mortgage redlining, and racial steering. Blockbusting, the practice of inducing a white homeowner to sell to a minority buyer in order to frighten others on the block to sell their houses at a loss, is also prohibited. It is not necessary to show intent in order to prove discrimination; policies, practices, and procedures that have the effect of excluding minorities, women, handicapped persons, and children are illegal, unless otherwise deemed reasonable. Title VIII, as amended in 1988, covers persons who believe that they are adversely affected by a discriminatory policy, practice, or procedure, even before they incur damages.

The law applies to about 80 percent of all housing in the United States. One exception to the statute is a single-family house sold or rented without the use of a broker and without discriminatory advertising, when the owner owns no more than three such houses and sells only one house in a two-year period. Neither does the statute apply to a four-unit dwelling if the owner lives in one of the units, the so-called Mrs.-Murphy's-rooming-house exception. Dwellings owned by private clubs or religious organizations that rent to their own members on a noncommercial basis are also exempt.

ENFORCEMENT

Enforcement of the statute was left to the secretary of the Department of Housing and Urban Development (HUD). Complaints originally had to be filed within 180 days of the offending act, but in 1988, this period was amended to one year. HUD has estimated that there are about two million instances of housing discrimination each year, although formal complaints have averaged only forty thousand per year. The U.S. attorney general can bring a civil suit against a flagrant violator of the law.

According to the law, HUD automatically refers complaints to local agencies that administer "substantially equivalent" fair housing laws. HUD can act if the local agencies fail to do so, but initially was expected only to use conference, conciliation, and persuasion to bring about voluntary compliance. The Fair Housing Amendments Act of 1988 authorized an administrative law tribunal to hear cases that cannot be settled by persuasion. The administrative law judges have the power to issue cease and desist orders to offending parties.

HUD has used "testers" to show discrimination. For example, a team of blacks and whites might arrange to have an African American apply for a rental; if turned down, the black tester would contact a white tester to ascertain whether the landlord were willing to rent to a white instead. That testers have standing to sue was established by the U.S. Supreme Court in *Havens v. Coleman* (1982).

Under the administrative law procedure, penalties are up to $10,000 for the first offense, $25,000 for the second offense, and $50,000 for each offense thereafter. Attorneys' fees and court costs can be recovered by the prevailing party. In 1988, civil penalties in a suit filed by the U.S. attorney general were established as up to $50,000 for the first offense and $100,000 for each offense thereafter.

TITLE IX PROVISIONS

Title IX of the law prohibits intimidation or attempted injury of anyone filing a housing discrimination complaint. A violator can be assessed a criminal penalty of $1,000 and/or sentenced to one year in jail. If a complainant is actually injured, the penalty can increase to $10,000 and/or ten years of imprisonment. If a complainant is killed, the penalty is life imprisonment.

Under the laws of some states, a complainant filing with a state agency must waive the right to pursue a remedy under federal law. In 1965, a couple sought to purchase a home in a St. Louis suburban housing development, only to be told by the realtor that the home was not available because one of the spouses was African American. Invoking the Civil Rights Act of 1866, the couple sued the real estate developer, and the case went to the Supreme Court. In *Jones v. Alfred H. Mayer Company* (1968), the Court decided that the Civil Rights Act of 1866 did permit a remedy against housing discrimination by private parties.

The effect of the 1968 Fair Housing Act, however, has been minimal. Without a larger supply of affordable housing, many African Americans in particular have nowhere to move in order to enjoy integrated housing. Federal subsidies for low-cost housing, under such legislation as the Housing and Urban Development Act of 1968 and the Housing and Community Development Act of 1974, have declined significantly since the 1980's. Conscientious private developers are confronted with the text of a law that aims to provide integrated housing but proscribes achieving integration by establishing quotas to ensure a mixed racial composition among those who seek to buy or rent dwelling units.

Michael Haas

Sources for Further Study

Kushner, James A. *Fair Housing: Discrimination in Real Estate, Community Development, and Revitalization.* Colorado Springs: McGraw-Hill, 1983.

Metcalf, George R. *Fair Housing Comes of Age.* New York: Greenwood Press, 1988.

Schwemm, Robert G., ed. *The Fair Housing Act After Twenty Years.* New Haven, Conn.: Yale Law School, 1989.

SEE ALSO: Civil Rights Act of 1866 (1866); Fourteenth Amendment (1868); Housing Act (1961); Civil Rights Act of 1964 (1964); Title VII of the Civil Rights Act of 1964 (1964); Housing and Urban Development Act (1965); Civil Rights Act of 1968; Indian Civil Rights Act (1968).

INDIAN CIVIL RIGHTS ACT

ALSO KNOWN AS: Indian Bill of Rights
DATE: April 11, 1968
U.S. STATUTES AT LARGE: 82 Stat. 77
PUBLIC LAW: 90-284
U.S. CODE: 25 § 1301
CATEGORIES: Civil Rights and Liberties; Native Americans

This controversial but important measure was designed to guarantee Indians living under tribal governments the same rights as those of other U.S. citizens.

A significant but controversial piece of legislation designed to guarantee the rights of individual American Indians came about in special Indian titles of the Civil Rights Act signed into law on April 11, 1968.

TRIBAL GOVERNMENTS

The existence of tribal governments and tribal courts had raised the issue of protection of the individual rights of American Indians living in a tribal context. Tribal governments have been considered to be inherently sovereign, because they predate the Constitution and do not derive their power to exist or to govern from either federal or state governments. Federal recognition or regulation of tribes does not make them part of the United States government or guarantee constitutional protection for tribal members. An 1896 Supreme Court case, *Talton v. Mayes*, determined that the Bill of Rights of the Constitution does not apply to tribes, because tribes derive and retain their sovereignty from their aboriginal self-governing status. The Indian Citizenship Act of 1924, which gave American Indians dual citizenship in their tribes and the United States, did not make the Bill of Rights applicable to situations involving tribal government.

There was little interest in the lack of individual rights for American Indians living a tribal existence until the 1960's, when national attention turned to civil rights. When the United States Senate began to investigate civil rights abuses throughout the nation, some attention was directed at tribal governments. In 1961, the Senate held hearings on civil rights issues on reservations, and investigators heard many examples of infringement on individual liberties and the lack of any way to redress grievances. Contributing to the problem was the fact that tribal societies emphasized the good of the group and were inclined to consider the good of the people as a whole more important than the preservation of individual rights.

An 1886 Supreme Court decision in *United States v. Kagama* determined that Congress has authority to govern the internal affairs of tribes and to make laws that directly affect American Indians. Therefore, Congress could impose restrictions on tribal governments and move toward granting greater individual protections to American Indians living on reservations.

CIVIL RIGHTS ACT OF 1968: TRIBAL INCLUSION
In 1968, when civil rights legislation was proposed to remedy the unequal protection of some groups in the United States, Senator Sam Ervin of North Carolina proposed bringing tribal governments under the constitutional framework of the United States. After a good deal of political maneuvering, Congressman Ben Reifel of South Dakota, a member of the Rosebud Sioux tribe, rallied support for the bill, and Public Law 90-284, the Indian Bill of Rights, or Indian Civil Rights Act, became law. This act was a set of special titles within the Civil Rights Act. It was intended to protect the rights of individual American Indians; however, it was controversial for its emphasis on individuals rather than the tribal group. The act was intended to preserve tribal autonomy while protecting the rights of individual tribal members. Largely as a result of tribal protests that the full Bill of Rights would severely upset traditional governing practices, a blanket imposition of the Bill of Rights on tribal governments was replaced by a more selective and specific list of individual rights that were to be protected. Those parts of the Bill of Rights that seemed to infringe on the special character of tribal government were omitted.

INDIAN BILL OF RIGHTS
The Indian Civil Rights Act prohibits tribal governments from interfering with freedom of speech, religion, press, assembly, and petition for redress of grievances. It specifically authorizes a writ of *habeas corpus* for anyone detained by the tribe, and it grants due process. This bill also protects the right of privacy against search

and seizure, using language identical to that of the Bill of Rights. The Indian Civil Rights Act does not guarantee persons free counsel in criminal proceedings nor the right of indictment by grand jury.

In addition to protecting individual freedoms, the Indian Civil Rights Act contains some provisions that impact tribal governments directly. The Indian Civil Rights Act permits tribal governments to establish an official tribal religion in order to allow the continuation of the quasi theocracies that form the basis of government in some American Indian communities. However, the act does require that individual freedom of religion be protected. The secretary of the interior is charged with the responsibility of drawing up codes of justice to be used in courts trying American Indian offenders. Assault resulting in serious bodily injury was added to the offenses on reservations that are subject to federal jurisdiction under the Major Crimes Act.

In an important victory for tribal autonomy, section 7 of Public Law 83-280 was repealed. Public Law 83-280, passed by Congress in 1953 in an attempt to abridge the rights of tribal courts, had given states the authority to extend civil and criminal jurisdiction over reservations. The passage of the Indian Civil Rights Act authorized the retrocession of jurisdiction already assumed by a state. A provision in the bill guaranteed the automatic approval of tribal contracts if the secretary of the interior did not act on a tribal request within ninety days.

CONTROVERSIES AND CHALLENGES
The Indian Civil Rights Act was controversial when it was proposed and has remained so. Many American Indians view it as an attempt to impose non-Indian values on tribal societies and regard it as a violation of tribal sovereignty, because Congress unilaterally imposed the bill on tribal governments and people. This raised many questions regarding the meaning of "consent." Tribes do not seek to be protected from misuse of power, but there are questions about both the legality and cultural implications of the Indian Civil Rights Act. The fact that Congress intended to bring tribal governments more within the constitutional framework of the United States caused a good deal of controversy. Tribes have questioned the legality of permitting Congress, which basically represents states, to have a direct role in the formulation and passage of a law for tribes. No mechanism was afforded for tribes to accept or reject

this legislation, although tribal cultures and customs are directly impacted by this law because it emphasizes individualism. Many tribal leaders feel the Indian Civil Rights Act restricts tribes in the exercise of their inherent sovereignty.

Since passage of the bill, numerous individual challenges to tribal authority have been litigated in federal courts, and many court decisions have favored the individual and weakened the concept of tribal sovereignty. More recent court decisions have tended to use tribal customs and traditions in interpreting the act. A landmark 1978 decision, *Santa Clara Pueblo v. Martinez*, supported a tribe's right to extend membership only to the children of male tribal members, as this was in keeping with tribal custom. The court ruled that it did not violate laws against sexual discrimination, because the Indian Civil Rights Act had a dual purpose of protecting individual rights as well as tribal autonomy.

Carole A. Barrett

Sources for Further Study

Clarkin, Thomas. *Federal Indian Policy in the Kennedy and Johnson Administrations, 1961-1969.* Albuquerque: University of New Mexico Press, 2001.

Deloria, Vine, Jr., ed. *American Indian Policy in the Twentieth Century.* Norman: University of Oklahoma Press, 1985.

Deloria, Vine, Jr., and Clifford M. Lytle. *The Nations Within: The Past and Future of American Indian Sovereignty.* New York: Pantheon Books, 1984.

Olson, James S., and Raymond Wilson. *Native Americans in the Twentieth Century.* Chicago: University of Illinois Press, 1984.

Prucha, Francis Paul. *The Great Father: The United States Government and the American Indians.* Lincoln: University of Nebraska Press, 1984.

Wunder, John R. *"Retained by the People": A History of American Indians and the Bill of the Rights.* New York: Oxford University Press, 1994.

See also: Indian Citizenship Act (1924); Indian Reorganization Act (1934); Oklahoma Welfare Act (1936); Termination Resolution (1953); Public Law 280 (1953); Housing Act (1961); Housing and Urban Development Act (1965); Civil Rights Act of 1968 (1968); Fair Housing Act (1968).

CONSUMER CREDIT PROTECTION ACT

DATE: May 29, 1968
U.S. STATUTES AT LARGE: 82 Stat. 146
PUBLIC LAW: 90-321
U.S. CODE: 15 § 1601
CATEGORIES: Banking, Money, and Finance

> *The act required creditors to provide clear and adequate information about the cost of borrowing and enacted protections regarding wage garnishment and loan sharking.*

The Consumer Credit Protection Act was signed into law by President Lyndon B. Johnson on May 29, 1968. The law had the longest legislative history of any consumer bill. It was introduced each year in the Senate beginning in 1960 but failed to receive committee approval for eight years. Despite the long struggle to get it passed, the final legislation was stronger than the original version.

BACKGROUND

Consumer protection began early in the history of the United States, primarily as governmental regulation of economic activities. The Interstate Commerce Act of 1887 was the first federal legislation that regulated an industry. It resulted in the creation of the first regulatory commission, which produced rules that were models for later legislation designed to ensure consumer protection. Legislation in the early twentieth century focused on the safety, purity, and advertising claims of foods, drugs, and cosmetics. The Federal Trade Commission was set up in 1914 to maintain free and fair competition and to protect consumers against unfair or misleading business practices.

After World War II, Americans were eager to buy new products. Because they had come to trust producers and believed themselves to be protected by government oversight, they had little concern about the quality or safety of products. Goods were produced as quickly as possible to satisfy demand. Advertising gained a new level of sophistication by playing to the psychological needs of individuals. In 1957, these tactics were exposed in a book called *The Hidden Persuaders* by Vance Packard, and the buying public became indignant. The consumer movement began to take shape.

The idea of truth in lending originated with Senator Paul Douglas, who believed that lenders deceived borrowers about the true annual rate of interest. The practice of charging interest on the original amount of the loan, rather than on the declining balance as an installment loan was paid off, resulted in a true annual rate that was sometimes as high as twice the stated rate. Consumers, who generally were not knowledgeable in financial matters and were unaware of the methods of interest calculation, were paying a high cost for credit. They were unable to compare the costs of borrowing from various lenders because there was no requirement of standard, accurate, and understandable disclosures of the actual cost of borrowing.

In 1960, Douglas introduced a truth in lending bill in the Senate. In addition to requiring disclosure of the dollar amounts of the loan, the down payment, charges not related to the financing, and the total financing charges, the bill also required finance costs to be disclosed as an annual interest rate, based on the unpaid balance of the loan. Retailers, banks, and loan companies objected to the annual percentage rate (APR) disclosure requirement. First, it was argued that consumers were accustomed to the monthly rates currently reported and would find the change confusing. Second, many sellers believed that the reporting of a much higher true annual rate of interest would result in reduced consumer purchases. Some argued that this would seriously hurt the economy. Other objections included the contention that the law would not do any good, since the cost of merchandise could simply be increased to hide the cost of credit, and that regulations in this area were the responsibility of the states, not of the federal government. In addition, it was feared that it would be costly and difficult to train retail personnel in the new credit procedures necessary to comply with the requirements.

Consumer protection supporters and activists were primarily liberal Democrats, and consumer protection bills were initially seen as part of a liberal agenda. Voting in committees was mostly partisan. This slowed consumer legislation in Congress. Business organizations also lobbied against most consumer legislation. Interference from the federal government was considered to be unnecessary and an infringement on their rights.

In 1960, John F. Kennedy campaigned for election as president as an advocate of consumer protection. Once elected, he proposed a "Consumer Bill of Rights," to include the right to safety (protection against dangerous products), the right to be informed (protection against fraud and misinformation), the right to choose (adequate competition), and the right to be heard (government responsiveness to consumer issues). Kennedy asked Congress to enact new food and drug regulations, strengthen antitrust laws, and pass truth in lending legislation.

PASSAGE THROUGH CONGRESS
In the version of the bill proposed in 1964, revolving credit arrangements, such as retail store credit accounts, were exempted from the annual percentage rate disclosure. The bill gained more acceptance, but it died because of strong opposition by the chair of the Committee on Banking and Currency, Senator A. Willis Robertson. In the 1966 election, senators Douglas and Robertson lost their bids for reelection so were no longer on that committee in 1967 when Senator William Proxmire reintroduced the bill. Senator Proxmire was more willing than Senator Douglas had been to bargain and compromise. The bill was debated in the Financial Institutions Subcommittee of the Committee on Banking and Currency. The bill cleared the subcommittee and the committee, then was passed by the Senate by a 92-0 vote.

Congress's attitude toward consumer bills was changing dramatically as a tide of consumer activism grow in the United States. The National Traffic and Motor Vehicle Safety Act of 1966 had proved to be a popular bill. Media coverage played an important role in the passage of that bill and helped gain attention for other pending consumer legislation.

Leonor Sullivan, an eight-term Democratic congresswoman on the Consumer Affairs Subcommittee of the House Committee on Banking and Currency, authored the House version of the truth in lending bill. After battling unsuccessfully to strengthen the bill in the committee, she fought vigorously on the House floor, where several amendments were added, making the bill stronger than the Senate version. The APR disclosure exemption for revolving credit was dropped. Restrictions were included on wage garnishment, whereby an individual's earnings are withheld from his or her paycheck for repayment of debt. Loan sharking was made a federal offense, with severe penalties when interest rates were charged in excess of the usury levels in each state. The bill also established a

Consumer Finance Commission to study the consumer finance industry. Publicity and strong public support for the bill resulted in the stronger House version clearing the conference committee.

TRUTH IN LENDING ACT

The main section of the bill is Title I, the Truth in Lending Act, which requires, before credit is extended, disclosure of the APR and all finance charges, as dollar amounts, along with other loan terms and conditions. Advertisements that included certain financing terms required further elaboration. Specifically, any advertisement that included the down payment, the amount of each payment, the number of payments, the period of repayment, the dollar amount of any finance charge, or a statement that there was no charge for credit also had to disclose the cash price or the amount of the loan; the amount of down payment or a statement that none was required; the number, amount, and frequency of payments; the annual percentage rate; and the deferred payment price or the total dollar amount of the payments. Additionally, the bill provided for the right of the consumer to cancel a consumer credit agreement within three days if a second mortgage was taken on the consumer's residence. The Federal Reserve Board was required to draft regulations that implemented the law. Regulation Z was issued on February 10, 1969. Regulations were to be enforced by nine different federal agencies, including the Federal Trade Commission, the Federal Reserve Board, the National Credit Union Administration, the Comptroller of the Currency, the Federal Deposit Insurance Corporation, the Federal Home Loan Bank Board, the Interstate Commerce Commission, the Civil Aeronautics Board, and the Agriculture Department.

NADER AND CONSUMER ACTIVISM

In 1960, when Senator Douglas first introduced truth in lending legislation, there was little support for consumer issues in Congress. The powerful business community and the credit industry were opposed to the bill. Politics, partisanship, and special interests stalled the bill for many years. The refusal of Senator Douglas to publicly question the ethics of members of Congress with special interests or to question banks' opposition to the bill helped enable the fight to go on for years without much publicity. Growing consumer support for protective legislation was in part the result of the consumer protection activities of Ralph Nader. Nader's investigation of short-comings in automobile safety resulted in General Motors (GM) having him followed and investigated. The public was outraged at GM's attempts to discredit Nader. Media coverage further fueled consumer demands for protection from unscrupulous business practices. The Ninetieth Congress, which finally passed the Consumer Credit Protection Act, was described by President Johnson in his 1968 State of the Union message as "the Consumer Congress."

SIGNIFICANCE

The Consumer Credit Protection Act was intended to protect unsophisticated consumers from the hidden costs of borrowing or buying on credit. The concern of business that customers would buy fewer goods and borrow smaller amounts when they became aware of the true annual cost of borrowing apparently was unfounded, although it is impossible to say what consumer behavior would have been in the absence of the law. Continued use of credit in the early 1980's, with its high inflation and high interest rates, seemed to indicate that consumers were willing to use credit at almost any cost. When inflation was high, consumers learned that delaying their purchases resulted in a higher cost of goods, leading them to purchase immediately even at high interest rates. They continued to use credit even when the APR rose above 20 percent. Interest rates generally dropped in the later 1980's, but credit card interest rates remained high. Consumers, however, continued to increase their credit card debt.

The original truth in lending bill of Senator Douglas was intended to introduce competition to the area of consumer credit. Douglas had hoped that with comparable APR information, consumers would be able to shop for the best rates. One of the results of the legislation appeared to be that some businesses ceased to advertise their credit terms and rates. Whether this was a result of the truth in lending act or the tight supply of money soon after the law was enacted is difficult to ascertain. The main purpose of the bill would not have been realized if creditors gave little or no information in attempts to avoid violating the law.

Businesses were concerned about the cost of implementing the regulations. Costs arose from training employees, redesigning credit agreement forms to comply with required standards, educating customers about the information being provided to them, and calculation of complex APRs. In general, businesses found that these costs were not as high as had been anticipated. The government provided rate tables to figure APRs, and training and education did not require much time for most businesses.

SUBSEQUENT LEGISLATION
In 1971, the act was expanded to include a restriction on credit card issuers that they could not send unsolicited credit cards to consumers. A fifty-dollar limit was put on a credit cardholder's liability if there was unauthorized use of the card (for example, in case of a lost or stolen card). If the issuer was notified before any unauthorized use occurred, the cardholder was not liable for any charges. The Truth in Lending Simplification and Reform Act of 1982 was passed with a revised Regulation Z that corrected several weaknesses and ambiguities in the original law.

Further legislation covered other areas of concern. The Fair Credit Reporting Act (1970) dealt with credit reporting agencies, their practices, and consumers' rights regarding information in their credit files. The Fair Credit Billing Act (1974) dealt with billing errors and procedures to handle them. The Equal Credit Opportunity Act (1975 and 1977) prohibited discrimination in the granting of credit and provided for prompt responses to consumers regarding the acceptance or rejection of their credit applications. This act especially benefited women, who had previously had difficulties obtaining credit. The law required that credit decisions be made on the basis of qualifications regarding financial status rather than characteristics such as sex, marital status, race, age, religion, or national origin. The Fair Debt Collection Practices Act (1978) protected consumers from deceptive and abusive debt collectors and established procedures for debt collection. The Electronic Funds Transfer Act (1978) established the rights and responsibilities of users of electronic funds transfers.

Rajiv Kalra

SOURCES FOR FURTHER STUDY
Blackburn, John D., Elliot I. Klayman, and Martin H. Malin. *The Legal Environment of Business.* 3d ed. Homewood, Ill.: Irwin, 1988.
Eiler, Andrew. *The Consumer Protection Manual.* New York: Facts On File, 1984.

Faber, Doris. *Enough! The Revolt of the American Consumer.* New York: Farrar, Straus and Giroux, 1972.

Nadel, Mark V. *The Politics of Consumer Protection.* Indianapolis: Bobbs-Merrill, 1971.

SEE ALSO: Interstate Commerce Act (1887); Securities Exchange Act (1934); Truth in Lending Act (1968); Fair Credit Reporting Act (1970); Equal Credit Opportunity Act (1974).

TRUTH IN LENDING ACT

ALSO KNOWN AS: Title I of the Consumer Credit Protection Act
DATE: May 29, 1968
U.S. STATUTES AT LARGE: 82 Stat. 146
PUBLIC LAW: 90-321
U.S. CODE: 15 § 1601
CATEGORIES: Banking, Money, and Finance

This law required lenders to provide customers with standardized credit information regarding finance charges and annual percentage rates.

In the late 1960's, Congress became concerned that consumers were confused by the many ways credit costs were charged. Rather than legislate the method for imposing credit charges, Congress proposed that credit terms be disclosed in a uniform manner. Ideally, uniform disclosure would provide consumers with the information needed to compare credit terms and make informed decisions on the use of credit.

The Truth in Lending Act was introduced in 1960 by Senator Paul H. Douglas. Eight years of discussion and disagreement ensued concerning the need for such disclosure information. The credit industry voiced much concern over the difficulty in computing an annual rate. The average sales clerk, they agreed, would be unable to compute it without substantially increasing the cost of extending credit. They further stated that consumers did not really care about annual rates and would be confused by the information.

In fact, they might be shocked and reduce drastically the volume of credit purchases made. These concerns were dispelled in 1966 when the state of Massachusetts passed a truth in lending law and none of these problems materialized; however, debate concerning the method of computing and when these computations would be required continued.

Finally, in 1968, the Truth in Lending Act was passed, establishing standard disclosures for consumer credit nationwide. Federal Reserve Regulation Z implements the disclosure laws laid out in this act and requires lenders to

(1) provide borrowers with meaningful, written information on essential credit terms
(2) respond to consumer complaints of billing errors
(3) identify credit transactions on statements of accounts
(4) provide certain credit card rights
(5) provide estimates of disclosure information before consummation of mortgage transactions
(6) provide disclosure of credit terms in adjustable rate mortgages and home equity lines of credit, and
(7) comply with special advertising rules.

Under these rules, the dollar cost of credit must be disclosed as the "finance charge," and the cost must be calculated as a percentage of the amount being loaned, according to a uniform method for computing the "annual percentage rate."

The Truth in Lending Act is primarily a disclosure law. Some people mistakenly believe it is the law responsible for governing such things as usury rates, late payment charges, and methods of rebating unearned finance charges. While this act requires disclosure regarding these practices, it does not regulate the practices themselves.

Because of the complexity of the Truth in Lending Act, ten years after its enactment more than 80 percent of banks were not in full compliance. This situation led to the passage in 1980 of the Truth in Lending Simplification and Reform Act. This act was designed to make compliance easier, provide simpler disclosures to consumers, and significantly reduce the number of lawsuits that were being filed for technical violation of the law.

Patricia C. Matthews

SOURCES FOR FURTHER STUDY
Brandel, Roland E., Barry A. Abbott, and Joseph E. Terraciano. *Truth in Lending: A Comprehensive Guide.* 2d ed. New York: Aspen Law and Business, 1991.
National Consumer Law Center. *Truth in Lending.* Washington, D.C.: National Consumer Law Center, 1995.
Rohner, Ralph J., et al. *Rohner and Miller on Truth in Lending.* Chicago, Ill.: American Bar Association, 2000.

SEE ALSO: Interstate Commerce Act (1887); Securities Exchange Act (1934); Consumer Credit Protection Act (1968); Fair Credit Reporting Act (1970); Equal Credit Opportunity Act (1974).

OMNIBUS CRIME CONTROL AND SAFE STREETS ACT

DATE: June 19, 1968
U.S. STATUTES AT LARGE: 82 Stat. 197
PUBLIC LAW: 90-351
U.S. CODE: 42 § 3711 et seq.
CATEGORIES: Crimes and Criminal Procedure

This legislation marked the beginning of a major federal effort to help states and cities in the control of crime.

In his 1967 State of the Union Address, President Lyndon B. Johnson first suggested the adoption of legislation that would become the Omnibus Crime Control and Safe Streets Act of 1968. Increasing crime rates and the riots in U.S. inner cities in the mid-1960's had generated widespread public concern over crime. In its original form, the proposed act reflected many suggestions of the Katzenbach Commission, which Johnson had appointed in July, 1965. The proposed bill provided for categorical grants to state and local governments. These grants would provide funds for police training, for innovative criminal rehabilitation programs, and for increased restrictions on guns and on electronic surveillance.

LEGISLATION

The bill that finally emerged for Johnson's signature was considerably different from that originally proposed—sufficiently different that Johnson delayed signing the bill for several days and considered a veto. Legislative support for the bill (which was approved by margins of 72 to 4 in the Senate and 368 to 7 in the House), combined with the upcoming Democratic National Convention, served to pressure the president into signing the bill. The revised legislation provided for block grants to states and eliminated any direct aid to cities; it also banned wiretaps and electronic surveillance by private individuals. Nevertheless, the bill sanctioned the issuance of warrants for electronic surveillance by cities, states, and the national government, and it eased restrictions on gun licensing.

ADMINISTRATION

Congress took the administration of the program out of the hands of the Justice Department and placed it in the hands of the Law Enforcement Assistance Administration (LEAA), a new agency designed with a three-person leadership. In an attempt to avoid partisanship, no two members of the leadership could be members of the same political party; moreover, all three top administrators had to form a consensus before taking any action. This design slowed the implementation of the program, however, and the leadership structure was revised.

OPERATION

Over a period of twelve years, the LEAA provided more than $8 billion to state and local governments. States and cities used these funds for modernizing equipment, communication improvement, criminal-identification facilities, and laboratories. Funding was also available for police patrols in high-crime areas, for training and recruitment of police, for criminal-rehabilitation efforts, and for crime-prevention programs. For several reasons, the largest portion of the funding usually went to equipment rather than personnel. A provision of the initial act limited funding for personnel to one-third of the total. States and cities were also often wary about using federal funds for personnel, because if a cutback in federal funds occurred, reductions in personnel would be more difficult than reductions in equipment expenditures. By the end of Jimmy Carter's administration, budget requests exceeded $400 million a year, and Congress essentially stopped the funding. In the early part of President Ronald Reagan's first term, Attorney General Edwin Meese presided over the final days of the LEAA.

Jerry A. Murtagh

SOURCE FOR FURTHER STUDY
Legislative History of the 1971 Amendments to the Omnibus Crime Control and Safe Streets Act of 1968. Washington, D.C.: Government Printing Office, 1972.

SEE ALSO: Comprehensive Drug Abuse Prevention and Control Act (1970); Organized Crime Control Act (1970); Racketeer Influenced and Corrupt Organizations Act (1970); Juvenile Justice and Delinquency Prevention Act (1974); Comprehensive Crime Control Act (1984); Violent Crime Control and Law Enforcement Act (1994).

NUCLEAR NONPROLIFERATION TREATY

DATE: Signed July 1, 1968; in force, March 5, 1970
CATEGORIES: Foreign Relations; Treaties and Agreements

The treaty, signed by ninety-seven nations, mandated on the nonproliferation of nuclear weapons.

Anxiety about the proliferation of nuclear weapons was the focus of a speech given by President John F. Kennedy in 1963 in which he said,

> I ask you to stop and think for a moment what it would mean to have nuclear weapons in many hands, in the hands of countries large and small, stable and unstable, responsible and irresponsible, scattered throughout the world. There would be no rest for anyone then, no stability, no real security, and no chance of effective disarmament.

Thirty years later, in 1993, President Bill Clinton addressed the United Nations with a similar appeal:

We simply have got to find ways to control these weapons and to reduce the number of states that possess them by supporting and strengthening the International Atomic Energy Agency. . . . I have made nonproliferation one of our nation's highest priorities.

AFTER WORLD WAR II: COLD WAR

The atomic bomb was developed by the United States during World War II. Enriched uranium was separated at Oak Ridge, Tennessee, plutonium was produced at Hanford, Washington, and the bomb detonation mechanism was designed at Los Alamos, New Mexico. The first successful test explosion was carried out in July, 1945, in the desert of New Mexico. Less than one month later, the cities of Hiroshima and Nagasaki were destroyed by atomic bombs, causing many casualties but also ending the war.

Once it had been shown that uranium and plutonium could be made into powerful explosives, several other countries soon developed their own bomb technology. The Soviet Union exploded an atomic bomb in 1949; Great Britain followed in 1952, France in 1960, and China in 1964. The hazards of radioactive fallout and radiation sickness had been dramatically demonstrated at Hiroshima. Nevertheless, the United States and the Soviet Union both embarked on military programs to build up huge arsenals with many bomb types and sizes.

In 1954, the United States detonated a hydrogen bomb at Bikini Atoll in the South Pacific. Its enormous explosive power was two hundred times greater than that of the Hiroshima bomb. A Japanese fishing boat, the *Lucky Dragon*, was contaminated by radioactive fallout when the wind shifted unexpectedly. The twenty-three sailors aboard suffered radiation poisoning, leading to worldwide protests against further testing. A group of Nobel Prize recipients, including Albert Einstein and Albert Schweitzer, wrote an appeal to the United Nations asking all countries to halt their bomb tests. Large antinuclear rallies mobilized public opinion against the escalating arms race.

Although the initial exploitation of nuclear energy was focused on producing weapons, there were found to be many nonmilitary applications for medicine, agriculture, industrial processes, and electric-power production. President Dwight D. Eisenhower launched an Atoms for Peace program in 1953 through the United Nations to publicize and advance peaceful uses of nuclear energy.

The International Atomic Energy Agency (IAEA) was created by the United Nations in 1957 with the dual mission of promoting civilian nuclear technology while restraining the arms race.

In 1958, President Eisenhower and Soviet premier Nikita Khrushchev agreed to a moratorium on nuclear weapons testing in the atmosphere. It lasted for almost three years. Renewed tension between the two superpowers arose in 1960 when an American U2 spy plane was shot down while flying over the Soviet Union. The Berlin crisis of 1961 further worsened political relations, and both countries resumed nuclear testing. The most powerful bomb in history was a 58-megaton device detonated by the Soviet Union in October, 1961.

The Cuban Missile Crisis of 1962 brought the world to the brink of nuclear war. President Kennedy threatened to seize several Soviet ships that were headed for Cuba carrying nuclear missiles. After several tense days, Khrushchev backed down and ordered the ships to return to Russia. The aftermath of this confrontation was the shared realization that the nuclear arms race could escalate into annihilation for both sides.

Subsequent negotiations between the superpowers led to a diplomatic breakthrough with the signing of the Limited Test Ban Treaty (or Nuclear Test Ban Treaty) of 1963, which prohibited nuclear explosions in the atmosphere, under the ocean, and in outer space. The 1963 treaty, however, still permitted underground explosions.

THE TREATY

Further negotiations between the United States, Great Britain, and the Soviet Union resulted in another major diplomatic accomplishment in 1968, the Nuclear Nonproliferation Treaty (NPT). The NPT stated that signatory countries possessing nuclear weapons would not transfer technology or materials to any other nation, while nonnuclear signatories pledged to refrain from trying to acquire nuclear weapons. When the treaty went into effect in 1970, ninety-seven countries had signed it.

Many smaller countries accepted the NPT because it was in their national self-interest to do so. They were spared the financial burden of acquiring a nuclear arsenal and could avoid the environmental hazards of testing. Furthermore, they hoped to reduce the danger that a regional border dispute might escalate from conventional to nuclear weapons. Countries that refused to accept the NPT in 1970 included France, China, India, Pakistan, Israel, South Africa, Argentina, and Brazil. They objected to the fact that the treaty allowed nuclear states to continue building up their arsenals without limit, while nonnuclear states were permanently excluded from joining the nuclear fraternity.

Signing the NPT was a voluntary commitment and could be revoked at will. By 1993, there were 161 signatories, including France and China, and no nation had withdrawn from the treaty, which was reaffirmed in 1995.

The Nuclear Nonproliferation Treaty made a sharp distinction between military and peaceful uses of nuclear energy. To provide an incentive for nonnuclear countries to support the NPT, the nuclear countries offered to share information about peaceful applications, including the technology of nuclear power plants. In return, the countries that received such aid agreed to allow on-site inspections of their facilities by the IAEA to verify that no weapons development was being done.

Many nonnuclear weapons states considered the IAEA inspection process an infringement of their national sovereignty. According to the 1970 treaty, states that already had nuclear weapons were not required to undergo inspections. Therefore, the original treaty was viewed as discriminatory, favoring the "haves" over the "have-nots." It was hoped that a broadened inspection policy, acceptable to both nuclear and nonnuclear states, would be negotiated in 1995.

POST-COLD WAR APPLICATIONS
After the defeat of Iraq in the Gulf War, the Security Council of the United Nations ordered a thorough inspection of all Iraq's nuclear facilities. Even though Iraq had signed the NPT and had been inspected twice a year, it had managed to establish two plutonium-production facilities. The IAEA board of governors strongly condemned Iraq's blatant violation of their NPT safeguards agreement, and the laboratories were dismantled. The incident demonstrated, however, that stricter inspection procedures needed to be developed.

The director-general of the IAEA, Hans Blix, recommended that satellite and other intelligence data should be collected and used to identify suspicious sites; that inspectors should be authorized to make unannounced site visits, without being subject to local visa requirements; that additional funding for personnel was needed, since the two hundred IAEA inspectors then engaged were inadequate for monitoring the more than one thousand nuclear facilities worldwide; and that the unified backing of the U.N. Security Council was needed to enforce the right of entry for investigators and possibly sanctions against violators.

In contrast to the experience in Iraq, the situation in South Africa provided grounds for optimism about the NPT's effectiveness. South Africa possessed deposits of uranium ore and was able to build facilities for producing enriched weapons-grade uranium in the 1970's. The country never conducted a nuclear test explosion but was thought to have accumulated a stockpile of six atomic bombs of the Hiroshima type. By 1991, when it became apparent that the widely condemned apartheid system soon would be dismantled, the South African government decided to join the NPT; it did so primarily to place its nuclear facilities under international control and out of the hands of the African National Congress. Shortly thereafter, the six bombs were dismantled, and the uranium fuel was converted back to its unenriched form. South Africa thus became a nuclear-armed country that relinquished its weapons voluntarily.

An unexpected form of nuclear proliferation occurred after the breakup of the Soviet Union in 1990, when Ukraine became an independent state. Ukraine returned all tactical nuclear weapons that had been stationed there to Russia but retained the remaining 1,650 strategic warheads with long-range missiles. Ukraine thus became an instant nuclear power with the third-largest arsenal in the world. It was hoped that an offer of international economic aid to Ukraine for industrial development would help in negotiating the dismantling of weapons.

When long-standing border disputes between neighboring nations remain unresolved, the incentive to acquire nuclear weapons increase. This was the case with Israel and the Arab states, with India and Pakistan, and with North and South Korea. In general, the nuclear nations restricted exports of nuclear materials and technology to these sensitive regions. Political and economic pressure from the world community, and even threats of military intervention, could also be brought to bear to maintain regional stability.

NONCOMPLIANCE AND THE NUCLEAR LEGACY

Nuclear proliferation normally is defined in terms of nonnuclear nations acquiring nuclear weapons. There is another side to this issue. From the perspective of nonnuclear countries, the United States and the Soviet Union had engaged in a world-threatening proliferation for forty years. Although the NPT in 1970 had called for "cessation of the nuclear arms race at an early date . . . under strict and effective international control," this did not happen.

A comprehensive test-ban agreement by the nuclear states—an extension of the 1963 treaty to apply the ban on nuclear explosions to underground explosions as well—would greatly have strengthened international support for the continuation of the NPT. By the mid-1990's, the United States had conducted more than seven hundred underground tests and the Soviet Union about five hundred. A voluntary moratorium on underground explosions went into effect in 1992, although it was quickly broken by China. It was hoped that a comprehensive test-ban treaty would eventually be agreed upon that would symbolize a formal end to the nuclear arms race.

The mass production of nuclear weapons left a legacy of radioactive contamination of the environment. Tanks of radioactive liquid at Hanford, Washington, plutonium contamination at Rocky Flats, Colorado, and residual radioactivity at the Nevada test site required costly cleanup. In the mid-1990's, Congress began to address the problem of compensation for armed forces veterans who had been exposed to excessive radiation. Similar situations existed in the Soviet Union and France. The disposition and safe storage of plutonium recovered from dismantled warheads also presented a difficult technical problem. An ongoing danger was the possibility that plutonium could fall into the hands of a dictator through theft. The best defense against the spread of nuclear weapons continued to be a community of nations strongly committed to nuclear disarmament.

Hans G. Graetzer

SOURCES FOR FURTHER STUDY

Barrillot, Bruno. "French Finesse Nuclear Future." *Bulletin of Atomic Scientists,* September, 1992, 23-36.

Blix, Hans. "The A-Bomb Squad." *World Monitor,* November, 1991, 18-21.

Boskey, Bennett, and Mason Willrich, eds. *Nuclear Proliferation: Prospects for Control.* New York: Dunellen, 1970.
Epstein, William. "The Proliferation of Nuclear Weapons." *Scientific American,* April, 1975, 18-33.
Gray, Peter. *Briefing Book on the Nonproliferation of Nuclear Weapons.* Washington, D.C.: Council for a Livable World, 1993.
Rathjens, George W., and Marvin M. Miller. "Nuclear Proliferation After the Cold War." *Technology Review,* August/September, 1991, 25-32.
Spector, Leonard S. *Nuclear Proliferation Today.* New York: Random House, 1984.

SEE ALSO: Nuclear Test Ban Treaty (1963); Seabed Treaty (1972); SALT I Treaty (1972); SALT II Treaty (1979); INF Treaty (1987); START II Treaty (1993); North Korea Pact (1994); U.S.-Russia Arms Agreement (2002).

AIRCRAFT NOISE ABATEMENT ACT

DATE: July 21, 1968
U.S. STATUTES AT LARGE: 82 Stat. 395
PUBLIC LAW: 90-411
U.S. CODE: 49 § 44715
CATEGORIES: Environment and Conservation

This amendment to the Federal Aviation Act of 1958 added a section titled "Control and Abatement of Aircraft Noise and Sonic Boom."

The tremendous growth of commercial jet aircraft traffic during the 1960's led to citizen complaints and lawsuits related to the noise pollution created by aircraft during takeoff and landing.

ROARING JETS, SONIC BOOMS
The problem was particularly acute over Long Island, New York, which was the confluence of flight paths for both Kennedy and LaGuardia airports, and over Washington, D.C., as a result of the proximity of National Airport to the center of the city. The introduction of commuter jets at National Airport in April, 1966, made

the noise problem considerably worse. Opponents had suggested using the new Dulles Airport, located twenty-six miles west of the city, for short-haul flights, and more than three dozen citizens' groups opposed allowing commuter jets to operate from National Airport. Nevertheless, approval for commuter jets was granted, perhaps because the principal users of this new service were people who preferred the convenience of arriving and departing a mere fifteen minutes from downtown Washington, D.C. As a result, during 1966, the modern, well-planned Dulles Airport served only 863,000 passengers, while pre-World War II National Airport accommodated 6,500,000 passengers.

By 1967, however, the complaints to congressional representatives became so severe that the House Interstate and Foreign Commerce Subcommittee on Transportation and Aeronautics began hearings with the aim of authorizing the transportation secretary to set aircraft noise regulations. Transportation Secretary Alan Boyd, chief administrative witness at these hearings, told the committee members that of all the subjects within the responsibility of the Transportation Department, noise abatement had become one of the most pressing. The secretary established study panels to investigate various aspects of aircraft noise such as aircraft noise research, aircraft operations, sonic boom research, airport and land use, and human response to noise.

Although there are special noise problems associated with jet aircraft takeoff and landing, the even more problematic noise known as sonic boom occurs whenever an airplane flies at a speed greater than the speed of sound (approximately 760 miles per hour at low altitudes). A sonic boom is a pressure-transient of short duration (about .25 seconds), analogous to the bow wave of a boat moving rapidly through the water. When the pressure waves from a supersonic aircraft are received on the ground, a double sonic boom is produced. The shock wave from the bow of the plane produces a large positive pressure increase, followed by a large negative pressure from the trailing edge. Since the pressure shock waves are produced during the entire time an airplane is in supersonic transit, not just at the moment it exceeds the speed of sound, the problem is severe over the entire flight path. Studies of sonic booms indicate that they can be quite destructive in occupied areas. They break windows, and cause structural damage and are extremely annoying to people.

During the late 1960's, the issue of sonic booms became prominent. Supersonic flight by military planes had been commonplace for more than a decade, but commercial airplanes that would routinely travel at speeds exceeding the speed of sound began to be developed. Three versions of the supersonic transport plane (SST) had been designed. Although none of these was operational yet, Anglo-French and Soviet versions existed as prototypes by 1968. A U.S. version of the SST designed by the Boeing Company was the most ambitious of these projects, having the largest capacity, the highest cruising speed (1,800 miles per hour), and the greatest estimated cost. Although the SST would be in competition with nonsupersonic jumbo jets such as the Boeing B-747 then being developed and tested, the only clear advantage to the SST would be its faster speed. Jumbo jets, which would be capable of carrying more passengers a greater distance for less money than the SST, were being financed entirely by the aviation industry, while the development of the American SST would require a massive government subsidy. In anticipation of the issues and problems that might occur when commercial supersonic transportation become a reality, the subject of nonmilitary sonic booms was addressed in the Aircraft Noise Abatement Act.

Setting Standards for Aircraft Noise

On May 23, 1968, the House Interstate and Foreign Commerce Committee, chaired by Harley O. Staggers, introduced H.R. 3400, to provide for nonmilitary aircraft noise abatement. It gave the Federal Aviation Administration (FAA) the power to set aircraft noise and sonic boom standards as part of its authority to certify aircraft for use. In their supporting report, the committee said the bill was intended to reduce all undesirable aircraft noise to the lowest possible level of disturbance consonant with the public interest and to afford the public present and future relief and protection from all unnecessary aircraft noise, including sonic booms.

On July 10, the House unanimously passed H.R. 3400 and sent it to the Senate. In reporting on this action, Congressman Staggers stated that this was a simple but important amendment to the Federal Aviation Act because, although the FAA had a program to reduce aircraft noise, it had no specific authority to set standards, rules, or regulations. H.R. 3400 provided this authority by charging the FAA with the responsibility of actively carrying forward a noise-reduction effort.

On July 1, the Senate Commerce Committee, chaired by Senator Warren G. Magnuson, reported H.R. 3400 without amendments. The committee believed that aircraft noise had become such a serious problem in so many locales that the problem must be alleviated. It reported that the first order of business was to stop the escalation of aircraft noise by imposing noise reduction standards. These standards required the full application of noise reduction technology, since a completely quiet airplane was not likely in the foreseeable future.

After receiving the final version of the bill from the House, the Senate passed H.R. 3400 and sent it to President Lyndon B. Johnson for his signature. The action came after rejection of an amendment that proposed that the FAA embark upon a two-year scientific investigation of sonic booms and their effects. It further banned all nonmilitary flights at supersonic speeds within U.S. territory except those conducted as part of the study. This ban would remain effective until Congress could review the results and determine whether the prohibition against supersonic flights should be continued.

PROVISIONS

As enacted, H.R. 3400 became an amendment to the Federal Aviation Act of 1958. The provisions of this amendment require the administrator of the FAA, after consultation with the secretary of transportation, to prescribe standards for the measurement of aircraft noise and sonic boom, and to prescribe rules and regulations to control and abate these noise levels. The act also directed the FAA administrator, in prescribing the standards and regulations, to consider all relevant available data, including the results of research, development, and testing and to consult with the appropriate federal and state agencies. Finally, the administrator was charged with considering whether proposed regulations were consistent with the highest degree of air safety as well as economically feasible and technically practical.

EFFECTIVENESS AND SUBSEQUENT LEGISLATION

Although the Aircraft Noise Abatement Act was an attempt to reduce aircraft noise by government regulation, and technological advances were required to meet mandated requirements, the restrictions were rapidly offset by the increase in the number of flights at almost all airports. Thus, aircraft noise continued to be a major environmental problem.

Prior to the passage of the Aircraft Noise Abatement Act, several congressional representatives, despairing of ever persuading the FAA to impose a ban of SST supersonic flight over land, introduced bills to ban such flights. In 1968, Senator Clifford P. Case introduced a bill that would have banned SST supersonic flight over any U.S. territory, but the bill was not passed. That same year, Congressmen T. R. Kuperfman, R. L. Ottinger, and ten colleagues introduced a resolution termed the "National Conservation Bill of Rights" that would have banned harassing booms. In February, 1969, Senator Case unsuccessfully reintroduced his antiboom bill, and in September of the same year, a nearly equivalent bill was voted down by the House. Although H.R. 3400, the Aircraft Noise Abatement Act, addressed the issue of sonic booms by authorizing the FAA to set limits on SST booms, the FAA declined to set such limits. It is useful to remember that the FAA had an interest in seeing the SST developed, and was therefore reluctant to establish limits on sonic boom noise, or even other aircraft noise. Senator Case likened this situation to "setting the fox to guard the chickens."

Because of the apparent reluctance of the FAA to set noise control standards, an attempt was made by Congressman John W. Wydler to add an amendment to the Noise Control Act of 1972 during debate of this act on the House floor. Charging that the FAA had not used its authority to set noise limits during the four-year interim since the Aircraft Noise Reduction Act became law, his amendment would place primary regulatory power with the Environmental Protection Agency (EPA). Congressman Staggers felt that the lack of aviation expertise in the EPA would ultimately endanger public safety. Consequently, this amendment was defeated by voice vote. Nevertheless, the final version of the Noise Control Act required the FAA, after consulting with the EPA, to set standards for the measurement, control, and abatement of aircraft noise and sonic booms. The EPA was directed to submit proposed control regulations to the FAA. The FAA, in turn, was required to begin proposed rule-making procedures within thirty days, and to hold hearings within sixty days. The FAA was further required to either approve, modify, or reject, the EPA's proposed rules. If any

EPA rules were rejected, however, the FAA was obligated to publicly explain the reasons in detail.

During the same House debate, an amendment to prohibit sonic booms over U.S. territory by commercial jets was once again introduced and defeated. This time, Congress was assured that work was in progress and that an FAA regulation of sonic booms would be issued soon. Officials believed that sonic boom prohibition should be done by FAA regulation rather than by act of Congress, because regulations are more flexible than laws.

The long-term result of the Aircraft Noise Abatement Act and the additional pressure put on the FAA by the section of the Noise Abatement Act that dealt with aircraft noise was that the U.S. development of a civilian SST was cancelled. The Russian and the Anglo-French versions have been operational since the 1970's. The cancellation resulted from an increased public awareness of the problems, combined with the untenable cost of the U.S. development program. The resulting FAA regulations, titled Federal Aviation Regulation 36 (FAR-36), forbade sonic booms over U.S. territory by civilian aircraft. Military craft are allowed to continue a limited number of supersonic operations over land areas.

FAR-36 also imposed rather strict noise limits, during takeoff and during landings, on aircraft certified for flight after 1969. Existing jet engines were consequently retrofitted to meet the FAR-36 standard, although airlines were initially reluctant to invest large sums of money on a retrofitting program. Nevertheless, a considerable proportion of the existing fleet was thus quieted. These craft were given promotional names such as "whisperjet" or "whisperliner" to alert the public to the fact that aircraft noise was being reduced. Additional noise reduction was effected by moving flight patterns away from residential areas where possible, adding sound barriers around airport ramps, and using zoning laws to create buffer regions near new airports.

George R. Plitnik

SOURCES FOR FURTHER STUDY

Shurcliff, W. A. *SST and Sonic Boom Handbook.* New York: Ballantine, 1970.

Strong, W. J., and G. R. Plitnik. *Music, Speech, and Audio.* Provo, Utah: Soundprint, 1992.

U.S. Environmental Protection Agency. *Report on Aircraft-Airport Noise.* Washington, D.C.: Government Printing Office, 1973.

U.S. Environmental Protection Agency. Office of Noise Abatement and Control. *Manufacturing and Transportation Noise.* Vol. 2 in *Public Hearings on Noise Abatement and Control.* Washington, D.C.: Government Printing Office, 1972.

U.S. Federal Council for Science and Technology. Committee on Environmental Quality. *Noise: Sound Without Value.* Washington, D.C.: Government Printing Office, 1968.

SEE ALSO: Noise Control Act (1972).

ARCHITECTURAL BARRIERS ACT

DATE: August 12, 1968
U.S. STATUTES AT LARGE: 82 Stat. 718
PUBLIC LAW: 90-480
U.S. CODE: 42 § 4151
CATEGORIES: Disability Issues; Health and Welfare

The act represented the first federal legislation calling for the removal of barriers that prevented the access of people with disabilities to publicly owned buildings.

In 1957, Hugo Deffner, a disabled man from Oklahoma City, was named the Handicapped American of the Year for his one-man crusade against unnecessary barriers that physically bar the access of disabled people to post offices, museums, houses of worship, concert halls, and other public buildings.

ANSI STANDARDS FOR ACCESSIBILITY
Four years later, the American National Standards Institute, in cooperation with the National Easter Seal Society for Crippled Children and Adults, issued American National Standards Specifications for making buildings and facilities accessible to and usable by the physically handicapped (the A117.1 ANSI standards). These

set forth minimal requirements for sixteen aspects of building design, including grading, parking lots, walks, entrances, doors, doorways, and rest rooms. These standards, although ground-breaking, are generally considered to have been incomplete and minimal because they contained few descriptive drawings, were nonspecific, and did not cover residential buildings.

These standards were distributed to all the offices of the Department of Housing and Urban Development (HUD) and incorporated into the construction manual of the Department of Health, Education, and Welfare (HEW), which made the standards applicable to all new construction under its responsibility. A national education program was also undertaken to ensure that state and local governments adopted the standard. As a result of public education, a small number of important structures, such as New York City's Philharmonic Hall and LaGuardia Airport and University of California campuses at Davis and Riverside, were built to accommodate the physically disabled.

STUDIES ON REMOVING BARRIERS

By 1965, thirty-four states had some legislation describing the removal of barriers, but most laws were not comprehensive and lacked enforcement provisions. Few buildings were built in compliance with these laws. In November of that year, the first federal law designed to further the removal of architectural barriers was passed. Congress amended the Vocational Rehabilitation Act (Public Law 89-933), establishing a National Commission on Architectural Barriers. The commission's objective was to determine the extent to which architectural barriers impeded the access of handicapped people to public buildings, to determine what was being done by public and nonprofit organizations to remove these barriers, and to prepare a proposal for further action.

After two years of study, the National Commission on Architectural Barriers presented its findings to Wilbur J. Cohen, the secretary of HEW. The commission, headed by Leon Chatelain, Jr., who was also president of the National Society for Crippled Children and Adults, found that the single greatest obstacle to the employment of the handicapped was the design of the buildings in which they would work. The commission also presented evidence that the public was generally unaware of and unconcerned with the problem of architectural barriers, despite the education programs.

Sixty-four percent of Americans polled did not even realize that architectural barriers were a problem because they had not thought about the issue. Of 709 architects surveyed, 251 were not even aware of the ANSI standards. Only three of seven national building materials suppliers were familiar with the ANSI standards, and none had any policies to meet them. There were still no standard specifications for accessible transportation.

The problems of inaccessibility mostly involved curbs and steps; inaccessible elevators; steep and narrow walks; gratings in walkways; doors that were too narrow, revolved, or were hard to open; lack of parking spaces for the handicapped; lack of accommodations for wheelchairs; aisles that were too narrow; public toilet stalls and telephone booths that were too small; and telephones, drinking fountains, vending machines, light switches, and fire alarms that were too high. Among the worst offenders were, ironically, Social Security offices in small towns, often located on the second floor of a building without an elevator.

In light of the lack of public concern, the commission recommended that federal legislation be enacted requiring all new public buildings funded by the government to be designed for accessibility to the elderly and handicapped, that all federal agencies plan and budget for architectural changes to existing buildings to improve accessibility, that similar laws be passed on the state level, that building codes be revised, and that a government agency be established to administer this new legislation.

PASSAGE AND PROVISIONS

These recommendations substantially were adopted by the House of Representatives as legislation H.R. 6589 in the summer of 1968. A committee then set out to resolve the slight differences between this bill and a similar one passed in the Senate (S. 222). An agreement was reached, and the Architectural Barriers Act of 1968 (Public Law 90-480) was signed into law by President Lyndon B. Johnson on August 12. 1968. Sections authorized the head of the General Services Administration (GSA) and the secretaries of the departments of HUD and Defense, in consultation with the secretary of HEW, to issue standards for public buildings. The heads of these agencies were given authority to waive the standards on a case-by-case basis and authorized to undertake surveys and investigations to determine general compliance. The jurisdiction of the law included buildings and facilities constructed or altered by, or on behalf of, the United States government; buildings leased after alterations in accordance with the law; and buildings funded by government grants and loans. The act was amended in 1970 as Public Law 91-205, making it applicable to the District of Columbia metro facilities but not to the trains themselves.

IMPLEMENTATION
The month before the Architectural Barriers Act was passed, William A. Schmidt, commissioner of the Public Buildings Service of the General Services Administration, had warned building owners and operators that unless they provided for easy access for physically handicapped people they would risk losing government agencies as tenants. Schmidt noted that this was no small matter. At the time, government agencies as a group were one of the nation's biggest tenants, occupying 6.5 percent of the space in buildings owned and managed by members of the National Association of Building Owners and Managers. Schmidt said that more than 10 percent of the people in the United States, or twenty-two million, were handicapped, including those in wheelchairs and the elderly. He demanded that these people be given equal opportunity for gainful employment and other normal activities from which they had been barred, literally, by the design and construction of government buildings.

Noting the lack of a program to ensure compliance with the Architectural Barriers Act, Congress enacted the Rehabilitation Act of 1973 (Public Law 93-112). This law created the Architectural and Transportation Barriers Compliance Board (A&TBCB), which was conceived to be the primary force to ensure the full implementation of the earlier laws. Modified by an amendment to the 1973 law, the A&TBCB was made up of the heads of the departments of HEW, Transportation, HUD, Labor, the Interior, and Defense and the heads of the GSA, Postal Service, and Veterans Administration.

In 1975, the General Accounting Office (GAO), responding to a request from Congress, determined the effectiveness of the Architectural Barriers Act. The GAO inspected 314 federally financed buildings and architectural plans for buildings, all of which were built, altered, leased, or designed after the 1968 act was implemented. None of them fully complied with the law, and most buildings showed halfhearted compliance. For example, wheelchair ramps were constructed, but they were too long, slick, or steep; doors were built wide enough for wheelchairs but were blocked by ledges. The GAO's report also cited inconvenient elevator controls and controls for heat, air conditioning, and lighting in bathrooms; high curbs; and water fountains that were too high. Although the government, private contractors, and building designers all agreed that the cost of incorporating accessibility features into new buildings was as low as one-tenth of 1 percent of total construction costs, little was being done. It was clear that the 1968 act had fallen short of its goals: It delegated authority too much, allowing different government agencies the discretion of implementing proper action, performing surveys, and waiving standards case by case. It also did not cover privately owned residential structures leased for public housing.

David R. Williamson, executive director of National Paraplegia, noted that when the Post Office was reorganized in 1970 and taken out of government surveillance, it was also (perhaps inadvertently) exempted from the 1968 law. When Williamson went to his local post office in Chicago, he could get into the front door but no further, because steps blocked his path to the main area of business. Usually, he had to request that a passerby go to a window to get an employee's attention for him. If no passersby were around, he would yell. The longer he waited, the louder he would yell. The entire process was frustrating and demeaning.

LEGACY OF THE ACT

Progress since 1975 has been slow but visible. The Center for Independent Living, established in 1972 as a workshop and growth center for the disabled in the San Francisco area, became a model for changing the environment to meet the needs of disabled people. After much time and effort was spent, the ANSI standards were revised in 1980. Descriptions of curb ramps, bathrooms, and kitchens were added, as were more figures and mandatory specifications. These additions corrected earlier deficiencies of this standard. Many reports, studies, and books have been published, so public awareness has increased. Many physical barriers have been removed. State legislation has improved, and the United Nations even had a special year to highlight the problem.

Frank Wu

SOURCES FOR FURTHER STUDY

Bednar, Michael J., ed. *Barrier-Free Environments.* Stroudsburg, Pa: Dowden, Hutchinson and Ross, 1977.

Lifchez, Raymond, and Barbara Winslow. *Design for Independent Living.* Berkeley: University of California Press, 1979.

Robinette, Gary O., ed. *Barrier-Free Exterior Design: Anyone Can Go Anywhere.* New York: Van Nostrand Reinhold, 1985.

Speck, Benjamin. *Caring for Your Disabled Child.* New York: Macmillan, 1965.

U.S. Architectural and Transportation Barriers Compliance Board. *Resource Guide to Literature on Barrier-Free Environments.* Washington, D.C.: Government Printing Office, 1980.

U.S. Congress. Committee on Public Works and Transportation. *Effectiveness of the Architectural Barriers Act of 1968.* Washington, D.C.: Government Printing Office, 1976.

SEE ALSO: Americans with Disabilities Act (1990).

WHOLESOME POULTRY PRODUCTS ACT

DATE: August 18, 1968
U.S. STATUTES AT LARGE: 82 Stat. 791
PUBLIC LAW: 90-492
U.S. CODE: 21 § 451
CATEGORIES: Agriculture; Animals; Food and Drugs

This law required uniform standards for poultry inspection and extended requirements to establishments not previously covered.

The Wholesome Poultry Products Act stipulates that poultry and poultry products must meet federal inspection standards. Prior to passage of this act, poultry processing plants were regulated by states or not at all. Poultry inspection processes therefore varied among states, resulting in some plants having modern equipment and sanitary conditions and other plants being less well equipped.

NEED FOR FEDERAL POULTRY REGULATION

The Wholesome Poultry Products Act requires that processors who prepare poultry and producers of foods containing poultry that are transported for sale across a state line meet federal inspection standards under the jurisdiction of the Department of Agriculture. Establishments that prepare or produce poultry for intrastate transport fall under the jurisdiction of state inspection. This act extended coverage of federal poultry inspection standards to establishments that had not previously been covered and provided a model for establishing inspection programs at the state level.

The objective of the Wholesome Poultry Products Act was to ensure uniform inspection across all states in the United States to increase consumer protection. Most poultry and poultry products produced in the United States move across state lines or through foreign commerce, so uniform standards among states are warranted. The act stipulates that "it is essential in the public interest that the health and welfare of consumers be protected by assuring that poultry products distributed to them are wholesome, not adulterated, and properly marked, labeled, and packaged."

HISTORY AND PREVIOUS LEGISLATION

The Wholesome Poultry Products Act followed the Wholesome Meat Act, passed in 1967. A consumer-protection movement had increased Americans' awareness of potential health and safety risks of meat-based food products. Consumer advocates and President Lyndon B. Johnson publicly supported improvements in inspection standards for food products in the United States. Once the Wholesome Meat Act was passed, the Amalgamated Meat Cutters joined with some members of Congress in requesting the poultry act. The meat cutters acted in part because they did not want to face regulation stricter than that applied to poultry processors. Later, a seafood act was introduced to complete consumer protection from animal foods.

Attention has been given to the safety of the practices of the meat processing industry since publication of Upton Sinclair's novel *The Jungle* (1906). That book alerted consumers to concerns about the safety of meat processing. The first law governing meat inspection, the Federal Meat Inspection Act, was implemented in 1907 as a direct result of Sinclair's book. Criticism of inspection practices of the 1960's may have led consumers to believe that conditions were still similar to those in the early 1900's. A resurgence in interest in food safety by policymakers led to the 1960's revisions of the meat act and the introduction of related acts, including the Wholesome Poultry Products Act.

Widespread consumer concern about the safety of the meat and poultry products available at supermarkets, commissaries, and delicatessens had the potential to substantially affect consumption. Because of the potential negative impact from consumer uneasiness, it was important to implement the new poultry inspection standards to restore consumer confidence in poultry products and to avoid substantial losses to producers of poultry and related foods.

Poultry products include, in addition to fresh and frozen poultry carcasses and pieces, canned and frozen foods containing poultry. The frozen foods industry had expanded by the 1960's to include prepared casseroles, dinners, entrées, hors d'oeuvres, pizzas, pot pies, and sauces. Also included in the 1968 Wholesome Poultry Products Act, and not previously included in standard inspections, were vending commissaries that prepare poultry products for off-premise sale. A commissary preparing such food items as casseroles, entrées, platters, and salads containing poultry was required to meet federally approved inspection guidelines throughout the facility.

The Fair Packaging and Labeling Act of 1966 was primarily targeted at nonfood items typically sold in grocery stores, but food and beverage packaging was affected by regulations for product weights or measures and manufacturer address requirements on packages. The Wholesome Poultry Products Act in some respects is an extension of the packaging and labeling act. The Wholesome Poultry Products Act requires that packaging be safe and free of contamination and that the poultry products being sold be represented accurately on the packaging. Specifically, labeling must not be false or misleading in terms of the origin of the poultry product, the quantity of the poultry product, or any additional ingredients to poultry offered in the package. Ingredients must be listed in order of quantity. Additionally, poultry packaging must disclose the name and address of the manufacturer, packer, or distributor. All required information must be placed on the package in a prominent place where the consumer is likely to read it.

The inherent nature of poultry is such that bacteria are easily bred when processing conditions are less than optimal. Under the act, inspections must be set up to detect disease or other types of contamination in poultry. When poultry products are condemned because of contamination or disease, the specific reason for condemnation must be scientifically presented.

PROVISIONS
The act states that adulterated poultry, which cannot be legally sold, is defined as containing additives that are unsafe as defined by the Federal Food, Drug, and Cosmetic Act; containing any poisonous substances; consisting of decomposed, unhealthful, or unwholesome substances; or having been exposed to radiation. Further, poultry processed under unsanitary conditions that may cause contamination is considered to be adulterated.

To reduce the chance of adulteration to poultry, federal standards were mandated for buildings that house meat and poultry packers, including preparers of frozen foods containing meats and poultry. The standards include specifications for plumbing and sewers, water quality, water temperatures, detergents for washing utensils, ceiling and floor surfaces, room sizes, lighting, and worker uniforms. These specifications were created primarily to increase the cleanliness of processing plants.

The secretary of agriculture or his or her delegate is authorized to enforce the Wholesome Poultry Products Act. As a result of the act, the Consumer Marketing Service of the Department of Agriculture provided training programs for state inspectors so that they would become familiar with federal standards and be able to implement uniform inspections. Each state was given two years after passage of the act to establish inspection programs. An additional one-year grace period could be granted to states making progress toward implementation. Penalties for noncompliance include an exclusion of the state from interstate commerce of poultry and poultry products as well as monetary fines.

IMPACT
In response to the inclusion of commissaries under the jurisdiction of the Wholesome Meat Act of 1967, the National Automatic Merchandising Association formed a Meat Inspection Committee. This committee worked with state agencies and the United States

Department of Agriculture to establish standard guidelines that would logically apply to commissaries, which differ substantially from slaughterhouses. The Meat Inspection Committee continued to work as the Wholesome Poultry Products Act was implemented.

Because most consumers in the United States obtain their poultry and poultry products from supermarkets or other retail establishments, the Wholesome Poultry Products Act of 1968 affects the purchasing confidence of many people. Exempted from the act are people who raise and slaughter poultry exclusively for their own use or who custom slaughter for people who have delivered poultry and will retrieve it for their own use. It would be virtually impossible to routinely inspect all small slaughterhouses such as these. Because inspections are not required and standards equal to those for commercial distribution need not be met, there is a greater chance that poultry processed in these slaughterhouses will not be safe.

Labeling requirements are waived for deliveries to certain consumers. For example, wholesale distribution directly to restaurants and hotels for use in their dining rooms is exempted, with the provision that the poultry is sound and healthy. The labeling exemptions eliminate burdens from industries that would not present packaging to the ultimate consumer for examination.

The cost of the Wholesome Poultry Products Act to the federal government is substantial. According to the act, the federal government provides half of the costs for establishing inspection training programs for the states. The states are individually responsible for the other half of training expenses. Traditionally, the federal government has provided inspectors free of cost to plants, a practice that is being continued by states. Although the initial costs of implementation of the act were substantial, the tradeoff in consumer confidence has the potential to offset the costs. As a result of the act, consumers are provided with more information about sanitary plant conditions, poultry quality, and specific product contents. This increased confidence in proper information and healthy conditions often leads to increased purchases and feelings of goodwill toward retailers of poultry.

Uniformity among poultry producers, processors, and retailers was expected to be achieved as inspection standards from state to state were homogenized. Implementation, however, proved to be a monumental task. Even though it would appear to be economically beneficial to leave the inspection process to federal representatives, the autonomous nature of states and industries provided motivation for them to become involved in the training of inspectors and the implementation of the act. By the original deadline for state implementation of federally approved poultry inspectors, forty-nine states had been granted a one-year extension, as they were making good progress toward meeting designated standards. North Dakota, the only state not to be given an extension, was notified by the Department of Agriculture that its progress toward an inspection program was not well enough under way, and federal inspectors were given jurisdiction to take over the regulation process there.

In actions related to the Wholesome Poultry Products Act, engineers were hired to redesign plants, plumbing and sewage facilities were updated and improved, and water treatment and purification systems were designed. All these changes have resulted in cleaner plants, safer poultry treatment, and better working conditions in poultry houses.

One of the biggest challenges after enactment of the Wholesome Poultry Products Act was to set into practice the authority of the Department of Agriculture to regulate the conditions of the act. Largely because poultry consumers receive access to information about the origins of the products they purchase, poultry houses were eager to comply with regulations and maintain positive public images. Although inspection processes are not foolproof, there are established practices to be followed by inspectors and plant operators so that safe poultry and poultry products will be delivered to supermarkets and served in commissaries.

Virginia Ann Paulins

Sources for Further Study

Hartley, David E. "NAMA Meat Inspection Guidelines: Commissaries, Labeling, and the Law." *Vend* 24 (1970): 23-26.

_____. "Status Report: State-Federal Meat and Poultry Inspection." *Vend* 23 (1969): 39-40.

Quick Frozen Foods. "Frozen Prepared Foods Must Meet Federal Inspection Standards." Vol. 32, 1972: 125-126.

Semling, Harold V., Jr. "Congress Seeks Stronger Poultry Inspection Law." *Food Processing-Marketing* 29 (1968): 85.

Sinclair, Upton. *The Jungle.* New York: Viking Press, 1906.

U.S. Congress. Senate. Committee on Agricultural and Forestry. Subcommittee on Agricultural Research and General Legislation, 1968 90th Congress. *Wholesome Poultry Products Act.*

SEE ALSO: Pure Food and Drugs Act (1906); Food, Drug, and Cosmetic Act (1938); Food Additives Amendment (1958); Food Security Act (1985).

WILD AND SCENIC RIVERS ACT AND NATIONAL TRAILS SYSTEM ACT

DATE: Both passed October 2, 1968 (both acts)
U.S. STATUTES AT LARGE: 82 Stat. 906 (WSRA), 82 Stat. 919 (NTSA)
PUBLIC LAW: 90-542 (WSRA); 90-543 (NTSA)
U.S. CODE: 16 § 1271 (WSRA), 16 § 1241 (NTSA)
CATEGORIES: Environment and Conservation; Land Management; Natural Resources

A system of national trails and a system of wild and scenic rivers was developed to preserve wilderness environments and to create places for public recreation and enjoyment.

In 1962, the Outdoor Recreation Resource Review Commission issued the final report of its congressionally mandated three-year comprehensive study of U.S. environmental resources. The report recommended that certain areas of the country be set aside and preserved in their natural state so that people of the future could enjoy pure and clean environmental beauty. Based on this report, President Lyndon B. Johnson signed policy papers directing federal agencies to initiate preservation of public lands. He also delivered a message to Congress on February 8, 1965, stating that he would submit a bill to establish a National Wild Rivers System so that free-flowing, undammed rivers would be more than just a memory. He also requested that the secretary of the interior recommend a plan for a National System of Trails.

WILD RIVERS: PROPOSALS AND DEBATES

In September, 1965, Senator Frank Church and thirty-one cosponsors introduced a bill for the Wild Rivers Act. Four months later,
the Senate passed its version of the bill and sent it to the House of
Representatives for passage into law. When the Eighty-ninth Congress adjourned in the fall of 1966, however, the House had not
heard the bill, which left the issue dead.

In January, 1967, the Ninetieth Congress began its session with
Senator Church and Senator Henry Jackson reintroducing the
Wild Rivers bill. This bill was unanimously passed by the Senate
in August and forwarded to the House of Representatives. The
House, which had been working on plans of its own, found that
there were four different bills, each of which contained a plan for
using and protecting wild rivers. In March, 1968, hearings were
scheduled on these four bills. Politicians, farm owners, electric
companies, and organizations such as the National Audubon Society, the Wilderness Society, and the Boy Scouts of America participated in the hearings, offering suggestions and registering requests for action about certain rivers. Although there was some
opposition to the concept, most people were in favor of the creation of a Wild and Scenic River System.

Following these hearings, a new bill was written to incorporate
the best points of all the plans. The new bill was introduced by Representatives John Saylor and Wayne Aspinall in July, and a vote was
requested. The governor of Pennsylvania did not want one of
Pennsylvania's rivers in the system, and he encouraged many members of Congress to vote against the bill. The vote was taken and the
bill did not pass. In September, 1968, Saylor and Aspinall reintroduced the bill with the river in Pennsylvania removed from the list
of protected rivers. This time, the Wild and Scenic Rivers bill won
its three-year battle through Congress and passed.

NATIONAL TRAILS: PROPOSALS AND DEBATES

In October, 1965, Senator Gaylord Nelson of Wisconsin showed his
interest in developing a national system of hiking trails, and he introduced his trails plan to the Senate. Six months later, Senator
Nelson submitted President Johnson's plan for a national trails system to the Senate, and seven other senators signed in support of
this second bill. In the House of Representatives, seven different
bills were introduced to develop trails. None of these bills had the

support needed for a vote, however, and they died when the Eighty-ninth Congress adjourned.

When the Ninetieth Congress convened in 1967, Senator Nelson and Senator Jackson proposed a new plan for a national trails system. Their plan was presented in February and was debated in the Senate that July. The debate was a long one, centering on such issues as which trails were to be included, whether or not it was important for trails to be continuous rather than segmented, and the meanings of such terms as "wild," "scenic," "pristine," and "natural." After several amendments were made, the Senate passed the bill and sent it to the House to consider for a vote.

The House had been working on nine similar bills in 1967 and had passed one of them by the time the bill passed by the Senate was received. In July, House members decided they preferred their own version of a national trail system. Keeping the number of the Senate bill (S.827), the House substituted the text of the bill it had passed for the original text, changed the title, voted, and passed the bill. It then sent the bill back to the Senate for approval of the changes. The Senate was not happy with the changes that had been made and requested that a special conference committee resolve the differences. In September, the Senate and the House were able to work out their differences and sent the bill to the president for his signature.

PROVISIONS OF THE WILD RIVERS ACT

On October 2, 1968, President Johnson signed the Wild and Scenic Rivers Act and the National Trails System Act into law. Eight rivers with ribbons of land were to be permanently protected by the National Wild and Scenic Rivers System Act, and twenty-seven rivers would be protected until they could be considered for addition into the system. The Appalachian Trail and the Pacific Crest Trail were protected by the National Trails System Act, with fourteen other trail segments designated for study for possible inclusion to the system.

The Wild and Scenic Rivers Act tried to accommodate as many diverse interests as possible by classifying rivers into three categories: Wild River Areas, Scenic River Areas, and Recreational River Areas. Wild areas are kept in their natural, wild state, and have very limited access points, typically footpaths. Scenic areas have limited road-access, and permit limited recreational facilities to be developed. Recreational areas are easily accessible to people and vehicles, and may have developed recreational facilities serving a variety of interests. These categories limit the use of different rivers in different ways, thus making the law more amenable to those people with interests in using land and water in ways that change the environment from the wilderness state.

As time progressed, the passage of this law allowed for many more rivers to be protected. From the original eight rivers listed in legislation, the list had grown to more than 151 rivers in 1992. Rivers would continue to be studied for inclusion in the system.

PROVISIONS OF THE NATIONAL TRAILS ACT
The National Trails System at first had three trail classifications: National Recreation Trails, Scenic Trails, Side and Connecting Trails; in 1978, a new category was added, Historic Trails. National Recreation Trails are readily accessible to urban areas. They may make use of utility rights of way, abandoned railways, stream valleys, and easements. They may be short or long, and may be used for one or more purposes, such as hiking, horseback riding, snowmobiling, bicycling, or skiing. Local governments or groups ask for their trails to be recognized in this category, and must guarantee that the trail will be maintained and accessible to the public for a minimum of ten years. Scenic Trails are primarily off-road trails for hikers. Although one would not expect to see motorized vehicles on Scenic Trails, campsites or shelters may be found along these long, continuous trails, and other activities deemed compatible with the trail's use may be allowed. Connecting or Side Trails provide additional points of access between Scenic or Recreational Trails. Historic Trails commonly follow routes of travel of a historic group of people, and often have points of significance linked by roadways.

The original legislation cleared the way for other trails to be added to these classifications. The National Trails System grew to include more than eight hundred Recreational Trails, eight Scenic Trails, two Connecting or Side Trails, and eleven Historic Trails by 1994.

IMPACT OF THE ACTS
The passage of the Wild and Scenic Rivers and National Trails System acts was a significant event for all Americans. By the 1950's, Americans were finding it difficult to find the great outdoors they

were hoping to enjoy because of rapid rates of land development. The designation of trails and rivers provided for access and availability of a high-quality environment and experience for U.S. citizens and visitors.

A significant element of these acts has been the designation of different uses of protected areas. Environmentalists have argued that, as a result of limited development or small borders of protected land, only certain elements of entire ecosystems have been protected. The compatible-use concept, however, has allowed enough support to be developed for bills to be passed that have enhanced conservation efforts.

Another significant result of these acts is the provision for public access to designated lands or waterways. Without protection, these areas would be developed as private property. Because of such laws as the Wild and Scenic Rivers and National Trails System acts, however, the opportunity to experience the environment in natural and semideveloped conditions is available to citizens of the United States.

Karen L. Barak

SOURCES FOR FURTHER STUDY

Callison, Charles. "The 90th Congress and Conservation—Much Good, Some Failures." *Audubon* 70 (November/December, 1968): 80-81.

National Park Service. *National Trails System Map and Guide.* Washington, D.C.: U.S. Department of the Interior, 1993.

National Trails Agenda Project. *Trails for America: Report of the National Trails Agenda Project, Summer 1990.* Washington, D.C.: U.S. Department of theInterior National Park Service, 1990.

National Wildlife. "The Wild Rivers: How Can We 'Save' a River?" 4 (February/March, 1966): 4-9.

Palmer, Tim. *The Wild and Scenic Rivers of America.* Covelo, Calif.: Island Press, 1994.

U.S. Department of the Interior. *National Wild and Scenic Rivers System, December, 1992.* Denver: U.S. Geological Survey, 1993.

_____. *Register of National Recreation Trails.* Washington, D.C.: National Park Service Recreation Resources Assistance Division, 1993.

_____. *Trails for America: Report on the Nationwide Trails Study.* Washington, D.C.: Author, 1966.

SEE ALSO: National Park Service Organic Act (1916); Pittman-Robertson Wildlife Restoration Act (1937); Multiple Use-Sustained Yield Act (1960); Wilderness Act (1964); Highway Beautification Act (1965); Eastern Wilderness Act (1975); National Forest Management Act (1976).

CHILD PROTECTION AND TOY SAFETY ACT

DATE: November 6, 1969
U.S. STATUTES AT LARGE: 83 Stat. 187
PUBLIC LAW: 91-113
CATEGORIES: Business, Commerce, and Trade; Children's Issues; Health and Welfare

This act defines substances as hazardous if they pose the unreasonable risk of injury or illness, bans certain products if they are deemed dangerous, and requires special labeling for others that may cause harm or injury.

The Child Protection and Toy Safety Act is the title of an amendment to the Federal Hazardous Substances Act of 1969. Under the authority of the Consumer Product Safety Commission, this act defines substances as hazardous if they present an unreasonable risk of personal injury or illness during any normal or reasonably anticipated use or abuse. Hazardous substances for children include toys or products that may present mechanical, electrical, or thermal hazards.

Mechanical hazards are found in easily broken or disassembled toys. Such toys may have sharp edges that cut, sharp points that puncture, or small parts that could be swallowed or lodged in the respiratory tract. Other mechanical hazards include exposed moving parts capable of causing amputations, crushing, fractures, or bruises to parts of the body, including fingers and toes.

Electric shock hazards may be found in electrically powered toys or toys that could conduct electricity, such as kites, which may become entangled in electrical power lines. Thermal hazards may be present from heated parts, substances, or toy surfaces.

Toys or products that present unreasonable risk of personal injury are banned from sale. However, certain inherently hazardous toys, such as chemistry sets, may be sold if product labeling gives adequate directions and warnings for safe use. Even with government and industry monitoring of toy safety, parents and caregivers have an important role to play in child protection. Adequate adult supervision ensures that children learn safe play habits and the responsible use of toys.

Cherilyn Nelson

SOURCE FOR FURTHER STUDY
Heffron, Howard A. *Federal Consumer Safety Legislation: A Study of the Scope and Adequacy of the Automobile Safety, Flammable Fabrics, Toys, and Hazardous Substances Programs.* Washington, D.C.: Government Printing Office, 1970.

SEE ALSO: Hazardous Substances Labeling Act (1960); Child product safety laws (1970's); Lead-Based Paint Poisoning Prevention Act (1971); Consumer Product Safety Act (1972); Magnuson-Moss Warranty Act (1975); Toxic Substances Control Act (1976).

FEDERAL COAL MINE HEALTH AND SAFETY ACT

DATE: December 30, 1969
U.S. STATUTES AT LARGE: 83 Stat. 742
PUBLIC LAW: 91-173
CATEGORIES: Health and Welfare; Labor and Employment

This act closely regulated the health and safety of coal miners; a 1977 amendment extended the act to include research on health and safety of miners, including those engaged in the mining of materials other than coal.

In the final days of 1969, the U.S. Congress enacted the Federal Coal Mine Health and Safety Act. The act grew out of concern for the miner as the most precious resource and first priority in mining. Deaths and injuries were a serious concern, and the legislation attempted to enforce more effective measures to improve working conditions for coal miners. Unsafe conditions were also a serious impediment to the growth of the mining industry, and mine accidents and diseases were an undue burden on commerce. The act made the mine operators primarily responsible for mine practices and conditions, and it directed the appropriate agencies to promulgate and enforce appropriate standards.

DEFINITIONS AND OVERSIGHT

The secretary of health, education, and welfare and the secretary of the interior were made responsible for enforcing the improved standards. The Department of the Interior's Mining Enforcement and Safety Administration (MESA), an expansion of the previous inspection arm of the Bureau of Mines, was formed to enforce the act. In addition, coal mine operators and miners were made responsible for complying with the standards. Agencies were to work with the states to develop and enforce state coal-mine health and safety programs. Finally, the act authorized expanding research toward preventing coal-mine accidents and diseases.

The 1969 act pertained to all coal mines, both underground and surface, and to the mining of all grades of coal, from bituminous to ignite and anthracite. Any individual working in a coal mine was considered a miner. An interim compliance panel was established with representatives from the Departments of Labor, Commerce, the Interior, and Health, Education, and Welfare (HEW) and the National Science Foundation. The panel was empowered to appoint examiners for hearings; the panel's decisions could be appealed by either operators or miners. The panel also had to make annual progress reports to Congress.

Promulgation of health and safety standards was mandated to the HEW secretary, although consultation with the Labor Department and other agencies was also thought to be necessary. Mandatory health and safety standards that were developed or revised had to be published in the Federal Register for a thirty-day comment period. If objections were filed and a public hearing was requested, additional time was allowed for that hearing. The final regulations were also published in the Federal Register. Only one year was allotted for developing the health and safety standards for surface mines and for the surface work areas of underground mines. When finalized and published in the Federal Register, every standard and regulation had to be sent to every coal mine operator and to the representative of coal miners at each mine; a copy was also to be posted on each mine site. The act also called for the formation of an advisory committee from the Office of Science and Technology, the National Bureau of Standards, National Science Foundation, and coal-mine experts. This committee was to direct the development of research into coal mines and to approve grants and research contracts.

INSPECTIONS
Representatives of the HEW secretary were also authorized to make inspections and investigations to obtain or disseminate information on health and safety conditions and accidents; gather information on mandatory standards; determine if an imminent danger existed; and establish compliance with regulations. The act specifically stated that no advance notice of inspections would be given and that inspections would be carried out at least four times a year. Investigators were given subpoena power and the right to hold public hearings with proper notice. Mine operators were required to report accidents and to prevent destruction of evidence. Provisions were made for confidentiality in the case of miners who informed the agency of violations and requested immediate inspections.

If an inspection revealed an imminent danger, a mine could be shut down immediately. Most violations, however, resulted in a notice that allowed time to address the problem. In cases where a mine operator refused to allow inspection, failed to comply with orders or decisions, or withheld information, the secretary could institute a civil action, secure a temporary or permanent injunction, or seek a restraining order. Operators could be assessed civil penalties of between $10,000 and $50,000 for various convictions of having knowingly violated and refused to comply with health and safety standards. Miners who willfully violated standards with actions such as smoking or carrying matches, could receive a civil penalty of $250 per violation. Fines and imprisonment were also possible for selling nonstandard mining equipment required by the regulations. Once a mine operation was shut down in consequence of orders under the act, the miners were entitled to their regular pay. Miners who reported violations or testified in hearings could not be discharged or discriminated against for this reason.

DUST LEVELS AND MEDICAL MONITORING

Unlike safety standards that were usually in place and easy to assess, health standards that would allow a miner to work underground for his adult life, without contracting pneumoconiosis (black lung disease) or other related diseases, were in a continual process of being refined. From the beginning, the HEW secretary was directed to post dust levels and the methodology for measuring those levels in the Federal Register. The act established an original level of 3.0 milligrams of respirable dust per cubic meter of air, which was to drop to 2.0 milligrams three years later. In cases where the operator, using available technology, could not achieve these levels, a permit for noncompliance was issued for a limited time of not more than eighteen months.

The act directed the National Institute for Occupational Safety and Health (NIOSH) to provide coal miners with periodic chest X-ray examinations, to begin within eighteen months after the law went into effect. The exams were to be provided to the miners at no cost to them by the mine operators. A second X ray was required three years after the first exam; if there were signs of pneumoconiosis, additional X rays were to be given two years later. Otherwise X rays were to be given at intervals not to exceed five years. Because of the high numbers of miners involved, X rays were given in groups and often scheduled for the workers in an entire mine. From 1973 to 1978, NIOSH interpreted X rays for more than 118,000 miners. Of these, less than 6,700 miners (less than 6 percent) had some stage of pneumoconiosis; 2,300, or less than 2 percent, were eligible to transfer to less dusty mining jobs. These low rates reflected the fact that many miners were new to coal mining.

NIOSH established a two-tier system of reading X rays and maintaining quality control. NIOSH was required to notify the Department of Labor Mine Safety and Health Administration of findings and to notify miners of any benefits due them under the act. Miners who showed evidence of various levels of simple pneumoconiosis were permitted to transfer to mining duties in areas with lower levels of coal dust; the specific levels and the procedures were well defined.

The 1969 act provides for autopsies for underground coal miners, regardless of whether they were active coal miners at the time of death. The procedures for the autopsies of coal miners required by the act were likewise well defined: Pathologists who submitted reports and tissue specimens were reimbursed $200 per autopsy, the cost of which was borne by the coal company. Generally, NIOSH conducted approximately three hundred autopsies per year.

An important portion of the act addressed claims for black lung benefits before and after December 31, 1972. The concluding portion of the act detailed efforts to be made in research, allocating grants, training inspectors, providing assistance to states, and making reports.

SAFE MINE CONDITIONS

Specific regulations were made for mines being managed with maximum safety of the miners. These regulations addressed criteria for roof support, ventilation, methane tests, daily reports, the presence of combustible material and rock dust, management of electrical equipment and cables, fire protection, blasting and explosives, haulage equipment, and many aspects of training programs, sanitary facilities, drinking water, and the like.

Among the regulations for underground coal-mine workplaces were prescribed levels of illumination within a miner's normal field of view of at least 0.06 footlamberts, a measure of reflectance, not candlepower. A new photometer developed for MESA to measure this light intensity provided a simple indication of whether light levels met regulations. The increased lighting requirements in turn increased the need to be careful with the added power cords necessary to feed the additional lighting equipment. By 1977, MESA had altered some light standards after recognizing that a drastic contrast in lighting intensity could be as dangerous as too little light.

The first extensive survey of noise levels in underground coal mines in the United States was made in 1970. NIOSH concluded that miners—who were exposed to pneumatic drills, heavy mining machines, and loading machines—generally had worse hearing than workers not subjected to excessive job-related noise. The 1969 act directed the secretary to establish maximum noise standards and to require a certified assessment of noise level in mines every six months.

In cases of underground mine fires or explosions, self-rescue equipment, which resembled a large gas mask in appearance and was intended to convert toxic carbon monoxide to carbon dioxide, was required. New MESA regulations required that miners be trained in the use of one-hour oxygen supplies and oxygen-generating units. It was permissible to carry a ten-minute device that would allow a miner to reach the one-hour canisters, located at various strategic places in the mine. These oxygen supplies improved on the previously used filter systems, which had not protected against oxygen-deficient air, carbon dioxide, high temperatures, and toxic gases produced by the increased use of plastics.

MESA also developed a point system for rating coal mines. Underground and surface mines were rated on different scales, which evolved into an intricate matrix of standards. MESA inspectors investigated dust levels, health and safety training, equipment and the management of it, accident and injury records, job-safety analyses by the company, employee supervision, protection equipment, maintenance schedules, health examinations, and enforcement of rules. Under its education and training mandate, MESA produced a series of films, some of which won industrial film awards.

SUBSEQUENT LEGISLATION
In 1977, the Federal Mine Safety and Health Act amended the 1969 act by extending its range beyond coal mining and calling for research to protect the health and safety of miners in all metal and nonmetal mines. In addition, two new mining programs were established: The Mining Industries Surveillance Program was to document the hazardous physical agents used in mining and to determine the toxicity levels for common levels of usage; the Health Hazard Evaluation Program was to conduct research on possible new health hazards in mining and to conduct scientific evaluations on specific hazards within 120 days.

John Richard Schrock

SOURCES FOR FURTHER STUDY
Dennen, W. H. *Mineral Resources: Geology, Exploration, and Development.* New York: Taylor and Francis, 1989.
Hoppe, R., ed. *E/MJ Operating Handbook of Mineral Surface Mining and Exploration.* New York: E/MJ Mining Informational Services, 1978.

Nelkin, Dorothy, and Michael S. Brown. *Workers at Risk: Voices from the Workplace.* Chicago: University of Chicago Press, 1984.

U.S. Congress. *Public Law 91-173: Federal Coal Mine Health and Safety Act of 1969.* 91st Congress, 1st session, 1969.

SEE ALSO: General Mining Act (1872); Occupational Safety and Health Act (1970); Mining and Minerals Policy Act (1970); Surface Mining Control and Reclamation Act (1977).

CHILD PRODUCT SAFETY LAWS

DATE: 1970's
CATEGORIES: Business, Commerce, and Trade; Children's Issues; Health and Welfare

Federal legislation prevented the marketing of potentially harmful children's products.

During the 1970's, the federal government of the United States undertook a concerted effort to improve the safety of toys and other products used by children. This effort was presaged by passage of the Child Protection Act of 1966, which prohibited sale of any hazardous substance that might cause harm to children, if it failed to display a warning label on either the product or its package. The Food and Drug Administration (FDA) was responsible for enforcing this act, which amended the Hazardous Substances Labeling Act of 1960. Prior to this act, signed into law on November 3, 1966, toy manufacturers were not held accountable for product safety or for reducing the risk of injuries sustained by children using their products.

CHILD PROTECTION AND TOY SAFETY ACT
On November 6, 1969, the Child Protection and Toy Safety Act was passed, extending the requirements of manufacturers by prohibiting any toxic, corrosive, or flammable toy or article that could cause personal injury or illness in children. In addition, if a product could cause an electrical, fire, or mechanical hazard to chil-

dren, a label was to be displayed on the product or its package warning of its potential danger. The law gave the secretary of health, education, and welfare the authority to ban what the FDA classified as a hazardous substance.

FLAMMABLE FABRICS ACT
The FDA was also responsible for carrying out the 1953 Flammable Fabrics Act, passed to ban nightgowns and children's clothing that would burst into flame when exposed to open flames. Unfortunately, the standards were not stringent. For example, if a six-inch sample of a material was held at a 45 degree angle from a flame for one second and did not catch fire, it passed the test. If the material burned at a rate of five inches or less in three and one-half seconds, it passed the test.

CONSUMER PRODUCT SAFETY ACT
On October 27, 1972, the Consumer Product Safety Act established the Consumer Product Safety Commission (CPSC), which was empowered to develop safety standards for most consumer products other than food, drugs, and automobiles. The CPSC was charged with protecting the public against unreasonable risks of injury from consumer products, assisting consumers in evaluating the relative safety of competing product brands, reducing the conflicts between state and local regulations, and promoting research and investigation into the causes and prevention of product-related death, illness, and injury.

TOY DANGERS
Prior to the establishment of the CPSC, the toy industry regulated itself. In 1968, the National Commission on Product Safety (NCPS) found in its final report to Congress that self-regulation by trade associations such as the Toy Manufacturers of America (TMA) and organizations that give seals of approval, such as Good Housekeeping, were ineffective. The TMA did not force its members to comply with its standards, and organizations such as Good Housekeeping were more concerned that advertising claims were truthful than with testing and certifying products' safety to children.

One toy safety advocate who testified before the NCPS was Edward M. Swartz, an attorney who represented several clients in court to obtain compensation for injuries suffered by their children as a result of playing with hazardous toys. At the 1968 NCPS hearings, Swartz demonstrated how dangerous toys could be to their child users. Swartz became an advocate on toy safety issues and wrote several books, including *Toys That Don't Care* (1971) and *Toys That Kill* (1986).

Swartz's research uncovered several unsafe products that were marketed in the 1970's having not been found to be dangerous by the CPSC. One product was the Wham-O Manufacturing Company's boomerang. Another unsafe product, marketed by PBI Incorporated, was a projectile toy that was advertised to the wholesale trade as a safe, flexible plastic toy, even though it had sharp edges and was potentially blinding. F. A. O. Schwartz marketed a fiberglass bow and wooden arrow set. The wooden arrows had rubber tips, but they were removable. The toy was advertised as being harmless.

During the 1970's, the Ideal Toy Corporation made a "Kookie Kamera" that was marketed as nontoxic and not intended for internal consumption. The product caused several cases of nausea, which may have led to vomiting and even asphyxiation as a result of blockage of the trachea in small children. Another product, the Newman Company's "Loonie Straw," was designed to be reusable. The problem was that instructions called for the straw not to be washed in hot water. It was intended to be used to drink milk, making it probable that bacterial germs would be bred in the unsanitary straw.

From 1973 to 1977, the CPSC received more than one hundred death certificates related to the ingestion of small objects. Forty-five of these deaths were related to toys and nursery products. In 1976, it was estimated by a CPSC study that 46,500 children under the age of ten were treated in hospital emergency rooms for injuries related to small parts. Twenty-five of forty-five deaths involving children's products were of children less than three years old.

During 1978, the CPSC received more than 180 oral and written comments from businesses, trade associations, and consumer groups regarding the safety of consumer products. In response, on August 7, 1978, the Consumer Product Safety Act tightened up safety regulations and required every manufacturer, distributor, or retailer who obtained information that a product either was unsafe or did not comply with the CPSC regulations to immediately inform the CPSC.

IMPACT ON TOY MANUFACTURE

The effects of regulation on how toys were manufactured and marketed were mixed. In 1980, the CPSC banned the sale of toys with small parts intended for children under the age of three if the parts could accidentally be swallowed or become dangerously lodged in their throats. By 1989, however, the CPSC still had not clearly defined what constituted a small part and if small-part toys should be banned in general. Toymakers still claimed that accidents being researched were isolated incidents; the CPSC concurred in most cases.

On the other hand, many products were banned because of the CPSC's enforcement of the Child Protection Act and Child Protection and Toy Safety Act. In the 1970's, products called crackerballs were categorized as hazardous substances. Crackerballs consisted of small quantities of gunpowder and particles of sand or flint in papier-mâché coatings. When thrown against any hard surface, they would explode with a loud noise. Lawn dart sets were required to carry warning labels, and they could not be sold at toy stores. In 1977, the CPSC required bicycles to have capped brake wires, treads on the pedals to prevent foot slippage, and reflectors for night riding.

One area of concern for product safety advocates was that under product safety laws, toy manufacturers were permitted to market products with labels recommending the age group for which the toy would be most suitable. The labels did not indicate that the toy would be hazardous to any child younger than the recommended age. As a result, many adults believed that the recommended age group was based on intellectual capacity or dexterity, not on safety standards.

In 1977, Parker Brothers marketed a product called Rivitron, a plastic construction toy for children aged six to twelve. After an eight-year-old boy died from ingesting a small part of the toy, the CPSC found the death to be an isolated case. Parker Brothers added chemicals to the toy rivets, giving them a bad taste so that children would be deterred from putting the parts in their mouths.

In 1987, the CPSC under Commissioner Terrence Scanlon seized goods valued at almost $4 million during spot checks. Seizures represented 1.5 million units of toys. James Florio, chairman of the House Reauthorization Subcommittee on Commerce, Consumer Protection, and Competitiveness, criticized the CPSC for being relatively weak during the 1980's. Florio and his committee believed that confiscating $4 million worth of products from a $12 billion industry showed ineffectiveness as a safety commission.

Many critics of toy manufacturers believed that the public was unaware of the dangers that children faced when playing with toys that were not being stringently monitored by the CPSC. On the other hand, toy manufacturers believed that regulations were too stringent and the public too demanding. They argued that many injuries to children were not caused by the children and their toys but by the lack of parental supervision.

TELEVISION ADVERTISING AND LONG-RANGE IMPACT

In 1968, Peggy Charren had founded Action for Children's Television (ACT). Charren was a critic of toy-based programs, which she believed were exploiting children and should have been scrutinized by the television industry and the Federal Communications Commission. In 1987, when Mattel announced a line of gun toys to be used in interaction with a television show, she unsuccessfully tried to stop the marketing of these products, claiming that simulating the shooting of a television figure would give children the wrong impression of real shooting. Charren's movement gave a new interpretation to product safety, expanding beyond physical features and taking into consideration the potential danger of marketing products that could lead to an unsafe situation or foster dangerous behavior.

Toy manufacturers were faced with other criticisms that may have led to decreased sales. In 1987, consumer advocate and attorney Ralph Nader found that television advertising manipulated child viewers to buy toy products that were not safe. For example, Nader found that plastic toy parts were more hazardous than were wood products, but that television advertising focused on plastic toys. Toy manufacturers responded that critics were more concerned with an antibusiness philosophy than with objections to the actual safety of toys.

Although the CPSC generally supported consumer advocates, in 1991 Toys "R" Us was permitted to sell wind-up dolls, even though children under three years of age could be injured by choking on some of the parts. Sale of the dolls was allowed because they were not intended for children of that age. Throughout the 1980's and 1990's, attorney Edward Swartz compiled lists of dangerous toys. Although many legal battles were won by the toy manufacturing industry, advocates such as Swartz, Nader, and Charren influenced the CPSC and the toy manufacturers to ensure that toys were safe. Toy manufacturers became more cognizant of their market and of the pressure that consumer advocates placed by lobbying legislators to strengthen product safety rules for children.

Martin J. Lecker

SOURCES FOR FURTHER STUDY

Dadd, Debra Lynn. *Non-Toxic and Natural How to Avoid Dangerous Everyday Products and Buy or Make Safe Ones.* Los Angeles: Jeremy P. Tarcher, 1984.

Heffron, Howard A. *Federal Consumer Safety Legislation: A Study of the Scope and Adequacy of the Automobile Safety, Flammable Fabrics, Toys, and Hazardous Substances Programs.* Washington, D.C.: Government Printing Office, 1970.

Oppenheim, Joanne. *Buy Me! Buy Me!.* New York: Pantheon Books, 1987.

Stern, Sydney Ladensohn, and Ted Schoenhaus. *Toyland The High Stakes Game of the Toy Industry.* Chicago: Contemporary Books, 1990.

Swartz, Edward M. *Toys That Don't Care.* Boston: Gambit, 1971.

_____. *Toys That Kill.* New York: Vintage Books, 1986.

SEE ALSO: Hazardous Substances Labeling Act (1960); Hazardous Substances Labeling Act (1960); Child Protection and Toy Safety Act (1969); Lead-Based Paint Poisoning Prevention Act (1971); Consumer Product Safety Act (1972); Magnuson-Moss Warranty Act (1975); Toxic Substances Control Act (1976).

NATIONAL ENVIRONMENTAL POLICY ACT

DATE: January 1, 1970
U.S. STATUTES AT LARGE: 83 Stat. 852
PUBLIC LAW: 91-190
U.S. CODE: 42 § 4321
CATEGORIES: Environment and Conservation

The law established national policies and objectives for the protection and maintenance of the environment in the United States.

Sometimes referred to as the environmental Magna Carta of the United States, the National Environmental Policy Act (NEPA) was the first law of its kind to require a comprehensive and coordinated national environmental policy that embraced public review of environmental impacts associated with the actions of federal agencies. Oversight of NEPA compliance was facilitated through the Council on Environmental Quality (CEQ), created through a provision of the act.

In response to widespread public interest in environmental quality during the late 1960's, Congress held separate House and Senate committee hearings to identify the best method for legislating a national policy on environmental protection. Among the problems discussed was the tendency of mission-oriented federal agencies involved in development to overlook environmentally preferable alternatives in their decision-making processes. Draft versions of House and Senate environmental bills were later integrated and approved by Congress as NEPA. Signed into law by President Richard M. Nixon on January 1, 1970, NEPA (PL 91-190) recognized the profound impact of human activity on the interrelations of all components of the natural environment, particularly the influences of population growth, high-density urbanization, resource exploration, and new and expanding technological advances. Language used in the bill embraced many of the philosophies of the conservation movement of the early twentieth century and later environmentalism of the 1960's.

PROVISIONS

Although other U.S. environmental statutes provide robust protection for the environment, such laws focus only on specific categories of resources. In contrast, NEPA serves as an umbrella statute that outlines a set of procedures and embraces the importance of public participation in federal decision making when the quality of the environment is at stake. NEPA does not demand explicit results such as limits on pollution emissions or specific actions to protect endangered species, nor does it serve as a substitute for other federal planning activities or regulatory processes. Rather, the act instructs that decisions be made on the basis of thoughtful analysis of the direct, indirect, and cumulative environmental impacts of proposed actions.

NEPA prescribes the completion of a series of steps for all actions involving federal participation that may affect the environment, emphasizing in spirit and intent the importance of public participation in safeguarding the environment. The first step in federal project review is completion of an environmental assessment (EA) with input from local governments, American Indians, the public, and other federal agencies. An EA documents influences on the environment associated with a proposed federal action, including the type and level of significant impacts. Following completion of the EA, NEPA requires that a second document be prepared for all actions going forward. A finding of no significant impact (FONSI) provides documentation in cases were actions have been determined to have no significant effect on the quality of the human environment. Federal actions that may significantly alter the quality of the human environment, including possible degradation to threatened or endangered species or their habitats, must be evaluated in greater detail. An environmental impact statement (EIS) involves additional analysis of pertinent social, demographic, economic, and ecological information and consideration of alternative courses of action. NEPA requires that the EIS process be carried out using a framework involving public input through a variety of mechanisms, including individual or group responses to proposed alternatives.

IMPLEMENTATION

Initially, NEPA implementation was difficult within agencies struggling to establish guidelines. Within the act's first two years, federal agencies had completed more than 3,600 EISs but were also involved in nearly 150 associated lawsuits. Although the number of EISs submitted each year has fallen, more than 26,000 have been written since 1970. These reports document actions ranging from the construction of highways to the development of facilities for holding toxic wastes. About 80 percent of EISs have been produced by a small number of federal agencies, including the Forest Service, the Bureau of Land Management, the Department of Housing and Urban Development, the Federal Highway Administration, and the Army Corps of Engineers. Although there is no formal tracking process, a much large number of EAs have been prepared for other federal projects and activities.

Critics argue that the EIS process is not cost effective in terms of human resources or dollars spent and that NEPA guidelines are often inconsistently applied. As an overarching policy, NEPA cannot prevent agencies from implementing unwise actions or even from concluding that other values are more important than environmental considerations. Despite ambiguity in its language, however, the act has been credited with significantly modifying the actions of both government agencies and private industry by preventing hundreds of activities with potentially severe environmental effects.

NEPA has raised awareness of the concept of environmental impact, highlighting the need for governments and citizens to be aware of the unintended consequences of federally supported actions that affect the human environment. NEPA has also assisted in creating pathways for other federal statutes that consider environmental issues in decision making, such as the 1980 Comprehensive Environmental Response, Compensation, and Liability Act (CERCLA), also known as Superfund. Having withstood consecutive regulatory reform commissions of the presidential administrations of Jimmy Carter, Ronald Reagan, and George H. W. Bush, NEPA stands out for its brevity and simplicity. Perhaps the best evidence of the act's success can be seen by the fact that it has been emulated by one-half of the state governments in the United States and by more than eighty national governments throughout the world.

Thomas A. Wikle

Sources for Further Study

Andrews, R. N. L. *Environmental Policy and Administrative Change: Implementation of the National Environmental Policy Act.* Lexington, Mass.: Lexington Books, 1976.

Burchell, R. W., and David Listokin. *The Environmental Impact Handbook.* New Brunswick, N.J.: Center for Urban Policy Research, Rutgers University, 1975.

Caldwell, Lynton. *Science and the National Environmental Policy Act.* University: University of Alabama Press, 1982.

Clark, Ray, and Larry Canter. *Environmental Policy and NEPA.* Boca Raton, Fla.: St. Lucie Press, 1997.

Creighton, J. L. *The Public Involvement Manual.* Washington, D.C.: Information Resources Press, 1979.

Eckstein, Otto. *Water-resource Development: The Economics of Project Evaluation.* Cambridge, Mass.: Harvard University Press, 1958.

Lake, L. M. ed. *Environmental Mediation: The Search for Consensus.* Boulder, Colo.: Westview Press, 1980.

Munn, R. E., ed. *Environmental Impact Assessment: Principles and Procedures.* Chichester, England: John Wiley & Sons, 1979.

Ortolano, Leonard. *Environmental Planning and Decision Making.* New York: John Wiley & Sons, 1984.

SEE ALSO: Multiple Use-Sustained Yield Act (1960); Clean Air Act (1963); Clean Water Act and Amendments (1965); Safe Drinking Water Act (1974); National Forest Management Act (1976); Department of Energy Organization Act (1977); Superfund Act (1980); Pollution Prevention Act (1990).

PUBLIC HEALTH CIGARETTE SMOKING ACT

DATE: April 1, 1970
U.S. STATUTES AT LARGE: 84 Stat. 87
PUBLIC LAW: 91-222
U.S. CODE: 15 § 1331
CATEGORIES: Food and Drugs; Health and Welfare

Cigarette advertising was banned from the American broadcast media.

The Public Health Cigarette Smoking Act of 1969 banned cigarette advertising from American radio and television beginning January 1, 1971. It also allowed the Federal Trade Commission (FTC) to consider warnings in printed advertising after July 1, 1971. Warnings on cigarette packages were changed, and under the act, the FTC was required to give Congress six months notice of any pending changes in rules concerning cigarettes. The legislation was signed by President Richard Nixon on April 1, 1970. After passage of the act, two voluntary agreements were reached between the

FTC and cigarette manufacturers. The companies agreed to list tar and nicotine content in their advertising and also agreed to feature the health warning label in print advertising.

The agreement was prompted by the pending expiration on July 1, 1969, of the Cigarette Warning Label Act (1966). The Federal Communications Commission unexpectedly announced in February, 1969, that if Congress allowed the 1965 act to expire, the FCC would propose a rule that would ban cigarette advertising from the airwaves. Several options were available. If Congress did not act and allowed the 1965 legislation to expire, the FCC could enact its proposed restrictions. Alternatively, Congress could have extended the 1965 ban or could have taken action on the health warning label, making it more or less stringent.

THE BATTLE IN CONGRESS

Antismoking forces hoped that Congress would not act, thereby allowing for the more encompassing regulations proposed by the FCC. Instead, the House Interstate and Foreign Commerce Committee held thirteen days of hearings two months before the ban was to expire. The arguments and many of the witnesses were the same as those heard in the 1965 hearings. In testimony before the committee, Warren Braren, former manager of the New York office of the Code Authority, made it clear that the National Association of Broadcasters (NAB) deliberately misled Congress and the public into believing that voluntary industry self-regulation in reducing youth appeal was meaningful. He revealed that television networks and advertising agencies regularly overruled Code Authority staff members in interpretation of standards. The Code Authority operated entirely on voluntary submissions by advertising agencies. Some tobacco sponsors simply had not subscribed to the code, and those that did made their own judgments on whether their commercials needed to be reviewed.

The bill that passed the House of Representatives on June 18, 1969, however, appeared to represent a victory for the cigarette industry. It prohibited the states permanently, and the federal agencies for six more years, from enacting regulations on cigarette advertising, in exchange for a strengthened package warning label. The House bill, however, sparked a severe backlash in the Senate and at the state level as well as in the private sector. *The New York Times*, for example, announced that it would require a health warning in any cigarette advertisement appearing in that newspaper.

The Senate Commerce Committee, chaired by Frank E. Moss, held a one-day hearing, with only five witnesses appearing. Speaking for the tobacco manufacturers in July, 1969, Joseph Cullman III, chairman of Philip Morris, told the Senate Consumer Subcommittee that the industry was ready to end all advertising on television and radio on December 31, 1969, if the broadcasters would cooperate, and in any event would agree to cease advertising by September, 1970, when existing agreements expired. The announcement by Cullman caught many broadcasters by surprise. They had proposed to phase out cigarette ads over a three-year period beginning in January, 1970. Cigarette advertising accounted for $225 million a year in revenue to broadcasters, and they had hoped that a gradual reduction would help in the development of contingency plans to recover a portion of the lost revenue.

BROADCASTERS VOLUNTEER A BAN

Meanwhile, the National Association of Broadcasters (NAB) Television and Radio Code Review Boards announced a plan on July 8, 1969, to stop advertising on radio and television beginning January 1, 1970. In addition, cigarette manufacturers were required to continue carrying warning labels on their packages. The agreement stipulated that member stations of the NAB would phase out cigarette commercials on the air beginning January 1, 1970. The Review Boards also said that they would prohibit cigarette commercials during or adjacent to any program that was primarily directed at young people and would further study ways to reduce the appeal of cigarettes to minors. The announcement amounted to a victory for critics of tobacco, most notably the FCC, which had threatened to ban all cigarette commercials from the airwaves.

The tobacco industry, in presenting its proposal, showed concern that broadcasters might sue for antitrust violations, on the grounds that the cigarette companies had acted in collusion. The industry included a request for antitrust protection in presenting its proposal.

A NEW WARNING LABEL

The bill that emerged from Congress on March 19, 1970, called the Public Health Cigarette Smoking Act of 1969, banned cigarette advertising from radio and television beginning January 1, 1971. It also agreed to allow the FTC to consider warnings in printed advertising after July 1, 1971. Cigarette package warning labels were changed to:

> Warning: The Surgeon General has determined that cigarette smoking is dangerous to your health.

Attitudes within the tobacco industry regarding the ban were mixed. It is commonly assumed in the industry that advertising does not increase the size of the overall cigarette market. Instead, it affects the competitive position of the various brands. The primary effect of the advertising ban, therefore, would be to freeze the market shares currently held by each of the brands. Print ads could still affect market share but were not believed to be as powerful. The money saved by not producing and placing advertising in the broadcast media would be substantial. As a bonus, the industry hoped that a cessation of cigarette advertising would yield a respite in the growing volume of antismoking advertising.

TOBACCO INDUSTRY RESPONSE

The tobacco industry's initial response to the broadcast advertising ban was to find alternative means to get its message to the public. Liggett & Myers, Philip Morris, and R. J. Reynolds all signed contracts with automobile racing organizations as a way to keep their brands on television, announcing that the races would be named after popular brands, for example the "L&M Continental Championship," the "Marlboro Championship," and the "Winston 500." Some industry observers saw this as an attempt at a "rear door" reentry by cigarette makers into the television market. Advertisers also positioned displays strategically at racetracks so that they would be captured by television cameras covering the events.

Publishers, unlike broadcasters, were not federally licensed and were not, therefore, limited by FCC regulations. Within one month of the imposed ban on broadcast media advertising, the number of pages of cigarette advertising in consumer magazines more than doubled as compared to the same period of the previous year. Although some increase was anticipated, its magnitude caught the magazine industry by surprise and created a controversy. This stemmed from the impression that the increase in cigarette advertising might convey in the light of the magazine industry's somewhat delicate position regarding health warnings. Congress had barred the Federal Trade Commission from requiring health hazard warnings in cigarette print ads before July 1, 1971, but not after.

ANTISMOKING CAMPAIGNS

Twenty months after the broadcast advertising ban went into effect, the FTC urged the government to buy broadcast time for antismoking advertising. Smoking had hit record high levels since the ads left the airwaves. In 1972, a total of 554 billion cigarettes were smoked, 3 percent more than in the preceding year. The tobacco industry apparently had survived the controversy that began with the 1964 surgeon general's report. Analysts correctly predicted that the industry would witness at least a decade of strong, steady growth. Some attributed this growth to the increase in the 25-to-44 age bracket, a group that accounted for a large proportion of cigarette consumption. Others argued that the ban had not yet had its full effect, since most young consumers had seen cigarette ads for most of their lives. John F. Banzhaf III, executive director of Action on Smoking and Health, an antismoking public interest group, stated that to date the greatest impact of the ruling was that antismoking messages were appearing far less frequently, since broadcasters no longer had to air them for free to balance cigarette ads. The effects of cigarette advertising were seen to be long-term, while the antismoking ads seemed to have an effect for a shorter period.

In the 1970's, public and medical research interest turned to the effects of smoking on nonsmokers. In 1972, the surgeon general issued the first report suggesting that secondhand smoke was dangerous to nonsmokers. In 1975, Minnesota passed the first state law requiring businesses, restaurants, and other institutions to establish non-smoking areas. The concern regarding secondhand smoke continued, with an increasing number of local governments and businesses restricting smoking in public areas.

The cigarette industry, in the meantime, continued to target new generations of smokers through print and billboard advertising, sales promotions, public relations, giveaways, and strategically place story displays. In 1988, tobacco companies spent more than one billion dollars on advertising and more than two billion dollars on promotion. The restriction on broadcast advertising and the required warning labels on packages and advertisements appear to have had a limited impact in the face of advertising that promises smokers increased status, social acceptance, and glamour. The cigarette industry has defended itself against charges of irresponsibility by claiming that individuals are free to decide whether to smoke and that it simply is meeting an existing consumer demand. The industry is particularly defensive regarding charges that ads are targeted toward children. It argues that ads do not encourage people to start smoking, but rather to switch brands.

Elaine Sherman and
Andrew M. Forman

SOURCES FOR FURTHER STUDY

Doron, Gideon. *The Smoking Paradox: Public Regulation in the Cigarette Industry.* Cambridge, Mass.: Abt Books, 1979.

Fritschler, A. Lee. *Smoking and Politics: Policymaking and the Federal Bureaucracy.* 3d ed. Englewood Cliffs, N.J.: Prentice-Hall, 1983.

Sobel, Robert. *They Satisfy: The Cigarette in American Life.* New York: Anchor Press, 1978.

Tollison, Robert D., ed. *Smoking and Society: Toward a More Balanced Assessment.* Lexington, Mass.: Lexington Books, 1986.

White, Larry C. *Merchants of Death: The American Tobacco Industry.* New York: Beech Tree Books, 1988.

SEE ALSO: Cigarette Warning Label Act (1966).

ORGANIZED CRIME CONTROL ACT

DATE: October 15, 1970
U.S. STATUTES AT LARGE: 84 Stat. 933
PUBLIC LAW: 91-452
CATEGORIES: Crimes and Criminal Procedure

A set of amendments to existing law and authorizations of new law enforcement entities to combat organized crime, the Organized Crime Control Act was a key element of the Nixon administration's "war on crime."

The 1960's were seen by many at the time as an era of increasing crime, disrespect for authority, and corruption. Richard M. Nixon's election as president in 1968 marked the beginning of a series of conservative policies designed to address those problems under the rubric of a "war on crime." The Organized Crime Control Act was a key element of that program.

In general, the act strengthened the ability of law enforcement authorities to gather evidence against organized crime, provided for the protection of government witnesses, revised explosives regulations, and increased penalties for "dangerous special offenders." The act also established a commission to investigate criminal involvement in gambling. Title IX of the act, known as the Racketeer Influenced and Corrupt Organizations Act (RICO), identified various illegal activities and specified penalties.

The legislation encountered some resistance from those who argued that it provided the government with unconstitutional powers, violating individual rights. The final version of the act included a provision establishing a commission to review federal laws and practices for potential infringements of individual rights.

Steve D. Boilard

Sources for Further Study

Philcox, Norman W. *An Introduction to Organized Crime.* Springfield, Ill.: Charles C Thomas, 1978.

U.S. Department of Justice. Organized Crime and Racketeering Section. *Racketeer Influenced and Corrupt Organizations (RICO): A Manual for Federal Prosecutors.* 2d rev. ed. Washington, D.C.: Government Printing Office, 1988.

Wallance, Gregory J. "Criminal Justice: Outgunning the Mob." *American Bar Association Journal* 80 (March 1, 1994).

See also: Interstate Commerce Act (1887); Anti-Racketeering Act (1934); Hobbs Act (1946); Omnibus Crime Control and Safe Streets Act (1968); Racketeer Influenced and Corrupt Organizations Act (1970); Comprehensive Drug Abuse Prevention and Control Act (1970); Juvenile Justice and Delinquency Prevention Act (1974); Comprehensive Crime Control Act (1984); Brady Handgun Violence Protection Act (1994); Violent Crime Control and Law Enforcement Act (1994).

RACKETEER INFLUENCED AND CORRUPT ORGANIZATIONS ACT

ALSO KNOWN AS: Title IX of the Organized Crime Control Act
DATE: October 15, 1970
U.S. STATUTES AT LARGE: 84 Stat. 941
PUBLIC LAW: 91-452
U.S. CODE: 18 § 1961
CATEGORIES: Crimes and Criminal Procedure

> *Commonly known by its acronym RICO, this law provided both criminal and civil remedies against persons who commit a variety of statutory and common-law crimes, and it became the primary statutory weapon used by federal prosecutors against organized crime.*

After twenty years of study and debate, Congress enacted the Racketeer Influenced and Corrupt Organizations Act (RICO) as part of the Organized Crime Control Act of 1970. The statute's primary purpose is to provide an effective means for government prosecutors to act against organized crime. RICO lay dormant for a decade, however, until its architect, G. Robert Blakey of Notre Dame Law School, convinced federal prosecutors to use it against the Mafia.

PORVISIONS: FOUR PROHIBITED ACTIVITIES

The general scheme of RICO is relatively simple. It applies to a defendant who, through a pattern of racketeering activity, has indirectly or directly participated in an enterprise whose activities affect interstate commerce. The critical phrases "person," "enterprise," and "pattern of racketeering activity" are broadly defined in RICO, reflecting a congressional intent to provide for the widest application of the statute in combating organized crime.

The Supreme Court recognized that RICO was to be liberally construed. The term "enterprise" thereby includes "legitimate enterprises" which have committed the requisite illegal acts. RICO prohibits four specific activities: using income derived from a pattern of racketeering activity to acquire an interest in an enterprise, acquiring or maintaining an interest in an enterprise through a pattern of racketeering activity, conducting the affairs of an enterprise through a pattern of racketeering activity, and conspiring to commit any of these offenses.

A "person," defined to include any individual or entity capable of holding a legal or beneficial interest in property, must conduct or participate in the conduct of a RICO enterprise through a pattern of racketeering activity, which requires at least two predicate acts within a ten-year period. The statute is thereby directed at conduct (the predicate acts) rather than status (organized crime). RICO therefore applies to anyone who engages in the proscribed conduct, regardless of who the perpetrator is. Federal prosecutors have generally exercised discretion in limiting RICO prosecutions to cases involving organized crime and securities violations.

The critical phrase "racketeering activity" is defined to include specific state and federal felonies. A veritable laundry list of predicate offenses includes murder, kidnapping, gambling, arson, robbery, bribery, extortion, and dealing in narcotics or other dangerous drugs. Also included as predicate acts are a number of federal crimes, including mail fraud, wire fraud, obstruction of justice, and securities fraud. In 1984 Congress added the distribution of obscene materials to the list of predicate offenses. Several other predicate acts reflect common perceptions of organized crime, such as bribery and sports bribery, unlawful transactions with pension or welfare funds, loan-sharking, interstate transportation of wagering paraphernalia, federal bankruptcy fraud, and violation of any law of the United States concerning drug transactions.

RICO is partially intended to strike at illegal activity that operates through formal, legitimate enterprises. An enterprise is defined to include any individual, partnership, corporation, association, or other legal entity, and any union or group of individuals associated in fact even though they do not constitute a legal entity. One of the most significant features of RICO is that members of an unlawful enterprise can be prosecuted for being part of an enterprise that commits a series of predicate offenses. It is no longer necessary to prosecute individual defendants for a specific crime, such as homicide, which may be difficult to prove.

RICO is distinguished from other criminal statutes because it includes in its penalties the forfeiture of illegally acquired gains and the economic bases of misused power. RICO forfeiture can be of any property that is traceable, directly or indirectly, to the RICO violation. Forfeiture is in addition to any other fine or imprisonment imposed. Criminal forfeiture was common in England, but it is not generally incorporated into the criminal laws of the United States. A freeze on a defendant's assets can also be imposed upon the filing of a RICO complaint by the federal prosecutor.

CIVIL RICO
Without much thought on the floor of Congress, an amendment to the proposed RICO statute was adopted, adding a civil remedy to the statute. RICO's civil remedy provision is the most commonly utilized provision of the statute. Its popularity rests on the fact that a victim may recover treble (triple) damages and costs of litigation, including attorneys' fees. In addition, the statute can be applied against any defendant who has committed the requisite two predicate acts within a ten-year period. It is widely used in cases of securities fraud, consumer fraud, and real estate development fraud. RICO has also become a standard pleading in business disputes. In January, 1994, the Supreme Court held in *National Organization for Women v. Scheidler* that RICO can be applied against antiabortion protesters. The Court held that RICO is not limited to crimes with an economic motive. Courts frequently use the civil and criminal RICO case-law interpretations interchangeably.

RICO's EFFECTS
RICO has been effective in the government's steady war of attrition against traditional organized crime; its record in prosecuting white-collar criminals has been mixed. Both the civil suit provision and the allowability of freezing assets have proved controversial. Plaintiffs seeking relief under RICO pursue its remedies and application to the fullest. They do not exercise the discretion and self-restraint characteristic of governmental prosecutors. Postconviction forfeitures are also receiving detailed scrutiny, although usually in state cases because of abuses in the use of the forfeited property. One final note is that roughly half the states have enacted "little RICO" laws modeled after the federal statute.

Denis Binder

SOURCES FOR FURTHER STUDY
Abrams, Douglas R. *The Law of Civil RICO*. Boston: Little, Brown, 1991.

Floyd, John E. *Rico State by State: A Guide to Litigation Under the State.* Chicago: American Bar Association, 1998.

Joseph, Gregory P. *Civil RICO: A Definitive Guide.* Chicago: American Bar Association, 1992.

Philcox, Norman W. *An Introduction to Organized Crime.* Springfield, Ill.: Charles C. Thomas, 1978.

U.S. Department of Justice. Organized Crime and Racketeering Section. *Racketeer Influenced and Corrupt Organizations (RICO): A Manual for Federal Prosecutors.* 2d rev. ed. Washington, D.C.: Government Printing Office, 1988.

Wallance, Gregory J. "Criminal Justice: Outgunning the Mob." *American Bar Association Journal* 80 (March 1, 1994).

Welling, Sarah N., Pamela H. Bucy, and Sara Sun Beale. *Federal Criminal Law and Related Actions: Crimes, Forfeiture, the False Claims Act, and Rico.* Eagan, Minn.: West Group, 1998.

SEE ALSO: Interstate Commerce Act (1887); Anti-Racketeering Act (1934); Hobbs Act (1946); Organized Crime Control Act (1970).

FAIR CREDIT REPORTING ACT

DATE: October 26, 1970
U.S. STATUTES AT LARGE: 84 Stat. 1128
PUBLIC LAW: 90-321; 91-508
U.S. CODE: 15 § 1681
CATEGORIES: Banking, Money, and Finance

This act caused policies to be implemented to ensure the proper maintenance and disclosure of credit information.

The Fair Credit Reporting Act (an amendment to the Consumer Credit Protection Act of 1968), was passed by Congress on October 26, 1970, and became law in April of 1971. Senator William Proxmire of Wisconsin was instrumental in the passage of this legislation.

NEED FOR THE LAW
Section 602 of the Fair Credit Reporting Act (FCRA) outlined the need for this law. First, the banking system is dependent upon fair

and accurate credit reporting. Inaccurate credit reports directly impair the efficiency of the banking system, and unfair credit reporting methods undermine the public confidence essential to the continued functioning of the banking system. Second, elaborate mechanisms exist to investigate and evaluate creditworthiness, credit standing, credit capacity, character, and general reputation of consumers. Consumer reporting agencies have assumed a vital role in assembling and evaluating consumer credit and other information on consumers. There is a need to ensure that consumer reporting agencies exercise their responsibilities with fairness, impartiality, and a respect for consumers' right to privacy.

OBJECTIVES AND PROVISIONS

The FCRA had four primary objectives. They were to establish acceptable purposes for which a consumer credit report may be obtained; to define the consumer's rights regarding credit reports, with particular emphasis on giving consumers access to their reports and procedures for correcting inaccurate information; to establish requirements for handling an adverse credit decision that resulted in whole or in part from information contained in a credit report; and to define the responsibilities of credit reporting agencies.

In general, it was the realization by Congress that consumer credit has had major impacts on economic activity as a whole that spurred the legislation. Consumers' inability to obtain credit for expensive items such as automobiles and large appliances negatively affected economic factors such as employment, production, and income, ultimately magnifying the business cycle, particularly in downturns. Financial institutions, as the grantors of consumer credit and the users of information supplied by credit reporting agencies, weighted their credit decisions heavily on the information supplied. Timely, accurate, and intelligible information was necessary for proper credit decisions. Consumers also needed to be protected from ramifications resulting from inaccurate, untimely, or improper credit information.

Consumers by far were the most heavily affected by the passage of this legislation. Consumers rely heavily upon consumer credit as a means of purchasing expensive items and raising their standards of living by purchasing goods for current use with future income. Reporting agencies faced higher costs as a result of the legislation but gained a greater reputation for accuracy and usefulness.

CREDIT INFORMATION AND CONSUMER ACCESS

The following information is usually contained within a consumer credit file: name; address; previous address; Social Security number; date of birth; employer; length of employment; previous employment; credit history including creditors, balances, and payment patterns; and public filings such as mortgages, chattels, marriages, divorces, collections suits, and bankruptcies. The FCRA made all information within a consumer's credit report accessible to the consumer.

Consumers can get access to their credit files in several ways. If a consumer is denied credit on a credit application, the lending institution is required to mail a detailed letter outlining the reasons for denial and including the name, address, and telephone number of any reporting agency consulted. The consumer may take this letter to the reporting agency within thirty days of the date of the letter to discuss and obtain a free copy of the report. A consumer who has not been denied credit may obtain a copy of his or her file from the local reporting service for a nominal fee. A consumer must provide proper identification in order to obtain a copy of his or her credit file. The FCRA identifies the type of material available to the consumer. The consumer has the right to know all the information in the file, with the exception of medical records. This includes names of people or companies that have obtained the report within the past six months and the names of those who received the report for employment purposes within the past two years.

PROVISIONS FOR CORRECTING ERRORS

The FCRA greatly benefits consumers by allowing them to dispute information contained within their files. Erroneous or inaccurate information can be contested and asked to be verified by the reporting agency. The consumer has the right to place within the credit file a consumer statement outlining his or her interpretation of negative information. This statement is then part of the file and is presented to future users. The consumer statement is usually limited to one hundred words. The FCRA limits the amount of time that unfavorable information can be reported on a consumer. Seven years is the maximum, with the exception of bankruptcies, which are reported for ten years.

In some instances, an investigative credit report may be compiled on an individual. It includes all the information mentioned above. In addition, it includes information on the character, reputation, and living style of the consumer. This information is obtained from interviews with friends, associates, and neighbors. The consumer has the same rights of access to this report as to an ordinary credit file.

RIGHT TO PRIVACY

The final major area that the FCRA addresses is consumers' right to privacy. Credit information is basically for use by the consumer, the reporting agency, authorized credit grantors, employers, and insurance companies. To restrict dissemination to proper users, those who request credit information must prove their identity and their reason for wanting access to a consumer's credit file. For users who obtain information under false pretenses, the law provides for fines of up to $5,000, prison sentences up to one year, or both. The same penalties apply to officers and employees of reporting agencies who misuse information. Consumers are allowed to pursue civil litigation against reporting agencies and are entitled to compensation for any financial injury, extra penalties imposed by the court, court costs, and attorney fees. Consumers can discuss complaints with credit reporting agencies by contacting the Federal Trade Commission.

IMPACT ON REPORTING AGENCIES AND LENDERS

Consumers were not the only parties affected by the FCRA. Reporting agencies assumed a more clearly defined fiduciary responsibility to act in good faith and trust. Their goals are to maintain timely and accurate files on consumers, handle disputes in a timely manner, and investigate complaints and inaccurate information on consumers. They must also ensure the confidentiality of their information while still making it available to the proper users. Failure to follow proper procedures and guidelines can result not only in consumer complaints but also in lawsuits, fines, or even imprisonment for employees of reporting agencies.

Consumer credit grantors also were affected by the FCRA. Lenders need to be careful when disclosing credit information. It must be both timely and accurate. Letters denying credit must be sent out on time, and procedures need to be in place to handle direct requests made to the organization. Lenders need to be careful with outside requests so as to not be viewed as credit reporting agencies. The final area lenders must address is the use of information for decision-making purposes. Many lenders place great weight in consumer credit decisions on the information obtained from credit files. It is essential that lenders have reliable information in order to make proper credit decisions. Lenders also use credit reporting agencies to screen borrowers. This works in two ways for lenders. It improves their credit quality by eliminating marginal borrowers and also gives them access to potential new customers. Lenders are bound by privacy laws and are forbidden to give copies of reports to consumers or other lenders.

CONCERNS FOR PRIVACY AND ACCURACY

In the years since passage of the law, many hearings have been held by Congress on concerns regarding the FCRA, such as privacy concerns, complaints about the difficulty of getting inaccurate information removed from credit files, the length of time to get disputed information reinvestigated, name mix-ups, and denials of credit based on the number of inquiries in a credit report. By 1991, consumer credit had increased sixfold since the act was first introduced, and the number of reports had increased fivefold. A revolution in computer technology had changed not only the shape of the credit reporting industry but also methods of record keeping and dissemination of consumer data. As a result of such hearings, the FCRA was later amended to enhance the proper maintenance and use of consumer information for credit, employment, and other related purposes.

William C. Ward III

SOURCES FOR FURTHER STUDY

Beares, Paul. "Regulation of Consumer Credit." In *Consumer Lending.* Washington, D.C.: American Bankers Association, 1987.

Cole, Robert H. "Regulation of Consumer Credit." In *Consumer and Commercial Credit Management.* 8th ed. Homewood, Ill.: Irwin, 1988.

SEE ALSO: Consumer Credit Protection Act (1968); Truth in Lending Act (1968); Equal Credit Opportunity Act (1974); Privacy Act (1974); Privacy Protection Act (1980).